DATE

**THE RADIANT CITY**

Published in 1933

**THE RADIANT CITY**

Republished in 1964

This picture is not symbolic. It is a large painting composed in 1930, at the same time as the ...tes for *The Radiant City* were being worked on in our studio. It is possible that there is a relation-

ship between these works despite their wholly different intentions. The human creative work stands midway between the two poles of the objective and the subjective, a fusion of matter and spirit.

THIS WORK IS DEDICATED
TO **AUTHORITY**

PARIS, MAY, 1933

LE CORBUSIER

# THE RADIANT CITY

ELEMENTS OF A DOCTRINE OF URBANISM TO BE USED AS THE BASIS OF OUR MACHINE-AGE CIVILIZATION

PARIS
GENEVA
RIO DE JANEIRO
SÃO PAULO
MONTEVIDEO
BUENOS AIRES
ALGIERS
MOSCOW
ANTWERP
BARCELONA
STOCKHOLM
NEMOURS
PIACE

Plans are not politics.
Plans are the rational and poetic monument
set up in the midst of contingencies.
Contingencies are the environment: places,
peoples, cultures, topographies, climates.
They are, furthermore, the resources
liberated by modern techniques. The latter
are universal.
Contingencies should only be judged as
they relate to the entity—"man"— and in
connection with man, in relation to us,
to ourselves:
a biology
a psychology.

THE ORION PRESS
NEW YORK

All rights reserved
Library of Congress Catalog Card Number: 67-12936
Manufactured in the Netherlands
First published in France in 1933
under the title *La Ville Radieuse*
Copyright by Vincent, Fréal & Cie, Paris
Translated from the French by
Pamela Knight (Part I)
Eleanor Levieux (Parts II, VI)
Derek Coltman (Parts III, IV, V, VII, VIII)
Translation © 1967, Grossman Publishers, Inc. and Faber and Faber Limited
This edition, making use of the plates from the 1933 edition, was printed in the Netherlands by
N.V. Drukkerij Koch en Knuttel, Gouda.

# DECISION

## MOBILIZATION OF THE LAND
## FOR THE COMMON GOOD

WE MUST UNDERTAKE THE REDISTRIBUTION OF THE LAND IN THE COUNTRY AND IN THE CITIES. LAWYERS SAY THAT THIS WILL TURN EVERYTHING UPSIDE DOWN. I PUT IT EVEN MORE CLEARLY: MOBILIZATION OF THE LAND FOR THE COMMON GOOD (THE REDRESSEMENT FRANÇAIS HAS PUBLISHED THIS THESIS).

THE PRESIDENT OF THE REDRESSEMENT FRANÇAIS WAS ERNEST MERCIER, PRESIDENT OF EST-LUMIERE (1928). HE WANTED TO FACE HIS COUNTRY WITH A CRUCIAL DECISION: TO EXPLOIT THE LAND OF THE NATION. THIRTY-FIVE YEARS HAVE PASSED!!! (1963).

# COMMENTARY ON THE OCCASION OF THE REPRINTING OF "THE RADIANT CITY"

*This work must be placed in its proper period. It offered, at one go, an organism (the Radiant City) capable of housing the works of man in what is from now on a machine-age society. This description serves as a key to a social and economic revolution. This revolution is as strong as a rising tide.*

*This book, written between 1931 and 1934, announces the three following events:*

*1. Those which will bring about agricultural exploitation.*

*2. Those which will assure the perfect functioning of linear industrial cities.*

*3. Those which will complete the tasks allotted to the radio-concentric cities.*

*All this is placed under the masterful government of natural conditions:*

> *sun*
>
> *space*
>
> *greenery*

*and its mission is the service of mankind:*

> *TO LIVE*
>
> *TO WORK*
>
> *TO CULTIVATE BODY AND SPIRIT*
>
> *TO TRAVEL ABOUT*

*(in this order and obeying this hierarchy).*

# CONTENTS

●

●

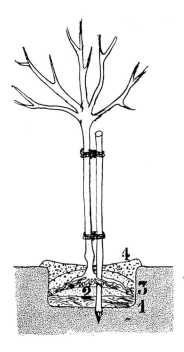

To plant a tree well: 1. good earth and basic manure
2. a covering of fine soil
3. very fine vegetable earth
4. subsoil and fertilizer

# 5th PART: PRELUDE

# 6th PART: PLANS

# 7th PART: RURAL REORGANIZATION

# 8th PART: CONCLUSION

# 1. MAGNETS...

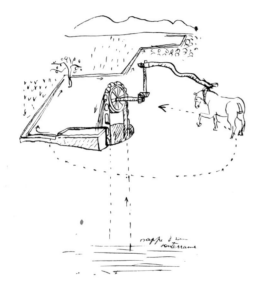

Spanish "noria," an age-old method of irrigation

... I am attracted to a natural order of things. I don't like parties and it is years since I set foot in one. And I have noticed that in my flight from city living I end up in places where society is in the process of organization. I look for primitive men, not for their barbarity but for their wisdom. America, Europe, farmers, fishermen. This means I go where men work to produce their food, and where they strive to find ways of making life a little easier. They also manage, without too much effort, to enjoy the pleasures of living in society – in work, the family and community. I am aware that as an architect and city planner I learn my trade from men, in their homes.

The city? It's already an empty shell. Its product is there all right, polished and superb, clear as crystal. The fruit of culture. But look at the refuse and scum. Look at the misery, the unhappiness and stupidity. People behave like children, negatively and destructively, without meaning to. What would we learn at a party? The closing prices? Gossip? And what would we do there? Engage in a useless exchange of uncertain remarks.

I go where order is coming out of the endless dialogue between man and nature, out of the struggle for life, out of the enjoyment of leisure under the open sky, in the passing of the seasons, the song of the sea.

I go where tools are being put to use: the primary tools that are required for the purpose of making existence possible within the limits of the day, the seasons, the years and the generations.

The phenomenon of invention; the law of matter; the chain reaction of progress; a rational, proportional growth; all these things take place in harmony, with the adverse effect of regulations and laws reduced to a minimum.

I am speaking of living men and present places, not of prehistoric times. Basic tools still exist, of course: wheel, knife, ax, saw. And many tools always will exist that have nothing to do with the mechanical age and the all-conquering machine.

I am aware that newspapers are being read every day, that houses have radios, that the priest celebrates Mass. None of this bothers me in the least: under these outside pressures man is more defenseless than ever before, his only means of expression being through his judgment, sensibility and taste. I see him better in perspective, he stands out more clearly. It isn't that I can see only the good qualities of my defenseless man, either. I have a very distinct, and necessary, understanding of his possible deficiencies, his faintheartedness, his continuing human weakness. So I can see at once the immense distance he will have to travel to attain with his simple brain a simple idea, the point of departure and the point of arrival. When the long distance has been traveled these two points meet. But in any event I, at the center of a natural order of things, have the point of departure: the gauge, the measuring tool.

As an architect and city planner, I measure my actions by this yardstick: my unit of measure is the measure of man. And I can keep a large range of relations in space by means of this basic binomial: man and nature.

●

This book is not a literary work written in the restful form of an impeccable progression of events, and in the serene study of things that have lived a long time and are no longer capable of change.

It describes the battering of life today; the rapid and violent growth of the modern phenomenon of urbanism; the explosion of accumulated anxieties and the outbreak of hysteria; dilemmas; a healthy, courageous and optimistic viewpoint; a belief in the future of a new civilization; the imminent awakening of contemporary thought; the joy of action and the commencement of great achievements; the certainty of a new confidence in basic human values; the possibility of reaching the basic pleasures.

Modern society is throwing off its rags and preparing to move into a new home: the radiant city.

Certain facts are known, certain definite principles and rules of conduct have been laid down. Not in any orderly fashion, perhaps. But they do form the component parts of a doctrine, something clear enough to serve as a guide. They are brief words, not revolutionary slogans, but they provide a solution to a revolutionary situation. For example:

The Plan must rule.

Disappearance of the street.

Differentiation between simple and multiple speeds.

What to do with *LEISURE* in the machine age; leisure could turn out to be the menace of modern times.

The use of land in town and country.

The dwelling unit considered as part of the public services.

The green city.

The civilization of the automobile replacing that of the railroad.

Landscaping the countryside.

The radiant city.

The radiant countryside.

The decline of money.

The basic pleasures: satisfaction of psycho-physiological needs, collective participation and the freedom of the individual.

The rebirth of the human body.

April, 1933.

●

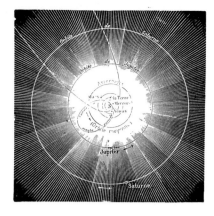

Solar system

# 2. BACKGROUND

the stupendous and extraordinary explosion of the bud

When a man has had the luck to spend a vacation in the midst of nature, far from city dwellers, surrounded by natural things unfolding imperturbably according to natural laws, and then he is transported abruptly to Paris, *to the city*, by car, rather

# 3. VACATION 1932

Harmony

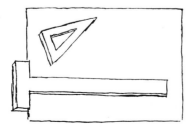

than making the return gradually by railroad car and station – man-made objects – the shock is severe, even traumatic.

While in nature life follows the seasons – birth, maturity and death, spring, summer, fall and winter – and each year nature cleans up, throws out and buries, we, the intellects of the universe, are pleased to live in streets and houses that are rotting (at least 60% of them), under obsolete laws, ruled by a system that is like a dead branch fallen from the tree of life. We crouch in a pool of dead things. The steps we take, our every movement and thought, right down to our incredibly grotesque kitchen equipment, are under the influence of antiquated junk. The single exception is our factories.

The guideline is there: nature.

Our crime is to have voluntarily abdicated our rights.

To walk over a clean surface, to look at an orderly scene. Live *decently*.

Only the tailor, the shoemaker and the laundryman help us to hold on to the right to remain the intellects of the universe.

August, 1932.

●

# 4. THE PLAN MUST RULE

By a strictly professional route I arrive at revolutionary conclusions.

Since I am a professional man, I make plans according to my professional concepts; this is where my judgment is good. If everyone did the same thing and the plans were coordinated by an authority in charge of the public interest, the result would, of course, be a Five-Year Plan, impossible to implement. Impossible because of our present social system! So now what?

Now what? Dilemma. The present social system preserves the status quo, opposes any action, eliminates or rejects proposals both pressing and necessary in the public interest. But it is *life* that guided us when we made our plans. Let's go along with *life*. The plan sets out its aims and calls for action. Let's change the system.

Such an act would be called revolutionary. There are those who would make the word "revolutionary" mean "destructive."

Untrue: it is a completely constructive point of view.

In simple terms, in a society waking up from the legitimate sleep that follows a period of intense activity, a new dawn is breaking – as has happened many times before in history.

Are we to predict and plan the details of each hour of the day? Absurd!

But we know that the sun has risen and another 24-hour day is ahead.

And the same for another 20 or 100 years.

So the game is worth the candle.

●

*"The cornerstone of all modern urbanization is absolute respect for the freedom of the individual."*
(*Reply to Moscow*)

June 8, 1930.

When I wrote this 1930 epigraph, I knew only one structure in the U.S.S.R., that of the leaders (I had made three trips). Lubinov controlling the various soviets and I myself (my idea or the idea produced by my lucidity) fighting the Architects' Soviet, the Moscow Soviet, the Labor Soviet. I saw those who gave the orders and those who obeyed them (they had the right to become leaders, just as in the jumble of Western freedoms, I have the *right* to become President of the Republic.) And I thought that in the U.S.S.R., just as in Paris, a basic human need had to be fulfilled, that of personal solitude. When the door is shut, I can freely enter my own world.

Such words, such a thought, such an act, are anathema in Moscow. I did not know this. Out of politeness I would have dropped my epigraph, which had suddenly, without my being aware of it, acquired an air of arrogance,

phenomenal arrogance,

enormous,

and crazy.

All this is typical of my lack of sophistication.

But is my epigraph completely worthless? It cuts right across established lines in the U.S.S.R. I am ready to retract it, if I have made a mistake.

Where is the mistake?

I think, and I weigh my judgments. That's the way I am. At certain times I need solitude. Even more than solitude itself, I need solitary action, I need to stand up, alone, face to face with the effort of my thought, to breathe deeply, to act, to prove, not to discuss. Discussion is for later, when I have thought, considered, formulated and proved. Then let the tide roll in!

If I am in error, how anxious I am to correct myself!

*Photo Brassaï*

when the door is shut. . .

●

August, 1932

## 6. UNPRODUCTIVE PROPERTY

Although the entire phenomenon of nature is one of uninterrupted movement, circulation, development, cycles, regularity and harmony, contemporary activity is hidebound by the esteemed and enduring institution of unproductive property.

I have always been afraid of giving my opinion on things I know nothing about. I have never found it necessary, till now, to discuss politics or economics. Today it is through my professional life that I encounter an obstacle: unproductive property.

Jean-Jacques Rousseau, in *The Social Contract*, accepted the principle of individual ownership, but he did state explicitly the double function of profit and duty: *land that can be cultivated or worked for some other purpose*.

Today we own land, but without any obligation to work it. In fact, a law which no one would dream of disputing gives one the right to work it or not, just as one wishes.

And from this have come both the *denaturalization* of property and the impossibility of doing the kind of work that makes men free, and that makes creative enthusiasm, civic trust and collective action practicable. We can make the plans and calculations for such work. But we will never be able to carry it through. Sheer madness! We seem to be out of our minds, and we are certainly accused of it!

Which one is wrong? The plan or the law? The program or individual neglect; life or death; action or inaction? Civilization or decadence; strength or degeneracy?

●

*Primo de Rivera* gave orders *for the construction of a road through Spain (Eastern Pyrenees, Barcelona, Valencia, Alicante, Murcia, Almeria, Malaga, Gibraltar, Cadiz, Seville, Madrid, San Sebastian, Western Pyrenees). The* National Circuit *is a 9-meters wide freeway, with banked curves, either macadamized or surfaced with a porphyry mosaic, its edges painted white. This was a country without one decent road; there were short stretches of paved road and goat tracks. Spain now has a* continuous road *that is the most beautiful I have ever seen, sometimes miraculous, a magnificent invention of modern times. It cuts right across land that has been under the plow for centuries. Unlike the cities and railroads, which give a false impression of everything, this road leads one directly into the soul of Spain. So far the road has caused no trouble to anyone.*

*In 1930 – the year that followed my tour of Spain – I didn't understand about the road. A show road, to impress foreign tourists? It wasn't finished. Now it is used and traveled. It is Spanish: a wonderful tool.*

*Fate?*

*I have always had this devouring curiosity to look into the effects of a positive action.*

Lunch at the inn in a small town.

I am going to ask a really serious question.

Is there one man in the Spanish government who, despite the paradoxical nature of the question, will understand its full significance, and who has the energy and power or influence to produce a strong proposal, more than that, a whole set of laws? Even more, to draw up and publish a doctrine that is neither contemporary, republican, socialist, nor communist, but just *human?*

Here is the question:

What, in the opinion of AUTHORITY, is the role played in the small towns and villages of Spain by the invasion of those light fixtures, made of bits of colored glass and beaten brass, and persistently displayed in shop windows in the hope of arousing the population's urge to buy? Ostensibly hand-crafted, these objects are in fact turned out by the thousands in factories, and *here*, in Spain, they are the poisons, vipers, vampires and scorpions of a civilization that should not be allowed on the *road* – they are contaminating and corrupt.

Electricity, progress? Yes, but how?

# 7. USELESS CONSUMER GOODS
# USEFUL CONSUMER GOODS

useless

Will you accept the fact that this kind of progress is the insidious destroyer of the only people in the world who live in a state of noble serenity – of inner life? (The Mediterranean coast, Barcelona, Tarragona, Valencia, Alicante, Murcia, Almeria, Malaga.) The symbolism of this invasion troubles me. Given the experience of neighboring countries, is it right to allow the unrewarding experiment of useless production and shoddy imitations to be repeated in a country that so far has remained unspoiled?

Spain has built her road, her freeway. It is the spring of a people following on a winter that was fruitful (it permitted them to sleep through the winds of mechanical change). It is a gesture, a sign, an action. Under the inattentive governmental eye, will the road become the carrier of machine-age refuse? The question goes deep, and the answer can end with Spain's sinking into the mud of the machine age, or with a clearsighted judgment and a *line of conduct*.

(Published in *Plans*, No. 8, September, 1931)

●

Liberty!

In Paris, in 1919, the great new religion was founded: *business!* Making money, organizing for the purpose of making a lot of money; business lunches, conferences, scientific management. The right man at the right place, etc. . . . .

Dialogue with my secretary:

"Can't you manage to arrive on time, at 8:30?"

She is very sorry. "I live in the suburbs, the stations are crowded, and if I miss my train I'm late."

"Oh, I didn't know you lived in the suburbs."

She began again, more boldly. "Look, you can't possibly imagine what it's like, all the trains are packed solid, morning, noon and night. And sometimes the men aren't too pleasant, we're all squashed together like in the subway and you have to look out!

"I catch the 7:45 and I have to walk nearly half an hour along muddy roads to get it. When it rains it's terrible and when it's windy it's worse, and in the winter it's still dark.

"I get up at 5. I wash my stockings and blouse, I press my dress and make my breakfast. . ."

"Why don't you do all that in the evening, after 6:30?"

She:

"6:30! I want you to know that at 5:30 the letters are ready for you to sign, but when I open the door you're talking with someone. At six you're still talking. At 6:25 you call me in and it takes you ten or fifteen minutes to sign them. You say to yourself: 'She can go home now.' But the letters have to be mailed. So I run to the post office. I can't possibly make the 7 o'clock train. I run to the station and the platforms are jammed and the trains full. I get on the next train, the 7:30 or the 7:45.

"When I get home it's 8:30 or 9. I have dinner.

"Then do something? I'm tired and nervous. I've been up since 5, and I just don't have the courage to start on something else . . ."

useful

8. **LIBERTY EQUALITY FRATERNITY**

I am beginning to be deeply interested in this daily round that reveals such a series of anxieties:

"Anyway, Sunday must be pretty nice in the suburbs, isn't it?"

She:

"Sunday! It's dreadful. I'm bored to death. You see, I never see anyone, I don't know anyone . . ."

"But that's ridiculous; nobody's alone like that in the world, especially a pretty girl like you."

She:

"I've been coming into Paris every day for ten years. My mother's pretty old, she often feels sad and depressed, and we have to be terribly careful about money. My mother knows a few people here and there that she meets when she does the shopping. We have a few relatives who live in other suburbs. What's the point of getting into a crowded train again, on a Sunday, to go and see them? We're too tired. And if we did, we'd find the same kind of people, stuck in the same kind of lives. Go for a walk? Of course we can, but the suburbs aren't much fun to walk in. It's not like the real country.

"I'd like to know some people of my own age. Men? Where would I meet any? Look, how can I make contact with anyone my age? In the train? If you knew what that kind of thing leads to . . . I've spent the best years of my life in the train. Ten years! Since I was seventeen. My youth and all of life's dangers have passed me by in the train. I often feel pretty low, and that can lead to the kind of adventure that only brings danger and bitterness and the rest. I keep telling myself that one day . . . something will happen, a miracle, a meeting. I haven't given up hope, don't worry!

"But life isn't much fun. *If you only knew how bored I get!*"

All this brought me up short. I had thought that life was cheerful, bright and amusing for these little Paris birds, so trim, with their heads in the air and their chic, miraculously made out of nothing.

The martyrdom of suburbanites. And something else again: the terrible solitude in the crowd of that vast urban agglomeration.

Oh, liberty!

\* \* \*

Equality!

In 1922, I began to walk into a dream that I never again left: life in the modern city.

I had made detailed plans for a contemporary city of 3,000,000 inhabitants. I had created new dimensions, I had made room for the basic pleasures: the sky and the trees, everybody's chosen companions. Sun in the room, a window filled with blue, awakening to a wave of greenery – there, *in the city.*

I had already made preliminary sketches for the Paris "Voisin" project, and I was going to show the final plans to the public, in our Esprit Nouveau pavilion at the 1925 Exhibition of Decorative Arts.

Inside me were new dimensions; I was living intensely through the intellect a new kind of daily life, active both physically and mentally, with the basic pleasures around me. I was thinking about the people who live in cities. In Paris I often walked through the district bounded by the Place des Vosges and the Stock Exchange – the worst district in the city and the most wretchedly overcrowded. Along the streets, on the skimpy sidewalks, the population moves in single file. By some miracle of group identification and the spirit of the city, *even here* people laugh and manage to get along, *even here* they tell jokes and have a good time, *even here* they make out!

I had created the prototype of a *classless city*, a city of men busy with work and leisure in surroundings that made these possible.

The chief architect of the city challenged me: "You want to destroy the beauty of Paris, the *history*, the past we have inherited from our forefathers. You're short-tempered and a pessimist, and you've made up your mind that the old ways can't go on. You tell yourself that a new life is beginning, and it's going to be different. But I think that things are just as they always were. All we need to do is widen a few streets here and there . . ."

The chief architect of the city performed his duties with the valuable aid of an official city car, a sedan driven by his chauffeur. And of one thing he was certain: traffic was perfectly normal. He even said: "And if it gets worse, we'll just get rid of the cars!"

At this time, M. Léandre Vaillat, who wrote a column on city planning in *Le Temps*, also accused me of wanting to destroy the beauty of Paris (in those parts of the city where he never set foot): "The most beautiful private houses of the seventeenth and eighteenth centuries are in that part of town, architectural gems . . . and the wrought ironwork . . ."

M. Léandre Vaillat lives in the west of Paris, on a broad avenue.

Last year another of the city's chief architects, who had been running a written and verbal campaign against my destructive ideas, told me: "Come now, you are forgetting that Paris was a *Roman* city, and that counts, you know!"

A million people are living in the slums of historical Paris. Another million are existing in the difficult conditions of the suburbs. A brick wall in the Cluny gardens, ivy-covered and crumbling, proves that Paris was once Roman . . .

Everything is fine. Our leaders will see that it stays that way.

Equality!

\* \* \*

Fraternity!

The important banker who is underwriting new and decisive city planning for Algiers, and who is thereby responsible for the very life of the city, said to one of my friends:

"You would like me to meet with M. Le Corbusier so he can tell me his plans and ideas for the future of the city? I know perfectly well who M. Le Corbusier is; as a matter of fact, I think very highly of him. But I can't see him. If I did, he might make me see his point of view and change my mind. I have no business changing my mind . . ."

This involves the entire reconstruction of the principal district of Algiers. A deplorable, fatal, tragic mistake is about to be made. In Algiers, I told the people of the city what I thought. I made them doubt the wisdom of the undertaking and I begged them to change these unfortunate plans. The very life of the city depends on it. Algiers has a future. Algiers will become the capital of North Africa. And North Africa is a vast potential in Western economy.

I submitted an overall plan, an idea that breaks right through the deadlock caused by the city's too-fast growth. I created a "radiant city." In this admirable setting – sky, sea, the Atlas and Kabylia mountains – everybody, each one of the 500,000 inhabitants making up the population of a future capital of modern times, will have the sky, the sea and the mountains marching past the apartment windows in an inspiring and joyous parade. *Everybody*. These are the results of planning.

flowers. . . for all of us ! ! !

slum            slum            slum

The center photograph
condemns a large part
of the vast program
undertaken by the City of Paris:
30 kilometers of urbanization
of the fortifications of Napoleon III.
    Remarkable property
    Available investment
    People to live there.
. . . . . . . . .
    Profit prevailed.
Nothing, absolutely nothing
was done in the public interest.
No kind of advance for architecture
no kind of advance for city planning.
This is a wasted adventure
But no one protests!

a big hotel on the Riviera
dinners and tangos:
business is good

# TATE OF MODERN CONSCIENCE

The chariot of death
In life after death, justice will come

I provided for the "basic pleasures."

But it is already too late: the money has been distributed. The whole thing would have to be done over again. This is unfortunate because, instead of a rather shaky financial operation, planning would bring a tremendous revaluation and one of the results would be to send money rolling into the coffers of the banks.

How rash and superficial we've been!

Money plays its own game: figures against figures and business against business. *Why is this being brought up?* The *urbanization* of Algiers? It will be thought about later, at the last minute, with technicians who will get their instructions – their orders – from the bank . . .

*Basic pleasures for everyone?* Time for that later, too, no time now. Stop rocking the boat!

Fraternity!

●

Goodbye, wheeler-dealers.

The Salvation Army's "Buttercup Day," on June 18, 1933, across the whole of France, symbolizes the maximum degree of success that can be obtained by this type of direct public appeal.

While diplomats and international experts are grinding to a halt in conferences that fail (the London Economic Conference), the rest of the world, ready to try something new, is reaching out for the basic pleasures. These should be defined. The civilization of money is dying. An appeal to the conscience of humanity. We are close to a simple word that could give us a line of conduct which would be like a trajectory through, above, every obstacle. Ignoring the ruins of our decaying world, it will point up the solution with simplicity, sureness and clarity. Instead of clinging desperately and fearfully to a drifting bark, the world will move into action, cooperating, taking initiatives, building, knowing the joy of creativity.

We need builders and we need a strong and simple doctrine.

And we must make up our minds to get rid of the rubbish.

The Salvation Army, having used money for necessities and not for appearances, found in the country a belief in simple happiness. These people who act in order to be part of a generous cause – and thereby discover one of the most precious values of the soul – succeeded in the end in touching people's hearts . . . They were respected. They were even loved. They opened the door to personal action, personal intervention and participation. They don't sit and watch life go by; they're out seeking their true fortune: the power of understanding. Pushing aside the display of riches which is measured by the disgusting piling of one franc on top of another, they take their chances on finding a varied and sometimes vast fortune: potentials of kindness, action or loyalty. That is the explanation: the Salvation Army has rediscovered an old currency that still works: spiritual values. And people thrive on it: the market has no power over it.

The big deal is disappearing and with its disappearance comes the inevitable collapse of the shady transaction, the effect of the wretched money web whose threads have slowly strangled conscience. This is where we have been led by this standard, this scale of hierarchies, this man-made measure that we have allowed to take root: money. In a comparatively short time – since the end of the war – the disease has spread: moral corruption, embezzlement, betrayal of trust. Percentages, middlemen, a shameful piling up of shady practices. Money: tips, graft.

Thieves and swindlers were not the only ones to be covered in the mud of money; gold can glitter too, and the weak ones believed they should run after it. The poor, or the not so bright, living or having lived until now within the limits of their family horizons, were shaken by the metallic clang. Every night the cinema mixed pearl necklaces, champagne, plunging necklines, greed and fantasy triumphs of money into idiotic love stories. They were trying to make money look respectable by association with an inevitably triumphant morality. Cinderella's happy ending was told over and over again: all those Prince Charmings as rich as Croesus had but one desire: to marry poor little typists. From one end of the social scale to the other, the conquests of heart and conscience, the virile actions of our mechanized and triumphant times, were all rewarded by a rush of riches. Hypocritically, virtue, and all the intellectual values, duly received compensation in the form of moneybags.

Foolish, stupid, moronic.

And finally, the instinctive sense of justice, which until now had entrusted Providence with the task of weighing the values of conscience, was thrown to the winds, and we all sat back and waited to be paid in hard cash for our actions. Decent behavior was going down the drain fast.

Money went down first.

However, there was some of it around, here and there. What happened to it? All one could do was to shout: "I am rich, I'm getting richer!" And then prove it.

An impersonal décor took over, in direct contrast to natural feelings, and jealousy, envy and greed were let loose.

A flower brings real happiness. The horizon and the sky comfort our hearts continually. They became insignificant. Physical fitness and the improvement of one's body give assurance and confidence. They were put off until later, until the money had been made. Reading opens up extraordinary possibilities; the mind, once the flood-gates are opened, leaps toward the gardens, the plains and seas of knowledge. Riches. Limitless riches, always growing, free and within everyone's reach. Nobody cared, nobody was interested, the wheeler-dealers moved in and with them a fine modern ignorance. Solidarity is one of our prerogatives. It is better to give than to receive. There is pleasure in giving. Put out one hand to receive a little, put out the other to give away more: then the circuit of life moves in a positive direction and leaves each conscience with its piece of contentment. All the doors were shut, and "holy selfishness" was born. The sport of the intellect, the fight, the struggle, the rivalry, the game, the freely accepted discipline of teamwork, the enthusiasm and excitement, the sacrifice made for one reason alone: victory! A remarkable human faculty, and the source of great exploits. A rightful force for heroism. All that is needed is that this capacity should not serve the cause of rape or cruelty – war and looting – but be directed toward initiative, construction and the very real need for beauty. So far, sport alone has attempted to achieve quality. This is one first victory, and an important one.

There they are, the basic pleasures. They are at our service, their stock-in-trade is within us, an inexhaustible fount of human possibilities. They are strong enough to finish off the old world and its money.

There will be leaders to show the way.

The way of enthusiasm.

(Six months before the Stavisky scandal.)

June, 1933

It is not noble to be poor, but it is a sign of nobility to be able to detach oneself from things.
(Krishnamurti, October 23, 1930)

(October, 1930)
Coste crossed the Atlantic

15

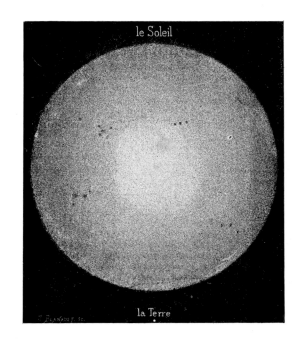

our law

# 2ⁿᵈ PART: MODERN TECHNIQUES.

1. MODERN TECHNIQUES.
2. A RALLY: THE CONGRESS AT LA SARRAZ, 1928.
3. OVERTHROWING SECULAR CUSTOMS.
4. EXACT RESPIRATION.
5. AIR, SOUND, LIGHT.
6. AN EFFICIENT HEIGHT FOR THE HOME.
7. "ARTIFICIAL SITES"
8. WHAT ABOUT AIR WAR?

# MODERN TECHNIQUES

1.

This much has been established. These are the marvelous fruits of a century of toil, the harvest of the first era of the machine age.

Here is no spiritual crowning, no mental fulfillment, no civilization. No: here are tools, a set of tools. Here are means of labor that allow us to begin putting the world in order.

We reduce everything here to the problem which concerns us: city planning. We seek to throw new technical values into relief, values having to do with the house, with the dwelling.

The dwelling takes a long time to change its form, modify its principle. When the dwelling changes, that means that new customs hold sway. New customs that appear only when the world has been radically upset. The dwelling changes only at the last moment, almost without the consent of the inhabitant, against the will of the passive forces of preservation. In the minds of most people, preservation expresses security.

Men have never been known not to take advantage of their discoveries and inventions, the vehicles of transformation. Men believe in the possibility of betterment. This betterment which changes habits is a disturber: it entails chaos, disorder; it rends; it brings face to face those two states which are ever present and ever in conflict: the active life and the passive life.

When inventions have multiplied and accumulated, based on one another like those of the nineteenth and twentieth centuries, the disturbance is no longer on the surface. It is deep, stirring, brutal. It is, in truth, a revolution.

The effect of inventions has been to shatter the ancestral statute. Everything has been broken, torn asunder. Social life is different. The life of the individual is threatened. A revolutionary situation requires revolutionary solutions. And to make a revolution there must be a doctrine.

A doctrine can be based only on extant facts: on the one hand, the machine-age revolution; on the other, the revolt of human consciousness.

•

# A RALLY:
2.
# THE CONGRESS AT LA SARRAZ

IAM-1
928

The Palais des Nations "affair" had begun in the spring of 1927, with the jury's verdict in the international competition for designs for the Palais in Geneva. It was disclosed when the proposals were exhibited in June (14 kilometers of plans) and it was brought to the public's attention by the illegal appointment of the architects in December, 1927. The Palais "affair" had upset the world of architecture, confronted by decisions so fundamental that they could either open up a new era or place a barrier before it. The affair had alarmed the thinking world (for in the open debate – the battle, actually – between the "Ancients" and the "Moderns," the League of Nations had just chosen the "Ancients"). Esthetic questions were not the only ones involved: The whole future was at stake. Architecture, *which is the expression of the spirit of an epoch*, delivered an ultimatum. The question was raised not only at Geneva; it was universally raised, everywhere, in everything.

Such tension created a spark. Spontaneously a gathering took place at a specific place, at a definite time: at the château of La Sarraz, in Switzerland. Principles had to be formulated, a battlefront had to be chosen. So the *International Congresses for Modern Architecture*" (CIAM) were born, in 1928.

These Congresses are alive. Step by step they accomplish their task. Today they have become the rallying point of the living forces in the architectural world. Some day, soon, they will be able to interpellate the authorities and send them summonses.

Session after session, the Congresses draw up a statute for the architecture of modern times.

It is worthwhile to print here the program which brought 42 delegates together that first time.[1]

PREPARATORY INTERNATIONAL CONGRESS FOR MODERN ARCHITECTURE
at the Château of La Sarraz
Canton of Vaud (Switzerland)
June 26-28, 1928

This first Congress has been convened to establish a general program of action aiming to wrest architecture from the academic impasse and to place it in its genuine economic and social setting. In the opinion of the promoters, this program should define the limits of the studies and discussions which future congresses should soon undertake, working on different aspects of the program. The mission of the present congress is to establish this series of programs.

Here I present only those aspects of the Congresses that enabled me to air the theories announcing the "Radiant City."

*A large part of world opinion has rallied to the cause of modern architecture. In every country there have been clear signs of it, and they are no longer merely fashionable passing fancies: modern architecture exists, led by a spirit appropriate to the machine age whose evolution has revolutionized society and which in every field has obliged us to create a new state of equilibrium.*

*Nonetheless, for discoverable reasons, a great number of professional architects, most of the leaders who are supposed to run our cities or nations, have remained apart from the real question. They cling to henceforth ineffective teachings, to habits of thought or of judgment which often even contradict the very goals which it is their mission to achieve. There is general confusion.*

*Now, the problem of architecture is the basis of social equilibrium today. It would be dangerous to remain blinded by habits. It is imperative that the achievements of modern architecture be made known.*

*The promoters, in response to the pressure of international public opinion and encouraged by the patronage of leading personalities, have invited a number of architects from all countries to the château of La Sarraz (Canton of Vaud, Switzerland), generously offered by Mme de Mandrot. The work which these architects have already carried out proves their real understanding of the tasks reserved for the future.*

*In its three-day work session, the Congress of La Sarraz intends to set forth the tasks of future meetings, which will bring together important members of the architectural and business worlds and of social and economic organizations.*

*The questions which justify the gathering of specialists from all nations involve an*

[1] I established this program in May, in the hope of showing our guests the direction I felt the discussions should take to avoid running aground on the rocks of individual passions which problems of esthetics inevitably arouse.

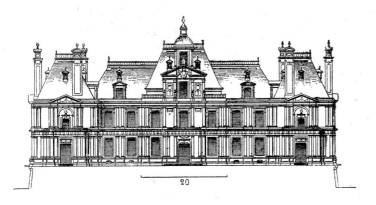

... obliges us to abandon architecture's
traditional methods

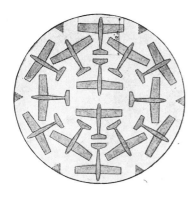

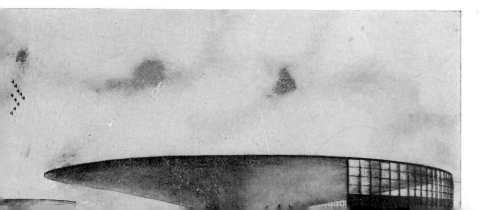

ne hangar
n, engineer

... supplies us with new architectural methods

examination of the changes which modern technique has worked in the fields of distribution and rationalization of labor, city administration, education and the role of governments.

*A group of six questions would seem to open up the way to a useful discussion.*

*The Congress should arrive at the formulation of the general programs of reform and innovation to be introduced into architecture.*

(The following concise analysis of the six questions placed on the agenda is intended to orient the discussion in a certain way and to elicit suggestions and useful rectifications.)

## QUESTION 1
### THE ARCHITECTURAL CONSEQUENCES OF MODERN TECHNIQUES

1° *Just as at certain times in the past, so today a structural apparatus (iron or concrete) exists bringing enormous freedoms and new elements to the home.*

2° *Recognition of this new circumstance:*

a) *Obliges us to abandon architecture's traditional methods;*

b) *Supplies us with new architectural methods.*

3° *These new architectural methods lend themselves:*

a) *To industrialization (through standardization);*

b) *To reform in the plan of the house;*

c) *To the demands of modern hygiene;*

d) *To constitution of the bases for a new architectural-structural and esthetic system;*

e) *Normally and efficiently to the efforts towards a new sort of city planning.*

4° *Not only does this new architectural system bring rational solutions to the problem of the house; but in addition, it suits every sort of construction, since it is capable of architectural expressions as fertile as those which made up the various traditions of the past.*

5° *It is possible to achieve architectural unity, the result of a new structural system born of modern techniques.*

6° *Every modern construction is based on a framework (iron or concrete) which, being independent and static, allows the standardization of its elements (industrialization) and, being independent of the floor plan of the building, leaves that plan entirely free and classifies the successive steps in the building's construction.*

7° *Support walls exist no more. There remain only exterior walls (façade) or inner partitions.*

8° *These partitions should be as light as possible since they hardly figure any more in the weight of the house.*

9° *Very light filling materials should be sought, since their weight is no longer needed in the static method of construction.*

10° *If the framework (resistance, toughness, casing, continuity) is a conductor of sound, then the principle of sound-proof (insulating) fillers must be adopted and the rules about the transmission of sound be applied. It is possible, without great cost, to obtain almost total sound-proofing in buildings with steel or concrete frames (the Pleyel studios).*

11° *The inclined roof is no longer a structural necessity. Steel and concrete normally furnish the flat roof. All superstructure in the form of garrets above the flat roof is superfluous (price), inefficient (dormers), and requires costly annual maintenance. The exacting theory of the flat roof (cold climates) requires water drainage inside the house (architec-*

*tural result in the arrangement of flat roofs): supporting walls and aedicules. The need to protect the flat roof from expansion leads to the creation of roof gardens. The flat roof, or roof garden, gives the dwelling a new and vital element (hygiene, sun, pure air, pleasure). In the city, the roof garden recuperates all the surface taken up by buildings.*

*12° The flat roof provides the city planner with new surfaces fit for traffic, to be used as promenades (in the air), cafés, stores (hygiene and classified traffic system).*

*13° The flat roof provides a pure city skyline (esthetically).*

*14° The static framework principle (iron or concrete) makes it possible to raise the house on pilotis and so to place the interior some distance from the ground. The posts being the least costly element of the house (in certain countries, the law requires that there be 60 centimeters of empty space beneath the flooring at ground level), it is more logical to extend these 60 centimeters to 2.5 meters, or 3 or 4 meters, and so recuperate almost all of the surface covered by the house which can be used for play, car parking or continuation of the garden beneath the house.*

*The entrance of the house is thus sheltered; only a part of the pilotis will be enclosed, that is: the staircase and, if need be, the garage. The cellar (there is no reason why it should take up all of the area under the house) will be dug beneath the stairway.*

*15° Pilotis provide the city with a vital solution, that of double superimposed streets: the lower one directly on the ground, for heavy vehicles; the upper one (a continuous bridge of reinforced concrete) for light, high-speed traffic (cars). The street's utility mains are hung, free and accessible for inspection, beneath the flooring of the upper street.*

*16° The needs of city planning (an area for planting, and desirability of setting houses back from the street) lead to the adoption of* indented streets (à redents), *by doing away with the corridor-street (the validity of this tendency will be borne out when man decides to build higher). It follows that two devices used in construction until now will be eliminated: the roof template (thanks to the flat roof) and the façade template. And the bow window too can be done away with, for the depth of a concrete building can be limitless, since it is no longer subject to the various limits imposed by the inclined roof.*

*17° The concrete or steel framework and the flat roof make it normal to build on indented plots; this leads to the prohibition of courtyards. Air shafts, however, will be tolerated and the maximum length of courtyards will be limited to, for example, 50 meters on each side. This in turn leads into the principle of* the redent (indented, or set-back, building).

the car ramp at the Fiat factory in Turin

## Question 2
### STANDARDIZATION

*1° Standardization already exists for the small hardware furnishings of the house and in the shape of certain synthetics or bricks. But all of the building trades (masons, carpenters, locksmiths, roofers, etc.) continue to work "to measure," and no two cases are alike.*

*2° Houses are built in the same way as in the past: in the open air, at the mercy of the seasons and the weather. The building trades have a lower production rate, what with unemployment in winter, than other industries do.*

*3° First of all, the number of building trades needs to be reduced as far as possible and the chief trades combined, if possible, into just one: that of the fitters. This means that construction has become industrialized and that most of the building's elements are produced* in a factory, *then carried to the site to be assembled. This is the solution of the "prefabricated" house.*

*4° Principle: it seems wrong to mass-produce a prototype (by standardization). To do that is to nip architecture in the bud.*

*What should be done is to mass-produce (by standardization)* a *living cell (or unit), that is: a complete element of the static system (posts and floorings), whose measurements are chosen so as to permit useful and varied interior arrangements.*

*5° The key mechanical element of the house is the* window. *Until now, the window has been a rather casual and cumbersome piece of woodwork. Reinforced concrete and iron mean the introduction of the long window, running the entire uninterrupted length of the façade. Since it can slide, the window is subject to no strain other than that of its vertical weight distributed evenly over its entire length. One pane of plate-glass would be enough if proper means were used to make it airtight. But plate-glass is very expensive. Yet the manufacturers tell us that plate-glass, a luxury item, can become an item of everyday use if it can be mass-produced in relatively small standard sizes.*

*6° Can architects adjust to a standardized, mass-produced window (if perfect)?*

*7° Standardization of the doors: wood, metal, paper, straw, etc.*

*If the doorframe is metallic, the door should be surrounded by a soft material (for adjustments after settling). Format: patterns should be established: 55 cm. space, 75 cm. space. For a double door: $2 \times 55 = 110$ or $2 \times 75 = 150$. Height: 2.05 meters, for instance.*

*8° It would be useful to standardize the overall dimensions of the staircase (5 meters) with reference to the cell.*

*9° In order to be able to standardize windows and doors, there must be a reform in the maximum height allowed for dwellings (for the cell), presently set at 2.60 meters. Obtain permission to set it at 2.10 meters, on condition that it be doubled for the living room: $2.10 \times 2 = 4.20$ plus flooring of $0.30 = 4.50$ meters.*

*10° In order to be able to standardize windows, cells, stairs, and all other elements, city planning should immediately apply the principle of* orthogonal arrangement of the ground, *the only means of achieving regular and standard distribution of labor.*

*11° Furniture must undergo important changes: the countless articles of* today's furniture *are inefficient and clumsy, forcing the architect to design outsized rooms. Except for chairs and tables, furniture should be reduced to sectional compartments, built to hold objects used by* human beings. *They can all be made on a common scale, with standard measurements. These standards should be determined. Henceforth these sectionals will be built into interior partitions. A study must be made of means to produce standard sectionals with their system of closing (steel, wood, cardboard, cement, etc.). Inside, these sectionals may be fitted out in any way, corresponding to different needs and varying from the most rudimentary to the richest.*

*12° The hardware fixtures used in building must be revised. They are too rudimentary, flimsy, not very ingenious. The construction of railway carriages (subways, sleepers, etc.) forces us to study the hardware problem in a clear way.*

### Question 3
### GENERAL ECONOMY

*1° An irrevocable economic phenomenon occurs: the birth of new building trades (electricians, fitters, metal workers, concrete mixers, etc.), simultaneously with the disappearance of certain other trades (roofers, tinsmiths, carpenters, stone masons, etc.). An irresistible economic tendency orients the building business toward industrialization (the ideal is to construct the house in the factory and assemble it on the site). This tendency has a worthwhile goal: the prefabricated house.*

2° *If building is to be industrialized (factory construction of elements later to be assembled), the dimensions of all the elements in a house must be revised so as to allow mass production* and, *by their multiples and sub-multiples, lend themselves to the various combinations which are* (or will be) *the proper domain of the architecture of housing.*

3° *This tendency leads to the birth of a new building trade:* the fitters. *The fitter will replace the mason, the tinsmith, the roofer, the carpenter, etc.*

The public must be informed about this tendency, so that extant industries and those to be created can be oriented harmoniously toward common goals.

4° *In order to inform the public and have adequate effect upon building corporations* (architects, contractors, and industrialists), *it would be useful to create a* central international agency *complete with a* review, for the concentration and diffusion of architectural inventions. *By "architectural inventions," we mean anything having to do with the establishment of common* (standard) *measurements and all that includes mechanical or constructive creations, architectural solutions relating to the elements of the house, to the internal or external arrangements of the house.*

5° *In addition to national languages, such an agency should dispose of a* universal, technical language.

The League of Nations should be approached with a view to making the teaching of a universal technical language compulsory throughout the world; *the effect of this moreover, would be to make all international contacts possible and easy. And this would mean a tremendous contribution to the pacification of the world.*

6° *The "International Bureau of Architectural Inventions" should be linked to specially equipped experimental laboratories in various regions so that architectural inventions could be verified with scientific exactness, with physics becoming one of the active branches of architecture. Government subsidies for limited construction of various housing developments* would be put to better use if they supplied the needs of these laboratories.

## Question 4
## CITY PLANNING

1° *Throughout the ages city planning has always made use of the most effective means which technique can provide.*

2° *Today, iron and reinforced concrete give us convenient means of carrying out the sort of city planning which responds to the profound social and economic revolution caused by the machine age.*

The social and economic revolution caused by the machine age confronts us with utterly new problems, affecting every part of every country.

3° *There is no* central agency *to guide and corollate the analyses which must be made and the initiatives which must be undertaken. There is general confusion, chaos prevails, danger is everywhere. It is imperative that in every country or region there be a plan to* create a permanent agency, *directed by a competent and responsible figure, able to give the country* its new statute.

For reforms are extended simultaneously to all cities, to all rural areas, across the seas.

4° *The new programs are of wider scope than anything that has gone before. And it happens that the nation's land, through successive sales and inheritances, is more than ever parceled out, along the most arbitrary lines. Countless sites, endlessly split every which way,* hinder any job of city planning.

February 6, 1934, in Paris:
awakening of cleanliness

23

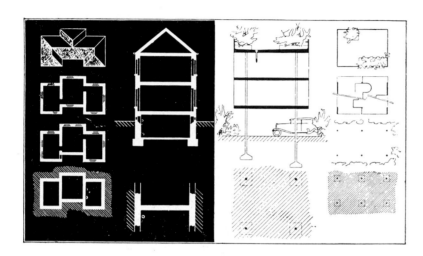

The architectural revolution is complete...

*So first there must be a* law decreeing the reconstitution of land, in city and country.

*5° This operation is directly linked to that of enhancing land values through works of public interest. There should be a law by which the basic price of a given property may be established and determining how, following works of public interest, the enhanced value may be shared between the owner of the property involved and the agency which took the initiatives in those works and bore their cost* (Law of the recuperation of enhanced values).

*6° Since new means now exist (steel or concrete), state or municipal ordinances setting limits on construction must be completely revised so as to allow maximum development of the resources provided by new techniques.*

*The first limit involved is that on the* height of buildings.

*7° But simultaneously the question involves the areas devoted to traffic and the areas planted (hygiene) between these buildings. So we may establish* the ratios *between areas used for traffic, for planting, and for housing, and another scale dividing cities into zones of population density per* hectare *(approximately 2.5 acres). This allows a flexible confirmation of the principle by which* the center of the city should be very densely populated, with a very great area devoted to traffic and plantings. *This will determine the types of tall structures which are to be built in the center of the city.*

*8° In some places the law already allows the city to develop freely by buying back a* protective green belt *circling the city and separating it from its suburbs.*

*9° In view of the urgent need to industrialize building, city planning will proceed to regroup blocks of buildings and traffic arteries along the orthogonal principle.*

*10° In view of the country's general economy, technical resources, traffic and public health requirements, city planning will make the roof garden compulsory and also, where needed, the street raised on pilotis.*

*11° In every instance, city planning should respect sports (hygiene, recuperation of nervous energy, etc.) by leaving room for them to be practiced very near the house.*

*12° Faced by hesitant authorities, always inclined to take short-range opportunistic measures, city planners will be guided in their layouts by the so-called "surgical" principle (layouts cutting across existing streets and blocks or boundaries), instead of the "medical" principle (aiming merely to widen existing streets or roads).*

## Question 5
### DOMESTIC TRAINING IN THE PRIMARY SCHOOL

*1° The architect's duties are badly defined. The problems of the dwelling are not clearly stated. The architect's clients, whose needs today are determined by a number of factors apart from living conditions, generally express their wishes very badly. This means that architecture inadequately fulfills the normal requirements of the dwelling; consequently, the country* spends huge sums to no avail. *Moreover, this fosters a tradition of* the expensive house, *which puts sound housing beyond the reach of a large part of the population.*

*2° Through primary school teaching, a sheaf of elementary truths could constitute the efficient basis of domestic training; for example:* general home economics, the relationships in which various elements of the home stand to one another and their harmony, principles establishing the function of furniture; the fundamentals of cleanliness and its moral significance, the effects of sunlight, the ill effects of half-shadow and darkness, a sufficient grounding in physics (resonance, heat, insulation, electricity, etc.), notions of mechanics (maintenance and functioning of mechanical elements), etc.

3° *The effect of such teaching would be to train future generations with a healthy and rational conception of what a house is. These generations (the architect's future clientele) would be in a position* to pose the problem of the house.

### Question 6
#### RELATIONS BETWEEN GOVERNMENT AND ARCHITECTURE

1° *"When building's all right, everything's all right." This saying clearly shows that the architect is the crux of economic prosperity.*

2° *Architecture today still operates within the traditions of the pre-machine age. Methods are old and the building industries are not in the least organized. Hence an enormous loss in yield and expense. In almost every country, the architectural vocation is inspired by academic rules.*

3° By definition and by function these Academies are preservers of the past. *They have established the dogmas of architecture according to the practical and esthetic methods of historical periods. The Academies corrupt the architect's vocation at its root. The viewpoint is false and the results are false.*

4° *Governments should, for the sake of the nation's prosperity,* withdraw the teaching of architecture from the monopoly of the Academies. *The past offers the pertinent lesson that nothing lasts, that everything evolves and that progress advances.*

5° *Governments, refusing to place their trust in the Academies, should revise the methods of teaching architecture and give as much thought to this question as to all questions whose object is to equip the country with the most productive and advanced agencies.*

6° *Because of the subjection of governments to Academies, most government work projects, which are among the most notorious manifestations of architecture, suffer from sterility and inefficiency.*

7° *This example from on high is harmful to the country as a whole, for it eventually stamps out the nation's living forces, sanctioning only the parasitic or senile ones.*

8° *If governments were to adopt the opposite attitude, a veritable renaissance of architecture would come about.*

9° *From the standpoint of the country's morale, the effect would be sound. For architecture is what is visible, what creates the country's appearance and molds the citizen's character. Civic spirit can be born of living architecture.*

\*     \*     \*

Here is the reaction of Paul Otlet (founder and director of the Musée Mondial in Brussels, and guiding spirit of the "Associations Internationales") to the Program of the Congress at La Sarraz.

"*My dear friend,*

"*I congratulate you on your Congress for Modern Architecture. I have just read the brochure. It is profound, simple, clear, broadly linked to the international social movement.*

"*Here and there, I should like to see certain theories completed and 'elevated.' For it is a good idea to formulate in this way, by connecting and grouping distinct points, the*

... withdraw the teaching of architecture from the monopoly of the Academies.

*overall complex of facts and ideas which should be at the foundation of a movement, an organization, an action: the theories.*

*"(Question 6). I should like to see it entitled: 'Relations between Society, Public Authorities and Architecture.' Society is the ensemble, both official and unofficial. One of the great problems today is to set forth and define the role of free social agencies, distinct from both individuals and the authorities.*

*"What you say under Question 1, 6 on architecture, should be stated more prominently, not as an argument but as a principle.*

*"Every modern construction is based on a framework (iron or concrete) which, being independent and static, allows the standardization of its elements (industrialization) and, being independent of the floor plan of the building, leaves that plan entirely free and classifies the successive steps in the building's construction.*

*"Now we need two things:*

*"1° A rational arrangement of all available space. 2° A perceptible harmonization of all that is visible. Upon whom is this double task incumbent?*

*"Upon architecture. Since it has already raised itself spontaneously to the level of 'City Planning,' let it prepare to accept this double mission. For the need is there, and no one claims to satisfy it completely.*

*"Space on this planet is becoming scarce: it cannot be wasted. Space is not only geometrical: every point in space exercises a multiple influence, for it is or is not occupied by something which does have physical, biological, human properties. Space saving (an indirectly active element, and not by any means a passive or a neutral one) is thus of the utmost importance, both quantitatively and qualitatively.*

*"From now on architecture has two sides: interior (living, place of work, room inside, even the clothes closet and the piece of furniture) and exterior (the street, the city). The common principle of architecture, which in no way limits it, must be made clear: to be the organization of space.*

*"And through an ordered space, the supreme mission of architecture is to watch over all* visible *ensembles, whatever they may be.*

*"Go down the list of those who could assume these two functions. There is no one. Neither the engineer, specialized in the technique of using energies and transforming matter; nor the artists of color, line and form, who have a particular and individualized goal and not a complex, general one: art is subordinated, then, to architecture.*

*"The word economy can be taken in its narrow sense, synonymous with economics; and in its broad sense, synonymous with organization. This second sense must be reaffirmed everywhere, in everything.*

*"The body of executive workers must be organized and all the intellectual branches of technique, but also the goals (or works, or functions).*

*"What goals, what works?*

*"A: Architecture is not fulfilling its mission as long as it has not provided a roof (tectum) for all that should be sheltered: men, things, actions. In this sense it should concern itself with collective services, with the agglomerations.*

*"You complain, rightly, that 'clients generally express their wishes very badly.' This statement itself is incomplete (Question 5). Who, in society, should be concerned with and responsible for providing the 'tectum'? Private individuals, associations, public authorities. But there should be one main authority to formulate and maintain, demand and recommend the social plan in this field. And that is architecture.*

*"First there must be a statement of the minimum of* tectum *per individual and per household, in terms of: a) the present degree of culture of the population in the twentieth*

26

*century and its rational and legitimate needs; b) then, the degree of technical possibilities of the most advanced technique; c) finally, the degree of economic possibilities (power of consumption, potentiality of consumption).*

*"B: Next, the minimum number of* urbs *must be determined (Question 4). Agglomerations, products of chance, should be transformed into urban centers, products of conscious and rational will. Architecture should determine the minimum of city planning: relations between built-up and free areas and volumes, between areas and volumes reserved to private individuals, to groups, to official departments; enumeration of the services, edifices and roads constituting a minimum. The whole calculable, in terms of balance sheet and profit, hence responsible terms; concrete points toward which particular progress and progress in general will tend, with coefficients that should be modified to correlate with progress itself; architecture (organized on a world-wide basis and possessing comparative data on tendencies and latent potential) periodically revising the terms. Architecture 'Guardian of Progress' in this field.*

*"Very good. Bravo to what you say.*

*"Stress it still more. Genuine organization of intellectual labor should go right to the heart of the question. All that the Institut de Paris (Coopération Intellectuelle) has done so far is on the surface.*

*"Every science should have its own international association, and it is up to this association, as you maintain, to organize that science.*

*"A distinction must be made between the interests of science and, next to them, those of the social function and, thirdly, those of men who teach a profession (protection, rights, economic and union defense).*

*"These three orders of interest have been confused; they must be made distinct, equipped with distinct agencies; then they must be brought to cooperate in a single organization.*

*"Now, in every field, the organization of science should be thorough: the data should include 'research and inventions,' synthesis and systematic arrangement, documentation (registration, preservation), dissemination (publication, demonstration), teaching, methods, villages and townships (unification), etc. All this is what the 'Associations Internationales' have done or should do, their relations with a Center of Centers, the Mundaneum.*

*"Excellent theories. Let us broaden them by the idea that adults need a systematic initiation. I am sending you my reports on universalist teaching and the didactic material. There should be an 'Architecture' section in the general encyclopedia.*

*"I have let myself go presenting these few remarks to you informally. Your subject is enthralling. Since you are going to found something, do not hesitate to lay the foundations for something huge, no matter how huge your first plan may already be.*

*" 'Architecture is the basis of social equilibrium,' you say.*

*"Yes; and what is more:*

*"The twentieth century is called upon to build a whole new civilization. From efficiency to efficiency, from rationalization to rationalization, it must so raise itself that it reaches total efficiency and total rationalization. The question is not so much to balance what is, as to construct what is called upon to be. Architecture is one of the bases not only of* reconstruction *(the deforming and skimpy name given to the whole of postwar activities) but of the intellectual and social* construction *to which our era should dare to lay claim.*

*"With my best wishes,*

Paul OTLET."

The greatness of the responsibility:
the municipium

This work program was accompanied by a plan of action: when an idea is clear, it can be expressed through diagrams.

At La Sarraz, we were going to start from scratch, amidst a confusion born of aspirations, battle plans, and the uneasiness of each nation. To our fellow delegates, whom the train or the automobile had brought so hastily to our meeting, we had to be able to say:

"We will advance step by consecutive, successive step; our needs will create new agencies that will act; we will have a plan of action." At the inaugural session of the Congress, this diagram was put up, expressing the battle plan:

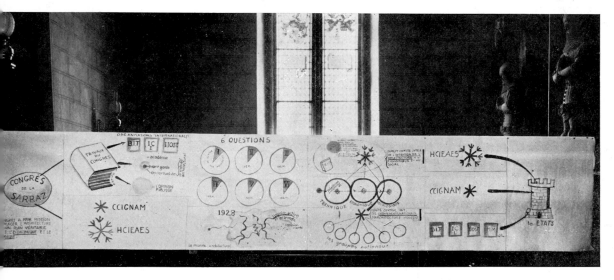

Here is the declaration by which the founding of the "International Congresses for Modern Architecture" was made known to the public:

DECLARATION:

*"The undersigned architects, representing national groups of modern architects, declare their agreement on the fundamental concepts of architecture, as well as on their professional duties to society.*

*"They lay especial stress on the fact that 'to construct' is an elementary activity of man, intimately bound to the evolution and development of human life. The architects' task consists of coming into agreement with the orientation of their epoch. Their works should express the spirit of their time. Thus they positively refuse to adopt, in their work method, those principles which have animated former societies; on the contrary, they assert the need for a new concept of architecture answering to the spiritual and material requirements of life today. Aware of the profound transformations which the machine age has worked in the social order and in social life, they recognize the inevitability of a corresponding transformation of architecture itself. They have met expressly to achieve the harmonization of extant elements: by reinstating architecture in its genuine role, which is an economic and social role, by withdrawing it from the sterile monopoly of the Academies, perpetuators of the past.*

*"Moved by this conviction, they declare their association and their resolve of reciprocal aid with a view to making good their aspirations, morally and materially, throughout the world."*

Château of La Sarraz,
June 28, 1928.

Attempt to cure the ills of today's social body? Tiring task, pointless work. Decrepitude, old age, dusk, decline of an outdated civilization.

What is needed is to equip a new, machine-age civilization.

Attempt to focus the argument on existing municipal ordinances? Out of the question: the only solution is a new body of ordinances. Modern techniques have revealed the way to other things. New things mutually coordinated by a biology which is whole, unique.

What are the existing regulations? The codification of a social state in balance with techniques – with the most advanced techniques then known: the techniques of stone, the simplicity of speed (the pedestrian and the horse). These techniques were mastered under Louis XIV; these speeds had been those of humanity for thousands of years.

The machine appeared.

From the slavery to which it has subjected us, it should lead us to emancipation. Tyrant though it is at present, it should descend to its proper rank: that of servant. What scope this would offer to our undertakings! All we have to do is set about it, decide that we want to create the conditions which are normal in the machine age.

A decision!

But this decision can be taken only if technicians have drawn up plans. A plan serves to show where one can go, to state what one wishes to do, to prove *that one can begin to fight.*

●

# CIAM-2 1929

The International Congress for Modern Architecture
2nd Congress at Frankfurt-am-Main
September, 1929
ANALYSIS OF THE FUNDAMENTAL ELEMENTS OF THE PROBLEM OF
"THE MINIMUM HOUSE"
Report by Le Corbusier and P. Jeanneret

The dwelling place is a distinctly biological phenomenon.

Yet the vessels, the rooms, the spaces which it implies are confined in an envelope of solid materials belonging to a static system.

Biological event, static event; these are two distinct orders, two independent functions. The mind which strives to solve one or the other of these riddles follows varied paths.

\* \* \*

The poverty, the inadequacy of traditional techniques have brought in their wake a confusion of powers, an artificial mingling of functions only indifferently related to one another, an exaggerated solidarity which is a hindrance. Methods of building have emerged from this, and been codified by the Schools and the Academies. These hybrid procedures are costly, they save neither matter nor effort; they can no longer respond to the severe economy of the present; the "Minimum House" cannot be achieved;

# 3. OVERTHROWING SECULAR CUSTOMS

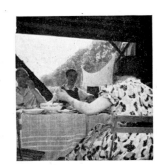

This summer house is a plank shack, 2 meters wide and 6 meters long, raised on pilotis. Modest and eloquent witness to the validity of "the minimum house."

Here my friends carved out a life at their ease; functions were given a precise statement and found an architectural reponse.

The lesson is that "the indoors" is extended toward "the outdoors." The economy of the cell and ease of communication. The participation of the fundamental elements: sun, sky, greenery.

This may be only a shack but it is also a proof. Proof that architecture and city planning are inseparable.

## THE MINIMUM HOUSE

biological event
static event

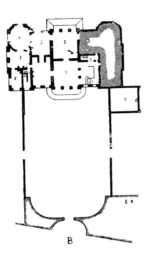

The sheer inadequacy of traditional methods to deal with contemporary problems...

waste is the ransom of discordance between the tasks proposed and the traditional techniques. This is true throughout the world. The impasse had led to the crisis in housing. We must find and apply new methods, clear methods, allowing us to work out useful plans for the home, lending themselves naturally to standardization, industrialization, Taylorization (mass production).

If our diagnosis of the sheer inadequacy of traditional methods were not more than enough in itself to impel us to look for new solutions, the history of architecture (our own past, or sometimes even the present in other climates) would show us that other methods of house construction exist or have existed which are infinitely more flexible, more deeply and richly architectural than those made popular by what is taught in the schools. (The lake house, the Gothic wooden house, the Swiss chalet [blockhaus], the Russian isba, the Indochinese straw hut, the Japanese tea house, etc., etc.).

*We must find and apply new methods, clear methods allowing us to work out useful plans for the home, lending themselves naturally to standardization, industrialization, Taylorization.*

If we do not sort out two independent events: *the arrangement and furnishing of the home*, on the one hand, and *the construction of the house*, on the other; if we do not differentiate between two unrelated functions: an *organized system of circulation*, on the one hand, and a *system of structure*, on the other; if we persist in the present methods by which *the two functions are mingled and interdependent*, then we will remain petrified in the same immobility:

*a)* Industry will not be able to take over the "Minimum House" and contribute its prodigious resources to the general economy.

*b)* Architecture will not be able to make plans adapted to the modern economy, and society, although it is in the process of regeneration, will be deprived of the "Minimum House."

By "the crisis in housing," we mean not only a quantitative crisis but a qualitative one as well. Man today is an animal deprived of its lair: he can only mope.

**An exact circulation is the key to contemporary architecture**

The running of a home consists of precise functions in a regular order. The regular order of these functions constitutes a phenomenon of circulation. An exact, economic rapid circulation is the key to contemporary architecture. The precise functions of domestic life require various areas whose minimum content can be quite precisely determined. For each function there must be a type of minimum "container," standard, necessary, and sufficient (the human scale). The order of these functions is established according to a logic which is biological, and not geometrical. These functions can be diagrammed along a continuous line; whereupon the interplay of the necessary areas and their proximities can be clearly discerned. It will be evident that the way these areas are connected has little in common with the more or less arbitrary shapes and areas of traditional houses.

Standardization is the means by which industry may take over an object and produce it at low cost, in great numbers and perfect quality. The domestic functions have these unquestionable characteristics: they are carried out on horizontal planes which are *floors;* they require a flow of light which in the daytime can be admitted only (theoretically) by the façades: *the façades are providers of light.* The partitions which mark off the series of "containers" necessary to the running of a home are in no way directly related to the walls; they are membranes, insulating or not. By its very definition, the **The façades are providers of light** façade-provider of light cannot carry the floors of the house. The floors will be carried independently of the façade, by posts.

30

From then on, with a classification: "*floors*" and "*light-giving façades*," the problem appears in all its clarity: to place at the disposition of the architect surfaces of free flooring covered by surfaces of free ceiling; on this available area, the architect will install, upon request, rooms (or vessels) connected to one another by a rational circulation. Sunlight will be provided by the façades, especially arranged for this purpose; openings can be made anywhere, vertically or horizontally, in these façades; and the depth of the house will be dictated by the height of the areas to be lighted between two floors. The flooring will be formed by a system of slabs or girders or flat vaults carried by posts which will either have foundations in the ground or be suspended from systems of bridges and hanging tongues; thanks to these, the number of posts may be decreased and the way opened for static methods which are not yet commonly used in building. The disposition of these posts or tongues will be dictated by an accurate computation of the distances to be spanned: what we consider the indispensable principle of the "free ceiling" (in order to achieve the "free" or "open plan") requires the elimination of visible crossbeams.

In order to permit industrialization, the spacing between posts and the spans of the girders will be standardized. The presence of posts inside the house (a presence which represents about .5% or .25% – the three-hundredth part of the surface built upon) can in no way bother the architect when he proceeds to make the plan of the house (size, shape of the rooms, circulation, arrangement of the furniture).

Modern materials, steel and reinforced concrete, allow the supporting, or static, function of the house to be realized with precision: that is, the framework.

*We feel that the house should be erected on an independent framework*, providing an *open plan and free façades*.

The masonry wall no longer has a right to exist.

In 1926, during a cycle of lectures at the Labor Exchange in Paris, Auguste Perret, speaking of *reinforced concrete*, stated: "It is madness to think of using reinforced concrete to build small houses: it is much too expensive. Only large buildings can be economically made of reinforced cement." Coming from an illustrious builder, this statement shows how widely opinions can differ.

We adopt another viewpoint; not of the present but of a near future: having demonstrated above that the ideal solution includes a *framework* and consequently an *open plan and free façades*, we say: iron and reinforced concrete lend themselves to these needs. Concrete and iron for big projects, and iron for scattered houses, *prefabricated and assembled*. Industry with all of the equipment and all of the methods for preparing iron and reinforced concrete already exists. Qualified and specialized labor is abundant; workshops, factories, mills are available. The open plan and the free façade are conducive to equipping the house in a rational way. Rational equipment (response to the biological function) brings an enormous saving on the area occupied by the dwelling, thus, a saving on the real volume and thus, on installation costs. The house that is rationally "equipped," by elements mass produced by big industry, means a considerable saving in operation and construction costs. But rational equipment, which replaces a good deal of furniture and makes things easier than ever before, can be arrived at only in terms of the free framework and open plan. So, the open plan and the free façade must be adopted and independent frameworks be created.

If that decision were paradoxically to be followed by greater expenditures, *this would merely be the result of industry's temporary lack of organization.* We would have to put

The floors will be carried independently of the façade

independent framework, open plan, free façade

camping . . .
savings,
precision,
efficiency:
where are
"the styles"
in all this?

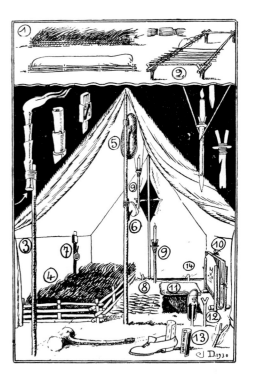

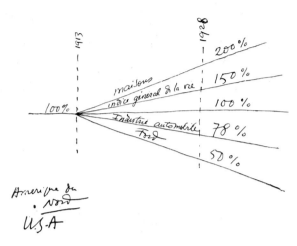

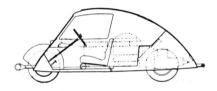

In 1928, Le Corbusier and Pierre Jeanneret conceived this car and called it the "Maximum Car." In 1935 the Société des Ingénieurs Automobiles held a contest for the "Minimum Car." The Société wished to present our "Maximum Car" in a supplement to its album.

. . . . . . . . . . . . . .

Cars have been made and driven since then, and no one has ever called attention to the "Maximum Car" of Le Corbusier and Pierre Jeanneret.

Normalization of standard measurements of equipment

up with this period of deficit, go through it and in a short time, thanks to industrial organization on the one hand and to perfection of domestic equipment on the other, we would attain an entirely new position in the history of architecture and simultaneously solve the problem of the *minimum house*.

Yet already, at this precarious stage of the question, we have achieved significant results: at the request of M. Loucheur, Minister of Labor, we drew up plans for totally industrialized houses, made with the most costly materials and executed in the most meticulous way. We extrapolated the house, so to speak, from clay and quarry and mortar; we transported it to the industrialist's factory, the Taylorization belt. And on the basis of one hundred houses, with contract price, we housed 6 people (father, mother and 4 children) in conditions completely different from the usual ones – and much better – for 38,500 French francs per house.

We maintain that this price, of 38,500 francs for 100 houses, could be reduced in the same ratio as that of mass-produced cars compared to cars individually made to order. For we actually produced the *prefabricated* house, and we did what the builders of cars and railway carriages do.

Walter Gropius has given us the American figures, revealing the present lack of synchronization between building and industry (the figures represent, from top to bottom, houses, general living index, the automobile industry and Ford).

\* \* \*

Modern architecture could get onto the wrong track, if it tried to build mass-produced standard houses (one, two, four, even ten standard models) and spread them over the country. The *raison d'être* of a whole mass of architects would be eliminated. But last year, at the La Sarraz Congress, our comrade Hoste cried: "If standardization and industrialization were to wipe out the architect's calling, I would accept this and say that we would not have the right to react against an ineluctable event." Rest assured, my dear Hoste: the architect's trade will not disappear; instead, it will be geared down, dispersed, divided into a considerable number of branches. In reality, the field of architecture has been prodigiously extended.

This is what we believe: As far as the "*minimum house*" (social tool that is indispensable to the present era) is concerned, architecture can center its attention on equipping the inside of the house. Depending on the problem (capacity), the size of the family, the sort of occupant (his way of life), the exposure to sun and winds, the topographical location (city planning), the architect of equipment can invent biological groupings within a static standard framework. Thus the industrial methods required here, as a result of the absolute transformation of existing elements, can be employed in any climate since they can be made to fit any and all local conditions.

The framework will be standardized; the elements of the house and the objects making up its equipment will be standardized around a series of varied models, worked out on an accurate human scale (stairs, doors, windows or glass walls, interior sectionals, etc.). The home appliance industry, until now confined to sanitation, heating and kitchen appliances, will expand indefinitely. And the task of a Congress such as ours will be to try, through the individual efforts of each one of us, to establish an international convention normalizing the various standard measurements of domestic equipment. This attempt at normalization (similar to that which has occurred in the field of photography) is closely linked with those questionnaires I and II which we sent you and which criticize the present regulations, concerning the dimensions of rooms, light surfaces, exits, etc.

To tell the truth, the industry toward which we are going to take a decisive step expects our studies to result in a revision of the dwelling's functions, with this short, concise (and so very revolutionary) phrase as a slogan: "*breathe, hear, see*" or again: "*air, sound, light*" or again: "*ventilation and isothermics (even temperature), acoustics, radiation of light,*" etc.

*Everywhere, in everything, in our daily research, we lack scientific certainty. Physics and chemistry are the territories which we must prospect in the search for sufficient truths.*

With such a program, as you can see, we are leaving behind the customs made sacred by tradition. We will learn more from the savages, from men close to nature whom the Academies have not touched; but above all, we will have to seal new pacts in the scientific world and in that of large scale contemporary production.

On the other hand, we are reassured as to the destiny of modern architecture, even though certain leftist circles are intoxicated or dizzied by certain words they consider fashionable[1]: those who are devoted to solving the problem of the minimum house will always (even in spite of themselves) be able "to act like gods" with pieces of wood, iron, cement or various assembled products.

Architecture will not be ruined by the "minimum house."

\* \* \*

One last word about these embryos of new systems which have caused a contemporary architecture to dawn (very palely so far!).

When we leave one function behind in order to take up another; when, for instance, we stop swimming in order to walk, when we stop walking in order to fly, we break up the established muscular harmonies and we fall – unless, by reacting with wisdom and perseverance, we create a new harmony wherein all the relationships are new but wherein coherence and unity of principle bring ease and proper functioning – real efficiency.

*Unity:* all evolution tends toward it. Everything can be in motion, everything can change overnight, but unity alone brings efficiency through harmony.

We have told you here of our belief in the need for a free framework, making the open plan and free façade possible. We note that this technical concept allows us to consider all the problems of architecture, from the minimum house to the apartment building, the office building, the skyscraper, and the palace (if that word doesn't offend your ears).

The idea is simple: in order to act, man needs horizontal surfaces protected from the rain, from temperature, from curiosity. That's all!

If we need horizontal surfaces, we will not build any more sloping roofs, which cannot be put to use: on the contrary, the possibility of placing gardens on the roof (to counter the effects of expansion) will mean profound changes in the general layout of the house.

Since we no longer have to lay foundations in the ground for the carrying walls; since on the contrary all we need is posts covering only .5 % of the surface built upon and furthermore, since it is our duty to make the house more healthful by raising its bottommost floor above the ground, we will take advantage of this situation by adopting the principle of "*pilotis*" or stilts.

What is the point of using pilotis? To make houses more healthful and at the same

---

[1] This is an allusion to the headstrong ideas of the "Neue Sachlichkeit," east of the Rhine, which proclaimed the decadence of the *art of architecture* and insisted that only an uncompromising functionalism could have a *raison d'être*.

when we leave one function behind in order to take up another . . . unless we create a new harmony

Pilotis

1934, America, first appearance of the elevated street

at the end of the interminable streetcars, subways, buses: the garden-city. The organized slavery of capitalist society.

time allow the use of insulating materials which are often fragile or liable to decay and so should be placed far from the ground and possible shocks.

But most of all: behold, they are available to work a thorough transformation in the system of traffic on the ground. This is as true of the skyscraper as of the office building, of the minimum houses as of the streets. *One will no longer be "in front of" a house or "in back of" it, but "underneath" it.*

We have to reckon with cars, which we will strive to channel into a sort of river with regular banks; we need to park these cars without, at the same time, blocking up the river bed. When we leave our cars we must not paralyze traffic all along the river and when we come out of our buildings, we must not obstruct the areas reserved for movement.

The President of the Work Soviet in Moscow, during the discussions prior to the adoption of our plans for the Centrosoyus, concluded in these terms: "We will build the Centrosoyus on pilotis because one day we would like to urbanize greater Moscow and solve the traffic problems."

The most indispensable functions of modern life require the installation of countless utility mains. If we agree that these mains should be able to climb freely from the bottom to the top of the house and come back down again (skyscrapers, offices, apartment buildings, villas, etc.) and that they should, as the most elementary common sense demands, be able to connect with their point of origin inside or outside of the city, and yet remain within sight for checking and within reach for repairs, then we will realize that the traditional wall and foundations are so many obstacles, and that burying pipelines under the ground is the most incredible nonsense of modern times. The framework with open plan means total freedom in placing mains. Pilotis make the "elevated street" feasible and thereby, the classification of traffic: pedestrians, cars and parking. And the city's utility mains will be installed like the working parts of a machine in a factory: accessible for inspection and repairs.

As a result, the entire surface of the city will be available for traffic. Moreover, new ground will be created: the roof gardens. What fortunate circumstances, if we know how to take advantage of them!

From this new building statute arise new architectural attitudes. Should we give it all up? Of course not! In the harmonization of the whole, let us create unity, let us tend toward unity! We feel that modern architecture is just beginning and that a new cycle has just become apparent.

As for the solution to be found for the problem of the "minimum house," we demand not mere methods of expediency, of temporary adaptation to existing but false situations, but rather methods which are harmonized with those of work as it should be done today. All we need is to get over the hurdle! But first we must make up our minds to get over!

## RATIONAL DIVISION INTO BUILDING LOTS

## CIAM-3

## 1930

3rd International Congress for Modern Architecture in Brussels, 1930
RATIONAL DIVISION INTO BUILDING LOTS
Report by Le Corbusier

The question raised by the Congress is restricted to one of low, medium, or tall buildings to be erected in the city.

Its object is to encourage or cause changes in the municipal ordinances of the various cities of the world.

First of all, I assert that the question can embrace only a part of the general problem of modern urbanization. Today more than ever an overall view is needed: it would be risky to try to settle certain minor points right now, only to have new questions, brought up immediately afterward, make them invalid.

The question before us includes two contradictory conceptions:

1° Agglomerations made of garden-cities, causing the dispersion of their inhabitants over a sprawling area:

2° Concentrated cities, built vertically, gathering the inhabitants in a joint social phenomenon and cutting the area of the city to a minimum.

Aside from this, two extreme forms of urban agglomerations must be recognized: the big city, and the small city.

Does the big city express a fortunate or a harmful occurence? What should its proper limits be: one million inhabitants? two, five, ten million? This time we do not need to answer: the phenomenon of big cities already exists; at certain times it represents a hierarchical occurrence of some virtue: the big city becomes a magnetic pole of attraction and from which, conversely, emanate the spiritual achievements resulting from intense concentration. The big cities are actually control stations.

Small cities are intentions of big cities left in a halfway state because of particular circumstances. Cities advance and succeed, or they vegetate: the destinies at stake are the result of innumerable factors. Vigilance or negligence, vital intensity or slackness. There is no better place than this to cry: "Opportunity only knocks once!" There is no hegemony of divine right; there is only the just reward for effort made, or the grace of the gods. Hegemony or decadence, such is the incessant hammering of life, the pathetic palpitation of every day. "Watch and be ever ready!" The antagonistic tide of destruction, decay or crushing defeat never ceases to batter the city.

Historical experience reveals that for military reasons, the area of certain cities had been vigorously, though temporarily, limited, by walled fortifications. But life was within the walls: its thrust made them burst. Today in the U.S.S.R., the program of national development has caused an absolute limit to be set on the area of the nearly 400 new cities which the Five Year Plan provides for. This area is limited to a fixed capacity of 50,000 inhabitants. The coincidence of peculiar and even tenuous circumstances justifies such a decision: we would have trouble finding parallel conditions in the old European countries. The U.S.S.R. is colonizing; in our countries, the territory has been occupied for a long time now.

\* \* \*

Cities are used for living and working. In the colonizing U.S.S.R., the link between working and living will be direct, since the city of 50,000 inhabitants is founded next to a factory or to a new lode. Let's not forget that the U.S.S.R. is a gigantic, barren territory, so that the birth of such cities is clearly a sort of colonization. Nor must we forget that in this case, the economy is state-controlled and that an authoritarian will makes decisions, imposes its discipline and its program (and there too, as the result of all-invading life, an evolution will follow, swift or slow, and which no one can predict).

In the world's present-day big cities, *working* and *living*, those two simultaneous

A roof garden at Ville-d'Avray

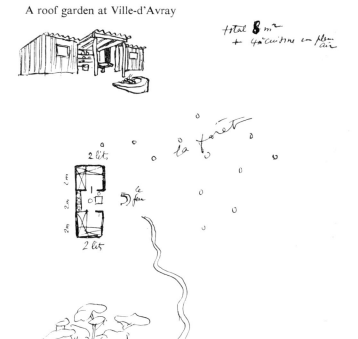

Four students built the "machine for living." would be worthwile extend it. This marvel efficiency may be in ocean-front pinegrove the Bassin d'Arcachon but couldn't the proble be stated and solved so to bring *joie de vivre* the big-city dweller?

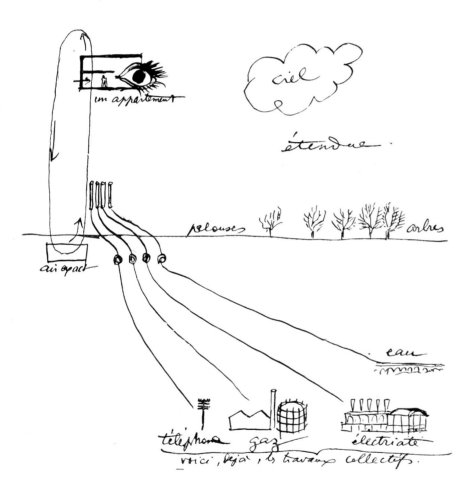

un appartement

ciel

étendue

pelouses    arbres

air opact

eau

téléphone    gaz    électriate

voici, déjà, les travaux collectifs.

functions (in the duration of the 24-hour solar day) are carried out in two different places; they form a complex whose organization, for lack of radical measures, is made virtually impossible by the crushing advent of the contemporary machine age. The question of transportation is decisive.

In small cities, the question of transportation is not of such vital importance.

* * *

The reaction of the big city upon the small one is proven, not absolutely but in general; the big population centers are thought-collectors and it is these centers which, after a more or less regrettable deformation, inspire what is undertaken in the provinces. Let's not forget that it is *ideas*, of whatever sort they may be, *that cause men to come together*.

The question before us (Brussels Congress, 1930) is confined to "*living*" and includes, where necessary, some considerations of the problem of transportation. But if it is a matter of big cities, then this last factor immediately takes precedence. If we consider the first side of the question: *living*, the problem is brought down to the human scale, that is: to a question of biology and a question of the sentimental sort.

The answer includes:

*A vessel* to hold each family, absolutely separate from other vessels containing other families. Problem of soundproofing.

*A flow of light:* We know that sunlight is indispensable, but we haven't enough detailed information as to the effects of its absence, of its direct or indirect radiation, of its being made to pass through a glass wall, etc. . .

*The consumption of pure air:* modern medicine (through a return to the fundamental cosmic notions) means to sustain the perhaps inexplicable but at any rate indubitable virtues of natural air. Supplying pure air inside the house is immediately linked to the techniques of heating and ventilation; outdoors, it is subject to disturbance of the atmosphere by dust, coal, gases.

*The time needed for upkeep of the home:* The verdict is clear, we must submit to the solar laws, the solar day; the solution must be found within the 24-hour limit, and within this 24-hour limit we must conquer the fatigue which has become our common fate. It is by organizing communal services that the city dweller will avoid pointless fatigue. But it is also by adopting the principles of a new modern consciousness, of a new doctrine of life, that the modern world will define its notion of happiness and will, as a result, be able to put aside the useless causes of fatigue. Conversely, the definition of a modern consciousness will let us discover which factors are most likely to "un-fatigue" us, that is: to satisfy, delight and comfort us. Enthusiasm replaces lassitude.

*Recuperation of physical and nervous energy:* In a word, this means the upkeep of the human machine: cleaning, draining the toxic substances, recuperating nervous energy, maintenance or increase of physical energy. The task thus formulated means that new services must be available indoors: physical culture, etc. . . . and outdoors: daily sports activities for everyone, children and grown-ups.

*Sentimental needs:* I express them insofar as they concern us, architects, in two words: *visual drama and architecture*.

By this I mean to indicate a group of perceptions, sensations, which are *of the nature of harmony*, and to demonstrate the need for them I confine myself to this negative observation: it is the lack of harmony, *cacophony* which has put human biology and the heart out of order today. We believe that we can get the better of these negative influences through the harmonious organization of contemporary architecture.

It is obvious how complex the problem is; there is more than just a single facet.

To consider only one facet would mean: disillusionment.

To correct only one rule would mean: having to bring up the whole question again in a very short time.

\* \* \*

If we can speak to the point about modern city planning today, this is only because the nineteenth century supplied us with *modern techniques. It is modern techniques which bring the solution to urbanization.*

\* \* \*

There is another revolutionary fact: *the new arrangement* of machine-age society; in truth, the profound transformation of secular customs, the intervention of new customs and the probability of still more new ones.

\* \* \*

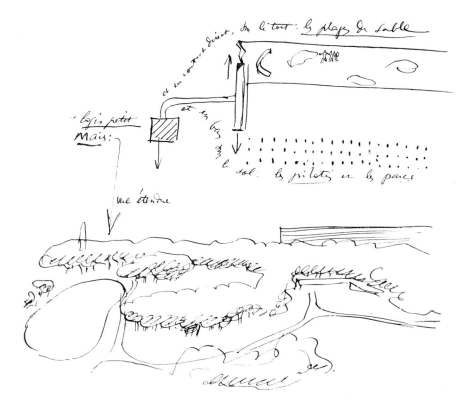

A third new earth-shaking fact: the search for a form of authority able to decide which general organization could develop the collective functions.

These various events occur simultaneously; at present they are stirring the masses violently or according to a more or less gradual evolution. Contemporary architecture and especially city planning are direct results of the social situation; this goes without saying. By means of personal inquiries let's keep up to date with the present evolution but, I beg of you, let's not get into politics or sociology here, in the midst of our Congress. They are too endlessly complex phenomena; economics are closely linked to them. We are not competent to discuss these intricate questions here. I repeat: here we should remain architects and city planners and on this professional basis we should make known, to those whose duty they are, the possibilities afforded by modern techniques and the need for a new kind of architecture and city planning.

*Hope in the present era:* A fundamental postulate, compelling us to do extremely subtle technical research, determines the form of social grouping from which our proposals for city planning and architecture will derive their inspiration. This postulate: *respect of individual freedom.* Actually, to be more precise, *restitution of freedom which has been lost,* an end to slavery. Architecture and city planning can gratify this profoundly human hope.

\* \* \*

Modern society is better prepared than its predecessor for collective disciplines. *Disciplines which are beneficial so long as they tend toward individual freedom.* But if they were to shackle it in any way, they would be hateful and would have to be cast off.

The essential topic of the Brussels Congress is: *garden cities as opposed to urban concentration.* Of these two contradictory states, one must be chosen, the one which avoids waste (of time, of energy, of money, of land).

The garden city leads to individualism. In reality, to an enslaved individualism, a sterile isolation of the individual. It brings in its wake the destruction of social spirit, the downfall of collective forces; it leads to annihilation of the collective will; materially, it opposes the fruitful application of scientific discoveries, it restricts comfort; by increasing the amount of time lost, it constitutes an attack upon freedom.

For the sake of one per cent of society or one tenth of one per cent – for the sake of the people who are well off and whose needs it can satisfy – the garden city plunges the rest of society into a precarious existence.

Whereas urban concentration favors the introduction of "communal services."

A mirage: *decentralization,* lowering population density to 300, even 150 inhabitants per hectare, with the pretext of giving the countryside back to the city man. Sheer illusion and falsehood, as the reality shows.

I believe that, on the contrary, the population densities of our present cities – 300 or 400, even 600 (overpopulated zones) per hectare – should be raised to 1000 by the prodigious resources of modern techniques. Then communal services can be multiplied, then genuine freedom can be achieved in the heart of family life, freedom instead of domestic slavery.

Outstanding problems of architecture and city planning.

So we come to take the implemental decision: the use of tall buildings. How tall will they be? 30, 40 or 50 meters; some people even propose a height of 150 meters, and more.

The question of elevators comes up as soon as a house is two stories high; the elevator is in fact the keystone of all modern urbanization, be it in proletarian sections or in wealthy sections (and moreover, such distinctions should disappear: the city, having become a human city, will be a classless city). It is a crime to make anyone walk up more than three flights of stairs. Now, by raising the question of the compulsory elevator, the elevator-cum-means of public transportation, we are also asking for a complete reorganization of the way building lots are divided, of the number of streets and of the way they are laid out. Until now, the custom has been to combine an elevator and a stairway to serve a maximum of two, three, or four apartments per floor. In that case, the elevator is run by the people who use it. Many people consider the elevator an almost superfluous item, a luxury, a symbol of wealth. If the elevator is to be truly efficient, the running of it should be entrusted to elevator operators, *both night and day.* At the rate of two or four apartments per floor, this is a witless, ruinous system. Suppose we adopt a healthy conception: professional elevator operators, day and night; fast elevators and, with this circulating material, this "vertical transportation" in existence, let's have a considerable number of floors; but instead of the two apartments which on every floor traditionally give on to a slow and perilous vertical system, we will suppose a system of intense vertical traffic, swift and sure, serving a great many apartment doors on each floor: 20, or 40, or 100. We say: 20, or 40, or 100 apartments on each floor, because

Elevators considered as vertical public transportation

Interior streets

we have arrived at the notion of "interior streets." So we have, within the apartment building, the introduction of corridors which become veritable *"interior streets,"* streets in the air, 12 or 24 or 50 meters above the ground. On the basis of a detailed study I propose, for example, to group 2,400 persons around a single vertical shaft with four elevators; each of these persons will have to walk 100 meters at most from the elevator to the door of his apartment. From then on instead of forty elevators accompanied by forty stairways, and perhaps by forty concierges, there would be only one stairwell with four elevators. The result is crucial, and obvious: we will *no longer have forty doors opening from the building* onto the street but rather, *a single door;* instead of having to make those forty houses open onto the street itself and consequently *having to build the houses directly on the street*, we will have only one door, and *from the street itself an approach road with "auto-ports"* (parking lots) will lead off to the single door. Thereafter, the problem of automobile traffic is on its way to solution. This means a complete reversal of the economy of streets, of the situation of houses and streets in respect to each other, of the hitherto interdependent function of house and street. The house no longer needs to rise above the street; the street is no longer at the foot of the house!

Auto-ports

The street is no longer
at the foot of the house

\* \* \*

The interior street has existed in embryonic form, in two or three apartment houses built last year in Moscow. It was considered undesirable to continue its application, because children made a deafening racket in the corridors and the neighbors could see directly into the apartments opening onto the corridors. Certain circles in Moscow, subdued by this failure, are thinking of abandoning the principle of the interior street and coming back to that of the separate stairway for every two apartments. The time of dangerous decisions has come; let's remain calm, let's react against panic: so the interior street did not work in Moscow? I say: let's not give up the principle of the interior street but instead, let's try to create the new organ which is the interior street; a new problem for architecture has come up here. How can we organize the interior street? That is what we must work out: *we must create that organ.*

Thanks to the principle of "interior streets," the usual number of streets in the city can be diminished, both as to surface and as to length, in the ratio of 10 to 2 and even of 10 to 1; *this is a tremendous reform.* In all events, the city planner is well aware that there are too many streets in today's cities; that intersections occur too frequently; that most of them should be eliminated in order to facilitate traffic in the ratio of 10 to 3 or of 10 to 1, etc. The city streets which were *on the ground*, in the open air, will then be transformed into *interior streets* serving every story of, say, a 15- to 20-story building. The police (the policemen) who today are spread in countless numbers over every intersection in the city will be released. But let's keep a few policemen; we will entrust them with guarding and keeping order in the interior streets. Instead of being on the street, *outdoors*, the policemen will be in the street, *indoors.*

The apartments grouped around the din of Moscow's internal corridor are uninhabitable. Yet we know that practically total soundproofing of buildings has been achieved, thanks to the labors of Gustave Lyon; it is possible, in every apartment giving onto an interior street, to provide a tomblike silence. It would be childish, therefore, to abandon the principle of the interior street because of noise.

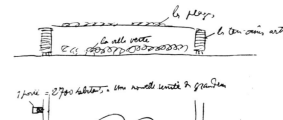

a session of CIRPAC (executive committee of the CIAM) at the Palace of the Generalidad in Barcelona 1932.

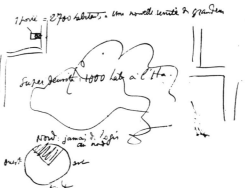

# 4. EXACT RESPIRATION

...But in the **LUNG,** the space which can be occupied by air is greatly increased thanks to the pulmonary alveoli which cover an estimated area of **200 M²**...A sheet of blood formed by the many fine links of the arterial capillaries covers an area of **150 M²;** it is renewed with every contraction of the heart, that is: **70** times a minute. The heart's right ventricle pumps about 180 grams of blood into the pulmonary artery, so that every 24 hours about **20,000 Liters** of it enter the lungs and will come into contact with **10,000 Liters** of air..."

(WINTER, 1931-1932) Everywhere I suffer from the discomforts of heating (in my studio: stoves; in government offices: central heating; in public buildings: central heating or hot air).

Distinguo: "Exact respiration" is not merely a matter of favorable temperature and purified air.

The U.S.S.R. writes me: "In the cities we are planning, there will be neither dust nor toxic gases." (Really!) And the U.S.S.R., stigmatizing "exact respiration" as a monstrous and unnatural idea, wanted our Centrosoyus Palace* in Moscow to be filled with *stagnant air*.

We've started something: let's get on with it!

Why should we let piddling considerations – the fear of words – stop us right on the threshold of modern techniques, right where we can find the solution to contemporary problems: the home, the factory, the office, the club, the assembly hall?

A matter of lungs. Air gives the lung its *raison d'être*. Let's talk about "exact air"!

For the past several years, while pursuing step after new step the genuine goals of architecture – or, to put it more exactly, having my eyes opened little by little to the duties of architecture, to the sacred and solemn tasks of architecture – I have realized that the key to life is the lung: a man who breathes well is an asset for society. I have arrived at the site of synthesis, the constructive idea, certainty: the need to provide exact air. And I have found the means to do it.

The invention? The discovery that if architecture follows certain paths, it can provide city dwellers with good, true God-given air, for the salvation of their lungs.

I have met with opposition on all sides, from "poets," from "friends of the people," from specialists. Yet I have persevered and attained utter certainty. I will tell the story of my research.

It is only at this very moment, as I am writing, that, putting down my pen and opening the medical student's physiology textbook, I come looking for facts with which to impress. I am sure of finding them there. Here they are, clearly and simply explaining our duties.

"The lungs are the essential organs of respiration; it is within the lungs that dark blood is transformed into red blood ... transformation which occurs thanks to a gaseous exchange between the blood and the air outside ...

"... with every inhalation or exhalation the lung absorbs or rejects about half a liter of air; as we accomplish 16 respirations per minute, we absorb 8 liters of air per minute, 480 per hour and, rounding off, about 10,000 liters every 24 hours.

"... the air which is inhaled has the composition of the air outside; thus it includes 21 volumes of oxygen and 79 of nitrogen, between 3 and 4 ten-thousandths of carbon dioxide and from 5 to 15 thousandths of water.

"... 750 grams of oxygen are retained by the lung every 24 hours; this represents about 530 liters.

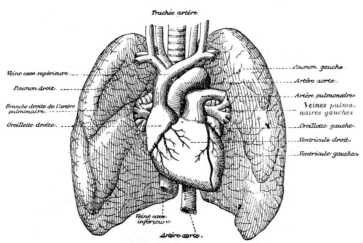

Fig. 246. — Rapports des poumons.

*Trachée artère*

*Veine cave supérieure*
*Poumon droit*
*Branche droite de l'artère pulmonaire*
*Oreillette droite*

*Poumon gauche*
*Artère aorte*
*Artère pulmonaire*
*Veines pulmonaires gauches*
*Oreillette gauche*
*Ventricule droit*
*Ventricule gauche*

*Veine cave inférieure*
*Artère aorte*

* The Centrosoyus, which is being finished now, will house the 3,500 office workers of the Ministry of Light Industry.

"In the same period, about 850 grams, representing some 400 liters, of carbon dioxide are exhaled.

"... The oxygen which is thus retained diffuses into the blood and the hemoglobin of the red blood corpuscles seizes it to carry it to every part of the body. This is the phenomenon called *respiration of the body tissues*. In this way oxygen is used for combustion deep in the cells, for their nutrition and their reproduction.

"... The lung is an exchange center; here the blood brings its volatile impurities to get rid of them, on the one hand, and on the other, picks up oxygen to carry it to the body tissues.

"... Lack of air causes death."

\* \* \*

The air of the cities is not God-given air. It is the devil's air. Doctors reveal the results of their analyses:

*Study of number of bacteria found in 10 m³ of air, analyzed at very nearly the same times:*

1) Altitude of 2,000 to 4,000 meters; and also, 100 km out to sea . . . .  0
2) Thoune Lake, altitude 550 meters . . . . . . . . . . . . . . .  8
3) Near the Hotel de Bellevue (Thoune), altitude 560 meters . . . . . .  25
4) In a room at the same hotel . . . . . . . . . . . . . . . . . .  600
5) In the Parc Montsouris, in Paris . . . . . . . . . . . . . . . .  7,600
6) On the rue de Rivoli, in Paris . . . . . . . . . . . . . . . .  55,000

*(Study made by Miquel and reproduced in Dr. Martini's book.)*

\* \* \*

Trees absorb carbon dioxide. They give off oxygen. The tree is man's companion. *Soon there will be no more trees in the cities.*

\* \* \*

In Rio de Janeiro, in Buenos Aires, in Algiers, the air is saturated with humidity. In certain seasons, it is overwhelming. Residents of those cities tell you: "Our work is much inferior to yours; we are crushed by the humidity in the air."

So it is that certain regions on this earth, although they are overflowing with natural riches, have a climate hostile to man, to the functioning of *the human lung*. There man is defeated, in the midst of his riches.

The normal temperature of air fit for breathing is 64.4° Fahrenheit.

In Moscow, in the winter, the thermometer can read 40° below zero! A gap of 104.4°! And in Paris, it often reads 23° above.

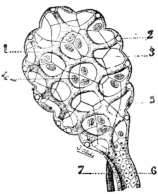

Fig. 253. — Circulation à la surface d'un lobule pulmonaire.

1 et 2. réseau capillaire ; 3. paroi de l'alvéole ; 4 et 5. noyaux des cellules épithéliales. 6. bronchiole. 7. vaisseau sanguin afférent.

Fig. 253. Circulation at the surface of a pulmonary lobule.
1 and 2, capillary network. 3, Alveole wall. 4 and 5, nuclei of epithelial cells. 6, Bronchial tube 7, Afferent blood vessel.

the tree is man's companion

the Opéra in Paris: one of the "finer" districts

41

The death penalty is demanded for General Sanjurjo, and life imprisonment for the other defendants.

The Public Prosecutor, Mr. Martinez Arogon, takes his place at the right of the Court.

It is very hot; the windows have been left open, as have the doors, so as to create a draft.

*(Le Journal).*

Summertime: unbreatheable air makes judges judge badly, makes workers work badly, paralyzes committees, assemblies, parliaments. Deficit everywhere.

mountain air

In Port Said, 104 above.

Man resists extremes of cold more easily than extremes of heat.

But then where is Utopia, where the temperature is 64.4°? We built a little house in Chile, in a paradise on the ocean shore: the air there is always at 64.4°. This spot is almost unique.

And why the devil do men insist on living in difficult or dangerous climates? I've no idea! But I can observe a worsening situation:

The variety of climates had forged races, cultures, customs, dress, and work methods suited to the obtaining conditions.

Alas! the machine age has, as it were, shuffled the cards – the age-old cards of the world. Since the machine age, the product of progress, has disturbed everything, couldn't it also give us the means to salvation?

Multiplicity of climates, play of seasons, a break with secular traditions – confusion, disorder, and the martyrdom of man.

I seek the remedy, I seek the constant; I find the human lung. With adaptability and intelligence, let's give the lung the constant which is the prerequisite of its functioning: *exact air.*

Let's manufacture exact air: filters, driers, humidifiers, disinfectors. Machines of childish simplicity.

Send exact air into men's lungs, at home, at the factory, at the office, at the club and the auditorium: ventilators, machines so often used, but so often used badly!

Let's give man the solar rays which will penetrate the all-glass façades. But it will be too hot in the summer and terribly cold in the winter! Let's create "neutralizing walls." (And "sun control.")

Oslo, Moscow, Berlin, Paris, Algiers, Port Said, Rio or Buenos Aires, the solution is the same; it is unique, since it answers the same needs: nourishing the human lung.

A "neutralizing wall" enveloping the building and sheltering it from the cold outside.

A circuit of exact air inside the building.

To achieve this, a bi-partite thermal power station: one which, in winter, in the cold countries, sends dry warm air, unfit for breathing, into the space between the two glass panes of the neutralizing wall; the other which produces "exact air" all year long, air freed of dust, disinfected, humidified exactly and brought to a constant temperature of about 64.4° Fahrenheit.

Of course the air which goes through the thermal power station is outdoor air, ordinary air. Let's not forget that prudent city officials cause the floods of water which supply the city's residents to go through a purifying station. They have done this because otherwise, danger hovered over the population, the ravages caused by epidemics.

All we need do is decide how big the thermal power station should be and build dwellings in groups of corresponding size.

Every minute 8 liters of exact air will *go through* the rooms and into the lungs of the city dweller.

\* \* \*

What distance has been covered between present customs and the recommended method?

This distance is a gaping void between today and tomorrow. We must leap over it. Today great masses, at work and at rest, are preyed upon by a fatal illness. This cannot go on! Tomorrow those masses *will breathe!* The transformation will be worked by inventions of architecture and city planning providing an answer to everything:

Lung, ear, and eye;

pure air, silence, and the joys of the heart ("basic pleasures");

elimination of dust, of mosquitoes and flies;

insulation from exterior noises;

reconstitution of a natural environment: *living air*, greenery and sky and the desired dose of sun on the skin; and, *in the lungs*, the living air of wide-open spaces.

The pressure of two storm-subject summer months is gone! The misery of cold in the home is over!

For all, for everyone.

The cities can be rescued from the threat of air warfare.

All that is needed to achieve this is to PUT THE GROUND TO USE.

\* \* \*

With "exact respiration," the municipal regulations of hygiene are unusable.

The home can become something else when supplied with "basic pleasures." We – we and the public – are ignorant of the material benefit of *living air* moving on a circuit through the home.

I place my man in a new environment: he is strong, smiling, healthy. Illness suffers a crushing defeat.

I make a drawing:

In front of every apartment, contiguous glass walls constitute the façade (A, A, A. . .). The home is behind it, in depth (L). The interior street leads to the door of each home (R). If the building complex has an east-west orientation, the homes are placed on either side of the interior street. If it is oriented north-south, homes will be placed only on the south.

This *depth-wise* disposition of each home is a departure from the traditional way of stringing out each home all along the façades, *T, T1, T2.*

Several ways (shown in section) of grouping around the interior street can be adopted. Either: homes 1 and 2 around an interior street. Or: homes *1a* and *3a* on either side of an interior street. With living air *Av* not even the least little nook is left stagnant.

Let's read the new solution: with *LT*, I express the most intense utilization of traditional methods. For 16 homes, for instance, the building would have a length of *mn*. With the new arrangement *LN*, the building will have a length of *m'n'*, or in other words, one third as much.

Whereupon the traditional city which extends over an area *VT* will extend only (new city) over *VN:* one third as great an area.

sea air

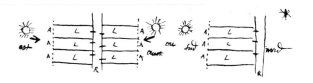

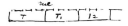

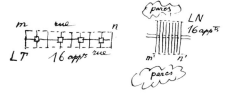

la ville étendue    la ville resserrée
Elle est Verte

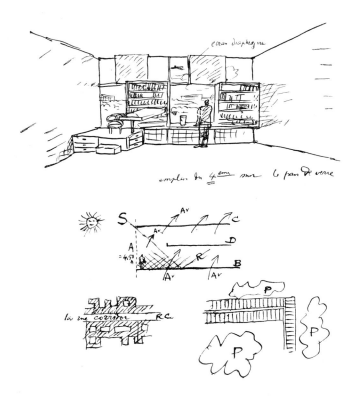

Here is the architecture:

the façade (triumph of modern techniques) is entirely of glass. It exists only to the south, the east, or the west: *never to the north!* (temperate regions of the northern hemisphere); for the southern hemisphere we have only to interpolate; and for the hot regions of the northern hemisphere, there could also be façades to the north, and the southern and western ones will be equipped with *brises-soleil*, or sun-breakers (interpolation in the southern hemisphere).

The glass façade will be *hermetic*. No opening! A glass prison? Stop and think: the view is right there, from the edge of the floor to the edge of the ceiling and from the lefthand wall to the righthand wall; the sight to be seen is in front of you, in the foreground (parks and open spaces), and not at the end of a trench-like street. Better still: go and see for yourself, wherever the glass-wall façade has already been carried out.

The glass wall is equipped with "diaphragms" for shutting out light at will. (Venetian blind-, shutter-, or screen-diaphragms already known to modern technique, or to be created in terms of a well-stated problem.)

We intend to make a big improvement (see below): an efficient height for the home, a new height, a height of 4.5 meters, divisible into twice 2.2 meters.

I draw the glass wall 4.5 meters high *(A)*, the floor *(B)*, the ceiling *(C)*; the subdivision at a height of 2.2 meters *(D)*. I bring in the sun *(S)*, I indicate its refraction *(R)*: the home is flooded by sunlight whose invigorating effects are undeniable but about whose exact action upon our organism and our surroundings we ordinary mortals are ignorant.

Finally, since exact air is mechanically distributed by pulsation, making it possible to bring life to limitless volumes of buildings, we can adopt a reasonable height of, say, 50 meters, for apartment houses. As a result of this vertical solution, open spaces, or parks (P), become available in front of the house and behind it.

A novel situation, in striking contrast with the universal custom of *corridor-streets* RC or *stagnant-courtyards* CS which gave rise to the *"cities of despair,"* all the cities of the first machine age.

\* \* \*

"Exact respiration," cornerstone of the urbanization of today's cities! The motivating idea (respiration) led to new architectural and city planning devices. But in addition to fierce opposition from every sort of technician, it was necessary to conquer the anxiety and uncertainty which often lie in wait on difficult days and plunge men into despondency. One day in 1931, our act of faith was vindicated: at the urging of Gustave Lyon (great scientist and great-hearted man), the laboratories of the Saint-Gobain Glass Factory undertake a series of decisive experiments. Exact respiration (neutralizing wall and internal circuit) is confirmed by experimentation! From then on, at the disposition of heating experts and technicians, there exist at Saint-Gobain two reports, 1931 and 1932, which relate the phases of these experiments.

The report begins:

"*After having studied the acoustical phenomena which occur in theatres and determined the methods by which their acoustics could be improved, Monsieur Gustave Lyon, vice-president of the Board of Directors of the Pleyel Company, continued his research by studying the ventilation and heating of these public halls. He was led to organizing this ventilation and this heating along a closed circuit, through the movement of a constant quantity of periodically purified, humidified and heated air. Whereupon, with a view to applying this process to all occupied premises (apartments, offices, assembly halls, etc.), he came to study a proposal made by Messrs. Le Corbusier and Jeanneret, architects, which consists of separating the ventilation circuit from the heating circuit for the sake of greater comfort. The first circuit would be realized inside the rooms and the second in the space between two fixed panes set into the window frame or even replacing the partition (which is then called "neutralizing wall") separating the room from the outside; in this space hot air would be made to circulate, to counter exchanges of heat between the inside and the outside. His first calculations having led M. Lyon to satisfactory results, he then made a summary verification on a small scale, on a double pane; this confirmed his calculations.*

"*Then these attempts were pursued by the engineers of the Saint-Gobain Company, on panes of ordinary dimensions, in a specially installed room . . .*"

"Glaces et Verres," 1932
*August-September issue*

The same issue of the review explained:

"*When the Soviet government entrusted Messrs. Le Corbusier and Jeanneret with the construction of the Cooperatives House (Centrosoyus) in Moscow, the two architects thought of using, instead of an ordinary heating system, a new process which they called the 'neutralizing wall' and which consisted of protecting the inside of buildings from any change in outside temperature by means of an air circuit introduced into the building's envelope, constituted by a double wall of glass, brick, or any other material.*

"*The Centrosoyus is composed of offices and work rooms for 3,500 employees. The buildings under construction have all glass façades. The double windows (common in Russia) or 'glass walls' which the architects have planned in this case can compensate for calorie loss to some extent. But no matter how powerful a traditional heating system may be (hot water or steam central heating), drafts are inevitable and comfort is thereby compromised, particularly since in Moscow the temperature may go down to 40° below zero. A traditional heating system equipped to handle such extremes wastes fuel and is, moreover, extremely expensive to install.*

"*As early as 1916, at an altitude of 1,000 meters, Le Corbusier had already conducted a conclusive first experiment with a 5m × 6m pane letting light into a living room.*

"*In 1927, in their League of Nations Palace project, the architects introduced a new heating conception for the large Assembly Hall.*

"*In 1929, after his successive trips to Moscow, the tropics and Argentina, Le Corbusier formulated the definitive statement of his theory of 'exact respiration,' including the building and equipping of 'neutralizing walls' and the installation of an indoor circuit of 'conditioned air' already accepted in America and in Paris, as a result of Gustave Lyon's work.*

"*But this theory, which upsets the heating industry's habits and the habitual notions of architecture, was not accepted in Moscow, where it aroused as much anxiety as it did interest.*

"neutralizing walls"
(St-Gobain experiments)

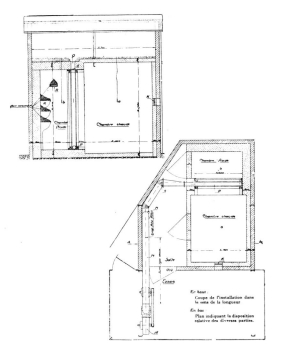

60% of the façade is covered
with stone . . . afterwards!

after this fine bit of work, all the
rest is made airtight with curtains!

the Cité de Refuge of the
Salvation Army in Paris:
hermetic building

modern apparatus for
making conditioned air

extract from the prospectus of an important
French firm of locksmiths:
industry exploits human stupidity!

*"Finally, in 1931, Messrs. Le Corbusier and Jeanneret based their plan for the Palace of the Soviets (crowning the Five-Year Plan) on the definitive technical and architectural version of their process. And they were able to establish the precise methods of a new economy of building valid in all latitudes and for all needs, by bringing together lighting, heating, ventilation, structure and esthetics.*

*"This, because meanwhile, the Saint-Gobain laboratories had backed them up twice with precise experiments carried out according to their data . . ."*

\* \* \*

And in spite of that . . . *sentiment* rebels, reason abdicates before . . . words! Here is the voice of Moscow:

*"Sometimes his imagination carries him (Le Corbusier) toward Soviet Moscow, and in that case, to a series of questions about the organization of collective living, he proposes solutions of vital interest. Sometimes he turns back toward Paris, and in his mind's eye he sees the nervewracked big-city dweller under present-day capitalism who must be rescued from noise and chaos, from the crowds and the stench of the streets: then he proposes the ineffectual measures of the most radical city planning.*

*"When we read H. G. Wells's descriptions of the city of the future, where the sky is replaced by a roof stretching over the entire city, where the sun is replaced by a constant and factitious light, where the artificial temperature is always even, we imagine a highly intelligent man, cloistered in his study, feeling the inevitable approach of a collectivist era and, in a rush of impotent wrath, striving to compromise the future by every means; all of Wells's works in which he tries to imagine the society of the future are pervaded by this tendency.*

*"But when we read a few passages from Le Corbusier's report, we come away with the impression that he consulted none other than Wells about the problems of urban organization.*

*"'The adoption of so-called "exact respiration," a system based on the production of what it has been agreed to call 'exact air,' should allow each resident to enjoy pure air and to maintain even temperature and humidity in his rooms. The system consists of this: within the building pure air circulates in a closed circuit at a steady temperature of 64.4°. As to the isothermicity of the translucid walls, experimental laboratories will be able in the near future to give us a new translucid material whose isothermal properties will be equal to that of the thickest wall. From then on, we will witness the inauguration of a new era: buildings will be altogether hermetically (Le Corbusier's italics. S. G.) closed, the use of air in the rooms being provided for by the closed air circuits mentioned above. Windows will no longer be needed on the façades; consequently neither dust nor flies nor mosquitoes will enter the houses; nor will noise. Experiments on the absorption of sound, especially in buildings of steel and reinforced cement, must be pursued!'"*

*"We repeat: it was our feeling that so morbid a fantasy could have been engendered only in the stale air of a solitary study, by an intellectual representative of bourgeois society who can see no other way of escaping the noise and stench of the big cities. It is therefore strange and startling to hear these same themes uttered by Le Corbusier, one of the foremost practical workers in the field of reconstruction of material culture."*

*Report by S. Gorny on my "answer to Moscow"*
*concerning the urbanization of that city.*
*October 25, 1930.*

What a pity that the Russians bring questions of political doctrine into the problem of the lung. More than any other country, they are faced with the weighty technical problem of efficient air, since their continental climate is more demanding than ours.

Being sure of my views as to indoor respiration, I am calmly going ahead with my research in the direction of the radiant city!

●

*RECAPITULATION:* All cities have fallen into a state of anarchy, following the irremediable development of a machine age. They need to be thoroughly straightened out. Today's regulations partly contradict today's housing requirements; it is forbidden, for instance, to avail oneself fully of the progress made by modern techniques. Moreover, these regulations impede any and all initiatives of sufficient scope to revolutionize the city's outdated organization.

Transformation of current regulations can occur only *when architects and city planners have made new proposals based on new techniques.* THERE MUST BE NEW ARCHITECTURAL AND CITY PLANNING PROPOSALS.

There is another imperative for these transformations: this is a new social situation brought on by the machine. Its effects and its consequences will be the concern of a forthcoming International Congress for Modern Architecture.

For today, and as far as this 1930 Brussels Congress is concerned, certain questions should call forth precise answers. These answers, supplied by technicians, physicists, doctors, etc., will shed new and decisive light on the future work of architects.

Anxious to answer the many questions raised by the effects of the machine age upon housing conditions, today's architects have already been led to make new proposals. The specialist's answers will bring them certitudes. *But even now, so as not to lose time, architects can suggest new and fundamental ideas for housing and city planning.*

Aside from the two other questionnaires drawn up by the Brussels Congress, this one will provide answers to the questions raised here:

AIR — SOUND — LIGHT

as well as diagrammatic architectural proposals *anticipating* the urgent changes which the machine age requires and an intelligent arrangement of social life within the big cities will soon dictate.

The members of the Brussels Congress *have called upon a large number of specialists.* The results of this appeal, concerned with *hygienic living conditions for the individual,* will guide architects and city planners in their projects.

Just one more word: The International Congresses for Modern Architecture were created for the purpose of solving the problems of contemporary architecture. The

Building in Paris: the "glass wall," bearer of daily joy, result of modern techniques.

# 5. AIR - SOUND - LIGHT

Internatioeal Congress for Modern Architecture
3rd Congress, Brussels, 1930

# INTERNATIONAL QUESTIONNAIRE

first congress, at LA SARRAZ in 1928, inaugurated this international organization. The second congress, at FRANKFURT in 1929, like that at Brussels in 1930, took up the problem of "the minimum dwelling." No genuine solution can be found to this problem of world-wide urgency unless and until certitudes have been gained *beforehand.*

a) The architectural revolution through modern techniques is now complete, in the more advanced circles (new materials, new processes, transformed layout, etc.).

b) We need to know in detail the reactions in the world of architecture and the discoveries in the fields of physics and chemistry.

c) We still need biological certitudes, to be supplied by doctors.

d) Finally, we need to know how the contemporary social situation tends to work out.

The present questionnaires should answer points b) and c).

QUESTIONNAIRE I. – For doctors: trees and greenery, exact constant temperature, noise, sunlight, artificial light.

QUESTIONNAIRE II. – For fitters of heating and cooling systems: (AIR).

QUESTIONNAIRE III. – For physicists: soundproofing, solar radiation, isothermics (even temperatures).

QUESTIONNAIRE IV. – For architects: new living cells; new grouping of cells; new layouts on the ground; new densities.

# QUESTIONNAIRE 1. — FOR DOCTORS*

## 1. QUALITIES OF OUTDOOR AIR

a) What is the exact influence upon the human organism of trees and lawns, of bodies of water (green surfaces, ponds, swimming pools, lakes)?
1. In summer.
2. In winter.

b) Do the exhaust fumes from cars which seem to destroy trees all the way down the street have a harmful effect upon the health of the inhabitants? What effects?

## 2.

"Exact air," replacing current heating or refrigeration practices, is prepared in thermal power stations attached to each residence group. Outdoor air is there made dust-free, disinfected, brought to the desired temperature, given a suitable degree of humidity. It is pure and ready to be consumed by the lung. It is distributed through a permanent circulation.

Question: Does "exact air" at a constant temperature of 64.4°(?) in summer as in winter, and constantly moving through the home, have a favorable effect upon the organism?

a) Should it remain at the same temperature all year long, or should it vary with the changes of season?

b) Should its degree of humidity be constant or modified according to seasons, climate and external conditions?

Examples: Paris, Rome, Moscow, Rio de Janeiro.

c) In regions of humid air (Buenos Aires, Santos, Rio, the colonial areas, etc.) will the presence of exact air indoors bring an improvement in the health of the inhabitants? Will it make for better working conditions?

d) The above questions a), b), c) imply the construction of *hermetic buildings*, that is: without any windows opening onto the exterior, and with an all-glass (transparent or translucent) façade.

Under these conditions, the inside of the building is completely protected from flies, mosquitoes, smoke and fumes, and dust. What do you think of this, in terms of private and public health?

## 3.

a) Do the clamor and intermittent noises from the street have any effect upon the organism of people who are subject to them while working or sleeping indoors? What effect?

b) Do noises from the immediate vicinity (radio, phonograph, people in apartments next door) have any repercussion upon the nervous system of other inhabitants?

c) In other words, does silence act in any way upon the organism? How?

## 4.

a) Is direct sunlight favorable to the organism? What effects? (Here we mean light that does not pass through glass.)

b) Does the absence of the sun's rays (northern exposure, or cast shadow) act upon the organism? How?

c) Does windowpane glass (plate or ordinary glass, or crude glass tile or glass brick) transform the effect of the sun's rays? How?

If so, do the sun's rays retain any useful properties?

d) There is a newly invented special windowpane which lets ultraviolet rays pass: is it desirable? Is it indispensable?

e) Since new techniques can lead to the construction of glass walls (all-glass façade), every room will have one wall that is entirely of transparent or translucent glass, letting in light.

Is the presence of such a glass wall desirable?

e) Does sunlight, when it passes exclusively through hermetic glass walls, penetrate sufficiently? Or must a device be created which would allow intermittent penetration of direct sunlight?

## 5.

a) Theoretically, is artificial light harmful to the organism? The question covers all places lighted solely by artificial means (offices, washrooms, etc.). In this case, is it harmful to spend a *limited* amount of time daily in such places?

b) Does the absence of sunlight indoors encourage the development of bacteria?

c) Are there certain sorts of artificial light which have more desirable effects than others? Which ones (aside from any consideration of cost)?

d) Concerning individual hygiene in the home, is there anything you would like to say about the use of certain sorts of artificial light?

* Certain of the following questions may seem childish. It was our wish here to evoke the structure of fundamental elements which constitute the human *environment.* If essential things had not been forgotten today, would we have let our cities sink into chaos?

# QUESTIONNAIRE 2. — FOR FITTERS OF HEATING AND COOLING SYSTEMS

### AIR

Program: It involves offices, luxury homes, average homes, working-class homes. All climates: Moscow, Paris, Berlin, Rio de Janeiro, Buenos Aires, New York, Tokyo, Rome, Madrid, etc. We wish to introduce the principle of "*exact respiration*" inside public buildings, offices or homes. "*Exact respiration*" is represented by a closed circuit of air with constant temperature and constant humidity. This air is dust-free and ozonified. All opening windows are eliminated with the possible exception of a few usefully disposed openings to act as portholes (so as to be able to lean out). So the buildings would be hermetic. The façades would be made of glass (clear panes, translucent glass, reinforced glass, glass brick or any other translucent material). If the façades are made of glass and if there is a permanent circuit of exact air moving through the house, then it will be possible to build rooms smaller than those required by official regulations and, consequently, to build smaller and more efficiently and cheaply.

Thereafter the question is this: can a human being live normally (the life of modern people), at his office and in his apartment, in a circuit of exact air?

a) Is *manufactured* exact air, distributed through a closed circuit, really *feasible*?

b) Should its temperature and degree of humidity vary during the seasons? What variations?

c) At what rate should the air in the circuit be totally or partially renewed with air taken in from outdoors?

d) What is the acceptable norm of "liters of air per minute" per person, according to the sort of premises involved:

1) Small rooms for roughly one, two or four people (office or apartment);

2) Larger premises for 50, 100, 200 people (banks, branch offices, workshops, etc.).

3) Meeting halls for 500, 1,000, 2,000 or more people.

e) Given this answer (capacity of the closed circuit, "air-minute-person"), what should be the normal output of an "exact air" factory? Once this normal output is established (maximum economy, determining the choice of machines (power) and the maximum length suitable for round-trip tubing), determine the normal volume of the buildings which can be grouped around a *model factory*.

1. Apartment buildings.
2. Offices.
3. Mills, workshops.

(So the question is to establish the norms for a model factory of exact air with optimum output, and the new unit of size for the group of buildings served by the factory.)

f) Once harmony has been established between the model factory and the size (in cubic meters) of the building to be supplied, what is the approximate *per person cost*, supposing an average calendar of temperature extremes but including the need to start up boilers in winter and cooling methods in summer?

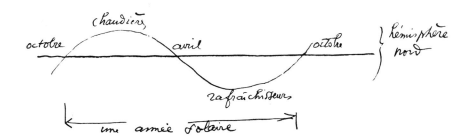

g) What is the per person cost, calculated normally in the same conditions, for the functioning of an ordinary central heating system?

1. Given the per person cost of the unit of exact temperature (warm in winter, cool in summer), can we suppose that this system of exact ventilation is applicable?

a. to the home.
b. to the office.
c. to workshops and factories.
d. Is there a saving over ordinary systems of central heating?

# QUESTIONNAIRE 3. — FOR PHYSICISTS

### SOUNDPROOFING
### SOLAR RADIATION
### ISOTHERMICS (EVEN TEMPERATURES)

A. Leaving aside the many so-called "insulating" materials put out by modern industry, can you formulate a simple law by which all transmission *of sound* from one room to another may be prevented, supposing that each of these rooms is in a big building made of steel or reinforced concrete (materials which are transmitters of sound)?

B. C. Can you indicate the translucent materials which could play a role equivalent to that of windowpane glass (without necessarily being transparent) for letting light indoors, but which could insulate the indoors against the effects of outdoor temperature *in a way comparable to the insulation afforded by a masonry wall?*

Or, in the case of ordinary windowpane glass, can you indicate a construction method leading to the same insulation effects?

If the materials which you indicate let sunlight through, more or less, can you indicate their coefficient of penetration by the sun's rays?

The answer may deal not only with existing materials but also with materials to be modified or created.

If we are to suppose that through radiation the sun's rays considerably heat the air indoors, can you recommend methods which neutralize the effects of this radiation (this concerns plate-glass windows in the summer)?

up by the best methods, what is the new population density which results for residential neighborhoods? (Paris complains of having 800 inhabitants per hectare in certain overpopulated districts; Berlin has 400; London boasts of having only 150. But should modern urbanization tend to reduce or, on the contrary, to increase population density?)

\* \* \*

# QUESTIONNAIRE 4. — FOR ARCHITECTS

This questionnaire does not take into account any presently enforced regulation. Its aim is to propose new architectural methods which will vitally affect the very way in which cities are built; the answers will cause the current regulations concerning building cities and dwellings to be modified.

On the basis of city planning, we can suppose, to begin with, that the construction of apartment buildings today relies upon outdated traditions. The dwelling place becomes a huge complex serviced by a vertical system of elevators run by specialized elevator operators.

This questionnaire, one of three drawn up during the Brussels Congress, was not received with favor by the delegates. They felt it was too much "up in the clouds."

Nonetheless, I managed to have it adopted by the Congress and was authorized to send it, in the name of the Congresses, to the persons concerned.

Until now, unfortunately, my everday occupations had prevented me from attempting its distribution.

*By inserting it now, I can hope that here and there it will reach the specialists called upon to answer it. And I hope that these responses will "snowball" into a great number of answers.*

At any rate, five years have gone by and significant experiments have already been completed.

a) How far apart should we space the vertical elevator shafts serving the living cells?

b) What is the number of floors you consider conducive to good mechanical and architectural functioning in the construction of apartment buildings?

c) What is the maximum distance you think a resident of any corridor in an apartment building should have to cover *between the elevator and the door of his apartment?*

d) Supposing that the principle of communal services expands more and more (nurseries, gymnasiums for daily physical culture sessions, food supplies, laundry – all services which will facilitate the running of the home and proportion-

ately reduce the real volume of apartments), what is the minimum living area which you would allot *to each resident?*

e) With a plan allowing maximum exposure to the sun and considering the needs both of architecture and of traffic (cars should never park along a street but only in lots linked to the streets and placed at the foot of the elevator systems), what is the most convenient schematic shape for the housing complex? The solution should comprise, insofar as possible: the shortest approach road, the greatest area of greenery, and the shortest distance to be covered on foot inside or outside the buildings.

f) Considering the above answers, and on the basis of one hectare of area built

**?**

Address it to:

M. LE CORBUSIER
35, rue de Sèvres
PARIS 6e

Answer this Questionnaire.
Share your observations,
your experience, your theories.

# 6. AN EFFICIENT HEIGHT FOR THE HOME

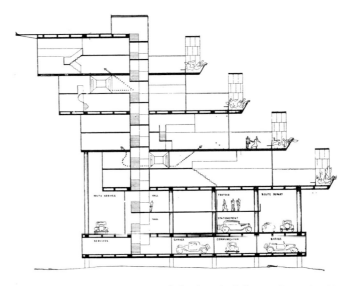

One of the four buildings, of 300 families each, on the Oued-Ouchaïa plot in Algiers. Devices boldly conceived in terms of the sun. An efficient height for the home revolutionizes the structural economy.

Here we touch on one of the critical points of harmony: first of all, the *pleasing* height of the box which serves as our shelter. Next comes the question of *useful* height. A height which is pleasing, first of all, to our human gestures: the height of a lair: clearly a biological function. Then the useful height, which determines the volume of air to be taken into our lungs and the quantity of light streaming in through the façades; a height which is actually determined by the condition of techniques. Two techniques: a) that of ventilation; b) that of means of construction (statics and resistance of the materials used).

Let's get this question of usefulness out of the way: the situation is altogether new, revolutionary, because of the effect of modern techniques.

1° Systems of conditioned air, living air, new air, of punctual and exact respiration, regardless of the height of the home, mean that the human lung is sure of being nourished with a perfection unheard of until now, both qualitatively and quantitatively.

2° The building's free framework provides a free façade. As a result, one of the four walls of every room is transformed into a glass surface admitting a stream of light under conditions unknown until now.

Let's look at the past: for the construction of (medieval) timbered houses – a construction similar to that using iron or reinforced concrete (though on a lesser scale of resistance) – an economic and efficient height had *naturally* been adopted: 2.20 meters. In the course of my continuous travels, I have observed how this rule has held good down through the centuries; natural organizations were everywhere dominant: the peasant's house. Examples remain to bear witness: the chalets of Bavaria or the Tyrol; Swiss or Scandinavian chalets; Gothic or Renaissance wooden houses in Rouen, Strasbourg, Zurich, Toggenbourg; the Russian isba, etc...

But I observed something else when, convinced that it was imperative to come back

51

## "CIAM"

to an efficient height for our contemporary home, I suggested "villa-buildings" (Salon d'Automne, 1922). This is what had caught my attention: standing on the sidewalk of a Parisian street, thinking that we would have to build tall houses (50 meters) in order to recuperate the ground devoted to traffic and to our sentimental needs (open space, sky and trees), I felt that the holes formed by opened windows one next to the other every 2.50 meters made up a network, a webbing, a mesh that was much too tight to be able to extend all the way up the great height of future buildings. Already, instinctively, in the 1922 Ozenfant house, we had made a main room 4.50 meters high, which at the back was divided into two heights of 2.20 meters. Already, in 1923, the hall and the living room of the La Roche villa had been partially subdivided into half-heights of 2.10 meters. These architectural results were surprising: you entered a scale agreeable to the human shoulders. Then I had noticed that certain Paris streets built after 1800 had shops 4.50 meters high and divided, in the back, into twice 2.20 meters. So much confirmation, so much inducement. This time we feel the question, deeply and emphatically. We carry out the "*Esprit Nouveau*" stand at the International Decorative Arts Exhibition in 1925: a living cell. It is a glass-walled room of double height which, at the back, is subdivided into two half-heights. I remembered then that in 1919 I had designed the "Citrohan" house – a model for mass production. It was already of that type. From then we are obsessed with carrying out this type of home, or cell, "for real." The desired opportunities slip out of our grasp each time; finally, here comes the *Werkbund's* exhibit in Stuttgart, the Weissenhof buildings. There we build the "Citrohan" house (1927). The Cook house in Boulogne, in 1925-26, had offered a brilliant demonstration of the principle.

The idea had materialized with proofs verified everywhere in the past and in folklore, proofs accumulated in our professional experience.

From then on, our city planning projects take on certainty. The living cell-unit is feasible, handsome, economic, efficient. The city can be raised up high, in conditions of brilliant cellular organization.

In 1933 the *Congress for Modern Architecture* is held in Greece; we travel through the Islands, the Cyclades. Here the profound life of past millenia has remained intact; the wheel does not yet exist. Perhaps it never will exist, the topography is so rough. We discover the eternal houses, living houses, houses of today which go far back in history and whose plan and section are exactly what we have been thinking of for a decade. Here in the bosom of human measure, here in Greece, on this soil redolent of decency, intimacy, well being, of what is rational forever guided by the joy of living, we find *measurements on the human scale*.

\* \* \*

The real question is here one of *harmony*. Reader, had it occured to you that a figure (that two figures), representing the city ordinances about the maximum height of the home, could hem in your happiness? The *omnipotence of harmony*, of this adjustment to our human dimensions, of this setting which shelters us, *resides in the figure which determines the height of the home*.

\* \* \*

Municipal regulations, because they follow events in the life of a city (means of construction, form taken by the ownership of land, layout of blocks built between streets, overcrowding in the home, etc.), consecrate an existing state of affairs, or one which has existed.

But one day, when enough events have taken place, the regulations become obsolete, paralyzing the city's ever-changing signs of life. Then the time has come to change the regulations.

* * *

We are calling for a new, efficient height for the home.

We base our plea on a synthesis of new technical possibilities and of the just and unquestionable claims of human biology and human psychology, thus:

a) Flood the home with the sun's rays. The glass wall of the façade takes up one entire side of the home. If we adopt 4.50 meters as the height of the home, the glass wall will be of the same height; consequently, the sun's rays will penetrate far inside, very deep into the home. So, we can make the home deep; so, a home that is relatively narrow. As a result, a good many homes can be placed along the façade: the street will be shorter and the city more compact. Behind this glass wall 4.50 meters high will stretch the "room to live in," that vast essential area where the human animal can feel at ease – adequate room, circulation, movement. The minimum home, as it has spread so tremendously these past few years in Germany, in Czechoslovakia, in Poland, in Russia, is no longer a place to live in: it is a cage. It is harmful, it is inhuman, it imprisons life within minimum limits, life that needs room. The *maximum* living room must be created.

b) Behind the hermetic glass wall (with portholes that can be opened occasionally), we introduce "exact respiration," living air, new air. From then on the city ordinances no longer need stipulate "the cubic content needed for good ventilation." Ventilation, by its very nature, is complete in no matter what cubic content, even the smallest.

c) We emphasize a conquest of modern times: electric light. We raise the question! Must we detest artificial light, in certain limited places, and perpetuate today's inextricable situation? Must we stubbornly, stupidly shut our eyes to the fact that, six months of the year, we live much of the day in artificial light? Or, on the contrary, having recognized that properly installed electricity conveniently bathes certain places in light, will we agree to get washed and shaved, for instance, by electric light (which we are constantly doing anyhow on winter mornings, afternoons and evenings, in rooms whose windows give onto the street)? Will we agree to a kitchen flooded with properly conditioned electric light when already, what with the building lots approved by unenlightened regulations, our kitchen must be lighted this way in spite of the window futilely open – onto a courtyard's well of shadow? Will we agree that whereas present regulations say that toilets must be ventilated by a window which remains obstinately shut a good part of the year, it would be immeasurably better to connect them to an "artificial" system of forced ventilation, etc., etc...?

"Artificial!" This word has the gift of upsetting sensitive souls. When I was young and I designed my first house (I was 18), on the builder's contracts I crossed out the

In Vézelay, 16th century and modern times and modern people
(height of 2.20 meters)

Why this astonishing freedom?

Why this sweeping generosity,

... and this intimacy?

word *artificial*, applied to the cements which were to be used in building; I wrote in *natural: natural* cement, and not artificial cement. It was explained to me that natural cement was very risky, that therefore it was dangerous to use it in cases where calculations should be justified by a punctual resistance of the materials employed; I was further told that science had created artificial cements, that is: compensated cements, all of whose elements conformed to the most favorable conditions, where all flaws were artificially eliminated. Later, I realized that drinking water was "artificial," that wines were "artificial," that different sorts of flour were "artificial." That meat and fish were kept under "artificial" conditions (freezers). Etc., etc. And I came to understand that the root of this word was ART, which designates the best way of doing things, that is: "the application of knowledge to the realization of a conception" (dictionary definition). And that in this way, man, through his creations, brought himself into harmony with the perfections, the constants of nature.

d) We recognize that certain events of daily life, being better lighted and better ventilated than ever before, can take place in a very limited space: everything that includes immobility. We multiply the number of these limited spaces and the benefit derived from them by cutting in two our height of 4.50 meters.

2.20 meters? But that is the height given to all living space aboard an ocean liner, be it a cabin or a luxury suite. Still another useful verification!

I conclude: if we agree to the reduced height of 2.20 meters for the accomplishment of certain domestic functions, we can give every man rich or poor a living room 4.50 meters high, splendid and magnificent, dignified, encouraging and beneficial: modern man will have ceased to be a beast in a cage!

\* \* \*

Let's take advantage of the chance that was offered us in Burgundy to verify once more the architectural splendor of the new efficient height of the home: 4.50 meters – a verification which, coming this time from feeling and not from reason alone, suddenly, and owing to exceptional circumstances, links the most venerable past to the most active present.

It was in Vézelay, where Saint Bernard preached the second crusade. A majestic site: at the tip of a spur jutting from deep in the hollow of the valley, the basilica, notable achievement of Romanesque art. A street climbs up to it. On either side of the street, houses as old as time, whose windows open onto distant horizons.

The architect Jean Badovici, director of *L'Architecture Vivante*, has bought up some of these crumbling houses. He brings in the modern spirit. Here is his own home: an old, old house with an oak-beamed ceiling. The height between stories is 2.20 meters. He breaks through one floor; in this way he connects two stories; he turns them into a modern living unit. Never mind archeology! He settles in with the instruments of the present day.

A few of us are gathered there, living and active beings of today: Fernand Léger, the painter; Guegen and Bonheur, poets; Zervos, director of *Cahier d'Art;* Ghyka, painter. We are in a lair for men. On our shoulders are ceilings that suit us. Our eyes find varied and contrasted prospects; our steps have a lively movement. Everything is minute, but everything is big. It is a jewel-box on the human scale. It is a place of well-being, of calm and diversity, of measure and proportion, of thoroughly human dimensions. Harmony. All of us unanimous in recognizing and proclaiming this.

* * *

We ask that city ordinances be changed to allow an efficient height for the home: 4.50 meters, divisible into twice 2.20 meters.

●

Because a proper human scale (that which has the true dimension of our gestures) has conditioned each thing. There is no longer old or modern. There is what is permanent: the proper measure.

### 7. ARTIFICIAL SITES

an enlightening term:
"artificial building sites"

To build houses, you must have sites. Are they natural sites? Not at all: they are immediately *artificialized*. This means that the natural ground is limited to but one function: withstand the strains, the weight of the structure (law of gravity). Once this is done, we say "goodbye" to the natural site, for it is *the enemy of man*. A home on the ground (beaten earth) is frightfully unhealthful; you no longer find it anywhere but in

Brittany. Many savages have immediately created artificial sites (a floor raised above the ground) to avoid floods or scorpions, etc... The natural ground is the dispenser of rhumatisms and tuberculosis. France is perhaps the only so-called "civilized" country which still allows a parquet or tile flooring to be laid directly on the natural ground. Everywhere else a gap of 60 centimeters is required between the ground and the bottom floor.

This triple sketch perfectly expresses the theory of "*artificial sites*" which is the means to countless solutions for the urbanization of today's cities.

But oh! sloth of the spirit, oh! fear of reality! You would think sometimes that man had remained more of a scorpion than a spirit, inertia keeps him so flattened to the ground. The notion of artificial sites becomes productive, evident, demonstrable, particularly in risky and apparently insoluble cases, like Algiers or Stockholm, Montevideo or Sao Paolo, wherever the topography seems to baffle every initiative; like Rio de Janeiro or Zurich where occupation of available ground has reached saturation point. But also, like Buenos Aires or Paris, where the cancer of inhuman distances preys upon the city's vital functions.

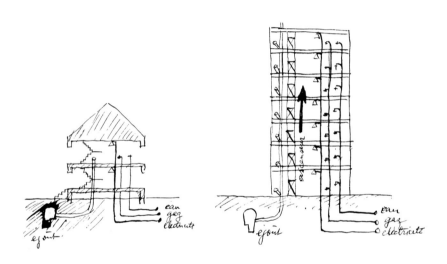

Let's give the sloth of the spirit another jolt:

I build my little villa in the suburbs.

I have built three artificial sites. I reach them on foot, by a stairway. I supply these artificial sites with water (for my bathtub, my washstand, my sink and my radiators), with gas (for my water heater and my stove); with electricity to give me light, etc...

And I send my refuse down the drain, into the sewer.

But the city dwellers do better than that: they erect apartment buildings six stories high!

They place six artificial sites one above the other. And they equip them with modern utilities: water, gas, electricity; and drains.

Ladies and gentlemen, organized society has been making artificial sites from the beginning!

And I am called a madman because I plan to carry this tradition further by increasing the number of these superimposed and equipped artificial sites, because modern techniques make it possible to perch 20 or 30 or 50 artificial sites on top of one another, a thing which until now was not feasible (stone walls and wooden floors).

But I can do still more: I can provide these artificial sites with rational circuits for getting about, indoors and outdoors. And thereby, bring happiness (the "basic pleasures") to the city's inhabitants. Never will the city fathers forgive me for that!

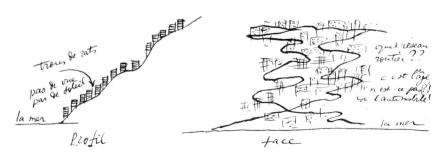

Algiers today

This for Algiers,

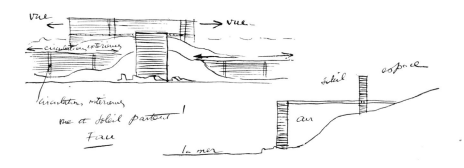

and that for Stockholm

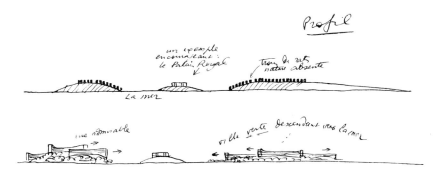

For Rio de Janeiro, where the ground available between the jagged mountain spurs is entirely occupied, artificial sites step in miraculously, without bothering anyone – a horn of plenty spilling its inestimable splendors from bay to bay and moreover, spilling millions, billions into the community coffers.

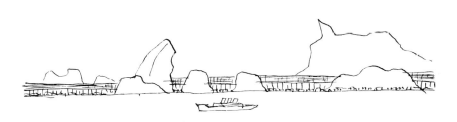

And for Paris or Antwerp, the "green city" and its basic pleasures.

These basic pleasures are dreams come true – the chimerical dreams of ordinary garden cities. Here then are "artificial" garden cities, *efficient* ones: instead of *horizontal garden cities*, we have created *vertical garden cities*. The vertical solution has all the advantages.

And instantly, the events of urban life are organized: traffic problems are solved; "communal services" eliminate waste and bring the urgently needed benefits of emancipation to the running of each home.

vestige of Roman times. Will this aqueduct, on a scale so much larger than that of the houses, destroy the site? Of course not! The aqueduct has created the site!

Here I certainly have the right to insert this memo on Algiers (1932) . . . which the city's authorities did not heed at all:

"*URBANIZATION OF THE CITY OF ALGIERS:*
"Valorization of the ground: an example:

"We have adopted the principle of replacing the construction of horizontally extended garden cities by the construction of '*vertical garden cities.*' The horizontally extended garden city is a financial disaster for the community; the '*vertical garden city*' *yields an enormous profit for the community and for the municipality* (if the latter agrees to order that the necessary work be done) . . .

"*ALGIERS:* There is an almost inaccessible site, available and free of buildings, located in the heart of the city: the hills of Fort-l'Empereur (elevation roughly 150 to 220 meters). It is impossible to reach these sites by streets with a normal incline of 5 to 10%, or to arrive conveniently in front of apartment houses which would have to be built on plots shaped by the zigzagging of these streets. Using modern techniques, we can reach these sites very easily, by approaching them from above, by means of a horizontal highway, elevation 150 meters. With room to house 220,000 people, these sites could be fixed up so as to afford exceptional comfort, "super-comfort" (see the plan). The prerequisite is to underwrite the preliminary expenditure for the horizontal viaduct, elevation 150 meters.

"The following figures are conclusive: in horizontally extended garden cities, for the average family (6 persons) you count, let's say, 300 m² of land at 75 Francs per m², or 22,500 Francs. So housing 220,000 people means:

$$\frac{220,000}{6} = 36,000 \text{ families.}$$

36,000 families (of 6 persons) × 22,500 Francs of land = 810,000,000 Francs.

*CONCLUSION:* If it is made valuable by a convenient approach (the most marvelous approach that Algiers could dream of), the presently sterile and therefore worthless land at Fort-l'Empereur could be worth 810,000,000 Francs. The authorities who launch this operation will be able in this way to pay for the approach viaduct and wind up the operation with a profit.

Another example of valorization of the ground:

a) *Horizontal garden cities.* The indispensable elements of each living unit are: the flooring of the ground floor *with foundations*, an intermediate flooring, a *waterproof* ceiling. The average cost of these three elements is 450 Francs per m².

b) *Vertical garden cities.* Concerning the Algiers project, let's consider the big highway, elevation 100 meters, linking Saint-Eugène and Hussein-Dey. It provides for lower-level traffic on the ground beneath the pilotis of the viaduct; at its summit (elevation 100 meters) it has a model highway 24 meters wide, with a floor of garages beneath. The rest of the viaduct is formed by flooring which is superimposed every 4.50 meters and which actually constitutes so many layers of superimposed floors of vertical garden cities. These floorings carry out what we had in the first case (a), that is: a floor with foundations and a waterproof ceiling with optional provision for an intermediate flooring.

What is the cost price of this standard element of vertical garden cities? Calculations give us this answer: with the traffic beneath the pilotis PAID FOR AND THE UPPER HIGHWAY ALSO PAID FOR, the square meter of flooring costs 320 Francs. This is the flooring of houses in superimposed garden cities. So the square meter of housing in a superimposed garden city means a saving of 130 Fr over the cost of each square meter in a horizontal garden city.

All along the viaduct proposed here, there are 4,500,000 m² of newly created superimposed sites; 4,500,000 m², each yielding 120 Fr profit give the community 540,000,000 Fr. *Such is the saving which can be realized through an urbanization based on the vertical garden city principle*, as opposed to the horizontal garden city.

But to these advantages must be added the saving which is henceforth made possible because the highway replaces a subway (300,000,000 Fr.).

The final item of *profit is that made by renting out an entire floor of garages* placed beneath the highway.
Such is the profit to be realized through the viaduct, which can shelter 180,000 people. That's not all.
*There remains another saving*, hence another advantage of the viaduct system: the overall cost of building *all of the roads and approach streets* (with all their upkeep, water, gas, electricity installations) *which would have to be built for horizontal garden cities with a capacity of 180,000 people;* this represents a vast road network.

But let's note here that the dwellings built in the viaduct (detailed studies have been made with strictest care) fulfill optimum conditions of inhabitability for the city of Algiers, that is: an admirable view of the sea or of the hills; immediate communication with the upper highway (elevation 100 meters) and with the lower highway beneath the pilotis: the viaduct dwellings are located precisely where most high-speed traffic is.

Here, one question: Assuming that the highway (elevation 100 meters) should be built all at one time but that the intermediate floors of the vertical garden cities can be built later and arranged as housing units as need requires over the years, can the necessary financing for the construction of the viaduct be arranged if, as security, there is a contract with the municipality or the government?

Forecasts are based on the possibility of having, in twenty years' time, to house a working-class population of 180,000 with optimum comfort, and 220,000 other people in extra-comfortable conditons on the Fort-l'Empereur sites.

There is a multitude of arguments, just as valid, for urbanization of cities in a modern way, based on rational use of modern techniques.

This, for instance:

Opportune use of the "Glass wall façade"
     of the "Open plan inside"
     of "Exact Respiration"

By applying these new techniques, we can *triple the normal* depth of the apartments, letting in daylight on both sides of the building (access to the apartments by an "interior street"). Housing blocks will be built one third as long.

Result: the street will be one third as long,
    the city will extend only one third as far.

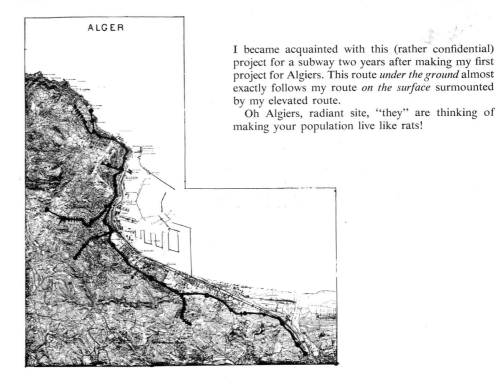

I became acquainted with this (rather confidential) project for a subway two years after making my first project for Algiers. This route *under the ground* almost exactly follows my route *on the surface* surmounted by my elevated route.

Oh Algiers, radiant site, "they" are thinking of making your population live like rats!

Project for a subway
(Administration's proposal)

This, in the middle of the ocean, on a ship: tennis, a swimming pool, sunbathing, conversation and amusement: Ships are 22 to 27 meters wide.
So are the buildings of the Radiant City. On the whole expanse of the city, above the sea of trees, new ground would be gained in this way.

Time saved, economy of 2/3 on means of transportation, of road construction and maintenance, etc.

Here we set the play of consequences in motion; everything is connected. Modern times are coming!

●

... And in spite of everything, I believe "*that the day will come!*..."

Here's something to reassure us! We are promised new joys!

The magazines and newspapers are full of pictures and descriptions. And the poison gas factories work to build up huge stocks. The chiefs of staff announce:

"*Not one existing city will be spared: fire, collapse, death by gas. Nothingness! the city razed to the ground!*"

*Before* 1914 they assured us that a war with modern weapons would be so horrible that never would anyone dare to unleash it.

Once it was unleashed, wise men everywhere wrote: "Modern war (mammoth matériel) is a *war of decision*. The war will last 3 months."

And they stipulated: "The devastated areas should be rebuilt in 3 months."

So that in the spring of 1915, the sun would shine softly once again on fresh countryside and brand-new towns and cities.

There are leaders who see the future this way.

Five years of war. Fifteen years of panic, crises, disasters and despair. The twentieth year, there is revolution everywhere: all that remains is to inter an expiring civilization and buy more picks and shovels and brooms to demolish, then sweep away the debris.

Clean up and build.

Build the modern era. Raise up the machine-age civilization. See, understand, decide, act.

Will FEAR (the air war) be the providential key which, once wound up, will start the necessary action?

\* \* \*

The facts of the case are unequivocal: here are the present-day cities.

Where are the inhabitants? They are dead! They didn't even have time to flee, for the attack was unpredictable.

What must be done, to hold out against war from the air?

Here is the gist of the unexpected verdict [1] made known by the chiefs of staff:

"Given the present state of city planning, only those cities which are conceived along the lines of the Radiant City are capable of emerging victoriously from an air war.

"Because in the Radiant City, 100% of the ground is free and only 5% to 12% of the surface has buildings on it; now, those buildings are 'on pilotis,' which means that air circulates, that there is continuous space, that the wind will be able to dissipate the gas.

[1] Read: *Le Danger Aérien et l'Avenir du Pays*, by Lt. Col. Paul Vauthier, Paris, 1930; and *Bautechnischer Luftschutz*, by Dip. Ing. Hans Schoszberger, Berlin, 1934.

# WHAT ABOUT AIR WAR?

60

"Apartment buildings in the Radiant City are 50 meters high; thus a number of floors are situated above the gaseous mass; the inhabitants will take refuge on the upper floors and no longer in cellars made specially impervious to gas. Besides these *casemate installations do not exist.* And how could they be installed in sufficient numbers to shelter the population of a big city? Moreover: if gas should happen to infiltrate into the underground shelter . . . then it becomes a tomb!

"Densely populated buildings covering only 5% to 12% of the city's surface can, with a normal expenditure, be equipped with bomb-resistant armored platforms (roofing); and on the last floor there can be shock-absorbing devices to take care of falling projectiles.

"Armor-plating as roof protection is inconceivable in ordinary cities with low population density and with more than 50% of the ground covered by buildings. Traditional and current means of urbanization (corridor-streets, countless courtyards) are ideally vulnerable to air attacks: reservoirs of (stagnant) gas, perfect target for every bomb; fire, and nothing to stop the spread of fire.

"In the Radiant City type of city, the danger of fire is eliminated; the scattered arrangement of the buildings considerably limits the effectiveness of bombs; damage is limited solely to the places which suffer a direct hit.

"Finally, everywhere in the Radiant (green) City, 88% of which is made up of parks, there are open-air swimming pools; hydrants can direct this water in streams to smother the layers of gas."

I add: the so-called "exact respiration" plants, widely spaced, very well sheltered and almost invulnerable, can effectively parry gas warfare.

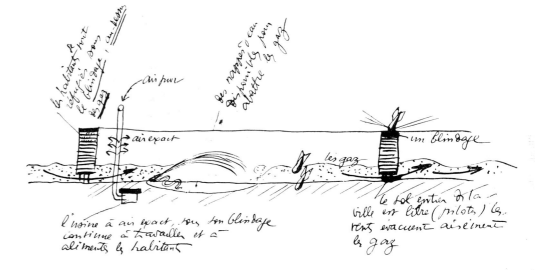

\* \* \*

By placing this discussion of air war at this point in the book, we have anticipated a little, for it takes into account plans which will not be described until further on.

Yet, like a sinister apotheosis, it crowns these chapters devoted to *Modern Techniques.* The evocation of its frightful reality thrusts us dramatically into MODERN TIMES.

Through the evocation of horror, attention must be attracted, public opinion mobilized at last, the power of decision torn from negligent city fathers; the obscenity and infamy of war must become the pretext for rallying enterprising souls and overthrowing secular customs, and be the herald of the Radiant City.

•

. . . life!

# 3<sup>rd</sup> PART: THE NEW AGE.

1. LEISURE, AN IMMINENT THREAT.
2. THE SOLUTION TO A CRISIS: HEAVY INDUSTRY MUST TAKE OVER ARCHITECTURE.
3. WHERE IS THE MONEY TO COME FROM?
4. LAWS.
5. THE BASIC PLEASURES.

# 1. LEISURE

Carotte blanche
des Vosges

Carotte rouge longue
obtuse sans·cœur

White Vosges
carrot

Round-ended
red carrot

Growing carrots and turnips is not a means of entertainment. It is a job. Modern man, tired from his work in an office or factory, is not going to rest himself by turning to backbreaking agricultural work.

That's romanticism!
(as honest men admit)

As soon as production is reorganized, the leisure time made available by the machine age will suddenly emerge as a social danger: an imminent threat.

Inevitably, and in a short space of time, the increased introduction of mechanization will mean extra hours in everyone's life unoccupied by work. If the workers' hours of daily obeisance to their machines are reduced to five or six, and if (as we hope) we succeed by means of a methodical and progressive overhaul of the present urban situation in clearing away the accumulated anomalies cluttering our cities as they stand, then we shall be left with a number of free, vacant hours every day. How many hours? A great many. If we add eight hours of sleep to the five required for work, we are still left with eleven unoccupied hours!

This is one of the most disturbing problems facing contemporary sociology.

The necessity for transforming this still vague notion of "leisure time" as quickly as possible into a disciplined function is therefore immediately evident. We cannot leave millions of men, women and young people to spend seven or eight hours a day in the streets.

So that we are faced with the extremely urgent task of creating living quarters in our cities that are capable not only of *containing* the people that live in them, but also, and above all, of retaining them.

Even when this task has been accomplished, however, the gap will remain no less gaping than before. It is at this point that a means must be found to enable contemporary society to haul itself up out of the hell or the purgatory of the first machine age: recovering his dignity, which is still being trampled underfoot today, modern man will be able to "*live*" at last, by which I mean to salvage his body, attain a harmonious existence within the family group, draw comfort from absorbing activities of the mind, and take part at last in communal activities, in communal, disinterested projects, in projects no longer implacably subjected to the laws of money.

Body, family, studies, meditation, collective activities, all these are vast functions requiring buildings and sites: architecture and city planning.

It is for this reason that we, the professionals in these matters, have a duty to study the vital questions of the day, even though they may have no direct bearing upon the work we actually have in hand.

\* \* \*

The sun governs our lives by determining the rhythm of our activities: a 24-hour cycle.

This means, to put it quite simply, that these new functions now appearing on the social horizon will have to be performed in the immediate proximity of people's homes, since the distance that they can travel is necessarily limited, on the one hand by *time*, and on the other by each individual's degree of resistance to fatigue and his physical capacity. The notion that it would be possible to equip sites outside our cities suitable for these new functions of the approaching machine age is therefore illusory. The human wear and tear involved will render all such ill-considered attempts valueless. We cannot expect each and every member of the population to maintain his or her soul in a permanent state of heroism. The functions we are discussing are all intimately connected with the home: they are an extension of it. The home and its extensions are circumscribed by a limitation that it is impossible to stretch beyond a certain point: distance.

Having reached a clear awareness of these things, there came a day when I expressed my conclusions in the following formula: *sport should be a daily matter and* IT SHOULD TAKE PLACE DIRECTLY OUTSIDE THE HOUSES. A hair-raising proposition? A wager? It seemed so at the time. And yet, with that idea firmly screwed inside one's skull, it was possible to search, to keep on searching . . . and to find an answer. A few years later, after many studies based on these very necessities, I arrived at the idea of cities of the "Radiant City" type. The sportsgrounds were directly outside the houses.

What is sport? Daily, disciplined, regular physical activity. A food as indispensable as bread itself. Everyone – men, women, children – at any age and on every day of the year, can "take off his jacket" when he gets home, go down in front of the building where he lives and play a game of basketball, of tennis, of soccer; can join his comrades in the races, the watersports, the walks that, given the immense, indeed the limitless areas of space available, will revivify their lungs, improve their circulation, strengthen their muscles, and fill them with joy and optimism. For such are the fruits of sport or physical training. And what a gulf there is between the valid promise of such a city and the specious nature of sport today.

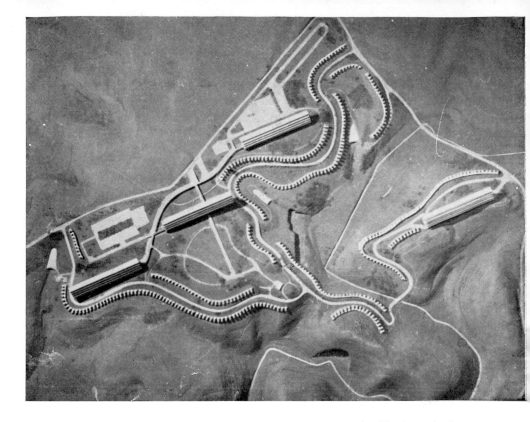

Algiers, estate of Bahradjah, 108 hectares of hills and valleys. 1800 families housed: the 108 hectares remaining unencumbered: walks and sports facilities provided.

I will explain what I mean: the notion of "sport" has penetrated deeply into the contemporary consciousness; it contains a diversity of elements all of which are well worth our interest: the element of aggression first of all, then that of performance, of competition; strength, decision, flexibility and speed; the element of individual contribution as well as that of teamwork; a discipline freely accepted by the individual. So many profoundly human values that emerged at the very moment when the human animal was being crushed, subjugated, torn apart, denatured by its subjection to the machine: everything that lies at the very heart of human nature, the primordial level of man's being, had been trampled on.

But alas, the cities we now have are unable to provide any but the most superficial of satisfactions. We have built *stadiums*, arenas in which games are provided for the populace, – ten, twenty, thirty consummate athletes performing for five, ten, twenty thousand paying, passive spectators who remain in one spot, yelling and stamping, for hour after hour on concrete benches. Sport as we know it today is the cause of innumerable illnesses contracted from exposure to sun, rain or cold by these crowds who have assembled to live a vicarious dream of valor.

A transition. We must look upon the sports stadium as a transition.

Modern city planning will accomplish the miracle of putting the crowds themselves on the playing field.

\* \* \*

Family life ought to develop in the joy of sunlight and space.

There are some people who attempt to delude themselves as to the degree to which our lives can be made bearable by fantasies. Our *liberty* having been proclaimed by various decrees or constitutions, these people allow their minds to be lulled by a fictitious belief, a salutary one of course, that all our undertakings, our actions and our gestures (as opposed to those of the animals, plants or minerals that constitute the remainder of the tangible universe of which we are part) make up an infinite variety of freely chosen activities and voluntarily selected occupations.

Looked at with a more realistic eye, however, men's lives are spent mainly in a daily humdrum of routine: and we should be bitterly and dangerously shaken were we able to see clearly to what an extent this is so. There are only a few of us who are concerned with this matter. They are the ones who know how to "read." How to read situations. Let them judge then, if they are also wise, how far these realities that appear so subtle and difficult to grasp, how far this humdrum daily life is efficient and how far deficient.

For that life is the inevitable product of past decisions and dispositions. And it is either *efficient* or it is *deficient!*

Past decisions and dispositions. Taken by whom? Oh, for the most part simply by the line of least resistance, by the forces of social wear and tear, by laziness, by the average mind, by the crowd instinct for avoiding responsibility. The heavy tide of life that carries men and things alike more quickly to the scrapyard, and therefore clears the way more quickly for the succeeding springs of newer things and other generations.

Efficient or deficient? We need someone with proper qualifications to appraise such questions. The government, for example. But almost everywhere in the world we find that the authorities governing us are fossilized, denatured. Who is observing and recording the fact that the trees in our cities have been killed off by the toxic gases in our streets, and that they have been replaced? That our handkerchiefs end every day as dustbins of

"Sport" as catered for by modern officialdom. No improvement since the Romans: roaring crowds and a great deal of pneumonia!

black filth? That, according to statistics, the third generation of families living in large cities has become barren and childless? That men who live in cities leave the place where they live, a compartment giving onto a street, only to appear shortly afterwards in the compartment of the office building or factory where they work, having in that short interim done nothing but walk on asphalt or stone sidewalks, or read their papers while crushed together in the compartments of a subway train or in streetcars or buses belonging to "public transport" companies?

And that they lead this robot-like existence every day of the year and every day of their lives?

That herds, consisting of millions of heads of men, have in this way strayed from the paths of nature and wandered into those of artificiality? And that these men, members of a species developed over thousands and thousands of years (both biologically and psychically) according to established relations with the sky, with fresh air, with the sun, with greenery, with water, with physical activity, have now been torn out of that framework and are wasting away in an entirely unnatural environment?

Who is to decree that this way of life is deficient?

Who is to decide that it must be changed?

It is a product of decisions and dispositions taken in the past! . . .

Let us propose other dispositions.

\* \* \*

To a healthy body, to a mind kept in a continual state of activity and optimism by daily physical exercise, the city, if the right measures are taken, can also provide healthy mental activity.

This would take two forms: first, meditation in a new kind of dwelling, a vessel of silence and lofty solitude; secondly, civic activity, achieved by the harmonious grouping of creative impulses directed towards the public good. These things are not fantasies. Here and there, in times and places where circumstances were propitious, history has recorded realities of this kind. Let us make our own times propitious, and build the places.

Architecture and city planning will thus become extensions of the ethical, sociological and political sciences. Politics will thus resume their true purpose, which is to lead towards the realization of a given era's destiny – society and implements.

\* \* \*

The term "leisure" is idiotic here, and yet it's not so bad at that! The imminent threat of so many leisure hours makes a disciplined approach indispensable. It would be possible, for example, while considering the five hours per day that must of necessity be given over to the nourishment and maintenance of the social body as a sort of normal tax on our time, *to imagine the remaining hours of every day as the normal work of people in the machine age.* This would involve a higher conception of the term work – as we speak, for example, of Pasteur's or Marconi's *work* – or, more simply, as I, for example, look upon the writing of this book as *my* work; as even the humblest member of society,

the privileged: those who perform while others watch!
Yet everyone is capable of playing too . . .
Result: strength, initiative, daring, character.

In the Radiant City, everyone has the right to expect this either on his doorstep or on his roof.

Priene (a Greek city, 4th century B.C.). The gymnasium is one of the city's essential institutions, and the inhabitants do not go there merely as spectators but to perform. In the stadium, races; in the palaestra, jumping, javelin and discus throwing, boxing; around the palaestra, an area where one walked, talked, rested (the philosophers' exedra).

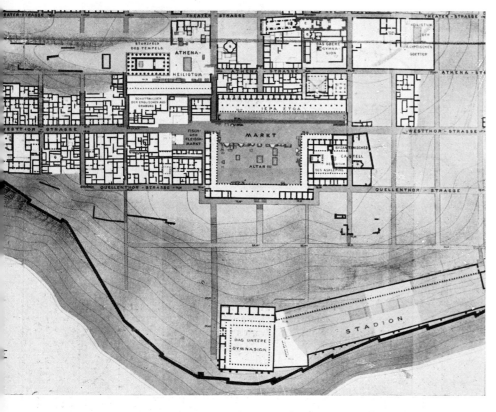

Along the strip where the word "Stadion" is printed were the plane trees: a country element within the city.

# SOLUTION OF A CRISIS

2.

playing about with some piece of cabinetmaking or an idea he has had, would have the right to look upon those things as *his work*. True work, the work of the machine civilization: men would have reconquered their freedom.

And these freely chosen forms of work would be carried out in joy as *leisure activities*.

A healthy body maintained in that state.

Meditation. Civic activity.

It is recognized that industry is submerging us with products that are irrelevant to our happiness. We have been propelled by machines into a false adventure, into a misadventure: these machines that can produce ten or twenty times as much as we ourselves ought to enable us to work at least five or ten times less. Modern industry, organized according to the laws of *supply* has inundated us with *useless consumer goods*. Wandering down this primrose path, allowing one thing to lead to another, we have finally allowed ourselves to be taken over entirely by what we call *free competition*, which is to say a form of slavery, which means that any effort is immediately countered by an opposing effort (a force equal to the original force): we have become merely a flock of rams, horns locked together, all trying to push one another backwards. The flock's strength is drained away, yet it is not moving, it remains always in the same place: we can make no progress!

Free competition has been forced to invent advertising, the traveling salesman, the prospectus, the exhibition, product prizes, etc: all those competing have to summon up all their energy to cancel out the efforts of their competitors.

It is indisputable that this frightful competition gives rise to the most violent emulation and effort.

*But is it also certain that the human spirit is incapable of creative enthusiasm when faced with fruitful tasks?*

An economy based on *demand* would put an end to the reign of the traveling salesman and the advertising agent, but it would necessitate a program. A *program!* Everything lies in that. A program for *the production of useful consumer goods.* Though not a narrow and exclusive one. The mind must always be left enough elbow room to satisfy its deepest purposes: quest for quality, supremacy, struggle and competition – but on the fertile soil of disinterest.

Our program will concern itself with consumer products of a useful nature and with the redirection of industry onto the path towards its true aims; with providing work for all and guaranteeing every man his daily hours of freedom; and with providing physical sites and quarters designed to permit the man of today to enjoy this new freedom without constraint, instead of being hemmed in like a hare in an ever-dwindling square of wheat at harvest time.

Let us imagine for an instant that quite suddenly, as a result of some sudden acceleration in social progress, the man of today has five extra hours of freedom at his disposal out of the eight or ten previously allotted to his work. We should be faced with social disaster, for no preparations have as yet been made to absorb such a vast flood of latent energies.

What we must do, therefore, is to study *modern man's daily existence.* We must decide what the occupations are going to be – communal tasks and individual duties – that will fill the space between two sleeps, *each day,* beginning with every sunrise. We must *concern ourselves with man,* not with capitalism or with communism; with *man's happiness,* not with company dividends; with *the satisfaction of man's deepest instincts,* not with the race for success being run between the managements of two companies or corporations.

Our task is to put man back on his feet, to make sure that his feet are firmly on the earth, his lungs full of air, his spirit bent upon *constructive* communal efforts and also animated by the joys to be derived from useful personal activities. What we must not do is to reduce him to the state of a fixed and faceless asset to be coldly stockpiled in the interest of some anonymous trust.

*We must concern ourselves with man!*

Which means, to design and lay out the sites, to construct the vessels that will be capable of containing useful activities. In other words: *city planning* and *architecture.*

Now that we are faced with the new phenomenon of *the highway,* which is at this very moment opening up the prospect of a brilliant new civilization that will supplant the railroad civilization now in its twilight, the concept of *city planning* must be applied not only to the great cities but also to the towns, to the countryside, to the country in its entirety.

We can no longer limit our attempts in this field to the cities alone. The whole notion of a city is being torn apart, diffused, spread by a natural process of dispersion, by the road, out across the countryside. An upheaval is due to take place in the cities: a large section of the urban populations will take to the roads, will be forced to move out, back towards the land, in order to substitute a more normal way of life for the disaster that has overtaken the cities. For these people, as a result of abortive urban development, the city has become a place of torture, a rack, the desert of disillusion, all that is *inhuman.*

Yet no city dweller who has once experienced the salutary effect that the city can have upon man's mind will ever consent to move out of his city in order to bury himself away once more in the spiritual desert of our country life as it is today. On the contrary, the movement is at present in the opposite direction: it is the dismal countryside, now stripped of all attractions, a harsh and demanding stepmother, that is today writhing its way towards the city, dramatically swelling the latter's flanks with hypertrophied suburban growths. The country today is harsh, unattractive and tyrannical: the *money civilization* by which modern society has been blackened and deflowered has extended its grip to the peasant and made his life a barren, sooty thing as well.

In order to halt the exodus from the country, and insure that the country as a whole is restored to more harmonious proportions by a flow of population back to the land, *we must develop the countryside,* develop it as a place where work appears a blessing, a happy combination of machine and hand and mind. This is one of the noblest tasks facing our age. It will require foresight, imagination, love, a reaffirmation of human purpose and dignity, and moderation.

The cities, in this entirely new organization of society, will conserve the honor of being the prophetic centers of the human tournament, centers of combat, of the quest for quality and quintessentials, centers produced by profoundly human processes where those who are marked with a certain sign will come to fulfill their destiny in a true sense of the word.

Such is the program.

What does it imply?

1934. A view of the *Radiant Farm*

Prefabricated in a factory, assembled on the site, adapted (needless to say) to the particular requirements of any given region, little by little it will give the countryside a wholly new aspect: gay, clean, and alive.

living-room in the *Radiant Farm*. A working tool of the modern age.

It implies deciding exactly what our tasks are: *plans*. Plans for the cities and plans for the country, for equipping the entire country for the future. And all these calculations and blueprints to be based on one value and one alone: *man*. A program on a human scale, a program of harmonization, of harmony, of moderation, of beauty, when all is said and done.

It means replacing the violent, savage, cruel and ruthless civilization of *money* with another based on *harmony and collaboration;* one in which each member of society will feel himself a vital agent in this enterprise that will *restore the face of our country*, that will illumine our countryside with those symphonic images that enable the human spirit to draw strength from its active collaboration with the forces and beauties of nature – nature, our indisputable and immutable mother.

It means that we must lay hands on our cities as they stand and destroy their misery, their ugliness, and their horror; we must make them *human;* we must take the road out into the countryside, revivify it, give it a soul; we must seize upon the providential advantage offered us by the communion that exists between man and nature; we must equip the countryside! Such is the program that will lead to a prodigious production of *useful consumer goods*.

\* \* \*

Such is the market now open to industry. A truly open market. No longer: competitor against competitor leading to immobility, sterility and human misery. But a program of human liberation calculated to galvanize the constructive spirit in men, to rouse them to enthusiasm.

What will happen to industry? All its machines, as well as its labor force, will be able to return to work as soon as the indispensable changes in program have been made. All that is required is that we should decide what the new industrial programs are to be, or to clarify and simplify present trends. Speaking metaphorically: *heavy industry must seize control of all construction*. "Construction" being every form of material endeavor that is undertaken in the service of man. And we already know today that houses and cities and garden cities can break away from the age-old routines of yesterday – the old conception of the workshop – and emerge properly equipped, glittering new, from the factory, from the workshop, faultless products of smoothly humming machines: houses, cities and garden cities as bright and spanking-new as though they had come "straight from Paris," as desirable as the dazzling products of sterile competition that are now displayed in annual automobile shows.

For the whole point of the matter lies here: we must realize that all our out-of-date masonry can be replaced by a new economy, an economy that can in its turn be given a place in our tradition through the prodigious, the meticulous, the dazzling work now being accomplished by machines: industry must take over the task of construction. *Useful consumer products:* new cities and garden cities. Human constructions of the machine age. Wide-ranging programs, unity of action, universal effort, the participation of all, understanding of what is being done, the appearance of new working sites, faith and enthusiasm.

A new civilization to replace that of Money: cooperation, collaboration, participation, enthusiasm.

The construction of a whole new framework for our lives that will enable us to achieve the aims for which we are working: understanding, support, enthusiasm!

The crisis solved.

modern equipment

"City planning is a way of MAKING money.

"City planning is not a way of spending money.

"City planning brings in a profit.

"City planning is not a waste of money.

"Eras deprived of technical innovations are attacked by stagnation.

"Eras with formidable technical innovations at their disposal inaugurate great constructive epochs.

"Replacing an outmoded object with a new object of equal efficiency costs the sum total of that operation.

"Replacing an outmoded object with a new object four or ten times more efficient brings in a profit of three or nine times the value of the object replaced.

"Any attempt to move the center of Paris outside Paris would mean the destruction of the city's greatest asset, the destruction of money's greatest power, and the result would be economic disaster.

"But to replace a now rotting center with a new center four or ten times more efficient than the old one would be to bring in a *profit* equal to four or ten times the cost of the operation. It would be to create, by a decision, by a *conception*, a *diamond mine* in the heart of the city.

"It would mean a fourfold or tenfold increase in buying power. And the profit achieved by the initiator of this change – the State – would serve to cover the expense of redesigning the outer parts of Paris: the elimination of the suburbs.

"Modern construction techniques would permit us to build ten times *higher;*

to reduce the built-up area of the center to only 5%

thus leaving 95% free for traffic and pedestrians;

to increase the greatest present density by four;

to pay compensation to the present owners equal to the full value of their property (and even more);

to create the new road and transport network necessary for easy access.

"A capital city must contain a business center *in the center*, a fact dictated by simple geometry, since no other positioning will eliminate devouring, wasteful distances. Towns are meant to live in, business centers to work in: these are two distinct functions, consecutive not simultaneous, representative of two distinct and categorically separate areas. The center of a capital cannot be displaced: the laws of geography, geometry, biology and economics makes this quite clear.

"I repeat: the city center is a fundamental *asset*, the value of which can now be vastly increased by the modern techniques at our disposal.

"It is madness to think of doing away with it." [1]

\* \* \*

The above lines were written in March, 1929; they were concerned with the replanning of central Paris, taking into account all the existing facts: that Paris is a capital, that it consists of infinitely subdivided private properties, etc . . .

And the reply of the communists, or rather of the apprentice communists who are floundering around like blind mystics trying to understand an austere doctrine that is, in fact, worthy of a much more considered understanding, their reply formulated in over-hasty and misguided commentaries is: "All attempts at improvement of assets are

[1] At the time these lines were being written the Congrès du Nouveau Paris was in session, and Auguste Perret was asking that the center of Paris be demolished and turned into "a garden for nannies in which we could go and amuse ourselves"!

3. # WHERE IS THE MONEY TO COME FROM?

pointless, since a modern society will have the entire national territory at its disposal without any need for financial considerations."

What does that mean? That as a result of a governmental decree nationalizing all private property, and of state capitalization, any task can thenceforward be undertaken and accomplished *without costing anything;* that all the difficulties involved in the planning of a new civilization will have been swept aside at one fell swoop: the credit system has been nationalized, and private property has been abolished! Henceforth there will be money to burn! The country will be swamped with money, inundated with it; it can be manufactured in whatever quantities the decrees of authority require!

Such are the fantasies of those weak-minded people who believe in the spontaneous generation of money.

*   *   *

Alas, there won't be one more cent available than there was before. Money is simply an economic relationshp, *the relationship between production and consumption.* Credit (and that means the credit used to finance large-scale construction work), is a levy on the work that is to be undertaken, on the labor ahead.

It is therefore the *work* that is needed, and work subjected to the hardest and severest law of all – the law of nature itself: *economy.*

Money is only made available (created), if the product costs slightly less to make than the price charged for consuming it. This margin represents the *money available* – if we ignore the animal needs of all members of society for food, clothing and a place to live – for financing the reconstruction and re-equipment of the country.

Every day I produce a certain number of man hours of work, possibly with the aid of machines. I help in the creation of some consumer product *indispensable* to the life of society: wheat, shoes, clothes, drinking water, heat, books, films, theatrical performances, music, pictures, or whatever. Every day I contribute a certain quantity of product to the collective stock, *for which I am paid.* But every day too, I eat, I wear things out, I destroy, *and for that I pay.* But dependent on me, indissolubly associated with my own producing entity, I also have a number of social annexes: my children at school, my wife running the house, my old parents who can no longer work, my dog, my cat, my canary. All these also eat, wear things out, destroy things every day, *and I pay for them too.*

On the one hand, for my daily expense of productive energy (my work in collaboration with machinery) *I am paid.* On the other hand, for the inevitable destructive processes attributable to me (to me and my family) *I pay.*

In addition, I must also pay my share towards subsidizing the existence of those who govern me, of the people who sweep my street, of the people who provide me with street lighting, of the doctors who look after my health and the health of my family.

So that my humble, and obligatory, participation in the national economy is a matter involving heavy responsibilities: *I am a group all on my own!* Yes indeed! For the fact that I live in society makes my work the sustaining element of a social group. If I don't work, and work every day, then my group (family, government, police, local council) and I will perish.

And if the place where I live – my city – must be rebuilt because it is unhealthy; if my government deems it wise to construct ports, or railroads, or highways that will enable the products I need to reach my mouth, or my eye, or my ear, then it is also essential that between the wage I am allowed for my daily work and the sum that I pay daily on my own behalf and that of my group there should remain a surplus available for that purpose.

People may say: but that's of no importance, since all that is required is that the

the family = a group

(the Negro painter Sidi Kalibe in the heart of the Sudan, bard of the native way of life there, an extraordinary talent, died prematurely.)

surplus required from my participation should be made over to the community by official decree! The State will make the necessary currency!

What with?

With decrees, with pieces of paper signed in the name of the State, with mere signatures in fact!

And what do they signify, these signatures? They *say* that *this piece of paper is worth a thousand francs.*

That those thousand francs are to be used to pay the workers who are to undertake the construction work necessary to the life of the nation.

And what are those workers going to do with those francs they have been given? They are going to buy wheat (bread), shoes, clothing, drinking water, heat, books, seats in movie houses or theatres or concert halls, a painting, or a copy of a painting.

*Those thousand francs therefore represent existing merchandise, part of the national stock.*

Who built up that stock? Workers who have performed certain tasks and then *handed over to the State* the fruits of a certain portion of their work, which is to say, a certain number of minutes or hours *from each of their workdays.* All well and good.

But be careful! Two alternatives now present themselves.

*First alternative:* the State has signed so many of these thousand-franc notes that when the recipient of one of them goes to the merchandise distributor and asks to have it changed into goods, the latter will say: "I am extremely sorry, but I just don't have that quantity of goods available, I have scarcely half (or a quarter) of the note's full worth to give you." Whereupon, throughout the country, everyone will immediately say: "What's all this? With a thousand-franc note signed by the State I can only get 500 or 250 francs' worth of the things I need to live." The currency signed by the State is therefore counterfeit. My group (children, wife, old parents, dog, cat, and parrot) and I are only going to be getting half rations or quarter rations of food. We are going to be hungry. We shall only be able to buy shoes once every two or four years; our feet are going to get cold; we are going to fall ill, and so on . . .

*Second alternative:* the State will say: "I want all those I pay with thousand-franc notes to get a thousand francs' worth of goods for those notes. Therefore the national stock must contain enough goods to meet the notes. Therefore all you workers (i.e. everyone) must increase the number of minutes or hours during which you work exclusively for the State. I want the balance sheets to be true. I insist that the goods to meet the pieces of paper I say are worth a thousand francs should *exist.*"

So that according to the wisdom of the programs devised (apart from the production of the food, clothing, etc. for the workers themselves) to create products for the public good – government, ministry of works, police, ports, railroads, highways for the transportation of products – according to the wisdom of these programs *we shall have to give a certain number of* WORK MINUTES *or* WORK HOURS *per day to the State.* It could be one or it could be the other: either minutes *or* hours! Either a *normal* participation in work for the good of the community, or a *crushing* participation in it, either reasonable liberty or slavery.

We must never forget one fact: our lives are ruled by the daily 24-hour cycle of our sun. So that between every rising and going to bed, every day, every 24 hours, according to the wisdom or otherwise of the programs (the plans) devised by the authorities, *we shall spend our time as we wish or be slaves.* Though it need not be absolutely the one or the other. The reality could lie anywhere along the entire scale from joyful liberty to crushing slavery: EVERYTHING DEPENDS UPON THE WISDOM OF THE PLANS.

Money cannot be created by governmental decree!

It can only be created by the sagacity, the ingenuity, the efficacity and the reality of the plans that are made. An efficient economy will provide us with freedom. Waste will produce slavery: it will entail the obligation for *everyone, every day,* to throw hours of their work . . . down the drain.

I am talking here of an ideal society that has already provided itself with a planned economy and swept away all the parasites present in the society we know today. The lesson is this: that the only possible solution is wholly dependent upon the wisdom and economic efficiency with which the value of the elements now in our possession is increased. To increase the value of what we have, the antithesis of waste, that is the lesson.

Earthly paradise cannot be created by governmental decree; it must be the result of intelligent management.

Only wise planning can open its gates to us.

\* \* \*

WE MUST THEREFORE IMPROVE OUR ASSETS!

equipment to help men in their work and prevent wastage.

* * *

And in the matter of city planning, in the matter of architecture, consider, consider, I beseech you, how deeply our lack of rational planning has plunged us into the most appalling waste.

There are some senseless, insane, thoughtless people who have dared to say: Waste? What's wrong with waste? *It's magnificent! That's what creates work!*

I think I have shown clearly enough above WHO PAYS for that work.

* * *

I must here give at least two *startling* examples of the harsh reality I have been demonstrating, for this is not the sort of matter that lends itself to a *black and white* or *heads or tails* kind of proof, but one in which everything is a question of *nuance*, of passing by imperceptible shadings from an acceptable and tolerable state to an unacceptable and intolerable one.

*First example.* In Moscow in 1930 the fad of the moment was for "deurbanization."

"The murderous stone-cannon of the city, the stifling, the crushing of the city dweller is a purely capitalistic manifestation."

Therefore the city must be smashed into ten thousand pieces and scattered across the countryside, in the woods, in the meadows, so that the houses will be in the heart of nature itself. Thus, man will have returned to the first wellspring of his inner harmony.

"All well and good," I replied. "But what about the work of the city (for the question of rural exploitation is in no way involved here), the work that must be accomplished within the 24-hour daily solar cycle?"

Their answer was that they would build whatever roads were necessary to link all the scattered houses to the city center. Everyone would have a car. They were going to manufacture however many cars, however many roads proved necessary, etc . . . (It was in this same year that Ford decided it would be possible to institute one day a week of *destruction* [leisure] *"in order to increase the flow of trade and industry."* Paper money, credits, further credits, confidence, hysteria . . . and then, one fine day: "But where are the *available* goods in the national stock, the *actually existing* products that this vast quantity of circulating currency is supposed to represent?" The goods simply weren't there: they had been consumed a long time before. Or, to be more exact, they had never been made. The hours or minutes of daily work necessary for the production of the merchandise that was needed to meet such a quantity of circulating currency had never been levied. It was mere paper, mere "bubble" money. And the bubble burst. Suddenly, brutally, this house-of-cards economy collapsed, and the U.S. was filled with hunger marchers, etc . . .)

But to return to the U.S.S.R. Plans were drawn up, propaganda films were screened for the benefit of committees. People were encouraged to entertain an idle dream: "The cities will be part of the country; I shall live 30 miles away from my office under a pine tree; my secretary will live 30 miles away from it too, in the other direction, under another pine tree. We shall both have our own car. We shall use up tires, wear out road surfaces and gears, consume oil and gasoline. All of which will necessitate a great deal of work; there will be a titanic demand for labor; enough for all: no threat of unemployment looming in the future, never again' . . .

Then, one fine day, authority, which is the door of reason against which all dreams, just and chimerical ones alike, must eventually knock, authority in the U.S.S.R. said: "Enough! It's all over! And stop that laughing!"

The mystic belief in deurbanization had fallen flat on its face!

* * *

*Second example.* Algiers in 1931, 32, 33 and 34. The future of Algiers. The reawakening of North Africa. The awakening of Africa. Algiers, the capital of Africa.

It was a city full of excitement; it was preparing to live an epic of modern times; it was preparing to increase to immense proportions within twenty years.

But the cliff on which Algiers is built no longer had a single square centimeter free for the construction of new houses.

Never mind! Let us build garden cities outside the old city, they said; let us open up new roads that will wind indefatigably away, far, far away, through inimical terrains. On the rails we build there will be streetcars; on the roads there will be buses, cars, motorbikes, bicycles; and under the earth, there will even be a subway.

Every day, so much tire rubber will be worn out; a certain amount of electrical energy, of gasoline, of oil will be consumed. Contractors will pour in to build the roads and the private houses; industry will be employed in the production of rolling stock, etc; trade agencies will multiply; so will engineers, so will architects. People will come to Algiers, they will live in Algiers and build homes for Algiers! Algiers will begin to attract the attention of international industries and trade.

Such were the pipe dreams with which the authorities flattered their egos.

But who was to pay for it all?

Who, amongst the inhabitants of Algiers itself, amongst the Berbers of the hinterland, amongst the fellahs farming the countryside, amongst the workers in French factories exporting goods to Algiers, amongst the workers in foreign factories exporting goods to Algiers, *who was to provide the daily tribute* of man hours necessary to pay for the wastage that would result from such foredoomed plans?

One fine day, the city would be forced to say: my municipal and territorial taxes, my subsidies from metropolitan France (also obtained by taxation) are no longer sufficient to provide the money necessary to pay for the work that has been executed, and my population cannot "sweat" the money necessary to meet the need of daily upkeep created by a misguided plan.

(What is meant by taxes? Simply man hours given daily by every member of society to pay for the errors of the plan. Hours of work *given* every day!)

* * *

This money that we hear being clamored for in these times of present trouble, this money that is so generally lacking, can in fact be created only by demanding a number of *supplementary* working hours from every member of society, hours in excess of those required to provide a subsistence for every member and for those forming an integral part of his group. Or, if it is not acquired by levying supplementary working hours, then it is acquired by taking back some of the fruits of hours already worked, by taking them back on behalf of the ogre, the State (hours or taxes, both = money). The State is an ogre because it has a frightening appetite: naturally, it wastes so much!

* * *

However, the question we were asking ourselves about the large-scale construction work we are discussing was this: "Where is the money to come from?"

Our reply to this question ought to be another question – *the real question:* "What *kind* of work are we discussing?"

Everything depends on the answer to that!

* * *

Well, what is in question here is the kind of undertaking that will provide our

the dam

The *Normandie*
Megalomania?

The lock at
Panama

machine-age civilization with the indispensable equipment that it so urgently needs. The continuing use in a machine-age civilization of pre-machine-age equipment (houses, streets, cities, farms, infinite subdivision and arbitrary distribution of property), provokes, maintains, extends and amplifies wastage of all kinds to the danger point. A large part of the labor that we all perform is being used, as things are now, to meet the cost of innumerable different kinds of waste (repayments to the State, taxes).

The provision of all this indispensable and urgently needed equipment should take place as the result of a prodigious catalytic process – the SOLUTION provoking a sort of *precipitation, a crystallization, a reduction from 5 to 1, from 10 to 1, of the aggregate of movements, material and hours invested.*

It is no good looking elsewhere. This is the only possible source of the money required: a murder first, an execution – the death of waste. Then, when the ground has been cleared, it will be time for carrying out the great catalyzing plans.

Disorder must be destroyed by the thunderbolt powers of the mind, and it must be replaced by order.

That is how money is made.

Not by wild dreamers printing pieces of paper.

To maintain and encourage waste on the pretext that it provides work and reduces unemployment simply means: either taking away a portion of everyone's daily bread, or else forcing every member of society to throw hours of work, every day, down the drain.

\*   \*   \*

Life is precise, strict, and economical.

The law of nature makes it so.

And our human creations – the artifical world that is now an indispensable part of man's future – must follow this universal law: Strictness and economy.

That is where the money must come from.

●

## 4. LAWS

The laws of nature and the laws of men.

Since man is a product of nature, the laws he lays down for himself must accord with those of nature.

The laws of nature *exist*. It is useless to criticize them.

But it is possible, if one accepts them wholeheartedly, to reach an awareness of how prodigiously simple and at the same time how prodigiously rich in powerful and varied effects they are. The spirit animating them is mathematics; the play of numbers projects its consequences throughout the whole extent of time and space. The laws of nature are always there to urge us on towards the creation of human laws that will in their turn be prodigiously simple and yet prodigiously effective.

Let us now enjoy the deep joys awaiting those who are willing to explore the laws of nature and discover the spirit animating them.

We live in the presence of three spheres:

Our dictator: the sun.

The globe on which we live out our destinies: the earth.

And a companion forever whirling around us: the moon.

This single fact already sets limitations upon all our activities:

The 365 days of a solar year, the inevitable track upon which our bodies, our hearts, our minds must move: a year, four seasons: the intense cold of winter; the tender hopes

## 1. THE EARTH IS OUR CLOCK.

of springtime; the burning heat of summer; the melancholy twilight of the fall.

Things are born, reproduce themselves, then die after they have handed on their life. And all this within strictly prescribed temporal limits: the law of nature.

The 24-hour cycle of the earth divided between sleep (conscious inaction) and work (conscious action). But in summer the day is longer than the night; and in winter the night is longer than the day.

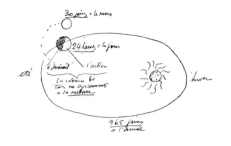

Every 24 hours we experience a period of sleep in which our joys, our sadness, our hope and our despair, all fade away. And every morning we awake with fresh energies and a refreshed vision of the world.

The life of man is an alternating thing: action, then cessation of action, *once every day*. The nights rain down on us implacably; the sun that imposes the darkness on us is infinitely far away: victorious politician or tattered hobo, *all* men must sleep, always, every day of their lives! *The 24 hours of the solar cycle* constitute the measuring rod of all human activities; they are what give our lives their scale and their perspective. Every 24 hours, *human activity stops*. That is the cycle.

The 30-day cycle of the moon creates the twelve monthly divisions of our year. Woman, that power in conjunction with which we work, is ruled by this lunar month. We, the men, are ruled by the solar year: it is spring that stirs our bloods.

The 30-day rhythm of the month, the 365-day rhythm of the year, the 24-hour rhythm of the day: these are the yardsticks of our lives, our time, our clock.

One, thirty, three hundred and sixty-five, *those are the units by which all our undertakings must be measured*.

●

Sun and water.

Active and passive.

Harmony, rivalry, conflict, a treaty of alliance, reproduction.

In short, a day well filled and full of variety: 24 hours of admirable and fruitful activity.

At night, everything sleeps. The water of the earth, infinitely subdivided, performs its habitual act of charity: the world's thirst is slaked.

4:00 A.M.: The sun appears over the rim of the plain; the dew lies on the grass, in the hollow of every leaf. Since the sun sank the evening before, the cool of the night has turned what was vapor in the air to droplets lying on the ground.

8:00 A.M.: The dew has left the ground, summoned by the sun as it rises into the sky.

10:00 A.M.: The scattered waters, now ascending, are driven far up from the earth by the luminous arrows of the sun, which, as they strike the ground, are transformed into caloric power: a force is produced that presses down upon the plains and lifts the vaporous layers up on its shoulders into the sky. When they reach a certain height, these vaporous layers break up, separate, then subdivide into regular clusters. The clusters take more definite shape and draw towards their separate centers: they are now small clouds floating over the plain. From where it flies above them, an airplane can discern their tactics: they are a team, they are a formation, a task force: they are appearing everywhere. They are the water's army.

Noon: The sun is in its glory. Its arrows strike vertically down into the earth; and they light furnaces upon it. These fires are not all of the same kind: here forests, there rocks, elsewhere sandy regions, in some places hills and in others plains. There are big fires and little ones. The giant of heat is now stretched to his full height, his feet crushing

# 2. MALE AND FEMALE

the hot ground: he gesticulates, walks up and down in the land, and waves his arms. The army of the water rallies its forces, brings up its reserves. Violence threatens, rivalries become apparent, the certainty of conflict emerges, and a battle is imminent. The air is filled with an electric charge.

The army of the water masses for an attack: colossal vertical clouds billow high into the sky and obscure its face.

5:00 P.M.: The first lightning flash streaks down, followed by tremendous thunder. All is terror and lashing rain, while darkness covers the unleashing of the storm. The animals are afraid.

6:00 P.M.: The earth is refreshed. The sky is clear. The sun, larger and clearer now, dips towards the plain again. Its movement becomes apparent, the speed of its descent almost alarming. The sky is green along one of its edges, red along the other, but clear as crystal everywhere. The birds are singing.

The apotheosis of a great day.

A pastoral symphony.

Nature!

\* \* \*

This prodigious spectacle has been produced by the interplay of two elements, one male, one female: sun and water.

Two contradictory elements that both need the other in order to exist: the one has no reason to exist, as far as performing its terrestrial function is concerned – a limited purpose in relation to itself, but total for us – except in relation to the other.

●

To our insufficiently sagacious eyes, it appeared that the foliage prolonging the movement of the branches, stems, or trunk of a tree or a plant were disposed around it like a symmetrical crown; that the leaves of a tree stood as motionless and quiescent around a tree trunk as the petals around a moon daisy, or the scales around an artichoke.

But now, the advance of technology (photography and clockwork: slow-motion film) shows us that each of those innumerable leaves is an eye hypnotized by the sun, an eye always wide open, continually turning so as to look the great solitary traveler who passes from East to West across our sky once every day always in the face.

It is the sun that governs us.

That tiny leaf, all those billions of leaves, free to move in the air, but held fast to their stems by a petiole and a stipule, all turn completely on their axes once every day; the stipule produces an intense muscular effort, and on the screen, magnified four hundred times and with its movement speeded up twenty thousand times, we can see it contracting, twisting into painful wrinkles, contorting itself in unremitting obedience to the commands of the sun.

This tiny and pathetic adventure, lived out daily by a tiny little leaf, by the billions of tiny leaves that form part of the complex existence of hedgerows or great forests, always obeying and turning their faces to the great warm star, proclaims the fundamental law of this earth we live on: that the sun is our dictator.

●

The airplane has disappeared, flying back up the estuaries, up along the great rivers, flying high above the savannah, looking down at the virgin forests.

A new eye: the eye of a bird transplanted into the head of a man.

# 3. THE SUN, OUR DICTATOR

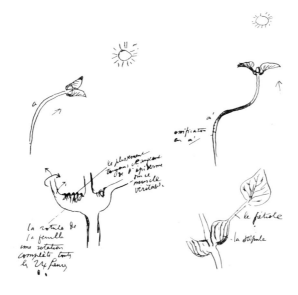

# 4. CHARACTERS

A new way of looking: the aerial view.

What the rational intelligence had acquired in the way of knowledge by analysis, by comparison, by deduction, suddenly becomes a matter of total and first-hand experience for the eye. And to see is a mode of perception unutterably more forceful than simply conceiving with the brain. *To see with one's own eyes. Actually to see!*

Standing on our own two feet, with our eyes a little more than five feet from the earth, a distance that has become the basis (the geometrician's tool) of all our mensuration, of all the sensations that affect us, of all the perceptions that unleash the poetic tide in us, with this *human height* as a foundation (feet on the ground, eye such a short distance above it) we have established our accepted scale of dimensions: all our notions of height and of extent. Ever since Adam, our first father! And on this basis we have observed and noted the characteristics of the reed, of the tree, of the mountain.

But now the airplane has endowed us with a bird's-eye view, and we find infinitely more general characteristics *hitting us in the eye*.

The characters of the various regions of the world have thus been made suddenly and overwhelmingly evident. We can now gauge their diversity. We are confirmed in the belief that character is one of the essential components of the created universe. And that since the order of that universe is so beautiful and the characters that compose it so clear-cut, we too should base our own human creations on the eminent values to be observed in character.

Instead of diffuse and confused elements, we must create characters. And these varied characters will combine amongst themselves to provide us with rich yet clear symphonies: counterpoint and fugue.

The music of our constructions – and by music I mean the poetic emanations they create – will be produced by the interplay of the characters we have created. Isn't that how it works in Aeschylus too?

. . . In the immense delta of the Parana, the reed beds form tranquil atolls. In the savannahs, the palm trees rocket up into the sky in slender groups that provide a violent contrast to the impenetrably matted growth of the virgin forest. And the airplane can even reveal the movement of the water present in the subsoil, disclosing the patterned progress of the green veins it creates across the yellow of the plain . . .

Nature is a thing of mathematical characters and inevitable consequences of purposes.

And the purposes are determined by the characters.

●

Now we come to the law of water.

First suspended in the sky, the water falls to earth in gentle rain or lashing storms. It brings nourishment to whatever is in need of it. Then what remains unused continues on to fulfill its inevitable purpose, which is to complete its cycle.

Water is fluid, and what is fluid is mobile. It flows according to the laws of gravity.

First the rivulet. It flows to meet another rivulet, then another. Width is added to width: simple arithmetic. Now they are a stream. The stream meets another stream. Again their widths are added; more simple arithmetic. Now there is a great river rolling towards the sea, relentless and powerful. Now it reaches its delta: the powerful flow becomes infinitely subdivided: still simple arithmetic. It gently pours into the sea. The estuary. The open sea.

The circulation of water is an invariable phenomenon; it is simply a matter of addition.

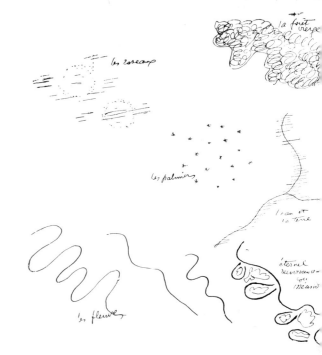

# 5. 1. HARMONY, THE LINK
## 2. ACCIDENT
## 3. THE LAW OF THE MEANDER
## 4. THE LINK OF HARMONY AGAIN

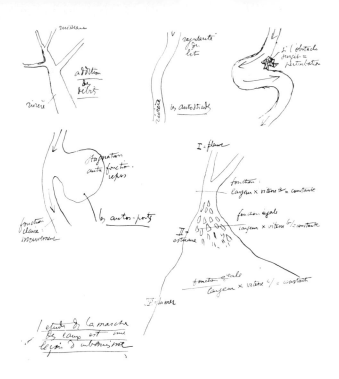

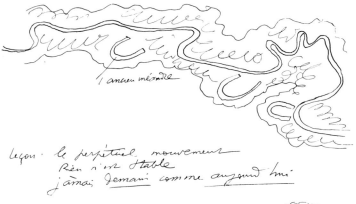

# THE WORLD'S SEASONS
# AND MEN'S SEASONS

Each stage of the process, rivulet, stream, river, delta, is a simple function of two elements in combination: size and speed. Each is a function of the other. And their product is *constant*.

This simple and beautiful lesson ought never to be out of our minds when the time comes for us, as city planners, to establish the correct bed for that new fluid of the modern era: the automobile.

Water circulates; it flows down to the sea. And its progress is *unbroken*. Though there is an interesting exception to this statement: when water meets with a depression or hole on the route of its descent, it makes it into a lake. This is a new event: a lake, a hollow filled with water, a place where the water is *stationary*.

We should keep this effect in mind for the day when we are forced to consider the manner in which our automobiles are to be allowed to become stationary too: parking – a lake of traffic.

\* \* \*

Now, the airplane suddenly reveals an irregularity in the smooth flow of the water towards the sea.

An obstacle has barred, or at any rate obstructed, its path: a rock. The symptom does not belie the effect; the malady develops; an interplay of consequences in time and space is set into developing motion. A meander has begun to form. For a moment, it remains merely a tiny break in the flow. Then, the process of erosion has already begun, slowly eating away at the clear and simple law that governs the downward flow of water: thrust aside by the presence of this obstacle, turned off its axis, the water is directed against the opposite bank. It bites into it, wears it away, causes it to crumble. But then, forced back in the opposite direction, it begins to do the same to the other bank, further down.

Deserting its straight line, the water is now flowing in a zigzag contrary to the simple law of gravity.

Instead of flowing normally down to the sea in a straight line, the river will be held up in its course by this abnormality, a meander.

\* \* \*

To the airborne observer, the great rivers of South America offer a startling revelation: the meander. And more than that: meanders within meanders.

In the sphere of human purposes, the meander would prove a profoundly demoralizing influence, if it were not suddenly and miraculously broken through.

For our human achievements too can sink into the silt of the meander; civilizations can disappear, our greatest works be engulfed, hegemonies be swallowed up. These things happen when the necessary energy is not forthcoming at the moment when it is required: history records the outcome, the page turns. A death has occurred.

\* \* \*

Nature, however, cannot stop; she must find a solution to everything, even to maladies as perilous as this. *When the time comes, the meander is dispensed with;* the river breaks through and returns to a straight course once more. Though, even so, this new route will still be encumbered for a long while with parasites, with evil vapors, with fevers and rotting decadence.

And so it is also in architecture and city planning; in sociology and economics; in politics.

●

The curve of human life is a brief one. That of a historical period may stretch over two, three or even five generations. The period begins to take shape; precursors become aware of this and herald its approach. Then it makes itself truly apparent; the signs become more and more unmistakable. Its rules are hammered out by those who are aware of what is happening. One day it will all come to pass! Then, without any further efforts, long years of fruitfulness flow by. Then come the signs, the warnings, of decadence; and suddenly decadence is there. Collapse is imminent. Already the prophets are heralding yet another cycle . . .

At what favorable or ill-omened times do our own individual destinies occur? Have we been born twenty years too soon, or twenty years too late? Am I, personally, just too old, or just too young, when the decisive hour strikes? Or was I born at exactly the right time?

The world's seasons and men's seasons are on two different scales, and because they do not always coincide, men's lives are also a matter of good fortune or bad fortune, disappointed hopes or joy, fulfillment or impatience.

Conjunctures and conjunctions!

●

The primary form of life consisted of cells that could reproduce by themselves, dividing themselves up, multiplying, and forming an amorphous, quivering, but purposeless mass.

Then an intention appeared, an axis began to form in the center of this motionless agglomeration. A current, a direction became apparent. An organism was born.

Then further ramifications followed. Life was pursuing its natural impulse towards *organization*. This impulse towards organization exists throughout nature.

I am flying across the immense reaches of a wild South American country, one only colonized very gradually, back towards its capital, Buenos Aires. In seven hours, I shall see, from high above, the furthest settler's farm, then the hamlet, then the village, then the small town, and finally the capital city.

My reactions will be guided by a strangely eloquent and very visible framework, because the formation of all South American towns, ever since the conquest, has always been based upon a very viable, living unit: the Spanish *cuadra* (square) with sides 110 meters long (an urban unit extremely well suited to control and exploitation; it is determined by the length of a man's stride and the distance he is able to see).

I shall see how the planning of towns in this country was first *organized*, then how it flowered. But then, from four thousand feet up in the air, I shall perceive the strange, the appalling disease that occurred: the wasting away, the decline of an organism that lack of the necessary vigilance has allowed to be drained of its vital and indispensable energy.

\* \* \*

Here is the first farm, isolated in the heart of the pampas. The settler arrived, halted his wagon and team, then drew a *cuadra* of 110 meters square in the earth. And there he settled himself at his leisure, within the bounds of that human truth: a simple geometrical figure of suitable dimensions.

\* \* \*

Here is Posada, a hamlet on the banks of the Rio. The *cuadras* run all along the river bank; one senses that it is easy to move about amongst them and that the little houses are a pleasure to live in as they nestle amid the surrounding greenery and gardens. Between every group of three *cuadras* a track leads away from the river into the fields; these tracks are intersected by others at right angles to them, and these larger squares with sides of 330 meters are an admirable size for market gardening and neat orchards.

\* \* \*

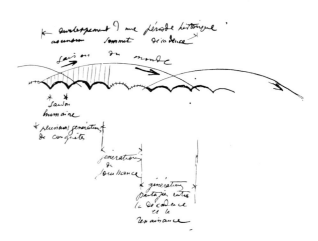

# 7. OPPOSING THE LAWS OF NATURE: DECLINE AND DEATH.

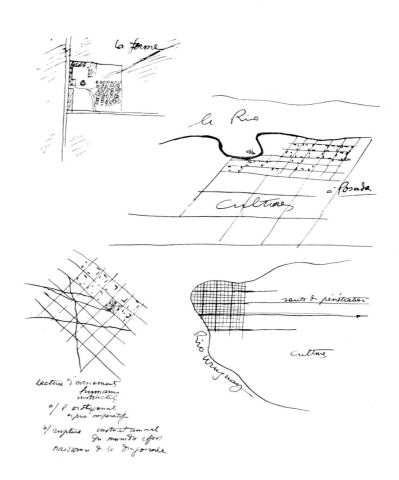

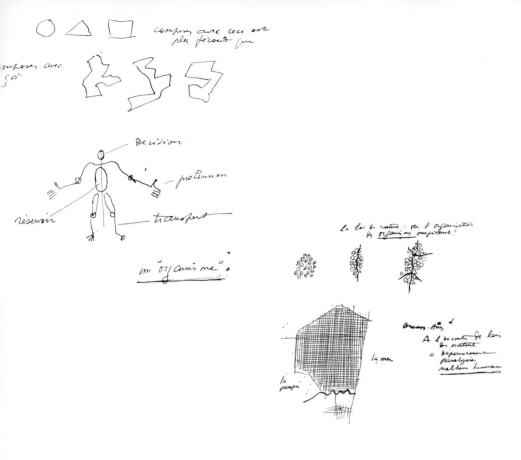

# 8. INFINITE COMBINATIONS

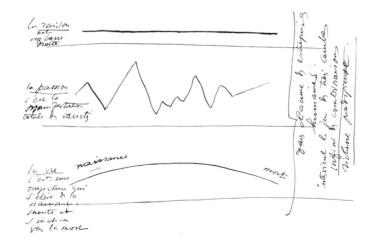

In the plain, we are now flying over another, similar agglomeration. Only here, cutting diagonally across the right-angled grid there are also cart tracks that lead off into the distance, towards the pasture lands and the fields sown with crops. Thus, tentatively at first, the diagonal has begun to make its appearance in the original, arbitrary system of *cuadras:* a manifestation of the instinct for the short cut, for the law of least resistance, which we must always be prepared to make use of when it brings with it economy.

\* \* \*

On the Rio Uruguay, in the province of Corrientes, a town has grown up in a bend of the river. It is an organism in the prime of life, in full bloom. Its lines of force and of direction are all clearly apparent. There is city planning for you!

\* \* \*

At the end of the journey lies Buenos Aires. Its innumerable inhabitants, invading the city in a gigantic and sudden tidal wave, have been forced to settle themselves in too quickly and as best they might. The surveyors have simply traced out as many *cuadras* as were needed: "If you want them, come and get them!" An immense scab, a sort of skin disease that has developed unchecked and is still growing beyond all proportions: 14 by 18 kilometers of it. A fine disease! Paris is but a pimple beside it.

The diagnosis is clear: through lack of forethought, a primary cellular structure has been allowed to develop without the introduction, when the proper time came, of the requisite organic structure. Where nature would have made immediate haste to give such a mass a proper structure, to organize the requisite channels of supply, evacuation, and energy (viscera, lungs, bones, limbs), human heedlessness has allowed a primary organic form of life to exceed the dimensions proper to it. The mass has collapsed into decay and become a stagnant pond. Buenos Aires is nothing more than a mass of protoplasm!

●

An infinity of combinations is possible when innumerable and diverse elements are brought together. But the human mind loses itself and is fatigued by such a labyrinth of possibilities. Control becomes impossible. The spiritual failure that must result is disheartening. For human intelligence enjoys following the intricacies of such permutations, and is delighted when we stake almost nothing and contrive to sweep the table clean.

But an infinity of combinations can also emerge from the extraordinary fecundity of relationships possible between only three or four elements, even when each of those elements is so strongly characterized that its own individual attitude and unity can be recognized in each of the combinations. Then we have what may be termed the firework display of human, of intelligent miracles. The distinction I am making here could be illustrated by a 14th of July crowd on the one hand, whirling and milling in the streets of Paris to the sound of neighborhood bands, and on the other, three dancers on a stage offering us a different and dazzling synthesis of movement every second by means of a controlled exploitation of gestures.

Look now at us, at mankind, endowed by heaven with three precise and totally different characteristics that are able to go on producing new effects from their continual inter-reactions to all eternity: reason, which is an unbroken straight line; the nature of our earthly destiny, which is a long curve rising from our birth then falling to our death; and passion, which is individual, ever varying, and irrepressible.

Any city, and the underlying plan of that city, is also governed by those three powers. Where are the fortunate conjunctions that will decide the future of that city? But those conjunctions may also, alas, be unfortunate ones too!

82

Unheard – of things exist.

Fabulous events take place.

We neither see them nor sense them.

They are there, but beyond our perceptions.

Nevertheless, there exists a universe, already immense and marvelous enough, that is made up of all that we can see and perceive. And to that universe we have given the name "Nature."

By this we mean our environment, the sphere in which, and upon which, we act and meditate.

Everything in that environment passes through us, through each of the individual personalities that make up mankind.

And whatever we are able to deduct or conclude from that environment, whatever our minds can piece together, in their turn, into another system, a system *that is ours*, is *human creation*, is a work of art – in whatever domain.

On the one hand, nature: a cone opening away from us towards infinity. Its point transfixes us; its contents are always flowing into us.

On the other hand, another cone, also opening away towards infinity: human creation.

Between the two cones, where their points meet, stands man. Man the perceiver and man the revealer: the focal point.

A note: It is worth remarking that come what may, man's eye – his most powerful instrument of perception – is immutably fixed at a height of 5′ 3″ off the ground. And our feet rest immutably upon the earth. This height of 5′ 3″ is the measure by which we – *mankind* – *perceive the dimensions of the universe.* (Note 1.)

●

Man must struggle with nature in order to survive. Some people, with the aid of sublime fictions in some cases, would like to persuade themselves that we can cause nature to abandon its antagonism by a voluntary act of faith on our part, and that a state of equilibrium can be achieved automatically by such means. Happiness is not a reality, it is a fiction, it is a relation, a tension. It is a force drawing its energy from one thing – a thing that is in us, and therefore subject to change – and directed towards another – which is contingent and therefore likewise subject to change.

Man is a product of nature. He has been created according to the laws of nature. If he is sufficiently aware of those laws, if he obeys them and harmonizes his life with the perpetual flux of nature, then he will obtain (for himself) a conscious sensation of harmony that will be beneficial to him.

All man has to go on are the laws of nature. He must first understand the spirit of them, then apply them to his environment in order to create out of the cosmos something *human*. In other words, a genuine new creation for his own use.

Nature is wholly mathematical in substance, but our eyes perceive it as a series of chaotic spectacles (for the most part).

And for this reason, in order to save himself from this chaos, in order to provide himself with a bearable, an acceptable framework for his existence, one productive of human well-being and control, man has projected the laws of nature into a system that is a manifestation of the human spirit itself: *geometry*.

In this artificial universe he is able to live at ease, whereas he is doomed to suffering and rude shocks as soon as he leaves it.

On the one hand, the mathematics of the universe; on the other, the human environment.

# 9. MAN, THE FOCAL POINT

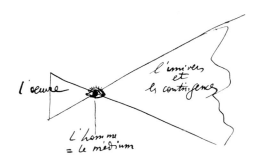

*Note 1 . ( 1964.)*

   *This journey, which took place in 1929, was made by airplane. The airplane was of wood, and my pilots were Mermoz and Saint-Exupéry. First airplane flight over South America. "Be prepared, Monsieur Le Corbusier; the airplane has now endowed man with an eye that can look down from 12,000, from 30,000 feet above the ground." For years I have been using an eye that is 30,000 feet above the ground!*

   *Another subject for astonishment: I shall be able to leave Paris at midnight and arrive in New York yesterday at one hour before midnight (when my plane – which can already fly at 500 miles an hour – can do 900 miles an hour).*

*(signed: L.-C.)*

# 10. THE PURPOSE OF INTELLIGENCE

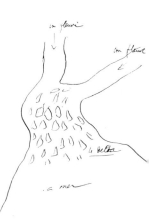

# 11. INEFFECTIVE CREATION
# EFFECITVE CREATION

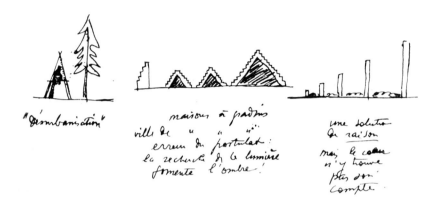

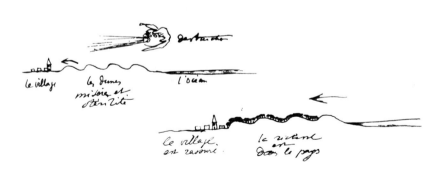

When, in Moscow, in 1930, the idea of "deurbanization" was given symbolic expression in the image of a man in a thatched hut or log cabin beneath a pine tree, the last stage of error had been reached. The laws of nature had been stood on their heads: men are creatures born to live in groups, to live closely with one another, to collaborate; it is nonsense to try and make them into hermits living in the depths of woods.

Deurbanization, garden cities, "satellite cities," etc... all these are ineffective forms of creation.

\* \* \*

When, in 1913 and 1930, attempts were made to create a stepped house, then a stepped city, on the basis of that natural postulate, the need for sunlight, and when, through an error of concept that led to combining various architectural features that were intrinsically contradictory rather than complementary, plans were drawn up for the construction of pyramid cities, those concerned fell straight into a paradoxical trap: their search for sunlight produced greater darkness. And the further this principle was applied to the far greater dimensions of our modern age, the more this contradiction became blindingly apparent: the city's very heart was a thing of darkness, and the streets remained the time-honored gutters they had always been. The result was simply Pelion on top of Ossa, a desert of heaped-up stone without greenery, without anything to relieve its utter harshness, a Babylonized Hoggar inimical to man. Ineffective creation! Creation against the laws of nature: the projected combination of the various architectural elements selected led only to impoverishment and heartbreak!

\* \* \*

When in Germany, before Hitler, there was an attempt to build according to the laws imposed by the sun, when the great pyramid was broken down into smaller units well separated from one another, this was a move towards freedom: those responsible were on the verge of achieving the solution they had aimed at – sunlight in their houses.

But the order they imposed on things was systematically sterile: spaces in the form of corridors, unvaried and wearisome parallelisms, a sky impoverished by stark and ill-balanced silhouettes.

From below, the human eye was deprived of the plastic riches that it must have.

Such starkness produces an uneasiness in the soul; the mind becomes anguished when starved of form.

Another example of ineffective creation.

\* \* \*

When, under Louis XV, Brémontier had the idea of sowing pine trees on the Gascony sand dunes that were being blown inland by the Atlantic winds and threatening to bury whole villages beneath their advance, he achieved his goal immediately. But more than that, he restored a whole region of his country to humanity. And more than that still, as a result of the timber and resin industries that grew up he provided a means of subsistence for a new population. It was an *idea*, an effective creation.

\* \* \*

When, more than a thousand years ago, the Dutch set themselves to creating productive and habitable land in regions that were then still below the level of the sea – the Low Countries – what they did was to link together into a single coherent system some of the principal elements of their geographical situation: they harnessed the winds and the sea, their enemies, and made them their allies.

This eminently simple combination is clearly expressed by a section through the edge of any polder: a trench (a canal); the earth dug from the trench piled up to form a dyke. All along the dyke, windmills pumping out the water and powered by the winds off the sea; an Archimedean screw sunk beneath the polder, turned by the power of the windmill, and raising the water up till it can pour out into the canal. The polder dries out; the water from it flows along the raised canal back out to sea.

A prodigious conception. A whole new country was born: inestimable wealth, lush pastures, gardens, and farm lands. The productive powers of nature used to combat her hostile powers.

A well-played match. Effective creation.

* * *

Today, if we consider the new machine age as it lies before us in all its present confusion and state of crisis, we shall see that it is possible to attempt some enterprise similarly governed by right reason.

Let us read the lessons of the past, and let us consider the present:

This disc, which is a diagram of how the 24-hour day of artisans was divided up in the past, shows that man's vital equilibrium was maintained by the long hours he spent with fingers, mind – and even heart – absorbed in his work. While the serpentine line of the graph below the disc shows that each individual *participated* in the adventure of production.

The second disc, which represents the situation in the machine age, shows that if the economy is properly planned, then the hours consumed by the task of production – in collaboration with machines – will be greatly reduced. Immediately, we glimpse that gaping void awaiting the modern age, that imminent danger: leisure. Every day, there will be a great number of hours unoccupied. What is to be done?

The sharp peaks of the graph below reveal how much more those individuals concerned with the mechanical aspects of the machine age will participate in the work of production than the rest – the managers, the engineers, the inventors, all absorbed in their tasks of management and technological improvement. Their participation will be of sufficient magnitude to give these people *an interest in life*.

But the vast mass of workmen and laborers can never find any way of participating in the great machine adventure. They will have no center to their lives. They will be the have-nots in a new sense; there will be a void inside them.

We must plan for this leisure time. Cities and countryside alike must be reconstructed. The sites and buildings necessary for the basic pleasures to be brought into these people's lives must be constructed. The last graph of all, in which that wavy line depicting the universal participation so necessary to society has been re-established, shows how this social void must be filled.

But this means a prodigious architectural and urban redevelopment program. And also, in consequence, the conscious organization of disinterested human activities: the bringing-up of children, education, body, spirit, heart. Total participation. Individual activity and collective activities. Goals assigned for human existence. True pleasures.

It also means, for those who know how to construe events and recognize the instruments required by our times, it also means the solution to our crisis: *the production of useful consumer goods*.

* * *

Thus, the idea of the Radiant City was born, over a period of years, from observation of the laws of nature; from a comprehension of simple and true events; from the recognition of natural movements, activities, and even aggression.

The Radiant City, inspired by the laws of the universe and by human law, is an attempt to guarantee the men of a machine civilization all this world's *basic pleasures*.

●

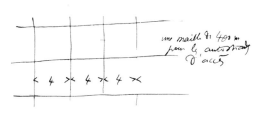

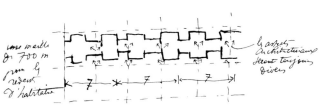

# 5. BASIC PLEASURES

man-made
park
(Mertens)

lyricism of nature

For all men, in cities and in farms:

> *sun in the house,*
> *sky through their windowpanes,*
> *trees to look at as soon as they step outside.*

I say: the basic materials of city planning are:

> sun,
> sky,
> trees,
> steel,
> cement,

in that strict order of importance.

Yet when I look about me, I see city authorities – reputedly the most modern in the world – planning towns that will deprive men, *for a century to come*, of the BASIC PLEASURES!

\* \* \*

The city of Stockholm, whose future seemed to be in such very good hands, has just hurled a flagrant proof to the contrary into our astonished faces.

I say that the people there are madmen. For we are certainly not the madmen, we who are seeking for a real solution.

We say that slum neighborhoods should be demolished, just as they do. But we want them demolished so that "corridor streets" and central courtyards (wells) can be thrown onto the garbage dump forever.

The city of Stockholm, according to the published verdict of its international competition for the replanning of Norrmalm, has just announced its intention of perpetuating *corridor streets* and *central courtyards*. And by way of making a start on this noble enterprise it has given its prizes to plans that can have no other effect but to demolish the present Norrmalm, with its corridor streets and courtyards, only to construct more corridor streets and courtyards in its place. There will be neither trees nor space. And as for the admirable site on which the town stands – hills sloping down to bathe in a sea all bays and inlets – *nothing has been done with it at all; it is to be made null and void!*

The basic pleasures, by which I mean sun, greenery and space, penetrate into the uttermost depths of our physiological and psychological being. They bring us back into harmony with the profound and natural purpose of life.

\* \* \*

But we must not forget a second group of basic pleasures: action, *participation* in collective work, the realization of which by communal effort is an undertaking that represents concrete benefit for all and the elimination of one of the greatest causes of unhappiness amongst the humbler members of society.

These are the supreme joys that each individual can earn by a spiritual or "maternal" participation in working for the collective good.

*That is what citizenship is!*

The country, or the city, or the village, has decided to undertake the realization of a plan. OF A PLAN! The foundations of new buildings are dug. The buildings themselves rise towards the sky. The surrounding countryside and the site itself add their powerful contributions to the composition. The sight of the finished whole fills the heart with enthusiasm. And the details, this man's room, then this other room, and then yet another – all the rooms, every room – offer to each and every inhabitant a new destiny, a noble future . . .

Ah! to participate in such an enterprise, to see an achievement of the communal mind and heart come into being and then to fruition in that way, to feel that we are not, after all, a lot of blindly bustling lice, despicably hanging on like grim death to our own egoistic enjoyments, but thinking beings, beings capable of decisions and of action!

That we have achieved sublimity by our own intelligent decision!

That the elders of the city, or of the country, or of the village, have thought boldly and then taken *the decision!* . . .

And that now we are committed to action!

*Basic pleasures* as well. The highest joys. There can be no greater goal than that of finding the means to mobilize enthusiasm and to give to every man (including the lowliest) the certain knowledge that he is an active being, that he is creating and raising a work of harmonious creation.

The responsibility – if officialdom fails us – lies with those who were afraid, who are afraid! They are cowards who will be condemned by the hearts of the people for abandoning their posts in the face of the enemy.

The enemy: laziness and fear.

●

A city should give joy and be a source of pride.
The materials of city planning are:
sky
trees
iron
cement
in that order of importance and indissolubly.
(Conference at Oslo, 1933.)

lyricism of human inventions (This was, in fact, so successful – the Alhambra of Granada unless I'm mistaken – that it was later copied on many occasions . . .)

the sun rises every day . . .

# 4<sup>th</sup> PART: THE "RADIANT CITY"

# THESE STUDIES ARE BASED . . .

Statistics . . .

A diagram illustrating how the populating of Berlin has hurled itself towards the center of the city. A striking image!

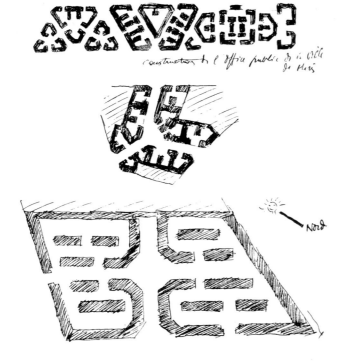

A denunciation of "illusions" or lies.

Revealing and accusing sketches of some recent attempts at planning inside the city of Paris.

These are the only too famous H. B. M. along the old fortification line, an architectural as well as an urban-planning disaster, monstrosities created under the very noses of the populace and the country. One is left stunned! No one protests! Yet thousands of families have been buried in these brand-new hovels. Thousands of families will never see the sun!!!

These studies are based on an unalterable, indisputable, essential foundation, the only true basis for any attempt at social organization: *individual liberty*. Where the planning of collective life threatens to demolish the liberty of the individual, we must respect it; at a time when the consequences of machine-age evolution seem daily more likely to destroy it, we must revive it; it is our aim, in this rich new era, to create an even greater measure of individual liberty now that modern technology is providing us with new and fabulously powerful means of progress.

This present work is not the development of an arbitrary structure, an exposition of some idealistic system, or pure speculation on the part of a brain that has wilfully set itself above the struggle of life. The ideas it presents are all derived from that struggle: they are the products of our age. Their spiritual direction is that of our age because they have been developed from the actual, carefully observed, tangible, material conditions of the world we live in.

The powers that be in Moscow once sent me a questionnaire asking me to give my solutions for the future of the Russian capital. It was possible to answer that questionnaire in everyday language: it was simply a matter of expressing one's ideas on the subject. So I did that. But as I was dictating my replies, there were images, rough plans, sketches beginning to take shape in my mind. For what am I, after all, but a technician trained in the techniques of architecture and city planning? "The simplest sketch in the world is worth more than a long report." Sketches could provide *the proof*.

And so it was that, after I had dictated my replies to the questionnaire, I undertook the execution of twenty or so sketch plans, without those plans having any direct connection with the questionnaire. The questionnaire was concerned wholly with Moscow; the plans dealt with the phenomenon of social organization in machine-age cities – in the cities of our time.

Would this second, and independent, line of argument confirm or contradict my answers to the original questionnaire? It seemed to me that it would be a fascinating line of inquiry. The two arguments seemed to fit together rather well, the second shedding a singular amount of light on the first and adding a great deal of technical truth.

Those twenty plans could have been extended to fifty, or a hundred: the problem, looked at from the outside in, then from the inside out, ricocheted back and forth in a thousand different ways, each time revealing a new reality that had to be isolated and considered as a living fact. It would take so much time, though. And unhappily I do not have much time: work of this sort must always be done in hours more or less stolen from the exigencies of everyday life. My consolation is this: what I provide here is like an opened fan – the future may open it even wider, may increase the number of branches, and even cause those I have envisaged to grow.

\* \* \*

Why publish this *Reply to Moscow*? My report and my twenty sketch plans have already been sent to the Russian authorities. I know that they will be welcomed there by minds anxious to discuss their implications. I also know that in Moscow they have, more or less – amidst the cartoon crowd of gesticulating figures that tend to run the affairs of this world – established the reign of intelligence. Besides, the Russians are an artistic people – a fact that certainly does no harm to a nation's affairs when it is a matter of choosing a line of conduct, a concept of life. My work will not remain – I trust – in some Soviet desk drawer until the next ice age.

But as I examined and re-examined, in my laboratory, the fundamental elements that go to make up a modern city, I found that I was dealing with many present realities that are no more peculiarly Russian than they are French or American. After my research programs in 1922[1] and 1925[2], after my books *Urbanisme* (1925) and *Précisions* (1930), I continued my advance through the undergrowth, or through the virgin jungle: I found new angles, I cut my way through to fresh vistas, I discovered truths that seem to me – in all humility – fundamental. At least, I mean they are the foundations of my system: architecture in everything, city planning in everything. My *Reply to Moscow* became the logical sequel to my previous researches. Its publication (for the title itself – *Reply to Moscow* – was merely a casual one) was a continuation of my efforts towards a manifestation of the new spirit of our age.

\* \* \*

But then, one fine day, the title *Reply to Moscow* was submerged by something larger and deeper. It became a question of humanity as a whole. And then I chose the new title: *The Radiant City.*

For the task before us is to satisfy men's hearts.

Every day the anxiety and depression of modern life spring up afresh: the city is swelling, the city is filling up. The city simply builds itself anew on top of itself: the old houses towered in a cliff at the edge of the streets; the new houses still tower in new cliffs along the same streets. All the houses are on streets, the street is the basic organ of the city, and the house is the individual, infinitely repeated mold. The street becomes appalling, noisy, dusty, dangerous; automobiles can scarcely do more than crawl along it; the pedestrians, herded together on the sidewalks, get in each other's way, bump into each other, zigzag from side to side; the whole scene is like a glimpse of purgatory. Some of the buildings are office buildings; but how is it possible to work well with so little light and so much noise? Elsewhere, the buildings are residential; but how is it possible to breathe properly in those torrid canyons of summer heat; how can anyone risk bringing up children in that air tainted with dust and soot, in those streets so full of mortal peril? How can anyone achieve the serenity indispensable to life, how can anyone relax, or ever give a cry of joy, or laugh, or breathe, or feel drunk with sunlight? How can anyone *live!* The houses are cliffs facing one another across the street. Worse still, behind the houses that face the street these are more houses still. They are built around courtyards. Where is the light? What do I see out of my window? Other windows, only six or ten yards away, with people behind them looking back at me. Where is freedom here? There is no freedom for men in this present age, only slavery. A slavery to which they themselves consent, and which is no longer even confined within set limits. To live, to laugh, to be master in one's own home, to open one's eyes to the light of day, to the light of the sun, to look out on green leaves and blue sky. No! Nothing of all that for the man who lives in a city. The man in a city is a lump of coal in a brazier; he is being burned up simply for the energy he produces. Then he fades and crumbles away. Every year, fresh contingents flood in from the country to replace those who have been burned out.

The houses look out onto the streets, or the houses look out onto a court. Offices too. Workshops as well.

More, the office, the workshop and the houses are heaped pell-mell on top of one another: din, smells, noise, a bubbling poison brew. How does one live? How does one laugh?

More recently, there has been a reaction, one made possible by the railroad. The laborer, the clerk and the shopgirl have been whisked out of the city along steel rails.

I prefer New York! It's hideous, but it's honest. It is the city of *hard labor*, but it doesn't try to hide the fact . . .

[1]. Salon d'Automne: "*Une ville contemporaine de 3 millions d'habitants.*"
[2]. Pavillon de l'Esprit Nouveau, Expos. Inter. d'Art Décoratif: "Plan *Voisin* de Paris."

The hour has struck, everywhere. It is time to equip our machine-age civilization. The mechanism is infinitely complicated; what does that matter?

Like an exploding shell, the city has shot out in all directions, pushing its tentacles out as far as the eye can see. At dawn, then again in the evening, the laborer, the clerk and the shopgirl sit in their railroad cars and are pulled along the rails. Their little houses are surrounded by greenery, away in the country. What could be nicer? They can really enjoy themselves – every Sunday. That's only one day out of seven, but never mind. So on Sunday, there they are, all alone in their little green nests: their boy friends, their girl friends, live on the opposite side of town, in another suburb. So on Sundays, the laborer, the clerk and the shopgirl still tick off the hours without living and without laughter. Or rather, there they are back in their railroad cars riding those steel rails again. Suburbs? Suburbs are broken, dislocated limbs! The city has been torn apart and scattered in meaningless fragments across the countryside. What is the point of life in such places? How are people to live in them?

Suburban life is a despicable delusion entertained by a society stricken with blindness!

The world is sick. A readjustment has become necessary. Readjustment? No, that is too tame. It is the possibility of a great adventure that lies before mankind: the building of a whole new world . . . because there is no time to be lost. And we must not waste time on those who laugh or smile, on those who give us ironical little answers and treat us as mystic madmen. *We have to look ahead, at what must be built.* Awe-inspiring experiments are already taking place before our very eyes: America (the United States) has already rushed into the machine age "before the plaster was dry" as it were. By which I mean that they have advanced into this new unknown like true pioneers and had the courage to improvise. They had no way of foreseeing what the consequences would be, and today they are already finding themselves trapped in many dead-end streets. There is very little happiness to be seen over there; no modern consciousness has been precipitated by all that has happened. America's magnificent, gigantic lesson is a negative one. Nevertheless, the U.S.A. has earned our respect: *they are people who have worked.* Russia and Italy are both building new regimes at this moment. Moscow, in particular, is attempting to turn a people long allowed to lie fallow into a living nation; they have started from scratch, and are now, with astounding energy, working out a whole new code of living. I am not judging the results, I am not even attempting to evaluate them. How could I begin to do so? Though I have now been to Moscow three times, it was never as anything but a spectator perpetually stumbling into some new pit of ignorance. These things are too vast, too complex, too difficult to define. They are beyond my capacities – as indeed they are sometimes beyond the capacities of the men who brought them about. Life has done its work: the storm, then the fresh shoots. And we are part of the process, much less masters of events than is sometimes believed. How are we to gauge these events? And yet, everywhere where it is feasible to do so, we must in fact gauge, evaluate, judge. For only then can we invent, decide, and act. We must do so.

\* \* \*

I am an architect and a planner of cities, and I shall remain so.

Architecture and city planning are the healthy fruits produced by a sound society.

Fruits? Does that mean that any action on our part would be premature at this moment? That we should wait for some more or less distant autumn to arrive? Not at all. The machine age is already a century old. It has brought about the destruction, the desolation of a whole world; it has brought misery and danger in its train; it has already

# 2. INVITATION TO ACTION

NOTE: This series of ten chapters dealing with The Radiant City is taken from the new review *Plans.* The articles appeared during the years 1930-31.

carried out the more painful half of its task: the breaking down. And it has affirmed the essence of its positive principle: the new functions ahead.

Architecture and city planning, if we consider the material facts now facing us, are the answer to the essential functions required of modern man. What is modern man? He is an immutable entity (the body) endowed with a new kind of consciousness. Define that consciousness! Yes, I shall do so. But we must also return to a clear awareness of what it means to be man the physical entity, man the body, for our present awareness of ourselves in this respect has been falsified by exaggeration, vanity and self-interest. We must measure afresh the consequences of being bodies; it is a task that all those who really desire to make the true destiny of the machine age a reality must face as a matter of personal experience.

The architect who is attempting to build a house (a home) for any member of mankind today must be guided by a modern consciousness. That same modern consciousness must also be the basis of all our proposals for the reorganization of the great cities in which we are to live together in our millions.

Modern techniques have created an architectural revolution. This architectural revolution is now virtually complete. It is the product of mathematics and machines. I say *virtually* complete because the results of this revolution can only so far be observed in certain significant prototypes scattered over the face of the earth and occurring only in those places where human intelligences have analyzed, formulated, built and produced concrete proof; just as scientists analyze, formulate and achieve proofs in their laboratories.

The outlines of an international architectural theory, one based upon science and technology, are already apparent. Little by little, this theory will be realized. And this revolutionized concept of architecture is adequate to meet the demands of the modern consciousness. It is from this consciousness that it proceeds. But a solitary man living in his solitary house is nothing; he does not exist. Men in a city are legion; there are millions of them. Architecture, having accomplished its own revolution, can no longer do anything to help modern society; it is doomed to stagnation as long as it has no program (official social status) and no environment (its precise urban function must be formulated). Cities are made by planning, and architecture can do nothing without such plans. For the houses it creates are in cities; they are the cities themselves, as we shall see.

Though the purely technical architectural proofs do exist, scattered here and there throughout the world wherever some new spirit has been enabled by an act of faith to erect a modern house the corresponding modern city still does not exist in its entirety except on paper: the act of faith that would permit it to rise from the earth and live must be performed by government. And governments turn a blind eye to the need for city planning. They have no awareness of what such planning requires in the here and now: foresight, preparations. They are busy controlling the past, and the floodwaters are steadily rising. Imagine what we must feel when faced with such neglect! When we know that there are working drawings of planned cities already available, pieces of paper on which *human happiness already exists*, expressed in terms of numbers, of mathematics, of properly calculated designs; plans in which the cities can already be seen, entire, functioning, with all the new organs necessary to the machine age already throbbing with life, governed by the rational requirements of the modern consciousness; the financial mechanism is in intimate accord with the technological data; the practical methods contemplated for their realization are a direct consequence of the financial mechanism. This being so, when one considers the fact that one gesture on the part of government could establish human happiness as a fact of city life, then one feels an urgent need to speak out, to explain, to tell in straightforward words what exactly this city quivering

93

In the Asian steppe

We must try to define the modern consciousness. We are invited to do so by our architecture and city planning: the external form that consciousness adopts.
Despite the frightful confusion of the present age, we shall dig deep till we find the truth. And that truth will be a *man*; a man searching passionately, as man has always done, for his point of balance. By means of ingenious – but possible – calculations, we must bring the falsified equation we see today (the relationship of man to his environment) back to its true form:
city = house = man (culture + deep traditions + climates + history + economic conditions + technology).

The "city of panic"                                    In the jungle

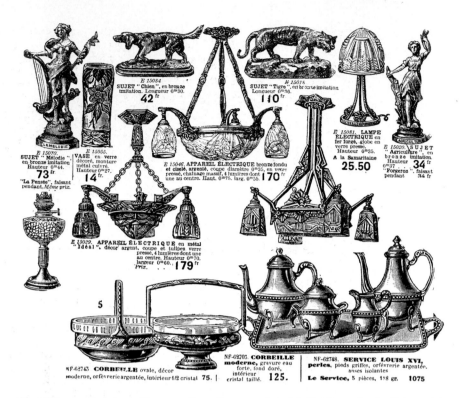

Waste! I am not outraged because these things are bought. But I am deeply distressed to see Authority remaining indifferent in the face of such sacrilege: the time lost in manufacturing these tomfooleries! A healthy, aware, strong nation ought to say: enough!

with life on a piece of paper is. The piece of paper is a plan. And a plan is something that can be used to build with.

\* \* \*

The problem is to create the Radiant City. The Radiant City already exists on paper. And when once a technological product has been designed on paper (calculations and working drawings), *it does exist*. It is only for spectators, for gaping bystanders, for the impotent, that the certainty of its existence lies in the execution. The city of light that will dispel the miasmas of anxiety now darkening our lives, that will succeed the twilight of despair we live in at present, exists on paper. We are only waiting for a "*yes*" from a government with the will and the determination to see it through!

I shall explain the plan for this city, and the explanation will be neither literary nor an approximation. It will be technical and rigorously precise.

The general characteristics of the plan are as follows: the city (a large city, a capital) is much less spread out than the present one; the distances within it are therefore shorter, which means more rest and more energy available for work every day. There are no suburbs or dormitory towns; this means an immediate solution to the transportation crisis that has been forced upon us by the paradox of the city + garden cities.

The garden city is a pre-machine-age utopia.

The population density of the new city will be from three to six times greater than the idealistic, ruinous and inoperative figures recommended by urban authorities still imbued with romantic ideology. This new intensification of population density thus becomes the financial justification for our enterprise: *it increases the value of the ground.*

The pedestrian never meets a vehicle inside the city. The mechanical transportation network is an entirely new organ, a separate entity. The ground level (the *earth*) belongs entirely to the pedestrian.

The "street" as we know it now has disappeared. All the various sporting activities take place directly outside people's homes, in the midst of parks – trees, lawns, lakes. The city is entirely green; *it is a Green City*. Not one inhabitant occupies a room without sunlight; everyone looks out on trees and sky.

The keystone of the theory behind this city is the *liberty of the individual*. Its aim is to create respect for that liberty, to bring it to an authentic fruition, to destroy our present slavery. The restitution of every individual's personal liberty. Waste will also have its throat cut. The cost of living will come down. The new city will break the shackles of poverty in which the old city has been keeping us chained.

Its growth is assured. It is the Radiant City. A gift to all of us from modern technology. Those are the outlines of this new city. And I intend to fill in those outlines later, down to the smallest detail.

\* \* \*

Over the ravaged landscape that we are attempting to transform by our foresight and our efforts into a modern and organized world, there hovers the shadow of war. Men's malice, their ingenuity, even their genius, are being secretly mustered at this moment in an attempt to guarantee the success of the coming war. It will be a chemical war, a bacteriological war. Death will come from the skies: aerial warfare. The aerial defense experts have already told us what will happen: all our cities – yes, Paris too! – will be annihilated in a great whirlwind of explosions. They then add: everything can be saved if we rebuild our cities. Their conclusion is: our cities are too old; they are crumbling away; they are uninhabitable; they are full of lurking disease; it is impossible to move around in them any more: traffic has reached its ceiling, and the reign of speed is leading to total immobility.

Now, however, modern city planning, by resolving the problem of how to provide a machine-age city suited to the purposes of a machine-age society, is also resolving the problems created by the need for aerial defense. We are answering a call for help from our chiefs-of-staff. City planning is – once more – an adjunct to the science of war.

\* \* \*

The world is in the midst of an economic crisis. A tragic crisis that is only just beginning. The machine age seems to be closing the circle and completing the disaster. *"At last!"* exclaim the poets in love with their sunsets along the ancient banks of the Seine, those river banks so packed with history (a history itself packed with acts and actions, but they forget that), *"at last, the great brute and brutality itself have been brought to their knees. The machine age is dying of its own accord. De profundis! Poetry will now bloom anew."*

Our modern factory equipment now produces so much that it is consumers we need more of. The only consumer who is able to consume all this product is the producer himself. How can you expect him to consume what he himself has produced without demanding an increase in his wages? The consequence is an increase in the cost of products, then another increase in wages, etc.: a vicious circle.

The authorities – international commissions, economic experts, diplomats – are all either looking for new markets or trying to protect those they already have. Before long, there is not enough work to go round, then the threat of war, the threat of misery for all.

\* \* \*

Drive through France in a car, along the national highways, along the by-roads; drive across Paris in every direction (not along the Champs-Elysées), eastern Paris, southern Paris, northern Paris, central Paris, and the west too; go out into the provinces and take a close look at the streets of Bordeaux, and Rouen, and Lyons; stop for a look at the little towns, at the villages, at the farms (in Normandy, in Charente, in the Massif Central, in the Dordogne): the houses are out of date; many of them are threatening collapse, others actually are collapsing, others are very unhealthy to live in.

Take an average, a cross section, and the caption you will have to add to it will be this: *A large section of this country must be rebuilt*, because if it isn't rebuilt it will fall down anyway[1].

\* \* \*

Nor is it any good thinking that people living in these old houses in the country will be kept healthy simply by *fresh air*. Statistics show that the mortality rate is higher in the country than in the towns, in the small towns than in the cities. Fresh air is no antidote to decaying homes.

Go and take a look at Germany, at Poland, at Russia, at the Balkans, at Italy, at Spain: in differing degrees, you will find the same threat everywhere.

Statistics also show something else: in the whole of France, the only two cities in which the birth rate is higher than the death rate are Strasbourg and Metz. Strasbourg and Metz were largely rebuilt during the German occupation.

The houses of Europe are centuries old; they are obsolete, antique, rotten. They are about to fall down. They are too badly built to last much longer. One of my friends, arriving home at night in his car after the headlights had failed, drove into the wall of his house; it wasn't the car that was destroyed but the wall: it collapsed in its entirety! Often, we try to make improvements in houses that are a hundred years old. And what

[1] This article was sent in to the editors of *Plans* on October 10, 1930. It was in November of the same year that so much publicity was given to the buildings that collapsed at Fourrières, in Lyons.

Proof that a healthy turn of mind could lead us towards a general renewal of our material and spiritual economic systems. Try to work out the consequences: such an attitude could be far-reaching and pull us out of the hole we are in.

We must pull things down . . .
And throw the corpses onto the garbage heap.

happens? Everything crumbles away and tumbles down. When the Garonne overflowed its banks last winter, it mowed down whole villages like a scythe slicing through hay.

With different coefficients, all the countries of Europe ought to be reconstructing all their cities, their villages, and their farms.

What a program of work and what a market that would mean! Think how many consumers there are longing to put their names down on a waiting list for that commodity: a place to live.

I therefore say this: If we rebuild Europe with stone, with mortar and bricks, then the crisis at present holding us in its grip will remain completely unresolved.

But I also say: houses must no longer be built with stone, with bricks, with cement, with sand and water; they must be built inside, *in factories*, not out in the open under a burning sun, in drenching rain, in the frost of winter. In what factories? In the factories and workshops of heavy industry, of the metal and wood and synthetics industries. These factories already exist, completely equipped; they are lying idle. If we do this, then our buildings will be subjected to the rhythm of modern methods of work, to the discipline of timetables, of machines and of our construction programs. In these factories – as we know – a *single* automobile would cost two hundred thousand francs, whereas mass production brings its cost down to thirty thousand. We may therefore assume that the price of a building will be reduced by half. The same will in consequence be true of the individual home. And we shall be able to reduce these figures still further when, in the course of sketching the details of *the Radiant City*, we have addressed ourself to the question: *what is a home?*

\* \* \*

These, then, are the truths of the present moment: if we can bring ourselves to look our present crisis in the face, if we wish to save industry and throttle the growing unemployment, *we must rebuild the country by constructing "prefabricated houses" in factories*. The *prefabricated house*, erected and bolted together on its given site, whether it is 60 feet high or 600 feet high, will not, I scarcely need say, be at all like the old stone-built house. It will provide a different sort of home – a 20th century home. A new word, *domestic equipment*, with the help of many different industries, will become a genuine source of happiness, for happiness is liberty, time saved, freedom from unpleasant tasks. And happiness is also meditation, and the activities in which those hours saved are spent; it is a thousand individually initiated activities – liberty itself – enabling people to demonstrate that they are *themselves*. And it means a suitable setting for our meditations; more than that, an harmonious setting, a setting full of all the luxury implied in the word *fitting*.

Industry will build the *prefabricated house* and equip it. It will do so with the same minute and meticulous attention to economy in the matters of space, materials and ease of movement as industry now lavishes on the ocean liner, the automobile, or the airplane. These last three are proofs of what can be done in this way.

But, before building the prefabricated house we must plan the cities.

And in order to make the modern home a reality, we must first define its aims. These will all add up to one general aim: a home that will conform to the modern consciousness.

\* \* \*

Architectural revolution? *Already accomplished.*
Industry, practical production techniques? They already exist.
City planning? The authorities.
Machine-age housing: must satisfy the latent needs of the modern consciousness.

The philosophic postulate? Yes, there is one - the keystone of the whole structure.

The present neglect, apparent in all spheres of life, seems to me to lead inevitably to the simple question: *Who am I?*

Revision.

Affirmation of the individual.

Recasting of the social structure.

. . . . . . . . . . . . . . . . . . . . . . . .

By bloody revolution? Not necessary.

By clarity of mind, sanity, good sense, ideals, faith and energy.

By character.

\* \* \*

We need a definition of the modern consciousness. Without it we cannot keep any clear image before us of the man for whom we are building the modern home; we cannot form any clear idea of the social obligations that must form the basis of the city's official regulations and statutes; we cannot demand of the authorities, in the name of this modern consciousness that has determined the form of the modern home and defined the city, that they issue the decree, the law, the act that will set this great work of construction in motion and raise the contemporary city that we need.

\* \* \*

The world is not coming to an end. Neither Europe, nor the United States, nor the U.S.S.R., nor Asia, nor South America, is in its twilight. *The world is coming back to life.* We are in the midst of a Renaissance. The Great War: the first fissure. It has been carefully plastered over; but let no one imagine that everything is now settled. No, the world is not old. It is full of energy. More than that, it is full of faith. A new faith is in the process of evolution. A great adventure is beginning; great changes of fortune are imminent; the surge of change will be both wide and deep. We are about to see new things. There are minds – a few, already – that have been grappling with new dimensions, with new relations between things. We have a constant: eternal man, who practically speaking does not change. But the curve of progress has suddenly made a prodigious leap. There is a new perspective in the world. I am certain that all we are now envisaging in the present, or for the future, is in fact on too small a scale. We see things too small. But our minds, already learning to cope with the new dimensions ahead, have already freed themselves, have already torn themselves away from the table cluttered with the remains of a centuries-old meal: those rotting cities, those infinitely subdivided fields, that incoherent distribution of population, that morality now becoming as fragile as a bubble. Our minds are insisting on a clean tablecloth.

October, 1930.

The Green City:

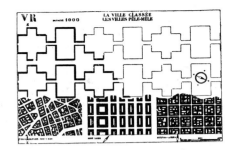

Paris, New York, Buenos Aires:

All on the same scale; comparison between a residential district in the Radiant City (with its superdensity of population) and similar districts in our present capitals.

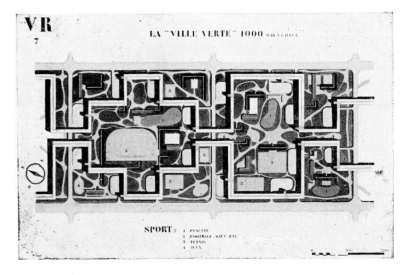

The Radiant City? Whenever we like!
One day, perhaps, those in power will be forced to show their accounts!

13th century. Notre-Dame de Paris

# 3. PARIS IN DANGER

Since my life is a perpetual enquiry into the matter of city planning, it is impossible for me to remain unaffected by the spectacle of Paris, our capital, bursting with prodigious life, sprouting on every side with the new buds of a renaissance, strangled by a tangled chaos of conflicting private needs and interests, and unable to express its vitality, unable to progress and develop except in such sadly stunted ways. How noble the energy expended, yet how disturbed the spectator must remain! This is why, in the midst of these laboratory studies, of which I am attempting here to give the results, harried more and more each day by the speed with which time is flying by, I am inserting these pages on Paris.

Impelled by the pressure of daily reactions to events, I must say: *PARIS IS IN DANGER!*

\* \* \*

"You're being very melodramatic, Monsieur," the unconcerned will tell me.

But if I could prove that this phrase really expresses a pathetic situation, one I find reflected in the anguish that oppresses me every time my thoughts turn to this city that could well fade away, decline, become paralyzed, and die a horrible death, if . . . If we do not act, if we cease to believe in life, if we let ourselves think that Europe is sinking into a twilight, if we deny the tradition of our city, if we capitulate! . . .

But that could also raise itself up once more, tall on that age-old soil, and cry out to the whole world the strong and joyous message that the world expects of her.

Paris, the seat of Cartesian reason, the field of great artistic battles; Paris, the awesome source of potential culture; Paris, which has always known how to judge, which has always, having judged, known how to act when the moment came. No, this city will not decline into a sleep, for such a sleep would be the end of it. Paris will not cease to be!

\* \* \*

I want to tell you how much I love Paris: a place throbbing with life, yet also a clear, desert atmosphere in which great forces are pitted one against the other in a "tournament of purity." The pure idea is always the champion, and all around lie the corpses, the not-quite-good-enoughs that have succumbed in the struggle! So violent is the struggle, so powerful the mass of age-old verities always ready to crush a new idea, that the only contenders who can possibly emerge triumphant are those who can laugh and sing no matter what, those who work on doggedly in the clear knowledge that their efforts are the product of a total lack of self-interest. They are the madmen of this world, the followers of art for art's sake, the only activity guaranteed to bring happiness in its train.

The seed is sown; the shoot appears: then it is trampled back into the ground. Another root goes down, the work continues underground; then a new shoot rises, followed by a second destruction. There are too many of us trying to champion our ideas all at the same time: a simple clever remark, the fruit of centuries of cultivation, is enough to cover one's name with mud. The experience is repeated over and over again; people consume their youth in the struggle, and even the prime of their lives. One has to fight for twenty years in order to achieve success. The "twenty-year war," waged by a single warrior (oneself) against an army of past feats. I know of no harder city in the world. Paris, maternal but happily harsh, we are able to sink strong roots in your hard soil, deep, slow roots that enable us to win the tournament of purity!

Such is the precious soil of Paris. Is this tension only a recent product of machine-age disturbances? Were things easier before Stevenson? I do not know; we were not there; and the man who has reached shore quickly forgets the raft that bore him through the raging waves; he turns his eyes to the future; he hurries to go on with life; he begins to build. We have no historians of the bad days. That is why there are no monuments to the unknown soldiers who have fallen in the Great Tournament.

Paris the Cartesian city, Paris refusing all confusion, Paris means clarity.

\* \* \*

On the Gulf of Lion there stands a dead city: Aigues-Mortes, a seaport now filled with sand, a town lying between reed-filled lagoons and salt marshes. It was built from scratch by Saint Louis to permit the embarkation of his armies setting out on the Crusades. The wall is still intact, with all its military defenseworks. These defenses are meticulously executed, accurate and ingenious; the stones are clean, the cornerstones still sharp. The walls shine with a spiritual light. Aigues-Mortes is a product of Paris, built for a Parisian by Parisians. Reason is all-powerful within its walls; yet it has a kind of smiling radiance too. And this is what we continue to find all through our history: *foresight* and the *radiance of pure mind*. In other words, a tough problem overcome without brutality, ease of manner combined with severity, and this severity, which occurs throughout the world history of all the arts, leads to a certain rigidity. This rigidity is the aristocratic sign of exactitude and perfect judgment. Is this rigidity too dry, too pedantic, a source of impotence? Not at all: though it will not bend either to the right or to the left, it nevertheless possesses the suppleness of the tightrope walker. It is mathematical expression, a pure profile, a line.

The interior of Notre-Dame, Fouquet's paintings, the fort of Vincennes, Clouet's drawings, the Pont-Neuf, the Place des Vosges, the Pont Royal, Nicolas Poussin, the Invalides, the Place de la Concorde, the Arc de Triomphe, the footbridge of les Arts, Ingres, the Bibliothèque Sainte-Geneviève, the Tour Eiffel, Cézanne – these are examples of the rigidity produced by severity. Our heritage from all the ages of Paris. The tightrope walker's rope stretched from the steeple of a church to the roof of the town hall isn't a straight line: it is a curve along which each point is a point of balance in the extreme tension of the whole, a shaft of wit. If you explore the rest of the world and make comparisons, then you will appreciate the truth of this.

Paris, in the heart of the Ile de France, is a place given over to the arts. The line of Paris is the straight line, correctness, all that is *well made*. Once again, you only have to take a look at the rest of the world to know the truth of that.

\* \* \*

What moves me in Paris is its vitality. She has been living on her present site now for more than a thousand years, always beautiful and always lauded, always new and always being renewed. The standard of progress has long been planted in this great tiltyard where the champions of Purity have jousted through the ages. Paris is alive!

But here is the reason for my anxiety: I am afraid for her because no one, in the places where decisions to act are taken, is concerned with carrying on the tradition of Paris. At this moment, the city is racked with disease; it is becoming impotent and senile on all sides. No Colbert to prescribe for it, no surgeon to operate. Not even a diagnosis!

\* \* \*

Am I overbold and presumptuous to speak of the problem in these terms? By what right do I dare to offer my opinion? On what grounds are my convictions based? I will tell you: life has a savor that can only be sensed by the nose; neither reasoning nor will are of any use in the matter. There are perceptions more subtle than either simple sight or simple touch that can suggest a direction for our actions: and we follow them. We follow because we know we are obeying the commands of life. Of life itself! But it is the action, the movement, the enterprise, the destined purpose of the passing moment

Jean Fouquet (15th century). A painter who knew how to paint and possessed lucidity and foresight (Portrait of Charles VII).

*Photo Giraudon*

Pol de Limbourg (15th century). The fort of Vincennes at the gates of Paris.

*Photo Giraudon*

"The straight line is not French." So writes the city-planning reporter for *Le Temps*.

History. Historic Paris, tubercular Paris.

that we must be able to seize! The signs are there for us to read: the propulsive force of the age we are living in. If only we can allow ourselves to be carried away by that force we shall be strong; otherwise we shall molder away, we shall rot. The signs before us now are explicit: the developments now occurring in our cities are heralding the irresistible, irrepressible floodtide of the machine age; the new age is making its presence felt, it is making itself apparent on every side, it is raising its head everywhere, it is pushing everything before it, knocking things down, pushing them aside, making itself master; it is transforming the old scale of dimensions that we have accepted for centuries, it is forcing a new concept of duration on time itself. Everything is exploding, and everything should be a source of joy in this new spring: action, optimism, work, achievements, pride, grandeur, collective enthusiasm, joyous impulse, conquests, risk – a wild and healthy adventure. But the forces of reaction are mobilized too, their weapons bristling behind the wall of immobility that they will defend in the face of universal suffering. The forces of reaction are aroused; their method is to appeal to public opinion. In order to crush us, to defeat those who want to act, the people who are satisfied with things as they are call out to the millions of poor wretches whose lives are oppressed and blackened by their decaying city: "Poor wretch, these people want to tarnish your time-honored reputation for good taste; poor wretch, there are vandals, men without heart, who are trying to destroy the beauty of your city, to annihilate the magnificent history that resides in the places where you live in poverty!" These people are attempting to capture public opinion, through the newspapers, through the magazines, with speeches. The forces of reaction are up in arms.

Just the moment when the decks should be being cleared for the great epic of our times, cowardly panic is the order of the day!

The city is decaying more and more quickly; from now on, the city is an absurdity.

The high tide of the machine age is spreading destruction everywhere. The Parisian no longer knows where the enemy is. As soon as spring comes, if he is rich he sends his children away from the city; the city is losing its soul – the joy of its populace. This has happened in the past twenty years, because blinkered views have obscured the true horizons of the city's future. Paris is abdicating, denying its past tradition every day. Paris is in danger.

\* \* \*

Let us talk about the taste of Paris, the temerity of Paris, the spirit of synthesis that reigns in Paris. It must be made clear how much the world expects a gesture from Paris that will bring light into the world. And we, the professional architects and city planners, we must set forth the certainties upon which the Radiant City is founded.

The prestige of Paris: the taste of Paris. The tightrope walker's rope is a good image; it conjures up the idea of a narrow path and hair-raising balancing acts, and it is these alone that draw forth shouts of admiration. The tightrope goes straight from one point to another; it is like the result of a vast saber stroke. Yet in depth, it is a curve – a mathematical curve on which any given point is an exact balance between its own weight and its distance between the two attached ends. Mathematicians define it as *the curve of a thread in equilibrium*. It is impossible to imagine a greater severity combined with so much flexibility. The tightrope is a line of perfectly balanced points.

The chaos created everywhere by the rising tide of the machine age imposes new choices, fresh decisions, at every moment. In the present ubiquitous state of doubt, it is always the exaggeratedly simple lines of thought that obtain favor with peoples who want to act: the two extremes of any question are worked out, and then they choose – *black* or *white*. Having chosen, then begun the work consequent upon this decision, they perceive their error. Whereupon, without so much as a blush at such a contradiction, they leap from black straight over to white. The movement is always to the contrary of what went before; a new school of thought is perpetually in the process of ousting its predecessor. Since the war, we have had a breathtaking series of "isms": expressionism, constructivism, functionalism. Extremes, always extremes! But Paris has always remained the home of the *juste milieu*. Life is not over there to the right, not over there to the left; it flows in the middle, between those millions of points that make up one cutting line, the boundary where the two opposing tides of extremist opinion meet. And Paris, which is an estuary for the creative powers of the world, lies on such a line of violent encounters: in equilibrium. If we wish to express the hard truth of life, then it is no good yawing continually from port to starboard, we must dance on the razor's edge, the line of equilibrium.

That is the strength of Paris where all the tempests rage.

(Except that the academies, needless to say, have no idea of it.)

* * *

The temerity of Paris. That first great Gothic nave – Notre-Dame. From small stone to small stone, the vaultings convey their efforts down through the buttresses, through the flying buttresses, through the pillars, down to the foundations. A bold use of limitations, a magical economy of means: successes in the midst of danger. And it was like that for centuries, in every sphere. The same image still haunts my mind: the razor's edge, the perilous line of the correct solution. The strength, not of Cyclopean masses of masonry, but of an audacious and hair-fine equilibrium. The same is true in the esthetic sphere. One evening, in commemoration of the armistice, the Place de la Concorde was floodlit. It was a spectacle that had never existed before; the architects who built the palaces lining the square could never have hoped for such a transparent expression of their thought. Under the black night sky, from the Palais Bourbon as far as the Madeleine, from the balustrades of the Tuileries to the Arc de l'Etoile, and then, in the center, the Obelisk, we saw the purest, the most tightly stretched straight lines combining into an harmonious and graceful whole. Each line was etched in light, brightly gouged into the black shadow behind; the overheavy roofs, the confusion of minor details outlined against the sky, none of that remained; we could see nothing but selected, razor-sharp lines: the expression of the architecture itself, a starkness of striking intensity. We were seeing intensity itself. Everything lies in that: almost nothing. We saw straight lines like the arrows of Apollo flying through the night. And between them – the relations that are architecture. That was two or three years ago. This year, the genius of the place is no longer visible; the number of projectors has been doubled, the spaces between the columns have been lit up, and the symphony of lines I have been describing is no longer being played. Mere floodlit buildings, nothing more.

The temerity of Paris: those great outlines created by Louis XIV, and of which we are so proud. Paris is in danger if we allow ourselves to believe, as we gape in wonder, that it was we who made them.

The temerity of Paris: those cannon-straight avenues blasted by Napoleon-Haussmann through the age-old remnants of a worm-eaten city. Paris is in danger if we allow ourselves to believe, in our stupidity, that it was we who did the blasting.

The temerity of Paris: the Tour Eiffel, the sign of Paris, a symbol dear to the hearts of those who think lovingly back to the capital from the depths of pampas or steppe, from African desert or American West. But Paris is in danger, yes, in danger, because we forget today that without Rodin and other bold spirits Paris would have demolished the Tour Eiffel, just as it demolished the Palais de l'Industrie, and the Galerie des

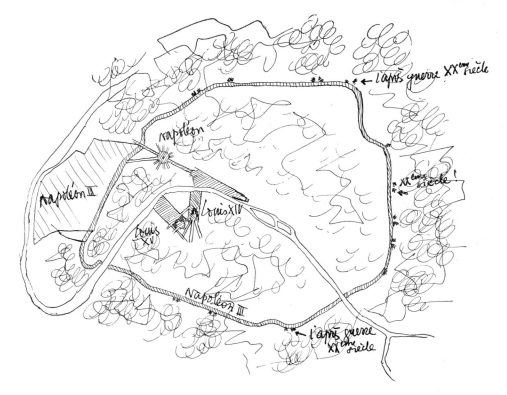

The Third Republic has accomplished a great deal of admirable anatomical construction in Paris: transportation, roads and innumerable public services. In the matter of city planning, regression all along the line. This sketch depicts the accomplishments of the Bourbons and the Napoleons. But those little scribbles at the gates of the city, obstructing our access to the national highways, those are the work OF THE TWENTIETH CENTURY POSTWAR PERIOD! ! ! Fear, confusion, diffusion and absence of strong and genuine responsibilities = the collapse of all enterprises, dust scattered to the wind: none of our social or technical problems even touched.

The Middle Ages builds its skyscraper, with small stones and *without cement*.

The Third Republic buries the skyscraper inside a dense mass of tall middle-class houses. Great cliffs along the line of the medieval streets: corridor streets and a stone desert.

How to have air, light and greenery all around us again. A vast new design, a vast new destiny for the city. Cities can now be seen from airplanes; tomorrow we shall all go in planes; we already ride in cars; our houses are made of steel and reinforced concrete. No, no, no, shout the "friends of Paris" in the name of History. History? But History is *life;* its thrill has never reached these people.

Machines. It did Paris great harm to demolish the Galerie des Machines in order to uncover the architectural poverty of the Ecole Militaire: a murder in order to show off a little ghost! With the exception of the Tour Eiffel, Paris has destroyed all its late nineteenth century architecture – buildings that were inspiring examples of discovery, of adventurousness, of audacity.

\* \* \*

Travel abroad. Visit other countries, other continents: the world is counting on Paris. All the cities of the world are equally sick, battered by the rising machine-age tide, bewildered by the new turn of events. The cities of the world are living in an anguish of uncertainty. Think: everywhere you look, governments have established academies. These academies are so many morgues: vast intellectual deep-freezes full of corpses. The doors are tightly closed, nothing can get in from outside. The only communication they have is a telephone line to their respective governments. Danger everywhere: we are living in perilous times when governments take the advice of their academies. The governments, unaware, are calmly watching their cities suffocate to death. Who will dare to smash the academies and insist on the governments using their powers in this matter of city planning? Perhaps the voice of the masses will make itself heard one day. But the matter is so urgent!

Travelers of the world, you know that a great gesture from Paris would set this adventure afoot throughout the world. The building of our machine-age cities!

\* \* \*

No more evasions. No more saying: we'll finish the program begun by Louis XIV little by little (that was what was said and written on the occasion of the opening of the Boulevard Haussmann – January 15, 1927). How can we dare to say that, to write it! No, we must conceive, struggle, decide, act! While there is still time! For instead of conceiving the Paris necessary to our most indispensable social functions, we are letting things slide into disaster while multiplying the number of people employed in keeping the peace by a hundred! It is terrifying! Every day, Paris takes another step towards petrifaction: people are allowed to rebuild their great buildings on the same sites, on the same old streets. Are there no young men any more? Is there no program anywhere? Has the trajectory of our great traditions been broken? Are we beaten, vanquished, on our knees, unable to help ourselves? We are being ruled by cowardice! Whose cowardice? Not ours. And we are legion . . . we would be legion if we could count ourselves. And that is what we must find out how to do. We must count heads, combine and blow the conservatives with their academic notions sky-high.

The dimensions, the place and the financial conditions of our problem have already been posited by the very fact of modern social development. New dimensions already exist, and it is according to these new dimensions that the new organs of modern life must be measured. The situation is clear: the city is in the grip of a deadly sickness. Diagnosis is possible: we know where, how and with what we must act. The possible improvement of the land as a financial asset is a direct invitation to the financiers to act immediately. The figures tell us that nothing is impossible; what must be done can be done. The age of architecture has begun. Today, architecture is involved in all the thousand and one little things that go to make up a great city's life. What is needed, in Paris, is order. Who will give the order? Those capable of carrying out such a program already have the facts in their hands. As always, they are ready to take the risk, they are prepared for the labor pains, for the drudgery involved in this change; they are curious to see the future, they have a thirst for harmony, they are ready to give their work in the cause of the idea.

102

\* \* \*

A unique moment is now upon us: the life of the city could depend upon it. Everything, if we neglect this chance, may now slither down into mediocrity. Paris a mediocrity! It isn't possible. Paris abdicating her position because of a few tired spirits unable to pull themselves out of their armchair sinecures! These people are in a blue funk, they are wiping drops of cold sweat off their faces because they believe in themselves as responsible people, because they are holding back progress out of a genuine conviction. Paris knows when to hold back, we know that. She allows no enthusiasm to cloud the purity of her thought. Paris has always known how to exercise restraint until the hour of peril is upon her. But when the danger comes, then Paris must throw herself into the battle.

\* \* \*

The building of the Radiant City can be a joyous adventure, an active, productive task carried out with enthusiasm, with faith, with a love of beauty, with an architectural grandeur inspired by the new programs, and on a new scale of greatness!

Paris is truly in danger; for if Paris doesn't move, Paris will become senile.

January, 1931.

●

"Whoah, my beauty!"...

(it applies to city planning too)

Paris was transformed on its own ground, without evasion. Each current of thought is inscribed in its stones, throughout the centuries.
In this way the living image of Paris was formed. Paris must continue!

ici, l'académisme dit: Non!

(Sketches for lectures in Buenos Aires, 1929).

# 4. TO LIVE! (TO BREATHE)

## SUBURBS MUST BE ELIMINATED AND NATURE BROUGHT INTO THE CITIES THEMSELVES

An immense melancholy fills me when I return to Paris, to the boulevards, to the dismal railroad-station approaches, to the streets – the sheer corridors, the blackness of them, the hidden sky.

(August, 1930)

Architecture, city planning,
our happiness,
the state of our consciousness,
the equilibrium of our individual lives,
the rhythm of our collective duties

are all governed by the *24-hour cycle of the sun*. The sun is in control. Of everything: thought, action, movement, functions, undertakings, obligations, all these are contained, inevitably, within the exact boundaries established by two sleeps. Each morning life begins afresh, and our energies are renewed; every evening, our eyelids close, and sleep performs its inexplicable miracle.

24 hours! That is the yardstick and the rhythm of human life; the unit to which everything must conform.

All problems of distance, dimension, and distribution have to be solved within those precise limits: 24 hours.

\* \* \*

A home? It is essential that those hours be capable of including the entire domestic symphony.

A home? Body and mind. Biology and feelings. Action and repose. Fatigue and recuperation. The daily balance sheet: active and passive. The image of a balance sheet contains a certain threat. What if every evening there is a deficit? That means a victory for death, the loss of paradise. But if the sheet balances every evening, or – even better – shows a profit, then that means the new life: light and joy!

But now we are coming down to the fundamental reasons for living. Yes, indeed we are!

\* \* \*

Government, AUTHORITY, the partriarch, the head of the family, the chief of the tribe, you who know (or ought to know), are you aware of what a home really means? What is it you are governing? What is it you are administrating? Results, effects, things already in the past, relics and remains. And the CAUSE? What constitutes the foundation of a balanced human life? Do you know, are you concerned to know, what that foundation ought to be today, or what things ought no longer to be tolerated today? All your efforts are centered on one problem: finding work for us. (And you allow the masses to manufacture no matter what, *for their own misfortune.*) Guardian power, you must learn to see more clearly. At this moment, you should be exclaiming to yourself: "*It is time I reached the bottom of this question.*"

\* \* \*

*Home* or *city*, it is all the same thing: both are manifestations of the same unity. If we conjure up an image of *the city*, then we can envisage the undertaking before us in its entirety. And we know that in undertaking the construction of the city we shall be giving work to everyone in it, which means that we shall be able *to banish, to forbid* all sterile, self-strangling and stupid work. That, today, is the UNDERTAKING before us: a word pregnant with tremendous possibilities for action and success! But we must not allow our thoughts to be chained too close to the earth; we must have a vision of the things before us. A vision – our eyes following the trajectory of a well-balanced equation. We must dare to affirm the results of these calculations; we must have a goal before us. And that goal is to wrench ourselves free from the appalling depreciation steadily destroying our present way of life. Everything is ready for this undertaking, everything has been tried and proved in advance by the sciences. All over the world, the calculations, the plans, the graphs, the prototypes and the proofs already exist.

Our opponents will put up a stubborn resistance to this, saying: "That is all impossible, it is too vast, it is an inconceivable task!" Answer: Gentlemen, we were able to carry on a major war for five years, one that involved the mobilization of millions of men, the feeding of millions of men, the construction of cannons and dreadnoughts, the creation of an aviation industry, the fabrication with clockwork precision of the storms, the tempests, the hurricanes, the typhoons unleashed by bombs and shells. We were able to create the necessary propaganda, the great "wartime press": all the newspapers combined, every 24 hours over a period of five years, to prevent our energies from flagging; they controlled public opinion entirely. We were able to perform miracles of transportation: the Americans were able to send a million men with all their equipment across an ocean full of torpedoes. We even created an espionage network and a counter-espionage system. There was no human energy we did not press into service, whether spiritual or material: biceps, doggedness, dreams, theories, earthy common sense, idealism and brutality; savage fury and religion. We even mobilized our churches! We conscripted Jesus Christ!

\* \* \*

Whenever they are confronted with any suggestion for reform expressed on paper, one that has been drawn up with a set square and lacks the usual superficial contortions forced upon us by our present "adaptations" to things as they are, sensitive souls bristle with antagonism and accuse us of trying to Americanize them. *Right angles are American.* That is the weapon with which they try to club us down. Shortly after the war, aroused by our campaign on behalf of order and against the chaos being caused by our "donkey tracks"[1] as a result of the automobile invasion, the city-planning columnist of a large Paris newspaper denounced us with the words: "the straight line is German and the curve is French." The right angle and the straight line not French? That is nationalism gone mad.

This takes me back to 1922 and to the state of mind I was in while creating "*a contemporary city with a population of 3 million.*" The task before me then was the inauguration, by analysis, by mathematical calculation, and also by an overwhelmingly powerful intuition, *of a new scale for our cities.* My researches had been long, patient, methodical; their results were ineluctable; *they had to be faced.* But then, how disturbed

---

[1] "The Donkey Track" *(Chemin des Ânes)*, which was the first chapter of *Urbanisme* (Crès et Cie), was a demonstration of how the great cities of Europe developed, day by day, along the urban transport channels determined by the first carts. Though these channels were originally guided by a sure instinct (the law of least effort), it will easily be understood that any new and *concerted* transportation developments must be conditioned by that entirely new phenomenon in human history – the high-speed vehicle.

*Living in order to work!* This means breaking our backs, driving ourselves mad, moral bewilderment, a prodigious hiatus between us and the realities of nature, plunging into a black abyss of artificiality. So men have grouped themselves together. Why? In order to struggle together for an improvement in their lives? No! In order to suffer. To have gone so far, to have allowed ourselves to drift so far in our cities – all our cities – that the human mechanism has run off the rails, so that we are mere hunted animals!... Flowers! We must live surrounded by flowers!

Flowers, sun, joy. Who is going to wear these beautiful bathing costumes created by our big stores? And how soon?

Sport? Only for the players (20 players for every 20,000 spectators). Where is the sport for the 20,000 spectators? Our aim: sport for everyone. That is the question.

I was by my discoveries! They were agonizing weeks to live through. In my head, in my vision, my notion of things, a whole new set of dimensions had been born; I was living them, I was feeling and perceiving everything through them. I was compelled to cross Paris again and again in every direction, to look again at all its avenues, not just at the streets of the Temple neighborhood where we were setting up the diorama in our workshop. The city crushed in upon itself, that absent sky, the deep, black, cataclysmic fissures of the streets all stifled me. But on the other hand, I was filled with a great anguish lest the immense open spaces that I was creating in our imaginary city, spaces dominated by the wide sky on all sides, should be "dead" spaces; I was afraid that they would prove full only of boredom, and that the inhabitants of such a city would be seized by panic at the sight of so much emptiness. [1]

It has taken eight years of worrying for me to find out where I should go to look for the answer to this problem. And the answer is: what are the true functions of the machine-age man? What if I can manage to fill my modern man's 24-hour day completely; what if, moreover, I can manage to make his life comfortable; what if, better yet, I can contrive to make him a gift of personal liberty within this collective organization, restore that liberty to him, amplify it, extend the areas of its effectiveness, and give him the opportunity to indulge in the activities that this increased liberty will give rise to? Once more, as always, the city planner must place the figure of a man before him, consider that man and talk to him.

We work in order to live. We do not live in order to work. Or at least, this postulate appears to be the norm. Has today's reality quite simply stood it on its head? The machine (born in about 1830, coming of age in about 1930) is able to do a large part of our work for us, and ought to have led to our liberation; the machine reduced the amount of necessary human work. But, without our becoming aware of it, for the human mind is only too prone to let itself drift in this way, new needs were also created. But, having begun as reasonable, permissible and pleasurable, these needs became insane, innumerable and unjustifiable. So that we have been led into the position of *living in order to work*.

If reason regains the upper hand, if the patriarchal AUTHORITY that governs us can find a way of imposing some sort of classification, a ban on the production of idiotic merchandise and the prevention of waste, then we can begin to work again (normally) *in order to live*.

Have the necessary preparations been made to provide occupations for the leisure time ahead? If the Paris worker leaves his work at three in the afternoon, *will he find* anything prepared to enable him to use his free time . . . on something useful, healthy, pleasant and exhilarating?

Answer: the harsh, inhuman city, pitiless to children and grownups alike, has not changed. *It would be dangerous* if all our afternoons became free after work. What would we do? What would the masses do?

*There is no residential neighborhood within the city.*

\* \* \*

The necessary explanations about the modern CITY – the Radiant City – are infinitely complex: each question ricochets back onto the others in every direction.

[1] "A contemporary city with a population of 3 million." Salon d'Automne, 1922. A stand 27 meters long, a diorama of 100 square meters. Graphs of the population densities of this "green city." Proposals for "villa-apartments," etc.

106

I shall therefore leap, at this point, feet firmly together, straight to the solution: here is a fragment of a residential neighborhood in the Radiant City. The population density is 1,000 per hectare (slightly less than 2½ acres). (London can boast only 150, Berlin 400, and Paris sadly admits to 800 in her most overpopulated neighborhoods.) *A thousand people to the hectare!*

The present city authorities are trying at all costs to thrust us out into suburban garden-cities (150 to 300 people to the hectare). My own proposal is that we should pile the city in on top of itself, *intra-muros*, and increase its population density to 1,000. At the Congrès du Paris Nouveau, the City Planning Commission considered the possibility of a Greater Parisian Zone 100 kilometers in diameter! We must eliminate the suburbs, eliminate and ban these garden-cities with their mock nature; then we shall hear no more about the transportation crisis. And then, on top of Paris as it is, costive, shut-in and stifling, let us build the GREEN CITY = THE RADIANT CITY. *Nature brought inside the walls of Paris.* A nature neither more nor less artificial than that of the garden-cities, but useful inside the city. But how can it be done? Listen:

(I am borrowing the dry terminology of the technical report.)

*Habitable surface available per individual (for his home).*

Let us begin with the figures envisaged by the Loi Loucheur: 45 square meters per 6 inhabitants; i.e. 7.50 m² per person. This Loucheur-type domestic unit can be occupied by 6, 4, 3 or 2 persons. If we suppose an equal space available in all of these four cate-

One of the beautiful sections of Paris, Saint-Augustin. This photo is on the SAME scale as the plan (on the right) of a popular section of the Radiant City. The density of Saint-Augustin, before the war, was about 200 to 300 per hectare. It was sterile, tight, shut in, selfish – pre-machine age.

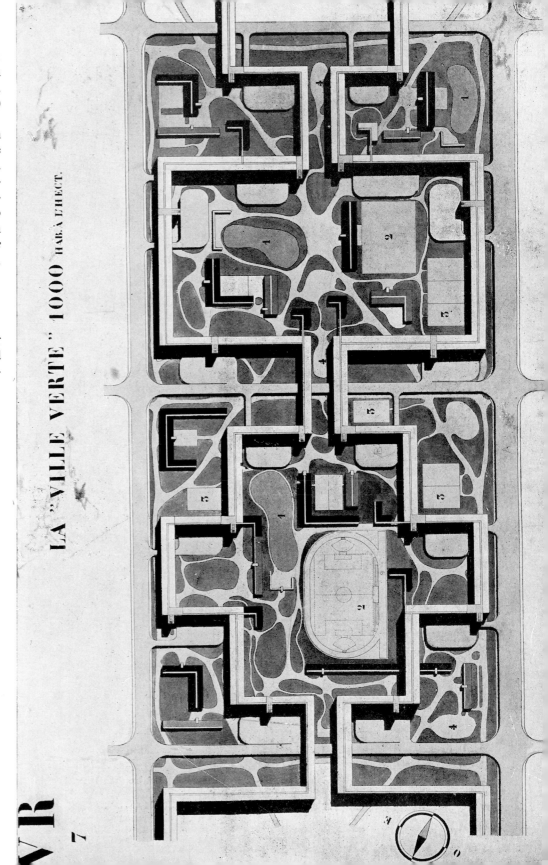

LA "VILLE VERTE" 1000 HAB. A L'HECT.

VR 7

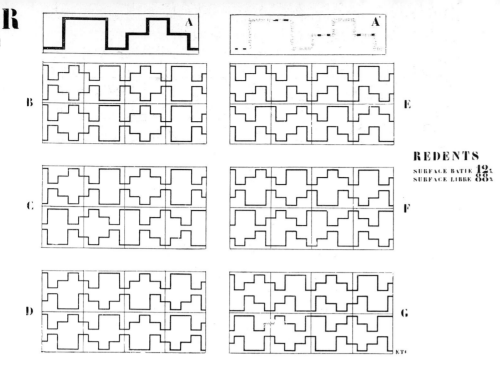

REDENTS

SURFACE BATIE 12%
SURFACE LIBRE 88%

One basic pattern (for apartment buildings without streets or courtyards). Here are six different variations on that pattern. Then we can start on another pattern, then another, etc.

Same scale: The Radiant City, Paris, New York, Buenos Aires. Note the white spaces in the Radiant City. Now color them green.

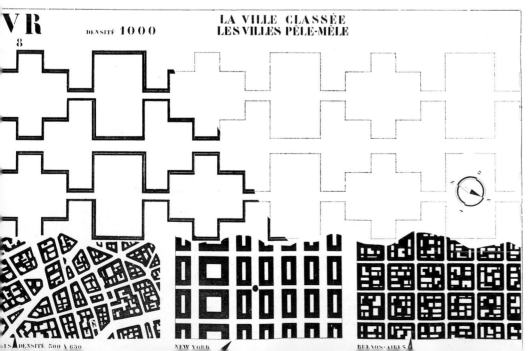

gories, we arrive at the following:

in a unit occupied by 6 people: 7.50 m² per person
„        „        4  „  : 11.25 m² „    „
„        „        3  „  : 15    m² „    „
„        „        2  „  : 22.50 m² „    „

giving an average of 14 square meters per person.
14 square meters per person. Magnificent!

With the modern techniques at our disposal, and now that the architectural revolution has been accomplished, we could produce some astonishing housing projects on this basis. Let us repeat, and repeat to satiety, that possibly two million of the population are now living in housing that is in direct contradiction to all the laws of natural domestic economy. Their lives are one long and suffocating martyrdom.

We have, of course, eliminated the "corridor-street" – the street that now exists in all the cities of the world. *Our living quarters have nothing to do with the streets.* More than that, we have deliberately (though not merely for the sake of it) gone against the present tendency to envisage the pedestrians running to and fro on raised walks *in the air* and the traffic occupying the ground. *We have allotted* the ENTIRE GROUND SURFACE *of the city to the pedestrian.* The *earth itself* will be occupied by lawns, trees, sports and playgrounds. Almost 100 per cent of the ground surface will be used by the inhabitants of the city. And since our apartment houses are all up in the air, raised on pilotis, it will be possible to walk across the city in any direction. In other words: NO PEDESTRIAN WILL EVER MEET AN AUTOMOBILE, EVER! And that is something absolutely new. Though it is a whole story on its own, and one that will be told in a later chapter called "The Death of the Street."

Thus, the parks, the sports grounds, the entertainment areas, etc, are all around the houses. And *under* the houses, there will be covered playgrounds. The houses will cover 11.4 per cent of the surface of the residential areas. That leaves 88.6 per cent open to the sky. In this way, one of our aims has been attained: SPORTING ACTIVITIES WILL TAKE PLACE DIRECTLY OUTSIDE THE HOUSES. No more courtyards, ever again. Instead, an open view from every window (though there won't be any windows, of course, only walls of glass).

# STANDARDIZATION LAW AND UNITY

*We shall be driven to despair by the uniformity of everything!*

*Yes, it is a danger. But here is a striking example taken from nature that will help us in the planning of our Radiant City. I had this simple, simplified vision of our world one dismal December day in 1930. There was sooty snow falling in the streets of Paris, night had already fallen at three in the afternoon; it was a sight to make the heart sink:*

*The Good Lord accomplished an amazing thing when he tilted the Earth's axis of rotation into the ecliptic.*

*1° The earth is spherical: therefore it would seem that any given point on its surface ought to be strictly identical to any other given point (same distance from the center).*

the apartment blocks will be built up on pilotis and not touch the ground (and these piles will be of use in case of gas attacks). Moreover, the buildings that cover 11 per cent of the residential areas will all have *roof gardens* on top of them (solariums, in case of aerial warfare). These roof gardens will be used for walks, for sports training, etc.

The fundamental calculations are as follows: you take a given city area; you build apartment houses on it that will provide accomodation for a thousand people per hectare and leave your surface area intact – 100 per cent. To that figure you add the 11 per cent surface of the roof gardens. Total: 111 per cent of the surface area of the city brought into use, exploited, producing a maximum yield, reserved for the *pedestrian alone*, so that he can enjoy himself, walk, run, play, breathe, soak up the air and the sun, revive his body, and even better than that: make his body a thing of magnificence. And as for the speeding traffic, the iron torpedoes that fill our lives with so much anxiety at the moment – *he never meets them at all!*

Further on, I shall describe how our roads will have left the ground, and how, by a correct use of speed, we shall all save time in the Radiant City.

To live! To breathe!

February, 1931.

*To preserve this*, in our disease-ridden old neighborhoods (and in fact, there is very little of this very pretty wrought-iron left now); it would in any case be simple enough to give these things away to the people who like them so much.

## TO CHOOSE

between these two attitudes:

or:
being able to do this outside our apartments in the Radiant City: we come home from work and change; our friends are there waiting. High spirits, physical activity. And then we can go on to think about the "serious" things afterwards.

An engineer in a factory deciphering his graphs. The curves he sees reveal reality. His calculations enable him to make use of this knowledge. And all this takes place quietly, carefully, honestly, naturally. Yet it permits him to convert the most audacious dreams into *reality*.

... elevated motives supporting theories.

LOTISSEMENT

— Oui... un wagon... j'dis pas... mais pour les temps un peu humides ça vaut pas une péniche.

(Dessin de L. KERN.)

**HOUSING ESTATES**

*"Yes, a railroad car's o.k., I guess. But when the weather's a bit damp . . . Well, it just don't match up to a barge."*

# 5. TO LIVE! (TO INHABIT)

## THE MODERN WORLD TO BE PREPARED. HOW TO APPRECIATE WHAT IS HAPPENING. EQUIPPING SOCIETY.

The buildings produced by architecture and city planning are the material objects in which the spirit of any epoch is beyond all question made manifest.

It is impossible to localize the efforts of an epoch and think of it as operating solely in the spheres of engineering, commerce and industry. The psychology of the masses is also deeply stirred. A new sensibility emerges. And an adequate environment must be provided for this new sensibility.

Everything must be brought into harmony.

The machine age: the first satisfaction accorded to popular demands: the 8-hour day.

But then, in 1930: world crisis, overproduction. The machine doing the work of ten men, of a hundred men.

If it had been possible to make predictions in 1830, men would have said: the machine is going to replace manpower, therefore men will work less.

Our needs at that time were limited by the money available after the expenses of a normal working day had been deducted from the receipts. It was a wholly artisan world; life was a sedentary thing, and the wear and tear to which things were subjected was extremely small. When the sun set to rest, so did we. The peasant lived in an indisputable state of pauperism. There was only very little industrial production: there was almost no industrial consumption at all. And in consequence, there was almost no trade at all either.

Since then, new appetites have arisen that the machine is able to satisfy. Technical progress, indeed, gave rise to them and sharpened them.

A hundred years later, an agricultural or industrial worker has acquired a radio that will enable him to listen to Beethoven and Stravinsky (and *Manon* too!), the most important lectures, the orations of heads of state, etc . . . The movie house assails him once a week with yet another superlatively ostentatious lesson in luxury living and comfort.

Competition, the *struggle for life*, the necessity for earning our daily bread have accomplished miracles. The book, the newspaper and the magazine can truly be said to have transformed the world. And I don't mean Gutenberg's book, I mean the books printed on the printing machines of 1850. And can we say that there are, that there will ever again be, any limits to such incredible inventions, to this fantastic menu that is being set on the world's table?

Yes! And yes again! The 24-hour cycle of the sun sets a limit to the degree of our satieties. When the world has had enough, when it is unable to consume any more, to swallow any more, then it ceases to buy. Crisis! What is the solution?

To produce less. To see that the machine *liberates* the individual worker with the work it performs instead of subjecting him to further slavery! Fewer working hours: 6 hours a day; perhaps only 5. We must master the machine; we must refuse to let it crush us any more.

And another thing: the economic and social boom that followed the Great War, that began during the war itself, has made woman a worker too and uprooted her from her former position at the center of home and family life. This tendency (especially strong in Russia: female emancipation and freedom = ideal = illusion) is perhaps leading us into *error*. If the wife goes back to her home, to her children, then there will be less labor on the market. The result would be less industrial unemployment. But take care! If the husband's working day is reduced to a mere 5 hours, then we must be careful not to force the wife back into the 12 to 16 hours of household tasks from which she has recently so energetically escaped. What is sauce for the goose is sauce for the gander: only 5 hours of housework per day as well.

Already we have the basis of the problem that faces us.

The problem is to design a city for husbands, for wives, and for children, *in which the average working day is only 5 hours.* We have to organize a whole new way of life. And that is a problem we have to look into closely. But before we do, one more word:

I am about to show you some working drawings for this new city. But how are these new designs to be superimposed on the city as it stands today?

*It is a process involving the replanning of private property.*

Who is going to dare to do that, even when the necessity has been understood and admitted? Who is going to impose the principle? Who is going to see that it is put into well-regulated practice? Authority! Where is it? There is no authority in existence sufficient to undertake the necessary tasks of our age. *The necessary authority must be created.* All of which sounds very disturbing! Of course it does! But who amongst us in these exciting days wants to keep his eyes shut and his head firmly ensconced on the pillow of the status quo? Each one of us? Everyone! Very well, then this is the moment when we must dare to cry: *Out of the way there!* The moment to exhort the world to action.

\* \* \*

*I have laid it down that the cornerstone for any form of organization in a machine civilization must be a respect for the liberty of the individual.*

Our working drawings have led us to the following conclusions:

The city dweller, as a pedestrian, must have the entire ground surface of the city at his disposal. The ground surface of the city is made up of parks. The city is one uninterrupted park. *No pedestrian ever meets an automobile;* the automobiles are there of course, but in the air, passing by behind screens of foliage. (This will be gone into later.)

The city dweller who owns an automobile will be able to keep it in a garage at the foot of his elevator.

Anyone who wishes to take a taxi, wherever he may be in the residential district, need never walk more than 100 meters to find one. And when he returns home, whatever the hour of the day or night, he will be taken up to his apartment by specially trained elevator operators.

From the door of his elevator, the longest distance that he will have to walk to his own front door will be less than 100 meters, along a corridor that will be *an indoor street.* The outdoor streets of the city (for traffic) will be curtailed to an astonishing degree. As we shall see shortly. Most of the city's streets will now be *inside the buildings.* There will be 12 or 15 of them, one on top of the other, the highest being 47 meters above ground level. The policeman, if he is still needed, will be able to say goodbye forever to his old beat in the heat of the sun or the rain, battered by storms and bustling crowds: he will now be employed on the indoor streets, *streets that actually run inside the houses.*

2,700 people will use one front door. Though in fact, if one looks at it another way, the idea of the house will have lost its present form. People will live in apartment houses with no breaks between the units, a ribbon of housing winding in an unbroken pattern across the city. The interior streets will be inside the ribbons, the roads outside. And wherever it is convenient, the roads will cross the lines of apartment buildings. The houses will not form obstructions at ground level because they are built up on pilotis. The ground surface is left entirely free. And, as I have already mentioned, the longest horizontal distance along an inside street from the door of any elevator to the furthest apartment door is 100 meters. Once over the threshold of his apartment, the city dweller will find himself in a self-contained, *soundproofed* cell. The apartment will be impervious to all outside noise; even a hermit in the depths of a forest could not be more cut off from other men. This is a new architectural fact made possible by the new science of acoustic isolation. It is something that has already been accomplished, that exists; Gustave Lyon has done it, I myself have done it . . .

Detail of "recessed" apartment pattern. At E, the elevator shafts (each capable of serving 2,700 residents). At F, the "interior streets" (the principle of which will be explained later). At H, apartments running the whole way or halfway across the thickness of the building according to the direction in which they face (no apartments facing North).

At A, the raised motorways. At B, the auto-ports.

At C, on a lower level, the paths for pedestrians.

Also visible are the nurseries, kindergartens and schools; all a long way from any kind of traffic.

Motor vehicles? The pedestrian never meets them (see p. 119).

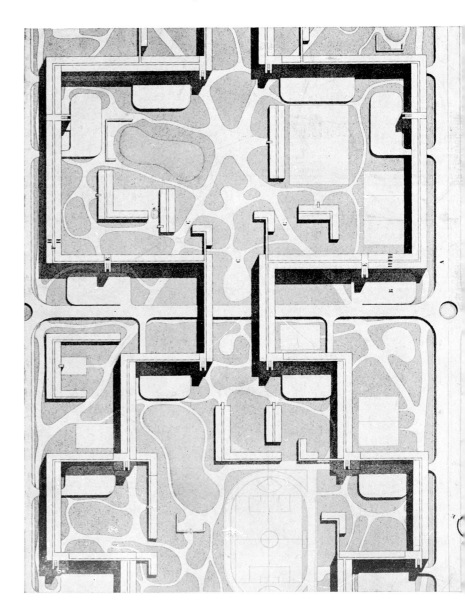

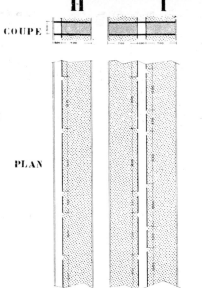

**COUPE** H I

PLAN

These two cross-sections are taken through one story of an apartment building; the "open-air street" or the "interior street" is shown in white. The façade is *plate glass;* the depth available for the apartments themselves is about 7 meters (it can vary from 6m. to 9m.) Type H will be employed if the recess has a North-South orientation, type I if it has an East-West orientation.

# CELLULES INSONORISÉES
## ET
## "RUES EN L'AIR"

On the right, an example of "recessed" apartment house patterns. Below, sections taken through A, B and C on the plan. In all three cases (K, L and M) it will be seen that the anxiety produced by the "corridor street" and interior courtyards has been eliminated. Instead, we have immense green spaces; sky everywhere.

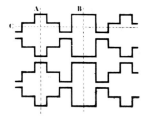

COUPE A   K

COUPE B   L

COUPE C   M

**REALISATION DE LA "VILLE VERTE"**
**DENSITÉ: 1000** HABITANTS À L'HECTARE

And once inside his home, this same city dweller, through the sheet of glass that constitutes one entire wall of the apartment, can look out on a magnificent vista of parks, of sky, of space and light and sun, stretching out below him (and I am talking about the average worker, not about millionaires).

Each occupant has 14 square meters of floor space at his disposal. Here are the figures according to which this figure of 14 m² per occupant has been established:

*2 occupants*
14 m² × 2 = 28 m²

| | |
|---|---|
| Room 4 × 4 ...... | 16 m² |
| Bedroom 4 × 2 .. | 8 ,, |
| Bathroom .......... | 4 ,, |
| | 28 ,, |

*2 parents and 1 child*
14 m² × 3 = 42 m²

| | |
|---|---|
| Living room 4 × 4 | 16 m² |
| Parents' bedroom | 8 ,, |
| Child's room ...... | 10 ,, |
| Bathroom .......... | 4 ,, |
| | 38 ,, |
| remainder | 4 ,, |
| | 42 ,, |

*2 parents and 2 children*
14 m² × 4 = 56 m²

| | |
|---|---|
| Living room 4 × 4 | 16 m² |
| Parents' bedroom | 8 ,, |
| 2 children's rooms | 20 ,, |
| Bathroom .......... | 4 ,, |
| | 48 ,, |
| remainder | 8 ,, |
| | 56 ,, |

*2 parents and 3 children*
14 m² × 5 = 70 m²

| | |
|---|---|
| Living room 5 × 4 | 20 ,, |
| Parents' bedroom | 8 ,, |
| 2 children's rooms | 20 ,, |
| Bathroom .......... | 4 ,, |
| | 52 ,, |
| remainder | 18 ,, |
| | 70 ,, |

*2 parents and 4 children*
14 m² × 6 = 84 m²

| | |
|---|---|
| Living room 6 × 4 | 24 ,, |
| Parents' bedroom | 8 ,, |
| 2 children's rooms | 20 ,, |
| 2 bathrooms ...... | 8 ,, |
| | 60 ,, |
| remainder | 24 ,, |
| | 84 ,, |

*2 parents and 5 children*
14 m² × 7 = 98 m²

| | |
|---|---|
| Living room 6 × 4 | 24 ,, |
| Parents' bedroom | 8 ,, |
| 3 children's rooms | 30 ,, |
| 2 bathrooms ...... | 8 ,, |
| | 70 ,, |
| remainder | 28 ,, |
| | 98 ,, |

*2 parents and 6 children*
14 m² × 8 = 112 m²

| | |
|---|---|
| Living room 8 × 4 | 32 ,, |
| Parents' bedroom | 8 ,, |
| 3 children's rooms | 30 ,, |
| 3 bathrooms ...... | 12 ,, |
| | 82 ,, |
| remainder | 30 ,, |
| | 112 ,, |

The areas left unaccounted for (4 m², 8 m², 18 m², 24 m², 28 m², 30 m²) will be used partly for efficiency apartments, partly for the communal services provided on each floor. And it was using this figure of 14 m² per occupant that we were able to arrive at the extremely high population density of 1,000 to the hectare in the residential areas.

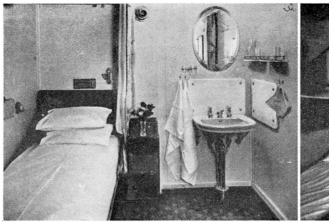

* * *

That is not all:

We shall also be able to build special nurseries for very young children outside the apartment houses, actually in the parks; though they will be *directly* connected to the apartment unit in which the parents live by a corridor sheltered from the elements. These nurseries will be surrounded by greenery. They will be run by qualified nurses and supervised by doctors – security – selection – scientific child-rearing.

Second-class cabins. These pictures are not intended as examples of how to build our houses. But they show the results of strictly observed economy.

The schools too will be outside the apartment houses, set in the midst of the parks. For each pair of apartment units (one on each side of a double elevator shaft, each of which will be used by 2,700 people) there will be a kindergarten for children between the ages of 3 and 6, then a primary school nearby for children between the ages of 7 and 14. The schools will be reached by an avenue running through the park for a distance of from 50 to 100 meters.

The sports grounds will be at the foot of the apartment houses: soccer, basketball, tennis, playgrounds, etc. . . . walks, shady avenues and lawns. Each residential unit of 400 by 400 meters will have a swimming pool from 100 to 150 meters in length.

For rainy days, there are the covered playgrounds extending the whole length of the apartment buildings. Paths and walks everywhere. Limitless opportunities for walking. It will be possible to cross the entire residential area from end to end, in any direction, either entirely in the open air or entirely sheltered from sun and rain. It will be as though the houses have been surrounded by a new Bois de Boulogne.

This picture, taken from a woman's magazine, suggests new social customs, an escape from hypocrisy and certain conventions.

And that is still not all: on the roof gardens, there will be sandy beaches for the occupants to sunbathe on in magnificently pure air 50 meters above ground level. And not little beaches either; they will be from 18 to 20 meters wide and several kilometers in length. Spaced out along these beaches there will also be pools and open-air hydrotherapy establishments. Beds of flowers and shrubbery too. All made freely available by modern scientific techniques: flowers, trees, shrubs all around the sand and the lawns on the rooftops – (trees, flowers and grass all grow remarkably well on roof gardens) – tennis courts, games of all sorts, etc. . .

* * *

But now we come to the keystone of modern housing methods: directly above the pilotis of the apartment houses, and running all along them for several kilometers, there will be a whole floor devoted to the provision of communal services (Note added in 1963: the communal services have been moved up to the seventh floor – halfway up the height of each block).

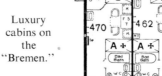

Luxury cabins on the "Bremen."

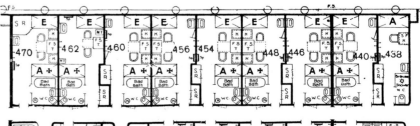

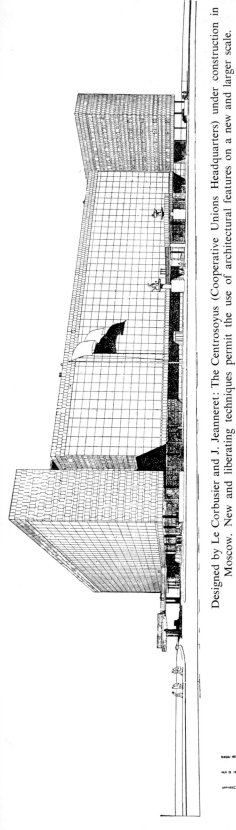
January 28, 1935, the newspapers say:

The "Normandie," a new super ocean liner, will carry 4,000 passengers.

To attend to these passengers: 628 stewards, 25 chambermaids.

Linen in use: 38,400 sheets, 19,200 pillowcases, 14,570 tablecloths, 130,000 towels, etc.

Glasses and tableware: 2,160 carafes, 47,000 glasses, 56,800 plates, etc.

Provisions for one crossing: 70,000 eggs, 7,000 chickens, 16,000 kilograms of meat, 24,000 liters of wine, etc.

Bakery on board.

The ship has seven stories of living quarters, 13 elevators with operators on permanent duty, etc.

(I suggest we moor a tired liner on one of our new housing developments as a demonstration of *what can be done!*)

The Centrosoyus in Moscow. New techniques based on entirely new methods of thought provide adequate lighting and fresh air inside enormous buildings.

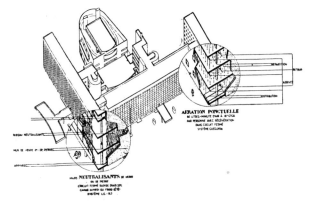

What about delivery trucks? Obviously food supplies and consumer goods will have to be brought into the residential areas. So where are the service roads for them? Under the raised highways. How do they reach the buildings? At certain given points where unloading bays are provided for them. These unloading bays occur regularly along the line of buildings, each one under the aegis of a separate catering section. There will be one unloading bay for every 3,000 to 4,000 residents; and a separate catering department for every 3,000 to 4,000 residents likewise. Each catering manager will thus be assured of a very sizeable clientele. And there will be a cooperative organization to see that the profits from this catering business will be used for the benefit of the customers themselves. Each catering section will have at its disposal an area of floorspace 18 meters wide and from 200 to 400 meters in length.

What functions will these catering departments perform? Primarily, they will see to the storing of incoming food supplies in storage rooms and deep-freeze rooms. These foodstuffs will arrive directly from processing plants or from the country, from the breeder, the hunter, the fisherman, the market gardener, the winegrower. They will be sold at low retail prices reflecting the elimination of the middleman. Adequate refrigeration will assure storage without waste. And what about les Halles? What about buyers and representatives? All done away with! And also done away with, at the same time, will be the insane chaos of carts and trucks thundering daily into the central markets of today from suburbs or the railroad stations. No more individual delivery trucks plying between the central market and the butcher's shop, or the small dairy, or the small grocer's, etc. No more traffic in from the suburbs and out again. No further need for the housewife to trudge out shopping in the rain, then trudge back again with all that heavy shopping. *Do away with les Halles?* Yes! That must be made quite clear. But doesn't that also mean doing away with thousands of little private businesses? Of course! That is clearly one way to exorcise waste in the city, and therefore to bring down the cost of living. I repeat: new techniques make social reorganization essential.

Also situated in the 3,600 or 7,200 m² of the catering departments are the laundries. No more laundry trucks cluttering the streets to and from the suburbs! Each laundry will have from 3,000 to 4,000 customers. This means a great increase in efficiency. We must remember that ocean liners, *at sea*, all have laundries that cater for clienteles of 1,000, 2,000 or even 5,000 passengers. [1] The catering department also has its kitchens. By means of service elevators specially designed for the purpose, it will be possible to deliver hot meals in insulated containers to any apartment in a given block. The menus will be distributed every morning; an hour later, a member of the catering staff will come round to every apartment in order to collect the day's orders. (This is only an example of the possibilities; things could be arranged in many different ways.)

The catering department also has its dining rooms. Does this sound unattractive? Why? Millionaires have been known to eat in hotel dining rooms or in restaurants. Workers have been known to eat out on a Sunday in suburban taverns, or in mountain or seaside diners during their vacations. And though some may have died from time to time, it was never from eating out! On the contrary, they enjoyed it!

[1] The "Aquitania" can carry 5,000 passengers on its transatlantic crossings.

Eating in a restaurant does not necessarily cause instant death. And besides, no one is going to force you to eat in them.

Moreover, if the members of its cooperative society so wish, any given catering department can extend the range of goods it sells at will.

It will also provide a household cleaning service. You have only to pick up a telephone...

(I have already explained myself at length on the theme of the home in a Great City in *Urbanisme*, 1925, *Almanach d'architecture moderne*, 1926, and in *Précisions*, 1930.)

\* \* \*

But let us not wander too far from our apartment buildings, our ribbons of housing winding through the parks of the Radiant City. Will it be possible to live comfortably on the proposed basis of 14 m² of floorspace per occupant?

On the great ocean liners in which passengers are confined and cabined for periods of from 10 to 15 days (though they are provided with the amenities of promenade decks, deck games, libraries and bars – all of which the Radiant City offers on a far larger scale even in its most modest neighborhoods) I must point out that the *luxury suites*, which are intended only for the most exceptionally wealthy passengers, measure only 56 m² for 5 to 7 persons. This means that they provide only 11 m² or 8 m² per person *in luxury class*. For one passenger, or two: 15 m²; which means either 15 or 7½ m² per person. For 2 or 4 passengers, 24 m²; which means either 12 or 6 m² per person. [1]

The ocean liner can only continue to function within these astonishing physical limitations because its communal services are rigorously organized, because the living quarters are stripped of all parasitical elements, and because life aboard (and I am deliberately limiting myself to luxury accomodations only, even though the theories I am arguing for are concerned with low-cost housing) is governed by an intelligent use of innovations that *permit a solution of the space problem*, on the one hand, and that REJECT ALL WASTE, on the other.

There is another subject that leads us towards the possibility of further domestic reorganization: home life today is being paralyzed by the deplorable notion that we must have furniture. This notion should be rooted out and replaced by that of *equipment*: domestic equipment designed to meet our material and, I would even say, our *spiritual* needs. Indeed, I would go even further: on the spiritual plane, we should be ignoring the industries of the Faubourg Saint-Antoine and all the knickknacks they produce, and listening at this moment to the exhortations of Diogenes.

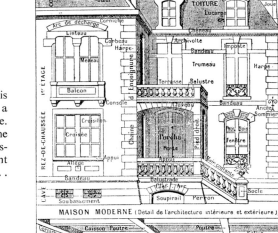

So who needs the knick-knack industries? This is real luxury, a luxury that reflects a new way of life and opens up new perspectives. Death to all industries stuck in a rut.

...while Larousse is still offering this as a picture of a house. This image from time past deserves our respect, but time present is now upon us...

1. Figures provided by the "Bremen."

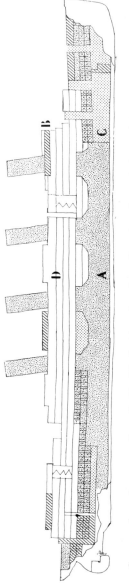

Cross-section of an ocean liner. Inside this floating city where all ought to be confusion and chaos, everything functions, on the contrary, with amazing discipline. The four main services (A. engineers; B. crew; C. stores; D. catering) are all separately located. Why should a city apartment house not attempt to provide us with the same comfort as a ship?

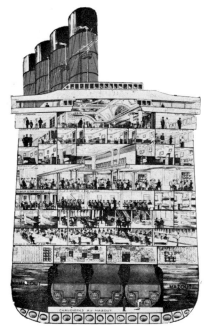

Cross-section of a "floating apartment house"

And even if this means that such knick-knack industries will be forced out of existence or obliged to undergo a complete transformation, that is another question altogether, and one which cannot in any case be considered as a reason for holding up the march of progress. Ever since the mid-nineteenth century, these industries in the Faubourg Saint-Antoine (i.e. since the beginning of the reign of speed) have been totally abusing our credulity, so that it is now wearing very thin. With their traveling salesmen, their department stores, their catalogues and their insidious advertising claims they have created the standard of mentality now referred to as "bourgeois." And in so doing *they have purely and simply created the present housing crisis:* cost of building, cost of furniture, subjecting our minds to the so-called "bourgeois" code. It has created our present housing crisis by flouting all true human standards. We let them persuade us, poor devils that we are, that they could turn us all into "princes of the blood." Yes, we allowed them to get away with it! But now it is time to call a halt! It is time we found out what we are really living for.

With 14 m² of floor space per person we shall now be able to have properly *equipped* homes. Since we shall only work 5 or 7 hours a day, we shall have time on our hands: let us use that time to create everything we need for our physical and moral health. Let us allow ourselves to respond to the deep and simply human aspirations that lie within us.

TO LIVE! To breathe.

TO LIVE! To inhabit.

Dignity, action, health, serenity, joy in living, all these can be part of our lives in the Radiant City.

*Curtain!*

. . . . . . . . . . . . . . . . . . . . . . . . . . . . . .

Now we are back in real life – I am thinking of all those who live a doomed life in our slums, back in our present indescribable filth! Chaos!

Chaos! Chaos!

March, 1931

Salon de l'Auto, 1930. A national celebration, or almost. The entire Place de la Concorde floodlit. The temporary exhibition stands have nibbled away all the streets in the entire neighborhood, as far as the Invalides, everywhere! And we tolerate it, we accept it: the automobile, crowning glory of our national industries!

Automobiles and more automobiles! While the old city stands all around them, totally unchanged. And those who govern us, the people who are making their speeches to inaugurate this exhibition of industrial progress have absolutely no idea that there are a great many changes that must be made, or that we must begin making them without delay.

The governments of the world are giving no thought to what CONSTRUCTING AN ERA entails. They are too busy scraping the barnacles off their leaky old ship of state. The sign outside the government house should read: BUILDING CONTRACTORS. In fact, it reads: MAINTENANCE AND REPAIR WORK.

For the ministers in power never have time to think: TOMORROW. They are too busy "expediting" *current business* (a horrifyingly apt expression).*

*Written in 1930.

It is well known that some of our city districts are full of tuberculosis. Even total demolition would not be enough to eradicate it. The doctors say: they must be burned! In my street, in a single apartment house, there are two or three little stores and apartments where tuberculosis kills a man or a woman every two or three years with monotonous regularity.

The highway network sketched out here will provide facilities (complete, efficient, necessary and adequate) for a city of one and a half million inhabitants. Each square of the network in residential areas measures 400 by 400 meters.

RÉSEAU DES RUES SUR PILOTIS

The age of the horse-drawn vehicle stops with Haussmann. Till then, from the beginning of civilization, cities did not need to take anything into account when designing their ground plans except the human pedestrian and the horse – except very low rates of speed that were naturally in perfect harmony with our biological functions.

The first carriage appeared IN THE CITY in about 1650! From that moment on, the history of Paris has continued to reverberate with vituperative tirades on the subject of traffic congestion. Louis XIV found himself up to his neck in it: he tried to straighten out the city's winding streets; he went in for wholesale rectification; he decreed not only that the city should have a new ground plan but that it should be redesigned *on a new scale*. A new doctrine was born: intelligence pitted against the hand-to-mouth, day-to-day conglomeration of chaos. Louis XIV was the Sun King, he put forth beams like the beams of the sun; and the beams of the sun are straight as arrows flying straight to their goal . . . Now, two centuries later, the automobile age owes it to itself to raise a monument in commemoration of the Great King.

6. **DEATH OF THE STREET**

This crossroad represents a fresh development in the history of mankind: death on tap; or at least a permanent threat of it.

During the horse age, the great cities served to provide a lodging for the sovereign and the princes . . . as well as for the people, the working classes. For the princes, the city meant clarity and intelligence: order and government, broad views, discipline, wide vistas: architecture. And this is what history clings to, these titles to splendor: the beauty of an architecture inspired by a *noble intention*.

And the people? Like worker bees or ants, they came and went, crawled in and out, slept in their tiny honeycomb cells, and bustled about in constricted, tortuous alleyways. The "Rights of Man" were still to be proclaimed. The aristocrat still retained his power of life and death over his serfs. From the huddle of hovels, from the depths of grimy lairs (in Rome – the Rome of the Caesars – the plebs lived in an inextricable chaos of abutting and warren-like skyscrapers), there sometimes came a hot gust of rebellion; the plot would be hatched in the dark recesses of an accumulated chaos in which any kind of police activity was very difficult. Soldiers would be sent to flush the conspirators out, to massacre, to burn; "order was restored." Occasionally, it was arranged that the city should burn down. History is more or less silent about such things: it prefers to recount the splendors of the courts. Christianity alone, spreading from hearth to hearth, from floor to floor, was able to mobilize a new state to oppose the State. And one day it toppled the whole structure. St Paul of Tarsus was impossible to arrest while he stayed in the slums, and the words of his sermons were passed like wildfire from mouth to mouth.

Then, the Rights of Man, *the Revolution*. Exactly the same process. Until one day, Napoleon III said: "This can't go on, it's too dangerous. I want all this cleared up, I want this impenetrable warren sliced up into sections, I want straight avenues opened up that my cannons can fire along. Then we shall see if they can still get up these revolutions of theirs." Haussmann obeyed those instructions. Napoleon's cannons brought a new speed into city life. Seventy years later – now! – the automobile age owes it to itself to raise a monument in gratitude to Napoleon-Haussmann. [1]

But the age of the automobile has arrived. And it would be pointless for me to tell you what that means: you have only to walk out into the street *to see for yourselves.* Human biology is now in the grip of a new speed. Our legs (alternating movement) have been replaced by the wheel (continuous movement); our bottoms run on four wheels; the horse has become a horsepower unit. Instead of a horse, we have 5- or

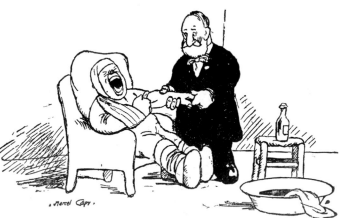

**CIRCULATION**

Le docteur. — C'est à la suite d'un duel ?
Le piéton. — Oui !... avec un autobus !

Dessin de M. CAPY.)

Thank you, Capy!

**TRAFFIC**

(CARTOON BY M. CAPY)

Doctor: *Were you involved in a duel?*
Pedestrian: *Yes, with a bus!*

[1] I have no particular affection for commemorative bronze monuments. Nevertheless, I cannot help envisaging a very "noble composition" at this point: Louis XIV offering his hand to Napoleon I, who is in turn giving the other to Napoleon III. Behind them, Colbert and Haussmann, likewise offering each other their hands, smiling with satisfaction at the thought of the great tasks they have accomplished. These heroes are all represented nude and wearing breastplates, showing that they are to be looked upon as supermen. This group, surrounded by fronds of victorious palms, is supported by a single pedestal connecting it directly to the earth . . . and its realities. This pedestal (also in bronze, similar to the Colonne Vendôme but in full relief) is composed of various representations of automobiles and buses: Renault and Citroën taxis, Voisin, Peugeot and Panhard cars, etc.; all these vehicles being driven by their above-mentioned creators (in bronze); they are at the same time paying homage and being honored. At the four corners, the arms of the city of Paris surmounting a cartouche on which is carved: "From a grateful city of the machine age to the city authorities of a distant, pre-machine-age past who made its continued existence possible."

This group of statuary would be used to embellish one of the working-class neighborhoods: the Marais, Grenelle, or the Gobelins.

I almost forget to mention that with their free hands, Louis XIV, Napoleon I and Napoleon III are holding above their heads a large scroll bearing the motto: "KEEP AT IT, FOR GOD'S SAKE!"

10- or 15- or 40-horsepower vehicles that whisk us off, not at twice the speed we went before, but at ten times, at twenty times, at forty times that speed! ! !

So?

Our city authorities think that everything will work itself out in the end.

It won't. Nothing will work itself out. We have to build new cities.

Consider this aquarium containing 100 fish (in a small space), some of them large, some small. They are all swimming at more or less the same speed. The aquarium is functioning properly and the fish go on living their fishy lives. Now replace a third of the fish with fish that swim at *twenty times the speed of the others*. The result will be a massacre, the complete destruction of all the fish, large and small, *because the aquarium is too small for such high speeds*. The little fish are the pedestrians in our cities, the big fish are the cars, the buses, the streetcars, etc. . . and other vehicles that will probably or possibly occur in the future.

THE AQUARIUM IS TOO SMALL!

Our streets no longer work. Streets are an obsolete notion. There ought not to be such things as streets; we have to create something that will replace them.

The "Rights of Man" have been proclaimed. We ought to be thinking out how to *provide good homes* for ALL MEN. Because after 150 years of waiting, after 150 years of mounting irritation, those men might very well decide to demand the materialization of these rights with which their ears have been continually filled in bloody and brutal fashion. A proper home for everyone. That too is something new, something *entirely new*. A fundamentally new problem. We must refuse to afford even the slightest consideration to *what is:* to the mess we are in now. There is no solution to be found there. We should simply end up in the same state as our present city authorities, who are just as clever as we are and infinitely better informed. As Sodom burned, Lot's wife turned to look behind her and was turned into a pillar of salt. Our city authorities, having been given the task of "keeping things going" from day to day, have been similarly petrified by the effects of this immense and age-old society of ours which is now dying, which is burning, which is crumbling away, which is dragging and will continue to drag with it into disaster all those who persist in clinging to its ruins. We must tear ourselves away, we must become completely indifferent to this now inevitable catastrophe. The only thing to do is to take a sheet of clean paper and to begin work on the calculations, the figures, the realities of life as it is today:

1° Classification of speeds. Normal biological speeds must never be forced into contact with the high speeds of modern vehicles.

2° Creation of one-way traffic. No *high-speed* vehicle should ever be subjected to the possibility of meeting or crossing the path of other moving objects. "One-way traffic" should become an automatic element of high-speed locomotion put into universal

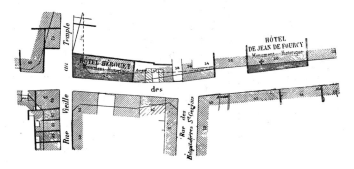

And because we want to pull down our already rotting neighborhoods, we are accused of blasphemy and madness. Here is one example from amongst a hundred of "road widening" in exactly the same neighborhoods but drawn up, in this case, by the authority of the Crown. This was in 1829. They simply demolished the beautiful old town houses. And today we simply make the road more tortuous or narrower in order "to save the beautiful old town houses." The treasures of the past (as you can see!) have been destroyed, all the houses have been pulled down and rebuilt. But NOTHING will be solved like this ! ! !

UNRECOGNIZED HEROES
And they talk about flying the Atlantic!

Et l'on parle de la traversée de l'Atlantique!

Houses contain pedestrians. Outside, they walk at 4 kilometers an hour. Yet at present they must walk on the same level as vehicles that move at 80 or 120 kilometers an hour! Here is a suggested solution:

A wretched kind of "modernism" this!

The pedestrians in the air, the vehicles hogging the ground! It looks very clever: we shall all have a *super* time up on those catwalks. But those "R.U.R." pedestrians will soon be living in "Metropolis," becoming more depressed, more depraved, until one day they will blow up the catwalks, and the buildings, and the machines, and everything!
This is a picture of anti-reason itself, of error, of thoughtlessness. Madness.

↓

→

A portion of "the city of 3 million inhabitants" (1922). Ground, earth, grass, trees, air, sky, all visible! Already wide-open spaces made possible by super-densities. Already the "green city." The green city is possible: man's victory over the machine.

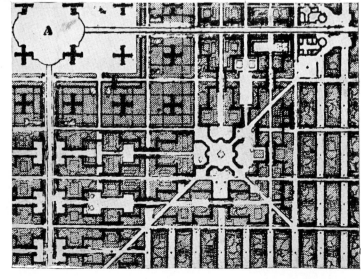

effect (and should not merely imply innumerable quantities of round signs stuck up on posts with white letters against a red background); crossroads (traffic meeting on the same level) should be eliminated.

3° High-speed vehicles must all be employed for specifically designated purposes.

4° The functions of heavy vehicles.

5° The liberation of pedestrians.

\* \* \*

I

*Classification according to speed: high-speed vehicles (traveling at 80 km. an hour) should never meet pedestrians traveling at 4 km. an hour: men, women, old men, children, people rushing to work, people out for a stroll, alone, with others, in groups, in processions, watching where they are going, dreaming, etc...*

The French Revolution (The Rights of Man) made the first gesture in this matter: it decreed the creation of sidewalks in order to put a stop to the abuse of coaches running down pedestrians. Since they had to be created, this means that sidewalks did not exist before that. They were therefore created at the expense of the street itself. As the threatening bulk of the coach became steadily more of an encumbrance, *so the street (the part reserved for traffic) became narrower!*

*And that was that!* The coach became an automobile, a bus, a streetcar, a truck, a railroad thundering through the streets of Paris at night into les Halles; the population increased *tenfold* (from 500,000 to four million); the nineteenth century Business World came into existence (a new economic system in time and space that created an absolute necessity for high-speed travel); *yet the street did not change!*

The necessity for speed! More and more high-speed vehicles appeared on the roads. So many, in fact, that eventually a man on foot in the Paris rush hour can walk through the busy commercial sections of Paris *as fast as a vehicle capable of traveling at high speed! ! !* Paris is suffering from apoplexy!

The street has become a demon beyond our control. DEADLY DANGER on every side as soon as we step over our thresholds. The newspapers have instituted a new column: TRAFFIC ACCIDENTS – a *daily* list of the injured and the dead.

And all over the world, in the United States (San Francisco, Chicago, New York), in Germany (Berlin, Cologne), in England (London), in France (Paris), solutions are being suggested. And all the solutions come to the same thing: SEPARATION OF TRAFFIC ACCORDING TO SPEED. *The pedestrian, from now on, will be confined to raised walks built up above street level, while the traffic lanes remain at their present ground level.*
Madness! !

I appeal to our human STANDARDS to rescue us from such a suggestion! Is man to spend his life from now on gesticulating up in the air on a series of (inevitably) narrow platforms, climbing up and down stairways – a monkey up in the tree tops! If he possessed the agile feet and the miraculous tail of a monkey it might make sense. But in fact it is madness. Madness, madness, madness. It is the bottom of the pit, a gaping pit of error: the end of everything.

These proposals have so far not progressed beyond the drawing board of course. But on paper they do manage to appear sensible, modest, rational, OPPORTUNE, FEASIBLE and financially acceptable.

But they are not! They are not feasible, they are impermissible, and they would never work. None of them has been made into a reality, anywhere in the world. NO, we cannot be made to climb about on catwalks.

In the plans for the Radiant City, I have proposed that the pedestrian should quite simply be given sole possession of the entire ground surface of the city, the e-n-t-i-r-e ground surface, as though he were living in the heart of the countryside. And I have put the roads up in the air, 5 meters above ground level.

NO PEDESTRIAN WILL EVER AGAIN MEET A HIGH-SPEED VEHICLE.

\* \* \*

## II

*Creation of one-way traffic.*

The illustration at the right of this page shows ten different types of traffic intersection. These probably constitute all the various kinds of normal intersections available to us. Each one of them provides a *perfect solution*. We can let loose as many high-speed vehicles as we like in these traffic lanes and they will never have to meet one another or cross one another on the same level. As I stated, explained and proved in *Précisions: traffic is a river;* traffic can be thought of as obeying the same laws as rivers do.

People will say: "That's easily said! But all your intersections are right angles. What about the infinite variations (excessively acute or obtuse angles, crossroads, multiple intersections) that constitute *the reality of our cities?"* But that's precisely the point: *I eliminate all those things. That is my starting point.* With the high-speed traffic of today we are obliged to take that as our starting point, otherwise we shall never get anywhere. To be or not to be! I can already hear the storms of protest and the sarcastic gibes: "Imbecile, madman, idiot, braggart, lunatic, etc...!" Thank you very much, but it makes no difference: My starting point is still the same: *I insist on right-angled intersections.*

The intersections shown here *are all perfect*. We shall see, in a later chapter, how it is possible, for example, and with the utmost ease, to provide transportation services for a skyscraper accomodating 30,000 employees. Why have our city authorities not suggested this solution themselves? Because they have not accepted the fundamental postulate: *first and foremost, right-angled intersections.* Any schoolchild in any primary school could perfectly well work out the solution to any one of these intersections in his turn, once that postulate has been accepted. I would even recommend to schoolteachers or parents that they should initiate their charges or their children into this game, *the intersection game,* for it is certainly productive of ingenuity.

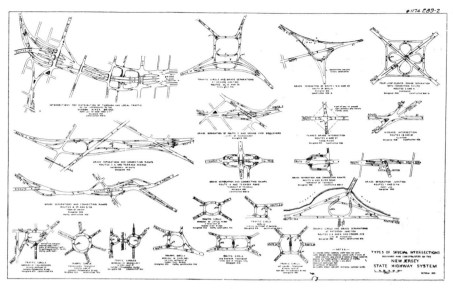

Last-minute confirmation: in the U.S.A., a special committee is studying possible solutions to the problem of automobile intersections. These sketches look as though they were taken from a biology textbook rather than from the hidebound results of the various Grands Prix de Rome.

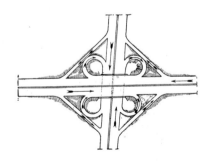

M. Causan's intersections.
*Arts et Métiers,*
December, 1929.

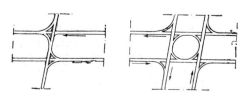

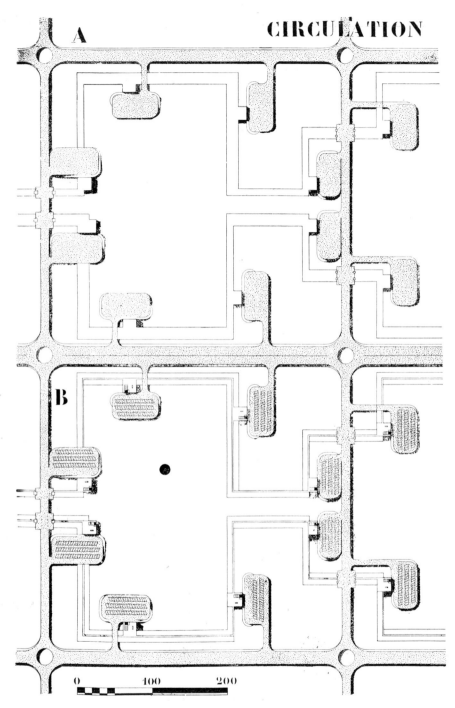

A

CIRCULATION

B

```
0        100       200
```

Residential neighborhood: traffic network. The shaded portions are the highways. The large plat-forms with rounded corners are the auto-ports. The white squares beside them are the catering ser-vices' unloading bays. The fainter key pattern represents the apartment blocks. One effect of this separation: high-speed vehicles in a "riverine" network free of all obstacles, dams or accidents, units measuring 400 by 400 meters. The highway sends out a distributary branch towards each auto-port, and each auto-port is *in front of the door of the apartment building*. And that door serves 2,700 residents.

Anecdote: While we were preparing the twenty plans of the Radiant City intended for the Brussels Congress and for Moscow, my partner, Pierre Jeanneret, who is a passionate automobile lover, happened one evening to begin a methodical series of drawings depicting all the possible solutions to the right-angled traffic intersection. "Now there's a thing," I said to him, "your solutions ought to be exactly the same as those of our mechanic from Suresnes." When I got back home, I looked at the December, 1929, number of *Arts et Métiers* containing the article in question, which was entitled: *An Essay on City Planning by a Layman*, and signed N. Causan. There were all our intersections, printed in black and white. Who is this Monsieur Causan, this layman? M. Causan is a garage mechanic who repairs automobiles and engines. One of those live-wire mechanics full of bright ideas with which the roads around Paris abound. He had come to visit me in 1929 and brought me a copy of the *Arts et Métiers* issue that contained his article. We had an excellent conversation; I found myself in the presence of a sound and lucid mind, questing and inventive. How many of them there are, all around us! But they are isolated, lost in their fantasies; they are recreating the world, but their joys are private ones. While between this active mass, this leaven capable of creating an impulse and provoking collective collaboration within the community, between these people and the *Authority* that decides in fevered debate the future of technical problems that it understands only poorly, there is a gulf. . . The gulf that lies between a new era that has not yet organized its forms of government and a dying era whose masters spend their time haranguing one another, with great eloquence.

\* \* \*

III

*Assignation of specific aims to high-speed vehicles.*

*a)* To transport loads quickly from the door of one apartment house to the door of another.

*b)* To be immediately available for use at all points throughout the city.

From one door to another. Are there a great many front doors in the city? In the city as it is today, alas, yes. One apartment house door with its *concierge* provides access to from 6 to 12 apartments containing from 36 to 72 occupants. Given such conditions, the automobile problem is quite intractable; the front doors *are all side by side* – a door every 10 or 14 meters. The automobile ought to stop right in front of any given door; it ought to be able to stop *in front of all the doors. Which means that the traffic lane must run directly alongside all those doors; which means that it is directly beneath the houses; which means that the houses open out onto the traffic lane.* And that is what we can no longer tolerate: TO LIVE! To breathe – TO LIVE! Homes to inhabit. The present idea of the street must be abolished: DEATH OF THE STREET! DEATH OF THE STREET!

In the Radiant City, one door provides access and egress for 2,700 residents. It is not merely a door, therefore, but also a *port*. A harbor for automobiles to drive into in front of each door. The automobile leaves the main traffic lane (which is a steadily flowing river of vehicles) and enters the appropriate auto-port. Instead of 75 doors opening onto a street, there is *only one door, well away from the street*.

The street has disappeared in fact. It has been replaced by the highway with its unbroken flow of traffic. *No vehicle ever parks on the highway.* A motionless vehicle on the side of the traffic lane would create a bottleneck in the flow, paralyze the rest of the traffic. But what possible cause could a vehicle have to stop in this case? None. *The highway is inaccesible on foot*. Pedestrians cannot leave the natural ground level of the city (the parks) except by means of the elevator that will take them up to the auto-port platforms (a maximum walk of 100 meters) *on which all vehicles are parked*. The pedestrian walks out of the apartment house elevators straight into the automobile parking lot *which is outside his front door*. And if, by some miracle, there should be no taxi available at that moment, then the catering department, which is directly behind the main door of the building, will immediately order one for him (by telephone – look at São Paulo in Brazil, behind the Automobile Club).

In the residential areas, these airborne highways are 12, 16 and 24 meters in width.

Let us take a look at them in cross-section: each highway has two lanes with a thin median wall between the two lanes: jockeying for position, violent and dangerous attempts at overtaking are things of the past. The auto-port, facing the main door used by the 2,700 occupants, is on the same level. Underneath it is the garage for private cars belonging to the residents of the apartment house. Directly beneath the main door into the apartment building there is a similar door opening out onto the parks. This is the entrance for pedestrians into the main hall of the catering section.

Through this lower door for pedestrians only, the occupants of the apartments have access to a direct and yet sinuous network of pedestrian walks criss-crossing diagonally and orthogonally at the same time. Where does this fluid network of paths lead to? *Everywhere* in the city, *by the shortest route*. The pedestrian is able to take the most direct route to any part of the city, on foot. The paths that make up this fluid network are slightly sinuous, but only slightly: in fact, the pedestrians' diagonal and orthogonal networks are direct routes. The sinuosity is there only in order to provide a certain charm, an element of pleasure, a feeling of being out for a stroll.

We should also note that every 400 meters the pedestrian network passes through an underpass beneath a traffic lane running at ground level – a point that has not been mentioned until now. This new traffic lane is inaccessible to pedestrians because it runs between iron fences rather like those that are used to enclose our present parks – the Luxembourg, the Tuileries, or the Parc Monceau. These enclosures reserved for the pedestrian, all measuring 400 by 400 meters, are linked together by underground passages as wide as you like, pleasant to walk through, bathed in light. These enclosures are the parks. Within the parks are the schools and the sports grounds. We walk along beside a swimming pool 100 meters in length and designed in the shape of a natural lake; on one side it is bordered by a sandy beach; at one point, curving away from the main body of water and forming a tranquil bay, there is a paddling place for the younger children. Then there are the tennis courts, the running tracks, the soccer fields. From time to time we glimpse the graceful silhouette of a highway amongst the foliage of the trees; the cars are driving along it quite silently (rubber against cement) at whatever speed they choose. No more horns: what would be the point? Along the center of the pedestrian walks there runs a sort of continuous marquise, rather like the ones that keep the rain off modern railroad platforms, or off the invalids at Vichy as they go out for a stroll. These marquises are the pedestrian's umbrella. The umbrella itself – a totally "bourgeois" accessory – no longer has any reason for existence in the Radiant City. (But that's the merest side-issue of course.)

You are standing in the Jardin du Luxembourg. There are trucks driving by along the Rue d'Assas on the same level as you. But they don't worry you: they are hidden by the trees and shrubbery. The entire ground surface of the Radiant City is like that.

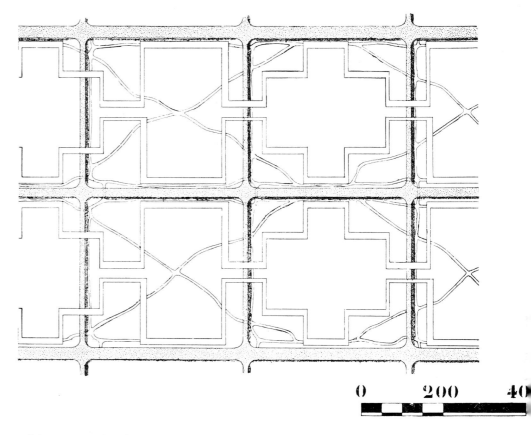

0   200   40

Highway network. Highways every 400 meters, in the air, 5 meters above ground level. Ground occupied exclusively by pedestrians. At ground level, in the parks, the 2 slightly winding networks, one orthogonal, one diagonal, reserved for pedestrians – direct access to all parts of the city.

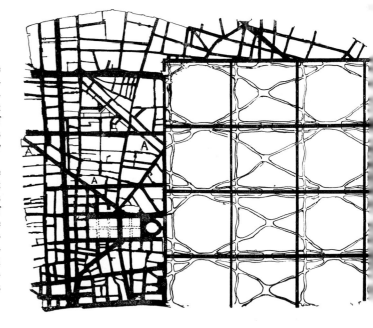

The truth that must be understood: here, as a contrast, is the road configuration around les Halles set against the road network of the Radiant City. This shows the new *unity and simplicity* to be attained.

An odd feature: It will be observed that in the street network of ancient Paris there exists a network of larger streets that come singularly close to our 400-meter units. It is the innumerable tiny streets and their intersections that constitute a hell for automobiles and residents.

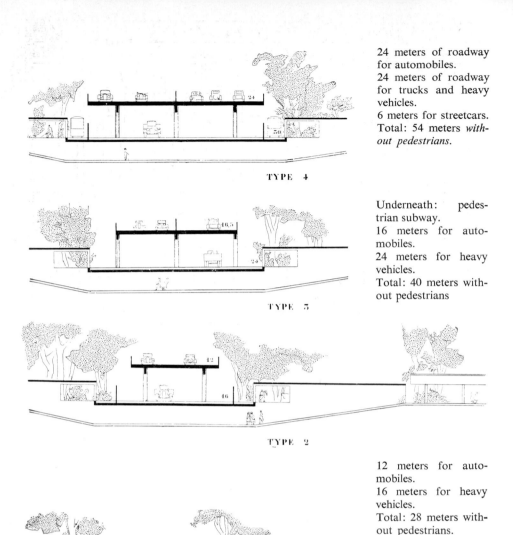

24 meters of roadway for automobiles.
24 meters of roadway for trucks and heavy vehicles.
6 meters for streetcars.
Total: 54 meters *without pedestrians.*

TYPE 4

Underneath: pedestrian subway.
16 meters for automobiles.
24 meters for heavy vehicles.
Total: 40 meters without pedestrians

TYPE 3

12 meters for automobiles.
16 meters for heavy vehicles.
Total: 28 meters without pedestrians.

TYPE 2

In the parks, running along the axis of the orthogonal and diagonal pedestrian paths, concrete awnings.

TYPE 1

There are also large trucks running along underneath the highways. Where are they going? To deliver food and consumer goods to the catering departments. As you see, special bays for them to unload these goods have been provided at intervals all along the length of the apartment buildings, beneath the pilotis. That is where they are heading for. Without disturbing anyone, without getting in each other's way, without interrupting or paralyzing any of the city's functions, they then quietly load or unload their merchandise.

In the Radiant City, the streetcar has regained its right to existence (whereas in the city as it is today, the streetcar is a critical cause of disturbance). Here, they run on their rails at ground level, to the left and right of the service roads under the highways. There are stops beside every underground passage. At these points, there are breaks in the park fences where shelters for waiting passengers have been provided. The bus will no longer be needed in the Radiant City. For though the bus is the most marvelous and adaptable form of mass transport for *cities in chaos* (Paris in particular), in an *ordered* city, the streetcar, which is much less costly, will regain its pre-eminence, provided it is subjected to certain improvements.

And the city's sewage system? In the open air, easily accessible, easily repaired, running beneath the surface of the highways. At last ! ! ! Or else in a corridor built underneath the pedestrians' walks, under the marquises, always in the dry and again easily accessible. The nightmare of our present Parisian ditches finished forever! The intestines of the city, one of its vital organs, will be finally rescued from the perpetual threat of destruction.

So the classification of the various vehicles has been accomplished: pedestrians, cars, trucks, streetcars. The street no longer runs alongside the houses; the houses are no longer cliffs overlooking a street. Man as he should be has returned to his norm: he lives *on the earth;* when he walks, he walks with his feet on the ground. The life-giving joy of the trees, of the flowers, of lawns, of the sight of a wide-open sky, of birdsong, of rustling leaves and a delightful calm, these are the gifts that careful calculations and scientific plans can confer on us.

*The Living Earth*, as J. N. Forestier, the guardian of Paris's trees and the architect of the Bois de Boulogne, used to say with emotion; (he has recently died; but while he lived he never ceased to celebrate the manifest yet ultimately mysterious benefits conferred on us by nature; and his life work, in many cities on this earth, was to make those inhuman mountains of stone flow once more with the green sap of our mother, the earth).

\* \* \*

We have ceased being animals hunted down through a desert of stone. Man's own imminent death in the Great City has been replaced by the *death of the street*. An improvement!

April, 1931.

●

NOTE: The various solution are dealt with in detail in our working drawings for the replanning of Antwerp (Left Bank). These will be found in a later section (L-C and P. Jt.).

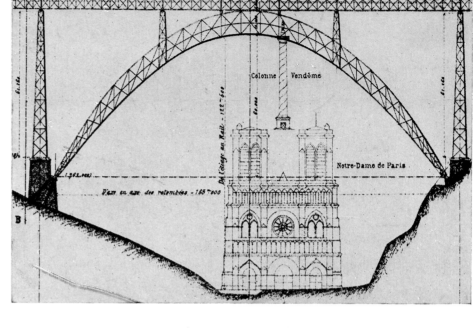

The 19th century: Eiffel, the Pont de Garabit.

# 7. IS DESCARTES AMERICAN?

The skyscraper: an explosion sprung from a budding century under the influence of new fertilizers: steel and cement. Cloudscrapers in fact, they're so high! Delight and amazement on the part of those big kids, the Americans. It has become a free-for-all, a contest, "the skyscraper game." The latest sport, a new form of competition. The prize is the publicity obtained. A skyscraper makes a good advertisement: *the biggest in the world.*

Result: the vast, romantic amphitheater that is now the gateway to America's immensity: Manhattan. The bewilderment of the French bourgeois, who thinks: strange attitude to life they have over here. An esthetic of chaos (romanticism again), an ethic that prizes confusion, a license to unleash disorder. Chaos, violence, primitive strength, the glamor of a besieging army, signs of power, pride in their own strength, national awareness, racial awareness, skyscraper-propaganda, a challenge hurled at the Tour Eiffel: the New World master of the Old. Everything tottering on some brink (and a lot of other things tottering all around the skyscrapers); something is really happening. What? "Let us pay no attention, it's all right for them; but we, after all, we have always represented *moderation and wisdom . . .*" (the indisputably uneasy reaction of our own "sages"; *sage* = man-with-head-in-sand). But there it is: skyscrapers are the fashion. The anarchy of youth is on their side. Skyscrapers mean anarchy.

The skyscraper has *petrified* the cities. In an age of speed, the skyscraper has congested the city. A statement of fact: the skyscraper has reinstated the pedestrian, exclusively. The pedestrian crawls at the feet of those skyscrapers like a beetle at the foot of a steeple. The beetle is hauled up the inside of the steeple: the inside of the steeple is dark because it is surrounded by other steeples; gloom, despair. But right on top of the skyscrapers that are higher than all the others, there the beetle becomes radiant: he can see the ocean and its ships; he is higher than all the other beetles. And indeed, that is where he generally is: up under the academic cupola surmounting his bizarre steeple. The cupola flatters him, he really rather likes it. He agrees to pay all kinds of money in order to have this stopper on his skyscraper intricately carved.

Gilded stopper on a Manhattan skyscraper. They are polishing up the Negro king's tiara.

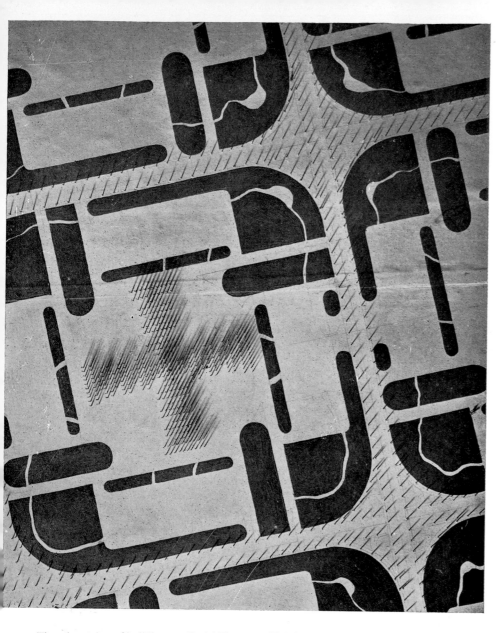

The advantages of building on pilotis! The ground is left free, in every direction. In Moscow, in 1929, the President of the Work Soviet decided after a three-hour conference: "We shall build the *Centrosoyus* (our project) on *pilotis*, as a first step in the urbanization of Greater Moscow." Here is the high-speed traffic network, based on a square unit of 400 meters by 400 meters. Heavy traffic runs between the pilotis supporting the highways. The pilotis of the skyscraper can also be seen. The four rectangles surrounding the skyscraper can, if necessary, be used as additional parking lots.

For the skyscraper is bizarre: at the very top, you will find Brunelleschis or Michelangelos of the first or second Renaissance, or masterworks copied from Rouen or Amiens (final fruit of medieval spiritual unease; now, instead of saying Mass beneath them, we do business). Up and down the façades, perpetual outcrops of stone that keep out all the daylight but provide opportunities for creating "styles"; behind these "styles," it is almost impossible to work; darkness and gloom; hence, electric light. At the foot of the skyscraper everyone is trampling on everyone else, because at ground-level there is no room at all; *the skyscraper has been built above yesterday's streets.* The skyscrapers are therefore all packed together; and they are too small. America *bristles* with them. Is it good, is it wise, to be *bristling* with anything? Is it beautiful to bristle? Is such hirsuteness in a city even mannerly?

If only all this were merely a Hollywood mock-up made of plaster! Alas, it is made of steel, it is built on granite, and it is faced with stone from top to bottom (why face it with stone, I wonder?). You can see it in Manhattan, you can see it in Chicago. A vast mishap.

Several years ago, a society was formed in New York for the purpose of demolishing Manhattan!

\* \* \*

PURPOSE OF THE SKYSCRAPER

*To decongest the center of the city by increasing the population density in order to diminish internal distances.* A contradictory postulate, though now imperative, and at last made miraculously possible by the advent of the skyscraper.

*To create a business center for a region or a country. By a hitherto unheard-of concentration of population (superdensities), to shorten internal distances, and save time (within each 24-hour sun cycle); to restore the ground-level of the city in its entirety to traffic of all kinds (decongestion); in fact, to create an entirely new relation between the new population densities and the ground surface necessary for efficient traffic systems. To help in the separation of varying speeds: stationary (offices), lowspeed (innumerable pedestrians), highspeed and superspeed (cars, streetcars, subways). To guarantee that this place intended for intensive labor is provided with silence, fresh air, daylight, vast horizons (wide views, "breadth of vision"). To bring decent living conditions and a light-filled atmosphere to places where everything at the moment is rottenness, filth, milling crowds, din, disorder, delay, fatigue, wear and tear, and demoralization. To create the nobility, the grandeur, the serene dignity made possible by suitable proportions. To provide a sublime expression (the mature fruit of machine-age evolution) of this century's strength. To bring back the sky. To restore a clear vision of things. Air, light, joy.*

Everything here is paradox and disorder: individual liberty destroying collective liberty. Lack of discipline.

\* \* \*

Nineteenth century architecture is underestimated. It was *discovery*, it was *change*, it was the unknown that lay ahead, the surprise of tomorrow, movement itself. Change and *movement itself*, these are what create souls. The nineteenth century was an age of hypothesis. Between theory and practice, what difference is there? What distance? What length of time must pass between the theory and the putting into practice, between the spiritual revelation and the reform? The divinatory flash and the reform are contiguous, the one follows the other automatically, they lie end to end. But if this reform continues without cease, if it becomes a bombardment, if it gives us no respite, if it overwhelms our normal capacities for assimilation, then we give it a different name: we call it revolution. The word revolution conveys a simple fact, it describes an event that is in itself unconnected with the uproar, the conflict, the violence of physical battle; it is a word signifying simply that something else has replaced something that has ceased to exist. Condorcet created the word *revolution*. And he did so several years after the fall of the Bastille (dictionary definition: "is used for changes taking place in the affairs of the world.").

The nineteenth century was swept by a desire for the grandiose. When man is torn from his state of inertia, thrust into new undertakings, swept up by a wave of initiative, bound to the prow of some new development that is hurtling forward like an avalanche, ever faster, ever vaster (consequences engendering consequences – the snowball principle), then he rises to sublimity. He finds himself *in the position to* . . . He becomes capable of fulfilling these new responsibilities. He becomes farsighted, a demiurge; he succeeds, he triumphs. What dazzling and radiant moments, what treasurable instants those are, however fleeting, when the lightning flashes out before us, our certain guide! And when that vision is followed by a full awareness of its meaning, then a new stage has been reached.

The nineteenth century was a time of fervor: *new discoveries were made each day.* There was no time to think about whether a discovery *would make money*, about whether it could be used as the foundation of a "Limited Company with a capital of . . .". The reality of the latest discovery, the possibilities of tomorrow's hypothesis, the budding dream, it was all one and the same thing: fervor, enthusiasm! A passionate race towards the most spiritual of goals. Masterworks: the product of disinterest. "Big money?" Such brutish considerations had no place in this race; in the sphere that we are concerned with here, the reign of precise calculations was inaugurated, "modern techniques" were hammered out. The old world was abolished: from then on we were able to build with *steel;* steel and glass; and then, later on, reinforced concrete and glass. From then on, nothing in the outward aspect of our material creations could resemble the aspect of the past. But the constant remained: emotion produced by beauty or harmony (as you wish).

Tour St-Jacques; Medieval Paris.

An American university (can you believe it?). What childishness!

129

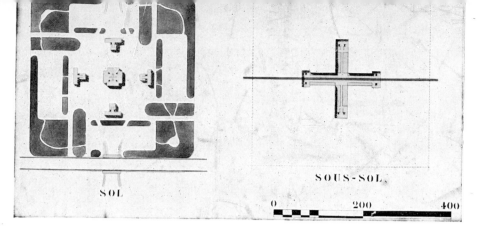

SOL  SOUS-SOL.

0    200    400

Ground-plan of skyscraper: 100 per cent of the ground surface reserved for pedestrians. The five entrance halls with elevators. Total liberty of movement between the pilotis.

Skyscraper basement; subway running through; platforms 150 meters long; communal staff amenities: restaurants, stores.

Traffic system of a skyscraper (from Plates for *The Radiant City*).
(Double scale.) Cross-section of skyscraper at highway level (5 meters above ground). Motorway unit 400 m × 400 m square. All one way. No intersections; all combinations of access possible. Veritable traffic machine – silent, quick, worthy of the internal combustion engine. On this level the pedestrian does not exist.

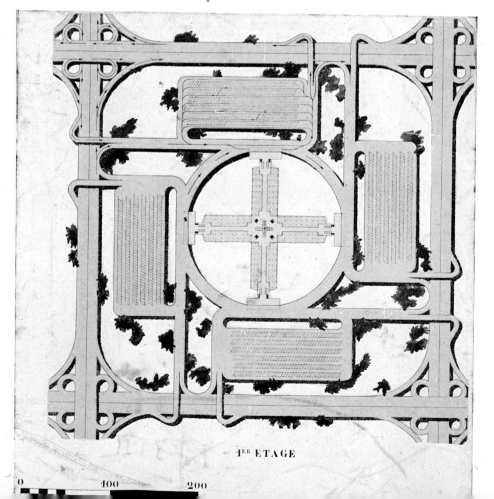

1ᵉʳ ETAGE

0    100    200

At the various Expositions Universelles in Paris, nineteenth century France was able to see with its own eyes the new children of that age: the palaces of iron and glass.

The Académie was shaken into awareness, then into action, and saw to it that all these things were demolished, for it is only too true, alas, that the pure air of high achievements is poison to mediocre minds. Almost alone of all these works the Tour Eiffel still survives, together with a few bridges (bold, slender, intelligent and beautiful) over mountain torrents or great rivers.

During the nineteenth century we lived through a great era, a pure and lyrical age of architecture based on mathematical calculation. Since then, everything has fallen into an appalling state of mediocrity again. We the young, the newcomers, accused by our contemporaries of fomenting revolutionary ideas, we place an infinitely low value on what we are doing. Few people are aware of this, since the works of our spiritual forebears have all been destroyed – those works that would have shouted the truth to our faces every day.

\* \* \*

Napoleon I founded the *Ecole polytechnique*. I should like at this point to attempt the task of rendering the notion of what is called *calculation* readily comprehensible:

Every day, laboratory experiments are undertaken in all the countries of the earth by individuals of different races, culture, and education. The object of these experiments is to express in human terms the hidden facts that determine the specific qualities of matter and the forces that act upon it or in it. In order to measure these things, numbers were created. With the help of numbers we have arrived at a universally accepted notion of distance, time, weight, and temperature. A fixed vocabulary now exists to describe that part of the universe which we have succeeded in comprehending.

The relations of quantity to weight, of weight to distance, of distance to time, of time to temperature, etc., have been observed. We now know what happens *in a given form of matter* when it is subjected to such and such conditions. There are signs (letters and numbers) to symbolize each of the many results that have been observed: these are called formulas. A formula is a limited power, an ineluctable and circumscribed entity. It can be used to perform only one task, its own, and it performs it exactly. A formula can thus be used in place of a reality that is itself too cumbersome to deal with. Given this, the permutation of these formulas can be achieved *instantaneously* on any blank sheet of writing paper, instead of necessitating *a long period of time* spent in the heat, the danger or the congestion of a laboratory.

Battle is joined: the formulas either conflict or form an alliance. They enable one to express a thought, to realize an intention, to pursue a desire. The dream, the hypothesis is measured against the reality of life. Each of these formulas is a sign on a piece of writing paper, but that sign is as unyielding and as clear-cut as a diamond. Such formulas cannot be kneaded together like so much flour and water. They contain the laws of the cosmos, and they will not finally solidify into a unity until the mixture reaches a perfect conformity with all the universal laws involved. No poets are less different from one another than the mathematician, the inventor, and the artist (the true artist!). Everything comes to the same thing in their mediating hands: a reabsorbence of chaos into harmony.

This purely intellectual labor of calculation, which nevertheless calls for intuition, for genius, this drama played out wholly on a few sheets of white paper, is as it were a transubstantiation of raw natural elements (hardness, softness, elasticity, brittleness, tension, heat, noise, violent chaos and disorders that pain the researcher even in imagination), into signs that are words with clear and reliable connotations, that are capable of expressing the world. This accomplished, man is no longer a digger of earth, a miner, a downtrodden Nibelung; he is a demiurge. He has the power of decision over *future events*. Once his calculations are finished, he is in a position to say – and he does say: "*It shall be thus!*" The power of calculation is such that the imprudent might be tempted to raise altars to it forthwith, and worship it.

But beware! It is only the mirror of our own very human divinity, and strictly circumscribed by our own limitations!

And yet, the discovery and first use of such calculations galvanized the nineteenth century into hitherto undreamed-of progress.

*Numbers were created to measure things.* The nineteenth century had instruments of measurement at its disposal so vastly different from those available in previous areas, *that numbers attained a wholly new value*, and the true science of calculation was born.

\* \* \*

Here is the solution provided by such calculation to the problem of the business center of a great city: superdensity: 3,200 occupants to the hectare (allowing 10 square meters of office floorspace per worker).

Skyscrapers built in quincunx or checkerboard pattern, one every 400 meters. The distance between these buildings will therefore be much the same as the average distance between our Paris métro stations. It is worthwhile here to try to visualize what huge, stupendous spaces the introduction of these skyscrapers will create. Their horizontal projection, by which is meant the plan of any given story, will represent no more than 5 (five) per cent of the ground area allotted to each building.

Despite these unexpected empty spaces, it should be noted also that the internal distances of this city center will be *four times less great* than those at present existing in even the most overpopulated of Parisian districts (800 inhabitants to the hectare).

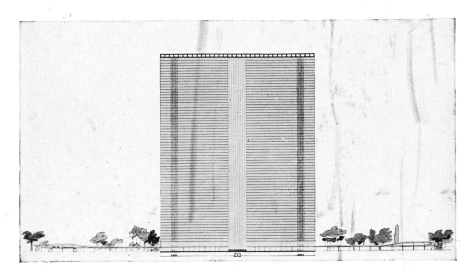

Vertical section of skyscraper: subway; ground level and elevators; raised highways. Then, sixty floors of building. At the top, the armored platform against aerial bombardments

Still from Pierre Chenal's film *Bâtir* – Model by Le Corbusier and P. Jeanneret, *Esprit Nouveau* 1920. Salon d'Automne. 1922. Pavillon "E.N." 1925; Int. Bau-Austellung, Berlin, 1931.

These skyscrapers are all built in the shape of a cross [1] in order to avoid central courtyards: *there are no courtyards anywhere.*

This form provides the maximum possible area of façade, therefore the maximum area of windows, therefore the maximum quantity of light. The offices are never more than 7 meters in depth, measured from the totally glazed surface of the façades: therefore there are no dark offices.

The cruciform skyscraper also provides a maximum of stability in relation to the thrust of high winds [2].

It is constructed of steel and glass. The vertical girders will spring up from the foundations to a height of 220 meters. The first floor will occur not less than 5 to 7 meters above ground level. Between the piles thus left to form a veritable forest in certain areas of the city's surface area, it will be possible to move about quite freely. Apart from five entrance halls for pedestrians, the space underneath the skyscraper is left vacant. Here again, as in the residential neighborhoods, the pedestrian has *the entire ground surface at his disposal.* He never meets a motor vehicle: all motorized traffic is provided for elsewhere.

All motor vehicles are up on the highway network, which again, as in the residential neighborhoods, is based on a unit measuring 400 by 400 meters. Each skyscraper is built in the center of one of these 400 by 400 meter squares. The highways run 5 meters up in the air (as before). From each of the four highway sections making up the square, a branch road leads off to the road network serving that particular building (thus avoiding any two-way traffic or the need for vehicles ever to meet). These four branch roads lead in to four separate auto-ports. Opening into each auto-port is a loading and unloading bay, of which there are likewise four per building. These four auto-ports provide parking for a thousand cars at the level of the bay itself, a thousand more on the ground beneath, and another thousand still in the auto-port basement. Total: 3,000 cars per skyscraper – far more than will be needed!

The roundabout linking the four parking areas will permit access to any of the four bays in each building from any of the road sections making up the 400 meter by 400 meter square.

At ground level, in the parks, a network of diagonal and orthogonal "landscaped" paths for pedestrians. Beneath the highways, the 400 by 400 meter square is repeated at ground level, though here enclosed by iron fences. Between these fences, underneath the highway, are the traffic lanes for heavy trucks (as before). This is also where the streetcars run.

The Cartesian
skyscraper:
steel and glass.

[1]   During the past few years I have reworked the design of the cross-plan skyscraper and evolved a more living form with the same static safety margin: a form dictated by the direction of the sunlight (Geneva – Right bank; Antwerp; Barcelona). There are no longer any offices facing north. And this new form is infinitely more full of life.

[2]   I have given all the appropriate information about cruciform skyscrapers, their construction, their plan, their effects on city planning, their contribution to the beauty of a city, in *Urbanisme*, 1925, and in *Précisions*. I shall not, therefore, repeat these details here.

In the Radiant City, the streetcar (either in its present form or in that of small trains) has been restored to its former eminence (economy and efficiency). The streetcar network does not coincide with the 400 meter by 400 meter highway network; it consists simply of a series of parallel tracks at 400 meter intervals, and therefore includes no intersections. Every 400 meters, the streetcars stop opposite two skyscrapers. There are breaks in the iron fences at these points occupied by sheltered platforms. Simple but functional.

There are wide underground passages, 20 or 30 meters in length, running underneath the streetcar lines and the heavy traffic lanes. (For pedestrians.)

Underground: the subway network of the Radiant City will then take the passengers on to particular buildings, the basements of which will all include a subway station. The line itself will follow one of the branches of the cross; on either side of it will be the platforms, and beyond the platforms will be located the communal services provided for the personnel working in the building: restaurants, shops, etc.

We do not yet know whether, before long, we shall have air-taxis from the Radiant City airport landing on the tops of the business center skyscrapers. It is possible. There will be runway platforms available 25 meters wide by 150 to 200 meters in length. The problems involved have already been largely solved by naval aircraft carriers.

All this works miraculously well "on paper," because the problem has been clearly stated and the necessary calculations made. Since it is the result of calculation it must, therefore, be feasible. Whenever you like! I have already given details [1] of the way in which the operation should be financed, and of the legislative foundation required for the immediate realization of a business center at the heart of a great city. Moreover, my thesis has been accepted by some of the most highly placed figures in the Parisian banking world. Which means that I am not entirely out of my mind [2].

And since 1930 we have been receiving unexpected support from chiefs-of-staff in charge of the country's aerial defense.

\* \* \*

In opposition to New York, to Chicago, we offer the Cartesian skyscraper – translucent, cleancut, gleamingly elegant against the sky of the Ile-de-France.

Conflicting spiritual attitudes: the French tradition – Notre-Dame and the Plan Voisin ("horizontal" skyscrapers) versus the American line (tumult, bristling chaos, first explosive state of a new medievalism).

[1] *Précisions*, Collection de l'Esprit Nouveau, Crès et Cie, Paris (Reprinted: Vincent, Fréal et Cie.).

[2] And moreover, we should now (1934) be able to dispense with the help of the great financiers. The *Plan* has now extended its effects to the nation's entire working economy (see "*Prélude*" 1933-34).

In place of a porcupine and a vision of Dante's Inferno, we propose an organized, serene, forceful, airy, ordered entity. From below, it could be sublime. From the air (we are all now learning how to look at cities from above), it will be *a symbol of the spirit*. It will be the city of the modern age: a new scale of things. I insist on this notion of *order* because it is my answer to the deformed and caricatured lyricism of those "preachers on behalf of life" for whom *life* is no more than accident. For me, life means something brought to perfection, not something botched. It is mastery, not an abortive chaos. It is fecundity (the total splendor of a lucid conception) and not sterility (the dungheap into which we have been plunged by all those thoughtless admirers of the miseries now existing in our great cities).

Instead of New York (magnificent and milling clamor of the machine-age giant in its adolescence), I propose the Cartesian city; I propose the era of "*horizontal skyscrapers*" (a glance at the accompanying pictures will make it quite clear what I mean). Paris, *city of the straight line* and the horizontal (man does live on the horizontal plane), follows that line in its style of architecture.

There are those who may laugh at this. But let them go and look again at the façade of Notre-Dame, and at everything that came after it, right up to (though excluding) the academic domes of the past fifty years. The essential grace of Paris lies in its straight lines (and not in its curves, despite the balderdash being talked during the present reaction).

September, 1931.

●

(1963):
.... Car j'installe, par la science
l'hymne des cœurs spirituels
En l'œuvre de ma patience".
            Mallarmé

Still from Pierre Chenal's film: skyscraper rising against a Parisian sky.

To be raised above the mass of average things was not a sign of arrogance but an expression of dignity

The *chief* architect of the city of Paris:
"Paris cannot change . . . Paris has its history! You forget too easily that Paris was once a Roman city!"
"Bravo! And where is this Parisian Rome today?"
"Where? . . . Why look at the Thermes de Cluny. . ."

*(A hole and four collapsing walls in the middle of a garden. The whole thing more or less buried in ivy.)*

A friend of mine from Moscow, a technician whose job it is to solve a variety of Soviet city-planning problems, objected to my plans for the Radiant City when they were exhibited in our studio because they do not comply with present Soviet theory: "Large cities are an expression of capitalist rule; they are monstrosities intended as prisons for millions of suffering beings. All great cities ought to be split up, dispersed, scattered throughout the national territory in urban units of 50,000 inhabitants . . ." Such is the doctrine of "deurbanization" (¹) that is all the rage in the U.S.S.R. at this moment (²).

A few days later, my friend Paolo Prado, the coffee king of Brazil, told me the story of Augusto and his misfortunes. Augusto is his cook. Augusto's wife is a good-natured, rather simple, fat matron. Paramount, the American movie company, have very recently built some of their enchanted palaces in São Paolo, and the films to be seen in them are also enchantments. Augusto's wife has ditched her husband and gone off to Hollywood: she wants to live her own life there, to take her chance. One day, Augusto was late serving lunch. "Well, Augusto, what have you been up to in there?" "Ah, Senhor," the cook replied in tears, "as I stood there stirring my macaronis in the saucepan, I was seeing my wife's face again!"

Hollywood, Hollywood!

¹. The Russian language employs the French word.
². 1930.

# 8. A NEW CITY TO REPLACE THE OLD

Cities are magnetic fields; the area over which they exert their pull can vary, and according to the composition of this pull, according to the qualitative differences of its components, so attitudes, attractive power, function within a national context, property value, etc., will all vary from city to city.

The word city indisputably signifies the center of gravity for a geographical region, the natural center of gravity for a given producing area. But it also signifies, because of much more subtle attractive forces at work, the center of gravity for an even vaster, sometimes immense, spiritual hinterland.

135

There is a fundamentally human phenomenon that must be faced: man cannot, normally, live alone. He takes a wife, he puts down roots: he has a family. Immediately, a complex of other factors (security, struggle for material comfort, etc. . .) leads him to become a member of further groups. Whereupon we have the tribe, and the center of the tribe is the village (whether nomadic or fixed). Rival and competitive elements tend to break up the principle of unity on which any group is based to the advantage of the strongest. The strongest is often the ablest, the most intelligent. From men's contact with one another, discussion, comparisons, competition and the notion of quality are born. Quality attracts, fascinates, creates adherents. A place comes into being that is the center of this quality, where the quality is higher than anywhere else: the capital, *the head*. The head adorns itself with all the multiform jewels produced by human intelligence. The radiance of these jewels is visible from a great distance all around; the man who works in the fields, or the woods, or the pasture lands, one day feels a need to go and see for himself; he feels that he has his contribution to make; he uproots himself from his home environment and goes to the city, bringing to it his individual conviction and his varied potential of energy. The city swells, fills up, grows, employs those energies, burns them up, develops, asserts itself, enriches itself. It is the center of all tournaments, the center of culture. Drawn into this struggle towards quality, man becomes sublime; he gives himself to the limit of his capabilities; leaping from one pair of shoulders to another pair still higher, he achieves dominion. That is the story of human history, of human destiny: a conquest of quality. It is the reason why we have cities, places where nothing of what was normal any longer exists. The environment is natural, but the norm that reigns in it is new: seductive, utopian, limitless, infinite, profoundly human: the life of the spirit.

We should note and take care to remember this hierarchy, this social phenomenon in the form of a pyramid with a wide-spreading base of enormous area and a summit that is no more than a point, a summit that is one man: splendor of the human spirit. *Everything is concentration, nothing is dispersed.* It is a thing we should remember, a thing we should cling to an awareness of at those moments of terrible crisis in our great cities when the weak, true demagogues attempt the appalling task of turning that pyramid over, of balancing it with its base up in the air and its point underneath.

But let us go back to the U.S.S.R., to revolutionary Russia, which in this sphere, through a disastrous confusion of aims that will not – I am certain of it – fail to be defeated eventually by the foresight of Soviet organizers, is at this moment embracing the most decadent of all the theses evolved by our Western academic committees. For the U.S.S.R. is also intent on dismantling its great cities, just as our own city authorities are all dreaming of sending us out into the fields (their garden-cities) to scrabble earth around a lot of hypothetical onions and live out Jean-Jacques' eighteenth century fantasies (without his wit).

Forms taken by culture in great cities. The other face of human destiny: "Oh man, live dangerously!" Those who can have always ventured into the lists of the great tournament: the Spirit that uproots men from a life of quiet and spurs them on to higher destinies!

What is the phenomenon that is the U.S.S.R.'s real stumbling block, from their Carpathian frontier to the banks of the Kamchatka, the problem that is really tormenting the Kremlin organizers as they sit in the very center of Moscow, which is itself the center of Russia? COLONIZATION: the vast distance between cities (of which there are very few)

136

scattered across an immense, almost limitless, incomprehensibly vast territory. "*The countryside must be industrialized.*" Those are Lenin's words. Not *disperse the cities through the countryside*, which is something Lenin not only did not say but never even thought. What are these new towns we find in the Five-Year Plan with their 50,000 inhabitants? Simply walled camps, towns built from scratch for the express purpose of administrating a given district: centers of discipline, of education, of territorial exploitation, of spiritual culture. A *walled camp* is a material weapon of conquest. Colonization of virgin territory; that is the fundamental political phenomenon in Soviet Russia today. It was also, and outstandingly, the fundamental political phenomenon of the Roman Empire at the time of its greatness. The Romans' aim was to colonize the Barbarians by founding cities that would serve, having been conceived, designed and laid out according to rules of implacable rationality, as efficient administrative centers and radiators of enlightenment. Gaul, Germany, Spain, Africa, all these regions had their scattering of colonizing settlements. But the center of everything was still Rome . . . Rome was in a state of confusion, of chaos, of the most violent tension. Its rulers did not have either the power, the knowledge, or the time to recoup: Rome fell. The Barbarians overran the Empire and the whole world was plunged into darkness for EIGHT CENTURIES!

Now let us look at the Western world today: the outstanding phenomenon to be observed is the invasion of the city by the country, a direct consequence of the machine age, the irresistible attraction of modern culture: new light, new life, new . . . novelty and again novelty. It is an illusion, a spurious fascination if you like. But it is a fact. All the country lads with an eye to the main chance (and Augusto's wife) want to get a taste of all these novelties! So there they are, in the city. First phase: the city as a magnetic pole. Second phase: inside the town itself, the novelty of city life, pink, blue, dazzling, an irresistible glitter.

Why don't our novelists describe the lives of these people who have come into the city "to get a taste of all the latest things"? The lives of *those who didn't become President of the Republic?*

"I had a pal who thought he knew what was what, a restless kind of fellow who was bored working in this grocery store in Paris. City of Light? Not enough for him anyway! 'I'm off to try America,' he said." He left for Buenos Aires. Ah, America! The pampas, the open-air life, the Indians, the virgin jungles and the silver in the waves of the Rio de la Plata! After several weeks of frightful misery and worry in that terrible checkerboard city, he ended up with a job in an office. The office is at the bottom of a well, one of those courtyards you find in Buenos Aires hemmed in by 15 or 18 stories of stone, and he sits in a tiny cell, just over a yard square, under an electric bulb that has been burning all day and every day now for several years. And he works at the same ledgers, the same columns of figures as he did before. A guy from Paris who fell under the spell of America's open spaces . . .

There are guys like that who have come to Paris from all over the world. They emerge from the railroad stations onto the Boulevard Sébasto', the Boulevard de la Gare, the Rue de Rennes . . . Then they take rooms in the railroad hotels, or else they move in with others of their own kind or nationality, the predecessors who have done once what they are doing now, and what they will be forced to do later: *they all go to earth in the filthy warrens of our slums*, wild animals without claws shut up in cages whose bars are the four walls of squalid rooms. There they will remain, there they will

Forms taken by culture in scattered communities: "folk art." Perfect harmony achieved on a scale with *man*. Serenity of the pastoral life. Tools and equipment sufficient though precarious. . . But the locomotive is either on its way or already there . . . Death of "folk art," dawn of a new culture and accompanying distress.

Paris of the past, yet still close to us ... Poetry of yesteryear, now destroyed. Sacrilege, don't you agree? So it's happened to us in the past, and other things too will die, like these, when they have outlived their reason for being ...

produce their children; before long, the population of the city has risen to five million. How many of those five million are simply a dead weight on the city, an obstacle, a black clot of misery, of failure, of human garbage?

Some of the city's inhabitants are therefore useless. The population is too large. There are great numbers of people who are bored to death living in it, but who will not admit it to themselves *in order to avoid despair*.

The Russians, intent upon their present negation of the city, have coined the term "transplantation" to deal with these people. They are attempting to turn these masses of urban flotsam into colonial settlers. They expect these parasites to become pioneers.

But what about us? What can we colonize? Nothing. The country is already settled. Nevertheless, it is possible to use this already settled land better; to make it produce more; to achieve a more efficient balance between agricultural exploitation and industrial exploitation [1]. To establish categories – then a program. To investigate given situations. To make fruitful decisions. To establish or re-establish order by means of constant vigilance and constant action, by means of a humane concern for those in our charge and also a fatherly firmness. It is possible to administrate the territory better, in other words to assume the necessary responsibilities, to act instead of cowering, to take an interest in life itself instead of only in what we can get out of it, to salvage a disastrous situation, to light a flame, to throw light on a problem so that everyone is aware of its implications, to make plans for a social program at once perfectly balanced yet in constant motion, to vitalize things instead of petrifying them, to excite faith and confidence, to create enthusiasm, to awaken a spirit of citizenship, to govern.

Authority! We must establish a program, work on that program, realize that program. *We must spread the blessings conferred by order across the whole land.*

\* \* \*

Another aspect of the problem:

"Yes, Mister chief architect of the City of Paris, Paris was a Roman city once. But it is so no longer. *Not a single stone of that city remains.*"

It was also a medieval city; not a single medieval house still stands.

It was another city again under Henri IV, and in about 1925 the modest administrative offices of 'l'*Esprit Nouveau*' were in fact to be found in a tall cramped house that was a relic of the Vert-Galant's reign.

It was also ...

Buildings have been removed, cleared away, old ones replaced by new ones, badly adapted ones by better adapted ones. That is how progress is made and, more simply still, how life is lived. A few masterpieces have been preserved, because "divine proportion" always speaks to the heart and remains forever young.

Nor were conflicting private interests unknown. Because of private interests, or conflicts that no one had the power or the time to resolve, the biological beginnings of the city were also allowed to remain: the lines of the old roads radiating out of the city. Until 1650 there was not a single carriage in the whole of Paris: people on foot still had room to move. Then, as a safeguard against the ever-rising flood of carriages that was

[1] It was not until 1933 that a group of peasants, having read the issues of *Plans* in which these studies appeared, enjoined me to turn my attention to the countryside. "You have done your *Radiant City*; now we want a *Radiant Farm* and a *Radiant Village*." Whereupon I immediately immersed myself, for several long months, in the difficult problems of agrarian reorganization. And submitted the resulting plans to my peasants.

invading the city, the "Rights of Man" era created sidewalks for pedestrians. These varied from 60 centimeters to 120 centimeters in width.

Buildings threatening collapse were replaced by new ones.

In reality, what now remains of the history of Paris? Nothing. Or very little: a few churches, a few town houses, a few palaces. But what *percent* of the surface area? Perhaps *one tenth of a percent* of the total Parisian area. Yes, Mister chief architect of the City of Paris with your one tenth of one percent, the history of Paris has been preserved. After all, as far as the age of the Caesars is concerned you seem quite happy with that little piece of wall in the Jardin de Cluny. And who says that we too are not prepared to preserve (and very piously too!) that one tenth of one percent of Paris's history? We will preserve it, I assure you. But the rest, for the most part, is ROTTEN. Yet you claim *in the name of our respect for History* that no one should be allowed to lay a finger on the remaining ninety-nine and nine-tenths percent! Even though you issue permits every day, Mister chief architect, for people to build *on the exact sites of the ancient city. Even though a new city is even now being erected, with your approval, on top of the old one.*

It is being erected, moreover, according to the same, obsolete biological pattern, *in an age when traffic travels at twenty times the speed it did before.* That is the crime, sir, the unpardonable crime. IN THE NAME OF HISTORY! you say. Very well, in the name of History, according to the laws of History, to the moral of History and the lessons of History, an old city must always be replaced by a new city, and that new city must have *a biological organization that conforms to the necessities of the machine age in which we are living!*

\* \* \*

In the name of History: TODAY.
The glory of the PRESENT.

Louder songs. A hymn to shake the sky.
A new world: a high-speed world.
A new life: the machine age.
A new ideal: use of the machine to liberate the individual.
A new daily round: productive, recuperative, joyful, healthy: the daily round of the machine-age man in the Radiant City.
New cities for old.

Is there any obstacle to all this? Yes. The present form of private land tenure, which is invested with private rights antagonistic to the public right. But if the public right is infringed, then THE INDIVIDUAL SUFFERS.

*It must be the task of our jurists to find a way of initiating the indispensable changes in present land tenure that can alone provide the authorities with the means of performing their duties.*

Let us pose the problem:
We need a *residential city*, the center of the system and of our activities.
To live! (To breathe.) To live! (To inhabit.)
Also a *business center*. An appeal to reason.
Also a manufacturing center, workshops. Immediately we are assailed by the simplest of solutions. We have electricity at hand: motive power at the touch of a switch.

Forms taken by culture in areas of concentration. Flowerings of the human spirit. It is from such things that our leaders draw the faith that enables them to accomplish their tasks. These are the high peaks of human thought. Necessary human nourishment.

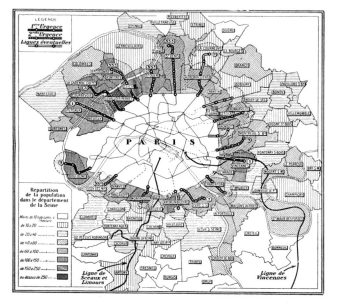

Is it a city or not? An ambiguity that must be resolved. Agricultural economy or urban economy? Agricultural worker or factory worker? For the love of God, we must know. We must have inventories, censuses, draw up a social plan, find out what we have to deal with. "What is the problem?" I can see nothing at the moment but a rising tide of bursting files and multitudes of hamstrung civil servants.

Paris has no PLAN!!!

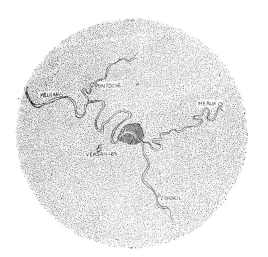

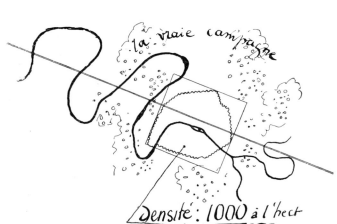

*la vraie campagne*

*Densité: 1000 à l'hect = "VILLE VERTE"*

By means of a PLAN, determine what Paris is and what it must become. Create Paris. Continue Paris.
Paris today, crammed to bursting, crazed, aimless, without a program, is dying. And the temptations lie in wait: *words!* "GREATER PARIS," 30, 50 kilometers in diameter: madness. My answer: concentrate Paris into a RADIANT CITY.

What is a workshop, or a factory? We must decide. We must also decide where our heavy industries are to be sited. Who knows? It is a question that may involve a great deal of re-thinking. The war and our present social crisis have already caused a great deal of ink to be used on this very subject. Let us, at all events, accept the magic power that resides in the word: REORGANIZATION.

The various elements of the city must be assembled according to living, efficient, and organic laws: contiguity, links, barriers.

Let all this be worked out on paper, in the form of rough sketches, then working drawings. Then we shall have a recognizable foundation, an orientation, a direction, a certainty.

*The certainty that an old city must be replaced by a new one.*

\* \* \*

Already we have said enough to plunge our urban authorities into a sea of skepticism, enough even to send them into fits of irresistible hilarity that would be Pantagruelesque were they somewhat less dishonest. – "Oh heavens, have you heard them, eh? Those wonderful city-planning prophets who want to build a new city on top of this one! Ha, ha, ha, etc. . ."

\* \* \*

Whereupon, since the city must after all be saved in some way from the disaster hanging over it, they suggest:

"Let's move out and build the city again somewhere else, nearby." (1st theory.) Or: "Let us build a series of satellite towns all around the city; the city will then be empty, freed from its present congestion, and the Parisian city dweller will henceforth be able to bask with delight in the calmer existence enjoyed by citizens of Meaux, or Orleans, or Nantes, or even Versailles." (2nd theory.)

And Paris itself? The center of Paris. One of these experts has already replied: "The center of Paris will become a village where we shall go to enjoy ourselves." ([1])

\* \* \*

Since this chapter has already offered only too many glimpses of prospects that cannot be qualified as anything less than disturbing, let us end it on a note of rather more gaiety by accepting the two theories outlined above and seeing what happens. Very well then, Paris has been emptied, and everyone is out in the country living the quiet life of the small country town (M. Homais). The City of Light is no more. In other words, the Marais district is empty; so is the Chevaleret district; and Menilmontant; and the Grenelle neighborhood; and the Gambetta neighborhood; and also, naturally enough, the whole of the district that stretches from the Louvre to Montmartre.

Empty. Nothing but rats and mice. As silent as an ambush. So who is going to dare to walk through these empty spaces that are now nothing but a hub for an immense wheel of satellite cities? The Cour des Miracles, on which M. Bailby has just finished building a movie house, will extend its influence, North, South, East and West, through-

[1] Auguste Perret.

140

out all these doomed Parisian neighborhoods. Theft will have become an industry, and an international one, since that is customary today. The police will have to be sent in! 40,000 policemen. Plus M. Chiappe with his sten-guns and his tear-gas grenades! And one fine evening, Parliament will exclaim: "But for heaven's sake, this has gone too far! This infernal jungle must be demolished!" And it will be demolished.

Well?

Isn't that enough? *It will be demolished.* At one fell swoop. It will cost a fantastic amount of money. And there in the geometric center of our ring of M. Homais's satellite towns there will be an enormous asphalt hole, a catacomb, a mantrap. Eventually, we shall have to plant it full of carrots and onions.

Un curieux dessin a été établi pour montrer l'intensité de la circulation par tramways, autobus et métro, à Berlin. Il montre la forme que prendrait la ville si les personnes qui emploient ces moyens de communication se fixaient à l'endroit où elles ont été transportées. On voit par là l'énorme afflux de voyageurs vers le centre de la ville. Et l'on en déduit la nécessité de transformer tout le système de la circulation aux endroits ainsi engorgés.

The market gardeners *in the center of the city* will have to go out to the *peripheral* markets in the satellite towns to deliver the carrots and onions that they once used to come in from their *peripheral* farms to deliver in the Central Markets. Etc.

*The center of Paris will have been demolished* and the operation will have cost fantastic sums of money!

*Demolition of the center.* That is what we have been insisting on ourselves for years. And now you are doing it! You are *actually doing it!* Because it is inevitable.

But we, unlike you, would do it quietly, section by section, rationally, with calm good sense. Then we would build our Radiant City. Where you are planting your carrots, we would achieve population densities of 3,200 to the hectare in the business section and 1,000 to the hectare in the residential section. We would be increasing the value of

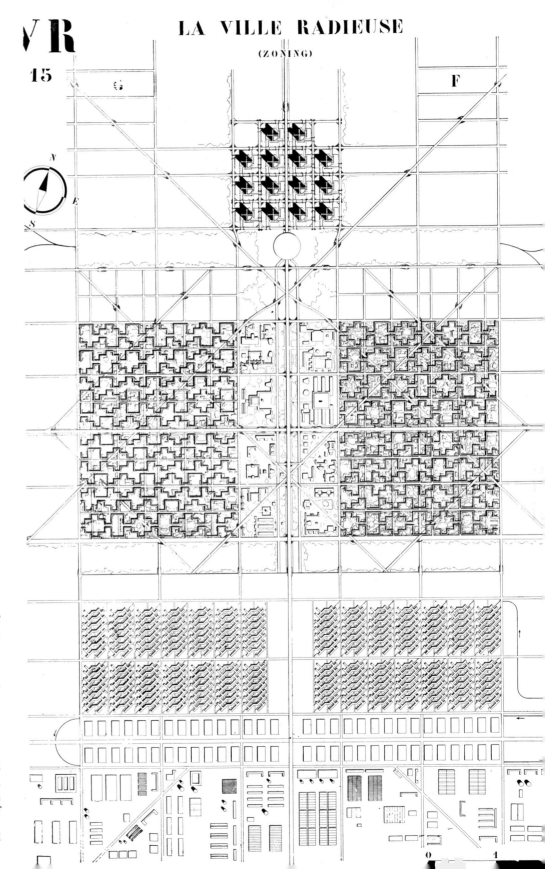

This gentleman has painted a dazzlingly pretty picture. He is delighted with it! (We must remember that organic life always develops away from the concentric, unicellular phase as the evolution of species progresses; it develops an axis, takes a direction, discovers aims.)

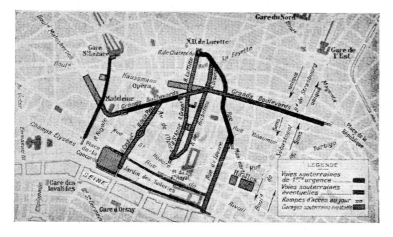

M. Bourdeix's projected plan for adapting Paris to new traffic conditions. I won't argue it out here, but I should just like to point out that if we implement this "reasonable suggestion" we shall find we have replaced one lot of buildings with another lot and *created a new Paris*. But before work starts, people will be saying confidently: "At least this won't demolish the whole of Paris; it shows respect for our beautiful city . . ."
It will have demolished everything!

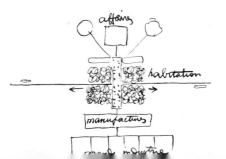

The principle is clear: housing is the primordial element. The various work and amusement areas should be so disposed as to avoid useless travel.

the land to an incredible extent. Instead of reducing the value of the land Paris is built on to almost zero out of sheer thoughtlessness, we would increase it threefold or tenfold. We would provide a magic new network for our new highspeed traffic. The pedestrian will be master of the city's entire ground surface. The city will be infinitely more concentrated than it is now, its inhuman internal distances (inhuman because they infringe the limits of mankind's 24-hour solar cycle) will be dispensed with. No more wasteful dispersion. Once concentrated within the Radiant City, Paris will have all the means at its disposal to provide the machine-age man with a full and fruitful daily life. In the beneficent calm provided by an organization that will spare the body sterile fatigue, and with the stimulus of energies concentrated and animated by civic enthusiasm, an eternal norm will have been rediscovered: we shall have reconquered the realms of the spirit!

Paris, the *City of Light*, will go on.

October, 1931.

•

(see the numerical tables on page 114.)

It is now time to offer a justification for these studies of mine, and I can think of no better one than their own origin: the cell.

What an abortive undertaking, mere idle cerebration, these somewhat miraculous and magical-seeming planning ideas would be, these suggestions for the reorganization of traffic, for repartitioning the land, for using the whole of the air volume above a city for living quarters, if, by some profound and gross piece of stupidity at their very conception, they had not been determined a priori by the fundamental notion of human happiness, which is: a man in the city, a man at home, comfortable at home, happy in that home. A man in whom, side by side with the subtler mechanisms of his sensibility, the coarser cogs of the animal envelope he inhabits are also performing their necessary functions adequately.

Functioning adequately on all the multiple levels of human existence: action, sensation, feeling.

On the day when contemporary society, at present so sick, has become properly aware that only architecture and city planning can provide the exact prescription for its ills, then the time will have come for the great machine to be put in motion and begin its functions. No decisions or enterprises, evolution or revolution, postulation of a theory of life, or constitution of a framework for society together with an exact delimitation of the AUTHORITY to govern it, can be sound and healthy unless they are based upon a human unit, a cell, that is biologically good in itself (in conformity with the individual's needs) and also susceptible of multiplication to infinity (by means of modern techniques).

Modern techniques! The time has come when they must at last be of some really fruitful use to us. But no! It is exactly at this point that we find Homais and the Academicians blocking our path.

Yet the time has come when our mastery of the means now at our disposal proclaims: The house that can now be built for modern man (and the city too), a magnificently disciplined machine, can bring back the liberty of the individual – at present crushed out of existence – to each and every member of society. And the result will be the formation of a serene soul in a healthy body.

· · · · · · · · · · · · · · · · ·

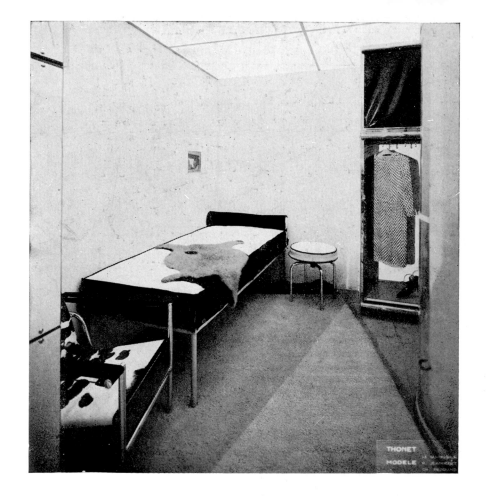

# 9. THE BIOLOGICAL UNIT: THE CELL

## OF 14 M² PER OCCUPANT

(1930 – BRUSSELS CONGRESS)

DEDICATED TO THE INTERNATIONAL CONGRESSES FOR MODERN ARCHITECTURE

The various sketch-plans relating to this problem were published as a whole in "PLANS" 1931: 1. bachelor apartment; 2. apartment for two persons; 3. and 3a. idem; 4. and 4a. couple and 1 or 2 children; 5. a couple and 2, 3, or 4 children; 6. a couple and 3, 4, 5, or 6 children; 7. a couple and 5, 6, 7, 8, 9 or 10 children. This work was carried out in collaboration with Charlotte Perriand.

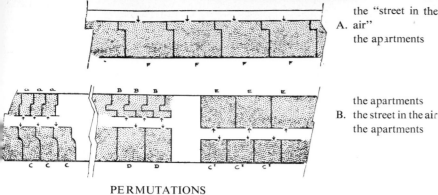

A. the "street in the air"
the apartments

the apartments
B. the street in the air
the apartments

## PERMUTATIONS

According to direction of sunlight: A shows the south-facing type of apartment; no quarters face north. B shows east- or west-facing types of apartment; the interior street runs between the apartments. Numerous permutations of apartments are possible, varying in form as well as surface area. These variations will permit the combination of bachelor apartments with others for families of 0, 1, 2, 3, 4, 5, 6, etc. children in the same section of any block. The depths of the apartments are determined by the effects of the "air-tight plate glass" forming the façades. Our "correct breathing" system (see *Précisions* 1930, Crès and Cie) resolves all problems of ventilation and temperature.

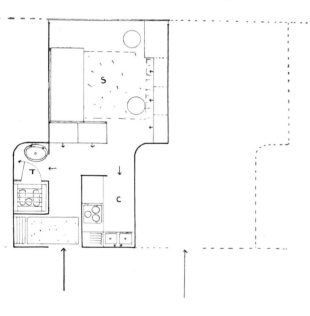

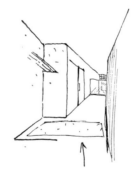

Entrance hall.
(Interior of living room not visible from hall.)

**1.** 1 × **14** m²

(see numerical table on p. 114)
Bachelor apartments

S: fitted living room.
T: washbasin and W.C.
C: kitchen

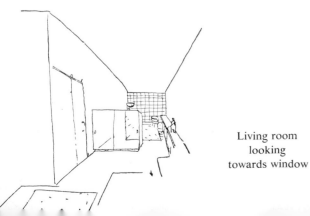

Living room
looking
towards window

Living room seen from window end

*Before undertaking my researches into the Radiant City, I had already satisfied myself to the point of certainty that a human cell of 14 m² per inhabitant could provide a basis for calculations that would lead to the expansion and flowering of men's lives in a machine age.*

*It is according to this basic assumption that all the solutions provided by the plans and theses already discussed have been evolved.*

· · · · · · · · · · · · · · · · · · · · · ·

*I dedicate these working drawings for the Cell of 14 m² per inhabitant to the* INTERNATIONAL CONGRESSES FOR MODERN ARCHITECTURE (CIAM).

· · · · · · · · · · · · · · · · · · · · · ·

Summer, 1930.

\* \* \*

The U.S.S.R. is methodically pursuing its researches into the correct planning of housing and cities. The inquiry is of great importance: we all have to decide whether to go *this way* or *that* – "urbanization" or "deurbanization." Oversimplified definitions, or even contradictory or paradoxical ones quite often, can serve as valuable resting points during the ascent. In the U.S.S.R., they have decided to "deurbanize." This seems to me to be a grave error, or the result of confused thinking. The present craze for *words* seems to have got out of hand. Yesterday, I received a letter from Germany on the subject of *Anticapitalist Architecture!* This is mere folly! Semantic floundering! It also appears that Milioutin, the People's Commissar, has published a book on the subject of how the ideal housing unit and city should be organized, a book that is to be used as a working contribution to the Five-Year Plan, in which he denounces my "Voisin" Plan as being *capitalist:* a business center must be capitalist ! ! ! Yet at this very moment we are building the vast *Centrosoyus* building (administrative center for Soviet co-operatives) in Moscow itself. This building is being constructed next door to the Gostorck, the Foreign Trade Center. And all around, the Russians are building, or are about to build, vast office buildings from which to administer their industries, business affairs, etc. In other words, they are building a business center. *In a very short time* the traffic situation in Moscow will be frightful. One look is enough to tell you that! If, instead of building this business center 7 or 10 stories high, they were to build it 50 or 60 stories high, then they could design a reasonable traffic system. In which case it would be nothing more nor less than another "Voisin" Plan: a Soviet "Voisin" Plan. We should avoid this playing with words: it's a dangerous game.

I am told that at the last meeting of the Congress for Modern Architecture (CIAM), in Berlin, last June, I was officially reprimanded because, it was said, I build only for the rich. Yet the congress was being held in Berlin on the occasion of the Bau-Ausstellung, in which Pierre Jeanneret and I, under the patronage of the magazine "Plans" were exhibiting our Radiant City – 40 meters of it! I had also, between 1923 and 1926, with M. Frugès, designed and built a number of standardized, industrialized workers' apartment houses . . . But for 6 years *we were refused water for them.* So that for 6 years the *Quartiers Modernes* in Pessac, already built, remained empty, since the law would not allow them to be either rented or sold without water! Though Pessac turned out to be an outstanding source of encouragement for the vast workers' housing projects later carried out in Germany, as well as for architects working on these problems in the U.S.S.R.

Public opinion in full cry, the authorities submissive, my colleagues protesting, the contractors all furious, etc... And all this despite the energetic intervention of two ministers, both of whom made personal visits to Pessac in an attempt to halt this scandal. (M. A. de Monzie, Minister of Works in 1926; M. Loucheur, Minister of Labor in 1929.) One day I must commit the curious history of Pessac to paper.

Mr. Milioutin, the People's Commissar, lives in a new model apartment house in Moscow that was built, with a great deal of talent, by Ghinsbour according to suggestions provided by the "apartment villas" with communal services of which I began to publish the sketches and studies in 1922.

The U.S.S.R. has for the moment adopted the figure of 9 m² per inhabitant as the numerical basis for the construction of its cities, a provisory measure of economy that is possibly very wise. But while the U.S.S.R. is preparing to *deurbanize* on the basis of 9 m² per inhabitant, I am proposing in my *Radiant City* to *urbanize* on a basis of 14 m² per inhabitant; my *urbanization* will be a Green City with a population superdensity of 1,000 to the hectare. In my estimation, the Russian figure of 9 m² will cramp the individual lives concerned; whereas my 14 m² will provide airiness, freedom, and elbow-room in which to organize things.

I give here some detailed plans of apartments, either for working-class occupants or others, designed on the basis of 14 m² per inhabitant.

These plans necessitate the installation of "correct breathing" or air-conditioning plants inside the buildings, an innovation that I consider to be fundamental, revolutionary, and extraordinary in its consequences [1]. This "correct breathing" installation necessarily implies that the façade of the building shall be of air-tight plate glass.

*Air-tight!* There's a terrifying notion for you! After I had submitted my answers to the "Moscow questionnaire" (attempt to establish a master plan for the city's reconstruction), one official reader wrote in his report (1930): "It seemed to us that a morbid fantasy of this sort could only have been engendered in the musty air of a private study, and in the brain of an intellectual representative of bourgeois society unable to conceive any other means of finding refuge from the dins and smells of a great city. It is therefore strange and startling to hear such theories coming from the mouth of Le Corbusier, one of the most eminent practical workers in the field of reconstruction, material culture . . .," etc.

Moreover, this entire Moscow Report is a vast melting-pot of undifferentiated and contradictory ideas that demonstrates clearly *how important it is that these arguments about housing and city planning should be clarified by theory before any construction work is actually undertaken.*

---

[1] The first time we suggested this was in our project for the Palais des Nations (1926-27). The second time, when it was couched in much more precise terms, was when we designed and built the *Centrosoyus* in Moscow (1928-29); though our air-conditioning system was rejected. Since then, in the answers to the "Questionnaire to doctors, chemists and physicists, heating and refrigerating engineers, architects," I have encountered further tough opposition. But this year, urged on by Gustave Lyon, the Manufactures de Saint-Gobain have begun a series of experiments based on our program that are very far-reaching and of critical significance. A report on these experiments will be issued shortly. The laboratory will be in a position to proclaim the truth, and a great step forward will have been taken.

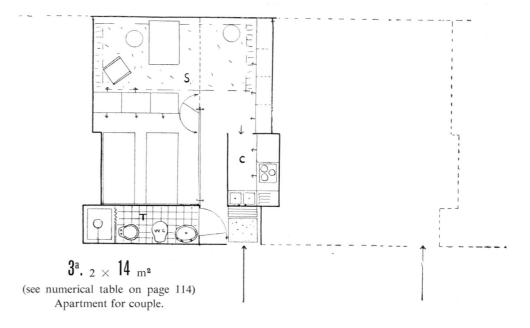

**3**a. 2 × **14** m²

(see numerical table on page 114)
Apartment for couple.

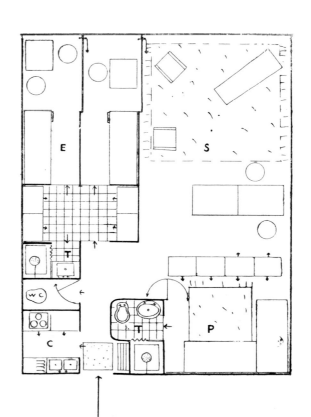

**5.** 4, 5 or 6 × **14** m²

Family with 2 children of different sexes or 3 or 4 children of both sexes.

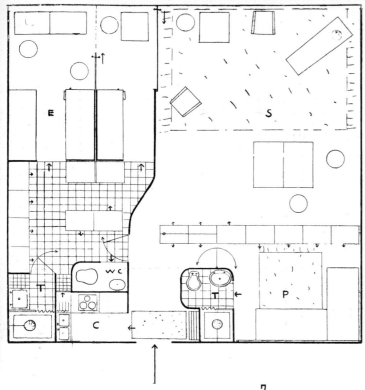

**6.** 5, 6, 7, or 8 × **14** m²

Apartment for family of 3 children of both sexes or 4, 5, or 6 children.
Ideal arrangement of closets.

Though I do, as the International Congress for Modern Architecture (CIAM) has remarked, build houses for the rich, I have also been constantly pursuing my researches into city housing and city planning for the past seventeen years (since 1914). And while working on these projects my thoughts have never been concerned with either the "rich" or the "poor," but simply with "man."

As for these apartments based on the figure of 14 m² per inhabitant, these working-class apartments if you like, I should be only too delighted to live in one of them myself. I will go even further: these are apartments designed for the working class, but in the present state of the Western world, the one person who won't want to live in them *is the worker!* He has not been educated, he is not ready to live in such apartments. The outcome of the Loi Loucheur has already demonstrated the sinister deficit with which we are hamstrung in this matter by the absence of any prolonged thought on the theme: "Construction – Occupation." We have an immense program of social education before us that must be put into effect very quickly indeed; the other nations of the world are all ahead of us.

July, 1931.

\* \* \*

*A later improvement – The cell of 10 m² per inhabitant.*
(1932-33-34)

The basic housing unit of 14 m² per inhabitant was evolved from data that included the current local regulations governing housing. These included a minimum height per story of 2 meters 60 centimeters.

**7.** 7, or 8, or 9, or 10, or 11, or 12, etc. × **14** m²

Apartment for family with 7, 8, or 9 children, etc.

Systematization brings liberty by means of order. And with order, poetry. Think of this apartment in relation to the roof beaches, to the sports grounds in the parks all around, to the sea of trees visible for 200 to 300 meters through the 12 meters of plate-glass window, to the clouds floating by in the immensity of the sky. Bright light, cleanliness everywhere. Efficient equipment to meet every domestic need. Last June, I suggested to Commander Peyron, head of the French Salvation Army, that we should overhaul the mechanics of the Loi Loucheur and introduce into it the one thing it lacks, the thing without which it has proved such an appalling failure: the necessary paternal concern that would allow us *to enforce, to guide, to instruct.* For then, the Loi Loucheur, which has brought us nothing to date but architectural disasters and social defeat, could achieve its goal, which is *to succeed.*

This can be improved upon. Our "correct breathing" air-conditioning system will enable us to create much more efficient designs based on a new height for houses of 4 meters 50 centimeters divisible into two stories of 2 meters 20 centimeters. With this diminished height, the floor area allotted to each inhabitant can be reduced to 10 m². A slight diminution in the volume of the whole building will also result, and, in consequence a further diminution in the city's area as a whole. But what is amazing is that the most outstanding result will be an improvement, an increase in the *joie de vivre* of the occupants, in the quality of comfort available. An increase of the basic pleasures. It was on this basis that we drew up our plans for Algiers, Stockholm and Antwerp. And on the same basis that we suggested a design to the municipality of Zurich for a most eloquent apartment house intended for 300 working-class families. And the design can scarcely be called unsuccessful, since the Socialist municipality of Zurich refused our plans with the words: "If we were to carry out these plans, the result would be a reproach to all the previous work undertaken by our own services (vast so-called "working-class dwellings"); it would mean throwing discredit upon ten years of assiduous effort!"

●

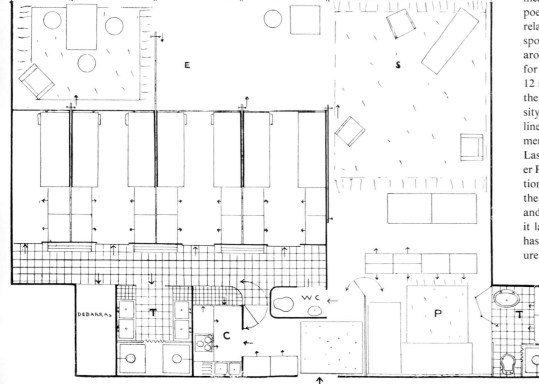

Things like this were being built at the same time as our railroads.

## 10. DECISIONS

The barrier, the point of breakdown preventing our present world from being transformed into an harmonious one, occurs precisely at the place where decisions must be made. We don't make the decisions, we haven't the "nerve" to decide, we are filled with anxious panic at the idea that tomorrow might not be the same as yesterday. So that everything in our present situation, the problem as well as the solution, is twisted grotesquely out of shape.

In the case of architecture, which is my subject, this grotesqueness is observable in the shape of the sites that are being covered with new buildings, in the orientation of those buildings, the treatment of their interior and exterior surfaces, the amputated dead-end streets that provide access to them, and in the very meanness of their dimensions. All architectural products, all city neighborhoods or cities ought to be *organisms*. This word immediately conveys a notion of character, of balance, of harmony, of symmetry [1]. Alas, our solutions are like the "square pigs of Mandalon." Mandalon

[1] Symmetry is used here in its original sense.

147

Organisms . . .
Perfect entities . . .
a function, a form..

is a large farm in the Alps where young pigs are fattened inside boxes that have an interior volume exactly that of a fat, grown pig. The pig grows inside this box, becomes stuck inside it, is eventually unable to move at all, continues to eat but can only grow to the shape of the box, and then, ripe for slaughter, is taken on a visit to the butcher, not even tottering on its own stunted legs, but helpless on a stretcher. This is an exact image of our architectural and city planning projects, compressed and deformed by the relentless interference of so many factors entirely foreign to the problem – by stupidities. "It is precisely in this difficulty," one of Paris's chief official architects has exclaimed, "that the thrill and interest of modern architecture lies!" The poor fellow is actually grateful for his blinders! Recently, I have been observing the flowering of modern architecture in Russia. While we, for the past thirty years, have been forced to knuckle down without respite to tasks both stultifying and degrading to our hearts and minds, Russia has begun demanding concepts commensurate with man's dignity, exhorting its architects, charging them with the task of developing the type itself, the pure organism. The creation of a new economy requires the construction of buildings commensurate with it: factories and dams, agricultural settlements, industrial cities, residential districts, office buildings and conference halls, clubs and stadiums, railroad stations and airports, etc. . . In Russia, the regulations governing these things have been entirely re-thought. The problem has been posited with all the strictness required by theory, with all the lucidity required by a viable program. In each case, the function has been clearly delineated: then the architect or city planner has created a *complete organism* to fulfill that function. Totally new entities are being born (1930). And this is how all other peoples have tackled such problems in the past, whether they were city dwellers or pastoral nations, as long as their period of virility endured. And Architecture was created. And the magnificence of its works was respected.

And it was in such works that the chain of tradition was first anchored.

Résumé: the grotesquely inadequate sites available in the West (privately held land infinitely subdivided) have forced us into the creation of orthopedic architecture. The vast spaces available in the U.S.S.R. allow architects freedom in their plans.

Two aspects of architecture: US – solutions, crippled in advance, that are fruitlessly draining away an exceptional reservoir of professional expertise that was once the glory of our nation.

THEM – creation of *organisms* in an era of reorganization.

DECISION – *To undertake a wholesale reorganization of land tenure in the country as a whole and the cities in particular. The lawyers say that this means calling all the beliefs by which we live into question. I have even expressed myself more clearly still:* requisitioning of land for the public good *(an article that was published by the Redressement Français), The President of the Redressement Français was Ernest Mercier, also President of the Est-Lumière* (1928). *He was attempting to make his country face up to a crucial decision:* the requisitioning of the nation's land. *Thirty-five years have passed since then! ! !* (1963.)

\* \* \*

"What are you doing in the city?" Nothing indispensable to that city? Then your life is boredom, your children are increasing the city's population, and as it increases, so more noises, more dust, more bustle and unease are created to do you harm, to poison the animal envelope you live in and force you to lead the life of a sick dog.

148

If you are in fact indispensable to the city, then you may well be burned up by it more quickly than you would be elsewhere; you may waste away and die very quickly indeed. But what does that matter! You will have been useful and you will have had the satisfaction of knowing it; you will have lived life knowing what you were about and you will have had your share of life's joys. You will have been a coal hurled into the furnace, and you will have given out your share of heat.

To the city's parasites, I say: go out and find some fruitful form of activity, some task in proportion to your particular destiny. The land is waiting for you. The railroad civilization concentrated the cities . . .; the budding automobile civilization (heavy trucks) will bring about a return to the fields. But:

Let us not accept the illusory solution of the garden-city, that palliative conceived in panic by authorities who, alarmed suddenly by the noise of the approaching storm, think that they can turn the linked energies of a great city into a scattered dust of up-rooted, immobilized and broken men. The fallacious benefits of an illusory countryside. The same stupid compromise that has already created the suburban commuter, drawn and quartered the city, and made innumerable people wretched at one and the same time: Gross Berlin, Greater London, Grand Paris, terms employed by Parliamentary reporters, local Governments, or speechmakers. Even the administrative heads of our railroads are telling us at the tops of their voices what a disaster it all is. Illusion, inefficiency, waste. The city must pull itself together, contract, become human again. And not with the help of philanthropic salvage operations but as a result of a simple and joyful reorganization founded on the 24-hour solar cycle that is our unalterable destiny.

The advent of the truck and the highway has now insured that the open spaces of our countryside will always lie open henceforth to displaced city dwellers. This problem, the purging of our cities, is one of the most onerous tasks bequeathed to us by the machine age. But the extreme difficulties it presents are no excuse for poking our heads into the sand. The railroad civilization created a myth of the city; a hierarchy was established on the basis of a numerically vast population of which each member was competing with and attempting to outbid all the others. We must pull apart this writhing conglomeration, peer into it, see what is really happening, make decisions and take all the necessary measures; we must drive out the nightmare that reigns in our cities, we must "put our house in order."

DECISION – *To take an inventory of our cities' populations: differentiation, classification, reassignment, transplantation, intervention. And implementation of the resulting decisions. The city is purged, contracts, rises skywards (the Green City); the suburbs disappear; nature lies quivering against the very flanks of the city; human life is lived out in the appropriate environment: the city for some, the country for others.*

(1963.) The pages above were written in 1930. The automobile was in its infancy. Long-distance trucks did not exist. The internal combustion engine had not reached the country. Things have changed in the past thirty years! ! !

\* \* \*

Infinite subdivision of property produced by splitting up family land equally between sons for generation after generation. We live in a machine age; but machines cannot be used here. (aerial view, Alsace, 1930.)

149

*Rome:* Palace of Justice, 19th century. Impermissible consumer product that reveals an abominable spiritual state (bad taste).

France, which may possibly be equipped for working, is no longer equipped for living. Its cities, its villages, its farms are all obsolete and falling down; in many cases, they are infected with tuberculosis. And though the remains do occasionally bear witness in a high degree to the virile and dignified life that was once lived in them, still they are of no practical use in the particular affairs of modern life. We are living in an antique shop; we could be living in the area of present-day realities.

I can appreciate as well as the next man the charm of a Louis XIV apartment [1], or the "truth" of a Normandy farm. These are delights to satisfy any cultured mind. The opportunities for such satisfaction are limited, however; the rest of mankind must perforce live in houses that lack such historical memories or perfection of style. But above all, I make my appeal to another sentiment: Sport. To be *one of the players*, not a spectator on a bench. The great divide lies between these two attitudes; one phlegmatic, the other passionate, and *alive!*

The question is, then, how to reconstruct the whole country, its cities and its farms! Is it possible? By what means? First let us consider whether it is not a matter of urgency to clarify our aims, to formulate the underlying reasons for our work. At the moment, we are in the grip of a mad greed for possessions, for useless consumer goods. All our productive efforts are being used to make such things, all our buying power to acquire them. With what result? A life of ugly stupidity. What must we look like to others, with all these gewgaws that clutter our homes and our persons, all the knickknacks with which we pack our stores, our houses, and our thoughts? Do we truly want them? No, they are illusions by means of which we hope to demonstrate to others the success of our businesses, the delicacy or even the opulence of our tastes. Worse still: we are being buried alive by these things, by this snowballing avalanche of novelties thought up by a humanity constantly threatened with hunger yet apparently under the impression that it is earning bread for itself when it is in reality merely sharpening its teeth. Every morning, we invent new consumer products "to keep trade and industry going" and to provide everyone with work. But luxury, that notorious superfluity, this flood of totally sterile, innumerable, unlimited, proliferating pieces of nonsense that we create to adorn our egos, costs money; and the money we are earning now is insufficient to pay for our daily bread and luxuries as well.

We must do away with all production designed to feed our greed for possessions and sterile consumer goods. We must halt production in these industries and set the productive labor forces freed in this way to constructive tasks: rebuilding the city.

Rebuilt cities: fertile consumer products that will in their turn produce physical health and mental calm, bodily and spiritual plenitude, joy in life. Instead of knickknacks, we must offer *joie de vivre at competitive prices, at equal cost.* To accomplish

---

[1] I have just spent seventeen years of my life in one.

150

this we must switch some of our producers over to a new, precise, calculable, determinable market to be created by regular stages according to a plan. I repeat: some workshops and factories must be temporarily closed so that they can be re-equipped for new kinds of production. We must open up the "building trade" to heavy industry and provide ourselves thereby with the most permissible and fertile of all consumer products: cities and housing.

This does not mean that we have the slightest intention of trying to turn metal turners, engravers and spinners into navvies and masons. Modern industry is capable of being turned over quite easily to the production of houses and cities. All we need is a program, a plan, and some re-thinking. And the building trade as it is now will be stood on its head, renovated, and given a new lease of life – that goes without saying.

The vital frenzy of the machine age once unleashed, then snowballing itself ineluctably into ever greater and greater excesses, has produced a vast glut of useless consumer goods: traveling salesmen, advertisements. *Signs of a profound disorganization and perversion of human labor*. The age of slavery is upon us. As soon as man's will is ruled by his tools, then man has sunk to the level of a slave.

We must find our way back to the wellspring of human nature. We must take an inventory of its needs. Final aim: *to satisfy those needs and those needs alone*.

It will be found that our houses are falling down. Not only the hovels of the poor either, but all the rest as well. Since the rate of machine production is going to increase more and more each day, this means that there will be more and more hours left free each day. These free hours have been termed *leisure*. And leisure has been made synonymous with amusements, with relaxation: movie houses, fishing, hiking, visits to amusement parks.

Such is the present failure to understand our twentieth-century situation. People blame Taylorism. It must be suppressed, they cry. Yet it enables us to do our work quickly, well, and without fatigue. It might even enable us to do a day's work in four hours if we could all agree to cease production of unnecessary consumer products. So that this, now, is the moment for action. We must shake man awake; grasp him by the scruff of the neck, bring him to life, galvanize him into action, transform his inertia into vitality, his passivity into participation. Participation in what? In the epic of creation that is lying dormant deep inside him. "Stop stultifying your soul with this sterile greed for possessions; you have a body: take care of it, revive it, make yourself beautiful. You have a spirit and a conscience: weak though they may be, press them into action!"

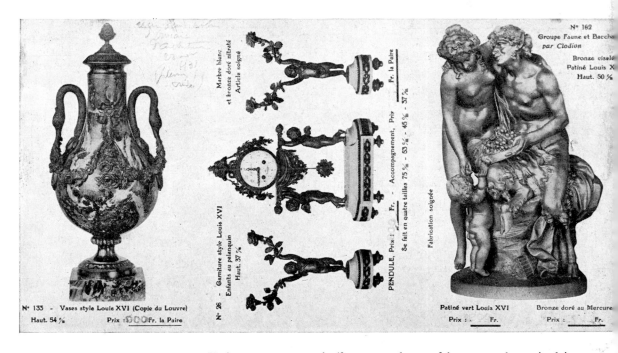

Useless consumer goods (from a catalogue of luxury goods received in November, at the height of our economic crisis!)

Alas, we have reached the point of dreading like some terrible misfortune the possibility of ceasing to be distracted hour by hour, moment by moment, by events exterior to ourselves. We cling to the most mediocre futilities for dear life. The newspaper, that destroyer of personalities which we read in the subway, in trains, at the meal table, in our beds.

*Chartres*: Eternally permissible product: the work of art, final end of human nature.

Where are the *places*, far from our factories and offices, where we truly enjoy ourselves in body and mind?

*They do not exist.* We are reduced to accepting day trips to Trouville or the seaside organized for us by a few philanthropists. No, let us herewith cease referring to these activities we aspire to as *leisure*. Let us rename them: *the daily activities of modern man.* Work will not stop with that accomplished in the factory itself, henceforth harnessed to the production of fruitful things; it will be followed by the work of restoring our bodies, by the spiritual and mental work that is the true wellspring of happiness. And all this implies the creation and equipment of THE MODERN CITY.

Authority must now step in, patriarchal authority, the authority of a father concerned for his children. Our great specialists in modern financial and economic maladies, constantly preoccupied with the task of stemming leaks in a civilization that has allowed its blind subjection to the power of money to make it ignore all fundamental human values altogether, will be of no use to us at all. We need to look deep into the hearts of men once more and offer them the spiritual food they need: the education that will enable their whole beings to expand and flower. Let all skeptics and snickerers keep away! We have had enough of their so civilized materialism and its pretty results: unemployment, ruin, famine, despair and revolution! We must build the places where mankind can be reborn. When the collective functions of the urban community have been organized, then there will be individual liberty for all. Each man will live in an ordered relation to the whole. In an ordered relation, not in slavish subjection to it as he is now. Each man will be his own man, free and happy, because we shall have released in him those interior forces that have no need of sterile personal acquisitions.

DECISION – *To establish a plan for producing permissible goods; to forbid with stoic firmness all useless products. To employ the forces liberated by this means in the rebuilding of the city and the whole country. Calling a halt to waste will permit their redirection into useful channels. Now that modern industry has reached a dead end* [1], *we must say: the time has come to concern yourselves with human ends, otherwise the country will crumble into disaster, into war, into despair, amid its obsolete cities and collapsing houses.*

\* \* \*

Conscience.

Where does Charlie Chaplin's greatness lie? In his eternal misfortunes? Yes, but his real triumph is that he *gives*, that he never ceases to hope and act, that his dedication and will-power never flag. That is why the masses have given him their hearts.

[1] On October 15, 1931, a banker said to me: "Big industry, Ford, Citroën, they must all be done away with; we must get rid of cities altogether. Production itself must go!"

*Failure* is reduced, even here, to no more than a mere mechanical necessity of the game that cannot prevent the player from always beginning again, from continuing to exist and act, from refusing ever to be beaten.

DECISION – *To believe. The masses will always go out to meet those who have something to give.*

\* \* \*

"What we need, Sir, is a despot!"

Do you too yearn for a king or a tribune? Weakness, abdication and illusion. The despot a man? Never. *But a fact*, yes.

The calendar is a succession of happy or empty days, of spontaneously occurring events, of unlooked-for incidents. A series of ripening boils!

What is the result? The result is that the city is walking on crutches. That it runs into more and more dead ends; that nothing is ever ready; that nothing ever fits. Feverish haste, precipitate action, incoherence, cacophony, submergence: our will is enslaved by the rush of events, all order swallowed up. The human idol you are yearning after could not stem this tide. Only *a fact* can do it. A PLAN. A suitable, long-pondered plan firmly founded on the realities of the age, created with passion and imagination, a work of human divination: man is a being capable of organization.

The mayor of a very large city said to me: "You cannot imagine the nonstop dramas we have to contend with every day. This morning, it was a man actually on his knees in front of me begging me to find his mother a place to live. Yesterday it was the medical council informing us that a whole neighborhood is rife with tuberculosis; or an apartment house is falling down; or an arterial road has been finally choked to death by streetcars and trucks; or the owner of a site that is indispensable for some project refuses to sell it to us. The necessity for an answer, not knowing what to do, having to decide; then finding out afterwards! There's not a moment's respite, and no hope of a solution."
There is no respite and no solution because there is no PLAN.

I shall tell you who the despot is you are waiting for.

*Périgueux* (Middle Ages): Permissible product.

The despot is not a man. The despot is the *Plan*. The *correct, realistic, exact* plan, the one that will provide your solution once the problem has been posited clearly, in its entirety, in its indispensable harmony. This Plan has been drawn up well away from the frenzy in the mayor's offices or the town hall, from the cries of the electorate or the laments of society's victims. It has been drawn up by serene and lucid minds. It has taken account of nothing but human truths. It has ignored all current regulations, all existing usages and channels. It has not considered whether or not it could be carried out in accordance with the constitution now in force. *It is a biological creation destined for human beings and capable of realization by modern techniques.*

And this plan is your despot: a tyrant, a tribune of the people. Without other help, it will plead its cause, reply to objections, overcome the opposition of private interest, thrust aside outworn customs, rescind outmoded regulations, and create its own authority. The authority will follow the plan, not precede it. Such and such a plan, such and such requirements for its execution: creation of an authority adequate to meet them.

The plan is an emanation of modern society, an answer to its needs, an urgent necessity. It is a product of technology.

Insist on the organization of that Plan. It alone is the despot you need.

DECISION – *Without paying any attention to what actually is, to what present laws or tastes or customs would permit, let all those who have an idea collaborate on a plan. And let us give up searching for this benevolent despot fellow.*

\* \* \*

The Kaaba, Tomb of the Prophet in Mecca, a moving collaboration of forms and colors with noble emotion.

I must now say goodbye to the reader of these chapters on the Radiant City. In conclusion, here are a few words from that category of men whose task it has been, in the appalling bedlam of war, to conceive plans, to give orders, and to succeed. Their words are terse:

"What is the problem?" (Foch.)

"A leader should have three qualities: imagination, will and technical proficiency. . . And in that order." (Pétain.)

"The world belongs to those who rise early . . ."

"The world belongs to those whose imaginations, capable of dominating and exploiting science, their servant, know how to sense truth, create ideas, see clearly, and be already in action when neighboring spirits are still numbed in sleep."

(E. Poidebard, Lieutenant-Colonel.)

\* \* \*

Leaving the museum in which the permanent Exposition Coloniale is housed, where I had seen the plans taken out of France on the old sailing ships by explorers intending to discover new lands and build cities in them, I made this note: *history is the lesson of movement, the balance sheet of human actions, the panorama of human adventure.*

\* \* \*

*The lesson of history is an order to advance.*

\* \* \*

Architecture and City planning!
We must equip the machine age!
We must use the results of modern technical triumphs to set man free.

\* \* \*

Such a subject is no longer strictly within my professional territory; it merges into sociology. My personal contribution in this matter will have been my refusal ever to relinquish my concern for its biological and psychological aspects: *a man before my eyes.*

November, 1931.

•

155

# 1929-1930

## 17 ILLUSTRATIONS OF THE RADIANT CITY

### EXHIBITED AT THE BRUSSELS CONGRESS
### OF CIAM. 1930

These plates, designed after my return from America, constitute the positive elements of a theory for the planning of machine-civilization cities. Being purely theoretical products, they have made it possible to express the fundamental principle of this matter in an ideal form, removed from the hurly-burly of everyday life. Can such a theory emerge from its utopian framework and confront the world as it is in reality? By examining any matter thoroughly with theory as one's guide, one acquires a degree of certainty as to what must be done. Each special case can then be looked into in the light of a fundamental postulate. This, it seems to me, is the only way to approach life. In the years that followed, these theories on the Radiant City were brought into direct contact with material reality: my Plans for Algiers, for Stockholm, for Barcelona, for Nemours, etc., etc.

A – Example of a recessed-line *(redent)* pattern capable of providing a startling architectural spectacle.

A – The same. Plan at ground level (pilotis), with unlcading bays for trucks supplying goods to the communal warehouses, etc.

Six examples of architectural combinations possible with this particular recessed pattern (other patterns could be chosen, providing different sets of architectural combinations, etc.). The "corridor-street," (an invariable element of all present-day cities in the world) will disappear. An architectural symphony (see the views of *redent*-pattern buildings on pages 283, 284, etc.)

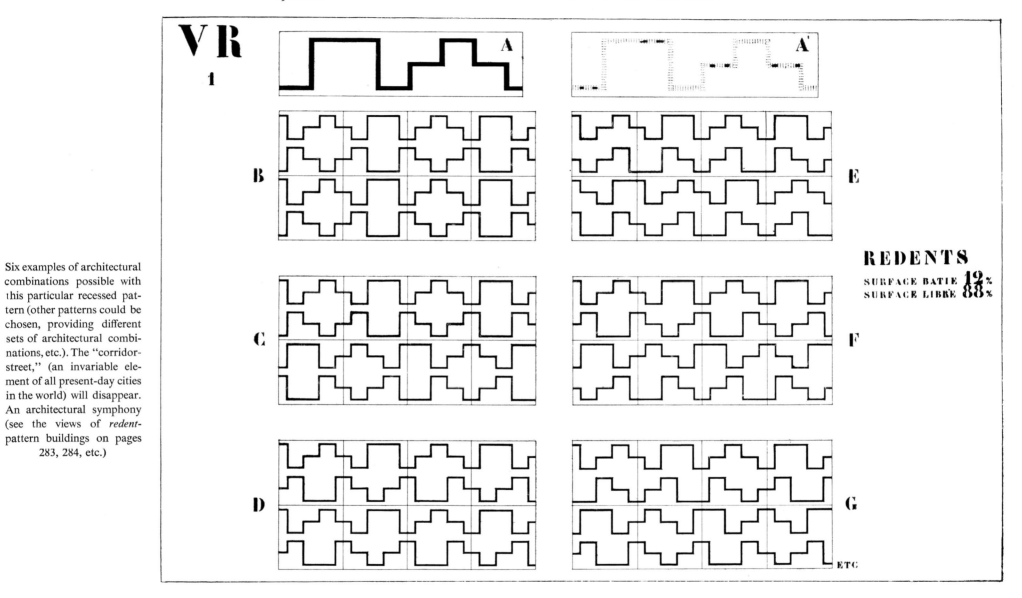

VR₁

REDENTS
SURFACE BATIE 12%
SURFACE LIBRE 88%

ELIMINATION OF THE DICHOTOMY: BUILDING-STREET
CREATION OF A PURE FUNCTION: HOUSING
SETTING UP OF A SERIES BY MEANS OF THE "RECESSED-PATTERN."
"RECESSED-PATTERN" SUSCEPTIBLE OF ARCHITECTURAL VARIATIONS

Traffic lanes (in yellow);
1. P. a) entire ground level for pedestrians;
b) highways and auto-ports 5 meters above ground level.
c) elevators (a public service);
d) horizontal interior roads;

2. P. elevator, service elevator and service stairs. pilotis, communal services; vertical shafts.

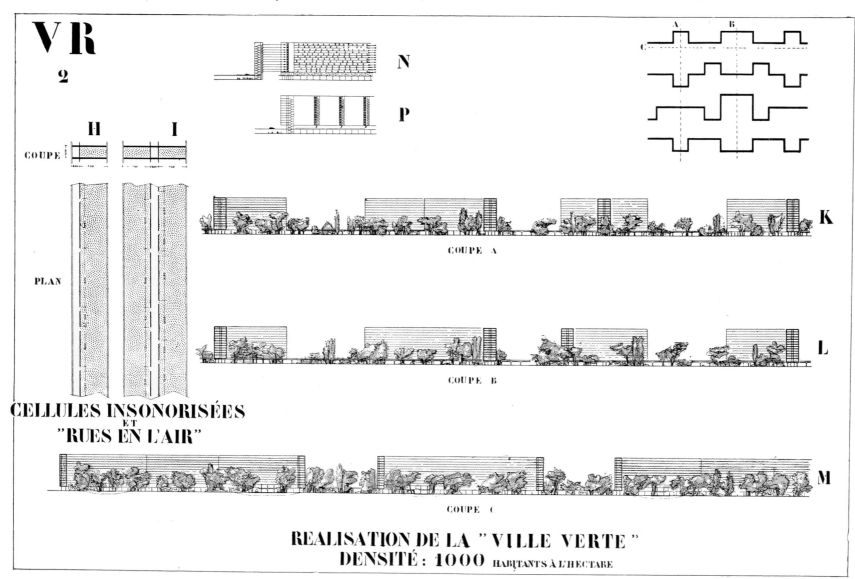

**VR**

**2**

H I

COUPE

PLAN

N

P

A B

C

COUPE A

K

COUPE B

L

**CELLULES INSONORISÉES**
ET
**"RUES EN L'AIR"**

COUPE C

M

**REALISATION DE LA "VILLE VERTE"**
**DENSITÉ: 1000** HABITANTS À L'HECTARE

Realization of the "Green City":
Ground left free (parks and pilotis).
Spaces of 200, 300, 400 meters.
Highways (5 m. above ground level).
Unimpeded views.
Height: 50 m.

Creation of interior streets:
H: building with north-south orientation; apartments on south side only.
I: building with east-west orientation; apartments facing both east and west.

— SKY, SPACE, TREES
— CREATION OF THE "INTERIOR STREET" OR "STREET IN THE AIR"
— 1. EXTERIOR TRAFFIC (SEPARATED): CARS, PEDESTRIANS
   2. VERTICAL TRAFFIC (ELEVATORS)
   3. INTERIOR TRAFFIC (MODULE: 100 M. MAXIMUM)
— THE WHOLE CITY ON PILOTIS = GROUND SURFACE LEFT FREE
— HEIGHT: 50 METERS

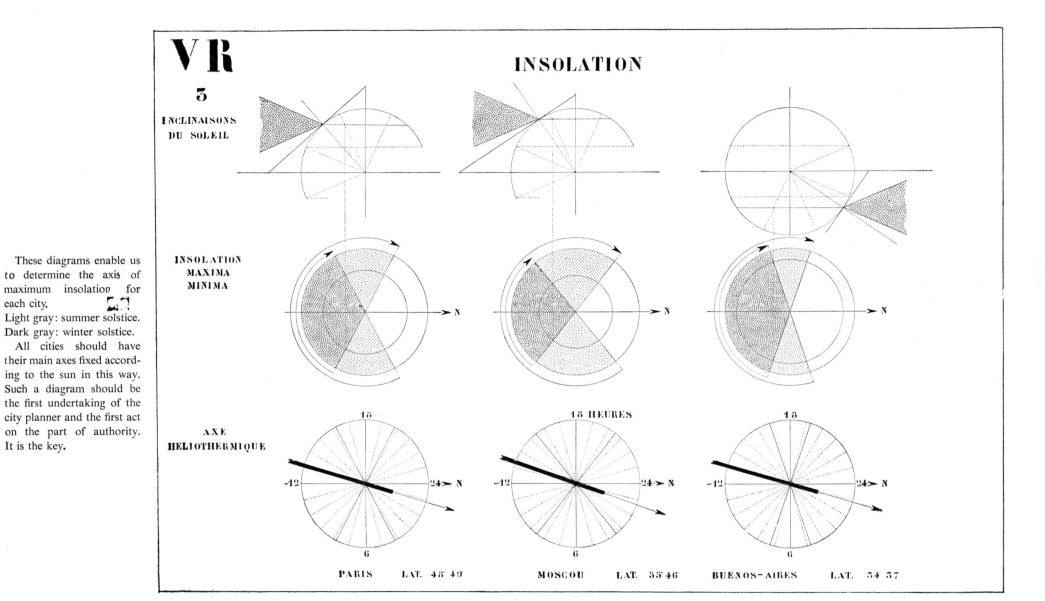

# VR

## INSOLATION

**5**

INCLINAISONS
DU SOLEIL

INSOLATION
MAXIMA
MINIMA

These diagrams enable us to determine the axis of maximum insolation for each city.
Light gray: summer solstice.
Dark gray: winter solstice.

All cities should have their main axes fixed according to the sun in this way. Such a diagram should be the first undertaking of the city planner and the first act on the part of authority. It is the key.

AXE
HELIOTHERMIQUE

PARIS      LAT. 48 49      MOSCOU      LAT. 55 46      BUENOS-AIRES      LAT. 34 37

— THE SUN
— NEED TO DETERMINE INDIVIDUAL HELIOTHERMIC AXIS
   OF EVERY CITY
— THE HELIOTHERMIC AXIS SHOULD DETERMINE
   ALL CITY GROUND-PLANS

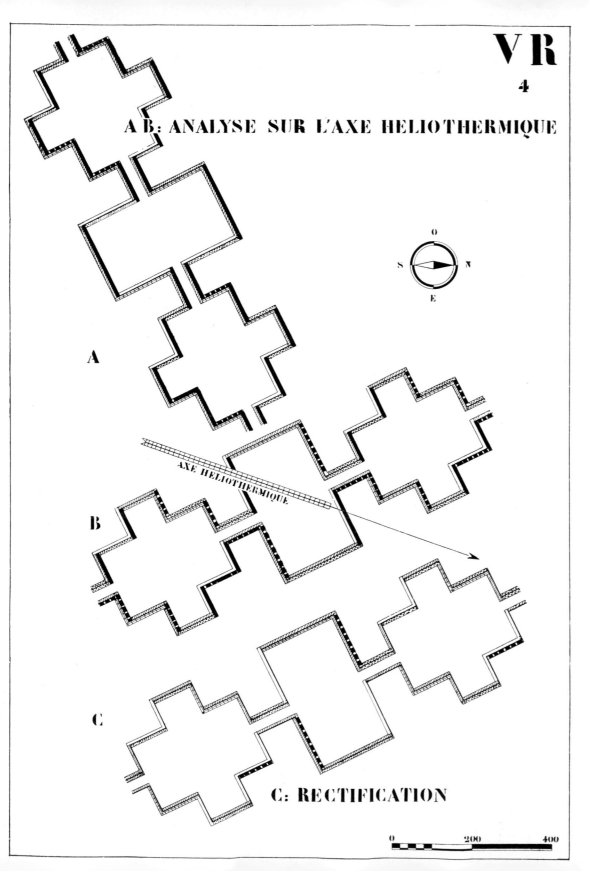

# VR
## 4

## A B: ANALYSE SUR L'AXE HELIOTHERMIQUE

A

AXE HELIOTHERMIQUE

B

C

## C: RECTIFICATION

1° One determines the heliothermic axis;

2° One adopts a recessed-line *(redent)* pattern with due regard to architectural questions, considerations of interior traffic, etc. (a critical choice; any pattern may be used provided it is serviceable);

3° One tries out the pattern in various positions with regard to the heliothermic axis until one has obtained the maximum amount of sunlight possible along the whole length of the pattern (inside and outside);

4° Two of these positions have turned out best (A and B). One then expresses the quantity of sunlight on the various portions by graphic means: black = bad; white = very good; dots or hatching = good. More practically, these results would be expressed by means of color: blue = bad; red = good; orange and yellow = middling.

5° This done, one can read the situation quite easily and decide what to do: one eliminates all the black (or blue) portions and is left with the final form one's pattern must take: no apartment will be without sun (C).

USE OF THE HELIOTHERMIC AXIS
ANALYSIS OF RELATIVE INSOLATION FIGURES
ELIMINATION OF NEGATIVE INSOLATION AREAS

0    200    400

1° Here, we have adopted a basic unit for the highway network measuring 400 × 400 meters (we even tried a unit measuring 400 × 200 meters on this particular working drawing, but it is pointlessly cluttered);

2° According to the proximity of any given neighborhood to the city's main traffic arteries, we have allotted the different sections of highway adequate widths of, variously: 24 m., 16 m., and 12 m.;

3° Next, one considers the intersections: this is a residential neighborhood, therefore the traffic is not abnormally heavy; we have illustrated one fairly important intersection, then other, simpler or very simple ones;

4° The highways run all the time through open parks, outside the houses. Occasionally, however, they do run through the buildings. We have indicated three different ways in which this can occur;

5° The highways are connected by branch roads to the auto-ports built up outside the main doors to the apartment units;

6° Inside each of these doors is a vertical transportation system. Each of the doors here serves 2,700 residents;

7° The auto-ports provide for the temporary parking of taxis or private vehicles;

8° Beneath the auto-ports are garages for residents' private cars. The garages are linked to the auto-port by two one-way ramps, one leading up, the other down.

a) recessed-pattern housing;
b) highway network (the 400 × 200 m. unit is unnecessary and should be discarded in favor of the 400 × 400 m. unit);
c) network of pedestrian paths:
1. orthogonal network,
2. diagonal network,
3. in addition, a "wilderness" network (not illustrated here).

RIVERINE SYSTEM
FOR HIGH-SPEED TRAFFIC: RIVER AND PORTS
(HIGHWAYS AND AUTO-PORTS)
ORTHOGONAL AND DIAGONAL NETWORKS
FOR LOW-SPEED TRAFFIC (PEDESTRIANS)
SEPARATION OF THE TWO
BY DIFFERENCE OF LEVEL

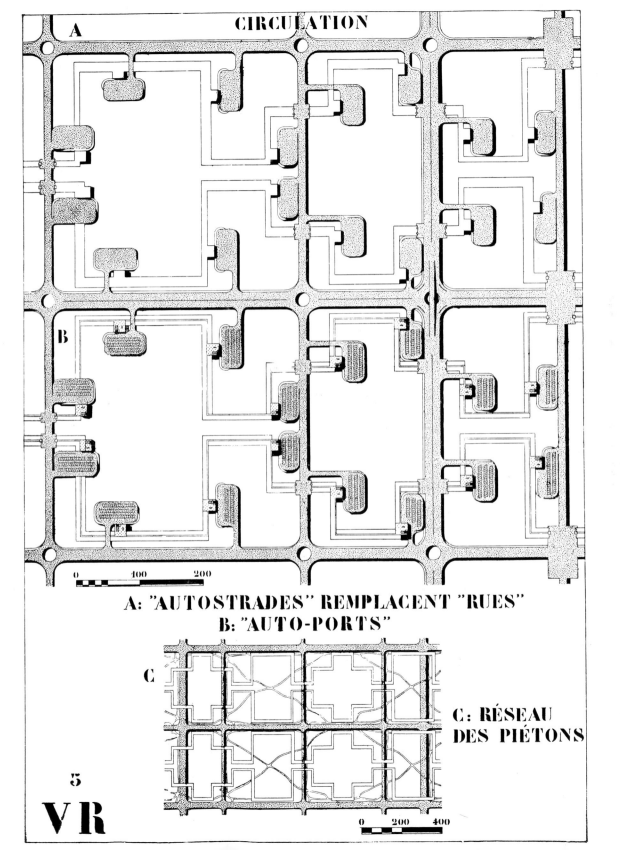

CIRCULATION

A

B

0    400    200

A: "AUTOSTRADES" REMPLACENT "RUES"
B: "AUTO-PORTS"

C

C: RÉSEAU
DES PIÉTONS

5

VR

0    200    400

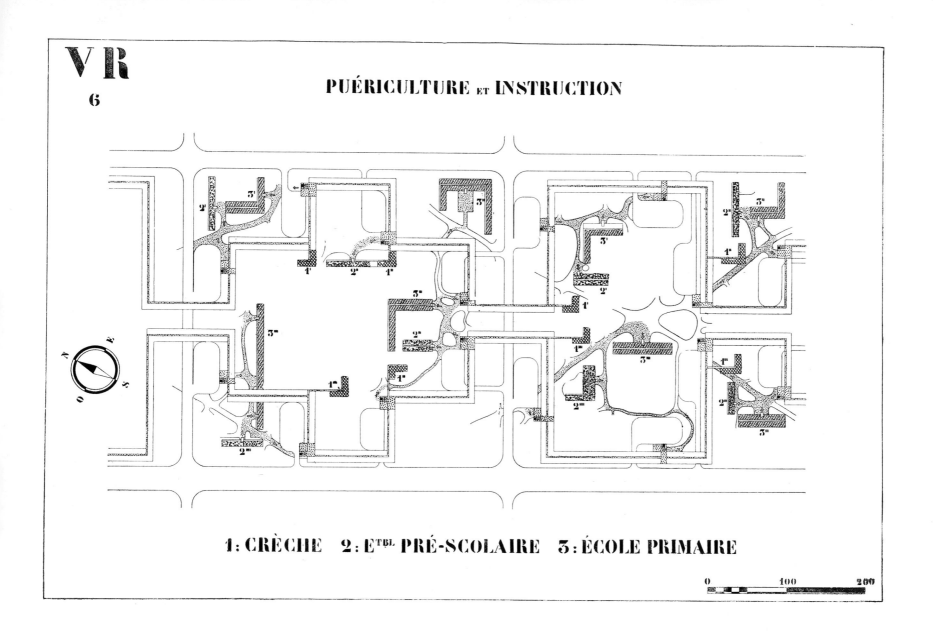

**1: CRÈCHE   2: ET<sup>BL</sup> PRÉ-SCOLAIRE   3: ÉCOLE PRIMAIRE**

0        100        200

Each main door (in this illustration) intended for 2,700 residents. Two doors: 5,400 residents. This figure seems to provide a useful size of "housing unit" (divisible, moreover, into 2 × 2,700). Each of these units is therefore provided with its individual set of services directly connected with family life: communal services (catering and household supplies), nursery (with a direct link to one of the interior streets 1¹); kindergarten, open-air playground in the park (2¹); primary school (3¹) in the park. Between the ages of 1 and 14, children will have all necessary educational establishments outside their own front door, in the park (none of the present-day street dangers).

DETERMINING THE BASIC HOUSING UNIT;
MODULE: MAXIMUM DISTANCE OF 100 M.
ON FOOT FROM APARTMENT DOOR TO
ELEVATORS. RESULT:
2,700 RESIDENTS
— HOUSING + COMMUNAL SERVICES +
NURSERIES + SCHOOLS.

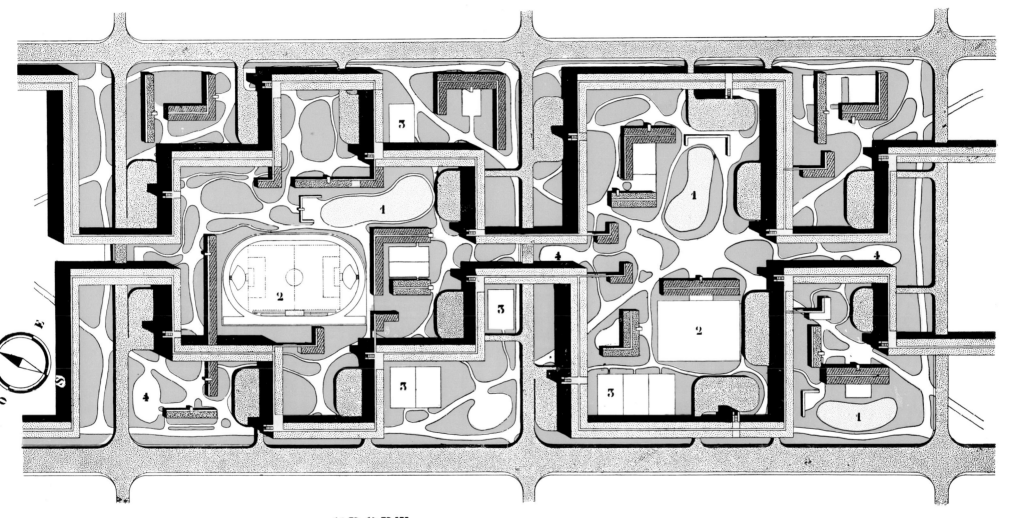

VR
7

LA "VILLE VERTE" 1000 HAB. À L'HECT.

**SPORT :**    1   **PISCINE**
2   **FOOTBALL, SAUT, ETC**
3   **TENNIS**
4   **JEUX**

0         100         200ᵐ

– THE GREEN CITY
– SPORTSGROUND DIRECTLY OUTSIDE
  BUILDINGS: 100 % of ground area
  BEACHES ON TOP OF BUILDINGS: 12%
  OF TOTAL GROUND AREA
  TOTAL: 112% TOTAL AREA AVAILABLE
– SUPERDENSITY: 1,000 POPULATION TO THE HECTARE

definitive
architectural
attitude: death of
the "corridor-
street."

Overall plan of one housing sector: housing, highways and auto-ports, total park. Vertical and horizontal pedestrian routes (in yellow). Landscaped (but direct) exterior pedestrian network. Sports facilities directly outside houses: complete stadium (2) + large swimming pool and sand beach (1) + tennis courts (3) + infants' playground (4) + covered play areas underneath buildings, + immense ribbon of sunbathing beaches on roof-gardens.

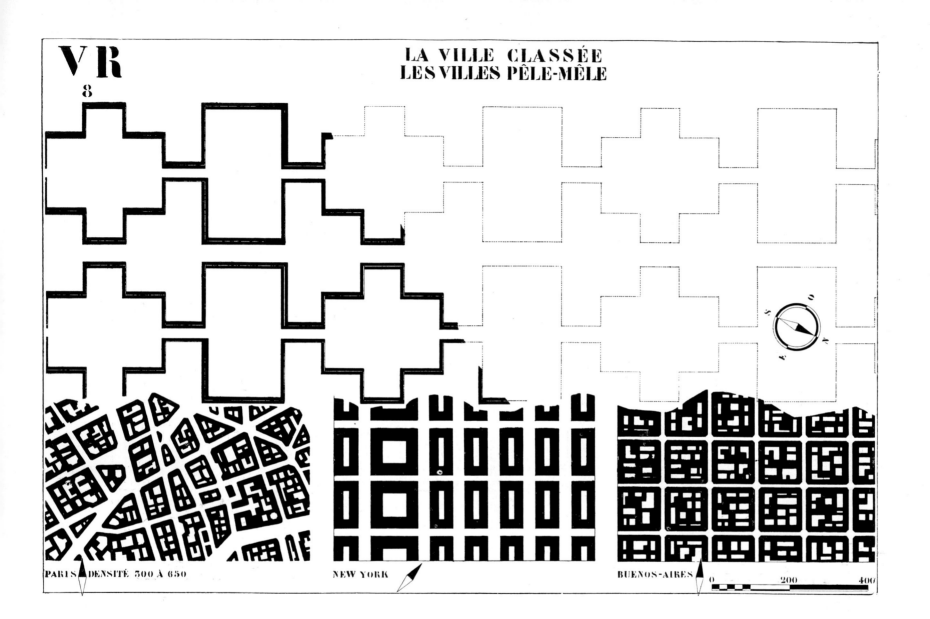

PARIS DENSITÉ 300 À 650

NEW YORK

BUENOS-AIRES

0    200    400

This diagram provides a clear expression of the prodigious reform implied in the Radiant City population figure of 1,000 to the hectare. It means a whole new way of life. (The plans of Paris, New York, Buenos Aires and the Radiant City are all on the same scale.)

— THE NEW SCALE OF
   URBAN HOUSING UNITS
— ELIMINATION OF THE STREET
— ELIMINATION OF THE COURTYARD

164

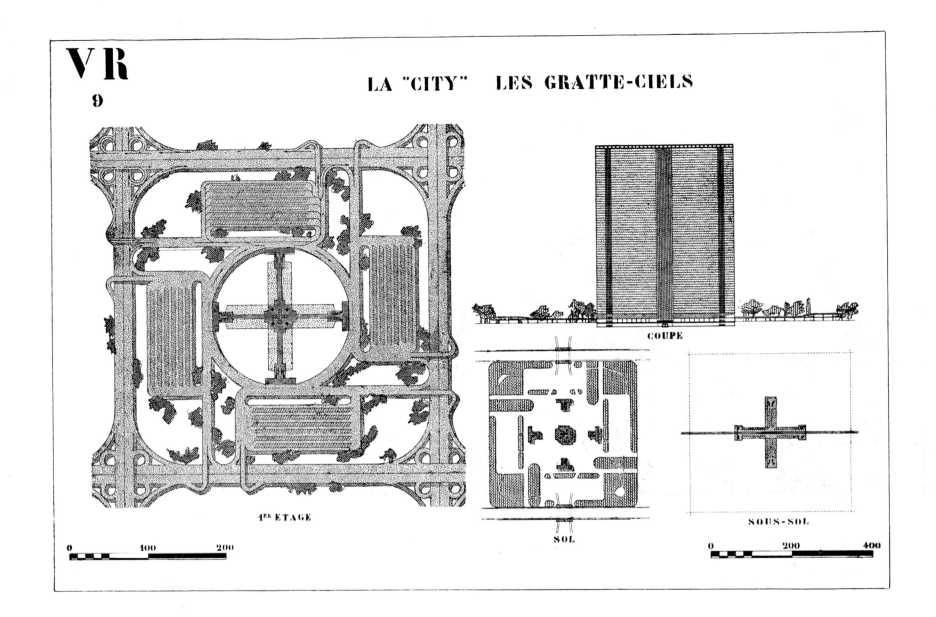

**VR**

**9**

LA "CITY"   LES GRATTE-CIELS

1ᴱᴿ ETAGE

0    100    200

COUPE

SOL

SOUS-SOL

0    200    400

SEPARATION OF TRANSPORTATION SYSTEMS:
1° UNDERGROUND: SUBWAYS
2° GROUND LEVEL: GIVEN OVER EXCLUSIVELY
    TO PEDESTRIANS, INCLUDING SPACE BETWEEN PILOTIS
3° HIGHWAYS AND AUTO-PORTS (5 METERS ABOVE GROUND LEVEL)

Creation of a vertical business center. Here, the height is 220 m. The building is cruciform (see chap. "Is Descartes American?"). For later improvements see next chap. PLANS FOR ANTWERP, BARCELONA, NEMOURS).

Illustrated here, organization of transport systems:

1° Basement: subway and communal services.

2° Ground level: pedestrians only (100% excluding the 5 entrance halls).

3° Highways and auto-ports: elevation 5 m. Perfected heavy traffic system. The 4 skyscraper entrances are approachable from any side of the square. The intersections are all ideal, one-way designs. Parking for 1,000 cars on platform 5 m. above ground. If necessary, 1,000 cars can also be parked under the auto-ports, then a further 1,000 underground.

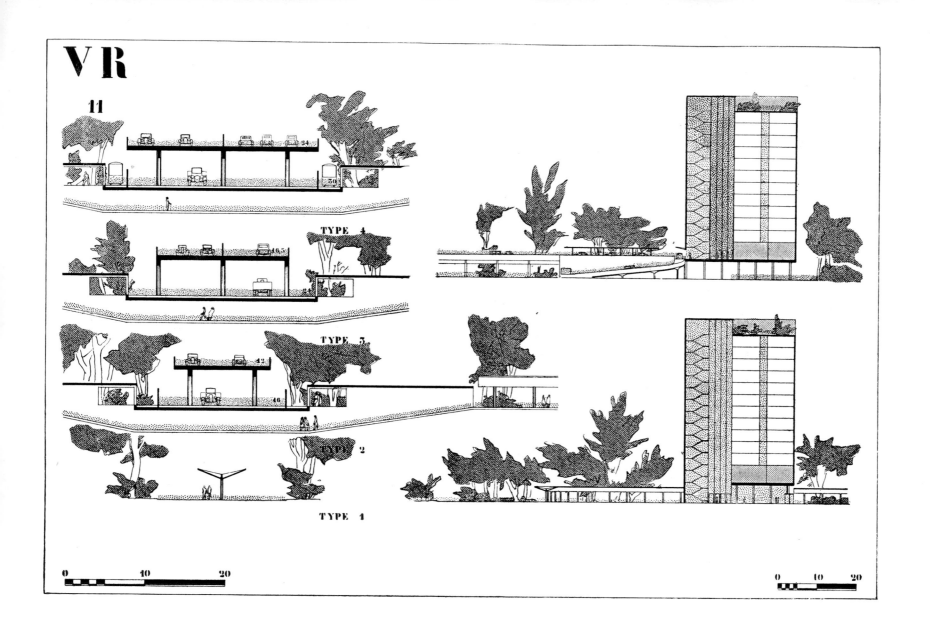

**VR**

11

TYPE 4

TYPE 5

TYPE 2

TYPE 1

0    10    20

0    10    20

— TRAFFIC MOVEMENTS
1° GROUND LEVEL: PEDESTRIANS
2° 5 M. ABOVE GROUND: CARS
3° ELEVATORS (PUBLIC SERVICE) HEIGHT: 50 M.
4° SUPERIMPOSED INTERIOR STREETS
5° ROOFTOP BEACHES (50 M. ABOVE GROUND)
6° COMMUNAL SERVICES (5 M. ABOVE GROUND)

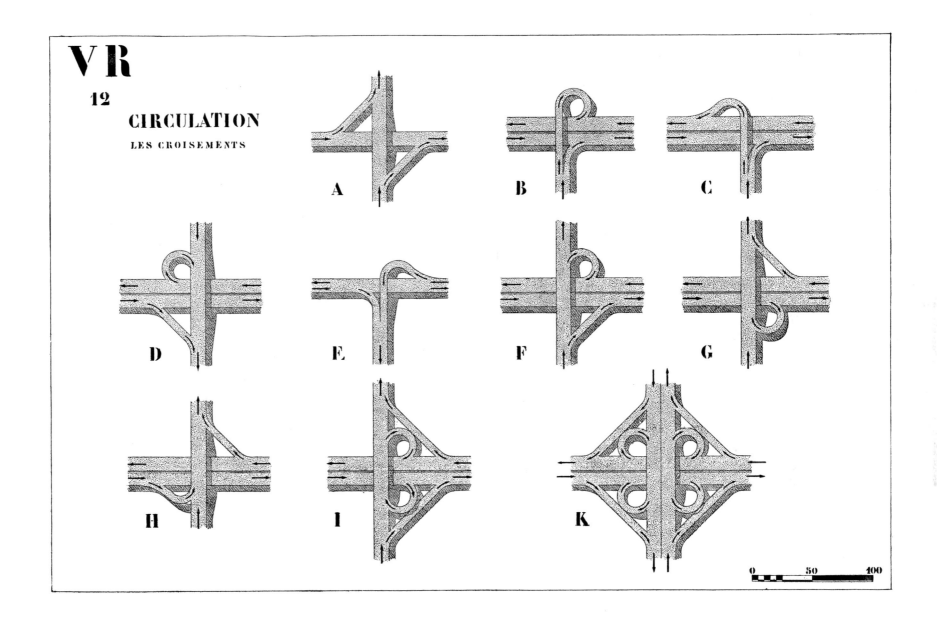

A    B    C

D    E    F    G

H    I    K

0    50    100

These are the forms of traffic intersection that should be used in planning new cities. The introduction of any extra branch road into or out of a right-angled (or almost right-angled) intersection makes any one-way solution impossible (without manned control). When such a situation seems imperative, the intersection should be divided into two linked intersections (see example, plate V.R. 15, p. 170: the division of a "star" intersection into two successive intersections, opposite the letter **B**). This is the primary condition for achieving a good automotive traffic system.

HIGH-SPEED TRAFFIC: ONE WAY

# VR
### 15

## LA VILLE

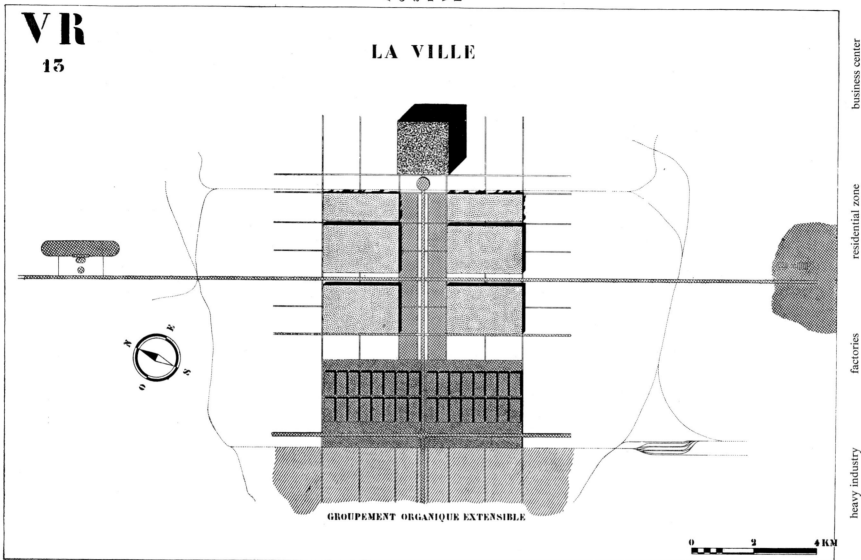

GROUPEMENT ORGANIQUE EXTENSIBLE

0   2   4 KM

business center

residential zone

factories

heavy industry

Central railroad station with air terminal on roof. The railroad station allows trains to pass through; it mustn't be a dead end.

At the two extreme outward limits of the city: grounds for mass sporting events.

To the right, the university.

ATTENTION! (1964.) Between 1931, the date when these illustrations of city-planning techniques were worked out, and the reprinting of this book now, in 1964, thirty-three years of further research have led me to the publication of more highly evolved proposals in the book *Les Trois Etablissements Humains* (*The Three Human Institutions*) (1945.) These three institutions are: 1. The Unit of Agricultural Exploitation; 2. The Linear Industrial City; 3. The Radio-Concentric City of exchanges. These together cover the entire needs of the whole country, infusing men's labor in a machine-age civilization with creative vitality.

Any concentrically designed city (all cities created in the past on ground plans determined by "donkey tracks"; also my own 1922 project for a modern city of 3 million inhabitants) makes regular, organic development impossible: a biological defect.

The essence of any city is the residential zone. Here, it can be extended without difficulty on either side, into the country. A considerable margin should be reserved from the very beginning for civic organizations.

By setting the business center and the industrial sector one either side, internal travel is diminished by half.

NOTE – This layout (symmetrical halves flanking a central axis) can be replaced, if necessary, by a non-symmetrical scheme in which the present axis is taken as a fixed boundary with the various city organs developing out from it on one side only, in the one lateral direction.

BIOLOGICAL ORGANIZATION OF THE CITY
PERMANENT POSSIBILITY OF EXTENSION

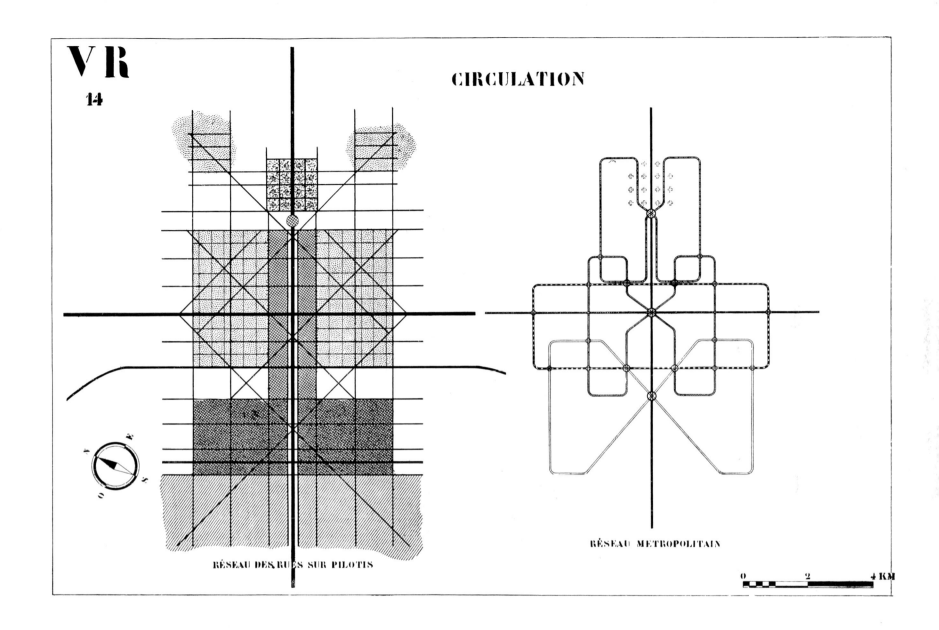

**VR**

**14**

RÉSEAU DES RUES SUR PILOTIS

RÉSEAU METROPOLITAIN

0        2        4 KM

— ORGANIZATION OF HIGH-SPEED TRAFFIC
— 1° HIGHWAYS: ORTHOGONAL NETWORK
        DIAGONAL NETWORK AT A HIGHER LEVEL
        AVOIDING "STAR" INTERSECTIONS.
— 2° SUBWAY NETWORK (UNDERGROUND).

The basic module once accepted (maximum distance from any given apartment door to elevators: 100 meters), the astonishing ground plan above is the result: this traffic network is both necessary and adequate to provide total facilities for a city of one and a half million inhabitants, all the various sectors included: residential, civic center, business center, factories and heavy industry. Necessary and adequate.

If one accepts the necessity for a subway system, then it is as well to keep it as well defined as possible, avoiding illogical muddle. Otherwise, the passengers will be confused.

169

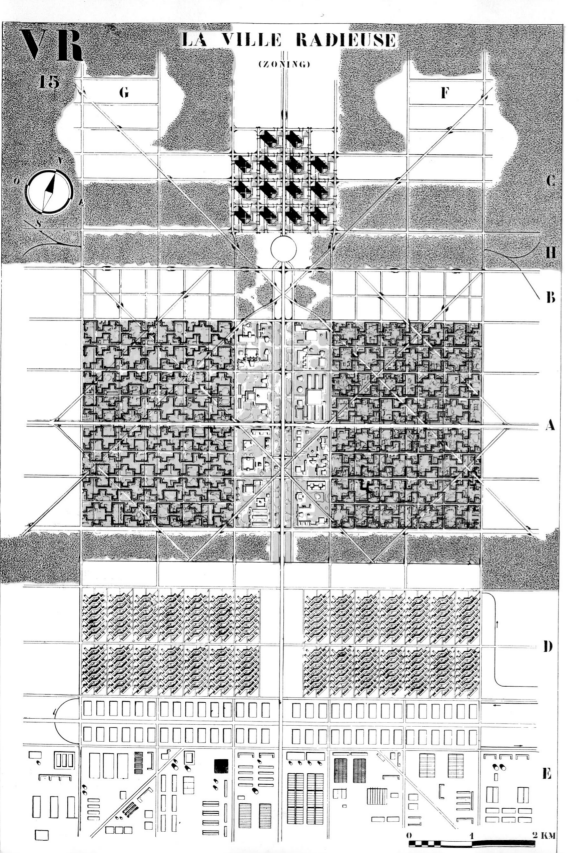

VR

15

## LA VILLE RADIEUSE

(ZONING)

G

F

Satellite cities. e.g.: government buildings or center for
social studies, etc.

C — The business center

H — Railroad station and air
terminal

B — Hotels
Embassies

Note: As has already been
stated (plate V.R. 13,
page 168), the biological
development of the city
can also extend laterally
from the vertical axis on
one side only (a ques-
tion of topography, pres-
ence of a river, etc.).

A — Housing

D — Factories

Warehouses

E — Heavy industry

0        1        2 KM

SYNTHESIS: THE RADIANT CITY

On top of the skyscraper: metal plating providing definitive anti-bomb protection (F).

The top story of the apartment buildings can also have this metal plating, or anti-bomb protection can be provided in an emergency by means of sandbags (G).
(H) Poison gas will spread out over the whole ground surface when dropped. It will be swept away by air currents (thanks to the pilotis). Also, the swimming pools will provide reserves of water that can be used to drive the gas off with hoses. The residents will take refuge in the upper stories (not in underground shelters).

It will be noted that the ground is free of all obstructions: no trenches for gas to collect in.

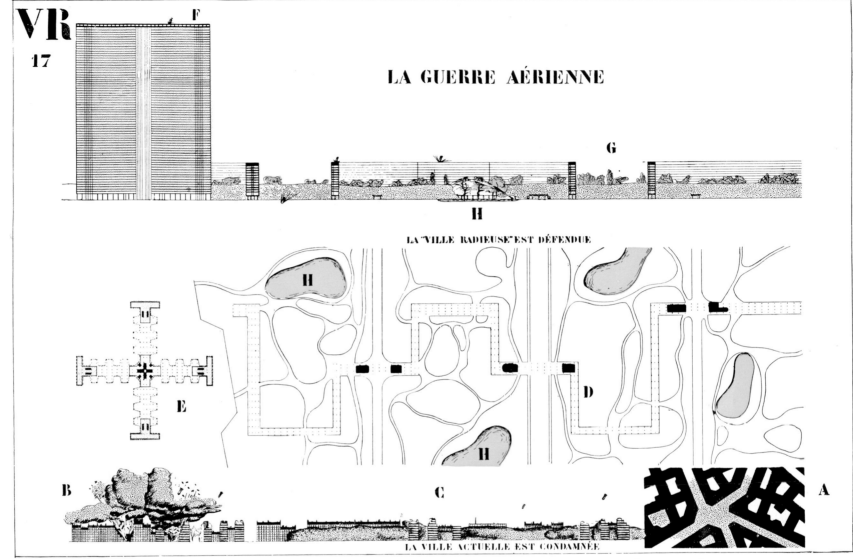

## LA GUERRE AÉRIENNE

LA "VILLE RADIEUSE" EST DÉFENDUE

LA VILLE ACTUELLE EST CONDAMNÉE

DEFENSE AGAINST

# AERIAL WARFARE

The "Report presented by Lieutenant-Colonel Vauthier, member of General Pétain's staff, Inspector General of aerial defense for the national territory" to the "Higher Committee for the Development of the Parisian Region," on March 14, 1933, advocates as indispensable measures several fundamental elements of the Radiant City. To wit:

Chapter II: *development of the Parisian region:*

Page 17: "given several solutions, all equally viable from an economic view, we should choose the one that decreases our vulnerability to aerial attack to the greatest extent."

"Center of Paris: what is needed is the undertaking of a very farsighted plan, to be executed in stages ... which will prevent rebuilding on present sites ...; diminish the proportion of built-up land ...; forbid corridor-streets and interior courtyards ...; isolate individual buildings ...; avoid buildings lining streets ... Stretch the city upwards (which means: "open it up": author's note).

Page 21: Anti-gas precautions. The shelters can be either high in the air (V.R. type: author's note) or underground. Anti-explosive precautions: protection can be organized on the tops of buildings.

Page 22: distribute the weight, not on walls ... but on pillars; pillars will not be destroyed by blast, and the building won't collapse.

Page 24: Les Halles, the central markets of Paris, are a very vulnerable target ... it seems practically impossible to protect them. In this case, dispersion seems the only answer.

Page 26: roads and streets ... It would be as well to forbid the construction of apartment blocks lining streets.

Page 28: There is already in existence an anti-aerial warfare technique in matters of architecture and city-planning providing precise and concrete rules ...

In 1930, Lieutenant-Colonel Vauthier brought out a book called "Danger from the Air and this Country's Future." Having examined the various suggestions then being offered for the redevelopment of Paris, he concluded in that work as follows: "Our preferences, in the matter of large cities, must go in every case to the Le Corbusier system. But the dangers of aerial warfare do require its revision in certain respects." (These remarks refer exclusively to the work I had submitted to the public in 1925 at the Esprit Nouveau pavilion. My plates illustrating the V.R., then still being worked on, had not yet come to Lieutenant-Colonel Vauthier's attention.)

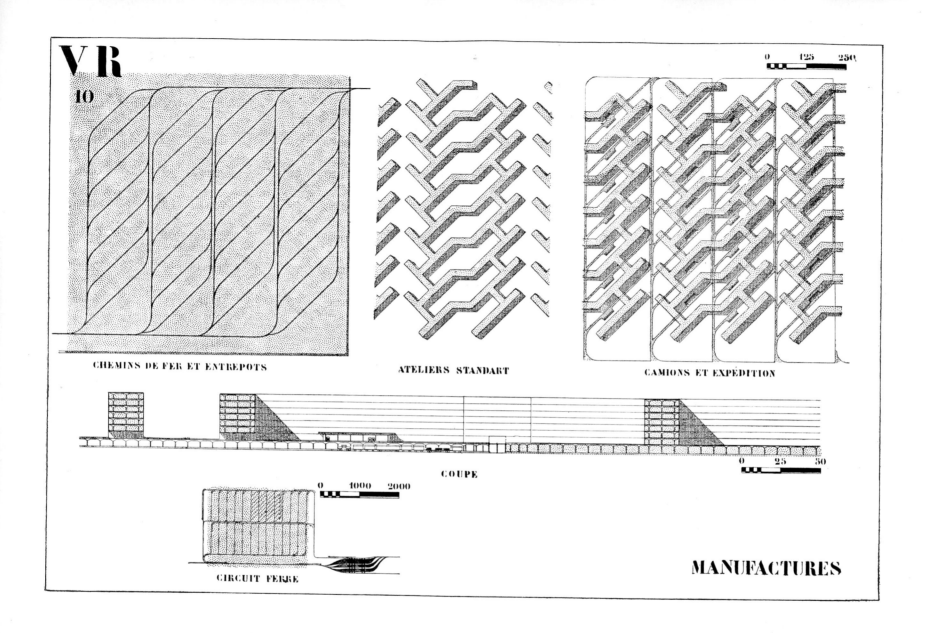

CHEMINS DE FER ET ENTREPOTS

ATELIERS STANDART

CAMIONS ET EXPÉDITION

0    125    250

COUPE

0    25    50

0    1000    2000

CIRCUIT FERRE

**MANUFACTURES**

— LIGHT INDUSTRY: STANDARD PREMISES
   CONSIDERED AS AN EXTENSION OF THE
   PUBLIC SERVICES
— RAILROAD ON GROUND LEVEL
   TRUCKS 8 M. ABOVE GROUND LEVEL
— WAREHOUSES BETWEEN RAILROAD AND TRUCK LANES
   COVERING ENTIRE SURFACE AREA

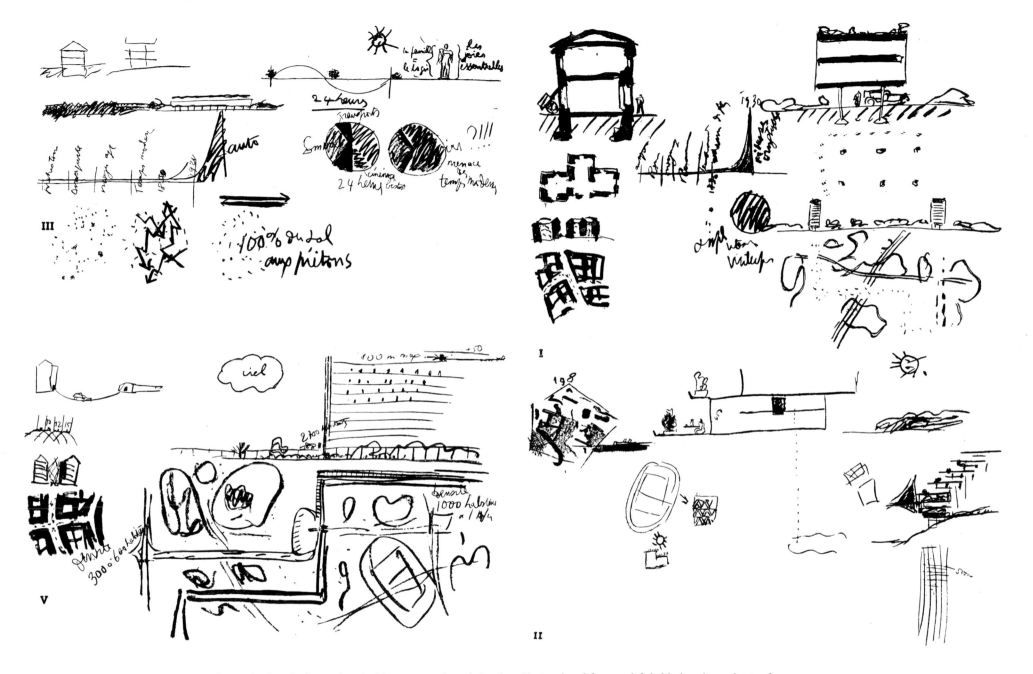

Improvisations in front of packed houses: words and sketches. Vast, colored frescoes left behind on huge sheets of paper.

These theories did not remain behind locked doors. They were published in various places and evoked passionate curiosity. I was forced to take up my pilgrim's staff and journey forth, often for great distances. Preaching a crusade? Who knows! Already there are many premonitory signs on the horizon.

Lectures given between 1925 and 1934:

| | | | | | |
|---|---|---|---|---|---|
| Paris | Basel | Barcelona | Rio de Janeiro | Oslo | Athens |
| Prague | Berne | Buenos Aires | Moscow | Algiers | Rome |
| Brussels | Frankfurt | Montevideo | Antwerp | Rotterdam | Milan |
| Zurich | Madrid | São Paolo | Stockholm | Amsterdam | |

173

"PRELUDE," in 1933, was the sequel to
"PLANS." Editorial board: Hubert
Lagardelle, Dr. Pierre Winter, François
de Pierrefeu, Le Corbusier. The texts
of this fifth chapter are taken from
issues of "PRELUDE" 1932-34.

# 5<sup>th</sup> PART: PRELUDE.

1. THE SPECTACLE OF MODERN LIFE.
2. PROFESSORS OF PREDICTION.
3. A NEW FORM OF GREGARIOUSNESS.
4. BOLSHOI . . . OR THE NOTION OF BIGNESS.
5. ROME.
6. MOBILIZATION OF THE LAND.
7. TRUTH FROM DIAGRAMS.
8. GENERAL MEASURES.

# 1. THE SPECTACLE OF MODERN LIFE

"We don't ask to be eternal beings, only not to see acts and things suddenly lose all their meaning."

(*Vol de Nuit* – Saint-Exupéry)

First of all, let us face the full and cruel meaning of our present state of awareness: *we don't know why we work!*

Put brutally, *it is for money*. The people who have found happiness in this world – the wise – have forced a breach in this heavy metal cloud and glimpse at least a corner of blue sky. They have assigned another goal to their work: quality. From that moment on, they are saved. But those people are few and far between.

Saved! The somersaults of the financial world will only disturb them secondarily.

Money – in our case, *gold* – can fail. Suppose someone does in fact discover a means of making gold. We should replace it with some other financial standard, of course; but in the meantime, what unforeseen ruin and disturbances!

Let us measure the full and cruel meaning of our present state: for some time now, we have been working merely for money.

A deceptive goal. It stimulates only a few of our qualities and leaves the most precious of them inactive. Worse, it encourages the defects in human nature.

Generally speaking, we would all be willing enough to change our credo.

But is another credo possible?

If society were to reorganize itself, to distribute the fruits of its labor in a new way, then our concern for money could diminish, and our energies, freed in this way, would find the roads opened towards goals set by higher passions.

The machine-age world has not yet harnessed the human passions. Quite the contrary.

In order to distribute the fruits of human labor differently, we must first organize that labor, set precise and fertile goals for it. Then, the advance of the great machine-age adventure could continue.

## YOU AGREE

You agree, do you not, that it would be wrong, despite all this, to try and halt this great advance that is at present deploying so powerfully, so ineluctably across the whole world? This advance unfurling so *cosmically* across the whole world – cosmically, because it has suddenly become an immense part of those natural forces that man has subjugated to date, to his own pain and distress at first, but before long to his joy and delight.

The fact that we are prepared to accept this shining new inheritance from our fathers proves that we are not afraid of what may come of it. This discovery, this great exploratory advance, forward, into the deeps, towards victory, is a matter of *joy* to us, not of fear, of anxiety, or of terror. *The future will bring joy!*

That thought itself is already a joy. There is joy in thinking of the future, joy already in imagining it!

From the conquest of money, which merely spurs on individuals, we wish to press on towards achieving a harmony in this age of ours that will summon all of us to the great task and bring satisfaction to everyone.

We must provide a visible goal to all the millions who are sinking every moment more deeply into doubt, into fear, and into despair.

By establishing a plan, the modern era can make its general goals clearly visible. The machine, that vast modern event, will be seen for what it really is, a servant and not a ruler, a worker and not a tyrant, a source of unity and not of conflict, of construction and not of destruction.

The participation of all in this social epic will necessitate a discipline. Is there anything more pitiful than an undisciplined crowd? And nature, which is all discipline, the logic of cause and effect – though sometimes that logic is contrary to the interests of mankind – nature cannot tolerate flagging energies; she will sweep them away, make them as nothing, reabsorb them and restore the rule of the unfeeling and ruthless elements once more.

Have you ever tried playing chess without rules? Or a game of football? Even the tiniest kid on the block will make an effort to master the rules of a game, for they are what give meaning to his actions, an interest to his movements, fuel to the resulting explosion of life.

## LET US LAY DOWN THE RULES

Let us lay down the rules for this age of ours.

They may all be subsumed in one phrase: *the creation of harmony*. We must provide all these forces that have so recently and so rapidly been unleashed upon us with a rhythm, an order that will permit us to harness them efficiently. And by efficiently, I mean so that everyone receives a merited share in their benefits. And by a merited share, I mean the right to eat, the right to expect a serene end to a life that has been filled with fruitful labors, and the right to know the reasons for all the daily actions we are obliged to perform.

To understand the reasons for our participation.

Which means seeing one's path lie clearly ahead.

Which means a *plan*.

A plan made with the object of achieving harmony between forces that have been unleashed upon the world by inevitable causes beyond our comprehension. We have struck our pick into the rock, seeking to find some good we sensed was buried there – and a volcano has erupted beneath us!

Work undertaken for the collective good must always command the interest of individuals. The necessity for *maintaining* the products of that work, provided a genuine profit results from it, will give rise to a freely accepted discipline and encourage *a spontaneous effort to maintain it that will be a proof of love*.

*Awakening of the* GOOD *in men*
*Sympathetic vibration of the artistic fiber*
*Outpouring of the creative spirit . . .*

Q. E. D.

## IT IS A SPIRITUAL TASK

Holland, a country won by conquest from the sea, a product of collective labor, is always scrubbed, kept neat, taken care of – when everywhere else people are constantly on the verge of discouragement, talking of giving up . . .

The new road to Valencia, in Spain, is also kept constantly clean and neat, winding tidily along between its flower-filled, well-tended verges.

The *Van Nelle* tobacco factory in Rotterdam, a creation of the modern age, has removed all the former connotation of despair from that word "proletarian." And this deflection of the egotistic property instinct towards a feeling for collective action leads to a most happy result: the phenomenon of *personal participation* in every stage of the human enterprise. Labor retains its fundamental materiality, but it is enlightened by the spirit. I repeat, everything lies in that phrase: *a proof of love.*

It is to this goal, by means of new administrative forms that will purify and amplify it, that we must lead our modern world. Tell us what we are, what we can do to help, why we are working. Give us plans; show us plans; explain those plans to us. *Unite us.* Speak to us. Are we not all *one*, within the serene whole of an organized hierarchy?

If you show us such plans and explain them to us, then the old dichotomy between "haves" and despairing "have-nots" will disappear. There will be but a single society, united in belief and action.

We live in an age of strictest rationalism, and this is a matter of conscience. We must awaken a conscience in the world. Conscience in everyone and about everyone.

It is a spiritual task.

The noblest of tasks also, and the only one that excites, or can excite, a passionate response in everyone. It is the truest task of mankind; its reason for being.

Spiritual satisfaction, spiritual joy—individually and collectively at the same time.

Such is the race we have to run: forward, forward-looking, big, living, and total. We must create excitement, exaltation, new talents, new heroes.

We must sweep aside the nervous panic that is now gaining a hold on us, smash the brake that some are trying to clamp down on this modern adventure, throw open our doors and windows to tomorrow. We must open our eyes to the spectacle of this modern age. The play is already well under way: the misers, the traitors and the cowards are already on stage; but so too are the debonair knights, assured of ultimate victory.

## THE SPECTACLE OF MODERN LIFE

The spectacle of modern life: we shall therefore accept any contribution towards success and action.

Despite what people say, the U.S.A. and Germany are still only in the chaotic first stages. It is said that these countries have reached the furthest limits of technological advancement. The furthest limits feasible within the framework of our present way of life.

But from the point of view of the way of life we want, there is no harmony at all as yet.

Production? It must be intensified to the maximum: mill and factory must function with the pure simplicity of mathematics.

In which case, no more than four hours' work per day, perhaps. And then, there will be new production goals: properly equipped cities, new housing, and the countryside (at last!) accessible to the wind of spiritual change that we have taken as the standard of all our efforts.

Three great new departures are implied by the Plan:

1. A new distribution of the 24 hours in our daily solar cycle: symphonic, logical, rich.

2. A decree that will permit work on the Plan to begin: a decree making the entire national territory available for redevelopment.

3. A reorganization of industry generally: taking over of the building trade – the metal industries and innumerable other industries, the ones producing articles henceforth classified as "superfluous" and prohibited, will be given over to the production of housing and suitable equipment for it. We shall prove that this is the only solution to the crisis that is now bringing the first cycle of the machine age to an end. Products of disorder: self-indulgence and a flood of useless consumer goods. Products of order: a lucid program and the manufacture of useful consumer goods.

## I CAN SAY NOW THAT PARIS FILLS ME WITH DESPAIR

I can say now that Paris fills me with despair. That once admirable city has nothing left inside it but the soul of an archeologist. No more power of command. No head. No powers of action. No genius.

The city's one great undertaking, its *low-cost housing developments*, has merely grafted onto each of its gates out to the provinces, onto each one of its exits, a bunch of cancerous ganglia; cancer of the pyloros. That's in matters of city planning. If I am to go on to architecture, well, it has to be said: there is nothing in the city that has moved a single step forward into modern life, nothing, not a window, not a room, not a staircase, not a courtyard. I cannot be accused of jealousy, since I am immune to that emotion, but the conditions were all there (authority, sites, capital and an authentic program) and the program has never even been started. No one has laid a finger on any of the old routines, the old customs; no one has built a single thing that was worked out beforehand as a theoretical solution, that would have opened up those avenues they have decorated with their pitiful trophies towards the future.

There is another municipal (as near as makes no difference) project that has been under consideration for several years behind a barrage of speculation: the *Triumphal Way* that is to be thrust into the funnel of the Champs-Elysées. What a spiritual disaster that will be! Paris will receive an enormous dagger thrust in her side – and it is hoped that the city will be able to escape through the resulting wound. City of Paris, thumbs up or down? Who wants this rich man's avenue intended to spread and multiply the pomps of the Etoile and its Triumphal Arch?

But there is more to the Arc de Triomphe than pomp. Let us shout aloud, at this moment when imprecision, even in the modern camp, is the password of the day, how masterly the conception of the Arc de Triomphe is, placed and designed as it was with a perfection that dazzles us every evening even now, floodlit with the radiance of revelation. It has all the French gift for lyric beauty in it: solidity, boldness, an almost cruel purity, lucidity of statement, mathematical religion. There is no other arch in the world that has that spirit. Strength and restraint. What modesty and what a blaze of trumpets!

In pious commemoration of the immense holocaust of the Great War, it was decided to lay beneath the flagstones of the Arch the body of an unknown soldier. A flame now flickers every night above that stone; the flame we see beneath the Arch, at the top of the hill. Nothing more humble could have been achieved than this, nothing more great imagined: to grasp and hold onto one's past, to make it live on today with one magical stroke, by the miracle of a great idea.

How, after that, can we have accepted the raising of even one other monument to that somber memory! The grocers have had their way . . .

Alas, alas!

The *idea*, that impalpable thing that has no time, no calendar, no schedule, but simply explodes when it will! And if it erupts from a soil deeply enough enriched with a powerful culture, with the experience and still-living sap of centuries, then it can produce effects of such intensity that it becomes a guiding light for all the world.

It is for lack of such ideas that the head and the heart and the arms of Paris are now languishing impotently beneath the weight of governing assemblies that are inept, stagnant, closed to reality. And so the City swells, struggles, and is sliding down into mediocrity.

. . . "Paris, city of all the world . . ."

## WE ARE IN NO WAY CONTEMPTUOUS OF THE PAST

One Armistice Day, in the evening, M. Citroën offered us that undreamed-of revelation: a floodlit Place de la Concorde. Not just lit up by its street lamps or the Republic's standardized little gas flames, but illuminated with all the floods of light made possible by electricity. The idea had come from America, the projectors from the war. It was (and continued to be every evening) one of the most astounding lectures on architecture that it would be possible to attend "in this wide world." Sublime straight lines, and oh, sublime French rigor! On that Armistice night a dumbfounded crowd, standing in the square, held in the grip of a grace unshadowed by a single jest – on the contrary, of a grace imperious in its command – that crowd was able to listen to *architecture itself*. The four-thousand-year-old obelisk and the centuries-old palaces, the starry sky, a postwar crowd, and that light, sprung from the twentieth century and suddenly creating a new dialogue between so many elements so disparate in time, all this led us to a clear appreciation of the parental influence and the modernity of spiritual works that can draw and merge everything into their unity: stone, soul, mind, the past projected into the future by the ever-renewed resilience of every new today.

No, we are in no way contemptuous of the past. What we want is to use the sympathetic vibrations of our sensibilities in such a way that past time shall become one with life today: action, enterprise, the proportions of all ages – eternal in our human hearts.

Paris functions by virtue of its past and also by virtue of that magnificent reserve of strength, its people: that constant transfusion of new blood that is poured into it by the provinces and even the whole world.

But I must now say that Paris fills us with despair, *because Paris has lost all enterprise.*

It is not death we find repugnant, it is the corpse. Cities: corpses fashioned out of aging or even brand-new building materials; and spiritual corpses propped up in the seats of power.

But life should excite us to passion!

## NOTHING HAS BEEN ORDERED, NOTHING HAS BEEN LAID DOWN

A port is alive; everything in it moves – the water and its burdens, the spirit of enterprise that hovers there. Docks, ships, journeys: poetry. If I were the Dutch, I should set up my college of architecture right in the middle of Rotterdam harbor [1],

[1] I have just returned from Holland. January, 1932.

in an old, disused steamship, so that the students would be able to see and feel that there is space between the earth and the sky to raise up the new housing and industrial equipment we need, and that the means are there for us to use: steel and concrete. And that these structures have a right to existence, that their presence would be pleasurable to us, since they would be accomplishing the real task we face today. And the teachers, too, inspired by the life of such an environment, would feel called upon to teach the future, and not what is already past, to draw from the past the lesson of perpetual movement and inevitable renewal.

Leaving or entering any modern city, by train, by car, or by plane, what a wretched and oppressive spectacle we see!

Fez, the holy city, has great gates in its walls that open onto the plenitude of unspoiled nature. The city, a work of the human spirit, has advanced into the countryside *in an opposing line.*

But what is this leprosy that is eating away the fields and woods, what is this dismal and suppurating zone – a creeping and purulent decay – that we find all around the immense peripheries of our own big cities like a shameful skin disease?

Why do our cities writhe out in tattered strands towards the countryside they intend to infect?

Why don't they rise up sheer from the ground, clear and glittering, straight and pure, calm and secure, dominating the iron or asphalt tracks that carry their substance out to far horizons?

Why are they rotten?

Why is not one of them *whole*, a form expressing a conception, honest, straight?

A city is made up of factories, of residential districts, of warehouses. Why are those factories, which house machines that are precision itself, all filthy and in chaos? A residential district is made up of houses; a house is an upright geometric prism. Why are those prisms not upright then, at the very edge of our wheatfields, or our woods or meadowlands?

Nothing has been ordered, nothing has been *laid down*.

Our cities are advancing into their futures without eyes and without guides, without plans, without controls. Decay. Skin disease, leprosy. The common spectacle of this modern age.

If I were the Municipal Council, I would say: the edges of the roads leading into the city, and the edge of the city where it meets the country, shall be green with grass and shrubs, yellow with ripening wheat, or flowered with gardens.

A simple edict, coldly promulgated. And penalties for infringements!

## THERE IS NO PROLETARIAT HERE

The Van Nelle tobacco factory in Rotterdam rises from the bank of a canal, beside a great curve in the railroad from Amsterdam to Paris, in the midst of meadows. The canal is straight, its banks smooth; the double line of railroad tracks glistens in the grass. On the horizon, a long way away across the flat meadowlands, the derricks in the harbor are outlined in bold profile against the sky. The road that runs into the factory, between the buildings, is smooth, flat, bordered with brown-tiled sidewalks; it is as clean and bright as a dance floor. The sheer façades of the buildings, bright glass and gray metal, rise up sheer, cleancut, and very high against the sky. There is no paint: all the iron has been pistol-sprayed with a protective coating of non-oxidising metal. [1] The glass begins at sidewalk or lawn level and continues

[1] A recent invention.

upwards unbroken until it meets the clean line of the sky. The serenity of the place is total. *Everything is open to the outside.* And this is of enormous significance to all those who are working, on all eight floors, *inside.* [1]

Because inside we find a poem of light. An immaculate lyricism. Dazzling vision of order. The very atmosphere of honesty.

Everything is transparent; everyone can see and be seen as he works. I am reminded of the remark made by a League of Nations diplomat in Geneva, in 1927, when he saw our project for the General Secretariat building in which there were five hundred offices that all realized these identical conditions: "But, Monsieur, diplomacy needs *chiaroscuro*!..."

The manager of the factory is there in his glass office. He can be seen. And he himself, from his office, can see the whole illuminated Dutch horizon, and, in the far distance, the life of the great port.

The immense refectory continues the pattern. The managers, the highest and lowest administrative grades, the workers, male and female, all eat together here in the same great room, which has transparent walls opening onto endless views of meadows. Together, all together. Everyone has tidied himself or herself up for the meal; there is not a single spot of dirt on the blue rubber floor covering that makes the atmosphere there even more limpid still. The workers, men and women alike, are all clean, dressed in unbleached smocks or blouses, their hair neatly done. How healthy everyone looks! I found it fascinating to observe the faces of those factory girls. Each one of them was an expression of the life within: joy or the opposite, a reflection of their passions or their difficulties. *But, there is no proletariat here.* Simply a graduated hierarchy, clearly established and respected. This atmosphere of a well-run, diligent hive is attained by means of a universal and voluntary respect for order, regularity, punctuality, justice and kindliness.

Then go and take a look at the machine rooms, at the machines themselves and the control panels, at the floor of the boiler-house, which is like the floor of a sitting-room, and at the mechanics who are all "Gentlemen"!

### PARTICIPATION

I have already remarked upon the centuries-old spirit of discipline created in Holland by the perpetual *necessity for maintenance* (the dykes, the windmills, the irrigation system of the polders, the canals, the boats, barges or tugs). The spade, the dredger and the paint pot are all in constant use. An example of everyday reciprocity: I keep up the place in which I work; my work interests me; so the trouble taken is a source of joy! A virtuous circle for once! All are united in a compact solidarity; all bear a larger or smaller share of the responsibility; participation.

Participation. That was how the Van Nelle factory was created. The architect was given a year in which to draw up a provisional plan; then they spent *five years*

---

[1] I am told that on certain days during summer, work in the factory has to be stopped because of the excessive heat. The transformation of the sun's rays into heat is not inhibited by glass. The architect added: "We ought to have had your neutralizing walls," your "correct breathing" air-conditioning system. Yes, this invention, the germ of which was already to be found in some of my prewar work, had not finally earned its key to the city until this year, 1932, thanks to the work of the Saint-Gobain laboratories. But modern architecture is constantly stumbling into similar obstacles in every other area as well. Because it is not concerned merely with decorative reforms but with a biological revolution. The new (architectural) entity must be *entire, a unit.* The contemporary architectural revolution should be allowed ten years' grace in which to harness all our new ideas and all our new techniques together into a single stream! If we progress with that stream: certain solution. If we hesitate for an instant: failure... and the hisses of the gallery.

working out the final form. Five years of collaboration: meetings to discuss every problem individually. And it was not only the directors and the architects and the managers who were at those meetings. The heads of the various departments were also present, as well as a skilled workman or clerk representing each of the specialized functions to be performed in the factory. Ideas can come from anywhere. In matters of mass production, it is well known how vitally important a minor short-cut can turn out to be. There are no small things, there are only correctly designed things that work.

Participation!

I can truly say that my visit to that factory was one of the most beautiful days of my life.

### PROOF OF LOVE

Next day, I was met at Amsterdam airport by the head of the new airline to the East Indies: "the East Indies Mail." Those who have never been fortunate enough to fly at 120 miles an hour over virgin jungle, estuaries, mountain chains and as yet unexplored stretches of territory, would not have had the same cause for emotion as myself when faced with a vast mural map, not just of Europe but of Africa and Asia as well, marked with red and blue lines representing the eight separate legs that are now being flown by this line. They would not shudder with excitement, as I did, at the idea that at that very moment those airplanes were actually flying along those red and blue lines, some on their way out, others coming back. It is noon, say; for that plane just taking off in Java, it is four in the afternoon; for another it is already sunset; for another, the sky is black with night; and for a fourth, the dawn is showing pale green in front of its propeller.

Listen to these amazing figures: the weekly mail of the Dutch East Indies amounts to 1,200 kilograms. (So much potential energy, latent acts and future struggles in so small a weight!) That was what the ships used to carry. Today, a fifth of it goes by plane. But that's not all: when the planes are carrying *two-fifths* of that mail (480 kg.), the East Indian airline (Amsterdam-Java) will be *paid for!* These figures make one wonder what further revelations, what similar breathtaking solutions might be provided by other sets of figures in other spheres.

The head of the East Indian airline said: "Little by little, we shall solve the problems of night flying, and that will cut days off the journey." The strips of color on that planisphere will change in number and in length. Today, the relays are as follows: Greece, Egypt, Arabia, India, Indochina, etc. A journey? No, a spiritual odyssey!

The office of the airline head looks out over the airport. Signal lights flash; airplanes land and take off. It has been done, Messieurs Voisin, Santos-Dumont, Wright, Latham, Blériot! And in twenty short years! It was only in 1909 that I was twisting my neck out of an attic window because of the noise of an engine suddenly tearing open the Paris sky: the Comte de Lambert was flying over the city. That evening, Paris went mad with joy.

Participation!

The deflection of a narrow and egotistical property instinct towards a feeling for collective action. To arrive at that happy result: the phenomenon of *personal participation* in every stage of the human enterprise. Labor retains its fundamental materiality, but it is enlightened by the radiance of the spirit. Everything lies in the meaning of the phrase: *a proof of love.*

We must guide, purify, amplify the realities that constitute our world today.
Decide what we are, what functions we can perform. What we are working for.

Make plans for us, show us those plans, explain them to us.

There is a power for enthusiasm in the human soul that can be made to explode.

January, 1932.

●

# 2. PROFESSORS OF PREDICTION

(In a recent interview for the British Broadcasting Corporation, the famous author H. G. Wells made an appeal for the appointment of Professors of Prediction capable of paving the way for us towards the future.

In response to this light-hearted request, *The Listener*, the B.B.C.'s own magazine, published a series of articles by various famous people replying to Wells on the subject of the need for such "prophets" or of what role they could perform.

Le Corbusier was one of the personalities asked to contribute, and we are happy to reprint here the article he sent in reply, an article in which our friends will find ample matter for reflection. *Editor.)*

### I DON'T BELIEVE IN SCHOOLS

I only believe in schools where the subjects taught are what is generally thought of as "exact," more or less reliable, more or less subject to verification: in other words, the very opposite of predictions. I don't believe in schools that are supposed to inculcate imagination; I am, in fact, a firm partisan of the necessity for closing them (Schools of the Fine Arts anyway). I have every confidence in the students, but I have a justifiable feeling of distrust with regard to the teachers. A teacher? A man who uproots you from that magnificent *school of doubt* provided by life itself, who is obliged by his *very profession* to develop a hard core of certainties inside himself so that he can then pass them on to his listeners. We know, for example, that Julius Caesar conquered Gaul and that Saint Louis wanted to reach Jerusalem. That's the sort of reality it seems to me useful to pass on to students in schools. But *teaching the future?* The teacher will automatically become a pontiff, whether he likes it or not; his students will make him into one simply by believing him; they are all around him, revering him, open-mouthed, insisting he cram them with positive information! The future comes. . . and life gives him the lie.

This is a perilous subject however: the whole problem of education. The situation at a glance: since the foundation of schools and academies, the sciences have made gigantic strides; the arts have foundered, the academic attitude has come into existence, together with the oppression it exerts and the stupidity of governments when they interfere in this domain. It is only outside such schools, at the feet of Mr. LIFE, the *only* worthwhile teacher, that creative thought has developed and expressed itself (with brilliance, energy and violence) in modern times. It is because of the teachers in certain schools that modern art has been labelled "revolutionary" when it is in fact the honest and licit expression of its age. Louis XIV was one of the most spirited and farsighted revolutionaries who ever lived, but because schools were not invented until after his time that epithet did not exist, or the reality either, and he, the King, was known as "the great classicist." What conclusion should we draw from this?

That the names of revolutionaries are the only names that history preserves – the names of those who were forced to revolutionize the age they lived in in order to express the vitality of that particular time, and who have thereby earned a place on the great list.

### THEY ARE LIVING OFF YESTERDAY

Though I am mistrustful of teachers, I am also, on the other hand, voracious when it comes to lessons, and as much so now as I was at the age of twenty. Lessons are things that emerge spontaneously from the works of men when they are immersed in life itself, whereupon they explode with dazzling force. When Mr. Wells spoke of Professors of Prediction, I think he was really talking about the ceaseless, continually accelerating explosions of events in these modern times, all the violent upheavals and transformations of a life that we only perceive through the work of those mediums the *inventors*.

In order to read the lessons of life, one has to be part of the general hubbub of excitement, in contact with events. More, one has to be a creator of explosions oneself, since it is an occupation that exercises the ear and eye, enabling one to perceive, to catch amidst the dazzle of racing events and facts, the exact moments of propitious conjunction between forces, the conditions most favorable to creations that will supply men's needs.

I am an architect and a city planner; *I make plans*. My temperament drives me on towards the joys of discovery; movement, growth, flowering, the very mechanisms of life itself are my passion. In consequence, since I have present reality always before my eyes, I make plans that express the face of the age we live in. In 1922, when I drew up plans for "a *contemporary* city of 3 million inhabitants," all my critics without exception talked about my "City of the *Future*"! My protests were in vain. I assured them that I know nothing at all about the future and understand only the present. Their reply was a cowardly stratagem: "Your concern is obviously for the future," which obviously implies the corollary meaning that "they" (everyone else) are concerned about the present. Lies! With all the modesty of a man still engaged on his search, I am concerned wholly with the present, with what is contemporary, with today, while "they" are living in *yesterday*, living off *yesterday*. That is the tragedy of the modern age. All the things Mr. Wells refers to are of today, not of tomorrow.

### THE REDEVELOPED COUNTRYSIDE

Let us translate this into material facts:

The automobile has eliminated distance, or, more exactly, it has modified the nature of the distances previously fixed by the railroad. The railroad had created its particular kind of civilization: that of great urban concentrations. The automobile is opening up a new civilization: *that of the highway*. The great cities, having become inhuman, can now flow out into country territory that has been rendered accessible and susceptible of colonization. Colonization not in the colonies, but in the countryside of France itself, everywhere. But before this happens, the countryside must be properly equipped, and the ATTRACTIONS of the city – all that affords men the caress of humanity, contact with whatever is believed to be best in human thought – carried out from the cities into *a redeveloped countryside*. The country must be redeveloped in preparation for the new highway civilization.

### GENUINE, INCONTROVERTIBLE, BREATHTAKING PLANS . . . .

In conclusion, this: for the past two years I have been living with an agonizing inner certainty. It began when I was summoned to Algiers to view the urban disaster that had overtaken that city, the choking, the strangulation, the imminent death agony of a city still so young, a city destined for such prodigious things. "What is to be done? The city is dying, and in a few years we shall have increased our population fourfold; there will be a million of us living here!" I drew up plans, after analyses, after calculations, with imagination, with poetry. The plans were prodigiously true. They were incontrovertible. They were breathtaking. They expressed all the splendor of modern times. They were the constructive counterpart of the gigantic destructive works of war. They used the same resources (techniques) but in another spirit. They mobilized the power of action to serve mankind, just as mankind so recently and so astonishingly permitted the mobilization of the world for purposes of destruction and murder.

Destruction, war? "Bravo, that's normal enough, it keeps industry and trade going . . .". People talk about these things, and do them, almost with enthusiasm. But construction, equipping the machine era, providing our time with the environment it so urgently needs: "No," the mayor told me, "your ideas are a hundred years ahead of their time." And again: "No," the great banker financing the redevelopment of Algiers said, "I will not see M. Le Corbusier. I know him of old, *he might be capable of convincing me*, and I haven't the right to let myself be convinced. It is my duty to place my capital only according to *tested methods*."

I have talked a great deal about myself. I am sorry. But I have been talking about a man "in the thick of it," an actor in these matters, a reader of life, a learner of lessons – and a *maker* of plans. Well, I think Mr. Wells will agree that *a man who makes a true plan* for the modern age is *doing something new*. He and I agree that such a thing could be prodigious, for a new era has been born. But the "fathers of the country," the guardians of the great families of mankind – authority – are afraid to act, to undertake anything, to risk anything. It's safer to copy. More comfortable to live off "yesterday."

## DISCOVERERS OF MEN

The result: Crisis and discouragement. *Whereas if they were to act: solution of the crisis and enthusiasm.*

In order to feel the excitement of these things, grasp them by the hair, seize the solution as it rushes by, it is not necessary to be a professor, it is necessary to refuse to be a professor. It is necessary to be a worker at a task: curious, nimble, courageous, always alert. The true professor, the true lesson, is the integral, forever renewed, that emerges from the storm we live through whenever the tension between nature and man becomes intolerable.

It is by *making plans*, not by *talking*, that truly fruitful lessons are taught. Professors ought not to be critics standing serenely above the world on their platforms, they ought to be workmen on the job.

There are some like that.

In place of the "Professors of Prediction" problem, I should like to substitute the problem of finding "Discoverers of Men," and I would suggest that instead of electing our leaders on the basis of electoral programs we should only entrust them with the function of governing us after they have given us proof that they have discovered one or more inventors – proof that they know how to discover men.

December, 1932.

●

# A NEW FORM OF GREGARIOUSNESS

### THEIR WORK IS BEING WASTED ON A FALSE ENVIRONMENT

Intelligent people accustomed to hard work do exist in this country, and form part of its essential technical machinery. But their work is being wasted on a false environment. They are playing a game of which the rules no longer hold good. Not only do they not get anywhere, they are cutting their own throats.

Change the environment, construct a new one, and those efforts will become productive; results will follow in due order, regularly, predictably. So let no one start pulling out his hair in despair and crying: "Then everything from now on is to be one long disruption; every moment from here to eternity is going to be a torture of violence, transformations, tearing apart and destruction." No. There are certain people who, by the very nature of their minds, because of their experience, their lives, their destinies, have had the opportunity to gauge and judge of these things; they have the power to create, to imagine, and to impose the results on the world; they possess the requisite passionate energy to face whatever perilous moments the days of the great transformation will have to offer. In the new framework of new methods these people are capable of setting up, the normal energies and the simpler work of the rest of society will find their quiet place, safe from the conflict, leaving the present impasse behind them, moving on towards the harmonious solution.

It is the realization of this harmony that is our problem.

### LIFE TOOK ANOTHER PATH

The traffic situation in Algiers – one of France's youngest cities – will shortly be impossible. "Oh come now! . . . Look at the Place de l'Opéra in Paris, the miracle of the D. system: buses, cars, pedestrians, sightseers and people in a hurry . . . Everyone needs to pass through it, and everyone does. You're just a dreary pessimist! . . ."

In Algiers, as in Paris, as in every city in the world, it is now essential that there should be a new system of stratification to cope with the new high-speed traffic. And a new theory of urban planning to create it. Everything is for the best in the best of all possible worlds, you think? Before he has reached Villeneuve-St-Georges, any long-distance traveler to Paris who has eyes is already staring at the leprosy of haphazard private building around our city with horror and stupefaction. Everywhere else, the country has been drained of people. No one wants to go back to it. Everything is for the best . . .

So what should we do, how should we start? The kind of urban planning that is needed to provide this new mechanized society of ours with a calm and balanced existence by respecting the *essential human realities* is costly, ruinous! And what about the new constructions (indispensable, urgently needed) the city ought to have? *They represent demands upon public funds so vast that we daren't even think about it.* "It's impossible, it's really so sad, alas!" And the sun, day after day, continues to set on that note of resignation. "Alas!"

A doctor – someone who knows – says to someone: "Your color, your eyes, would seem to indicate that you have cancer. See what can be done."

In public affairs, the sun sets every day on these inevitable, ineluctable expressions of resignation.

And then, one fine day, everything is one great groan, pale and shivering or burning with fever: Hitler, U.S.S.R., Mussolini, Dollar, Sterling, France-quatre-sous, etc ... Guns, fortifications, war. Everything has become so unreal that war, War, WAR has become possible, admissible, desirable: "Well, why not?" We have preserved the old stratifications, forgetting that beneath that stiffened, ageing framework of outmoded human organization – efficient working tools, means of keeping order, both things that are indispensable but naturally of limited efficacy if not renewed – life was still going on. Life went on developing, and now that framework is supporting nothing that is not already dead. Life has taken another path. It is elsewhere.

## THE PROBLEM IS MAN

It is therefore time to ask ourselves without more delay: "What is our problem?"

Our problem is man, just man as he is, placed by the laws of nature in that rich, perilous and total equation: INDIVIDUAL-COLLECTIVITY. For you, we, I, are all IN-DIVIDUALS whose every hap or mishap is a personal matter, and whose reaction to collective events constitutes at any given moment an individual joy or an individual misfortune.

Man the basis of everything, man the peak of everything. Man, the stake in the game. His destiny unfolds harmoniously in a symphonic progression: individual, man and wife, family, trade (mind and hands), all that lies within the grasp of his understanding. That is how the cycle of a man's life would unfold in an harmonious world.

## RETURN TO THE HUMAN SCALE

Yet what is the reality today? Man and war, crisis, unemployment, famine and poverty, inertia and decay. The play of natural forces has been warped by a frame-work of obsolete artifices: political frontiers fringed with bayonets and a scum of flotsam; distorted notions of patriotism, honor, "the great collective family," etc.; the negative forces of hatred! rivalries! suppurating sources of conflict; forces of destruction ...

Then comes the storm, the thunder, the lightning ...

In order to find a way out of the dead end into which architecture had been misled by the Academies, we have had to *find our way back to man, to the human scale, to human needs.* By this means we have been able to kill off all those "styles." And it was high time!

## A THEORY ... SOURCE OF HUMAN HAPPINESS

We have also been able to formulate a basic theory for housing. And free ar-chitecture from its shackles – create an architecture for this age. And by means of that other tool, *City planning*, based upon the architectural revolution that has been accomplished, we have been able to harness the power of modern techniques and create the collective, contemporary framework, the machine-age environment that will provide every individual with personal liberty and the basic pleasures. A body of theory does exist, in architecture and in city-planning, *that is a source of human happiness.*

Passing through the fogs, the storms, the floods, the earthquakes, we have made our way back to the value that matters: man. Having looked with fresh eyes at the problem before us, we have formulated a doctrine, created a new environment, accepted new methods. And a unanimity has been established throughout the world as to the truth of these postulates.

Human consciousness is in need of a revelation. We need a new framework for the contemporary consciousness.

We must therefore determine the exact nature of what may be termed *the basic pleasures.*

We must think what the advent of the machine means, accept all its efforts on our behalf, but insist that they are directed only according to our will.

Then we shall recover the liberties now lost; we shall recover a measure of free time each day. But what shall we do with it? We shall be bewildered by it. So we must also prepare our minds for this new adventure without delay. Leisure time! The reality is a crushing burden to anyone not prepared for it.

The leisure time ahead constitutes a threat to those cities that have done nothing towards preparing for it! Eight hours of each day without work to fill them – if we domesticate our machines successfully. This means that *architecture and city planning* will immediately become matters of the most urgent necessity: sites to be planned, grounds and buildings to be constructed.

We must prepare ourselves for new departures.

We must train men's minds to think on a new scale.

In this field of architecture and city planning – grounds and buildings – in this search for an environment to liberate our *basic pleasures*, we shall be forced to delve deep if we are to unearth the truth of contemporary life.

February, 1932.

•

# 4. BOLSHOI ... OR THE NOTION OF BIGNESS

"Bolshoi!"

It is a word (a magnificent one) and not a mere matter of party membership.

In 1928, I was called to Moscow to discuss the construction of the Centrosoyus there. I was taken into the office of Mr. Lubinov (now the People's Commissar, once mayor of Moscow, before that a peasant, and at this particular time President of the Centrosoyus). There was an interpreter there. The President delivered himself of a long speech in which the word "bolshoi," always delivered with great force, recurred again and again. The interpreter passed on the substance of this speech to me as follows: "The construction of this palace must prove itself to be an outstanding event in Russian architectural history, a history that only began with the Revolution itself. It is essential that there should be a visible quality of bigness in all the aspects of its design, a bigness achieved not simply by means of physical dimensions, nor by emphasis, but by a judicious regard to proportions. It is essential that this non-military building, the biggest that has so far been envisaged by our regime, should constitute a model: strict expression of function and dignity. All our projects now must come into the world under this sign: BIG, bolshoi ..."

I questioned the interpreter: "That word 'bolshoi' Mr. Lubinov kept ham-mering out, what does it mean?"

"Big!"

"So Bolshevism? . . ."

"Bolshevism means: everything as big as possible, the biggest theory, the biggest projects. Maximum. Going to the heart of any question. Examining it in depth. Envisaging the whole. Breadth and size."

Till then, I had understood from our newspapers that bolshevik meant: a man with a red beard and a knife between his teeth.

## THEY WERE UNCONCERNED WITH THE LESSONS OF HISTORY

At the time when I was a student – and more recently too – I often used to go over to the "Vert-Galant's" island to look at the Pont Neuf. From below, you get a very good view of it with its whole mass outlined against the sky: its two arms, to left and right, linking the road out to the Southwest provinces, the road to Toulouse, with the right bank of the Seine where the Louvre, the Kings' palace, stood. Architect: Du Cerceau, 1550. The Renaissance. Paris was Gothic. Lines of pointed roofs like the teeth of a saw; narrow streets fit only for cut-throats; a city that cramped any kind of impulse . . . Yet how eloquent the stones of that great bridge! The vast and sturdy spanning arches, the masterly cornice with its firm, powerful, opulent profile. There is a whole spiritual tide flowing through that work. 1550! Du Cerceau had taken a prodigious step into the future. For not only had he built a stone bridge across the Seine, he had also thrown a bridge of greatness over the spiritual realities of his time. Since Notre-Dame (three centuries earlier) Paris had only been marking time, thinking and not acting, shriveling up. The city had ceased filling the free spaces of site and spirit with its enterprise. Du Cerceau, architect to the King, created for his master what was needed: Bigness.

It is intoxicating, if you know how to set about it, by which I mean if you know, to stand on the Ile du Vert-Galant and look up at that bridge with the eyes and the soul of someone living in 1550: you see the carpenters building their wooden arches up and out over the water, the masons deep in their descriptive geometry on the banks, the arches rising towards their keystones, the platform advancing over them. You see the finished bridge; then the King as he comes to take possession of it, his brand-new, shining white, extraordinary, prodigious, luminous bridge, swelling with a new lyric majesty in that gothic city. Then you know what an impulse of the spirit can be worth, the value to any city of a truly big thought.

When I had climbed back up to the level of the town, I used also to ponder every time, with alarm, the fact that Paris in 1900 had ceased to see big, and that those who were responsible for the fate of the city were as lacking in bigness of spirit as they were unconcerned with the lessons of history.

But that charming French Renaissance, as we have just seen, achieved a great deal more at the time than merely being charming: it built the Pont Neuf, which is still standing, still one of the biggest and most admirable that Paris possesses. And it built it in an age when the stone had to be brought from the quarries to the river bank by teams of oxen.

Thirteen years after the Great War and Big Bertha, after the Atlantic has been crossed by air, after a hundred years in the machine age, an architect, with the full approval of the city authorities and as a *gesture of respect to history*, has just finished a project on the left bank end of the Pont Neuf executed in the style of Du Cerceau. That, you see, is the attitude they take to life! History says: "*Enterprise, belief and action.*" But what do they proclaim? Retreat, abdication, treachery . . . and lies. Yes, lies!

The work of that architect is *in the style of Du Cerceau*. It's a fake. A copy, an imitation. "This isn't Leonardo da Vinci's La Gioconda itself, it's a copy executed very exactly in the same style; the authorities have decided that it shall be hung in the Salon Carré, side by side with Mrs. Gioconda herself, as a token of profound and sincere comprehension! ! !" (I refer to the new apartment buildings at the end of the Rue Dauphine.)

## . . . LOOK BACKWARDS!

The city of Berne was the recipient of an impressive legacy from the past: its whole history expressed in three or four arcaded streets with some really admirable town houses, built for important personages of the past, running above them. But life is insatiable: in the twentieth century, it has become necessary to sell a great many socks, a great many souvenirs for tourists, a great many pictures of the Jungfrau, etc. By some malicious and Mephistophelian twist of fate, it has come about that this traffic is being carried on in the very houses that were once inhabited by the former rulers of Berne. It became necessary to "redevelop" them. So they were redeveloped. Shop fronts were installed with Saint-Gobain mirrors, and the floors had to be replaced. But it also proved necessary to strengthen the façades, which were too old: in other words – in fact – to replace all the old stones with new ones. The authorities, rightly disturbed by this, *insisted that the new stones should be copies of the old ones*, or at least that they should imitate the correct historical style.

So that the great streets of Berne are really made of new stone; they are *brand-new fakes of old streets*. The result of a spiritual decision. Little by little, one house after another, and as the result of an act of devotion towards its own history, Berne is becoming a fake. Yet the tourists continue to flood in, eager to swallow this lesson in fake history. And all this took place almost imperceptibly, irrevocably, because of a spiritual decision that had been made. That decision was: *to look backwards*.

## + SIGN OR − SIGN

A spiritual decision!

The quality of that decision.

The direction of that decision; forwards or backwards?

When people have finally come to understand the sad significance of these pilots' offices that occur in various spots throughout the collective social structure and which can influence by the way in which they are wielded, producing even the minutest or, quite often, the most shattering consequences, the entire mass of mankind's interests, projects, actions and – in consequence – consciences; when people have finally realized that quality and spiritual direction are the cause of happiness or unhappiness, of mediocrity or splendor, of indifference or participation, of a + sign or a − sign placed before the achievements of an era; and when they have understood that there are critical moments in the flow of human history when everything may depend on *the initial decision* – then they will not truly be able to bear a grudge against us for trying to see clearly into things, for dissecting, analysing, synthesizing, and then shouting our findings aloud, for making proposals and inciting them to action, for appealing to public opinion, for spreading new horizons before them crammed with projects and action and interest, for replacing what can now only be called our disenchantment with the word *faith*, and what is at present cowardly retreat with *will*.

"Bolshoi," BIG.

Bolshoi! Bigness of mind, and mustered on every side, all the forces of good and the assurance of a *joy in life* to replace the present snickering, treacherous, fallacious joy of *hoping to possess!*

Agreed, accepted!

So now, decisions must be made.

### ALAS, WE TOLERATE THESE ABNORMAL SITUATIONS

To see, to conceive, to think big in that total liberty we are invited by the human spirit to enjoy.

At each moment of the day, in every action we perform, we are given the opportunity of making a judgment. There are some disinterested, artistic, creative spirits that are wholly without chains and are in constant quest of harmony. I have an image that is always recurring in my mind: a plant, or a tree, growing in good earth, in the sunlight, unencumbered by any obstacles; good, solid, abundant roots; a fine trunk; noble branches; beautiful leaves, radiant flowers and fine fruits; grace of bearing, a supple and easy stance; an harmonious spectacle; a fine plant, a noble tree.

Nature's very essence.

It is possible for the works of man to grow and rise in just the same way. We ourselves are products of nature; we carry within us nature's own potential, nature's own forces, her spirit and her essence. Our fingers and our brains are capable of creating works that express her harmony, works of perfection and purity. That is only natural.

But it is also rare, for our spiritual plants are not often sown in good earth, and we trammel their growth with too many obstacles. It is only the disinterested spirits that know how to plant a seed and tend it without allowing themselves to be disturbed or troubled by customs, by criticism or impatience, by a thirst for immediate gain or hasty and ill-considered praise. They calmly follow the normal path towards their futures, and so their works, like them, are also *normal*.

I have proved a hundred times that the world today is in a state of abnormality and that we, alas, are all tolerating, accepting these abnormal situations and works.

### SATAN COULD NOT DO BETTER

Follow the free and inevitable injunctions of natural law. Act according to nature; seek the aid of the mother who created us in all our hypotheses! An attitude of indisputable honesty, faithful, safe and reassuring; an attitude you might expect to earn us the immediate, the automatic support of the whole world. Alas! It has earned us nothing whatever but abuse and stones.

To announce and express a farsighted work of construction by means of a plan is to be treated as a utopian and dangerous enemy of the established order.

Works of negation and destruction, on the other hand, will always find plenty of takers.

The director of a bank told me today: "There is a great political maneuver afoot. The basic aim is to involve the U.S.S.R. in an interminable war with the Chinese. This will produce two results: a great need for guns, munitions, boots, canned food, trucks and equipment of all sorts, etc., etc.; capitalism will be saved; the factories will all be started up again; the economy will revive; everyone will be happy; the slump will have been overcome; the capitalists now against the wall will be reprieved, and public opinion – well, public opinion will take a big contented step backwards and everything will go on as before. Second result: the U.S.S.R. will be out of the running for the next twenty years; a whole generation exhausted by war.

"Krupp's and Creusot's agents are already on the job, in the East, taking their orders. To date – and the thing hasn't begun yet – they already have orders amounting to 500 million francs.

"The big financiers have been working on it for months . . ."

"But the Russians have still actually got to march on the Chinese," I said. "They've still got to declare war! And they're not absolute idiots; they might see through it all . . ."

"Oh, a few millions placed in good hands, in nice, clean hands . . ."

My bank director, I might add, was utterly sickened by all this.

My thoughts turn to what the newspapers have to say: the press is in favor of Japan, which ten days ago invaded China; at the moment, the Chinese are taking it on the nose. No one really wants them to fight one another of course, but no one is stopping the troops being fitted out, the regiments and the artillery being landed, or mass war hysteria taking grip on the whole of East Asia.

There is a really marvelous opportunity out there to stir up trouble; the confusion produced by the great distances, ignorance of the consequences, and an ever-ready fund of human infamy.

It is worth noting that China and Japan have never fought a war before. But when the armies are all there, there will be stray shells, stray airplanes, a perpetual and acutely dangerous state of agitation. And then, we must remember that Europe and the U.S.A. have private citizens living out in the East, fathers and mothers with families, businesses and agencies whose vanity will have been hurt, who will have an obligation, a genuine one, not to allow their national prestige to suffer . . . These countries dependent upon the patriarchal solicitude of the great civilized nations cannot be left to themselves in this way . . . Some sort of police action will have to be initiated, internationally . . . The West, the U.S.A., will land contingents of 10,000 men per country – to begin with. That means 100,000 men, increasing eventually to 500,000, and the yellow races will be completely surrounded.

The mothers of these men we send will not feel the frightful, appalling shock of a war, a real war, a national war; the operation will be called: an expedition. "My son is out with the Expedition." Europe and the U.S.A. will not have to face the frightful, the appalling reality of a war. The moral stratagem will have succeeded.

Perhaps the League of Nations, having taken a quick health cure, will seize this opportunity to use the new troops and the new powers that we have been hearing about "In the name of civilization . . ." There are millions of Chinese there for it to equip and organize into voracious armies. Destruction. Oh, to destroy everything! To eat up the whole world!

And all the consumable products you could wish for will be eaten up: guns, canned food. And just try telling people, all of them, any of them that such a thing is an abomination. Those millions of unemployed who will have got their factories going again, that life throbbing away once more, flourishing stupendously at last after the despair of the present period, everything will clamor in reply: "For heaven's sake, shut up! Everything's doing fine again!"

I sit stupefied with admiration. Just a few men have organized all that. Standing the sick world on its head, they have actually performed this prodigious trick: providing everyone with bread and making hope spring afresh; consolidating the positions already won by a use of the present-day, anarchic modes of production that can only be kept working by waste . . . Trampling on the toes of the U.S.S.R. On their toes! If possible, playing them a dirty trick – and what a dirty trick! . . .

And I think: so that's governing! That's what it means to make a PLAN. What a plan!

"Bolshoi . . ."

"Bolshoi indeed!"

Satan could not do better.

. . . . . . . . . . . . . . . . . . . . . . . .

## BIG, BIG!

My work companion said to me: "But why can't they understand that instead of making munitions they could be undertaking the reconstruction of the world?"

"You forget one thing," I replied. "It is this: correct city planning throughout the world – the execution of a *Plan* – is a linear conception: the results would not be seen for four or six years. If you tell the masses that this is what we need, they will answer: "Bread, now, today!" The masses will work to equip an expedition to the East, in order to avert a national war, in order to rescue themselves from poverty, even though in doing so they are also rescuing capitalism. In order to realize our Plan, we should need new institutions, total political redevelopment. In saving themselves and saving capitalism, the masses are obliged at the same time to renounce the bright future that was about to dawn for them, and all their hard work will be used to deliver a stab in the back to the one country that has attempted the really essential reforms. Such is the balance sheet of this amazing, machiavellian, satanic maneuver. That, in short, is really knowing how to play chess. That's what it means to govern. To think big. Blood, mourning and shame. Such is their plan. And everyone will be forced to add their stone to it quite *naturally*.

So much the worse. Meanwhile, let us continue to draw up our plan for the machine era under this sign, *the only true one:* harmony.

Let us make our plans, plans on a scale with twentieth century events, plans equally as big as Satan's. Plans to trample Satan back into the dust!

Big! Big!

March, 1932.

# 5. ● ROME

Rome is a simple word. A sign expressing a precise concept. One of the forms taken by the character: CONSCIOUS STRENGTH.

Roman.

It's Roman.

That is enough: the idea has been placed.

Rome is like round, like full, like whole, like central, eminently geometrical, simple and essential.

Such is the fruit, after two thousand years of varying tumult, of one people's work: a living fact in the bottom-most depths of mankind's awareness. To pronounce that name is to release a latent power. To refer to that name, to take one's stance upon it, is a proclamation of great intentions; it means that one has chosen a noble path. Today, in the present universal state of spiritual prostration, it is almost a sign of arrogance, of pretentiousness.

Because the word Rome signifies also hearts of bronze.

The paradox is, though, that Rome also attempted, later on, to embody the Christian Word: "Love one another." The result was a violent distortion of the Christian Word. That Word was originally an appeal to individual conscience; but Rome is a center of empire, of command.

The Rome that sets our hearts beating is ancient Rome.

A simple, elementary, essential, unshaded idea: Rome is geometrical!

Here are the fundamental Roman forms:

They are so intimately the outcome of a dominating, organizing type of thought that they will always continue to haunt all human creations.

\* \* \*

Roman thought conquered the world; the Roman legions marched out to occupy the lands of the Barbarians; they laid down stone-paved roads of which the remains are still to be found all over Europe. Roman roads, we may be quite certain, always drive directly through the essential features of any landscape. At the natural center of any total site, you will find the vestiges of a sentry post. The sentry was in control of the entire countryside.

With them, the legions took military engineers who were also geometrician-architects and whose job it was to found and build cities. Roman cities were always laid out on the exact spot where it was necessary for a city to be if it was also to be healthy, sunny, well supplied, and easily defended. No Roman city is ever an error. They are often prodigiously poetic collaborations between nature and geometry! Think of all the Roman cities that were built all over the known world: Asia Minor, North Africa, Spain, France, Germany.

The Roman city is a city of ORDER. Disciplined, hierarchic, dignified. And the Roman camp too already possessed the same qualities. It was disciplined, hierarchic, dignified.

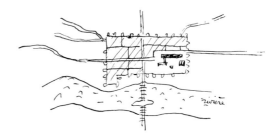

First, the form of the city: proportion.

Then its defense: walls.

Then its traffic system and division into compartments. Everything followed straight lines, because a straight line is the norm of action.

The public places: basilica of justice, temple and forum. Places of communal excitement; for they were places specifically designed to contain that communal energy that is the very essence and happiness of human groups. They are worthy of their function, in the highest degree.

The Forum is a meeting place for collective action: it encourages such action by the nobility of its ordered design and the charm of its proportions. Everything in it is synchronism and synthesis: Gods, judges, heroes, civic duty.

Respect for divinity, rituals, harangues and orations, the spell of human speech, appeal to men's virility and energies, justice, respect for virtue and deference to illustrious men.

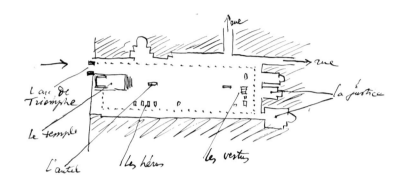

There is always a place for these things in a Roman city, an entire and magnificent place: the Forum. The Latin spirit is a spirit of orderliness.

\* \* \*

Family life was lived in security, inside the home, under the open sky of the atriums and in courtyards that were also partly gardens. Each family had its trees, its flowers, its trickling fountain. The women and children were in the gynaeceum, in safety. Strangers were never permitted to enter it. Noble, charming and worthy human habitations.

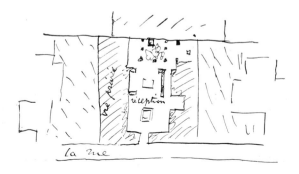

\* \* \*

For their great public spectacles, they built the circus.

Vast in its unity, overwhelming in its simplicity. Inside it, the crowd is a whole, a living, thrilling group – at one.

\* \* \*

Across the countryside, bringing down cool, pure water from the mountains, they stretched the long lines of their aqueducts.

The baths they built everywhere were vast and magnificent. A Roman had to be beautiful. To be beautiful one had to take care of one's body: stadium and baths.

The Romans built WHOLES. The creations of their architects and city planners were invariably WHOLES. And because of this, we today still express admiration for their achievements with the simple phrase: "They were Romans."

They conceived, they classified, they reduced everything to order: Rome meant enterprise. They invented Roman cement. The Republic, *res publica*, was the object of all their care. The public good was the reason for the city and also for their arrival in the city. Participation in it was their life. They were lucid, strong, simple and geometrical. They created cities that worked like machines: machines of which the product was action.

In the midst of the barbarians, Rome was a center of empire, of command.

Rome, conscious strength.

# 6. MOBILIZATION OF THE LAND

The "International Congresses for Modern Architecture" were founded in 1928, at Sarraz, as a result of the scandal aroused in professional architectural circles by the choice of architects for the *Palais des Nations* after the international contest in 1927.

The members of these congresses do not meet to defend their financial interests.

The statutes run as follows:

"The aim of this Association is:

a. To formulate the architectural problems of the modern age;

b. To represent the modern architectural idea;

c. To aid the penetration of that idea into technical, economic and social spheres;

d. To seek a solution to the architectural problem."

No one chooses to be a member of the International Congresses for Modern Architecture. *One is chosen* to attend, if one's work has earned one that honor.

The "Int. Congresses for Mod. Arch." have no drones attending them. Only creative energies are accepted; they are invited to attend the moment they appear on the architectural horizon, and in no matter what country. At the preliminary congress in Sarraz, in 1928, sixteen countries were represented by forty-two delegates. At the Athens congress in 1933, eighteen countries by over a hundred delegates.

## THE SICKNESS IS APPALLING

The 4th congress was at work for ten days. And a day's work, for those in responsible positions, meant from 12 to 15 hours. The congress began aboard the "Patris II," a beautiful vessel belonging to the Neptos Company, as soon as it left Marseilles. The Greek owners had forseen that there was going to be a great deal of activity on board: on the voyage out as well as the voyage back (7 days sailing in all), they put all the saloons, the deckhouses, and the dining-room at our disposal – any space that could be used as a place to work, as an exhibition room, as a conference hall. Typewriters clattering everywhere, committees sitting anywhere they could find, all over the boat. Two plenary sessions every day. The members' plans for cities were exhibited and discussed.

In Athens itself, the exhibition of the plans for the "Functional City" was housed in the Polytechnic. Or, more precisely, the exhibition of a first series of plans intended to provide a diagnosis of the state our cities are in at the moment.

Eighteen groups in different countries had all spent two years preparing this unique documentation: a veritable treasure hoard now it is assembled – there before our eyes, all on the same scale, all expressed according to an agreed convention of signs making it possible to visualize them with great clarity, were 42 cities revealed as though by X-ray. Were they sick or were they healthy?

This time, it was possible to see the answer. The sickness is appalling, uniform, general, typical: *our present cities are not organized to cope with the everyday realities of modern life*. The machine age is upon us: it has gnawed away our cities, rotted them, destroyed them. Laziness has closed our eyes; our fear of enterprise has paralyzed the world. The growth of this sickness is identical everywhere – a threat, a desperately frightening threat. Our cities have destroyed the joy of life. Those lucid drawings showed exactly how the privileged classes are able to bow out of the game and "with an easy conscience" stick their heads in the sand. But as a result, millions of human beings are henceforth being deprived of the *basic pleasures*. They will be deprived of them *all their lives* – every hour, every week, every month, every year of their lives!!!

The verdict of these plans at the 4th Congress is irrefutable.

## HARMONY: THE MODERN CAUSE

The Greek government had realized the significance of these sessions that were to take place in Athens.

The first reception given to the Congress, near Marathon, was attended by several ministers. And almost the entire government was to be seen on the platform in the Polytechnic gardens on the occasion of Le Corbusier's speech.

". . . I am accused of being a revolutionary. When I returned from Athens to the west (in 1910) and decided to attend the courses of academic instruction available there, I saw that they were taking the name of the Acropolis in vain, using it to justify their lies. I was able to gauge how far our Academies were lying by flattering our idleness: I had learned to reflect, to look, and to delve to the heart of a problem.

It was the Acropolis that made me a rebel. It was a certainty that stayed with me: Remember the Parthenon, remember its clarity, its clean lines, its intensity, its economy, its violence, remember its great cry in the midst of that landscape created by grace and terror. Strength and purity.

Today, then, it is a question, not of putting forward all the various imaginable points of view, but of knowing why we must do so, and of finding the means of combining into one whole, into one harmony, all the *essential things*.

And then, so that the Acropolis – that peak and culmination of human creative energies – may fructify the living forces within us, it is essential "in the name of the Acropolis," in the name of the harmony it embodies, that we should go on, with unflagging, uncrushable valor of soul, to *create harmony throughout the world*. Harmony: truly the great cause of modern times.

We must imbue ourselves with all the urgency of that notion: to bring harmony to the modern age. We must seek out one certain kind of men: the "harmonizers" of our times. We must discover, in our present misfortune, the key that will open the gate through which alone disorder and misery can be driven out. And that key is harmony.

In the name of the Acropolis, a harmony without weakness, without flaw, strong, and triumphant. We must make ourselves souls of bronze. Such is the lesson of the Acropolis."

## OBSERVATIONS

During the return voyage, on board the Patris II, the congress prepared, discussed and voted on their findings. The results were not called resolutions, but "*Observations.*"

In their final form, worked out in Marseilles, Zurich, Barcelona and Paris, they take up sixteen pages of typescript, and we do not have the space to print them here in their entirety. The value of this final draft lies in the fact that every word in it has been carefully weighed in order to express the maximum possible agreement between all the necessarily diverse tendencies represented by the very active members of such an international architectural conference: Catalan trade unionists, Muscovite collectivists, Italian fascists, and – an important point – sharp-eyed technical experts always on the look-out for a truth applicable to their own particular environment.

We shall therefore follow here the example of the "Beaux-Arts," which, for the same reasons, after an introduction by its editor, M. Brunon-Guardia, published in its September issue the first draft of this document, which was drawn up by the Resolutions Committee and read in closed session at sea, off the coast of France.

Those who would like to acquaint themselves with the whole of the work carried out by the 4th Congress will certainly meet with a warm welcome at the:
"*Secrétariat Général des Congrès Intern. d'Architecture Moderne*" 7, Doldertal, Zurich (Switzerland).

on board the Patris II

. . . . . . . . . . . . . . .

The International Congress for Modern Architecture, met here on board the Patris II on the voyage from Marseilles to Athens, in this city, and on the voyage from Athens back to Marseilles, from July 29 to August 13, 1933,

1° Devoted its labors to the replanning of cities in this modern age.

2° Its work was based on an analytic documentation compiled during the two previous years by groups from the following eighteen countries: America (U.S.A.), Germany, England, Belgium, Spain, France, Greece, Hungary, Italy, India, Dutch East Indies, Indochina, Norway, Poland, Switzerland, Czechoslovakia, Yugoslavia.

These groups provided plans of the following thirty-three characteristic cities: Amsterdam, Athens, Brussels, Baltimore, Bandoeng, Budapest, Berlin, Barcelona, Charleroi, Cologne, Como, Dalat, Detroit, Dessau, Frankfurt, Geneva, Genoa, the Hague, Los Angeles, Littoria, London, Madrid, Paris, Prague, Oslo, Rome, Rotterdam, Stockholm, Utrecht, Verona, Warsaw, Zagreb, Zurich.

The documentation was compiled according to precise and uniform methods laid down at the Berlin congress in 1931 and by the "Cirpac" committee in Barcelona in 1932.

a. Uniform scale.

b. Visual expression of the various constituent elements of the cities concerned by a convention of signs designed to produce clear expressions of the following factors: *Housing:* rich, middle, working-class, poverty-stricken. *Leisure. Places of work*: business centers, industry. *Traffic* in the city and its environs. *Relationship* of the city to the surrounding region.

3° The Congress limited itself strictly to the technical aspects of architecture and city planning. This attitude permitted them to envisage the problems revealed in all their simultaneous reality:

*Anthropocentrism:* Human biology and psychology (the individual).
*Sociology:* (Collectivity).
*General Economy.*
*Authorities:* Administration and Executive.

## FUNDAMENTAL POSTULATE OF THE CITY

The city is part of an economic complex. Its various characteristics have all been determined by individual circumstances throughout its history (military defense, administration, successive modes of transport).

New stimuli provoke a continuing development of the economic system (scientific discoveries, new forms of transportation, new industrial possibilities, new markets, etc.). The bases on which cities develop are thus continually subjected to change.

The tasks of the city planner are to direct urban development by the use of already existing elements and to prepare the city's future: destruction of unwanted remains, improvement of inherited spiritual assets, creation of urban elements that will benefit contemporary life, predictions that will make it possible to continue the development of urban life progressively into the future.

## RESOLUTIONS OF PRINCIPLE

1° The city should provide liberty for the individual and the benefits of collective action on both the material and the spiritual plane.

2° All urban planning should be ultimately based on the human scale.

3° Urban planning should fix the relations between the various places devoted respectively to residence, work and leisure according to the rhythm of the inhabitants' daily activity.

4° Housing should be considered as the central element in all urban planning.

5° The material elements at the disposal of the urban planner, and which it is his place to combine, are: sky, trees, housing, places of work, places for communal activity (including leisure activities), and traffic.

A questionnaire drawn up by a separately appointed committee has also made it possible to provide the answers given by members of the congress to a series of question relating, variously, to housing, to work, to leisure activities, and to traffic. All these documents still exist in their entirety in the Congress's files. The following is a résumé of the answers given to the questions about housing:

a. A house is made up of a floor on a foundation, a water-tight ceiling, and walls that may either let light through them or not. This unit may either be placed on the surface of the earth itself (spread out) or be superimposed in vertical columns of 10, 20, 30, etc. Modern techniques (steel and cement) will now permit us to create these "artificial sites."

b. By using modern techniques, houses can be made soundproof.

c. Aside from its habitable area, housing should include certain indispensable extensions (psychology and physiology): space, sunlight and greenery.

d. By taking advantage of modern techniques permitting us to increase the height of individual buildings, the city's past tendency to spread in area can be reversed: it can contract.

e. Building taller housing units will permit the introduction into the city, whether artificially or naturally, of green areas and natural elements (water, trees).

f. The safety, efficiency and hygiene of our cities have been disrupted by the invention of new high-speed vehicles. These have made the introduction of a new kind of traffic classification essential: the pedestrian should not have to share roads with automobiles.

g. Different kinds of traffic should not be allowed to mix. They should be separated according to their functions (speed and weight).

h. Traffic lanes should be independent of the means of access to housing units.

i. No housing should ever run alongside a traffic lane.

k. The new high-speed vehicles necessitate greater distances between intersections, and therefore a decrease in the number of streets.

l. The introduction of communal services in domestic life could lead to a saving in the area of the individual housing unit. Such communal services lighten domestic labor and free wives for more useful work.

m. The organization of such communal services will necessitate the building of housing units on a larger scale.

n. This new housing unit will be in accord with the new traffic system.

o. These new housing and traffic systems will provide space for a new system of green areas between the housing units.

p. The park outside each housing unit will contain the nurseries, children's playgrounds, primary schools, and areas for daily sporting activities or relaxation.

Collation of these requirements with the analyses of existing cities compiled by the Congress prompts the following observations:

q. When considered in relation to modern needs, our existing cities, whether of ancient or recent formation, present a picture of chaos.

r. Only very rarely do they reveal organic phenomena; they merely express the incessant accretions of private interests.

s. Although they are in a constant state of change, the changes do not take place in accordance with the requirements stated above.

t. Since the conditions that determined their growth no longer exist, the results of those conditions must be swept away so that redevelopment can take place.

From which we may conclude that:

u. In order to satisfy the constant developments of the economic factors involved, it is essential to design cities as adaptable organisms.

Fundamental measures to be considered:

The suppression of arbitrary limitations resulting directly from the contradictions of the economic system itself.

Forecasts of the future that will enable the future needs of the developing city to be met by a rational classification of urban elements without regard to private interests.

Mobilization of private property, whether built on or not, as a fundamental condition of any planned development of "Cities."

Any practical realization of these principles depends upon the development of the economic system. Research into the correct solution for this problem is not part of the architect's professional task. Architects and city-planning experts can only resolve the technical problems of urban redevelopment within the limits imposed on them by the economic system.

Since the city is only one part of an economic organism, instead of attempting fragmentary redevelopment of it within present administrative limits, we must draw up the overall plans for an entire and organic economic unit. The city should become once again the natural and normal expression of a region.

. . . . . . . . . . . . . . . . . . . . . . . . . . . . . . . . . .

## MOBILIZATION OF LAND

"Mobilization of private property, whether built on or not, as a fundamental condition of any planned development of Cities."

That is the sore spot probed by the 4th Congress in the conclusions they were inevitably forced to draw from their exclusively technical postulates!

Destruction of the legal system! Modification of age-old truths!

In order to provide liberty for the individual and all the benefits of collective action, on both the material and the spiritual plane, contemporary society must have the entire land surface of the country at its disposal.

"To have at its disposal" does not mean doing away with the concept of property, or stealing, or depredation. It means improving the assets represented by our land for the benefit of mankind. Let the lawyers find a way!

Mobilization does not mean nationalization. It means solidarity!

## NO MONEY, NO DECORATIONS, NO TITLES

Yet, the 4th Congress for Modern Architecture was very much a symptomatic event.

They were an élite, an authoritative body selected according to the sole criterion of professional ability, grappling with one of the great problems of the age; devoting two years of scrupulous, disinterested, passionate inquiry to it; each concerning himself with his own field of knowledge (each group its own city); delving into the very flesh of living and suffering cities; discussing, noting the recurring symptoms, arriving at diagnoses, getting right back to their primary professional duty: *Architecture = bringing happiness;* establishing a terminology for human needs; defining the "basic pleasures"; proclaiming that with the modern techniques at our command a solution is possible; providing those elements by means of which life in cities can become a thing of joy; concluding with simplicity:

*We must mobilize* (make available) *the country's land.* And then say, calmly, with conviction, modestly: "Research into the correct solution for this problem is not part of the architect's professional task."

So you see, an authority does already exist in the sphere of urban and national development (city planning cannot be limited merely to cities). And that authority has only one ambition: to do magnificent work, to create magnificent cities, magnificent countries.

No money, no decorations, no titles.

The International Congresses for Modern Architecture are one of the modern forms of beneficent authority that the world is waiting for. (That is the meaning of the initials CIAM.)

●

189

# 7.

# TRUTH FROM DIAGRAMS

## WHEN MEN WERE STILL ARTISANS

When men were still artisans, during the pre-machine-age civilizations, the 24-hour solar cycle revolved each day without shocks, without breaks or hiatuses, in an uninterrupted progress from cause to effect. Men's hands and minds were bound to their work in a permanent collaboration. Whatever the hands fashioned, they did so at the instigation of the mind; the raw material was transformed into a finished product by an unbroken process of initiative on the artisan's part. Difficulties, failures, and successes were all linked. The artisan's whole being was constantly stimulated, in other words. The man was *participating*. And that word, even all on its own, implies many of the elements essential to moral calm and satisfaction.

From sunrise to sunset, the hours flowed by without any sudden breaks. More: the father often worked side by side with his son. Trades were often a part of family life. And *quality* was one of the goals of life.

If this disk is taken to represent the 24-hour solar cycle in the days of "handicraft

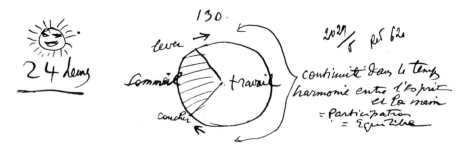

industry," the time that elapses between two sleeps is an *unbroken whole*. Moreover if zone A in the second diagram is taken to express the normal quantity of necessary and sufficient interest to provide life with a purpose (the feeling of being *active*,

responsible, creative, *participating*) ..., then the wavy line B, B[1], B[2], etc., indicates that despite the variations introduced by individual cases and characters, the average quantity always remains more or less normal.

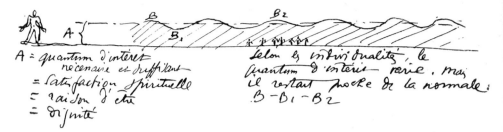

Revolution: the machine.

The machine makes machines: work is snatched out of men's hands and entrusted to machines, which *execute* it. A new and violent hierarchy is established, beginning with the head at the very top, then the technicians and inventors, then, lower down, the foreman, the skilled worker, and finally the unskilled laborer. For some (those at the top of the pyramid), the spiritual involvement is intense, well above average; for others, the involvement becomes so slight that it can no longer be felt; the result is indifference; no more participation; depression. The result: discouragement, boredom, demoralization.

There are certain trades, some new some old, that have not had these psychological depredations inflicted on them by the advent of the machine. But others – the major part of industry – have dug a vast pit of boredom all around themselves. *And I am not far from attributing the truly contemporary sense of the word* proletariat *to these very causes.*

## THE THREAT OF LEISURE

As soon as industrial production becomes planned, there will appear on the disc representing the 24-hour solar cycle of our imminent machine-age civilization a new sector unknown up till now.

The immense sector representing *the leisure time of the machine era.*

At the moment, thanks to our defective transportation systems, to our bars and movie houses, to our 8-hour working day, we simply struggle through the 24-hour cycle as best we may. And it's a pretty poor best at that.

What form will this new leisure time take? It is destined to constitute modern man's *real working day. A day that will be above all productive – on the human level:* body and mind. Maintenance of the body (physical and mental recuperation). Cultivation of the mind and spirit on every level (clubs and education). Manifesta-

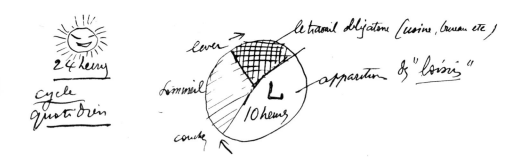

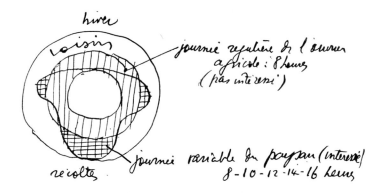

tions of initiative (handicrafts without thought of profit). Social use of individual aggression (sport). Family life.

The curves on our diagram can then be revised like this!

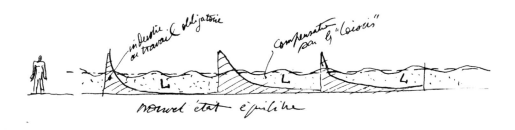

When his leisure time has been properly prepared for and organized, then the true man will appear:

1° Quota of collective labor (industrial production).
2° Physical culture.
3° Mental culture.
4° Family.
5° Sleep.

The gaping and demoralized void of our present way of life filled with satisfying leisure activity.

Man's day will be *productive*.

Result: disappearance of the "*proletariat*."

This diagram constitutes the essential framework that must underlie all the new departures to be undertaken by the authorities. It implies a total redevelopment of our cities (architecture and city planning).

So much for industrial society, which is ruled by the 24-hour solar cycle.

### THE RURAL WORKING DAY

The rural economy, on the other hand, is ruled by the 365-day cycle of the *solar year* (with its four seasons). Rural life and industrial life are profoundly different. The developments needed in our rural activity can be expressed by another diagram:

In the ordering of its daily round, country life implies (as it has always implied) an admirable state of balance between manual and mental activity. If the material conditions of life are assured, then there is no "proletariat" in the country.

Leisure activities will appear in a quite different light from those in industrial regions. Looking at the matter from the point of view of a rural society that is leading a life as harmonious as the one it is our duty to plan for industrial society, here too we shall find a sufficient and necessary interplay between complementary activities. But instead of relating these to a *daily timetable* (24 hour cycle), we must relate them to a *calendar* (yearly solar cycle).

The French countryside lends itself to large-scale, single-crop agriculture in only very few areas. Its topography, the variety and richness of its soil, and the high standard of education amongst its peasants, would lead us to urge French agriculture as a whole towards "garden" agriculture rather than large-scale farming, towards quality rather than quantity production.

This complexity (topography, variety of crops, etc.) requires constant vigilance and initiative on the part of the peasant, and represents, in fact, a contact so intimate on his part with the land he administers that it becomes impossible to avoid the conclusion that we should attach the peasant to his land with the most fundamental bond at our command: the family.

An indissoluble link between the peasant and his earth.

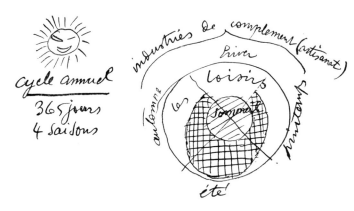

ATTENTION! (1964). Since 1931, when this article was first published, the machine has appeared on the rural scene and revolutionized it. A new page!

Therefore, to each family a plot of land. A plot of land such that one family will suffice to cultivate it: 20 hectares, for example.

The country timetable, unlike the industrial one, is not regular. The day is either overfull or empty according to the seasons.

In the busy periods (harvest), the peasant with a stake in the land is up against it. Some people would like purely and simply to eliminate the agricultural laborer. The agricultural laborer is a seasonal worker, therefore a nomad, and in consequence, often of dubious quality.

If country life is organized in relation to a "co-operative center," my diagram shows that the agricultural laborer could become a stable and fixed element in the village (the agricultural laborer does not live on the farm) and ceases to be a nomad. The co-operative center would therefore necessitate the setting up of complementary industries to provide work during the off seasons. It would include workshops for handicraft industries as well as the system's fundamental organs: communal market, communal silo, communal machines, the club, and lastly, the housing unit providing accomodation for the staff of the co-operative and the laborers.

## NEW UNITS OF SIZE

The outstanding task facing us at the present time is the devising and setting up, in all spheres, of *new units of size* that will correspond with the new machine-age phenomenon. This applies equally to the constitution of authority, to the material redevelopment of cities and countryside, or to the formation of new economic groups.

Let us consider, for example, what *authority* implies in its absolute form:

Some people are inclined to entertain chimerical dreams of a single and universal form of authority (whether on a world scale or on the local plane).

Let us imagine that this single authority has been created (I).

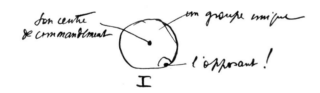

Scarcely will it have been formed when, quite spontaneously, a center of opposition will spring up on its fringes: a man, a group, etc. We may then assume that this new force will continue to grow until it has become equal in strength to the first (II).

Does this imply a state of balance?

We may be sure that it does not, for soon, and just as spontaneously as before, there will emerge from one or other of the two already existing groups a third unit that will act as a mediator, a pendulum (III).

It is this third force, by creating a constant state of imbalance, that permits life to express itself in the form of perpetual change.

Therefore, even the very simplest form of authority implies the existence of three elements.

## THE PYRAMID OF NATURAL HIERARCHIES

What is the specific characteristic of authority? That it is always recognized, appraised, and measured, according to its results. But who is to be judge? Units able to pass such judgments must be formed from those manifesting a capacity for that particular task.

All men work, practice a trade. All men are capable of making judgments about things concerning their own trades.

Men's trades must therefore form the foundation for our edifice of authority and power, for our hierarchy of responsibility. It is in the hearts of those trades that the eternal and fruitful struggle of creative effort versus academic sterility will be fought out.

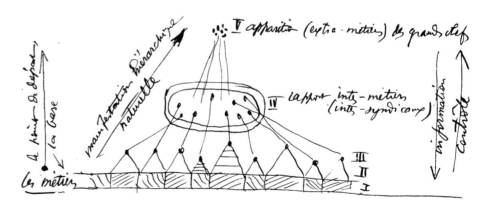

The diagram above may therefore be taken to express the various trades of society, one beside the other, forming the great foundation of society's labor (I).

From the heart of each trade will rise the pyramid of natural hierarchies (II) (this may entail the most violent struggles; but the conflict will never exceed its proper limits and spread outside the official decision-making groups).

The activities of the various trades should be simultaneous; that is the first step in a planned economy. On the next level, the qualified deputations of each trade (III) meet at an inter-union conference (IV) where the main problems of economic interdependence are hammered out and a state of balance achieved.

All of which means that the supreme authority (V) is freed from all problems stemming from technical insufficiencies. It is at liberty to concentrate on the country's higher purposes. For it is in the works of this supreme authority that the whole philosophy of a civilization will be expressed: *its direction and its purpose*.

## FRONTIERS...

Administration inevitably implies the notion of boundaries. It is not possible to administer an undefined territory. The definition of a territory is a direct function of the techniques available for frontier supervision. The more developed those techniques become, the more precise the frontier. The telegraph, the airplane, and the camera, have now made the frontier absolute.

How does the natural frontier arise?

First stage: the family.

Second stage: the tribe.

Later: the region.

A center of attraction has emerged: *centripetal* pattern.

But if another center of attraction should form, elsewhere, then a frontier is automatically formed between the two fields of attraction.

The administration intervenes: *centrifugal* pattern – the orders go from the center to the periphery.

Here too, a frontier is formed.

The administration does not excite aggression between two or more regional centers.

But a nation's *direction and purpose* – the philosophy of its civilization – may transform the normal state of the frontier, which is *a void*, into a deliberately artificial state that will lead two regions to conflict with each other, rise in arms, and eventually confront one another across their common frontier:

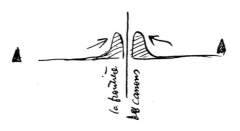

This is the frontier of dissensions. The threat today.

## CONVENIENT CENTERS OF ADMINISTRATION

Why are these threatening frontier conflicts so prevalent today?

Because the natural frontier, produced by normal administrative development, has everywhere been replaced by arbitrary boundaries that are the result of wars and coercive treaties: rape and violence.

It is also because the machine-age revolution that began in about 1830 was characterized in its initial phase by the creation of widespread disorder. The new forms of transportation introduced in the early machine age reduced the world's economy to chaos. Critical political situations, conflicts that no one was prepared for, suddenly sprang up overnight. Such were the fruits of the first hundred years of the machine age: tragic disorder.

First of all, a conclusion: our new modes of transportation demand the development of administrative units on an entirely new scale.

In the diagram I, A represents a country bounded by political frontiers and B another such country. Their common boundary has become a terrifying double wall of bristling bayonets that is draining, paralyzing, destroying both countries. A wretched, frightening, intolerable situation.

Before anything else, each of these countries must turn its attention back upon itself with a view to reorganizing its own economic and spiritual life. Convenient administrative centers must be selected and administrative regions organized around them. A new form of social aggregation will then ensue. What will its determining causes have been? Those permanent elements that dominate the machine-age adventure: climate; topography, geography, race. They are termed: *natural regions*. And it is possible that these natural regions may even overlap the present political frontier in some places (II).

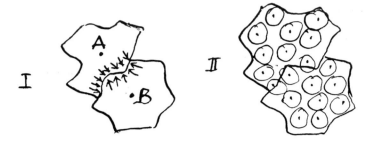

In this way, men will find a true foundation for their fundamental condition.

## THE SUN!

But the present state of the machine age demands developments proportionate to the new high speeds with which it has endowed our civilization.

At the moment, it goes without saying that everything is functioning quite well: railroads, ships, planes. And we have an effective system of communications: mails, telegraph, radio.

But we must not evade recognition of the one fact that is the prime cause of our present disorder: this system of transportation and communications is intense, but it is not *regulated* – it embraces currents of different voltages; it forces together, willy-nilly, potentials that are in reality contradictory. We have all the necessary means, yes. But nothing works because the various elements *have not been brought into harmony*. It is that harmony we need now!

Redevelopment on a world scale? Ideally, theoretically, on an extremely long-term basis, the concept is possible. But the distance to be covered before such a thing can be practically considered is vast, gigantic, quite impossible to cover in a single bound. We have to admit the necessity of transitions. And in any case, such a theory of world unity must always remain limited. As we have seen earlier, the single power unit, the single group is a chimera: its existence could only mean that man had ceased to struggle and that life itself had come to a stop.

As always, when attempting to place a "theory" back in its true frame, we must ask "what are the facts?" We must go on, again as always, to take our bearings on the controling factors in this matter: geography, races, climate, and even, for the present moment, those tyrannical interior barriers within mankind: languages.

Let us open our atlas, consider the world as a whole, and base our thinking on the primary and cosmic reality that controls everything: the sun.

Until some radical change takes place, it seems likely that the machine civilization must always be limited to those regions of the world where men are not subjected to the extreme heat of the sun or the extreme rigors of the cold. There is a limit, a moment, when because of excessive heat or excessive cold the minds and bodies of men are forced to evade the strict rule of the machine. Our map of the world reveals to us (to our great astonishment, I imagine) how *extremely limited* the regions of machine-age industry are. It is a lesson in facts.

The geographical configuration of the earth is also extremely eloquent. The obstinate wish to try and establish exchanges of manufactured products along lines of latitude (between the 40 degree and 50 degree parallels that ineluctably hem in the

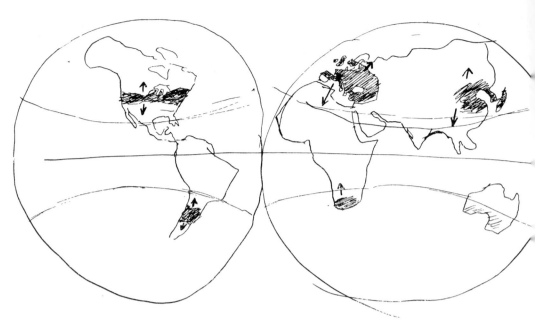

thin ribbon of machine-age activity) is chimerical: all we do is continually get in each other's way, compete with one another, bump into one another with our hands full! All the free space is to the north and south: the true line of trade is the line of longitude, a line of longitude, any line of longitude.

All this (I mean this foray into the field of world economy, which is a problem outside my competence) is only useful here in so far as it permits me to conclude with a final diagram (below) that offers a substitute for the previous one depicting our present threatening, bristling and cataclysmic frontiers. Here it is:

If we can manage to provide the peoples presently pressing with all their force against their arbitrary political frontiers with new axes of expansion, axes created by means of limited and organic federations, then the current of energy in those countries will turn back from the bristling frontiers, flow towards the new and fruitful axis, rush out towards its new objectives, and leave the frontier *empty*. The frontier will become once more the "no man's land" that, by definition, will protect the world from the present threat of national conflicts.

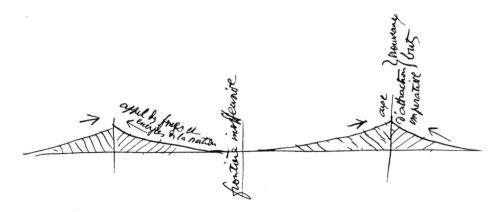

194

We must therefore make it our task to create new economic groups based on a *new unit of size*. The existence of closed, self-sufficing economies will preserve us from the present, world-wide, economic anarchy.

From top to bottom of the scale, from individual man right up to collective man (the nation), we must develop new methods of organization that will provide the necessary quantity of interest to give life purpose. We must re-group human energies according to a new scale of size and then assign them new goals.

NOTE. – The above thoughts on these themes date from 1931 to 1934. During the past thirty years (1934—1964) much has happened to confirm them (1964).

●

8.

# GENERAL MEASURES

March 1, 1934

A local bookseller has arranged my book

*"CRUSADE*
*"(OR THE TWILIGHT OF THE ACADEMIES)"*

in his display window side by side with Camille Mauclair's

*"IS ARCHITECTURE DYING?"*

Both labeled "Just Published."

"Is Architecture dying?" Such is the cry of alarm and despondency being raised in December, 1933.

## WE STILL HAVE TO BUILD IN FRANCE

*We still have to build in France:*

*Vast residential districts in our obsolete cities; demolition and reconstruction;*

*Buildings scattered throughout the city that will enable everyone, men, women and children, to occupy the leisure time soon to be made available by the introduction of a normal production standard to replace the industrial hotch-potch we live in at present. They will have multiple uses and will provide an opportunity for large-scale architectural solutions;*

*In the country, most of the farms need to be rebuilt (hygiene, rationalization, adaptation to new machinery);*

*The agricultural village should be redesigned according to a contemporary program;*

*All the cities in the world as they now stand should be fundamentally redeveloped in order to adapt them to the new phenomenon of high-speed traffic (internal combustion engine), (conclusion of the Athens Congress, 1933 – 4th International Congress for Modern Architecture); reality: beacons, stations, workshops, hangars, hotels and catering;*

*The waterway will recover its importance, modern equipment will be installed on its banks, and an immense resurgence of activity will result;*

*Transoceanic air travel will be made possible by the creation of a beacon network. Etc., etc . . .*

## THIS IS NOT AN ESCAPE INTO UTOPIA

Let me try to explain:

Our cities now, both as regards architecture and layout, are the expression of a social and economic phase that is now outmoded. A new era has begun, and a new ethical attitude is becoming more clearly apparent every day. We are living anachronistically; yet we feel ever more imperious and specific desires as time goes by: the satisfaction of those desires *means the construction of new sites and buildings: in the country as well as the city.* All of which takes a long time to design and even longer to formulate in practical terms. But is it not our duty, our most important duty, to formulate the natural requirements of our age and draw up plans to meet them?

This is not an escape into Utopia! I am concerned with our country and our people. Geographical region means topography and climate; people means biology and psychology. It is with this particular country that I am concerned. And just as any birth contains the forces of its own future – the factors that will determine its growth – in the procreative act, so our age was brought into the world by the advent of the machine and carries its own ineluctable, organic, and logical laws of growth within itself. All of which is beyond any checks that the academies or even the will of man can apply. It is nothing else than one of the seasons in the life of this world. And it is by observing and accepting the reality of the matter that we shall be able to make out the only road lying open to us: to avoid becoming the victims of events. When winter comes, we busy ourselves with precautions against the cold. When a flood threatens, we . . . ought also to take the necessary precautions (alas! we simply run away like a lot of rabbits, telling ourselves that this time must surely be the last!). When war breaks out, we defend ourselves.

Now that the machine age, after a century of invincible advance, is obviously here to stay, we should make up our minds to take our places among the new people of a new civilization. *And, since the machine is a reality entirely independent of human desires or wills*, in order to assure our futures we must confront it *as men*. Eating, thinking, feeling *men*.

Simply.

Man is a quantity we know, or one that we can at least *recognize;* for we have seen him recently being seduced away along a path contrary to that of nature. Today, he is suffering for it. The proofs are in our hands. Now we must return to the path of nature, and listen to her voice again.

When we have taken this simple decision – to become men again – then, and only then, shall we have our confidence, our certainty, restored to us.

And on this foundation we can base our plans.

## THE RAILROAD CIVILIZATION

Let me explain further:

We have just lived through a railroad civilization.

The horse (and cart) traveled at the time-honored speed of man himself: 4 to 6 kilometers an hour. In consequence, the country was harmoniously divided into short travel stages with many small towns as relay points. And all these scattered districts, obeying the human law that insists on all administrations, whether material or spiritual, having a head, looked towards a number of precise centers for guidance. These vital centers, the capitals of provinces, were determined by topography, placement of watersheds, and language differences (coming either before or after the event). Regions were formed, and well organized regulations controled everything within them according to the slow but regular rhythm of the horse's hoof. Advent of the railroad: 50 kilometers an hour, then 100 kilometers an hour. An historic intrusion into the life of our society so violent, so impossible to restrain, that the former, as it were molecular, form of the region was swiftly exploded by it. Spiritual as well as material freight could from then on cross the boundaries of the old regions immediately. The railroad created a new "culture." Above all, it destroyed the organization of the provinces. Think of the new biology created, for example, in France: the network of railroad tracks, determined by political considerations, was laid out from Paris and entirely in relation to Paris. Paris became the hub of an immense wheel which is the country as a whole. Let your imaginations work, and see those lines of iron rail as channels full of water, or molten gold: you will immediately realize what will happen all along the banks of those channels: excitement, activity, the bustle of life itself; and in the areas between the channels, the spaces drained of life and people, a great silence will fall. The railroad is built in 100-kilometer stages. The whole pattern of social aggregation in the country changed. Population and activity was concentrated in fixed and wholly arbitrary points (arbitrary with relation to the regions' fundamental functions: topography, languages, climate). And everything else was forced to change in consequence.

In Paris, in particular, the result was a prodigious invasion from the provinces, a catastrophic explosion of population. The provinces had listened to the railroad's summons: they had left their fields!

And at the points of concentration there occurred the accumulating miracles of the machine. Eventually, they became so attractive that they created the *city mirage*. (This is the latest cycle of the machine age.)

## THE DESERTED COUNTRYSIDE

But it was no more than a mirage!

The city does radiate an indisputable magnetic field in the spiritual sphere. It is a place so big, so full of miraculous things that lads out in the country begin to think: "It's time I went and tried my luck too!"

And they leave their farm in order to go to Paris and become President of the Republic!

So much ambition results in a great many failures. Failures who get left behind and sink to the bottom. For our country lad, even when defeated, does not go back to his farm. He stays. He has already put down roots, and the bright lights of the city have become necessary to him. Result: quite suddenly, Paris has 4 million inhabitants.

And the countryside is deserted.

## THE HIGHWAY ERA

For the past thirty years, 1900 – 1930, we have had the automobile. Though it did not begin to have any real effect until after the war, in about 1920. At this moment, the highway era is still only in its earliest stages: the railroad is declining, the highway emerging. By night, fantastic convoys of 20- or 30-ton trucks hurtling into the darkness at 90 kilometers an hour, each entrusted to the hands and the eyes of a single man, along highways now open to every member of society. By day, veritable meteors that do 100 or 120 kilometers an hour. Moreover, industry is not only already offering immediate delivery of mass-produced cars that will do 120 kilometers an hour, it is also prepared to provide us with others that do 140 as soon as the roads have been improved. The development of the highway during these past five years already threatens strangulation and disaster. Death-dealing machines entrusted to the reflexes of individuals, whether educated for such responsibility or not, are being hurled across the face of the country over roads that are still those on which a previous era of civilization developed, a civilization based on the horse and cart. The road, constantly swept by a stream of cars and trucks going at 100 kilometers an hour, is not fenced off: men, women, children, old men, drunkards, racing cyclists, cross-country runners, hens, geese or cows, heavy carts or traps, everything is to be found on it in one place or another, either going along it or cutting across it. And this deadly ribbon with its dizzying high-speed traffic runs straight through the hearts of our villages and small towns. So that what was once the center of a district, the mouthpiece of a district, *Main Street*, the time-honored nucleus of local life, becomes simply a section of death-dealing road! The town is cut in two as though by a saber stroke [1].

The highway era has been born. Yet neither the city authorities nor the government has so far taken any constructive measures to make life possible in this new age. The only tactics adopted have been ones of defense: policemen waving batons, red and green lights, bells, etc . . . Childish toys!

Nothing has been conceived, nothing done, to develop means of access and egress to and out of Paris, with its four million inhabitants and its hundreds of thousands of missile-like cars. No one has even realized that we have a new era to deal with.

And in this governmental void, the phenomenon is growing, developing, taking clearer and clearer shape. This is the beginning of the highway era. Look at the great railroad stations, the centers of our provincial networks, forces of concentration. They are losing their function and they are losing their passengers. Their future is already evident: the railroad will henceforth be used for long journeys only, from Paris to Berlin, from Paris to Madrid; trains will be huge missiles shot along fenced-in rails. And the rest – paradoxically – having become an obsolete pachyderm with

[1] Note: this was written in 1931-1934.

creaking joints, will be replaced by the automobile. For the automobile follows the roads; it *can take us from one front door to another front door* 5, 10, 100, or 500 kilometers away, *directly*. The car, the truck, the long-distance bus: new equipment that requires the development of a new transportation network for its particular needs. These vehicles will be able to take us from door to door – total efficiency. Instead of the concentration brought about by the railroad, they will provoke social dispersion. The city will move out towards the country. They will establish natural links; the country is once more accessible; a new highway civilization is being born that is the exact opposite of the railroad era. The *land* is being brought back to life! We only have to open our eyes and pave the way!

## REVIVAL OF THE LAND

I must explain further still:

Our house must be set in order.

At the moment, it is in chaos.

By house, I mean the city in its present inhuman state. And I'm not talking about the rich people's part of the city, because they always come out of everything all right, but about the city of the people, which is bound inevitably to its present wretched state simply by its own poverty.

The city must be cleared of all the dreams that have burned their wings, the miscarried lives, the dead embers of men and homes and communities that have accumulated around the city's bright furnace and are now stifling it with their dead and sooty weight. There are four million people living in Paris. Why not flatter the egos of our city councilors by increasing the number to eight million? Or twelve million? Or, on the other hand, why not make the city an efficient size once more by reducing it to *one* million?

During the past few years, we have been using the results of various analyses in a creative way to determine the final form of the Radiant City. The area within the old walls of Paris (Napoleon III's fortifications) could house eight million inhabitants in a "Green City." But in our opinion there is no need to concentrate eight million people there – quite the contrary! The problem of how to purge our cities of their inefficient population is the great question that faces city planners at the present time

We have been appealed to by some of our French peasants themselves, from their fields, but above all from their inhuman farms. Inhuman because unfit for human beings: rotted by saltpeter, undermined by obsolescence, threatening collapse, old, old old! These peasants have demanded that we design the *Radiant Farm* and the *Radiant Village* – new forms of agrarian stratification, a new kind of agricultural existence in keeping with the present age. Farms and villages that will be equivalent, in the matter of basic pleasures, to the seductive city herself. Unity, a state of equivalence to be established between the labors and joys of the city and those of the country. We have to break down the dualism, the rivalry, the opposition, the inequality between these two factors that have created two classes, almost two different peoples, within the nation. We must restore dignity to the city by cleaning it up and dignity to the land by the creation of a modern way of country life.

When we have done all this, then the land will attract people back to it naturally. *We shall not be able to empty the cities of their superfluous population until the land has been materially and spiritually redeveloped.* When it has, then it will attract all the people who are unsuited to city life back again.

## PLANNING EVERYWHERE

I must conclude these explanations.

The highway era and the reclaiming of the land.

We must construct highways, farms and villages. We must not forget that France's farms and villages are all quietly falling to pieces at this very moment: they are all one-, two-, three- centuries old. And they weren't built to last this long.

*We must have city planning in our cities and "city planning" in our countryside!*

We must decide what the true natural regions are, then revitalize them by means of the new contact between city and country that the modern highway can provide.

We must tear up the railroad in a great many places.

We must create a public aviation service and develop it.

We must open up the country by means of waterways, for the waterway is the true highway for freight and merchandise.

City planning everywhere.

Universal city planning.

Total city planning.

We must make plans.

In order to make plans, we must change laws: *we must make the national territory available. While avoiding any transfer of ownership, we must make property exploitable, available for the great task of equipping the machine era.* For the public good, in order to permit the realization of *carefully studied, deeply thought-out* projects, we must MOBILIZE THE LAND and bring speculative building to a complete halt.

We must rescue modern man from the chaos caused by the first wave of the machine age.

We must control the machine age; place man above the machine; restore order by means of city planning and architecture; use that order to re-establish the play of harmonious energies released by *labors of love:* happiness!

Miraculous architectural age! Everything is architecture! Architecture is the creation of order!

## STOP YOUR CROAKING, YOU ACADEMIC CROWS

*"Is architecture dying?"*

Oh, stop your croaking, you academic crows!

City planning is a three-dimensional science, and each dimension is linked to the others. It is not a two-dimensional science, as the town councilmen practice it and as the schools teach it.

Nothing that concerns the surface can exist otherwise than in terms of height.

Here is the key to all solutions.

# 6<sup>th</sup> PART: PLANS

1. DECISIVE DEMONSTRATION
2. PARIS:
    a) THE "VOISIN" PLAN
    b) 1937: VINCENNES
    c) PORTE MAILLOT
    d) 1937: KELLERMANN
3. SOUTH AMERICA:
    a) BUENOS AIRES
    b) SÃO PAULO
    c) MONTEVIDEO
    d) RIO DE JANEIRO
4. ALGIERS: PROJECT A
    —      B
    —      C
5. GENEVA:
    a) THE LEAGUE OF NATIONS PALACE
    b) THE "WORLD CITY"
    c) THE RIGHT BANK
6. ANTWERP
7. MOSCOW
8. ALGIERS, THE OUED OUCHAIA
9. STOCKHOLM
10. ROME
11. BARCELONA
12. NEMOURS

# AS A FRONTISPIECE TO THE PLANS
# DECISIVE DEMONSTRATION

Now that it has gone to print, I realize that the text of this chapter has already appeared, in my book, *Croisade*, 1933. Technical reasons prevent me from cutting it out now. Please excuse this weakness. When one realizes what a brimming, bustling, tumultuous life is the life reserved to the active innovator! In the very first pages of this book I have warned you that this is not a work of serenity, written in the calm study of a man of letters. Alas! that serenity is not for us!

On the Acropolis, in the silent bosom of this landscape straight out of prehistoric times, swells a discourse of pathos, almost a shout, short, clamoring, intense, violent, compact, massive, piercing, cutting, decisive: the marble of the temples carries *the human voice*.

Architecture: when all has been done, resolved, built, paid; when the house is finished, when life takes over the usefulness of the work, there is an explosion of delight before this agile machine-to-live-in. Here progress has spilled out its horn of plenty; the air is good, the sun enters through the wide windows, there is water in all of these pipes and every faucet is a miraculous fountain; light bursts from the wires and heat circulates in the arteries as in a living body ...

Suddenly silence fills the very depth of each being. We tremble at the voice that rises little by little, discoursing, revealing, chanting, describing something epic: the essential feelings which guide our gestures, our work, our greed, our daily struggle – those movements of the soul which are the very foundation of our existence; those happenings which make us suffer, cry, pray and shout our joy – all that is great, gay, sad, sweet, strong, tender, brutal.

And nothing remains of that clever construction but one fruit: our excitement.

Of all the works which accompany our life, rare are those which call forth that human voice; we undergo the vast hurly-burly, the crush, we exist in the still swamp from which nothing rises at all, not one syllable, not one word, not one speech.

If the Acropolis of Athens has a destiny, it is to cradle between Mount Pentelicus and Mount Hymettus the very sound of the voice of man and the justification of the actions of man. There we get to the bottom of the question, there we face the question itself.

For the true inflections of the human voice, once they have been revealed to the heart and the eyes, the ears and the touch, reveal in turn the worthy achievements that stand in the countryside, in the towns and the cities. In the name of the Acropolis, this wall surrounding a pasture seems noble to us and we appreciate the meaning of its line; this haystack, alive and throbbing with the caress of peasant hands, rises like a monument from the stubble; that hovel of mud and sticks becomes the confession of a sensitivity rich and pure; this bridge, that airplane, this corrugated-iron shack, that Spanish highway setting off the Mediterranean shores from the Pyrenees to the Sierra Nevada, this fishermen's boat and that dam down in the valley: in a word, these constructions informed with spirit are transposed from the level of utility to the level of mentality: speeches, words striking to the very center of our sensitivity.

What does it matter to us that the Parthenon is of the Doric order, or that the Propylaea have two Ionic capitals?

What are "orders"? Academic classifications. Don't mean a thing to me . . .

What matters is something else: what matters is the emotional power which, sprung from the depths and transcending usefulness, like a perfume rises and grips the passer-by: halts him and speaks to him of that thing which has no other purpose than to feed the inner flame. Our day has been made fertile, we have the courage to live.

*   *   *

In this time of turbulence in which we live, the first necessity dictated by a chronology of logic and fate was to tear ourselves away from the discourse of the devil, and drive back the devil himself as he paraded human achievements under a veil of lies and artifice. Academies, invoking the Acropolis of Athens (which, by the way, they had never been to see), wove the tissue of lies: lucre, vanity, boorishness, stupidity, insensitivity. The peoples of the North, the first to be committed to the adventure of the machine age, had been seized with a drive to devastate: a clean-up, we have to clean up! It was almost a religion: that of negation, of void, cleanliness, absence. It was a state of mind, a noble moral intention. Under such blows, true human creative force rose up in those who already possessed the substance of it . . . and here and there, the achievements of contemporary architecture appeared.

I say today that after this effort, for which we must thank the peoples of the North, the peoples of the South, of the Mediterranean, where the sun empties, washes, cleanses better than northern mists do, where the sun strips a block of stone until it has no moral value left other than that of proportion itself, I say that from Athens to Alicante, modern architecture can and must face the call of the Acropolis: iron, and sheet iron, and reinforced concrete and stone and wood can and must, by obeying their innermost law, bring and hold within the tension of great economy, the very word of architecture which is:

"What did you want to say to me?"

A human question, humble, poor, indigent, but full, *totally* filled with the reasons for our happiness. Architecture: decisive demonstration of our creative powers. It concerns a human voice: with the profundity of time, permanent and carrying a message forward, eagerly.

November, 1932.

●

# PARIS
# 1922
# 1925
# 1932
# 1934

1922
The two theses face to face: New York is not a city of the machine-age civilization. New York is countered by the Cartesian city, harmonious and lyrical.

How can we deal with the problem of Paris?

Paris is not merely a municipality, Paris embodies France, and Paris, throughout the world, is a place dear to all. A part of the heart of every man belongs to Paris . . . Why?

Because century after century for a thousand years, Paris was the temple of thought, of creativity, enterprise, daring. Now and again Paris went out of the bounds of her authority. Whereupon Louis XIV grew stern, ordered, fixed healthful limits. He wanted to govern something coherent . . .

Let's jump to the present. What a sad sight! Nothing is exact or supervised any longer, nothing is dictated or decided. Paris has become a monster crouching over an entire region. A monster of the most primitive biological sort: a protoplasm, a puddle.

This, the City of Light? Never! She is still that city, thanks to the undying miracle of beautiful acts. Whatever light is still upon the city is there because the light was turned on violently, clearly . . . two centuries ago, one century ago, by the Louis XIV's and the Napoleons. Stars now extinct but like those of the firmament, their light still reaches us although their flame is no more. Paris gleams

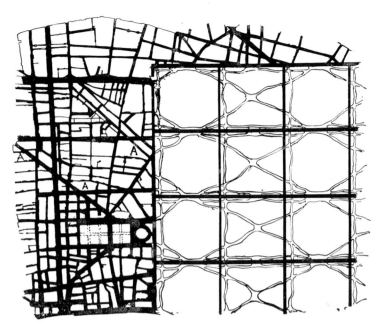

1922: Here the two networks appear:
In the era of the horse.                    In the era of the automobile.

We're demolishing? Yes, every day. But we must demolish well, and firmly and according to a healthy program.

today with the lights of the past. Throughout history, we trace the natural progression of the grandeur of urban undertakings parallel to the growth of technical means and of administrative authority. A curve regularly climbing up a graph could express this expanding strength . . .

The machine age intervenes: the city is overcome by multiple speeds; in one century the population rises from 600,000 to 4,000,000. We assume that measures will be taken on the same scale. No, they regress, the scale shrinks. There are no more visions, no more ideas. All that is left of the truth are patchwork repairs, decisions made from day to day. A terrible, overwhelming event: the War. A

unique opportunity: the postwar period. At last everything will harmonize with the scale of the present? No. Housing – a new onslaught, the housing crisis, the urgent demand for housing? Oh well, contracts are signed by profiteers, and suddenly, in ten years, on the finest sites available, the city is ringed around with 33 kilometers of buildings none of which, with a few exceptions, marks any progress in the housing question. Of all that makes up the very heart of this book: human psychology, collective psychology, civics, technique, industry, efficient methods, general economy –

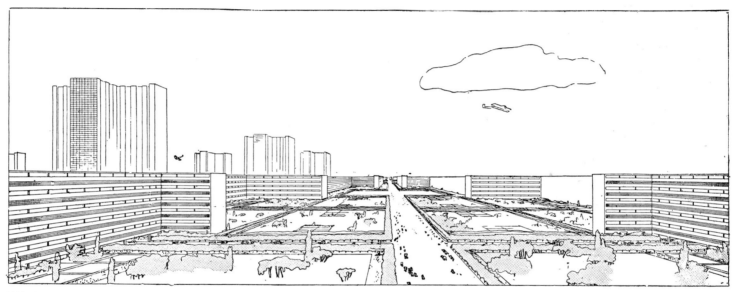

1932. Suddenly light is shed on the problem: three-dimensional city planning. The end of the corridor-street. In praise of the home. The home rules over the city. There are no more pariahs deprived of sun and of space. Equipment worthy of a machine-age civilization.

there is not even a hint on that miraculous occasion.

Meanwhile, the whole Paris region is allowed to foul itself with a mold of bungalows or one-story houses, scattered along little streets; and one after another, every twenty or fifty meters, these streets run into the highways leading to the provinces, highways where trucks and swift cars hurtle by.

Besides, Paris is rebuilding on the sly, from day to day, from top to bottom. Every day the authorities grant permits to demolish or to rebuild, sometimes with the provision that the sidewalk be widened by one, two or three meters. For each new house there is a number of automobiles, futilely seeking shelter along a sidewalk that is too short, and so obstructing streets that remain unchanged. The Paris of a newborn civilization puts on new clothes but does not alter the pattern set in the era of the horse.

In short, in short, in short!

Let us try to earn forgiveness for having dared to sully the splendor of the city!

Endless talk, complaints all day long: and the years go by and the city withers.

The lesson of life is that we must be bold enough to blunder, to set to work, to open up the wound to see what is inside. To begin, to turn to . . . Then catch our breath a moment, meditate, begin again. Try once more, continue stubbornly. Suggest, brave public opinion.

In 1922 the Salon d'Automne asks me to take part in its city-planning section. "You'll do a fountain in a square and, since you like imaginative things, in the back you'll sketch in the skyline of a modern city." "All right!"

A few months later I submitted the theoretical study of *a contemporary city with 3,000,000 inhabitants*.

During the exhausting hours of toil, in the middle of the night when we were bent over our drawings and despaired of ever completing them, I said to Pierre Jeanneret: "We've got to do these drawings carefully, old man, we've got to go all the way. Just say to yourself that ten years or twenty years from now, they will still be called upon as witnesses; better still, that is when they will be published."

Well! It is with impartial studies of this sort, that you win the anonymous heart of the public. In 1922, the blow was struck. And from then on, the door was open.

We have never ceased to go deeper into the question. And others have come, bringing their contributions. We await the verdict of public opinion.

And the city shall become a park (95 % of the ground) (see page 221).

1922-1925

We jump into Paris! We suggest beginning at one end. We open up the question. We ask the question. This "Voisin" Plan for Paris, a huge tapestry covering one of the walls of the city-planning rotunda in the Pavillon de l'Esprit Nouveau at the International Exhibition of Decorative Arts, is in line with the traditions of Paris. This is not an impertinence. This is a continuation of life (harmony in natural progression with the outline of the Invalides [Louis XIV] and with the Champ de Mars [Louis XV]).

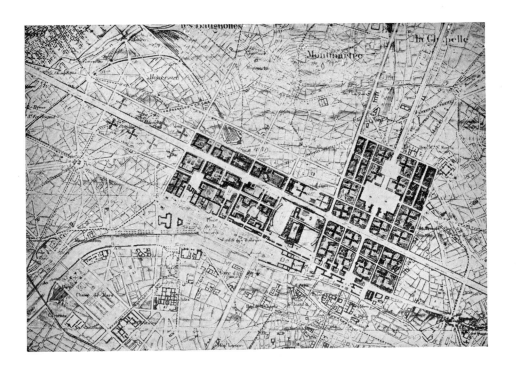

205

1922-1925. The "Voisin" Plan for Paris: 5 % of the area is built upon, 95 % is free. Super-density of 3,200 inhabitants per hectare. The slums are cleaned up, their value enhanced. Here the skyscrapers are cruciform, radiating light. Later corrections will be introduced (see Antwerp, page 265): henceforth *all* sides of the skyscraper will receive the sun.

Note added in 1964: At the center of this drawing appears, *for the first time in the world*, the "multi-level" traffic intersection. This drawing is forty years old ! ! !

In the name of the beauty of Paris, you say "No!"
In the name of the beauty and destiny of Paris I maintain, "Yes!"

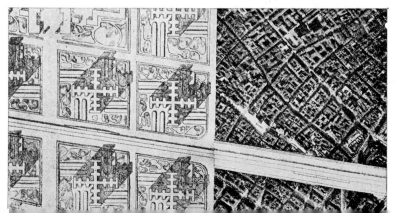

The district as it is today.

Such is the scale of modern times.

The axis of the undertaking was well chosen: you can see the Tour Saint-Jacques, which has been spared.

Above, in the future *place*, you see the Porte Saint-Denis and the Porte Saint-Martin.

From right to left, from east to west, you see the "great East-West throughway of Paris" which embodies the future of Paris and offers the City Council the chance to launch a gigantic financial enterprise, a "money-making" enterprise = a source of wealth.

Since 1922 (for the past 42 years) I have continued to work, in general and in detail, on the problem of Paris. Everything has been made public. The City Council has never contacted me. It calls me "Barbarian"!

207

Yes, Paris has got too small, we've got to make it bigger! but in order to make it bigger, we need a genius!

And if you need a genius, I offer my services... Here I am!

While I'm at it, if I pick up the Obelisk and carry it to Carpentras,

...let me move the Opéra, let me put it in Sologne,

...the Arch of Triumph in Normandy,

...the column of the Place Vendôme in Valenciennes,

...the Grands Boulevards in Brittany.

---

Quoted from Monsieur Jean Vallée:

In certain houses visited by the Public Health Inspectors, tuberculosis, in the space of ten years, had killed a number of human beings greater than the normal population of the building.

From Monsieur Juillerat, this other quotation:

Once tuberculosis has made its way into unhealthful houses, it's there for good; one after the other, all of those whom their fate has led into this den will be struck down by tuberculosis. Its greed is never appeased, it contaminates first the fathers and then the sons, the grandparents and then the grandchildren. The infected hovel will remain infected indefinitely.

And also this quotation from Dr. Surmont:

Of all the infections which decimate the ranks of humanity today, none causes greater damage than tuberculosis. In civilized countries, one seventh of all deaths may without doubt be attributed to tuberculosis.

Letter to the Prefect of the Département of the Seine.

Paris, March 8, 1934

Monsieur le Préfet:

A sense of duty and solidarity oblige me, today, to tell you about this touching incident:

I live on the rue Jacob and this morning I learned that at number 14 of the same street, the shop of a *bougnat* (coal-wood-and-wine dealer), the shopkeeper's wife died last night of tuberculosis. Her name is Mme. L...

In 1932, in the same shop, Mr. B... and his wife died of tuberculosis.

In 1930, in the same shop, Mr. R... died of tuberculosis.

In 1927, the two shopkeepers, man and wife (no one was able to tell me their names) also died of tuberculosis.

I was not able to pursue my inquiry any further into the past.

The four above-named couples were all sturdy Auvergnats who had come straight from the Auvergne countryside to Paris. It took no more than two years to finish off each of them at the age of thirty.

Obviously no one thinks of letting you know about this: least of all the landlord, who impassively rents his shop anew after each death.

Tomorrow another couple will arrive from Auvergne, and will die in 1936, of course.

I have taken the liberty of thinking that this little incident, rather touching in itself, falls within the jurisdiction of your department.

Very sincerely yours,

LE CORBUSIER

---

Let's cross out the suburbs, let's sweep away the provinces, Let Paris be all of France!

...and let everyone become a Parisian! (Mind you, that's not such a bad idea!)

Moreover, if I place the Gare de Lyon in Lille, and the Gare d'Orléans in Dunkerque, train traffic will be greater and will satisfy more travelers!

Then I set up a bus from the Madeleine to Marseilles!... from the Bastille to Perpignan!... 12 *sous* in first class and 9 *sous* in second!

And Paris will be all of France! France will be the capital of Paris! that's what I wanted to demonstrate!

...After that, I've got a right to rest a little!

"It's marvelous: Paris is upside down!"
(Commentary of the times.)

Here is what Paris knew how to do and was able to do! A titanic achievement. Hats off! Today Paris lives on Haussmann's work.

MY RESPECT AND ADMIRATION FOR HAUSSMANN

I don't like the roots of Haussmann's character: – a very practical man; "good-natured" and easy-going; a man who "will have all the luck." A born administrator. Nicely stereotyped tastes (. . . at the foot of the stairs, waterfalls and water nymphs, dolphins, statues bearing candelabra). The triumph of ostentation which, seen in the laces of Haussmann's time, was to overtake stone itself and ornamental plaster under our present-day academicians. Quadrilles and balls, visiting kings and emperors come to Paris – in the midst of the machine age, all of that was futility and insouciance and unawareness, perfectly in line with the "art" style of an "engineer" like Haussmann: for a change from sewerage, you make plaster naiads. Bourgeois grandeur, and idiocy through lack of feeling. Such affectation, such sham! It was all Napoleon III style, the true, the pure bourgeois style, the style of the era. What then? An unfeeling man. Because of all this, one cannot *like* the man.

(Notes pencilled in the margins while reading that very worthy book by Georges Laronze, LE BARON HAUSSMANN. Published by Librairie Félix Alcan.)

209

# ... THE WILL OF ONE MAN
# ... AND THE GRATITUDE OF THE MASSES

extracts taken at random from the book by Georges Laronze, LE BARON HAUSSMANN

Sensational events *which have just occurred.* Our fathers knew of them, our grandfathers lived through them. We ourselves were children when Haussmann died on January 11, 1891.

*"Paris is upside down!"* And that is why the city of Paris, a thousand years old, can live today in that new biological structure which Haussmann bestowed on it.

... A prodigious urban experience, an earthquake in the midst of Paris. Ruins ... then a new wonder of the world, Paris white and fresh.

## BALANCE SHEET

... Just picture an inextricable tangle of streets, whose names and uneasy turnings are reminiscent of tragedy and misery, the rue Saint-Nicaise, rue Transnonain, rues du Chevalier-du-Guet, des Mauvaises-Paroles, de la Vieille-Lanterne. As in the reign of Philippe-Auguste, the main crossroads of Paris is still formed by the rue Saint-Denis and the rue Saint-Honoré. Just yesterday, the rue de Rivoli ended at the Arc du Carrousel. From there, an opening cut through towards the Hôtel de Ville tries to climb up the slope of Saint-Jacques-de-la-Boucherie. Next come the Middle Ages, picturesque to be sure, but unhealthy and hard to reach. No boulevard Sébastopol, and no rue Turbigo. Let your mind's eye also do away with the boulevard Malesherbes, the boulevards Saint-Michel, Saint-Germain and Port-Royal, with the rues Etienne-Marcel, Réaumur and de Châteaudun, with the avenues which open onto today's Place de la République, and with those which make the Place de l'Etoile the noblest crossroads in the world. Change the streets of Paris into narrow, badly lighted alleys. Uproot fifty thousand trees. Imagine the pont d'Austerlitz, the pont d'Arcole, the pont des Invalides as wobbly suspension bridges. Take other bridges – National, Solférino, de l'Alma, d'Auteuil – and destroy them; destroy the town halls of several *arrondissements*, half a dozen hospitals and asylums, a number of schools, the Trade Tribunal, the churches of la Trinité, Saint-Augustin, Notre-Dame-des-Champs and Saint-François-Xavier; the Protestant church of the Saint-Esprit and the synagogue of the rue de la Victoire, the theatres called du Châtelet, Sarah-Bernhardt, and de la Gaîté; the fountains on the Champs-Elysées, at the place du Théâtre-Français and the place Malesherbes. Close the Parc Monceau and level the Buttes-Chaumont as well as the Parc Montsouris and for that matter almost all of the *squares* in Paris. Shrink the Bois de Boulogne, choke it with a wall; deprive the Bois de Vincennes of the wide avenues leading to it, of its lakes, of its gentle undulations. Turn the Champ de Mars into a desert and the Champs-Elysées into a cesspool. Strip the city of its admirable network of sewers. Let the city's inhabitants drink the polluted water of the Seine. In other words, withdraw from the capital a part of its natural territory, its arteries, its essential organs, withdraw air and life: and you have Paris as it was in 1853, when Haussmann was named Prefect of the Département of the Seine.

## MINISTER OF PARIS

But he had decided (the Minister, Persigny): "You are exactly the man we need."

An irresolute city council ... The transformation of Paris requested by the Emperor and badly needed. To carry it out demanded boldness and obstinacy. There was only a modicum of normal resources: so what?

The city council feared the proposed extension of public works. That would mean a new phase in the conflict between the Tuileries and the Hôtel de Ville involving, this time, even members of the council itself.

A battle shaping up, a battle to be fought every day, from one ambush to the next.

... Boulevard Sébastopol, so important that at first it was named Boulevard du Centre.

Napoleon continued to argue determinedly for open spaces.

The theory of *productive expenditures:*

Sure of all the means at his disposal, the Prefect guided the plow with a firm hand across the capital. As a song from a revue put it at the time,

"Every minute the hammer comes down

"On another part of town."

And already, even if the overall plan was not discernible, the ideas behind the layout of new streets were apparent. These ideas were the Emperor's – humanitarian, dynastic, grandiose all at once – as arranged by Haussmann. New arteries – those created a bit haphazardly in the quartier de l'Europe and the rue de Rouen (today the rue Auber) – would link the heart of Paris to the railroad stations and drain off some of their congestion. Other arteries would serve in the battle against poverty and revolution: as strategic routes, they would plunge into the centers of epidemics and uprisings, facilitating the arrival of a more tonic air – and of the armed forces. Like the rue de Turbigo, these arteries would connect the seat of government with the barracks and, like the boulevard du Prince-Eugène, the barracks with working-class districts. New *quartiers* in the west were specially planned to enhance the reputation of Paris; their splendid boulevards would lead, like the boulevard Malesherbes, for one, toward the suburbs which an aroused ambition planned to annex to the capital, or would form regular geometric figures: the Place de l'Etoile with the avenues radiating from it, that other star which was the Place du Roi-de-Rome, and the checkerboard framed by the Invalides and the Champ de Mars. Plans also called for routes made inevitable by a combination of these various requirements or by other, extant openings through the city: the boulevard du Palais and the boulevard Saint-Michel, extending the boulevard Sébastopol, and the branches of this fundamental artery which, in a flanking movement, would open up the montagne Sainte-Geneviève, starting point of the boulevard Saint-Germain and of important streets: Gay-Lussac, Monge, Médicis; the boulevards Saint-Marcel, Port-Royal and Arago completing the outer circle for the convenience of travelers and troops. And the boulevard Magenta and the boulevard Daumesnil would also lead to and from the train stations and, by plunging through the popular districts, would channel Sunday crowds to the woods at Vincennes.

And so, in the perennial holiday atmosphere of the capital, here was one more show for all to see.

It's marvelous: Paris is upside down ...

## AT WORK

So the entire city dies and is born. The hard echo of the pick, the rumble of falling plaster, the din of scaffolding sound a refrain to the rhythm of daily life. Everywhere heavy carriages or handcarts trundle furniture, and people expropriated from their lodgings carry bundles of household goods. If a few weeks later you return to visit the tomb of a defunct house, you find that even the ground on which it stood has been taken by a stranger – a boulevard bordered by straight lines of tall buildings, uniformly white, like soldiers on parade.

... Broad streets; paving stones replaced by macadam or those novel little blocks of sandstone; regular sidewalks; shelters; machines to sweep and water down the streets; the passage from one bank of the Seine to the other made easy by the construction of new bridges (de Solférino, de l'Alma) or the reconstruction of others (d'Austerlitz, Louis-Philippe, Saint-Louis, d'Arcole, des Invalides); the great number of more comfortable coaches; gas lamps stretching away in a blaze of light from street to street every night.

The broad collection basins for drainage where sluice-boats ply; where, far from the sewers the feed pipes for water supply are placed; a network like the system of blood circulation, transporting water along a multitude of arteries into each of the multitude of houses – this network will be 570 km. long by the time Haussmann leaves the Hôtel de Ville and will give him undisputed title to the gratitude of his fellow citizens.

The overall prefectural plan constituted the third network, and this, without the least aid from the government.

It provided for the creation or extension of streets serving the railroad stations – the rue de Rennes leading to the gare de l'Ouest, the rue La Fayette to the gare du Nord and the gare de l'Est – or the completion of crossroads – or radiating-squares: the commencement of the boulevard des Amandiers (to become the avenue de la République), the opening up of avenues to complete the Place de l'Etoile complex and that of the Place du Roi-de-Rome. Another intersection was to be created in the heart of the luxury city, in front of the new Opéra then being built; it would crown and complete the entire conception. To lay it out, meant following the rue Réaumur; while along the axis of the other part of the theatre there would be an avenue whose two extremities would soon be opened, as if the administrative district were holding out its hand to the district reserved for pleasure. The imperial plan baptized this the avenue Napoléon; it was to become the avenue de l'Opéra. And the Opera house itself was to be set in a horseshoe of two other streets, the rue Scribe and the rue Gluck. At that point a new intersection would come into being; a new boulevard would complete it. An impressive boulevard, a link with avenue Friedland to the west; in reality the Etoile would give birth to it. From there the new boulevard would cross the old faubourg St. Honoré – in a symbolic gesture it would sacrifice the house in which the Prefect himself was born, would cut across the boulevard Malesherbes and eventually, the goal of its long race, end at the boulevard Montmartre. So throughout Paris – the Paris of businessmen, the Paris of stockbrokers, the Paris of theatres and evening pleasures, the Paris of strollers – the new boulevard would bear the great name of Haussmann.

And then, all across the capital, the pencil traced countless arteries – some new, others lengthened or merely widened – so many gifts meted out by justice: to the west, the Chaillot district opened up once and for all, the Rond-Point des Champs-Elysées perfected by the extension of the avenue d'Antin, the boulevard Malesherbes thrust into the former community of Batignolles among the lands of Emile Pereire. In the center, the completion of several streets – Maubeuge, Drouot, Le Peletier, du Cardinal-Fesch; the latter was renamed rue de Châteaudun and isolated the church of Notre-Dame-de-Lorette. On the left bank, the avenue Duquesne, the rue des Saints-Pères, the boulevard Saint-Germain were all lengthened. To the north, the rue Caulaincourt was created – not without causing fierce opposition. Whereas to the east, a problem caused by the boulevard Prince-Eugène was solved by the boulevard de la Reine-Hortense (renamed, boulevard Richard-Lenoir).

The Bois de Vincennes, to the east, was a faithful replica, down to the last detail, of the Bois de Boulogne on the west – there was even a racetrack, inaugurated in 1863.

The immense Parc Monceau. Beginning in September, 1861, strollers appreciated its affected elegance, its artificial grotto, its imitation ruins, its gilded gates.

· · · · · · · · · · · · · · ·

Ever since the Emperor assumed his throne, Paris has destroyed in order to rebuild, and seen broad open spaces flooded with sunlight there where hundreds of insalubrious houses had jostled each other before. Admiringly, happily we find that in certain matters, a single mind can be more fertile than a throng of advisers.

Prodigious life.

His notion of art within order obliges him to demolish. His soul is given over to this passion, he invests all of his love in the transformation of Paris.

The dictator wears his watch on "a little gold chain worth easily eighteen francs." Speculators offer him sizeable commissions – and come away shamefaced.

. .  . .  . .  . .  . .  . .  . .  . .

It was during this period that he completed the boulevard Sébastopol and, on the left bank, stretched the boulevard Saint-Germain; that, on the right bank again, he leveled the areas overlooking the Seine and added the last touch to his network of bridges with the Napoléon III (later, the National) and Auteuil viaducts. At the same time, he considered new arteries along the approaches to the Luxembourg gardens, as well as others to prolong the rue de Rennes or the boulevard Haussmann, or to bring down the butte des Moulins. And from every corner of this Paris overwhelmed, down every street mended or transformed, appeared a startling growth of new monuments, like so many flowers: town halls as well as churches, theaters as well as hospitals, courts of justice as well as schools.

Lariboisière hospital was nearly finished, and the Hôtel-Dieu being rebuilt.

Poorhouses were founded, homes for the aged established, insane asylums planted in the suburbs of Paris.

The municipal pawn office opened branches. The Trade Tribunal, one of whose façades was a response to the Strasbourg wharf in the distance; the Palace of Justice rejuvenated, with its Empire stairway, its painted face gazing haughtily over the old place Dauphine; the Santé prison; the barracks of Lobau and the Cité des Celestins; acquisition of the Carnavalet mansion, future Museum of the City of Paris; the Sorbonne restored, as well as the lycées Bonaparte and Saint-Louis; the lycées Rollin and Chaptal, rebuilt; the covered markets, the slaughterhouse of la Villette.

An age of stone – and of air as well.

Three years of hard work and an outlay of 6 million francs had transformed the quarries of Chauve-mont into a fancy-dress spectacle: like other parks before it, the parc du Mont-Souris was given lakes and bridges and gentle slopes.

The prejudiced, in their polemics, refused to recognize Haussmann's efforts to provide the citizens of Paris with decent drinking water. And yet, his attempts became real feats, ranking him among the great masters. Do you realize that at the beginning of the Second Empire, the capital could consume no more than 134,000 cubic meters of water per day? And that of this amount, springs provided only 2,400 cubic meters and the well of Grenelle only 800, as against 100,000 from the Ourcq canal and 30,800 from the Seine? There were fountains, and there were Auvergnats (coal-wood-wine merchants) selling water, like precious goods . . .

Haussmann spent seventeen years at the Hôtel de Ville, as prefect; seventeen years working toward this goal.

Habit offered fierce resistance.

Company directors were disappointed.

The opposition vaunted the merits of the Seine's waters.

Although Haussmann left the Hôtel de Ville without having completed this task, the achievement belongs to him.

For every day, Paris is to receive 130,000 cubic meters of spring water. In the battle against epidemics, this means victory.

A crowd of people from every nation, had flocked to the Champ de Mars in compact throngs. But a curiosity just as strong had attracted them to Paris, new wonder of the world.

What prestige the Prefect enjoyed then, in the eyes of these august visitors! He personified the boldness of a city's efforts – and thereby, the glory of an empire. One after the other kings came to marvel at monuments, follow the splendid promenades amidst the flags of the Place de Grève (de la Concorde, today), and even in the sewers below. And Haussmann received them, Haussmann, the "préfet magnifique." Dangerous thrills for country cousins: they were flattered to have as their guide, their counselor even, this devil of a man who had rejuvenated the capital ten centuries old. Yet their smiles grew faint as all of this luxury was spread before them. "Before such a queen as Paris," the Emperor Alexander admitted to Haussmann, "we are nothing more than bourgeois."

And now enormous waves advanced to engulf the Prefect.

Faithful to his vision of a capital belonging not so much to the Parisians as to France, he sought to have the municipal budget ratified by the legislature. People wondered, warily, "What does that mean?"

The *Courrier du Dimanche* is suppressed; this puts an end to the biting criticisms from Alfred Assolant, Charles des Arnas, Pascal Grousset. But there remain the campaigns led in the *Figaro* by Lockroy, Ferragus, and Jules Richard; in the *Journal des Débats* by Michel Chevalier and Léon Say; in the *Temps* by Ulysse Ladet, Henri Brisson, and especially Jules Ferry, who has written the satirical "Comptes Fantastiques d'Haussmann"; in the *Opinion Nationale* by Guéroult; in the *Gazette de France* by Escande, J. Bourgeois, Charles de Lacombe and Boissieu. And there are still the campaigns led by the *Presse*, the *Union du Siècle*, the *Journal de Paris*, the *Nain Jaune*. In addition to these articles, a number of pamphlets appear: from the pens of Augustin Cochin, Dantès, Lasteyrie, Veuillot, Achille Arnaud, Fournel, Dr. Akerlin, Boileau, Horn. The letters and the salons of Ximenès Doudan, the Countess of Beaulaincourt, Madame Baroche buzz with carping comments. Street vendors offer, for fifteen centimes, *Paris deserted, lamentations of a Haussmannized Jeremiah*, ridiculing "the leader of the city, *the house man*." And the chorus of complaints keeps swelling -

archaeologists and poets, bourgeois and workers, royalists and republicans, *grandes dames* and *grands seigneurs*, former city councilmen and ministers-for-the-moment, toss in, pell mell, their doctrines, their prejudices, their nostalgia, their rancor, their anxiety for the future. Everything about the Prefect brings grist to the critics' mill – his financial management, his political opinions, his work, his private life. Feeling – the spirit of opposition, envy, then hate – goes out of bounds. There are people who insist that the waters of the Seine are healthful; who maintain that it is madness to cut a street leading from the Bourse to the Opéra, that is, from "an establishment open in the daytime to one that is open at night"; who hold that letting in more air will not make the city more healthful, for "the drafts will cancel each other out."

It is unthinkable to let a prefect stay in his post when his work is condemned wholesale by all parties.

"Or to accept streets dictated by megalomaniac stupidity. A child could have done that, by putting down his ruler anywhere on the plans. And avenues leading to – what? Towards the open fields of Ternes and the Etoile, where no one will ever live; or again, and which is of no use to anyone but the Emperor, from the Tuileries to the new Opéra! Besides, these avenues are so wide that it's absurd."

"We've all drunk Seine water without dying of it. And that, gentlemen, is the opinion of my doctor."

The end of family life. The Parisian has lost the right to live in his *quartier*, to die in the house where he entered the world. Even on Sunday, the demolition crews are at work, undermining his memories, effacing the house of his fathers and the enveloping silence of its mossy courtyard, his old familiar church, the lofty sculptured panels of the salon where he became engaged. And the destructive rage does not stop even there.

"I refuse to resign, I do not want to seem to be dodging last-minute problems. I want to present my accounts, liquidate the debt of the City and make my exit through the front door . . . I want to take complete responsibility for what I have done . . ." And rejecting even the possibility of retirement, he dictates the only remaining course of action: "I wish to be relieved of my duties . . ."

*He refuses. He wishes.* Even at the time of his downfall, he remains unbowed. And since he *refuses* to abandon his work, his *wish* is to be revoked.

From the pen of Girardin, in the *Liberté*, this cry: "History will not believe that the author of the transformation of Paris has been recalled." While the *Marseillaise* and the *Réveil* hail Haussmann in their own way: they demand that he be tried!

From then on, all those who surrounded him withdraw, leaving him alone.

That evening, in his home on the rue Boissy-d'Anglas, he has gathered a few intimates about the table. During this pleasant occasion, with his accurate memory, he makes the bygone hours come to life again. A sudden pain strikes his chest. His guests are anxious. The valet goes down, does not find the family doctors, comes back with another physician. Haussmann is still seated in his armchair, his features drawn; he breathes with difficulty. The doctor applies his stethoscope. This man of eighty-two, who is about to die, recovers lucidity enough to describe what he feels. The diagnosis is certain: lung congestion, caused by the cold weather, and there is no hope. He obeys the doctor, he goes to bed; but he smiles faintly: at the end of his life, ten minutes' rest. Then the Baron Georges-Eugène Haussmann, in his modest little bedroom, dies.

Now the dead man is carried slowly through the capital city. At the Place de la Concorde – that splendid crossroads where a prefect's order has caused the Champs-Elysées to add the foliage of the future to the city of kings – the 131st Regiment beats out a funeral march. Lancers, dragoons, an artillery battery present arms to the dignitary of the Legion of Honor. But neither France as a whole, nor even Paris itself is to render any other homage. Three masters of ceremonies bear cushions displaying the decorations which "le grand baron" has received from awe-struck nations. Behind the funeral coach there is nothing but heaps of flowers – wreaths and sheaves and violets sent by banks and imperialist committees. Some two or three hundred people follow the procession: members of the Institute, friends, a few city councilmen, like Alphand, who have come on their own initiative; and delegations from the Appeal to the people, their names evoking an Empire already remote. The government is not present. The Prefect of the Seine is not present. The city council has not sent any delegation. Even the onlookers all along the very streets and boulevards which Haussmann's imagination brought to life, gaze indifferently. Towards the corner of the rue Drouot, a member of the procession cries, with outstretched arm, "Ingrates!"

Was he a genius? Savior or tyrant? Benefactor or accomplice? Suffice it to say that in his time and in his duties, he was the man who was needed. After the Napoleonic wars, after three revolutions, after the tremendous tumult of ideas, France hoped for only one thing: to go on living. Moreover, it was the time of new vistas, new prospects. Industrialism was the only goal whose conquest would not require bloodshed. The new ideal? Let there be railroads, public works, stock speculation, competitive trade, market and fair all in one. Captains, philosophers, poets, relegated to the background. The country needed an administrator. Haussmann was nothing more than that. He was all that.

A producer, a man of achievements, that was Haussmann. His adversaries could justly criticize him for destroying more than was necessary, for his monotonous plans, for a certain vulgarity in his taste, and especially for the means he employed. But where any other man might have failed a hundred times, he succeeded.

# POUR CONTINUER LA TRADITION
## DE PARIS
### Manifeste de la Nouvelle Génération

Absorbant un crédit de 1 million 300.000 francs, la France officielle reconstitue, dans cette Exposition même, les sites historiques de Paris et documente l'opinion sur l'état présent de la ville

Maquettes des créations des rois et des empereurs ! Splendeurs des civilisations pré-machinistes ! Gloires que chacun connaît et que nul ne cherche à discuter !...

Autour de ces quelques vestiges précieux, qui ne couvrent pas le UN POUR MILLE de sa surface, la VILLE agonise, meurt de congestion, s'écroule de vétusté.

    La maladie règne.
    Le bruit nous écrase.
    Le soleil n'entre pas dans les logis,
    L'atmosphère est empestée,
    Les distances sont devenues critiques,
    La désespérance est sur des millions d'êtres,
    La vitalité même de la ville est ruinée,
    Le monde machiniste est sans demeure
         sans ville,
         sans outillage,
         sans équipement

Plus gravement, le développement de l'Époque Machiniste est étouffé.

**PARIS N'EST PLUS LA CITÉ DES TEMPS MODERNES !**

Serions-nous devenus des gardiens de musée ?

**IL FAUT FAIRE DE PARIS LA CITÉ DES TEMPS MODERNES !**

    Redonner à Paris les joies de l'action,
    Faire éclater le civisme de Paris,
    Renouer la tradition de Paris qui fut toujours *grandes vues hautes intentions* : CRÉATION

    Au cours de l'Histoire, Paris s'empare de toutes les techniques nouvelles, se transforme et domine l'événement

    Paris est un haut-lieu du monde occidental.

**PARIS EST UNE VILLE VIVANTE.**

**IL FAUT CONTINUER PARIS !**

La Revue PLANS, Gustave Lyon, Gabriel Voisin
E. Mongermon, Henri Frugès, Philippe Lamour
François de Pierrefeu, Docteur Pierre Winter
Fernand Léger, Brancussis, Blaise Cendrars
Delaunay, Jacques Lipchitz, 'Cahiers d'Art'
Christian Zervos, Jean Wiener, Albert Jeanneret
Maurice Raynal, Tériade, Pierre Chenal, A P
Ducret, Charlotte Perriand, Pierre Jeanneret
Le Corbusier

## A L'OCCASION DE LA DEUTSCHE BAU AUSTELLUNG DE BERLIN, MAI 1931

Here is the poster that created a scandal! It was put up in the entry hall of the 1932 International Building Exhibit in Berlin. The directors of the Exhibit had generously placed this hall at my disposition; at the last minute, two days before the Exhibit opened, I suddenly decided to expose my theoretical studies of the *Ville Radieuse* (the Radiant City) and certain instances of their application to Paris: I had felt that Paris, or France, should, in such an international exhibition, show something other than the past, even if it was the "splendid past."

Official circles resented my move terribly. This poster was considered a crime of *lèse-majesté*. It was torn off the walls.

... And in 1934, when the City Council was discussing our participation in the International Exhibition of 1937, one speaker cried: "Le Corbusier worked against the interests of France, at Berlin!"

The improvised stand at the 1932 International Exhibit in Berlin.

Our stand at Berlin, as Gropius and Mies van der Rohe were kind enough to arrange it at the last minute.

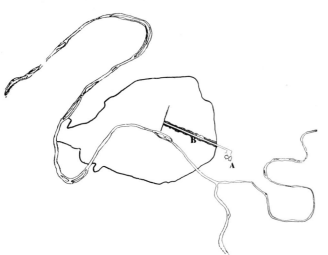

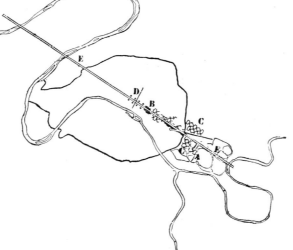

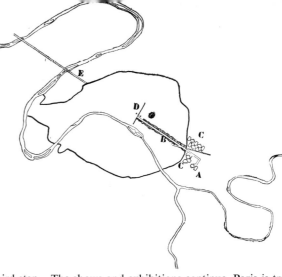

First step – the 1937 show:
 a) Exhibits
 b) First section of the great Paris throughway.

Second step – Ten years of successive home shows and city-planning exhibitions (World Research Center). E: the western section of the great throughway is begun.

Third step – The shows and exhibitions continue. Paris is transformed into the Green City all along the throughway. The Business City is under construction. The great Paris throughway is completed.

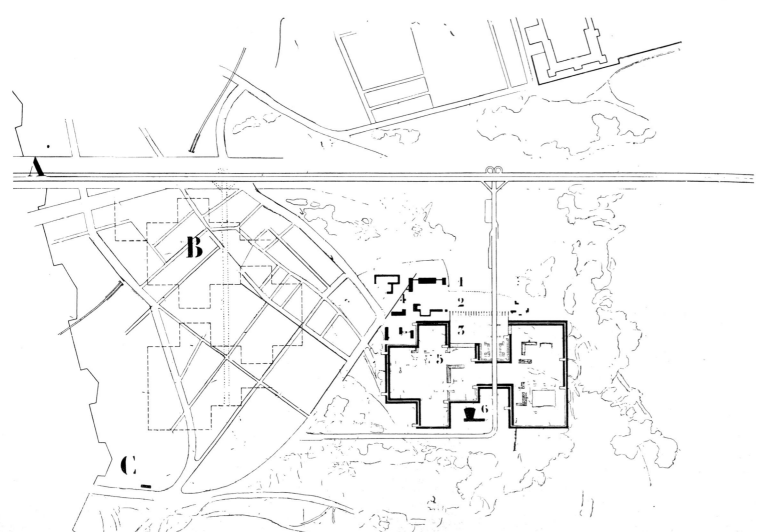

**1932.** PROPOSAL FOR THE INT.

# EXHIBITION OF 1937

(A 15-page pamphlet submitted to the Exhibition Committee on June 15, 1932.)

TO THE EAST OF PARIS, A GREEN CITY
CAN BEGIN TO TAKE FORM.
AND LITTLE BY LITTLE, IT CAN PENE-
TRATE INTO THE HEART OF PARIS.

"The Dwelling: an International Exhibition," title suggested as replacement for "International Exhibit of Decorative Arts." The problem was to choose a strategic spot (here, the Bois de Vincennes, to the east of Paris), for building a *redent*, or indented unit of the Radiant City, as a model worksite for the art of housing: techniques, organization, sociology, urbanization. Pursue the suggestion made by Maréchal Lyautey in 1927: join the east of Paris to the boulevard Sébastopol. Actually, our overall idea of 1922-1925: the east-west backbone of Paris, crossing the entire city: opening up, making way. And all along this backbone, the idea was to rebuild the city *as a city*, of the Radiant City type, reaching and clearing the center of Paris, siting the business city (the "Voisin" plan of 1925). To the west, parallel to the Champs-Elysées and its extension (the overly celebrated "Triumphal Route"), the great Paris throughway was to be pursued. In this way, the "Triumphal Route" would be rescued from compromise, ambiguity, absurdity, and all of the traffic hastily thrust into the *cul-de-sac* of the Place de la Concorde would be re-absorbed. The backbone would be joined to the eastern and western provincial highways.

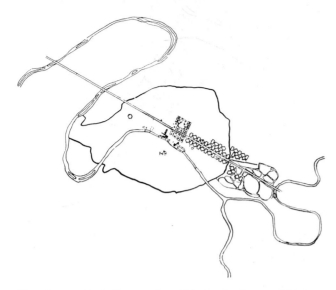

Fourth step: Paris lives again within its fundamental biology; historical Paris is saved.

Paris has withdrawn within itself, into a "radiant city": 80 % of the land surface is planted, 100 % of the ground belongs to the pedestrian. The suburbs have been reabsorbed: the transportation problem is solved. In the black area, shown here, Paris could contain 5,000,000 inhabitants (an undesirable eventuality, however). The effect of this rebounds, to salvage the "triumphal way" (!). The great throughway MN is joined to the big national highways HM, E and so forth. At A, the Exhibition, no longer useful, has become a housing *redent*.

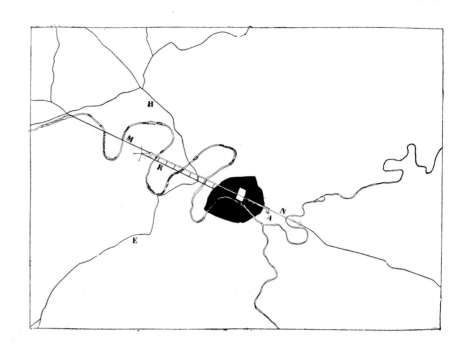

You planners who work in terms of vanity, have pity on 3,000,000 inhabitants.

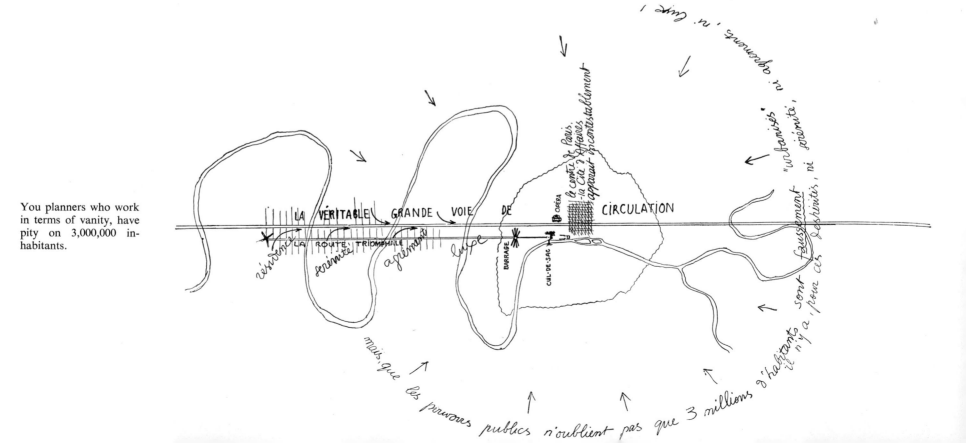

In the middle, the monument to Maréchal Foch, an island of silence.
The Maréchal lying, dead, upon a slab of stone.
A striking contrast in this scene of bustling life.

the large platform for pedestrians, a genuine forum.

the highway for rapid through traffic.

# 1930 - DEVELOPING THE PORTE MAILLOT

Mr. Léonhard Rosenthal placed this problem before ten architects, when there was a question of buying back Luna Park: private enterprise had to be coordinated with the urgent need to classify types of traffic at one of the most congested points in Paris: the western exit from the city, at the Porte Maillot.

Mr. Rosenthal insisted on erecting very high buildings intended to serve the automobile trade and thus preserving in its entirety the surface necessary for automobile traffic.

Finally, and quite naturally, in the process of developing this area, part of the solution should be in terms of monumental architecture: a monument to Maréchal Foch.

PM 2353

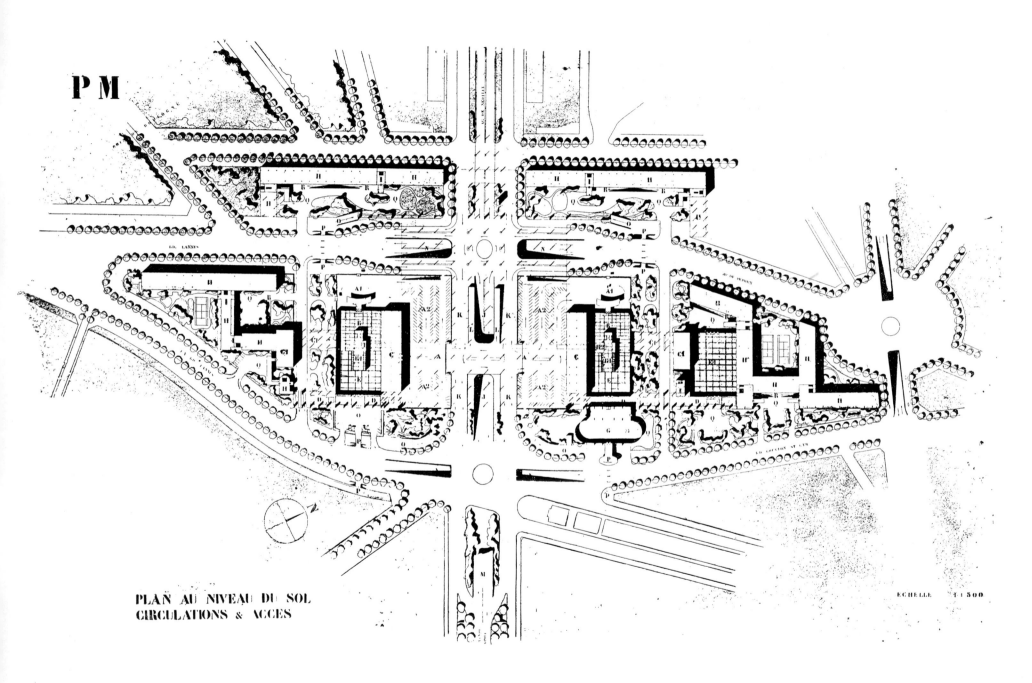

PM

PLAN AU NIVEAU DU SOL
CIRCULATIONS & ACCES

ECHELLE 1 : 500

Here was the chance to apply rigorous theories to an awkward case. Everything becomes simple if you possess a clear doctrine. Three problems:
1° a site of intense automobile traffic;
2° two business buildings with their own private automobile and pedestrian traffic, with parking;
3° housing, the start of a "Green City."
Here was proof that Utopia could become reality, that Paris could transform itself from top to bottom over the years and be endowed with the equipment indispensable to its existence.

**PM** 2554

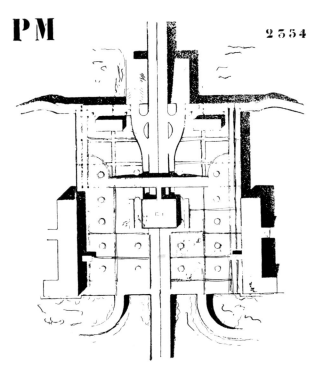

VARIANTE

Separation of the various automobile speeds as well as pedestrian speed can be achieved only through the use of different levels.
Then it all becomes astonishingly simple.

To the west of Paris, beginning of a "Green City." The houses have withdrawn from the edges of sidewalks and are placed at a distance from the roads. There are no more courtyards, front or back.

**PM**

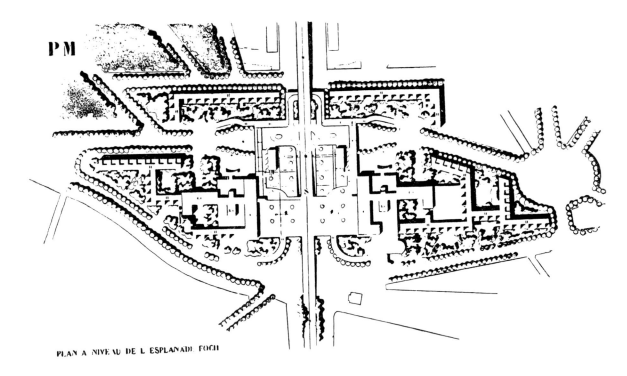

PLAN A NIVEAU DE L ESPLANADE FOCH

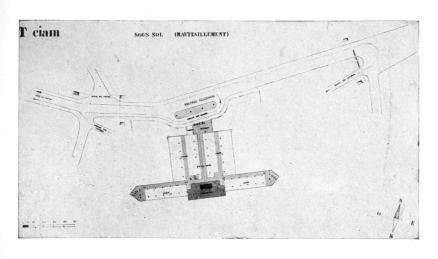

SOUS SOL (RAVITAILLEMENT)

at the level of boulevard Kellermann: where trucks unload (food supplies).

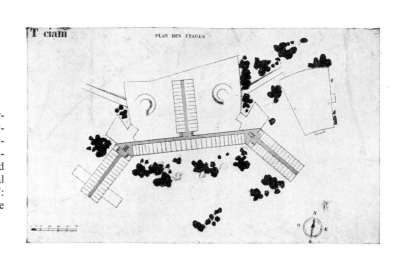

PLAN DES ÉTAGES

on successive floors: various groupings of apartments on the VR (Radiant City) principle. Above the pilotis: food supplies and communal services; below the roof: the school system; on the roof: heliotherapy.

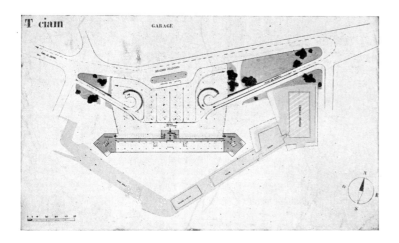

GARAGE

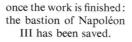

halfway up the substructure: automobile passage.

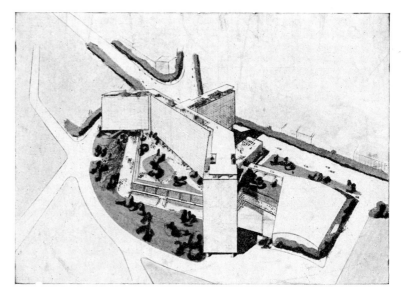

once the work is finished: the bastion of Napoléon III has been saved.

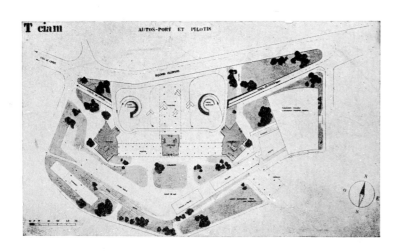

AUTOS-PORT ET PILOTIS

on the level of the bastion's crest: the grand esplanade beneath the pilotis; extensive view of the horizon and the zones of greenery which have been preserved. Sports: openair and indoor swimming pools, and sand beach.

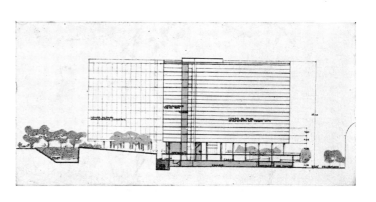

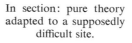

In section: pure theory adapted to a supposedly difficult site.

# 1937
# INT. EXHIBITION OF
# ART AND TECHNIQUE
### (BOULEVARD KELLERMANN ANNEX)
### HOUSING SECTION:
### "A MODERN WORKSITE"

And the idea is taken up once again, in 1934, submitted to the authorities, approved by the Trade Minister, by the Director for Fine Arts, by the Prefect of the Seine; then by the Paris City Council and by Parliament.

But in 1935: the wind is blowing the other way, etc. etc... What is to become of the idea?

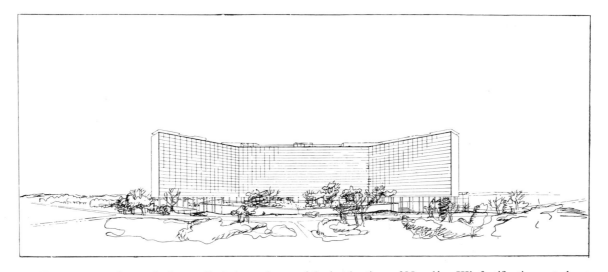

Realization approaches: a site is actually designated: one of the last bastions of Napoléon III's fortifications – today a 30-km stretch built up, filled in, vanished. More prominent than the others, this bastion had not yet been destroyed. *Piously*, we will preserve it; it will remain intact, with its imposing wall and its moat. We will save it – we who are accused of considering the past with contempt. Always, in all of our projects (Paris, Stockholm, Barcelona, Algiers, Moscow, and so forth), we have spared the worthy achievements. Better than that: we have pointed out what should be done to enhance them.

For our part, this international show would be the demonstration of a model worksite.

When all is finished, there will be "a housing unit" set in the middle of Paris, faithful to "Radiant City" criteria.

We have "depersonalized" ourselves, by asking the International Congresses for Modern Architecture (CIAM) to patronize this significant adventure.

This annex of the Exhibition: the *Home*, will be called La Tour de CIAM.

April 20, 1934.

The program includes thirteen headings:

Group    I: Concrete skeleton
—    II: Metallic skeletons
—    III: Façades – facings of all kinds, from opaque to transparent
—    IV: Isothermics
—    V: Sound-proofing
—    VI: Home equipment
—    VII: Vertical and horizontal traffic: people – goods
                telephones – mail
—    VIII: Communal services: hotels – labor – cleaning – restaurant – prepared dishes –
             food cooperative
—    IX: Child-rearing: – nursery – kindergartens
—    X: Hygiene: physical culture – hospitals – open-air and indoor swimming pools
—    XI: Leisure time: Sports: physical culture gymnasia – Library – club –
             popular art theatres – puppet shows
—    XII: Teaching
—    XIII: Historic CIAM exhibit: Frankfurt, Brussels, Athens
             (Architecture and city planning)

The planned buildings are large enough to house the above demonstrations *consecutively*, that is, next to one another, so as to make for conclusive reports.

SUMMARY: By organizing their part in the 1937 exhibition along these lines, the CIAM show that their aim is to furnish machine-age man with perfectly harmonized solutions to all problems touching on family life: the home, physical health, intellectual activity, and so forth.

This program implies extensive cooperation by technicians of all countries. The 1937 exhibition is really the appointed place for the gathering of creative energies. We felt that it would be particularly valuable for Paris to be the first city in the world to provide the occasion for a multiple study liable to lead to conclusions of vital social interest.

IN CONCLUSION: INDUSTRY ITSELF IS CALLED UPON, ITS COOPERATION REQUIRED. IN WHAT THE CIAM SECTION HAS CARRIED OUT, INDUSTRY WILL FIND NEW MANUFACTURING GOALS. AN ENORMOUS GOAL: THE HOME.

The home is a consumer article which is completely lacking everywhere, in every country. Thus, through its CIAM Section, the 1937 exhibition is sure to stimulate a magnificent double cooperation: industry, and the technicians of architecture.

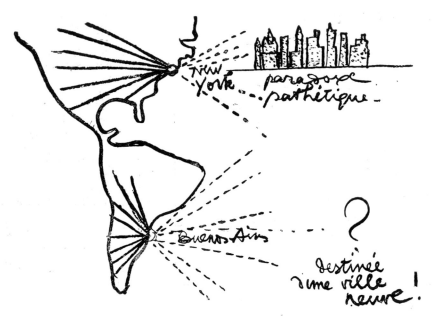

Sensing where countless causes of life accumulate – fateful geographic sites.

When you arrive in a city, or a country, or on a continent of which you know nothing; when the boat or the plane thrust you into a situation strongly marked by architecture and by city planning: if your mind is so formed that it rebels against academic classifications and naturally tends towards the construction of harmonious systems, then each sight which you discover and each system which is revealed creates a violent commotion within you; abruptly you cut across fine phrases and more or less beclouded explanations to come to the heart of the matter. You feel things accurately and you see clearly.

The The
Pacific. Andes. The hills and the Pampa. The site predestined for commerce.

After a two-week crossing, the New World, the lands of the Pampa would appear on the horizon and come to a sparkling head: the Business City of Buenos Aires.

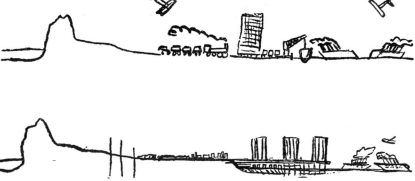

Yet here, on dry land, in Buenos Aires, there is no room.

But founded on rocks under the waters of the Rio de la Plata, the Business City could arise. (See *Précisions*, 1929, published by Crès in the Collection de l'Esprit Nouveau. New edition in 1960, published by Vincent, Fréal and Cie, Paris.)

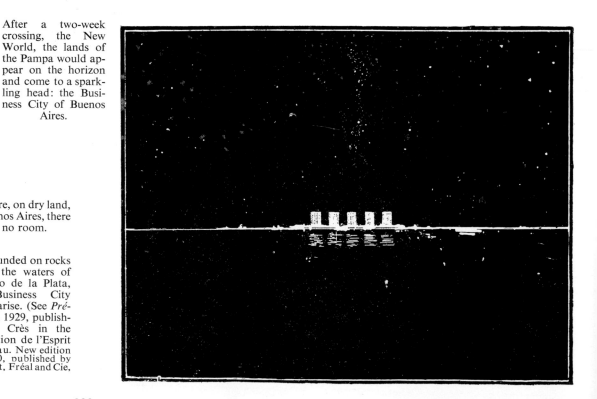

220

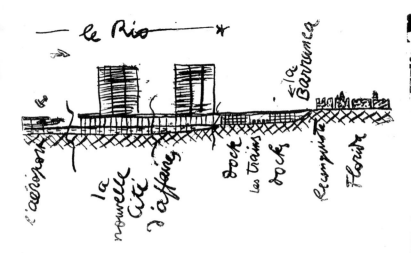

Sketch during a Buenos Aires lecture. "Ideas" can be expressed through diagrams.

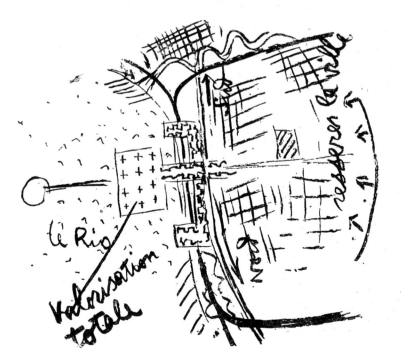

A battle of giants? No! The miracle of trees and parks reaffirms the human scale.

Buenos Aires, gigantic, protoplasmic, grown wildly in twenty years, must open the channels vital to urgent urbanization: waterway, railway; must reshape its cellular condition. Dictates of city planning.

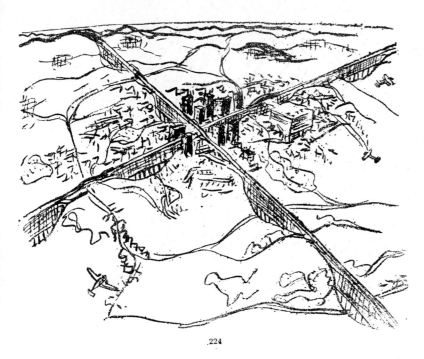

.224

The Prefect of São Paulo had told me: "We're lost; we don't know how to remedy the chaos of our city."
Answer: here is order.

Montevideo:
It would be so simple!
valorization,
efficiency,
architectural splendor!

This American trip, with its stopovers and its cities, and that emptiness of mind which the inertia of an ocean voyage creates, was an astonishing stimulant, a detector. Clear and clean-cut, ideas burst out "above the roaring crowd," above the day-to-day dilemmas; energy-ideas, nourished and fertilized by an already lengthy meditation on the state of architecture and city planning.

In Buenos Aires: "Your city is choking? Give it its vital axes, of deep and distant origin, in the hinterlands and the provinces. You have no land left at the critical point of concentration? Then take the sea, build on the water: there's nothing to it, it's easy."

In Montevideo: "Your topography is against you? Your old town slides down steeply to the port? There's no room? Then why not build artificial sites? And that labyrinthine, treacherous slope of streets not made for automobiles – get rid of it, lay out your great horizontal boulevard at the summit of your artificial sites."

In São Paulo: "You're completely tangled up in your valleys and your hills. You can't get across the city any more! Drain off your traffic! But do it from above, from up high, in the air above your city, where you're free!"

Rio and its enchanted offshore view! From the houses, no one sees it. There is no more land to build upon. Find communications? Open up new ways? Where? There are nearly a dozen bays, closed, isolated. If you walk through the maze of streets, you rapidly lose all sense of the whole. Take a plane and you will see, and you will understand, and you will decide.

This sketch, done in the plane: an idea is born.

Here a city planner of the classical school has once again proposed courtyards and corridor-streets.

223

Here you have the idea: here you have artificial sites, countless new homes, and as for traffic – the Gordian knot has been severed.

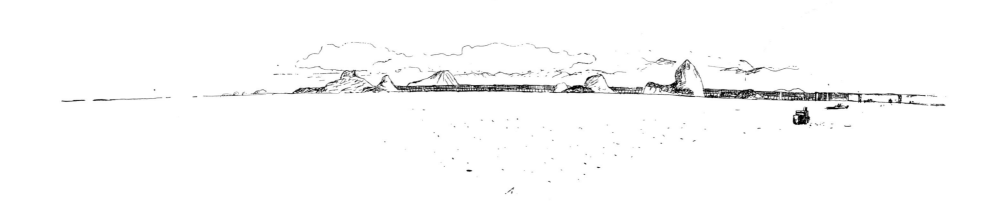

Architecture? Nature?
Liners enter and see the new and horizontal city: it makes the site still more sublime. Just think of this broad ribbon of light, at night . . .

In Rio de Janeiro: "You've no more land to build on? Your traffic is halted by each of those cliffs reaching down into the sea like so many fingers on the 'hand' of sheer-dropping mountains circling the bay?

"Create artificial sites, superimpose great numbers of them. Set yourselves up in the city, over the city. Glide above the city. Pillars of concrete, 'pilotis' will let you touch ground. Immediately you give new and mighty impulse to the city, you obtain immense benefits for it: you solve the problem of bay-to-bay, finger-to-finger communication. You place yourselves above the fingers that barred the way. There you are free, 100 meters above the ground."

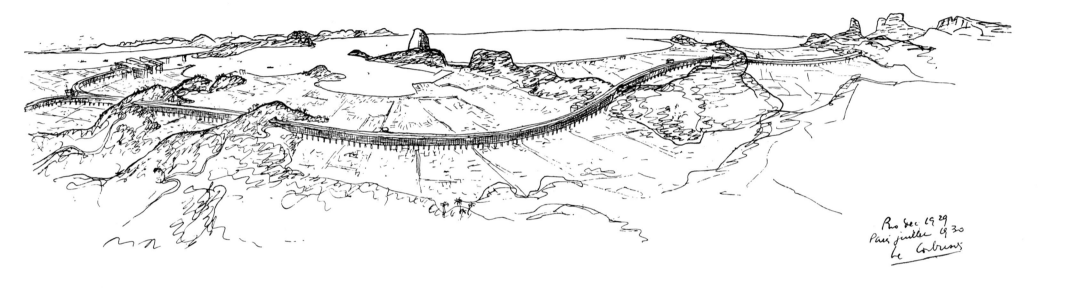

The viaduct highway elevation, 100 meters, launched from hill to hill above the city.

This is what is written on the plan:

"If you build 6 kilometers of highway at an elevation of 100 meters – highway carried above the built-up city by pilotis 40 meters high; the substructure up to a height of 60 meters is utilized as housing.

"6 km × 15 floors = 90 km of apartments.

"90 km 20 meters deep = 1,800,000 m² of apartments.

"If you allot each inhabitant 20 m² of living space you will house $\frac{1,800,000}{20} = 90,000$ inhabitants in the most favorable conditions you could dream of.

"If you rent this surface at 130 Francs per m² (as in Paris, for instance), there will be an annual income of 234,000,000 Fr which, at the rate of 10 %, is capitalized at 2,340,000,000 Fr and, at 5 %, by 4,680,000,000 Fr.

"Enough to pay building expenses – and do good business!

"This is how, through city planning, *instead of spending money, you can make money.*"

PROJECT "A" (PROJECTILE PROJECT)
1931

The Hussein-Dey district: the highway (elevation 100 m.) (houses 180,000 inhabitants)

ramp leading to

the seafront highway, elevation 10 m.

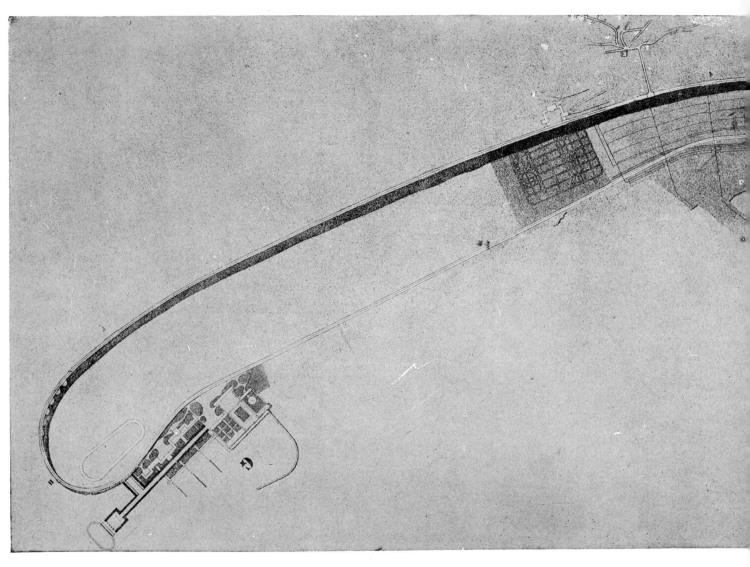

A new sports center and beach resort.

1931-1934: ALGIERS,

atic development of the merchandise harbor.

The highway
(elevation 150 m).
The *redent* of Fort-l'Empereur
(housing 220,000 people).

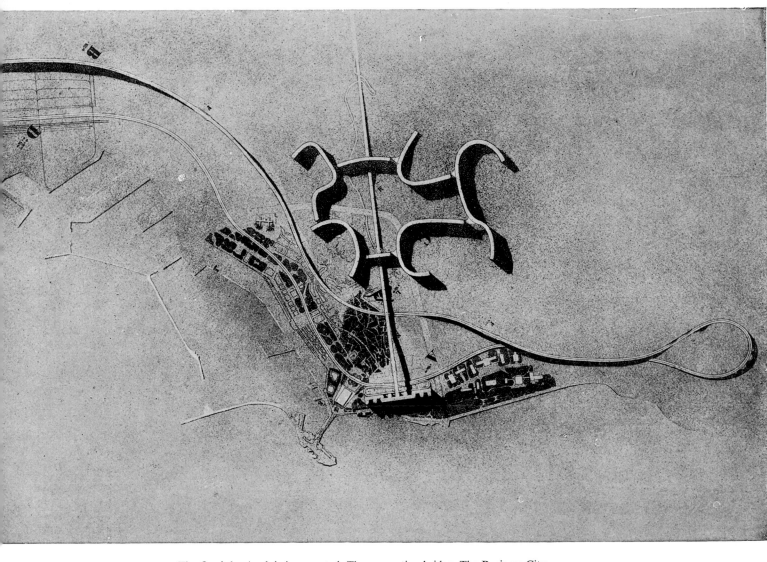

Saint-Eugène (outer district): Connecting ramp between the highway, elevation 100 m and the seafront, elevation 10 m.

The Quai des Anglais is respected. The connecting bridge. The Business City.
The new bus terminal.

# CAPITAL OF NORTH AFRICA

# LETTER TO A MAYOR:

TO MONSIEUR BRUNEL,
MAYOR OF ALGIERS.

"Paris, December, 1933

"With a firmness and broad-mindedness which have earned you as much admiration as envy, you govern a city of great destiny.

"The economy of the world is upset; it is dominated by the incoherence of arbitrary and harmful groups. New groupings, and regroupings, new units of importance must come into being which will give the world an arrangement that is less arbitrary and less dangerous. The Mediterranean will form the link of one of these groupings, whose creation is imminent. Races, tongues, a culture reaching back a thousand years – truly a whole. An impartial research group has already, this year, through the organ *Prélude*, shown the principle of one of these new units. It is summed up in four letters, laid out like the cardinal points:

$$\begin{matrix} & P & \\ B & & R \\ & A & \end{matrix}$$

Paris, Barcelona, Rome, Algiers. A unit extending from north to south along a meridian, running the entire gamut of climates, from the English Channel to Equatorial Africa, embracing every need – and every resource.

"Algiers ceases to be a colonial city; Algiers becomes the head of the African continent, a capital city. This means that a great task awaits her, but a magnificent future too. This means that the hour of city planning should strike in Algiers.

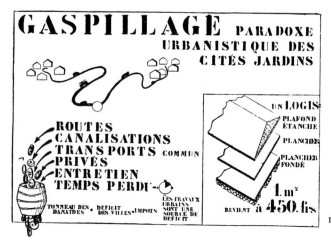

no comment

"Under your leadership, Monsieur le Maire, the problems have been outlined little by little. A group of civic-minded citizens – 'The Friends of Algiers,' led by the active and eminent barrister, Monsieur Rey – has begun investigating these problems, so new, often so misunderstood, so seldom set forth in their true dimensions.

"In 1931 this Committee did me the honor of urging me to come and talk to the public of Algiers about 'The architectural revolution achieved by modern techniques' and 'How the architectural revolution can solve the problem of urbanization in the big cities.'

"These lectures were held in the Casino's new auditorium. You yourself did me the honor of presiding over one of these meetings, and Mr. Peyrouton, Secretary-General of the Government (and now Governor of Tunisia), of presiding over the second.

"When I arrived in Algiers, the Honorable M. Rey urgently advised me: 'Whatever you do, do not talk for more than three-quarters of an hour: the people of Algiers are not used to keeping up with a lecturer longer than that.' I spoke for four hours, before a capacity audience. Three days later, I spoke again for four hours before a similar audience – except that this time, the corridors were filled with people who stood up to listen. For the people of Algiers realized that the hour of city planning had struck.

"Having thus established contact, and a very heartfelt one, with your city and its inhabitants, with the material conditions obtaining then and with the tendencies of the city's imminent development, I promised the 'Friends of Algiers' that – free of charge, of course – I would offer them an organizational plan; that, in a word, I would submit an idea.

"For over a year I worked on this idea, undertaking a thorough study of the question. In reality I sought not so much to adapt a plan to circumstances which were already present, as to discover how the city could and should be developed – along what lines, according to what order of size, according to the sorts of steps to be taken.

"Work like that comes under the heading of 'attack': you charge ahead, scouting for something, trying to determine where you direct your fire. Afterwards, you can control your fire.

"In 1933 I came back to Algiers to explain my plans.

"One must not labor under a delusion! You yourself, Monsieur le Maire, who were so courteous as to attend my talks, making a point of sitting in the front row – you told me: 'That's for a hundred years from now!'

"In my explanations before the public, I used clear drawings to set forth undeniable truths. But my listeners shook their heads as they filed out and concluded, 'If that were really so, and if it were possible, it would be done.'

"My project (a first step in coming to grips with so vast a problem), was a projectile project, intended to determine the line of fire.

"You will grant me this, Monsieur le Maire: when I came to Algiers for the first time, your administration had done a splendid thing: it had decreed complete demolition of the area called Quartier de la Marine. This meant that somewhere in the world, there would exist an entire and unencumbered site in the heart of a bustling city – a site available for any initiative which modern times should care to take. But no: the administration's agencies had also drawn up a plan by which, in place of the slums which crowded the Quartier at the time, blocks of apartment houses were to be built as custom demanded. On the very spot where Algiers could find the key to its urbanization problem, the administration (and the banks) had deemed it sufficient to replace housing units by other housing units.

"I did my utmost to show that something else was needed, that this spot was *the* site par excellence in Algiers. I urged: 'Here you must build a business city, the "City" of Algiers like the "City" of London, and here you must create highways, both seafront and perpendicular ones, to constitute the vital axes of Algiers.'

"Meanwhile, your city council appointed my worthy colleague, Prost, to draw up plans for the city's expansion. It named an engineer, Monsieur Rotival, to assist him. Now, M. Rotival – as he will tell you himself very nicely – is completely in favor of my ideas on city planning and seeks to apply them opportunely.

"So much has been achieved.

"Since then Algiers has received a number of other proposals. I myself, when you were in Paris last summer, took the liberty of delivering to you a reworked study of the 'City,' with the bus terminal and airplane taxi-station.

"Just recently, a Paris colleague, Monsieur Cassan, has submitted a plan calling for a seafront boulevard with a new harbor station and a bus terminal.

"Messrs. Prost and Rotival have conceived some bold solutions to the problem of linking the new Government Palace and city traffic.

"So efforts are being made, continuing and completing one another. Algiers is becoming a center of attraction. Plans are being offered on a different scale. We move from the old notions of city planning into modern times. My 1932 projectile project is no longer held to be valid only in the distant future. And today, boldly and faithfully pursuing the fundamental idea of my proposal, I am taking the liberty of submitting this 'City' to you once more – a City so vital, indispensable, a necessity for the near future, for right now.

"And in so doing, I maintain:

"That the Quartier de la Marine is situated on the very axis of the face of Algiers. As it stands today it is an obstruction which, until now, has split the city in two: on one side the Saint-Eugène district and on the other side, Hussein-Dey; the city is halved. It is decided that the obstruction should be removed (demolition of the Quartier de la Marine). But the administrative plan is to rebuild it. That is where the threat appears, that is the dangerous mistake. That is my reason for persisting, proposing.

"I say: on this site, a Business City. The financial profit to be derived from this operation seems certain (I am having it worked out in detail at this very moment). But the City idea is a 'compound' idea: if we let it, it will automatically make way for the conquest of the sites at Fort-l'Empereur.

"Monsieur le Maire, you know how thoroughly convinced I am that this thesis is right. I see in it the whole future of the city.

"If Algiers increases its population by another 100,000 or 200,000, where will it house these people? There is no more land left on the already crowded flanks of the cliff of Algiers! Well then, the city laid out as a Garden City? With those inhuman, time-consuming distances overflowing the fatal framework of the 24-hour solar day?

"Now listen: four hundred meters from the harbor of Algiers and therefore from its future harbor station (liners, planes, buses, railroads), four hundred meters away is Fort-l'Empereur, a site capable of accomodating 200,000 inhabitants. This land is at an elevation of 150 and 200 meters.

The air there is exquisite, the purest, the most healthful air (whereas the air down below, elevation 20 to 30 meters, is unhealthful). The view from Fort-l'Empereur is stupendous: one of the world's most remarkable sights: the Atlas, the Mediterranean, the Kabylia mountains. It is possible to build there in such a way that every housing unit benefits from these incalculable advantages. Speaking in 'city-planning' terms and therefore in 'human' terms, I have called these elements 'the basic pleasures.' By this I mean that air, light, space, and natural beauty, as they are felt at every hour of the day, of the season, of the year, of one's life are the advantages which take precedence over and dominate all others.

"Now, this land at Fort-l'Empereur, at the summit of the cliffs, can be reached only by using entirely new methods of urbanization. New methods but normal ones, easy, economical, reasonable.

"The two faces of a coin: heads, the 'City.' Tails, an area set aside for 200,000 inhabitants.

"Such is the proposal which I persist in believing favorable to the destiny of Algiers.

"With an important corollary:

"Unlike the muddle and jumble of a new residential area, the business city of Algiers does not cover even the fiftieth part of the available surface: 98 % of free land!

"At the very spot which constitutes the navigation axis for ships coming in from the open sea; on this cape, this prow, this nose on the face of Algiers, 98 % of the land is left free!

"This magnificent soil, on the historic site of Algiers, preceded by the Admiralty and the little port for pleasure craft, flanked by the Casbah (an adorable Casbah! which can be improved and which must never, never be destroyed!), led up to by the Arcades des Anglais – this soil, amidst the greenery of parks to come, can welcome the civic center which Algiers owes it to itself to create: Law Courts Financial Delegation, Employment Exchange, People's Hall, etc.

"Here is the trilogy:

"Civic center – 'City' – residential community at Fort-l'Empereur.

"Monsieur le Maire, you will admit that this idea is not for a hundred years from now. It is for the immediate present. As such, it can be tied in with the future solutions to problems which sooner or later Algiers, capital of Africa, southern point of the quadrilateral formed by Paris, Rome, Barcelona and Algiers, will have to take up.

"I still have hope of being heeded. I persist in my efforts with unshakeable conviction.

"With my most cordial good wishes,

LE CORBUSIER."

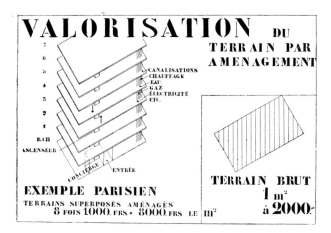

no comment

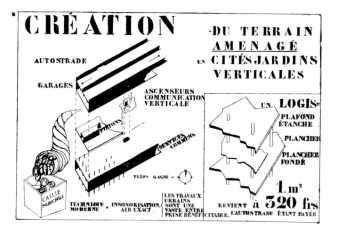

no comment

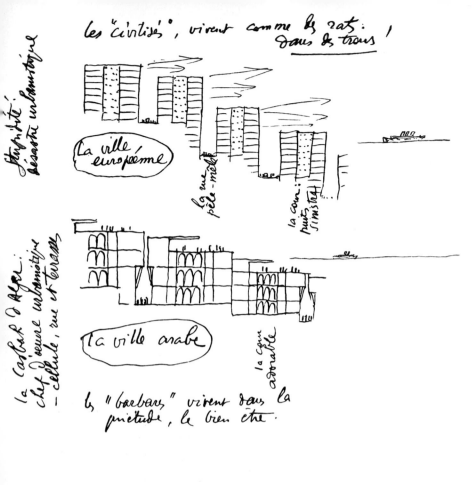

les "civilisés", vivent comme les rats. dans des trous !

stupidité désastre urbanistique

la ville européenne

la rue pêle-mêle

la cour: puits sinistre...

la casbah d'Alger: chef d'œuvre urbanistique — cellule, rue et terrasse.

la ville arabe

la cour adorable

les "barbares" vivent dans la quiétude, le bien être.

Pure and efficient stratification of the Casbah. Among these terraces which form the roof of the city, not an inch is wasted.

Harmful stratification (touching the walls of the Casbah itself) of the civilized houses: gutters and reverberating wells. Here is the problem backwards! Men have made streets, they have forgotten to make the homes!

## WITNESSES
### THE "BARBARIANS" SPEAK

O inspiring image!
Arabs, are there no peoples but you who meditate daily in the splendid sunset hours? Sky, sea and mountains. Beatitudes of space. The power of eyes and mind carries far.

See how, in the European city, the "civilized" people are holed up like rats in the deafening straits of stone!

O inspiring image!
Arabs, are there no peoples but you who dwell in coolness and quiet, in the enchantment of proportions and the savor of a humane architecture?

While the street is a channel of violent movement, your houses know nothing of it: they have closed the walls which face the street. It is within the walls that life blooms.

| the key | = the cell |
| | = men |
| | = happiness |

The street is only the bed for the rushing stream of passers-by.

O inspiring image! Arabs, you are at home within the hospitable and charming house, so clean, so measured, ample and intimate.

# WITNESSES

## THE VOICE OF THE DESERT

Since the doors of their houses are forbidden to us, we assumed that these cities were merely dried, sunburned crusts of beaten earth.

The airplane reveals to us a miracle of sagacity, of knowing and beneficent arrangements; within, living shells, as it were, open up to the luscious greenery of gardens. The elegant line of arcades reveals a genuine civilization in the midst of the land of thirst.

The aridity of rocks, pebbles and *pisé* (beaten clay and gravel).

An aerial view reveals sound biology, brilliant anatomy. This is Berrian, a city in the M'zab, surrounded by palm groves and stuffed with all the trees of paradise on earth.

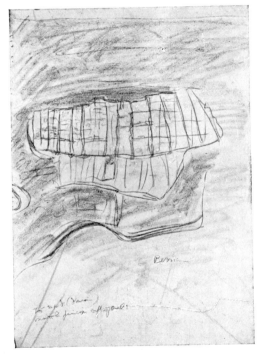

Hallway-street, nameless corridor, mute walls. Silence! But then, does something fine and beautiful go on behind such crudeness?

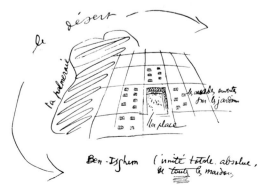

Ben-Isghem, another city in the M'zab. Such order, such decisiveness, such choice, such a sensitive instrument ready to serve man.

the key = the cell
= men
= happiness

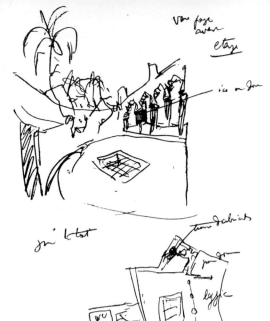

the silent street

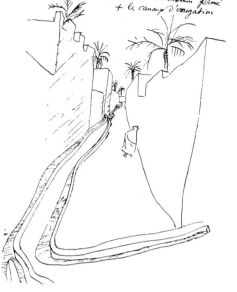

The layout of these houses has made them well-filled shells. No opening to the outside; all walls are party-walls. But within: a poem!

Each house is equipped in a standard way. Everything has been foreseen. In the spring, the Arab leaves the winter city, and 3 or 6 kilometers away he enters his summer house, in the palm grove, bringing with him only rugs and kitchen utensils. A masterpiece!

# WITNESSES
### THE MELODY OF THE OASIS

The palm grove of Ghardaia, summer residence, in the M'zab.

The roof of a house.

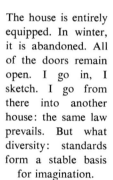

The house is entirely equipped. In winter, it is abandoned. All of the doors remain open. I go in, I sketch. I go from there into another house: the same law prevails. But what diversity: standards form a stable basis for imagination.

The garden of a house.

Whereas everything seemed to go against man: desert, stoniness, sun's infernal blaze, suddenly the most lilting melody is heard: architecture and paradisiacal verdure, streaming waters, coolness, flowers and fruit: palm trees, orange groves, apricot and pomegranate trees, green shadow and starry nights to worship, filtered through the date palms.

the key = the cell
= men
= happiness

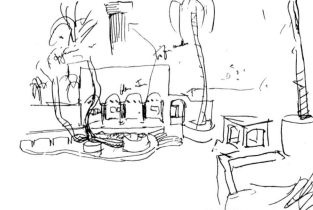

232

In the midst of trees, slopes, ravines, and sea, the Kabylia mountains appear. The ecstasy of natural splendors within reach of those who shall know how to attain them. Only 400 meters from the heart of the city!

For each house, the Arabs have conquered a view of the sea. The Casbah is nothing but an enormous stairway, a lofty gallery where thousands come each evening to worship nature.

The horizon at Fort-l'Empereur. As early as 1822, soldiers, who were forced to drag up cannon, built modern roads on a regular incline. These two winding roads are a giveaway: the rise is steep. Today, attempting to bring cars right up to the foot of their owners' houses is sheer folly: it means extending these zigzags. Yet that's what happens, what's allowed to happen! Algiers is a hopeless tangle.

*Drawing by Brouty.*

The horizon from Fort-l'Empereur.

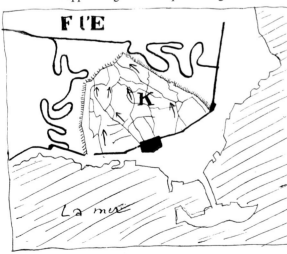

The soldiers of the French Conquest drew up handsome plans for the city. They knew how to plan. Today's Algeria, cities and villages, has these outlines of 1831 to thank. What has been done (or allowed to happen) in the last fifty years is pitiably shoddy, a denial of city planning.

F l'E: sites available at Fort-l'Empereur.
K: Casbah, where there are only steps, porters, donkeys and mules: *never a wheel!*

The sketch below demonstrates once and for all how the sites at Fort-l'Empereur can be conquered. Is the impossible possible? Yes! The Business City, 150 meters high; from there the viaduct (elevation 150 m.) which reaches the horizontal boulevard of the *redents*. Car elevators near the Business City. The boulevard of the *redents* is linked by elevators to the naturally uneven ground. Connection with the zigzagging footpaths.

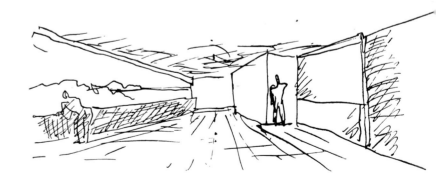

And this picture shows how the artificial sites to be created at the *redent* of Fort-l'Empereur can be used: terraces, hanging gardens, wide windows opening onto a dream landscape *conquered* through height. Do you still have doubts? Municipality, by creating the artificial sites at Fort-l'Empereur, up high, *in the God-given air*, you will open up a prodigious source of wealth, of *profit*. This will be manufactured money: healthy currency.

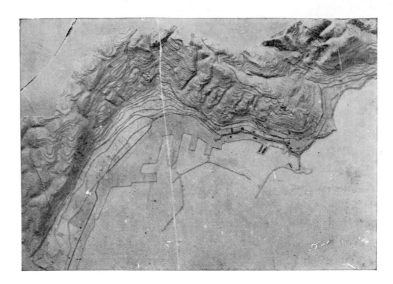

The Cliff of Algiers. We were the first to establish this relief map of the Algiers region. I say that any city councilman who looks at this relief map should recognize that never again will he copy Paris, nor Berlin, nor London, but that, building a twentieth century city, he will use modern techniques and leave the city free to welcome its real destiny. A similar relief map should be placed in every one of the offices dealing with the city's urbanization. At present they are content to study the problem on paper, on a flat surface, in a rebus of contour-lines . . .

The free but inaccessible lands of Fort-l'Empereur, 400 meters away from the harbor and the station.

The city of Algiers, crowded into its cliff-top space, dwindles hopelessly away into distant suburbs. The native and European communities make an unwonted and disorderly mixture, compromising the general economy of city planning. Here at Fort-l'Empereur, room for 220,000 inhabitants . . . if only the authorities will resolve to adopt the modern methods which will make its conquest possible . . .

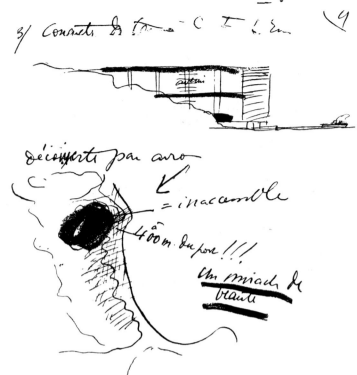

A treasure: the land
at Fort-l'Empereur.

The land at Fort-l'Empereur, in the very heart of the city.

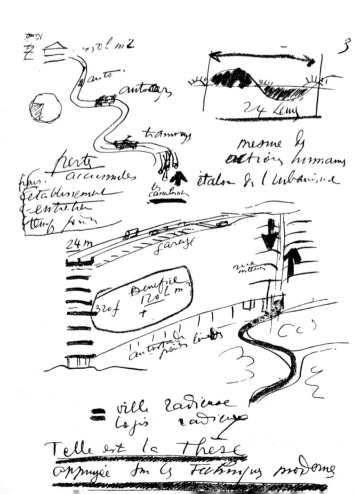

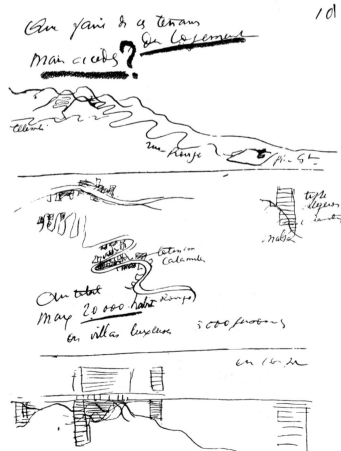

The great Project A highway, elevation 100 m., linking the two suburbs: Saint-Eugène and Hussein-Dey. You free the surface, you free yourself from submission to the cliff, and you house 180,000 people in optimum conditions, providing them with access to traffic.

If you urbanize in the ordinary way, you have a disaster. Given the impossible conditions governing access, you can't house even 20,000 people!

Conquest of the sites at Fort-l'Empereur:
1st step: on the side of the Quartier de la Marine, build the Business City.
2nd step: the connecting bridge, elevation 150 m.
3rd step: construct housing *redents;* artificial sites for 200,000 people.

Road
to
El-Biar

The housing *redent* at Fort-l'Empereur; the Business City

Everywhere else along the cliff, the mad meander of roads leading to the suburbs.

The seafront highway.

The highway, elevation 100 m.

# PROJECT "A" 1931-1932

### FIGURES FOR THE CITY COUNCIL'S FORECASTS

The preliminary project studied in March, 1932, includes the following:

1. Execution of a single highway 26 meters wide and 13,000 meters long, 10 meters above the ground.

2. Execution of a 14-story building 15,000 meters long, 26 meters wide, with a highway on the upper part.

3. Execution of a 31-story administrative building, with 22,000 m² of covered area.

4. Execution of other buildings, 23 stories high on the average, with an approximate covered area of 165,000 square meters.

The preliminary estimate submitted for this preliminary project is understood for a reinforced concrete skeleton with excavation of the footing blocks, set on ground with a resistance of 5 to 6 kgs. per cm², as well as for the execution of the highway terraces and pavements.

The average height between floors is 4.50 meters.

1. *Cost of material brought to the site.*

*a)* Each ton of super-cement . . .　360 Fr

*b)* Coarse sand, fine sand and gravel, pebbles, per m³ . . . . . . . .　52 Fr

*c)* Round steel reinforcing wires, % kg . . . . . . . . . . . . . . .　125 Fr

*d)* Framing and scaffolding wood, per m² . . . . . . . . . . . . . . .　500 Fr

*e)* Hollow rough-walling, 12 to 13 cm. high per ‰ . . . . . . . . . . .　1300 Fr

Why these curving forms at Fort-l'Empereur?

1. To view broad horizons in all directions;

2. To find the lowest-lying point on the undulating site, so as to increase the real volume of the buildings;

3. To respond to the landscape's invitation, an event of plastic creativity: response to horizons carries further; response to winds and sun is truer. A lyrical event. Of utmost importance, the climax of a rational procedure.

(The area enclosed by the *redent*, 1,200 meters × 800 meters, becomes a natural space once again, a landscape.)

> A city of Modern Times!
> Functional and
> architecturally splendid

PROJECT "A"

The highway, elevation 100 m.

The seafront highway.

The *redent* at Fort-l'Empereur.

The harbor station (the Casbah is visible; it has been respected).

The Business City.

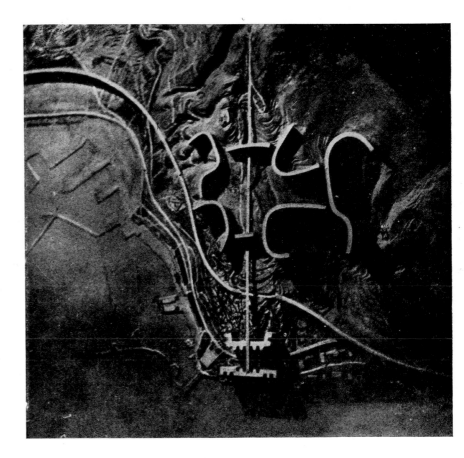

## 2. *Gross application prices*

### a) Reinforced concrete:

| | |
|---|---:|
| Cement 0.350 × 360 . . . . . . . | 126 Fr |
| Sand, gravel 1.250 × 52 . . . . . | 65 Fr |
| | 191 Fr |
| Labor . . . . . . . . . . | 55 Fr |
| Tool insurance . . . . . | 6 Fr |
| | 252 Fr |

Or 250 Fr per m³, on the average.

### b) *Round steel reinforcement wires*

| | |
|---|---:|
| ‰ kgs . . . . . . . . . . . . | 125 Fr |
| Losses . . . . . . . . . . . . | 7 Fr |
| Labor . . . . . . . . . . . . | 65 Fr |
| Tool insurance . . . . . . . . | 7 Fr |
| Per ‰ kgs | 204 Fr |

### c) *Framings*

| | |
|---|---:|
| Redemption of wood . . . . . . | 10 Fr |
| Labor . . . . . . . . . . . | 17 Fr |
| Tool insurance . . . . . . . . | 2 Fr |
| Per m² | 29 Fr |

### d) *Hollow rough-walling*

| | |
|---|---:|
| Bricks 12 × 1.30 . . . . . . . . | 15.60 Fr |
| Labor . . . . . . . . . . . . | 26. Fr |
| Tool insurance . . . . . . . . | 2.40 Fr |
| | 44. Fr |

| | | |
|---|---|---:|
| | Sum carried over . . . | 44. Fr |
| | Concrete 0.075 × 2.52 . | |
| Supplies | Steel wires 8.5 × 1.32 . . | 31.50 Fr |
| | Framings 0.6 × 1.0 . . . | |
| | Per m² | 75.50 Fr |

In view of various pressures, fairly short deadlines, installations, general expenses, taxes, etc., all of these elementary prices have been given an increase coefficient of about 2.

Thus for the 30-odd story building, for example, we obtain the following quantities per m² of flooring:

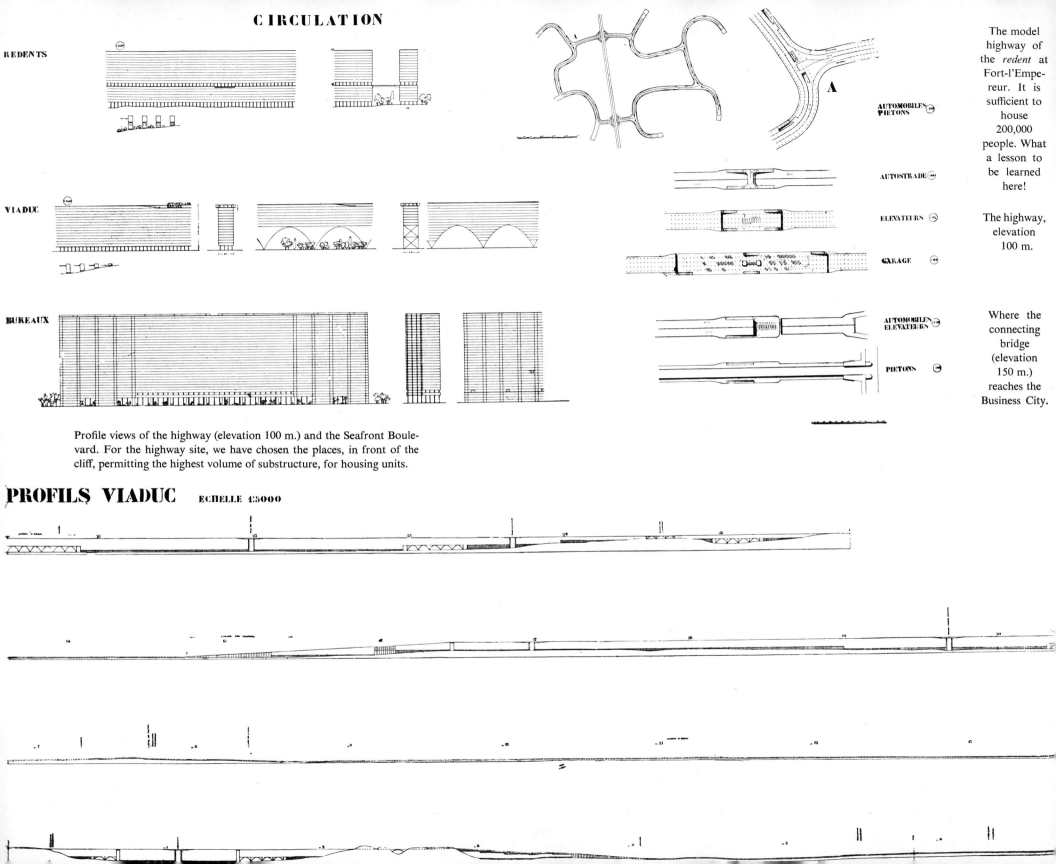

# CIRCULATION

**REDENTS**

**VIADUC**

**BUREAUX**

AUTOMOBILES
PIETONS

AUTOSTRADE

ELEVATEURS

GARAGE

AUTOMOBILES
ELEVATEURS

PIETONS

The model highway of the *redent* at Fort-l'Empereur. It is sufficient to house 200,000 people. What a lesson to be learned here!

The highway, elevation 100 m.

Where the connecting bridge (elevation 150 m.) reaches the Business City.

Profile views of the highway (elevation 100 m.) and the Seafront Boulevard. For the highway site, we have chosen the places, in front of the cliff, permitting the highest volume of substructure, for housing units.

# PROFILS VIADUC    ECHELLE 1:5000

LES BUREAUX
ECHELLE 1 1000

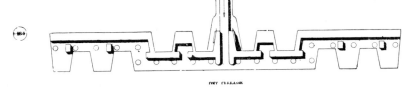

At the summit, elevation 164: cafés and gardens: what a stupendous view from up there!

Elevation 160 m: automobile distribution. In the center: big restaurants. In the wings: offices.

The garage beneath the skyscraper.

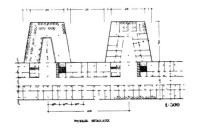

Elevation 156 m: garage for 400 cars.

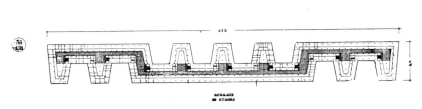

Example of divisions of office space: upper administrative echelons, individual offices, etc.

Elevation 38 to 152 m: model offices (all dimensions possible)

PROJECT "A"

Here, the Business City was conceived on too vast a scale.

---

Hollow rough-walling: 1 m²

| Average per m², for post, footing block and beam | Concrete ... | 0.170 m³ |
| | Steel .... | 22.65 kgs. |
| | Framing ... | 0.687 m² |

Excavations: 0.135 m³/m²

In this way we obtain the following unitary prices per m² of flooring:

| 1 m² hollow rough-walling, supplies included ........... | 75.50 |
| Concrete 0.170 × 250 ...... | 42.50 |
| Steel wires 22.65 × 2.04 ...... | (depends on quality) |
| Framing 0.687 × 29 ........ | 19.90 |
| Excavations 0.135 m³ × 12 .... | 1.60 |
| | 185.70 |
| | × 2,370 Fr per m². |

The other elements in the flooring on a 14- or 23-story basis have been calculated in an analogous way and yield results of this sort.

Obviously the coefficient of increased charges is extremely variable. The one allowed would certainly seem to be a *maximum maximorum*. It could perhaps be lowered to 1.40.

We attach the corresponding recapitulation.

### RECAPITULATION

1) *Single highway*, 13,000 meters long, 26 meters wide and 10 meters above the ground.
Average cost per m²: 1000 Fr.
Area: 13,000 × 26 = 338,000 m²
Approximate total cost: 338,000 × 1000 = *338,000,000* Fr.

2) *A 14-story building*, 15,000 meters long with a highway on the upper part. Average cost per m² of flooring: 330 Fr
Covered area: 15,000 × 26 = 390,000 m²

Cost per m² covered:
| 14 floors at 330 ....... | 4,620 Fr |
| Coating and watertightness | 50 Fr |
| Earthwork ......... | 30 Fr |
| Per m² | 4,700 Fr |

Approximate total: 390,000 × 4,700 = *1,833,000,000 Fr.*

(COST OF HOUSING 180,000 PEOPLE, INCLUDING ALL ROADS AND MAINS; THE 300,000,000 FR WHICH WOULD OTHERWISE HAVE HAD TO BE SPENT ON A SUBWAY SYSTEM ARE THUS ECONOMIZED.)

3) *Administrative building.*
Area: 22,000 m². Floors: 31.
Cost per m² of flooring: 370 Fr.

Approximate total cost: 370 × 31 × 22,000 = *253,000,000* Fr.

(IN PROJECT "A," THE BUSINESS CITY WAS CONCEIVED ON TOO LARGE A SCALE; IT IS REDUCED TO 100,000,000 FR IN PROJECT "C" AND, BESIDES, YIELDS A PROFIT OF 200,000,000 FR IN SITES MADE FREE FOR THE EDIFICES OF THE CIVIC CENTER.)

4) *Redents. Buildings.*
Covered area: 5,500 × 30 m = 165,000 m².
Average number of floors: 23
Average cost per m² of flooring: 340 Fr.
Approximate total cost: 340 × 231 × 65,000 = *1,290,000,000* Fr.

5) *Miscellaneous:* 36,000,000 Fr.

(COST OF HOUSING 220,000 PEOPLE, ALL ROADS AND MAINS INCLUDED.)

We obtain the following figures:

| 1° | 338,000,000 Fr |
| 2° | 1,833,000,000 Fr |
| 3° | 253,000,000 Fr |
| 4° | 1,290,000,000 Fr |
| 5° | 36,000,000 Fr |
| | 3,750,000,000 Fr |

(THE ABOVE IS A BUDGET TO BE STAGGERED OVER SEVERAL YEARS: FOR THIS SUM, THE CITY CAN HOUSE 400,000 PEOPLE, WITH ALL UPKEEP INCLUDED AND THE HOUSING AND TRAFFIC PROBLEMS GIVEN PERFECT SOLUTIONS.)

N.B. If American methods are used to carry out these projects – that is, a metal skeleton with special profile sections of steel, wrapped in concrete – the net cost per m² of flooring can be 25% lower.

*Technical and financial study carried out by the E.G.T.H. (Entreprises de Grands Travaux Hydrauliques, Paris), December, 1932.*

# VALORIZATION OF THE GROUND: AN EXAMPLE

We have adopted the principle of replacing the present fashion of horizontally extended garden cities by the construction of "*vertical garden cities.*" The horizontally extended garden city is a financial disaster for society; whereas *the vertical garden city yields an enormous profit for the community and for the municipality* (if the latter agrees to order that the necessary work be done).

ALGIERS: There is an almost inaccessible site, free of buildings, located in the heart of the city: the hills of Fort-l'Empereur (elevation roughly 150 to 220 meters). It is impossible to reach this terrain by streets with a normal incline of 5 to 10% or to arrive conveniently in front of apartment houses which would have to be built on plots shaped by the zigzagging of these streets. Using modern techniques we can reach these sites very easily – by means of a horizontal highway, elevation 150 meters. With room to house 220,000 people, these sites can be arranged so as to furnish superlative comfort (see the Plan). The prerequisite is to underwrite the preliminary expenditure for this horizontal viaduct, elevation 150 meters.

Here are conclusive figures: in horizontally extended garden cities, for the average family (6 persons), you count, let's say, 300 m², or 22,500 Francs; so housing 220,000 people means:

$$\frac{220,000}{6} = 36,000 \text{ families} \times 22,500 \text{ Fr of land} = 810,000,000 \text{ Fr.}$$

CONCLUSION: If it is valorized by a convenient approach (the most marvelous approach that Algiers could dream of), the presently sterile and therefore worthless land at Fort-l'Empereur *could be worth 810,000,000 Fr. If only the authorities would decree the execution of this project*, they would be able in this way to pay for the approach viaduct and wind up the operation with a profit, and all with the most reassuring simplicity.

\* \* \*

Another example of valorization of the ground: *Horizontal garden cities:* the indispensable elements of each living unit are: the flooring of the ground floor *with foundations*, an intermediate flooring, and a *waterproof* ceiling. The average cost of these three elements is 440 Fr per m².

*Vertical garden cities:* Concerning the Algiers project, let's consider the big highway, elevation 100 meters, linking Saint-Eugène and Hussein-Dey. On the ground, it provides for traffic under the pilotis of the viaduct; on the top (elevation 100 meters), it provides *a model highway 24 meters wide*, with a floor of garages beneath. The rest of the viaduct is formed by flooring which is superimposed every 4.50 meters and which actually constitutes *so many layers of superimposed floors of vertical garden cities*. These layers of flooring constitute what we have in the first (horizontal) case, that is: a floor with *foundations* and a *waterproof* ceiling, with optional provision for an intermediate flooring.

What is the cost price of this *standard element* of vertical garden cities? Calculations give us this answer: with the traffic beneath the piles PAID FOR AND THE UPPER HIGHWAY ALSO PAID FOR, the square meter of flooring costs 320 Fr.

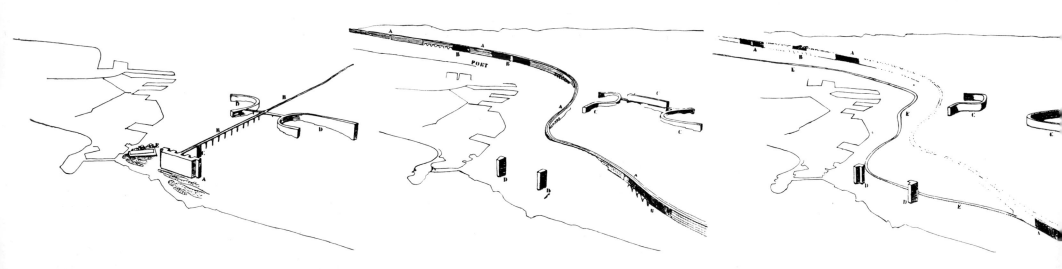

Construction of the four elements in the urbanization of Algiers.
Successive stages, over the years:
1) The Business City (A), first undertaking in the Quartier de la Marine. Then the connecting bridge (B). Then, substructure of two *redent* elements. Continuation of the road from the summit toward El-Biar;
2) Beginning the viaduct, elevation 100 meters. The platform at 100 meters is built; the substructures are raw, empty. Here and there, they are fitted up as housing units (B, second drawing). Up at Fort-l'Empereur, one housing volume (C) is erected, below the model highway. Etc.
3) Year after year, the substructures of the viaduct 100 meters are fitted up as housing units. The realization of the *redent* at Fort-l'Empereur is continued. Etc.

240

In the realization of this connecting bridge, application of the "Tensistruttura" methods invented by my friend Fiorini (Rome).

People of Algiers! Here we are on the highway, elevation 100 meters, driving along at top speed, looking out over a landscape that is sublime (because *we see it, having conquered it, having constructed it*). I am not deluding myself; but I say to you, people of Algiers, citizens of Algiers that, having erected this city of Modern Times for all the world to see, you would be proud, and happy!

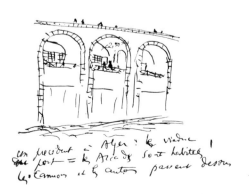

A precedent in Algiers: the Arcades des Anglais (see the photograph on page 234), which ever since their construction (about 1850) have sheltered a population of fishermen. Heavy traffic goes by above their heads: the biggest boulevard in Algiers is above their heads. Now, nothing here was conceived with particular efficiency for the housing of families. Whereas the viaduct elevation 100 meters is a model of housing under optimum conditions.

In July, 1934, guest of the Fiat factories in Turin, I find over the shops themselves at a height of 40 meters, the highway which was spontaneously conceived for Algiers. In 1920-21, in *l'Esprit Nouveau* I had hailed Senator Agnelli's noble conception for his Turin factory. Then, I had forgotten it. In 1934, I drove at high speed on the Fiat roof and observed that here the proof existed, for those who know how to see and understand.

241

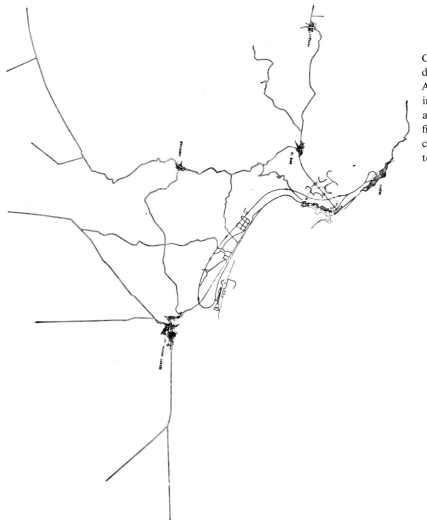

Going back to page 234, refer to the disturbing scale model of the cliff of Algiers. Here, on these two drawings, the future of Algiers is guaranteed. The city is pure, magnificent, healthy, light, swift. And the city is reattached to its region and to the major highways of Algeria.

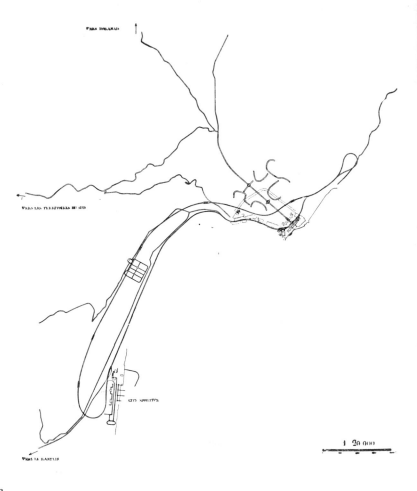

This is the flooring of houses in superimposed garden cities. So the square meter of housing in a superimposed garden city means a saving of 120 Fr over the cost of each square meter in a horizontal garden city.

All along the viaduct there are 4,500,000 m² of newly created superimposed sites; 4,500,000 × 120 Fr means profit of 540,000,000 Fr. *Such is the saving which can be realized through an urbanization based on the vertical garden city principle, as opposed to the principle of the horizontal garden city.*

To these profits, must be added the possibility of doing without a subway system, replaced by the highway (saving of *300,000,000 Fr*).

There remains the profit yielded by renting out an entire floor of garages, placed beneath the highway.

Such is the profit to be realized through the viaduct, which can shelter 180,000 people.

And *there remains another saving, hence another profit; the overall cost of the roads and approach streets* with all their upkeep, water, gas, and electricity installations, *which would have to be built for horizontal garden cities with a capacity of*

*180,000 people.*

It should be noted that the dwellings built in the viaduct (detailed studies have been made with strictest care) fulfill *optimum conditions for the city of Algiers,* hence for the inhabitants of the viaduct: *an admirable view of the sea or of the hills; immediate communication with the upper highway* (elevation 100 meters) *and the lower highway beneath the pilotis: the viaduct dwellings are located precisely where the most high-speed traffic is.*

Here, one question: Assuming that the highway (elevation 100 meters) should be built all at one time but that the intermediate floors of the vertical garden cities can be built later and fixed up as housing units as need requires over the years, could it be agreed that the treasury advance the sum necessary for the construction of the viaduct if, as security, there is a contract signed with the Municipality or the Government?

Forecasts are based on the possibility of having, in twenty years, to house a working-class population of 180,000 in optimum living conditions, and 220,000 other inhabitants in extra-comfortable conditions on the Fort-l'Empereur sites.

Here is the new Algiers. Instead of the leprous sore which had sullied the gulf and the slopes of the Saël, here stands architecture . . . architecture
is the masterly, correct and magnificent play of shapes in the light.

There are a multitude of arguments, just as valid, for urbanization of cities in a modern way, based on rational use of modern techniques.

This, for instance:

Opportune use of Glass-wall façade
      Open plan inside
      "Exact Respiration" (see conclusions reached by the Saint-Gobain Laboratories).

By applying these new techniques, we can *triple the normal depth of the apartments*, letting in daylight on both sides of the building (access to the apartments by an "interior street"). The façade will be one third as big.

Result: the street will be one third as long, the city will extend only one third as far.

Time saved, economy of 2/3 on means of transportation, on road construction and maintenance.

Etc. etc . . .

And this site at Fort-l'Empereur, which we will not disturb: views, mountains, Kabylia, violent movement of hills and ravines, lacework of pine trees, nobility of military ramparts . . .

Our grand *redent* will fit in here, like an airplane touching down onto the ground. And from the most modest ground-floor apartment (these sketches were done from the ground), to the superimposed villas at a height of 50, 100, or 125 meters, up in the conquered air, the basic pleasures will find here their most splendid expression.

243

52% of the surface covered by streets and courts!

52% of installation costs: sewers, water and gas mains, electricity, telephone; ballasting, asphalt or paving stones, sidewalks;

52% of daily upkeep;

52% of wasted surface, lost to consumption;

52% of the surface dusty, or dry, or terribly hot;

52% of traffic risks, of insecurity for the pedestrian;

52% of confusion, of sorts of traffic intermixed: trolleys, buses, trucks, cars, horses, pedestrians, children, old people, baby carriages;

 0% of greenery;

 0% of games;

 0% of sports;

 0% of well-being.

Such is the balance sheet of official custom and teachings!

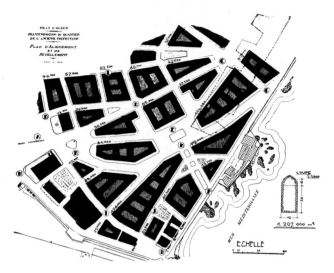

The administration's projects: Demolition and reconstruction of the Quartier de la Marine. This sector was an obstruction, cutting the city of Algiers in two. Dwellings are destroyed – but dwellings are rebuilt! The obstruction is put back in place! Corridor-streets, odd-shaped buildings. Catastrophe – typical of spineless proceedings!

Three events: 1) The worthwhile attractions of Algiers are safeguarded: the Admiralty point, the Casbah intact but cleaned up, the Arcades des Anglais (sole proof of an architectural conception – at the time of the French Conquest);

2) The disorder of the past fifty years which, little by little, is reabsorbed by the order of:

3) The construction of the city of modern times.

# CIRCULATION

This drawing is a lesson in nature, in urban biology: it expresses the network necessary, and sufficient, for the dazzlingly efficient traffic of a city with a population of 500,000 to 600,000. It shows what must be spent on public works, bridges and roads, to achieve the conquest of Fort-l'Empereur. This is enough, for 200,000 residents! Isn't it clear? What must be done, then, in order to convince people? On what must a reasoning be based in order for it to carry home?

Often, this is the answer: "It will be ugly!" (see drawing on page 241).

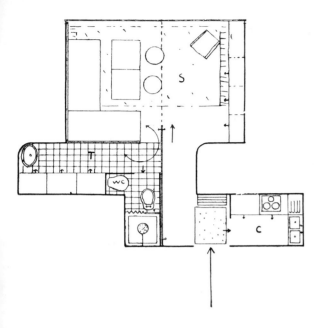

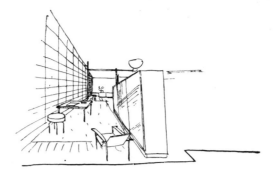

The advantages of the glass wall

Further study of the cell, 14 m² per person (see page 143) applicable to the housing constituted by the great viaduct, elevation 100 meters (see pages 144, 145 etc.); little by little, it can house 180,000 people. In recent years several other studies have been made of a similar subject and published in various magazines. They have resulted in establishing a new, efficient height for the home: 4.50 meters.

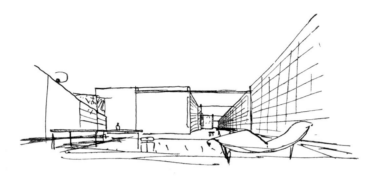

Independent skeleton,
open plan,
free façade.
Modern techniques leading to useful results.

The *redent* is curving because on an uneven terrain, the curved form means that the lowest point can be found and that consequently, the highest volume of structure can be attained. Curved, the *redent* is better able to embrace distant horizons. Curved, it contributes architectural eloquence and supple power, crowning the landscape with dignity.

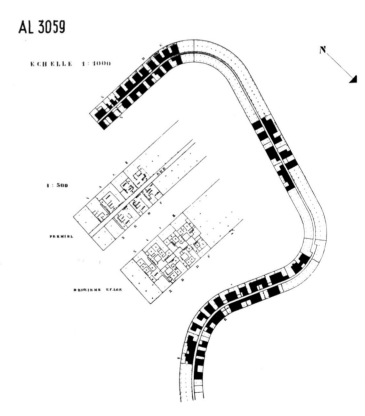

AL 3059

ÉCHELLE 1:1000

1:500

PREMIER

DEUXIÈME ÉTAGE

N

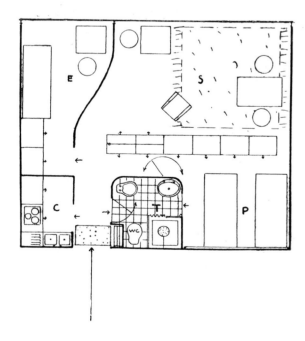

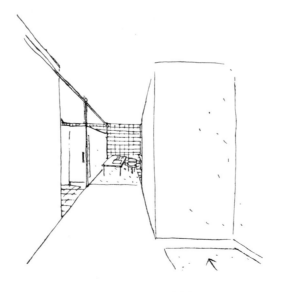

A fragment of "curved *redent*," Fort-l'Empereur type. No trouble with the reinforced concrete, the stakes are to be set once and for all along a curved alignment: each floor fits neatly above the others. Whereas, the "artificial sites," to be sold, are orthogonal; the houses, villas are squared. There is no faulty section.

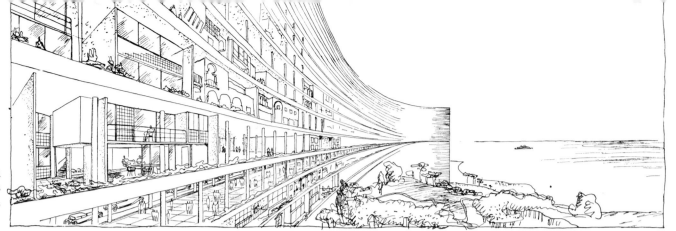

Sites are put up for sale, on every floor: sites with 10 meters of façade, or 15, or 20, or 30, with or without garden.

Here are "artificial sites," vertical garden cities. Everything has been gathered here: space, sun, view; means of immediate communication, both vertical and horizontal; water, gas, etc. thriftily supplied; ideally simple sanitation – sewers, garbage pails, etc. The architectural aspect is stunning! The most absolute diversity, within unity. Every architect will build his villa as he likes; what does it matter to the whole if a Moorish-style villa flanks another in Louis XVIth or in Italian Renaissance? The uneven terrain reached without effort, without difficulty. Footpaths wander over the very hilly

ground. Cars come, on the level, along this unique and perfect highway, abundantly furnished with garages below.

The artificial lots are created first: highway + floorings of the substructure. And these sites are put up for sale as villas with garden and limitless view. Then, the operation continues, with successive layers of superstructure.

In this way some 220,000 people will be housed "royally" at Fort-l'Empereur, gradually, as the need arises, and there each architect will plan each villa in whatever way he likes.

# AL 3342

# CITÉ JARDIN EN HAUTEUR

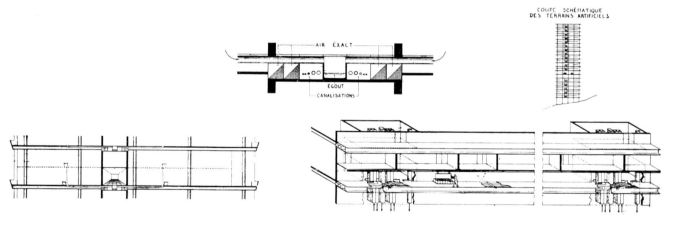

VOIRIE DES RUES INTÉRIEURES SUPERPOSÉES.

UTILITIES IN THE SUPERIMPOSED INTERIOR STREETS

Does there exist, in any city in the world, a system of roads and mains as perfect as this? As economical, as easy to reach? All of the pipes are accessible: perfect distribution of perfect air.

Garbage collection. What savings, what a reform compared to the senseless waste of horizontal garden cities. A miracle worked by reinforced concrete and steel.

The plan of the villa: main floor with patio and garden; upper floor opening onto the patio.

One example: a very small villa on a 15 m. × 12 m. site (180 m²).

People of Algiers, is there in your city even one apartment providing these basic pleasures?

Actually the most luxurious of first-class steamer luxury. But there is an even more amusing irony in this. In this plan, on the inaccessible land of Fort-l'Empereur we see that the principles

heights, the patio opening on to a garden surrounded by high walls, the view of the sea. Now, *that* is good regionalism!

M. BRUNEL,

Mayor of Algiers

ALGIERS

Monsieur,

"... When you did me the honor of visiting my studio to look at the plans which I had worked out in order to establish general directives for the urbanization of Algiers, I had the distinct impression (moreover, you did not disguise your feeling) that you thought these ideas worthy of better times; that is, of the future; that is, of some distant moment which you felt could be postponed for one hundred years.

"Let me say to you, Monsieur le Maire, that this opinion does not coincide with present reality. The events which should bring an indispensable equilibrium to contemporary society cannot be deferred for one hundred years but must be immediate, since right now there is complete imbalance between an all-engulfing machine age and man's total lack of adaptation to these new conditions of existence.

"No point in stressing the idea further, but I will take the liberty of saying to you now, from the very bottom of my heart, and also with utter awareness of a technician's responsibility, that the plans which I have conceived for Algiers are plans for today, and not for tomorrow. These plans for valorization can procure huge financial profits for the community, whereas in modern times, anytraditional concept of urbanization can only

entail ruinous expenditures, yielding neither profit nor an adequate solution.

"My project for Algiers is nothing more than a basic project. If one decides to look ahead and not behind, one can examine it with a critical sense of the circumstances and begin a fruitful and efficient study of precise local conditions, both technical and financial. It will also be possible to look for solutions, which although partial, tend toward the same goals, open up the era of major works, launch the true plan for Algiers and thus constitute not an entire operation but a first step, which can be followed by a second, then a third, a fourth, and so on.

"Monsieur Brunel, let me tell you plainly: every day the reality of the study which I have pursued ever since your visit is confirmed. This 'Utopia' must not be greeted with a shrug of the shoulders, when the truth is that it could become reality simply through a governmental decision.

"Through my city-planning studies, carried out for various capitals throughout the world, I have always urged: courage, enthusiasm and action. For I feel that the world today, and the nation in particular, are sunk in the most alarming period of inertia, the most dangerous period of stagnation. This age is heavy with portent. *By building*, you can direct events toward the solution and toward joy for some time to come.

"Please forgive me for having spoken so freely. I know how much you love Algiers and for that reason I tell myself that if, in spite of everyone, you change your first impression, you will agree that there are forces which it would be good to put to work, especially when they are disinterested. My disinterestedness where Algiers is concerned

is such that I offer my plans to the city of Algiers."

●

*Paris, December 10, 1932*

M. le Maréchal LYAUTEY

5, rue Bonaparte,

PARIS (6e)

Monsieur le Maréchal:

"... Modern techniques, an understanding of the spirit of the times, knowledge of the contemporary social milieu – all of these have led me naturally, and irrevocably, to solutions which, as I am well aware, go against certain extant legislation (some of it a thousand years old), and cut across certain sometimes secular regulations.

"The plan must rule; it is the plan which is right, it proclaims indubitable realities.

"Why are people frightened by it, why don't they want to carry it out?

"Because of deep-rooted customs and, especially, because of fear and laziness.

"As for customs, the law can transform them. As for fear and laziness, the government could get rid of them and could do something marvelous: *arouse*

*enthusiasm*. Arouse enthusiasm in every country and put an end to our doubts. And finally, give constructive purpose to our courage.

"We are filled with courage, we are valiant, but the authorities whose task it is to guarantee the nation's happiness believe that they can guarantee it best by leaving the dust of the past undisturbed. At certain moments such quietude becomes tragic and when you look at Algiers or at Paris and when you see the impasse looming up, is it madness or sanity, to want to do something about it?"

●

*Paris, December 10, 1932*

M. PEYROUTON,

Secretary General of the Government
(now Resident General of Tunisia)

ALGIERS

Monsieur,

"... I have written to the Governor and to the Mayor. I am considered mad. I am certain of being absolutely realistic and perfectly right. I express modern times: is that a crime? People try to make me believe that; I will never agree.

"You who are at the very center of Government, help us! There is a whole group of young people of Algiers who

are on my side and who want to see their city live.

"In a word, do we agree to be beaten beforehand? The defeat of those who dare nothing! Or, do we agree to set out to conquer something, certain of taking a giant step and of speaking, at long last, the language of our times?

"I could write you fifty pages, I will merely ask you this: help us!"

●

*Paris, December 14, 1932*

M. Justin GODARD,
Public Health Minister,

PARIS

Monsieur le Ministre:

"... I ask this question on behalf of Algiers:

"Is it a matter of indifference that, thanks to a conception counting on modern techniques:

a) 200,000 persons can be housed in optimum conditions concerning hygiene, view, sunlight and traffic?

b) 50,000 employees can work under optimum conditions with the advantages of silence and light, sunshine and view?

c) about 180,000 people (the harbor's working-class population) can live in the best possible conditions as to comfort and hygiene, and directness of access to the most vital sorts of traffic, etc.?

"And that these three operations, which represent the city's imminent growth, do not cause a deficit such as all traditional urbanization efforts entail but rather, a financial operation of such balanced efficiency that all the costs of exploitation, expropriation, collective improvement, contracts, etc., are actually paid for by the profits of the whole?

"We all know with what energy you have taken up the problem of the city dweller's hygiene and happiness. It is generosity which leads you forward in so arduous a task. It is my very firm belief that there is work to be done in Algiers. This work would solve the housing problem under optimum conditions for 200,000 people and, most important of all, *the era of large-scale public works* would begin at last. Algiers could become the point of departure for the indispensable transformations which all big cities today require.

Modern techniques will rescue them from the misery into which the machine age has plunged them."

●

*Paris, December 14, 1932*

M. CARDES,
Governor General of Algeria,

ALGIERS

Monsieur le Gouverneur,

"... The city planning of modern times is made totally helpless today by the weakness of the authorities.

"Louis XIV and Napoléon had foreseen and commanded. Today Paris is choking, coming to a standstill and

rotting where it stands. Weakness on the part of the authorities, ignorance of contemporary city planning, unawareness of the prodigious resources afforded by modern techniques. Rather than dare anything, critics prefer to clutch at the forms of an already vanished equilibrium. Rather than preverse the dust of lifeless ruins, I propose to take action.

"Acting, I bring plans drawn up by a technician. These plans bring equilibrium to today's big urban populations. The solution is immediately termed utopic by people who are determined to undertake nothing whatever. It is true that this solution, this plan delivers an ultimatum. It becomes evident that regulations, sometimes of a secular nature, are henceforth invalid. It becomes evident that notions which sometimes date back several centuries are incompatible with a normal and harmonious evolution. Above all it becomes evident that people are afraid to imagine, to undertake, to act, to invent and innovate, and that faced with all of these factors, and ignorant of the technical facts of the matter, the authorities prefer to mark time, so as to run fewer risks. And so a democratic inertia reigns over the nation, a

nonsensical situation causing anxiety, disturbances, rebellion and sadness.

"My studies of city planning have led me through the techniques of the machine age, through sociology and economics, through questions of finance, to this crucial and decisive point: the authorities.

"Today, one can dream of only one man: Colbert.

"Act, undertake, achieve.

"Monsieur le Gouverneur, the aim of my letter is simply to tell you that I am entirely at your disposition and that I should be happy to be of some use. I say this in all simplicity, without any fancy phrases, and because I love my era, which is a great era, and because it deserves to make an impression otherwise than with the proofs of negation by which we are crushed and strangled everywhere today."

●

The BANK, concessionary of the demolition and reconstruction of the Quartier de la Marine, replied:

"I am
acquainted
with M. Le Corbusier.
I value, I even admire what
he does. But I do not wish to
receive him. I cannot receive him.
For if I were to receive him, he
would be capable of convincing me. And I haven't
the right to be
convinced!"

**TACITUS: "HISTORIES"**

LXXVI. *While these fears made him hesitate, the other legates and his friends strengthened his will; at last Mucien, after a great many secret talks, determined to speak to him publicly in these terms: "All those who take it upon themselves to decide important matters should consider whether their undertaking is useful to the State, glorious to themselves, easy to realize or at least not too difficult; at the same time it must be determined whether he who gives advice is ready to share the risks; and finally, in the event that fortune favor the undertaking, to whom is accorded the supreme honor. Well then! I summon you to empire, Vespasian: is it for the salvation of the State? does it further your* glory? *that depends on you, after the gods. And you need not fear that I have adopted the mask of flattery: it is an insult rather than an honor to be chosen after Vitellius. It is neither against the over-sharp mind of Augustus, nor against the cunning old age of Tiberius, nor against the solidity which the long possession of empire imparted to the house of Gaius, Claudius, or Nero, that we rise to do battle. You made way even for the ancestors of Galba. But to lie any longer in torpor, and abandon the republic to those who wish to sully and undo it, would appear to all as apathy and cowardice, even if servitude were not as unsure for you as it is dishonorable.*

The die is cast!

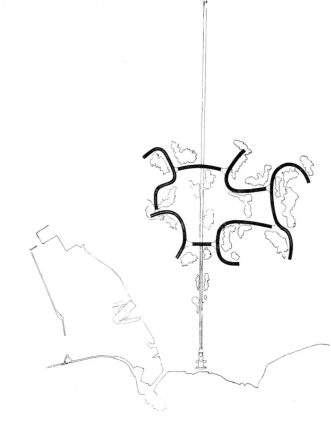

The territory of Fort-l'Empereur.

PROJECT "B" 1933 brought a new solution: the Business City in the Quartier de la Marine. The bus terminal occupied a part of these lands which had been freed. The connecting bridge toward El-Biar, across the *redent* of Fort-l'Empereur, was conceived according to Fiorini's "Tensistruttura" process. In the harbor, next to the harbor station, was a mobile landing platform for airplanes (last stage before the airport at Maison Carrée).

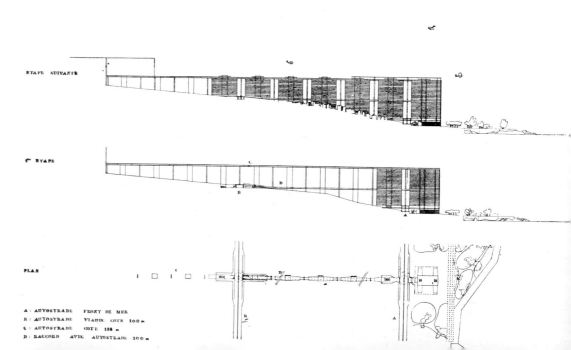

ETAPE SUIVANTE

1<sup>re</sup> ETAPE

PLAN

A : AUTOSTRADE FRONT DE MER
B : AUTOSTRADE VIADUC COTE 100 m
C : AUTOSTRADE COTE 158 m
D : RACCORD AVEC AUTOSTRADE 100 m

The *redent* of Fort-l'Empereur, as a "Green City."

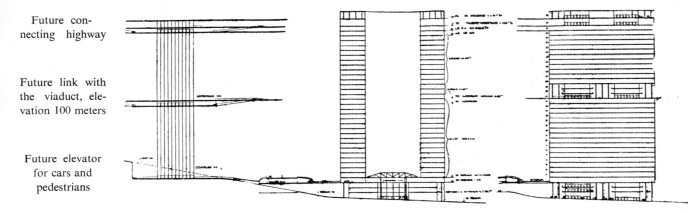

Future connecting highway

Future link with the viaduct, elevation 100 meters

Future elevator for cars and pedestrians

The artificial sites of the Business City

**PROJECT "C"** (1934) is, this time, a formal proposal sent to the City Council of Algiers on March 20, 1934. I was told: "You want to upset everything in Algiers." Here I reply: Project "C" is strictly limited to the operation now being carried out, the demolition and reconstruction of the Quartier de la Marine. It does not overstep those bounds by so much as one square centimeter. But it provides Algiers with the fundamental, essential elements of its civic life: the civic center. Here are the sites which I make available, here are the organs which I create, here is the money which I produce, here are incoming sums and no longer the bottomless hole of expenditures.
The future? Preparations have been made! The years can come!

The Hall, the Business City's Forum. And a view of the roads before the harbor, view of the Saël; a dazzling promenade. I appeal to the calm judgment of the people of Algiers.

# ADVISORY NOTE TO THE CITY COUNCIL

PARIS, March 20, 1934

To the City Councilmen
To Monsieur le Maire
City Hall,

ALGIERS

Messieurs:

I have the honor of submitting to you the Project which I have drawn up, Project "C", for the urbanization of the Quartier de la Marine, in Algiers.

I was not commissioned to do this study; may I remind you, however, that in 1931 THE FRIENDS OF ALGIERS asked me to submit my ideas on architecture and modern city planning to the people of Algiers. My lectures, delivered at the Municipal Casino and presided over by your Mayor, M. Brunel, and by M. Peyrouton, then Secretary General of the Government, were so successful that I was encouraged to draw up a general plan for the city's urbanization.

This project was not meant to be applied directly to specific cases in point but rather, to determine how the urbanization of the city could be undertaken on the basis of its peculiar and extremely complicated topography. This first project was submitted to the city during the city-planning exhibition in 1933 and through its publication in a great number of Algerian, French and foreign magazines.

The preliminary project, Project "A," was soon followed by Project "B." They showed the need to count on a synthesis of wide-ranging enterprises and to adopt new and larger scales in thinking "urbanization."

I believe I am right in saying that Algiers took this advice to heart since a proposal for a *Gare*

*Synthètique* (a multi-purpose station), appearing to answer these new needs, was quite recently submitted to you.

My Project "C" is an independent unit but one which can be linked to further urbanization tasks that will undoubtedly be required.

1) Project "C" is concerned solely with the Quartier de la Marine. It takes into consideration only these factors:

a) a distinctly limited site

b) a connection with the future multi-purpose station

c) its complete adaptation to the finance mechanism which you adopted when contracts were signed with the Real Estate Authority (Régie Foncière).

Its only innovation, then, is the technical plan itself.

2) It is apparent that the financing of Project "C" cannot be compared with that of any solutions considered until now.

Through the use of modern techniques, it allows the land in the Quartier de la Marine to be occupied in an entirely different manner, creating sizeable financial resources.

3) Project "C" answers the city's urgent organic needs, by creating a BUSINESS CITY. For how is it possible to picture the future of Algiers, destined to become the head of Northern and Equatorial Africa, without acknowledging the need to arrange a district fully equipped to expedite all of the transactions which will become the very *raison d'être* of the City of Algiers? To let little office blocks and business buildings spring up all over the city's present surface, among the residential areas, would be

a serious error since the demolition of the Quartier de la Marine offers an exceptional opportunity to group all such premises in one spot, with all of their technical resources, apparatus and organization: THE BUSINESS CITY.

Furthermore, the site of the Quartier de la Marine is extensive enough to include edifices whose construction or whose reconstruction will sooner or later be indispensable to a future Civic Center. Let me suggest: the Trade Tribunal, the Employment Exchange, the Financial Delegations, Chambers of Commerce, and so forth.

Isn't this an unhoped-for stroke of luck? This certainty that henceforth the Civic Center can count on the land it needs, at the most propitious place in the city?

If you agree to the idea of creating a Civic Center on the present site of the Quartier de la Marine, available next to the site of a future Business City, then you cannot deny that the city's land will have been put to use in the best possible way, since the very vitality of the city will be represented by buildings erected right at the crossroads of all contacts, which is also the site disposing of the finest view.

Finally, the Quartier de la Marine, if put to use in the way mapped out by Project "C", will become an incomparable architectural monument visible to all travelers approaching Africa from the open sea.

4) *Description of Project "C":* The documents submitted are as follows: Al 3,228, AL 3,229, AL 3,230, AL 3,233, AL 3,244.

Plan AL 3,228: The Roads of Algiers, from the Harbor Station to the Bab el Oued district. The Business City is located on the northwest edge of the Quartier de la Marine (6), and includes an immense Seafront Esplanade 300 meters long and 80 meters wide.

The BUSINESS CITY covers 1 hectare (2.47 acres). About 7 hectares remain available for distribution among the future edifices of the Civic Center.

Plan AL 3,233 suggests a way of parceling out the site to provide for the construction of the Palace of Justice (area built upon: 3,000 m²; lots: about 9,000 m²). Financial Delegations (area built upon: 1,700 m²; lots: 3,300 m²). People's Hall (area built upon: 4,700 m²; lots: 15,500 m²). Trade Tribunal (area built upon: 1,900 m²; lots: 4,500 m²). These structures give on to the Place du Gouvernement (whose

character has been preserved), on the one hand and, on the other, on to a boulevard linking the Place du Gouvernement and the great Seafront Esplanade. This boulevard serves the Palace of Justice and faces the searoads between the two existing Mosques.

The breastworks which today hide the two Mosques almost entirely are cleared away; the Mosques would thus be reset in their original décor at the foot of the Casbah and on the shore, and would be of the greatest historical interest.

Project "C" joins the future multi-purpose station to the Business City by a highway located at mid-height on the seafront arcades. This highway runs in between the two Mosques, then below the future Palace of Justice, only to rise to the level of the mezzanine of the Business City. After which it dips down again to join the present network of streets in the Bab el Oued district. It goes without saying that this highway is intended for greater things: in the future it could be extended both north and south to constitute the Seafront Boulevard which this city needs.

Thanks to this highway which will absorb automobile traffic and will, in the Square Aristide – Briand in front of the Opéra, be linked with the rues Constantine, Dumont – d'Urville and d'Isly, the important Boulevards de la République and Carnot will be freed of traffic. Wide sidewalks could be laid down before the arcades; between these sidewalks and the parapet, the city could plant a colorful tracery of flower beds and thus bring new life to its ancient arcades.

Finally, a corollary to the project shows how the lower parts of the Casbah could be improved if the rue de Chartres were widened and the rue de la Lyre made to open on to the Civic Center. Between the rue de Chartres, which is elevated, and the modified rue Bab-Azoun, which is on the same level as the Quartier de la Marine, there would be room for institutions serving the native population.

5) *Financial estimate pertaining to the project:* An outline of the financial operation to be foreseen when the time comes to reconstruct the Quartier de la Marine will be found in the "Financial memorandum, annexed to Project "C" for the urbanization of the Quartier de la Marine in Algiers."

The question is very simple. I have always felt that it would be most detrimental to the future of Algiers to plan on building apartment houses on the Cap d'Alger (Marine sites); intelligent urbanization should enhance the value of such a choice location. Project "C" arrives at financial conclusions that will certainly catch the attention of the authorities.

This Financial Memo merely mentions the super-profit to be made from the possible sale of the 7 hectares of land available for the Civic Center (page 3 of the Financial Memo).

The authorities of Algiers are in a good position to estimate what this profit could amount to. The 7 hectares can be sold for 2,500, 3,000 or even 4,000 Francs per m².

6) *Conclusion:* Having studied Algiers' case for three years, I have reached a certainty: I have the honor of submitting to the City Authorities drawings which express the essence of the technical and architectural project. These documents include the presence of the proposed multi-purpose station and the subsequent development of the Quartier de la Marine, the two in a perfect technical and architectural relationship. In this way Algiers would be assured of possessing the constituent elements of an important city: the edifices required for its administration and for its work.

All that remains for Algiers to do is to make a close study of the housing problem. In no way is the solution to these problems endangered by Project "C." On the contrary: Project "C" paves the way for the further urbanization of Algiers.

Should the Authorities of Algiers and its Technical Advisers wish additional explanations, I hope they will feel free to call upon me.

Believe me, yours very truly,

LE CORBUSIER.

●

PROJECT "C"

# SURVEY IN ALGIERS

Questions put to specialists in real estate operations in Algiers:

*a*) Sums to be had through renting the proposed installations?

*b*) What are the city's requirements as to office space?

RESPONSE:

Memo on "LA MARINE"

The Business City includes

| a ground floor | Shops | 2,628 | m² | | |
|---|---|---|---|---|---|
| elevation 166 | Cafés-Terraces | 3,490 | m² | | |
| hall lofts | Shops | | | 6,118 | m² |
| | Restaurants | 5,256 | m² | | |
| elevation 160 | Restaurants | 4,522.50 | m² | 9,778.50 | m² |
| mezzanine | Stores | | | 2,436 | m² |
| mezzanine | Garages | 4,800 | m² | | |
| elevation 100 | Garages | 3,116 | m² | | |
| elevation 156 | Garages | 5,272.50 | m² | 13,188.50 | m² |
| floors 1-16, 20-30 | Offices | 103,140 | m² | | |
| floors 18-19 | Offices | 7,600 | m² | 110,740 | m² |
| | | | | 142,262.50 | m² *(sic)* |

We group the ground-floor shops and the café-terrace together; for they seem to us to be worth about the same. Hard to judge. We charge 250 Fr per year per square meter. It is possible that the beginnings of the Business City will not justify such a price. Rents could then be lower, with gradual built-in increases. In fact, once the City is full, rent will rise beyond our figure.

We place the shops and restaurants of the hall's lofts and the restaurant (elevation 160 m) at the same price, 150 Fr per year and per square meter. Of course the latter will increase in value as time goes on, but not so easily as the really indispensable restaurants lower down. There too, leases with built-in provision for price revision.

The stores, it seems to us, are worth 100 Fr per m² per year.

We assume that the section has mistakenly placed offices on elevation 100 m (where the highway comes in), so we ascribe the area of these premises to the heading "Garages". The total garage area is more than 13,000 m², which we expect to house 1000 cars a month, at 100 Fr each, or 1200 Fr each per year. This will show how moderate our estimates are. The fact that, until the highway is built, the garages on elevation 100 m and elevation 156 m cannot be used affects our estimate very little or not at all. Their rental as office space gives roughly the same figures.

To office space we apply the figure of 100 Fr per m² per year. We suppose that the division into offices would come to about 100 Fr per m². An interest rate of 10% of this amount increases the rent per m² by 10 Fr per year, so that the overall price, once the division has been made, comes to 110 Fr. This price is purposely low, compared with prices in the few office buildings Algiers has already. The Hall of Agriculture, on the boulevard Baudin (Guiauchain-Perret) was rented out on the basis of 130 to 140 Fr per m² per year, and is completely full. The Bernabé building, also on the boulevard Baudin: 150 Fr per m² per year, is also full. The Garcia building (on the corner of the rue de Constantine and the rue Joinville), with higher rent, is full.

But three factors must be taken into consideration:

1) The need to attract tenants quite quickly with an intentionally low rent.
2) Unquestionably, the present business center is closer to the boulevard Baudin than to the place du Gouvernement. Which is why all the notaries, who used to have their offices near the place du Gouvernement, have moved toward the Main Post Office.
3) Office or store space which is badly situated or hard to reach is going begging at the present time. We have a fair amount of such unused space.

So we arrive at the following figures:

| | |
|---|---|
| Shops, cafés-terraces: 6,118 m² × 250. . . . . . . . . . . . . . . . . . . . . . . . . . . . . . . . . . . . | 1,529,500 Fr. |
| Restaurants, shops: 9,778 m² × 150. . . . . . . . . . . . . . . . . . . . . . . . . . . . . . . . . . . . . | 1,466,775 Fr. *(sic)* |
| Stores: 2,436 m² × 100. . . . . . . . . . . . . . . . . . . . . . . . . . . . . . . . . . . . . . . . . . . . . . | 243,600 Fr. |
| Garages: 1,000 cars × 1,200. . . . . . . . . . . . . . . . . . . . . . . . . . . . . . . . . . . . . . . . . . | 1,200,000 Fr. |
| Offices: 110,740 m² × 100. . . . . . . . . . . . . . . . . . . . . . . . . . . . . . . . . . . . . . . . . . . . | 11,074,000 Fr. |
| TOTAL | 15,513,875 Fr. |

Or, in round figures, minus annual expenses:

FIFTEEN MILLION FRANCS

PROJECT "C"

batteries of
elevators

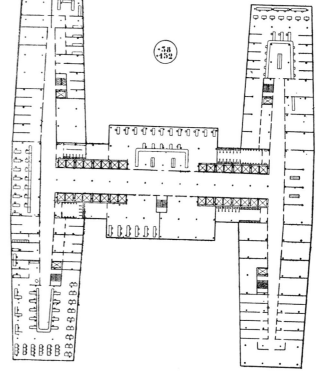

entrance with
elevators

limitless
office
installations

Ground-level plan

Upper floor plan

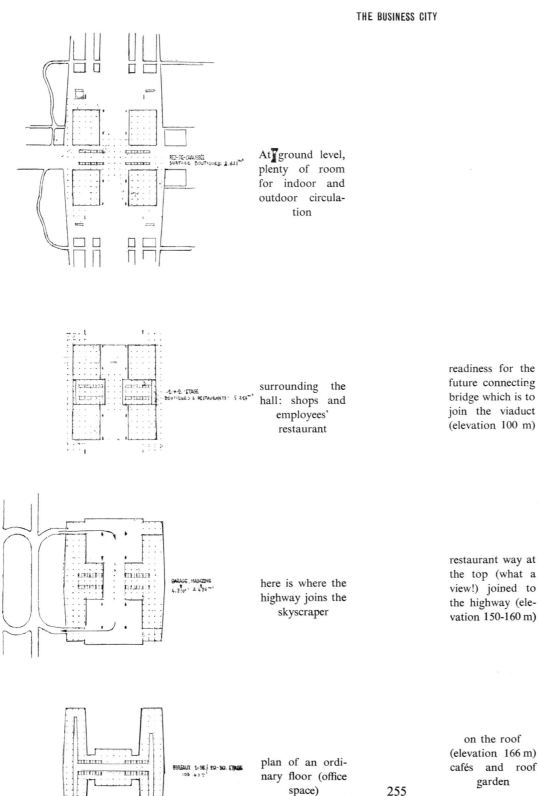

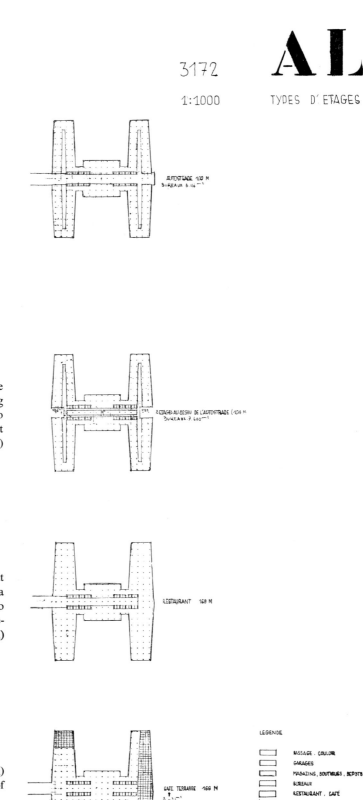

At ground level, plenty of room for indoor and outdoor circulation

surrounding the hall: shops and employees' restaurant

here is where the highway joins the skyscraper

plan of an ordinary floor (office space)

readiness for the future connecting bridge which is to join the viaduct (elevation 100 m)

restaurant way at the top (what a view!) joined to the highway (elevation 150-160 m)

on the roof (elevation 166 m) cafés and roof garden

255

According to your sketches, we feel that of the 12 hectares involved in the plans for urbanizing "la Marine," 7 hectares are used in a way nearly analogous to the way suggested by the Régie Foncière; analogous, that is, as to yield, but far superior as to pleasurable aspects. The skyscraper involves 5 hectares of land, and their cost must be added to the cost price of the skyscraper. On the basis of very approximate and unendorsed information, it appears that the cost price of the sites in the Quartier de la Marine would be, at most, 1,600 Fr per m². So the sum of 80,000,000 Fr must be found. Thus, if the skyscraper costs 100,000,000 Fr, its total cost price comes to 180,000,000 Fr.

A sum of 180,000,000 Fr which yields 15,000,000: that means a profit of 8.3%. With a rate as high as this, and estimates as moderate as ours, the operation is practicable. Even supposing, for instance, that we had 50,000,000 Fr of excess expenditures and extras, that would still leave us 6.4%, which is higher than the ordinary rate on a municipal bond issue.

We have fixed this estimate for our own sake, for it is impossible for us to give an exact answer to your second question. We have no idea at what rate the administration assesses the sites reserved for public buildings. Probably each case has to be treated separately. For "la Marine," the assessment would vary between the cost price of the land, with cost of completed roads and mains deducted (about 2,500 to 3,000 Fr per m²), and the price an expert can give for the urbanized land (4,000 Fr?).

As for your last question (b), for a basis of comparison we can refer to what the City of Algiers has built, and absorbed, as office space between 1929 and 1934.

| | |
|---|---|
| (French) Government........ | 18,000 m² |
| SHELL.................... | 5,000 m² |
| STANDARD (upper part).... | 2,000 m² |
| GERMAIN buildings........ | 2,000 m² |
| LEBON Co ............... | 5,000 m² |
| BERNABE building......... | 2,000 m² |
| Hall of Agriculture.......... | 3,000 m² |
| BLACHETTE House........ | 1,000 m² |
| GARCIA House............ | 3,000 m² |
| Miscellaneous buildings...... | 3,000 m² |
| TOTAL.... | 44,000 m² |

(These figures are relative. It is very hard to judge what portion of these buildings is lived in and what part is rented out as offices.)

So, between 40,000 and 50,000 m² of office space absorbed by Algiers. From these figures must be deducted the empty, badly situated apartments freed by the occupation of these offices, especially in the Government building.

So the skyscraper would have to be built in two stages, separated by a five-year interval. It might be good advertising to build the first half to full height: this would immediately show people how daring the whole idea is. Or else, build the whole building up to elevation 100, which would cost less.

But we feel that there is no need to build in two stages. All of it must be built, right away. The country's demographic development (a paradox for a classical economy) justifies our optimism.

J-P. FAURE AND LAFON

February, 1934.

FINANCIAL MEMORANDUM ANNEXED TO PROJECT "C" FOR THE URBANIZATION OF THE QUARTIER DE LA MARINE IN ALGIERS AND SUBMITTED TO THE CITY COUNCIL OF ALGIERS

1) Construction of a Business City.

2) Seafront esplanade.

3) Future erection of public buildings to fulfill the city's pressing needs.

1) *Business City.*

2) *Esplanade.*

The Business City includes the following premises:

| | |
|---|---|
| Offices......... | 110,700 m² |
| Garages, for 1000 cars...... | |
| Stores ...... | 2,436 m² |
| Restaurants and shops........ | 9,778 m² |
| Shops, cafés and terraces....... | 6,117 m² |

The Business City covers an area of 8,000 m² on the ground floor, and 5,272 m² on the floors above.

The construction cost, including rock-bed foundations, comes to 80,000,000 Fr; let's round off at....... 100,000,000 Fr.

This figure includes the skeleton, the façades, the tiled or parquet floorings, heating, and all of the communal services: water, light, telephone, telegraph, elevators, passages, etc... Interior partitioning will be incumbent upon each tenant; it can be made of any material and in any way the tenant likes, since the whole construction is borne by posts.

To the cost of the building must be added the cost of the land and of the surrounding esplanade which will set it off: about 15,000 m² for the building and the immediate area, 35,000 m² for the esplanade which, at the *cost* price of land in the Quartier de la Marine, would be on the basis of 1,600 Fr per m²........... 80,000,000 Fr.

Total cost price of the Business City...... 180,000,000 Fr.

This operation leaves some 7 hectares of land available as sites for various other buildings.

*Profit derived from the operation.* The prices on which the following calculation is based are minimal, and even below the average prices in Algiers today.

We figure:

| | |
|---|---|
| Offices......... | 100 Fr per m² yearly |
| Garages......... | 1,200 Fr per car yearly |
| Stores ......... | 100 Fr per m² yearly |
| Restaurants, shops ......... | 150 Fr per m² yearly |

Shops, cafés, terraces at 250 Fr per m² yearly. So the foreseeable income from rent would be:

| | |
|---|---|
| Offices......... | 11,074,000 Fr |
| Garages......... | 1,200,000 |
| Stores......... | 243,000 |
| Restaurants, shops......... | 1,466,775 |
| Shops, cafés, terraces......... | 1,529,500 |
| TOTAL......... | 15,513,275 Fr |

This income represents 8.3% of the cost. Even if building expenditures amounted to 50,000,000 Fr more than our expectations and the rate were consequently reduced to 6.4%, this rate would still be higher than that of an ordinary municipal bond issue.

3) *Sites available for public buildings in the civic center.*

Plan AL 3,233 suggests a *possible* apportionment of the site:

|  | Area built upon | Lot |
|---|---|---|
| 1) FINANCIAL DELEGATIONS...................... | 1,649 m² | 3,300 m² |
| 2) TRADE TRIBUNAL............................. | 1,902 m² | 4,580 m² |
| 3) PALACE OF JUSTICE.......................... | 3,273 m² | 8,728 m² |
| 4) PEOPLE'S HALL................................... | 4,706 m² | 15,510 m² |
| Employment Exchange, Chambers of Commerce, Produce Exchanges | | |
| 5) TERRACE WITH RESERVE PARKING LOT....... | 9,681 m² | |
| 6) NORTH-AFRICAN COMMERCIAL OFFICE WITH EXPOSITION.................................. | 5,674 m² | |

Number (6), located on the right of the Business City, and beyond the Quartier de la Marine, represents an outlook for the future.

By selling these sites to the proper authorities, a *super-profit* can be made, thanks to the way Project "C" conceives the urbanization of the Quartier de la Marine.

It is hard for us to estimate accurately the price that the authorities involved will be willing to pay for the sites of their future buildings. For the Quartier de la Marine, estimates would vary between the cost price of the land, with the cost of completed roads and mains deducted (about 2,500 and 3,000 Fr per m²), and the price an expert can give for the urbanized land (4,000 Fr per m²).

## MEMORANDUM

Is it wise to plan on building 110,000 m² of office space in Algiers?

A local survey reveals that new offices have been built as follows in the five-year period just ended (1929-1934):

| | |
|---|---|
| (French) Government........................................... | 18,000 m² |
| Standard (upper part)......................................... | 2,000 m² |
| Germain buildings............................................ | 2,000 m² |
| Lebon Co.................................................... | 5,000 m² |
| Bernabé building............................................. | 2,000 m² |
| Hall of Agriculture.......................................... | 3,000 m² |
| Blachette House............................................. | 1,000 m² |
| Garcia House................................................ | 3,000 m² |
| Miscellaneous buildings...................................... | 3,000 m² |
| TOTAL.................... | 39,000 m² |

This represents nearly half of the building program which must be mapped out for the future.

We feel, therefore, that the Business City can be built right away (in two stages, if necessary).

The country's demographic development justifies our optimism.

## COROLLARIES

Project "C" includes two important corollaries.

a) Developing the border area between the Casbah and the existing rues Bab-Azoun and Bab el Oued.

b) Linking the present square Aristide-Briand with the future highway which is to serve the harbor station.

c) Creating the highway relieving the harbor station, leading into the Business City and joining the coast toward Oran.

a) The existing rue de Chartres would be widened on its seaward side. The difference of level here could be used to advantage for the erection of a *redent* of big buildings to overlook the landscaped area which is part of the overall plan for "la Marine" and the space cleared away from it.

These big indented *(en redents)* buildings could be used by the Arab population for stores, offices, meeting halls, etc. In the gardens located on the level of the place du Gouvernement, Arab cafés could be set up, sheltered by arcades or peristyles.

This would also link the cathedral directly with the place du Gouvernement by a garden-lined route that would leave the bishopric as it is.

The last improvement of the Arab city would be accomplished by clearing a space around the two Mosques near the harbor. The cliff face which formerly surrounded the Mosques could be virtually re-created, so that the heavy breast wall which completely hides them today could be taken away.

Once the Quartier de la Marine and the immediate area are installed in this way, they will constitute a general civic center, effecting a properly nuanced liaison between the European city and the Arab city.

b) A one-way ramp starting at the Opéra would absorb all traffic coming from the lower quarters of Bab el Oued and from the rue d'Isly by way of the rue Dumont-d'Urville and lead this traffic with utmost smoothness right onto the highway which relieves the harbor station. This would free the boulevard de la République and the boulevard Carnot to become a magnificent garden spot, a seafront promenade whose crowning glory would be the arcades that offer passengers such a beautiful sight as their boat approaches the city.

c) Monsieur Cassan's proposed harbor station, which seems to be on a suitable scale, would be given clearance toward Oran by the creation of a mid-height highway running between the two Mosques and slowly rising to an upper level at right angles to the Business City; from there it would dip down again to leave the city in the direction of Oran. This highway is a new version of an idea presented by the earlier projects "A" and "B." Both of them felt that a Seafront boulevard stretching from Saint-Eugène to Hussein-Dey was indispensable. Facing the spot where the ramps of the place de l'Opéra open onto the highway, there could be a revolving platform for taxi-planes, built to the same measures as the Navy uses for its aircraft carriers. This location is currently reserved for big steamers; but in the future it would harbor private craft. So the shoreline of Algiers, all the way from the new sites planned for the City Hall to Bab el Oued, will become a genuine composite achievement of city planning with unquestionable architectural grandeur.

## A SUPER-PROFIT

(The figures used in this memorandum come from the study made by Messrs. Lafon and Faure, of Algiers, who of course point out that their figures are only approximate – and frankly pessimistic.)

The estimate was made by a very big firm which has already counted a margin of 80,000,000 Fr: this has been rounded off at 100,000,000.

The cost price of the Business City also includes the vast Seafront Esplanade which will be Algiers' finest ornament; this Esplanade accounts for 80,000,000 Fr worth of land.

In addition, we have further assumed that costs have been underestimated to the tune of 50,000,000 Fr more.

Even so, it is apparent that the operation would yield a profit of 6.4%.

In all truth we can say that the originators of Project "C" took the gloomiest possible view of the situation.

Resources, on the other hand, are calculated at a very low level; *the project's authors have even confined themselves to pointing out only the super-profit which could be realized by the sale of the sites which will remain available in the neighborhood of the Business City and the Esplanade. This land would be all of a piece, measuring about 7 hectares.*

*These 7 hectares can be sold, to whatever agencies or groups are interested, at prices ranging from 2,500 to 4,000 Fr per m²: in other words, they are worth between 175,000,000 Fr and 200,000,000 Fr.*

A glance at the administration's proposal suffices to show that in streets and courtyards alone, it *wastes 52% of the land; moreover, this absolute waste of land wastes money as well, for road building and upkeep of roads and mains.*

So, a modern urbanization proposal taking advantage of modern techniques speaks for itself, financially; whereas the urbanization proposal based on old methods forgets that the present day has new means at its disposal and new needs to satisfy.

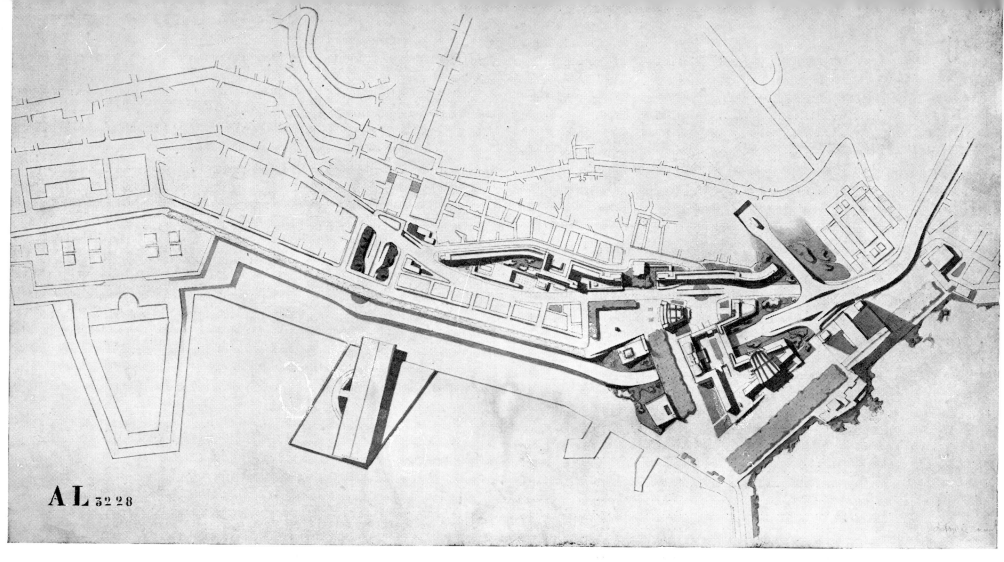

## PROJECT "C"

The new multi-purpose station proposed by Messrs. Renaud, engineer, and Cassan, architect, in 1934. The scale model is shown below, and the site is shown at the lower left of our drawing above. At last! a healthy reaction against the administration's urbanization proposal. Here is an idea on the proper scale!

Here is Algiers' Quartier de la Marine; located on the "forehead" (the axis) of the city's face, it gives the city a complete civic center. Thanks to classification of its elements, there is abundant room without disorder. The pedestrian rules the ground: esplanades, promenades, boulevards. Cars speed along to their destination. The shoreline of Algiers is on the scale of modern times. A symphony of architecture played on a natural stage.

The two Mosques, obscured today. will be seen in their original setting,

Like a sentinel, the old Arab palace forms a sharp contrast with the pure prism of the Business City.

The public became very interested in Project "C" for the Quartier de la Marine. Series of studies appeared in the city's newspapers (by Cottereau, J-P. Faure, etc.).

258

The seafront highway leading into the Business City and linking one end of the Cap d'Alger to the other.

At ground level, the Business City is a forum, both indoors and outdoors.

The Business City puts an end to congestion and opens up a stunning view.

**PROJECT "C"**

This is how our last proposal (1934) would place the shoreline of Algiers on the scale of modern times.

the tiara placed
on the head of
Algiers

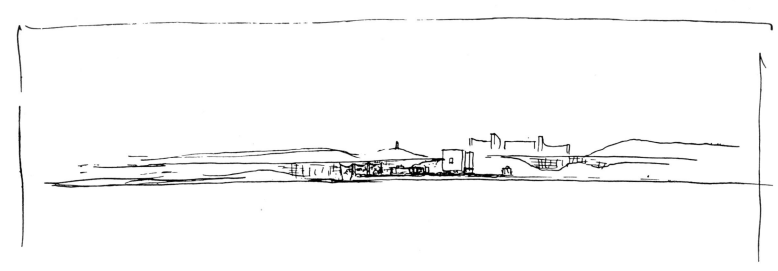

GOODBYE TO ALGIERS . . .

In 1294, the Florentine Republic passed a decree
ordering Arnolfo di Cambio to make drawings and
execute a model for the reconstruction of Santa-
Reparata (the future Duomo), Santa Maria del
Fiore.

"*Of such loftiness and splendor as cannot be
expected of human endeavors, so that there will be
nothing nobler nor more beautiful, with this in mind:
that any work undertaken for the Community should
be conceived with a grandeur befitting the grandeur of
the soul of all the citizens when they unite their efforts
in a single effort.*"

*Sunday, July 22, 1934.*

Now the "De Grasse" is on the open sea. Algiers drops
out of sight, like a magnificent body, supple-hipped
and full-breasted, but covered by the sickening scabs
of a skin disease. A body which could be revealed in
all its magnificence, through the judicious influence
of form and the bold use of mathematics to harmonize
natural topography and human geometry.
  But I have been expelled, the doors have been shut
in my face.
  I am leaving and deeply I feel:
  I am right, I am right, I am right . . .
  I suffer bitterly to see that men so devoted to their
  city still refuse to offer it the smile of art and the poise
  of grandeur.
  "O City Fathers! you who hold the fortune and the
  misfortune of your city in the palms of your hands!"

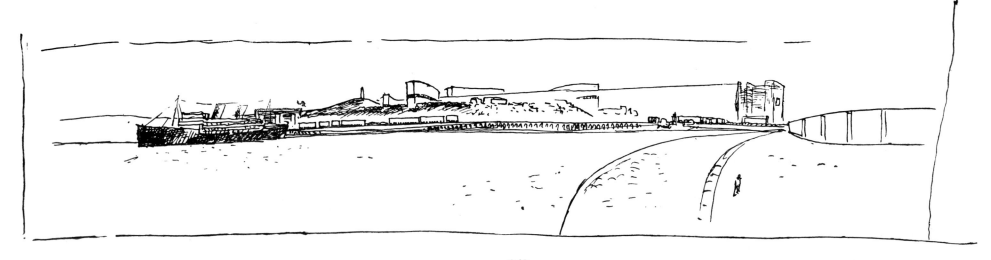

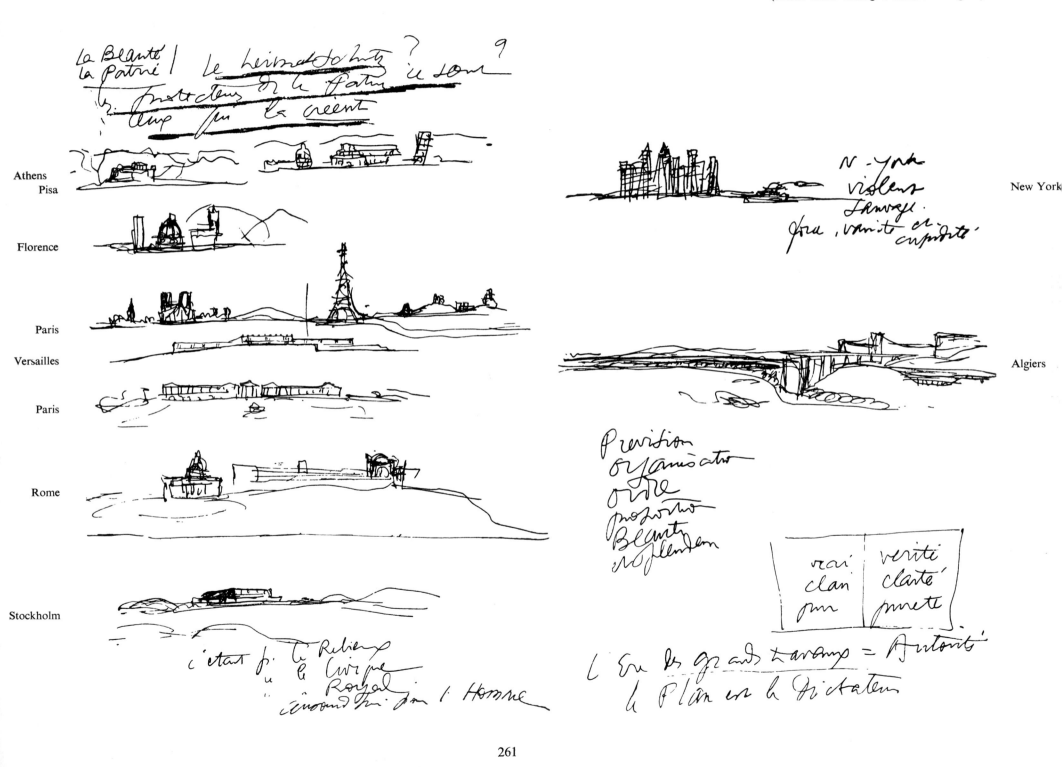

Athens
Pisa

Florence

Paris

Versailles

Paris

Rome

Stockholm

New York

Algiers

261

1927. League of Nations Palace, Geneva.
For the first time in centuries, architecture subtly and eloquently inserted itself in the site, absorbing its power to move us and in return, offering to it the symphonic elements of human geometry.

"Born" architecture shares the integrity of nature. It exalts each site, opens the soul of the site to us, is embodied in the site. Architecture is nature itself through human creative force.

1927. THE LEAGUE OF NATIONS PALACE
(first site, on the lake front)

# GENEVA
## 1927
## 1928
## 1929
## 1932

# NATURE
# ARCHITECTURE
# AND CITY PLANNING

Without disturbing a single element of the site – neither hills nor gently sloping lawns, neither woodlands nor grasslands.

When in 1927 the jury chose this design, one of its members, a M. Lemaresquier from Paris, discovered that our plans had been drawn... with printer's ink and not with India ink.

On this pretext, he demanded that we be excluded from the competition. And so, thanks to intrigue, we were!

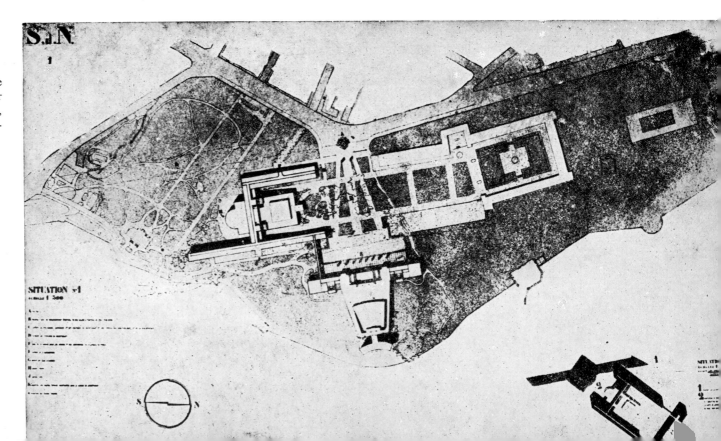

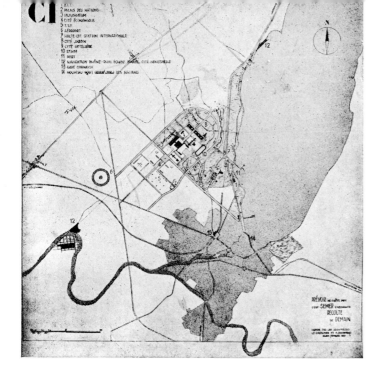

On this plan, submitted to the League of Nations, was inscribed: "It costs nothing to look ahead, to sow the crop for tomorrow's bountiful harvest."

1929. Plan for the World City, based on Paul Otlet's program (Brussels) for an international center of learning, outside of the League of Nations but in agreement with it.

Like the Wandering Jew, this World City seeks a home. In 1933, it became part of the plan for urbanizing the left bank of the river Escaut (Scheldt) in Antwerp (page 271).

Theory: every edifice is a biological being, whose life develops outward from within. The outside expresses an inside. It is the harmonious organization of whole events, as in a living body. And the site? Something else again! Just as an animal (or a man) adopts a different position or attitude depending on whether it is on flat ground, or on sloping or very rough ground, just as it moves into sunlight or into shade, just as it seeks to see straight ahead or on either side, just so an edifice takes possession of the site according to its needs, *adapts itself to the site, plants itself on the site*. In this way it is never mutilated: it remains whole.

This is the theory of reciprocal independence between building and site. (See pages 289 and 290 of this book, the Palace of the Soviets and the Centrosoyus. For that matter, see all of the statements in this book: architecture and city planning.)

All of this is the very opposite of the meanness into which two-dimensional city planning traditionally squeezes architecture.

## 1929. THE LEAGUE OF NATIONS PALACE

(second site, in the Ariana section, on the hillside)

Here we clearly see how theory relates architecture to city planning:

The first Palace project in 1927 (facing page) constituted a biological unit in terms of precise functions. Through sensitive appreciation of the site's natural resources, the unit fit freely and gracefully into the landscape.

1928: a different site! There is no reason to change the biology of the Palace. So the same Palace takes possession of the new site.

See the theory (in box, upper right).

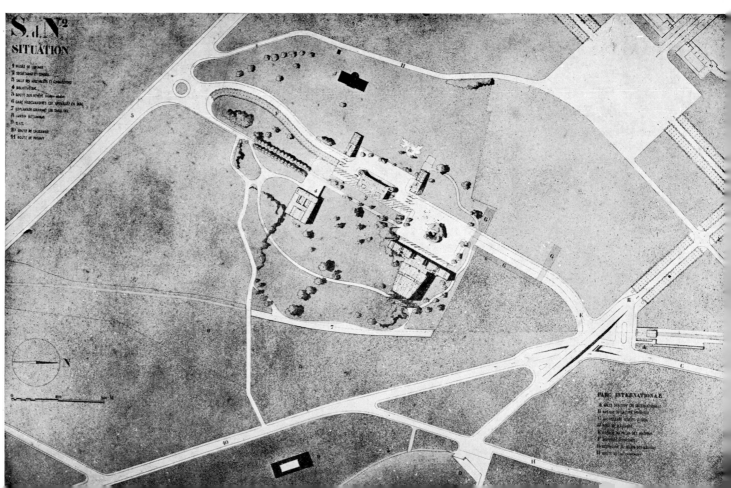

## 1929. THE WORLD CITY
### GENEVA (THE CITY)
### THE LEAGUE OF NATIONS PALACE
### THE I.L.O.
### THE REGION
### CONTACTS WITH THE EXTERIOR

Geneva cropped up suddenly on the map of the world. A calm city, attracting students and tourists, transformed into the center of world government. It would seem that to look ahead should not have been a crime! To look ahead: that is, to situate, reserve, safeguard. Discussions, stipulations, rectifications could come afterward.

We look for the right place for a world city, world information center. We find a hill, at the Grand Saconnex, available, admirable, the perfect spot for the acropolis of machine-age civilization. The topography is eloquent. A dazzling site, with such uncrowded horizons!

The League of Nations Palace is already fitted into the hillside, and at the summit we plan a new city; we lay out the roads of the future, straight and sober, like those of Louis XIV. We cause them to join the international routes: la Faucille to Paris, Bellegarde to Lyons, Lyons to Lausanne and from there – Berne, Basle, Berlin, the Simplon pass and Milan.

We prepare the entrance of the tunnel where the Rhine-Rhone canal is to flow. We make connections with the city of Geneva and better yet, within the city, above the lake, we connect the right bank with the left. We make connections with Annemasse, with Evian.

We have made a distinction: we have not confused the destiny of Geneva-the-city with the destiny of world government and its institutions.

Yet it was the people of Geneva and their officials who rejected our proposals out of hand. Our aim was disinterested enough: we offered our plans for nothing to Geneva and the League of Nations.

(Paul Otlet and I gave lectures; we exhibited the plans in a shed built at our own expense. We set up a diorama measuring 80 m² to give a clear image of the overall conception.)

264

A part of the large diorama exhibited in Geneva, in a shed set up in the Parc de la Perle du Lac.

All of these buildings, expressing flawless functions in the pures technicity, rise up in an orderly and purposeful design to compose, with the lake and the mountain peaks the moving symphony of Nature and Architecture.

"Born" architecture shares the integrity of nature. It exalts each site, opens up the soul of the site to us . . ."

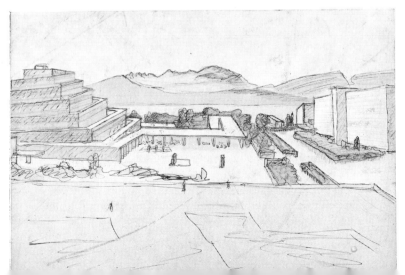

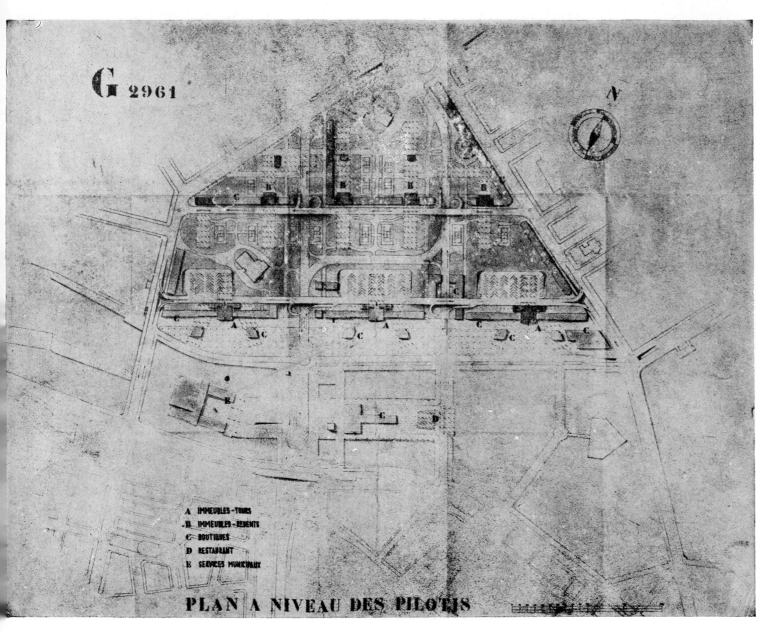

G 2961

A IMMEUBLES-TOURS
B IMMEUBLES-REDENTS
C BOUTIQUES
D RESTAURANT
E SERVICES MUNICIPAUX

PLAN A NIVEAU DES PILOTIS

# GENEVA, RIGHT BANK, 1932

The Saint-Gervais district is to be torn down and replaced by a new one. Certain vital lines of communication must be guaranteed. The cathedral's slope overlooks the Rhône; in the background rises the very beautiful Salève. As in every city set amidst the spectacle of natural beauty, the in-

habitants, from their homes hovering over corridor-streets, cannot even glimpse this beauty.

If the operation is to be financially worthwhile, a certain real volume of dwelling must be reached.

The "Radiant City" theories are applied: the ground is liberated; there is even provision for pleasantly undulating verdure, to screen pedestrian routes from fast automobile traffic.

The question is thorny: on every hand the realities of the present city crush you with their presence. And yet the solution stands out clearly.

COUNTER-PROJECT URGED BY THE CITIZENS' GROUP
FOR THE IMPROVEMENT OF THE SAINT-GERVAIS DISTRICT

(Extract from a pamphlet distributed throughout Geneva;
its cover made an appeal "To all who are interested in
the future of our City!")

Its appeal concluded:

• • • • • • • • • • • • • • •

"10. And now, it is up to every one of you to
compare, and to draw your own conclusions.

"... The residents and merchants of the endangered districts, and all of Geneva's citizens
must realize that they should have their say in this
matter and must wage a campaign to force the
Government to drop this senseless project.

"Doesn't wisdom often begin with fear of the
voter?"

And here is the project demanded by the
"voters." The protests were not directed at
our project but at the Administration's,
which had been inspired (ever so slightly!)
by ours!

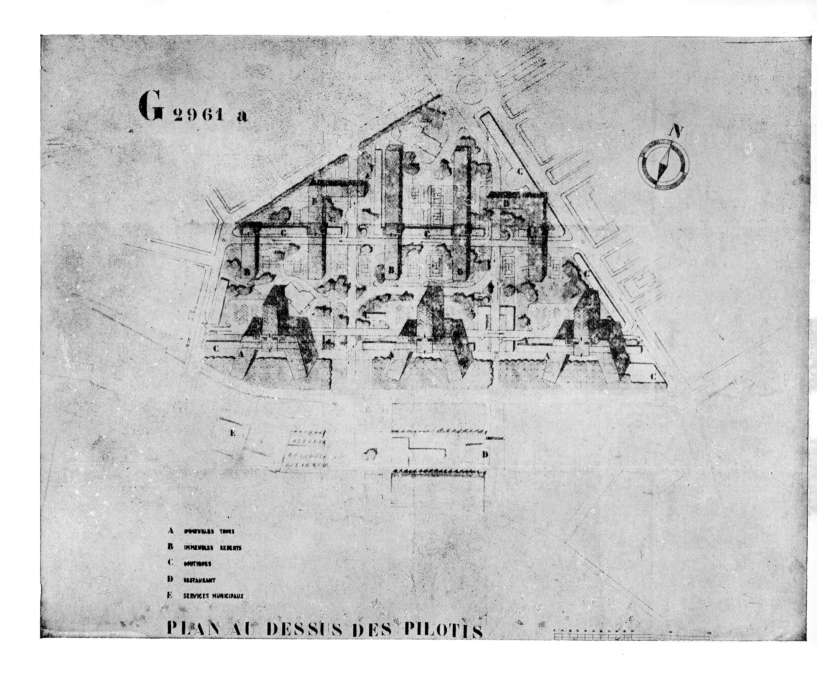

G 2961 a

A IMMEUBLES TOURS
B IMMEUBLES REDENTS
C BOUTIQUES
D RESTAURANT
E SERVICES MUNICIPAUX

PLAN AU DESSUS DES PILOTIS

Everything falls into place. The two churches are preserved, with their setting and their approaches. Shopkeepers have what they need all along the bank of the Rhône and the rue du Mont-
Blanc. The island is improved. The big transversal route for pedestrians, Corraterie-Cornavin,
fulfills urgent needs. Dwellings? Optimum conditions at last!

All this is just fine! One day our plan arouses a certain enthusiasm. Our victory is acclaimed.

But Geneva rejects us. Our name is enough in itself to condemn our proposals.

1927. League of Nations Palace.
1928. The Mundaneum.
1929. The World City.
1932. The Saint-Gervais district (right bank) . . .

# I CALL UPON VENICE AS A WITNESS

(PREAMBLE TO THE ANTWERP PLAN)

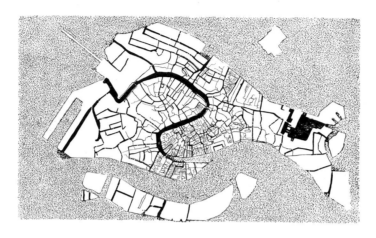

Two means of transportation: by foot on land, by gondola on the sea. Here: the network of waterways.

Venice is "shaped" by a lagoon.

Relative elevation + 0 is the basis of all measurements; there every measurement, even the crudest, is unquestionable; all disorder becomes order. So the plain of water – like the plain of land elsewhere – cannot be called a nuisance. Rather, a friend to architecture, one of its greatest props.

Here we see the thrust of multiple speeds, the big garage, terminus of overland roads. There is *not a single road* in Venice.

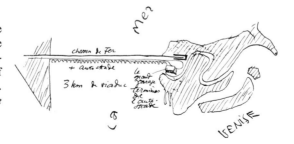

the garage is a blind alley.

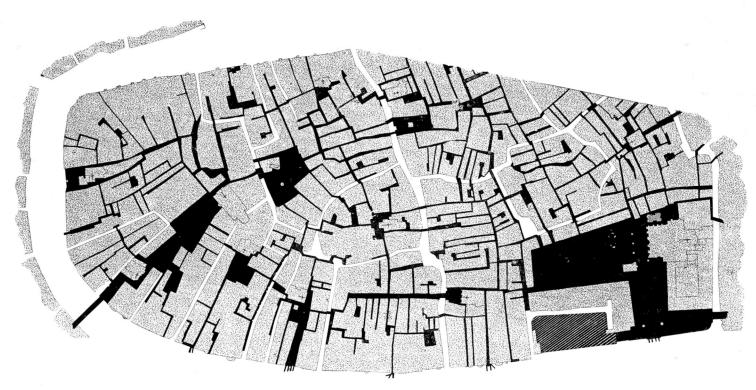

Venice: a) pedestrians
 b) gondolas
 c) public transportation (steamboats) on the Grand Canal
 d) international transportation (warships, liners, cargo ships) in the lagoon.

This drawing is a revelation: and accurate, made according to surveyors' maps. Doesn't it look like perfect biology? – the circulation of blood in a living being?

 The pedestrian is king: he has never lost his dignity.

Venice is a great inducement for us to continue studying urban organization in a machine-age civilization.

 (July, 1934)

The fundamental aspect of Venice is the classification of natural and artificial sorts of traffic: the pedestrian and the gondola. Nature has made this classification compulsory, and it means not only an economy of urban installations but a priceless gift to the inhabitants: joy, and peace of mind.

Thanks to the clearcut separation of two types of traffic, two types of layout – here, sidewalks; and there, canals – can be achieved simultaneously, without ambiguity or redundancy.

The system of sidewalks is miraculously thrifty, without losing any of its efficiency. A revelation! A lesson so stunning that I obtained survey maps and from the jigsaw puzzle of houses, I picked out the network of walks: a flawless circulatory system. Nothing is narrow any more. But what are the dimensions here, exactly? Streets 1.20 meters (under four feet) wide, or 2 meters, or 3. A street measuring 6 meters (under twenty feet) across is very broad indeed! The percentage of land set aside for traffic is at a minimum. The piazzas are so many mighty reservoirs, lakes for the crowd to flow into.

Have you noticed how gay and proud are the people of Venice? Gay because they are on their feet, free to go where they like, never in danger, never jostled, never bothered; happy to be alive and living in a city of serenity. But where are we at in this respect, in other cities where pedestrians and vehicles must coexist? There we haven't even the faintest idea of this Venetian happiness I'm talking about.

The "sheet of water" made the human scale inevitable: to get out of your gondola or into it,

you must climb steps properly placed and measured. This is an exacting function, and neither pomp nor academism can be admitted.

The intersection of waterway and walk is ruled by a strict equation between the height the gondolier needs in order to pass and the least possible disturbance for the pedestrian.

It could be shown (as in fact I did show, during the Fourth *Entretien d'Art* at the Ducal Palace in July, 1934) that Venice is a perfectly conceived machine, a clever set of precision instruments, an accurate product of true human dimensions. A functional city, Venice, extraordinarily functional, a model for today's city planners, witness to the strictness of the measures demanded by the urban phenomenon.

Venice, witness to functional strictness.

Daily, for hundreds of years, Venice has sustained the pride of its citizens because neither its birth nor its secular upbringing since were marred by accidents. Venice has been pampered by its officials, obedient to the dictates of its site. And through total cooperation of all the craftsmen who worked to build it and design its waterways, every object was turned out sharp and clean, polished and effective as a cherished tool. Even without its Renaissance *palazzi*, Venice would be an admirable creation of human hands.

In its most fundamental elements, Venice naturally forms an introduction to the urbanization plans for the new city of Antwerp, on the left bank of the river Scheldt.

# 1933
# URBANIZATION OF THE LEFT BANK OF THE SCHELDT IN ANTWERP

IN COOPERATION WITH HUIB HOSTE AND LOCQUET (FROM ANTWERP) AND PAUL OTLET (FROM BRUSSELS)

This study was as minutely detailed as possible, going into every nicety implied in the life of a new city with a population of 500,000. Every one of the solutions it proposed was completely new. We made 40 meters of the most accurate plans. The jury went by and its members shrugged their shoulders.

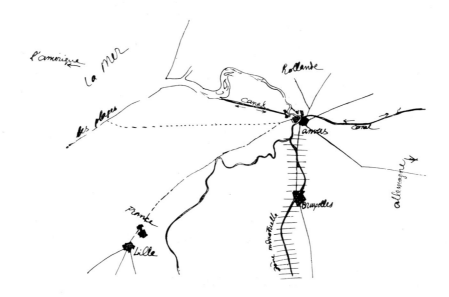

## INTRODUCTION

This project is presented by a team which has striven to consider every possible aspect of a complex problem, and to solve it through synthesis.

Assuredly, those who organized the competition deserve congratulations for having stated its terms in such a way as not to exclude any rational solution. But for this very reason, they forced the contestants to make a thorough study of the various factors involved. It is by such a study that the authors of the present project began, relying upon three sources of information:

1) The Imalso Company's program and report;
2) the numerous studies already published on Antwerp, its port and its urbanization;
3) the fine collection of documents recently assembled at the 25th Anniversary Exhibition of the Commission for a Greater Antwerp.

This statistically and materially substantial survey was supplemented by personal research. The survey acted as a catalyst and check system for hypotheses which, in turn, led to the individual creations included in the overall project.

Again and again we went beyond verifiable present reality to the upper realm of future reality, sure that this realm too could be checked with a maximum of probability. So the project is presented today from the four angles which are basic to any task of urbanization: 1) economic and social; 2) technical; 3) theoretic and general; and 4) esthetic.

We have confined ourselves here to indicating the aims and principles relevant to the plan.

1) THE PROBLEM: Since, on the left bank of the river Scheldt, there is a sizeable area on which no structure stands, which belongs to a single public body and is already connected to the right

bank by two tunnels, for what purpose should these sites be earmarked? Next, how may they be improved so as to combine a financially profitable operation with an organic contribution to Antwerp's growth?

2) THE SOLUTION had to fulfill this ambition: give Antwerp all of the elements needed in this twentieth century to make it the biggest port on the continent and, to the West, accommodate the very considerable agglomeration of men and firms which would be the prerequisite, the cause and the effect of such a port. This demonstration rests on Antwerp's continuous development ever since the city was liberated, and on its geographical location. Thus the plan consists essentially of a core of suggestions to further the city's development, in terms of both local circumstances and present demands of city planning.

a) Safeguard for today and for tomorrow, the greatest chances of expanding the city's harbor installations, and especially, provide for those which are still lacking.

b) Create a sizeable residential sector on the left bank.

c) Look to the possibility of establishing a World City there, in conjunction with a residential center organized as a model city.

d) Link this newly created area to the present city so as to make a balanced whole.

e) Next, in terms of the enlarged and harmonized functions of this new whole, improve and augment the city's present facilities and its means of communication with the surrounding area, with the rest of Belgium and with neighboring countries.

In this regard, we have reckoned with:

a) the consequences of the electrification of the Belgian railway system (now in preparation) and of its union with the electrified system in the Netherlands.

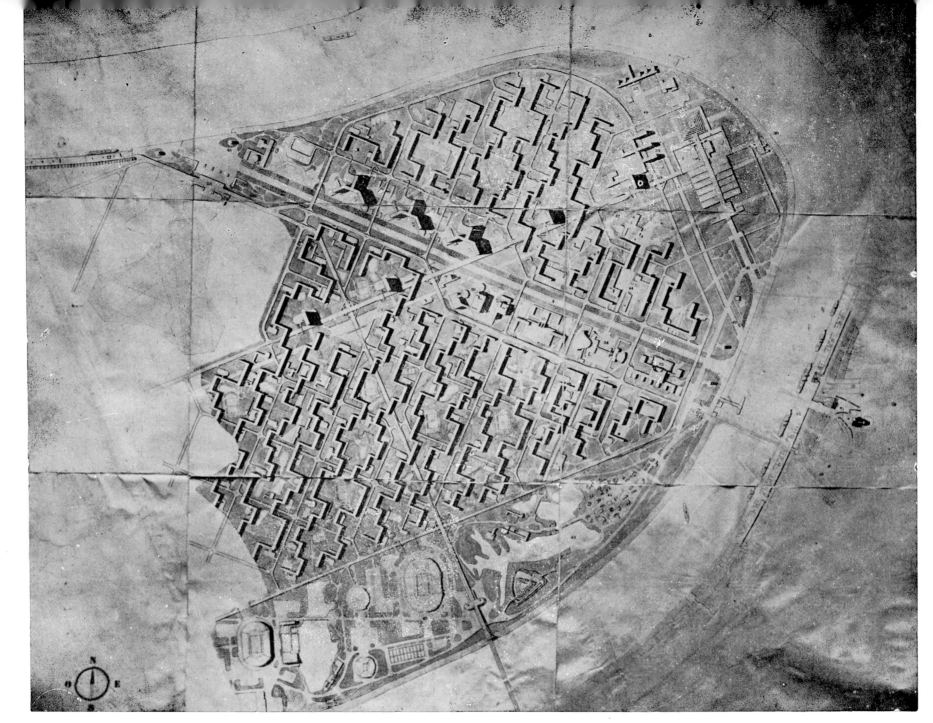

3108
Detailed
plan of
the New
City.

b) the creation of new highways.

c) the fact that the Brussels-Charleroi waterway takes on new significance.

d) the results to be expected from the Albert canal and from various waterways which, in one way or another, will make of Antwerp the great Rhenish port for which the Treaty of Versailles made provision.

3) CHARACTERISTICS OF THE PROJECT ITSELF: a) Habitat and traffic: exceptionally fine possibilities, because of the site and of the overall operations which circumstances allow us to envisage.

b) Travel and transport: 1) Navigation: free port, passenger port, port for perishable goods.

2) Automobiles: center, intersection of the great highways leading to or from Amsterdam, Paris, Berlin, Lille, Ostend, and London.

3) Trains: harbor station liaison.

4) Airplanes: Antwerp air terminal.

5) *Métropolitaine* (or shuttle) lines.

c) Completion of the panorama along the banks of the Scheldt.

d) A good deal of room allotted to the expansion of presently cramped installations and to promenades along the river which are lacking today.

4) ADVANTAGES OF THE PROJECT: It GOES WITHOUT SAYING that the project is altogether feasible even if the establishment of a World City were not considered.

To the advantages which the above statement of the project's solution and characteristics makes self-evident, must be added:

a) Maritime installations will be concentrated in the North, to avoid the drawbacks of wide-spread scattering.

b) The city will be liberated from its tangle of railroads; in addition, much of the land presently taken up by railway roadbed can be sold (1000 hectares, worth 1,500,000,000 Francs).

As with any urbanization plan, it will take time to carry out this one; it should be done by stages. But with such a plan to guide policy for a quarter or a half century to come, it will be possible to act rationally, through accumulated efforts. This plan is the fusion of Antwerp's needs and the CROWNING of the city's ambitions.

The project is based:

1) On historical data.

2) On the need to secure the "basic pleasures" for each inhabitant of the new city.

3) On exposure to the sun (not one home faces north).

4) On the classification and separation of simple and multiple speeds; *the entire ground surface is available to pedestrians.*

5) On the adoption of the elevator in a special way, that is: as a vertical public transportation service, in houses whose maximum height will be 50 meters.

6) On the "concentration" principle, instead of the "dispersion" principle, for the horizontal "garden city" is a deplorable error which leads to waste, precariously stretches the city's geographical area, and seriously weakens civic authority.

7) On elimination of the *traditional* street and construction of residential districts on an indented or in-and-out plan *(en redents)*. Only 12% of the city's area is built upon; the remaining 88% becomes parks devoted to sports and relaxation.

8) On the unitary principle that no inhabitant should have to walk more than 100 meters from the door of his home to the elevators leading directly to automobile traffic, or from within a park to

a conveniently located streetcar stop, shuttle station or parking lot.

9) Gone, the city which is merely a blighted crust pierced by deep ditch-like streets: now it is a vast park, a "GREEN CITY," built on the "RADIANT CITY" pattern. This means that its constituent elements will be able to accommodate "LEISURE ACTIVITIES," the most imminent phase in the evolution of our modern machine age. *To this impending problem, city planning must, at all costs, suggest solutions.*

Indeed, life in the machine age entitles us to expect, in the near future, a work day so shortened that of the 24 hours in the solar day, a considerable portion will be left free. Today's public officials have the obligation *to prepare facilities capable of occupying tomorrow's leisure time, devoted to recuperating physical and nervous energy* (sports practiced at the foot of each house, solaria and beaches as part of the roof-gardens, etc; room set aside for childrearing (to breed a healthy race and give the child special care starting at birth); places for study, for meetings and group activities, in appropriate rooms and halls. And finally, the freedom of the individual is guaranteed by the sound-proof home, flooded by sunlight and opening, not onto the traditional street but, onto the sky and an expanse of parks.

CHAPTER ONE

HISTORICAL DATA

We have not neglected the historical significance of present-day Antwerp, as clearly shown by the arrangement of the city's principal arteries: they radiate toward the cathedral and toward the time-honored port. Although our left bank project is guided by a number of rational conditions, we were able to effect a spiritual link *with the heart of Antwerp by means of a grand avenue* ending in a view of the cathedral.

Public buildings will rise all along this avenue, and at the other end of it the new harbor station, able to handle the tonnage of huge ocean liners, will begin. To one side of the avenue are the city's old and historic port and the cathedral; to the other, the river Scheldt escapes into the sea.

A new city like the one planned for the left bank *should have a reason for existing*. It may be said that since Antwerp dominates the estuaries of central Europe, it is fated to be the point of exchange between America, on the one hand, and central and eastern Europe, on the other. From there the city's influence, as the outlet of a great diagonal crossline, will extend into Asia Minor and the Persian Gulf.

So we can accept the validity of a *future international business city;* accordingly we have planned a line of office buildings (No 10), 150 to 200 meters high, stretching from the Left Bank Harbor Station all the way down the avenue de la Cathédrale.

This supposition is borne out by studies undertaken some time ago in Brussels and Paris; they came to the conclusion, in 1928 and 1929, that a "WORLD CITY" *(Cité Mondiale)* should be built, as an international center of information on philosophy, biology, statistics, jurisprudence, and so forth.

We have included the possibility of erecting such a city (No 11) on the appropriate spot.

Lastly, around the marshes south of the New City, there is land available for the creation of an international center (No 12).

CHAPTER TWO

"RADIANT CITY" PRINCIPLES APPLIED TO THE LEFT BANK

Modern techniques (steel, reinforced concrete, etc.) have brought *vast new measures of freedom to the city dweller; we may call them the "basic pleasures."*

Through efficient soundproofing, from now on, each apartment can be swathed in the most absolute silence, as the project's authors know from having already solved similar problems.

Thanks to modern techniques, the façade of each apartment can become a *glass wall* giving onto sweeping open spaces. In the present project, *these glass walls are oriented in strict accordance with the "heliothermic" axis*, whose direction is established by plan No 3115. Research into this axis for the Antwerp region dictates that not one apartment in the New City should face north; instead every apartment faces either east (sunlight from dawn to noon), or south (from 9 in the morning to 5 in the afternoon), or west (from noon to sunset).

We systematically eliminate the traditional "corridor-street" and build residential districts by *redents;* as a result, *there are no more courtyards* and since there are no more streets, no apartment is exposed to the noises of the street. Between each *redent* structure we leave spaces varying in width from 75 to 300 meters with, in addition, a view extending far into the distance. Lawns, trees and shrubs are planted on the remaining free surface (88%) of the city, and *within these parks there are playing fields and courts* (for football, basketball, tennis, and the like).

Moreover, each *redent* has its own open-air swimming pool over 100 meters long. *Thus sports can be practiced at the foot of each house.* This is a genuine achievement of modern times, fulfilling a recognized need. And each apartment building is raised *on pilotis* 5 meters high (see plans 3110 and 3111), leaving a covered playground where children will be safe from the sun's glare and from rain.

Furthermore, there is the endless ribbon of roof-gardens at the summit of each *redent,* 50 meters above the ground: here, with modern techniques, we can create sand beaches, which mean hydrotherapy, sunbaths, promenades. These are genuine beaches, 12 or 24 meters wide, with a splendid view and perfect exposure to the sun.

By conceiving the apartment building in this way, the urbanization of a city offers the inhabitants what are rightfully termed "the basic pleasures," joys of everyday, and of every hour in every day. They are fundamental to the happiness of the individual. The requirements of both biological and psychological functions are satisfied.

As we shall see later, *automobile traffic* in such a city *is completely separate from pedestrian movement;* traffic is localized in a network of elevated highways 5 meters above the ground. Which means that *pedestrians never have to maneuver around automobiles* and that children are completely out of danger, since all of the ground in the city belongs to them. *The ground has been won back.* At last we can use our legs again.

Within the parks, and attached to the apartment buildings are the establishments needed for *bringing up and teaching children. Three kinds of establishments form an integral part of the apartment buildings:* a) nurseries for infants; b) kindergartens for the two- to six-year-olds; and c) primary schools. These are no longer immense structures far from home. Instead, their size has been planned in terms of groups of about 6,000 inhabitants. Later we shall see that this figure represents from 2 to 3 residence units served by the general transport system.

In plate No 3116 VR 7, we see how the traditional idea of apartment buildings has been transformed by the creation of soundproofed homes which, instead of opening onto a stairway, at the rate of two apartments per floor, give onto "interior streets." Every 200 meters, each of these superimposed streets leads to an elevator shaft; the elevators are considered a means of public transportation and are run by licensed elevator operators. Each elevator meets the natural ground with its network of footpaths and walks; while 5 meters above the ground, it opens onto the "*auto-port*" platform where the elevated highway ends. Here and only here, parking lots, or "*auto-ports*," are to be found. The principle governing this layout is the following: *no inhabitant should have to walk more than 100 meters along an "interior street" in order to find vertical transportation services. On this basis, for a building 50 meters high,* figures show that each group of vertical transportation absorbs a population of *about 2,700* (at the rate of 14 m² of living space allotted to each inhabitant).

The result of this new traffic distribution is to channel automobile traffic into a system altogether different from that required by the traditional street. The latter, bordered by a continuous hedge of buildings, each with a façade 10 or 20 meters long, forced cars to pass directly in front of each door of each building and consequently meant that the street had to be right at the foot of the house: houses were placed right *on the street, exposed to the noise and dangers of traffic.* But the new conception channels cars onto elevated highways about 5 meters above the ground, according to a mesh of about 400 × 400 meters which is *completely independent of the dwellings.* This mesh branches off where necessary, and every branch ends in an "auto-port" right where the elevator comes up. So we achieve total separation of "multiple speeds" (cars) and "single speeds" (pedestrians). This is how we propose to solve a *problem without precedent* in the history of human civilization: that of multiple speeds. Until now they have spelled disaster for the city (see plans 3104 – 3107 – 3108).

For residential districts of the "RADIANT CITY" type, see plans 3110 – 3111 – 3116 VR 7.

### CHAPTER THREE

## TRAFFIC
### ESTABLISHING CONTACTS WITH THE CITY OF ANTWERP.
### NEW SYSTEMS ON THE LEFT BANK. INTERNATIONAL LIAISONS.

A. *Railroads:* Whereas the city of Antwerp was in the *avant-garde* of railroad development from the outset, it has let this system swell to such a point that today the railroad actually squeezes and stifles the city, at a time when it costs more to transport freight by rail than it does by truck. Antwerp's railroad system should be revised.

On plan 3102, we have suggested eliminating a certain number of rail lines, so as to free the city from their paralyzing effect.

What, then, is the traffic problem today in Greater Antwerp? First of all, to secure international liaisons: PARIS-BRUSSELS-HOLLAND; BERLIN-ANTWERP-HOLLAND; PARIS or BERLIN through ANTWERP via OSTEND. (See plan 3102.)

*Passenger traffic:* the system should be built all along the Scheldt's right bank to link the main lines to the present quays and go on directly to Holland. At the southern entrance to the city of Antwerp, it will fork off, through a tunnel under the river, to the *New Harbor Station*, able to handle big steamers (left bank, north of the new city). This rail line includes a Gare Centrale Rive Gauche (Left Bank Central Station) (No 13), then continues by way of Ostend. The rail lines to the left bank, at the exit of the tunnel beneath the Scheldt, will be *sunken but uncovered*. On the right bank fork, south of the city, there is to be a triple-branched station (No 14 – Gare du Sud, or South Station); on the Brussels-Antwerp-Amsterdam line, there is to be a second Gare du Nord, or North Station (No 15). In this way, the problem of rail traffic is solved. We should point out that the word "station" here means a simple *through-station:* for the trains are made up outside of the city, and they merely go through the stations. (The opposite of terminal, hence blind alley, stations.) Plan 3102/c shows how very advantageous it would be to eliminate a great number of rail networks which would be nothing more than useless obstacles.

Notice that the Left Bank Central Station (No 13), Right Bank South Station (No 14) and Right Bank North Station (No 15) are so situated as to be in direct contact with other networks which will be required in the future: shuttles, streetcars, highways, for the development of traffic in the New City and its connection with Antwerp. How this contact is established at the proper points is shown on Plan 3101.

*Freight traffic:* Plan 3102/b shows how freight lines are brought to the appropriate points. On the right bank, they absorb the freight of the present Harbor Station; all that is needed is to arrange the river quay (see plans 3107 and 3108, and the section drawing of this installation).

The freight network of the *New Harbor Station* (17) and of the new free port planned to the north of the new left bank city, is linked on the north to the Main Sorting Depot (19), on the right bank; from there, it fans out toward Holland, Germany, Brussels and France. And freight is shunted off from the free port (No 18) along network No 19 toward Brussels, Ghent, and other points south.

Here, we are submitting the idea of a "*Free Port*" and a *New Harbor Station* north of the new city, as a suggestion only; it includes the creation of a canal directly linking north-south navigation No 20, feeding into Brussels and the Charleroi basin. This canal would relieve the loop made by the Scheldt between the two cities, Antwerp and the left bank.

### PUBLIC TRANSPORTATION:
### "METROPOLITAINES" OR SHUTTLES, STREETCARS, HIGHWAYS

There are two problems:

1) Link with Belgian shuttle lines (plan 3103/a);
2) *Urban* shuttle service, between Antwerp and the new Left Bank city.

The *Belgian Railways* plan to electrify their lines and thereby to develop the rail system and possibly provide more frequent connections between Brussels and Mechlin (Malines) or Antwerp, Charleroi, Ghent, etc., by shuttle lines named "*Métropolitaines.*"

It is this Belgian network which must be accommodated in both Antwerp and the New City on the left bank.

The Belgian networks on the right of the river Scheldt will all end *in a belt around Antwerp,* along a ring installed on the site of the former fortifications. This ring will feed into the entire periphery of the city and its adjacent suburbs.

The new left bank will be linked to the Belgian shuttle line by the terminus of this part of the ring which, after tunneling under the Scheldt to the south (No 21) and north (No 22), will join the Central Station in the middle of the new left bank city. Moreover, the same tracks are used for the shuttle and the New Harbor Station's international railroad.

The line will leave the Central Station (No 13) to end at the New Harbor Station (No 17) and at the New City's western extremity: No 23. This circuit is called Line No 2.

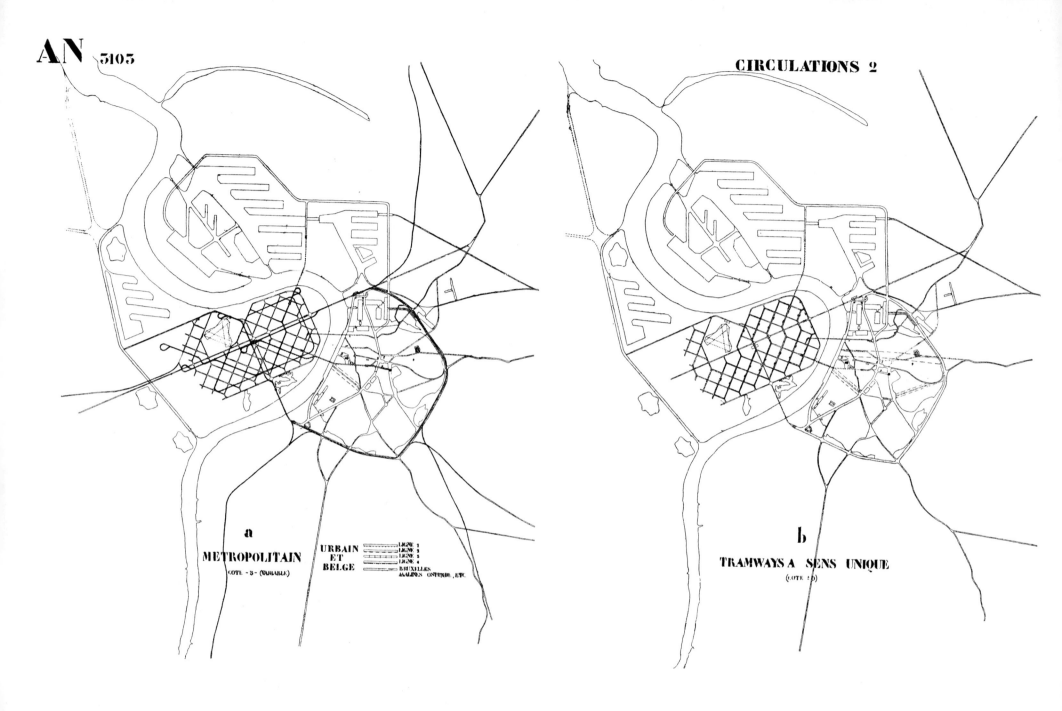

The various districts of the new left bank city are reached by the shuttle lines No 4 and No 3.
*Finally, line No 1 links the heart of the New City to the heart of Antwerp as far as the* place *of the present Central Station (No 24).*
This network makes possible the following combinations with the network of streetcars:
*Streetcar circuits* (plan 3103/b). These streetcars should serve the various districts of Antwerp and the New City.

In the layout of the city, the streetcars occupy a very precise position: on the ground beneath the elevated highways. They are separated from the parks in the residential neighborhoods by fences, and *each station is located only where the tracks meet a sidewalk.* Sometimes, where convenient, the station also coincides with the junction of a shuttle line, and is so arranged as to permit *direct connections between sidewalks, shuttle, and streetcars.*
At this junction, the sidewalk goes down gradually to a lower level beneath the streetcar tracks.

274

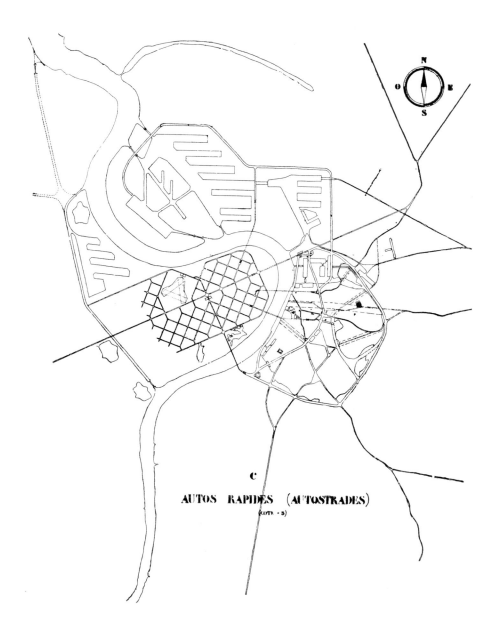

AUTOS RAPIDES (AUTOSTRADES)
(COTE - 3)

Cars travel on a network of elevated highways, 5 meters above the ground. Built of reinforced concrete, their overall length is surprisingly little, compared to the city's land surface and especially compared to the streets in the cities of today. Consequently, their construction and maintenance are far less costly than those of the traditional street, used simultaneously by pedestrians and every sort of vehicle – buses, trucks, and cars moving at various speeds.

These highways have but one purpose: *to allow cars to go from one entrance door to another.* Now, as we have already seen, thanks to a new conception, each door serves 2,700 people. The doors can therefore be spaced very far apart, and the highway reaches each one by branching off to it; each branch ends in a parking lot.

Plan 3104 gives overall and detailed views of these highways; plans Nos 3113 and 3114 show profile views and solve the question of intersections.

There are three sorts of these highways:
1) Normal: 12 meters wide.
2) Average: 19 meters wide.
3) Major: 25 meters wide.

These highways are divided down the middle by an uninterrupted stone parapet, creating two parallel one-way lanes without any possibility of penetration from one to the other. A rational layout automatically takes care of intersections. There is no longer the slightest need for supervision. Traffic flows uninterruptedly. At last a system of urban automobile traffic capable of answering the needs of the automobile.

*The resulting classification, of a realm set aside for pedestrians and another for cars, must not be underestimated.*

In certain cases, however, a car can rightfully cease to be a utilitarian means of rapid transportation and be used simply for pleasure. In every city there are certain places definitely set aside for pleasant walks and drives. The present project includes such places especially along the avenue de la Cathédrale (No 25). We will describe the width of this avenue later; on either side are to be public buildings, the most handsome of all those planned.

Another spot intended for leisurely promenades is the "World City" (No 26), to which a special report is devoted.

And finally, the two extensive parks set aside to the south of the New City, across from Antwerp, are perfectly suited to promenades. They are linked to the avenue de la Cathédrale and to the World City by the avenue de la Cité Mondiale – still another possibility for leisurely driving.

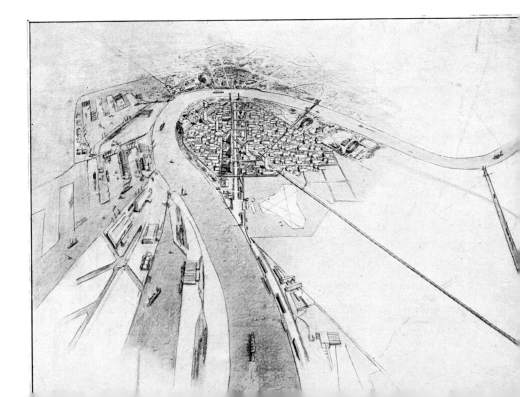

This slope is *landscaped;* the pedestrian goes down a sort of little valley banked with lawns and trees, so that the descent has none of the forbidding aspect of a tunnel.

Plans 3113 and 3114 show in exceptional detail exactly how these stations work, with their intersections and their various levels.

The streetcar tracks are divided into contiguous one-way networks, each one forming a complete circuit, as plan 3103/b shows.

When a city has a rational layout, the streetcar becomes the most economical, the most efficient means of transportation. For in the inextricable tangle of streets that plagues today's cities, the bus is nothing more than a marvelous *makeshift.*

*Highways for rapid automobile traffic. Plan 3103/c.*

Here we see the application of a *firm principle: the absolute separation of pedestrian movement – for which the ground is entirely set aside – and automobile traffic.*

275

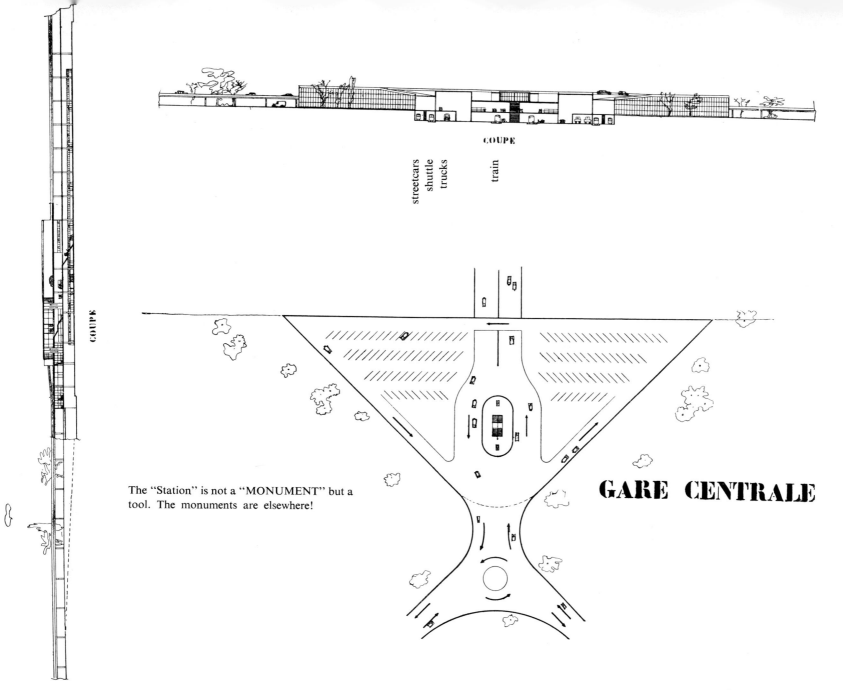

Parking lot above the station.
Highway.
Trucks.

COUPE

streetcars
shuttle
trucks

train

COUPE

The "Station" is not a "MONUMENT" but a tool. The monuments are elsewhere!

GARE CENTRALE

*Tracks and trailer trucks.* They should have a road network of their own, parallel to the streetcar tracks beneath the elevated highways but completely independent of them and never intersecting them.

What is the point of trucks in a city? To carry every sort of provision to each home. So it is easy to organize a rational scheme of food distribution in the residential districts (see plan 3105).

Trucks branch off from their one-way lanes toward *centers for loading and unloading.* These centers are regularly spread throughout the residential areas, at ground level, between the pilotis that support the houses. They correspond to the *Intermediate Floor of Communal Services.* In the future these services can be run by hotel syndicates taking care of housework in each apartment (upkeep, cleaning, cooking, possibly a catering service) and refrigeration of all food to be supplied to each home.

CHAPTER FOUR

CONSTITUENT ELEMENTS OF THE NEW LEFT BANK CITY

1) Living Conditions          2) Recreation

1) *Living conditions.* Part of the "RADIANT CITY" has already been described at the beginning of this report and we have seen that living conditions have been studied with utmost care.

The present project distributes residential neighborhoods evenly over the city. *There are neither poor nor wealthy neighborhoods* nor any sort of distinction made to mark them off; probably this classification will come about of itself. The idea has been to use all of the most perfected means of transportation *to link each individual's home to his job wherever it may be throughout the region.*

276

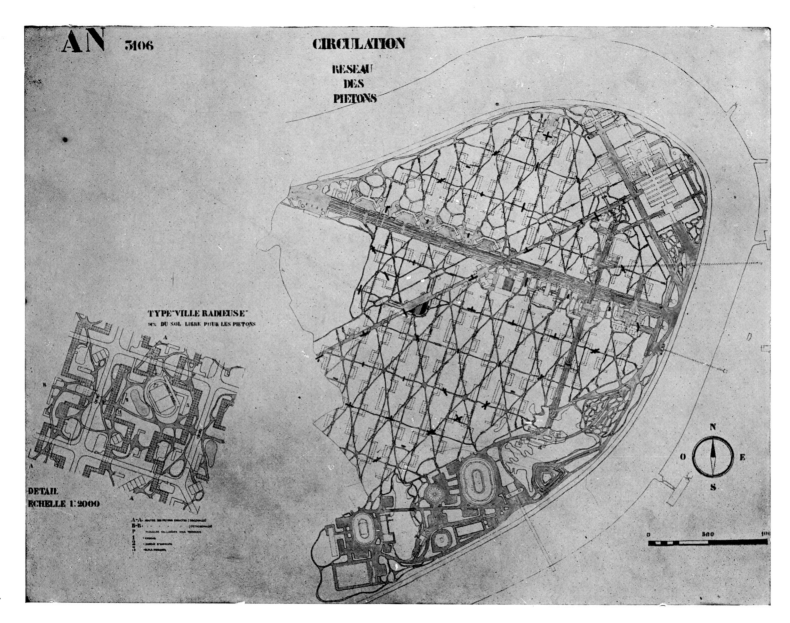

TYPE "VILLE RADIEUSE"
90% DU SOL LIBRE POUR LES PIÉTONS

DÉTAIL
ÉCHELLE 1:2000

3106 n° 5.

2) *Work*. Residents of the New City will work especially in the *Business City* which starts at the Harbor Station and extends along the avenue de la Cathédrale toward the Central Station (No 10). It is to consist of huge buildings 150 to 200 meters high, *without courtyards*, very well ventilated, very static, with excellent exposure to the sun and the most perfected means of transportation within and without (highways, auto-ports or parking lots, shuttle service, etc.).

This Business City is at one end of the New Harbor Station, *opposite the airport*.

The airport *has been placed in the city itself*, and not some distance outside of it. It has been laid out according to the most recent technical data and takes into account the area of limitation on the height of nearby buildings. *In practice, commercial aviation has shown that an airport placed outside the city is a serious mistake, canceling out the advantages of travel by air.*

Work of the intellectual type will be done in the "WORLD CITY," comprising all of the various institutions that can be created there.

Furthermore, the big public buildings which are to line the avenue de la Cathédrale will embellish the heart of the city, while making their services directly available to the city's inhabitants.

People will also work in the *New Harbor Station* and the *Free Port* next to it. There are direct connections between residential districts and these work districts – streetcars, shuttle service, highways, truck lanes.

And finally, the residents of the New City can go about their business in the important complexes of Antwerp's present or future ports, to the north of the New City or in the city of Antwerp itself (the present Harbor Station and Old City). Plans 3103 and 3101 show how direct connections will be provided.

First there is the already completed tunnel of the *Canal des Brasseurs* (No 27). Our project makes this tunnel emerge onto a special *place*, or outlet, in the New City; only afterwards does it open into the grand promenade-avenue de la Cathédrale. A special road forking off from the exit of the Tunnel des Brasseurs will link it to the New City's general network of elevated highways.

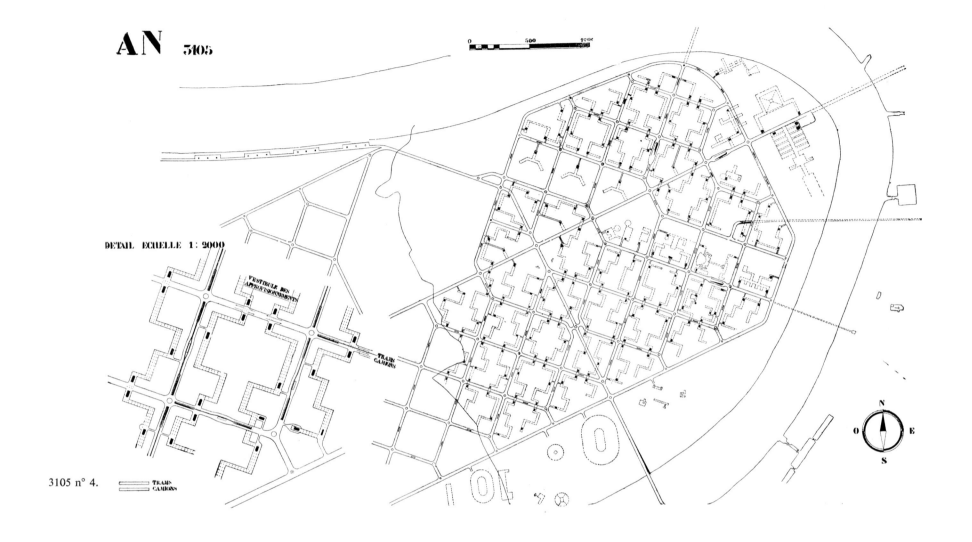

DÉTAIL ÉCHELLE 1 : 2000

VESTIBULE DES APPROVISIONNEMENTS

TRAINS CAMIONS

3105 n° 4.

TRAINS
CAMIONS

A second tunnel exists, at the quay Saint-Jean (No 28), *for pedestrians only*. In the New City, it ends opposite the promenades on the quay of the river Scheldt and right next to the main arteries, highways, streetcar tracks and shuttle lines. In the city of Antwerp, the tunnel will lead onto the new esplanade on the quays, at the head of a proposed opening to be cut through the more undesirable districts to the boulevards (towards the chaussée de Malines). And the tunnel's elevators can lead up to the Seafront Esplanade Station (the present Harbor Station, transformed). This Esplanade, offering a splendid view, is to run along the docks of the Harbor Station and from there, to the ramp leading to the streets which open onto the City Hall and the cathedral. So much for the two existing tunnels.

But we consider that it is imperative to create a new car tunnel, to echo the present pedestrian tunnel on the quay Saint-Jean (No 29). This new tunnel will emerge, in Antwerp, between the cathedral and the Central Station.

Obviously, these few tunnels in themselves would not be enough to serve the vast expanse of the new left bank city, whose population could rise, according to our plans, from 100,000 to half a million or more. So we have planned a tunnel running east-west: No 30, between the "WORLD CITY" and the future North Station. This tunnel would carry a shuttle line as well as cars and heavy trucks. To the northeast it is linked directly with the route for Holland (No 31) and to the southeast, with the highway going to Ghent and Ostend.

We have planned this passage as a tunnel so as not to obstruct the view of Antwerp from the loop of the river Scheldt. But the tunnel could undoubtedly be replaced by a suspension bridge one day, whenever it becomes apparent that Antwerp's present Harbor Station should be replaced once and for all by the left bank's New Harbor Station.

A tunnel for average traffic could also be placed at number 32, to link the left bank city to Antwerp's big Commercial Port.

Finally, we have planned a tunnel from one side of the Scheldt to the other, upstream from Antwerp (at right angles to South Station); this tunnel is to accommodate the international line of Antwerp's Left Bank Harbor Station and the Belgian shuttle. But for automobiles, streetcars, trucks and pedestrians, we have planned to build a suspension bridge across the river. The lower of its two platforms will be 22 meters above the Scheldt. Big ships do not need to come this far up the river.

So the inhabitants of the New City are assured of connections between the places where they work and their homes.

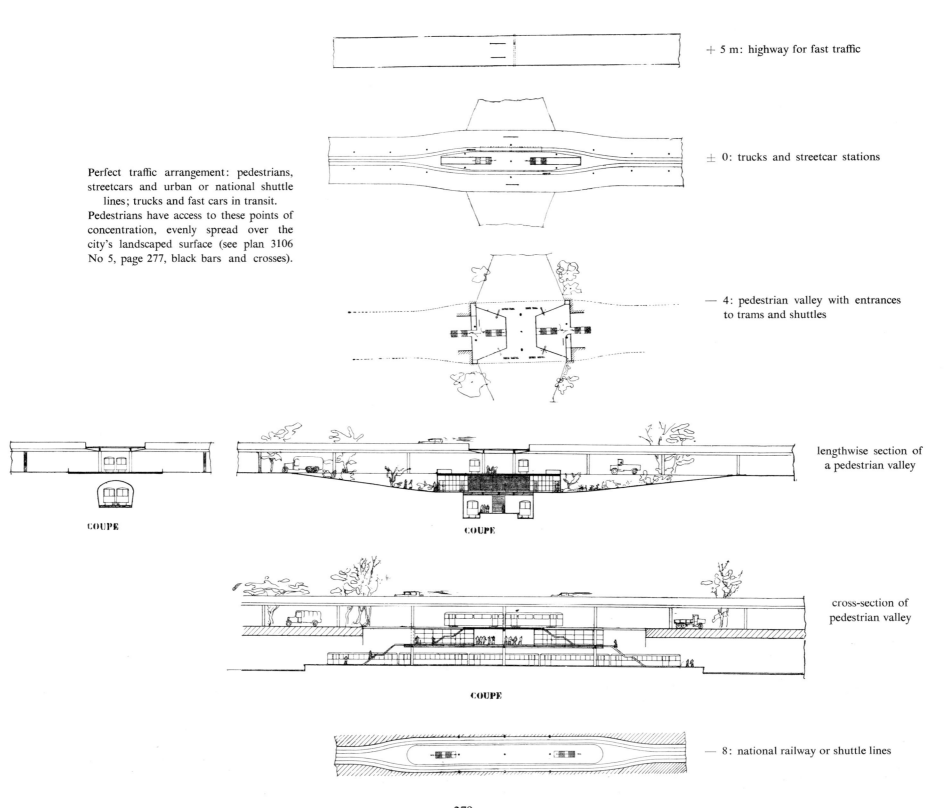

+ 5 m: highway for fast traffic

± 0: trucks and streetcar stations

Perfect traffic arrangement: pedestrians, streetcars and urban or national shuttle lines; trucks and fast cars in transit. Pedestrians have access to these points of concentration, evenly spread over the city's landscaped surface (see plan 3106 No 5, page 277, black bars and crosses).

— 4: pedestrian valley with entrances to trams and shuttles

COUPE

COUPE

lengthwise section of a pedestrian valley

COUPE

cross-section of pedestrian valley

— 8: national railway or shuttle lines

279

DETAIL ECHELLE 1:2000

AUTOPORTS

CIRCULATION VERTICALE

3104 n° 3.

CHAPTER FIVE

## RECREATION

The plan of the New City includes vast expanses of parks directly at the foot of each house ("Radiant City" type), and beaches for sun-bathing, as indicated at the beginning of this report (Plans Nos 3107 and 3108).

These elements, composing what we call a "GREEN CITY," are the very basis of the residential neighborhoods. They are part of the home, and it is thanks to them that the city dweller is guaranteed the "BASIC PLEASURES" we mentioned as early as line 2, Chapter Two, of this report.

In plan 3116 we see the complete mechanism of a residential district. It expresses a model solution, which can be varied in any way to suit local conditions – topography, etc. We do not need to dwell upon the means of recreation which the "RADIANT CITY" provides for the inhabitants, right next to their homes. To recapitulate:

*Sports practiced at the foot of the house.*
*Pleasant walks and places to rest, in the parks.*
*Children's playgrounds between the* pilotis *of the houses.*
Roof-gardens: therapy, sun-bathing, etc.
From the collective viewpoint, the city has the facilities needed to occupy a good deal of leisure time.

*First of all, the great promenades, for pedestrians and drivers,* all along the avenue de la Cathédrale (No 25), 120 meters wide. The big public buildings will rise on either side of this avenue. For instance: facing Antwerp, there could be the City Hall and Municipal Services, with room for banquets and festivities generally. Then the People's Meeting Hall (34), all sorts of group facilities, including halls for various purposes; next, a complex of museums (35) built along new lines.

Farther on is the department store group (36) giving onto the avenue de la Cathédrale and the thoroughfare which intersects it here, the avenue de la Gare Centrale (37).

At the end of the avenue de la Cathédrale is the airport, with its restaurants (38), and opposite, on the other side of the avenue, the casino with its riverside gardens (39).

Another community pleasure site is the grand avenue de la Gare Centrale running east-west from the "WORLD CITY" toward Ostend. There is no elevated highway above this avenue, which crosses the residential districts and goes by the Central Station (13).

The WORLD CITY itself, an outstanding architectural composition, is an exceptionally pleasant spot with superb views of the river, the New City and Antwerp. Try to picture the pyramid of the Musée Mondial, or World Museum (41); the walk which spirals around it up to a height of 100 meters successively reveals four horizons and culminates in a magnificent panoramic view. The avenue du Museé Mondial (41), along the axis of the Museum's pyramid, links the WORLD CITY to the parks and marshes to the south (42) and to the Olympic Sports Center (43). This avenue de la Cité Mondiale pours traffic into the Tunnel des Brasseurs. Then it crosses the avenue de la Cathédrale and from there leads into the parc du Sud at the site of the Zoological Garden (45) and the lakeside restaurants (46). Next to them begin the avenue which circles the lake and returns to the avenue de la Cathédrale, and the other branch of the avenue leading to the Olympic Sports Center.

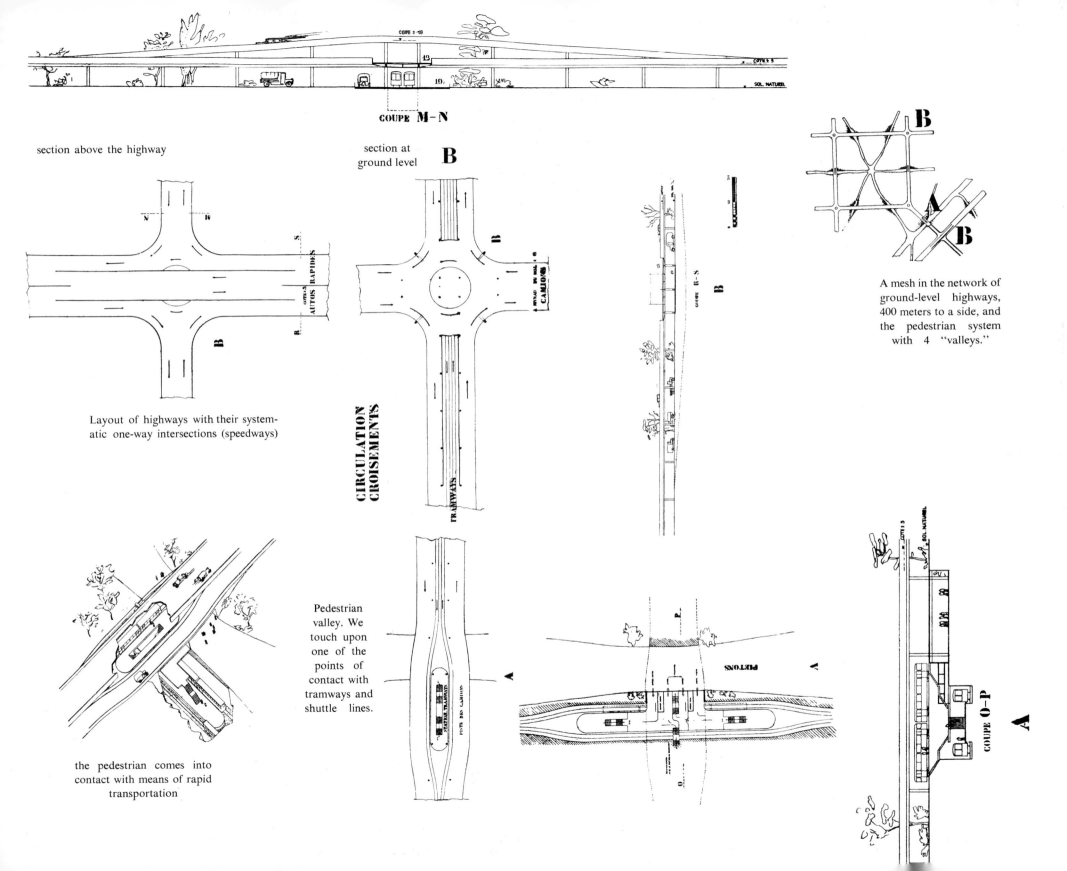

COUPE M–N

section above the highway

section at ground level

B

Layout of highways with their systematic one-way intersections (speedways)

CIRCULATION
CROISEMENTS

A mesh in the network of ground-level highways, 400 meters to a side, and the pedestrian system with 4 "valleys."

the pedestrian comes into contact with means of rapid transportation

Pedestrian valley. We touch upon one of the points of contact with tramways and shuttle lines.

COUPE O–P

A

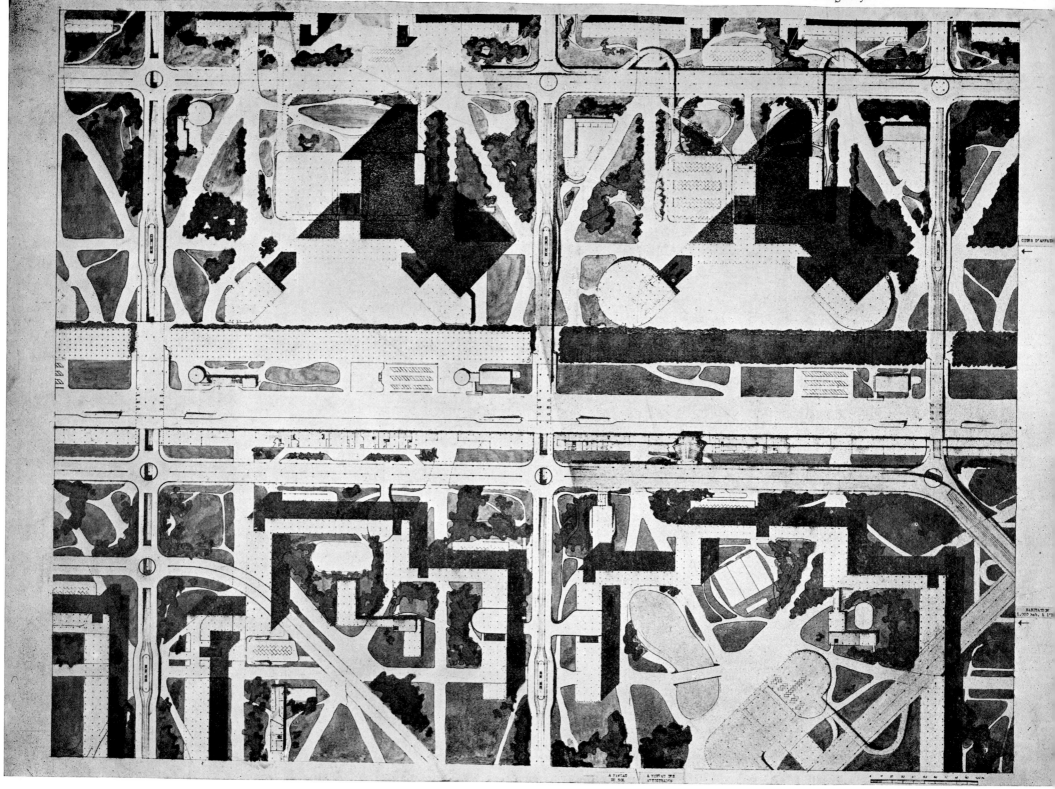

One portion of the avenue de la Cathédrale. We worked on this study for months. It is the strict representation of all the solutions found for countless individual problems, dealt with according to a systematic doctrine of city planning. It "works" everywhere!

High buildings perform general functions but man – the city dweller – is taken into consideration. Try it, let him walk around in every part of this plan: he is at ease here and finds stimulation and joy. The stroller finds pleasure; and the citizen, a source of pride.

The plan on the opposite page seen in perspective: the "corso," the main promenade artery, in the axis of the cathedral. It extends from the new to the old harbor station.

At the tip of the avenue de la Cathédrale, facing the old port of Antwerp, stretches the grand esplanade onto which the tunnel of the quay Saint-Jean opens (47). On either side of the esplanade stands a pylon with a beacon to guide pilots at night. Two other identical beacons stand at the other end of the same avenue (48).

Facing Antwerp, the esplanade turns into the main avenue of the World City (49), used only by pedestrians and by automobiles at reduced speed. This avenue crosses the GRAND CLOISTER (50) of THE WORLD CITY'S INTERNATIONAL EXHIBITION HALL (51), then continues in front of the WORLD CITY'S office buildings (52) to end at the University of World Science (53).

The ramp of the World Museum (54) is parallel to the above avenue. From the banks of the river, the ramp rises gradually to a point halfway up the World Museum pyramid, having meanwhile passed along the roofs of the Exhibition Hall (51), with their roof gardens, restaurants, and so forth.

It should be noted that very close to the sidewalks all along these promenades, especially along the avenues de la Cathédrale and de la Cité Mondiale, is a succession of cafés and shops on the ground floor or on an upper story set back from the edge of the building. This stepped-back story, forming a roof, is in itself a splendid upper promenade which could accommodate specialty or luxury shops.

In this way, the grand vistas of the New City actually compose a forum and thus perpetuate the time-honored traditions of every city that has ever been blessed with an intense civic life.

The plans show that everywhere along these imposing prospects there are meeting halls for clubs, night classes, motion pictures, lectures, theaters, and the like.

It should be further noted that this project includes several vast hotels which could provide still more meeting halls of all sorts. These hotels are placed about every 500 meters along both sides of the avenue de la Cathédrale, along the major Holland-Ostend highway and parallel to the avenue de la Gare Centrale. They are to be about 150 meters high, and are intended to serve the city's vital districts, from the WORLD CITY to the Central Station, the airport, etc.

CHAPTER SIX

THE PROJECT'S ARCHITECTURAL ARRANGEMENTS

First we must recall the reasons for the working out of this project:

To begin with, the solar orientation, made to coincide with a notable architectural axis: the avenue de la Cathédrale. Next, the network of elevated highways, each mesh a square measuring 375 meters on each side, serving the entire surface of the city in conjunction with the networks of shuttles, streetcars and trucks.

Then, the flexible mesh of pedestrian routes (diagonal and orthogonal meshes) covering all points of the city.

Once the city was given these complete arterial and capillary systems, the big principal arteries were introduced: avenue de la Gare, avenue de la CITE MONDIALE, avenue de la Cathédrale.

Then we established a ring of highways around the city.

Every part of the city gets a maximum of sunlight, since it is full of greenery: a "RADIANT CITY."

The pedestrian can walk fast or simply stroll, independent of any vehicle.

Streetcars and trucks can perform their functions without ever being hindered by intersections or the presence of any obstacle.

Cars can drive slowly up the grand avenues or speed along to every point in the city.

Finally, to establish contact with the exterior, Antwerp or the Belgian provinces or other countries, there are big through routes whose straight lines crossing the city classify its layout and give it a topography both distinct and varied.

We want to stress the fact that *the most absolute diversity will be the rule in this city, thanks to the infinity of possible combinations of its simple constituent elements.*

Never again will we have to look upon the depressing, stifling sight formed by "corridor-streets"; instead, we may look upon immense architectural ensembles, conceived in a harmonious crescendo.

With this in mind, we realize that the city's skyline will no longer be the work of accident or cacophony. Instead, it will take on unaccustomed splendor, accurately reflecting a new civilization.

In place of a bristling line of irregularly shaped roofs, *the roofs of all apartment buildings will be uniformly horizontal, at a height of 50 meters.*

The effect of this horizontal can be stunning. Remember that the natural wealth of verdant parks will provide endless diversity, so that the continuous line of cornices glimpsed through the trees at a height of 50 meters becomes a dignified and restful architectural achievement.

On this horizontal landing 50 meters up will stand the five big hotel buildings, rhythmically following one another every 500 meters down the Holland-Ostend highway.

The Business City's three skyscrapers, 150 or 200 meters high, stand obliquely in relation to this line of vertical prisms. We can enjoy the ample treatment of their façades and the cadence of their arrangement.

Next, we can appreciate the precision with which the four beacons mark off the avenue de la Cathédrale.

Then come the varied silhouettes of the public buildings lining this avenue: the opulent orchestration of the most pleasing architectural forms, a symphony of diversity. In a word, an intense architectural creation.

The WORLD CITY, set back slightly, is bathed by the waters of the river Scheldt; its axis converges upon the vital center of the old city of Antwerp, where the cathedral stands.

These grand architectural movements are set off by several big parks to the south and by the river which bathes them.

Ships approaching the New Harbor Station from the northern stretch of the Scheldt will, as they enter the loop, instantly have a view across the city's grand avenue to its venerable cathedral way at the other end, in the mist veiling the horizon. An effective spiritual link between past and present.

But the City of Antwerp itself, when the approaches to its old quay are improved, will receive the architectural benefits of the whole.

In conclusion, it is time to speak of the improvement of the City of Antwerp.

CHAPTER SEVEN

## IMPROVING THE CITY OF ANTWERP

It is impossible to go into detail about the day-to-day improvements which the city of Antwerp would need to make because of its relations with the New City which is to spring up on the other side of the river. But even at this point we can outline them to some extent.

First of all, it would be a good idea to clean up certain districts of the lower city, between the port Napoléon and the pedestrian tunnel on the quay Saint-Jean.

We plan to demolish the old buildings at the edge of the quay and replace them by a strip of greenery. But the historic setting of the City Hall and its *place*, and of the cathedral and its *parvis*, will be preserved. Opening up the areas immediately around these historic monuments would be liable to take all relative proportion and all grandeur away from them.

But the present Harbor Station could, on the contrary, be improved, by the construction of a Seafront Esplanade on the docks themselves, facing the avenue de la Cathédrale of the new left bank city. This Esplanade (No. 55) could be situated 10 meters above the quay and lined with roof gardens and kiosks and, behind these, cafés. It would be linked to the city by a big inclined walk going down to the *parvis* of the cathedral, and to the elevator of the quay Saint-Jean tunnel. As a last touch, several stairways lead down to the loading platforms behind the docks.

The esplanade could be a stunning promenade for the citizens of Antwerp.

On either side of the cathedral but not less than 150 and 250 meters away, two openings could be cut through the undesirable districts:

one toward the National Bank and the Palace of Justice (56); the other toward the boulevard d'Italie and the suburb of Deurne (57).

The latter opening affords a practical solution to the problem of the rue Carnot and the Chaussée de Turnhout, whereas costly expropriations of business buildings have done nothing so far to relieve the situation.

Very near the cathedral, the Schoenmarkt, reserved for slow traffic, could be widened, as an extension of the rue Leys which begins at today's Central Station.

Once the city's old *quartiers* were purged, the former docks would furnish an ideal site for a public playing field. The basin could be used for aquatic sports, and a football field, tennis courts, a stadium, club buildings, restaurants, and so on could be built (see plans 3107 and 3108).

Both plans show that the Van Dyck and Jordaens loading platforms have been connected to the exit from the great east-west tunnel of the New Left Bank City, on the same spot as we have planned the North Station. So this northern tip of the city becomes an important site of traffic classification: Antwerp's great interior boulevards, the Ring, the quays of the Scheldt, the route to Holland, etc.

CHAPTER EIGHT

MISCELLANEOUS: This study has not gone into detail as to the location of certain municipal and urban services which depend upon distinctly local circumstances and do not necessitate any particular provision in the plans. We are thinking especially of hospitals, and suggest this innovation: each residence group (or *redent*) could include not only school systems and a nursery, but a *Health Center* as well, where minor surgery could be performed and medical care given. As to the hospital itself (in this regard new ideas are coming to the fore), it could be established either in the city or outside, near the university medical centers.

Churches and all other places of worship can easily find room in the sizeable open spaces characteristic of the "GREEN CITY." The same may be said for theaters, concert halls, and the like.

There is no point for the moment in trying to decide where the cemeteries should be placed.

The present project points out the existence of an industrial zone south of the South Station, between the river and the railway tracks. This is the culmination of the great Charleroi-Brussels-Antwerp industrial zone.

Here we have planned to do away with the petroleum harbor and transfer it to a point north of the New Right Bank City. For this harbor we would use the present riverbed, on the other bank, transforming it into a basin by correcting the curve of the Scheldt. This correction was mentioned among the elements of the competition and helped us to select the site of the New Left Bank Harbor Station.

It is obvious that definitive technical improvements in the harbor of greater Antwerp go beyond the scope of this competition. Accordingly, we have confined ourselves to making a few suggestions or predictions.

*Le Corbusier and P. Jeanneret, Huib Hoste, Locquet.*

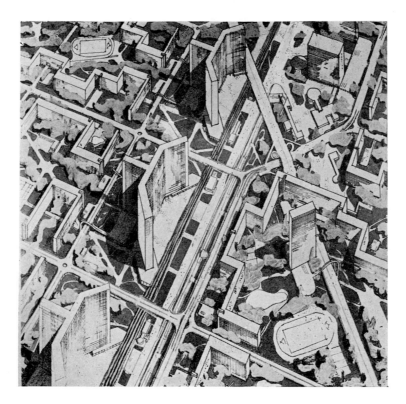

The plan on page 282 seen from another angle.

## THE WORLD CITY

The idea of a World City has been presented to the Belgian government. This project applies the idea to sites on the left bank of the river Scheldt, and suggests creating such a City as a satellite of Antwerp.

### I.

### DEFINITION OF THE WORLD CITY
### (ACCORDING TO THE MEMORANDUM).

"A permanent Universal Exhibition, a great fair, a market, a great commercial exchange, a central institute of information and education, acting as a veritable International University. Consequently, the World City is called upon: 1) to be a *practical instrument for international cooperation* in every field, just as the capital city of every country facilitates such cooperation on a national level; 2) by uniting all forces, to provide the occasion for the achievement of a MODEL CITY, because this city could be built according to a coherent plan, free of the historical contingencies which make older cities hard to transform; 3) to be a permanent symbol of the unity of mankind apart from any political, economic, social, intellectual or religious institution."

### II. ADVANTAGES OF THE WORLD CITY.

a) *Advantages of choosing Antwerp for the World City.*

There is an admirable site for such a city, relatively isolated by the fact that the river forms three sides of it. An island could easily be created by the construction of a canal (justifiable for its own sake) on the fourth side.

Moreover, the World City would be linked with:

1) a big and flourishing city, Antwerp; communications by tunnels, ferryboat, bridges and a shuttle;

2) Belgium as a whole by means of numerous railways, roads and highways, as well as by existing waterways or others which could easily be built;

3) overseas nations, because the most important transatlantic liners come right up to the banks of the river;

4) all parts, by means of an airport and other facilities for which the flat terrain is ideally suited. As to the geographical position, Antwerp is really the best possible site for a World City. As the Committee report puts it, "Belgium is the seat of a great international movement, the center of the quadrilateral formed by Paris, London, Amsterdam and Cologne, the world's most densely populated and active area. Antwerp can be reached from anywhere with remarkable ease."

Today the world is divided and hesitant, awaiting a unanimous signal to take up the task again

Air view of the New City.

The new transversal canal.

The new harbor station.

The esplanade on the docks of the present harbor station.

The World City

with vigor. The availability of an international meeting point and business center could make the new effort easier and keep things moving. In the sixteenth century, Antwerp was just such a place, its precious Exchange attracting delegations from every country. Antwerp can become such a place again in the twentieth century.

b) *Advantages of the World City for Antwerp.*

1) The wealth of a city has always been its population. Now not only would the city be able to make its demands upon a surplus of population but there would be shifts within the population, attracted by the World City. Antwerp could also call upon the exterior, upon everyone whom the World City would attract with its advantages of security, convenience, pleasure and beauty.

2) Neither the city nor the province nor the Belgian government would have to bear the World City's general sumptuary expenses for, as in the case of World's Fairs, they would be incumbent upon the various countries and participants. The site of the World City would become the property of a body which would enjoy fiscal autonomy and have recourse to loans to finance its undertakings. The very valuable site would be security for these loans, and interest would be raised by normal taxes levied on the "inhabitants" – including government bodies and international business associations – or beneficiaries of the advantages offered by the City.

3) The World City, far from being a burden upon Antwerp, would bring Antwerp precious sources of prosperity. Over the centuries Antwerp has been subject to the vicissitudes of the great current of trade: the World City would guide this current in a way favorable to the city and the entire nation, and Antwerp could put its port to full use. Antwerp would become a city to the fourth power: Port, Market, Industrial City and World City.

### III. HOW THE PLAN WAS ESTABLISHED.

Certain parts of the plan are governed by three sorts of desiderata: those of the World City; those of the site and the vicinity; those of the New or Model City.

1) *Desiderata concerning the World City.*

a) As to the structures needed, we referred to the enumerations given in the report of the Committee on the World City.

b) As to the location of each one, we have tried to conform to the basic diagrams because they express relationships of class and function.

For according to the ideological plan set forth in this report, the City's layout should comprise two fundamental axes, with the buildings reserved to national bodies along one and those for international bodies along the other. At the right angle intersection of the two axes stand the general buildings; both sides must contribute to the cost of their construction, as they house institutions on a world-wide scale, syntheses of economic, social, and intellectual life. Here we have the World Civic Center. All around it are developed the big residential districts with their communal services and all of the elements devoted, as was requested, to nature, to greenery and bodies of water.

These buildings and these arrangements appear on the plan.

But it goes without saying that because of the special, largely novel function of these buildings, each one should be studied with special care and arouse special creative efforts. Their distribution throughout the City and their approximate dimensions are, however, essential because of the activi-

Architecture in LA is
very trendy; sort of like fashion

There are ground breaking
buildings redefining what it means
to build.

A vast diversity of styles

Many studios, streets that
are curved.

DISTINGUISHABLE ARCHITECTURE IS
NESSESSESARY FOR IDENTITY;

1. TOPIC GENERATION : Triangulation

Los Angeles
GLITZ
BROADCASTING CAPITAL
ART DECO
(OLD)
THEATRICAL
ENTERTAINMENT
ARCHITECTURE
~~Public transportation~~
ASSOSIATION
THEMES
HISTORY OF CITY.
ARCHITECTURE.
DECAYING OR GALVANIZ
IDENTITY OF LA
IN GLOBAL ECONOM

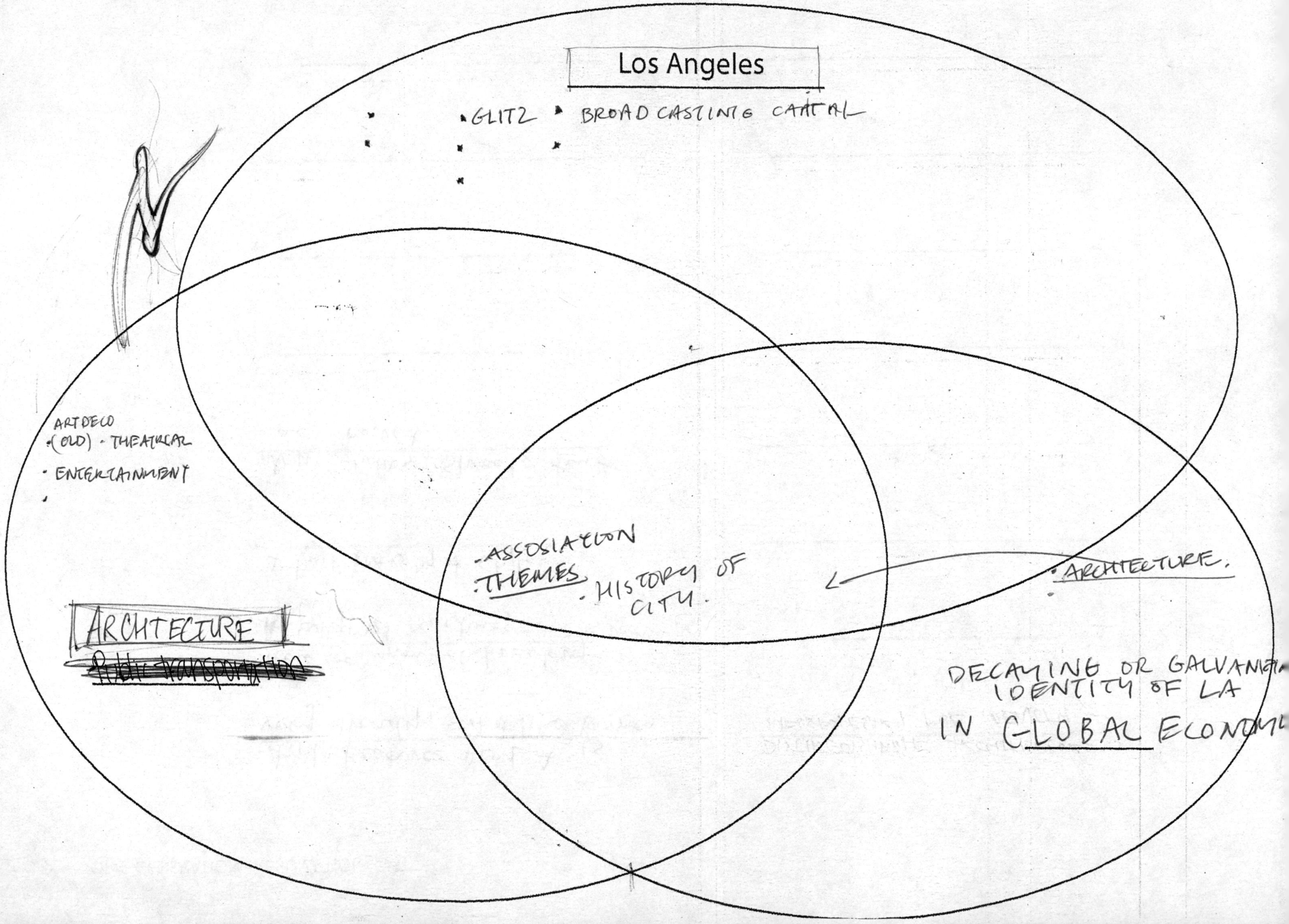

# AN 3112

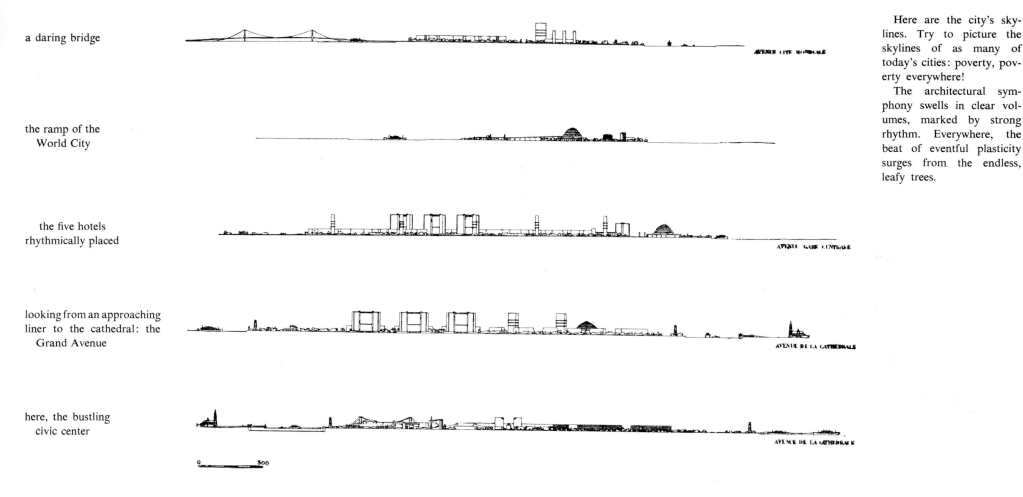

a daring bridge

the ramp of the World City

the five hotels rhythmically placed

looking from an approaching liner to the cathedral: the Grand Avenue

here, the bustling civic center

AVENUE CITE MONDIALE

AVENUE GARE CENTRALE

AVENUE DE LA CATHEDRALE

AVENUE DE LA CATHEDRALE

0 _____ 300

Here are the city's skylines. Try to picture the skylines of as many of today's cities: poverty, poverty everywhere!

The architectural symphony swells in clear volumes, marked by strong rhythm. Everywhere, the beat of eventful plasticity surges from the endless, leafy trees.

---

ties to which they are to be devoted, and this is why we have emphasized them.

2) *Desiderata concerning the site and its vicinity.*

They have determined:

a) the orientation of the general plan;

b) the way roads and mains have been joined to the city of Antwerp itself;

c) the general architectural character of the City as a whole, a City whose modernity contrasts with historical Antwerp;

d) transferral to the City of institutions which lack for space in present-day Antwerp but which should be held on to, as nuclei of broader institutions which could eventually be internationalized. This applies to the Zoological Gardens, Botanical Gardens, and Sports.

3) *Desiderata concerning the World City itself.*

They caused certain devices, certain edifices to be selected, as the result of combinations inspired by technical potentialities and those of the most up-to-date economics.

\* \* \*

Instead of dealing with these sorts of desiderata separately, we fused them into a synthesis. Our prime concern was to achieve unity, so that every part was subordinate to the whole. Unity was imperative not only if we were to meet the fundamental requirements of architecture and city planning but because the ideological plan of the World City, which we tried to carry out to the utmost, laid down this condition:

"To build in such a way that the mere sight of the unity and co-ordination of the buildings and other features of the World City persuades everyone – visitors, residents and workers alike – that it is possible to co-ordinate the activities of the world itself; and also, to build the City, as sign and symbol, in such a way as naturally to lead the mind to the exterior realities which are represented."

*Paul Otlet (Director of the World Palace, Brussels).*

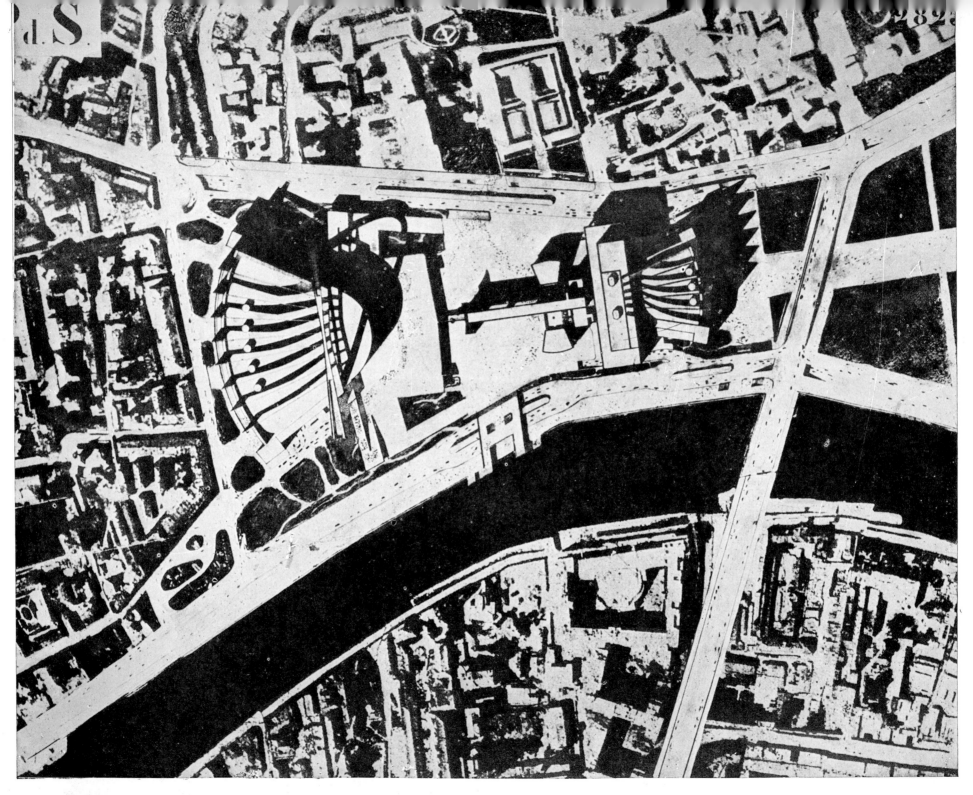

## THE PALACE OF THE SOVIETS

The Main Auditorium: an audience of 15,000. Open-air platform: 50,000 people, and perfectly regulated acoustics. Small auditorium: 6,500 people. Huge crowds can move about at their ease on the esplanade. Cars are on a lower level; the parking lot is beneath the auditoriums.

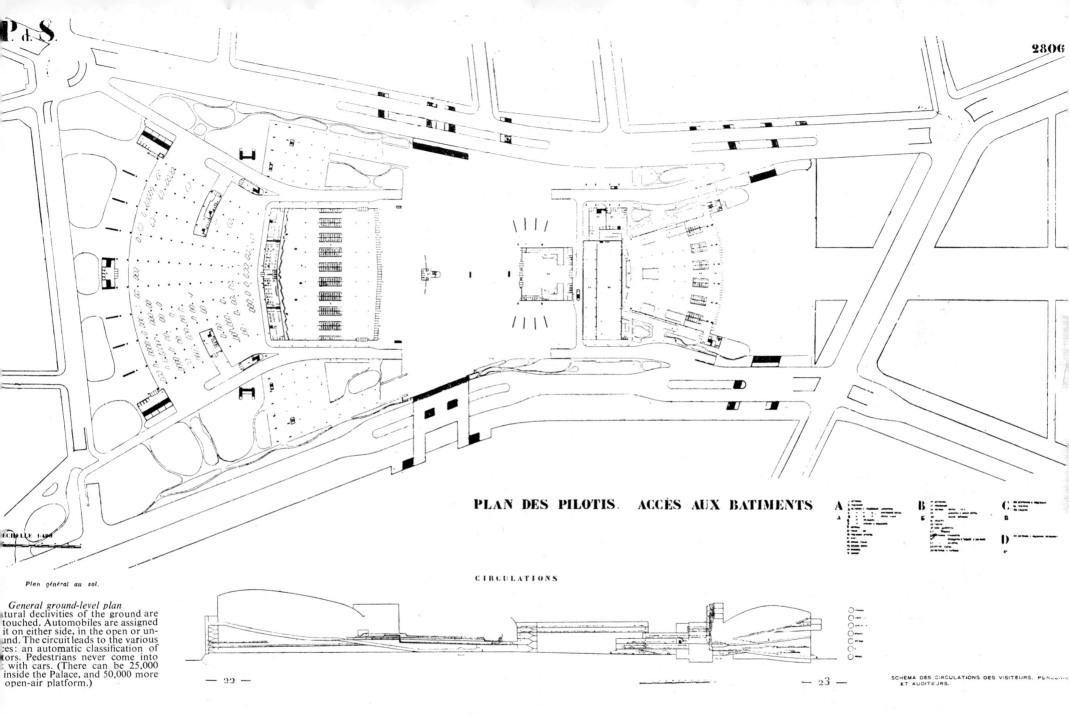

PLAN DES PILOTIS. ACCÈS AUX BATIMENTS

CIRCULATIONS

*Plan général au sol.*

*General ground-level plan*
tural declivities of the ground are
touched. Automobiles are assigned
it on either side, in the open or un-
und. The circuit leads to the various
ces: an automatic classification of
ors. Pedestrians never come into
with cars. (There can be 25,000
inside the Palace, and 50,000 more
open-air platform.)

— 22 —

— 23 —

SCHÉMA DES CIRCULATIONS DES VISITEURS, PERSONN...
ET AUDITEURS.

1932. PROJECT FOR THE PALACE OF THE SOVIETS, IN MOSCOW.

# MOSCOW 1928—1931 CLASSIFIED TRAFFIC SYSTEM

The ground is devoted to movement: pedestrians, cars.
Everything above the ground (the buildings) is devoted to stability.

No similarity between the two. The ground beneath the buildings must be freed, for regular
streams of cars and lakes of pedestrians. The streams flow directly to certain entrances; the pedestrians
are widely scattered. This makes for a new economy of layout.

The streams of cars can flow in sunken beds or along elevated highways. Starting 5 meters above
the ground, buildings take on definite shape. Distribution of traffic has been achieved below, on the
ground.

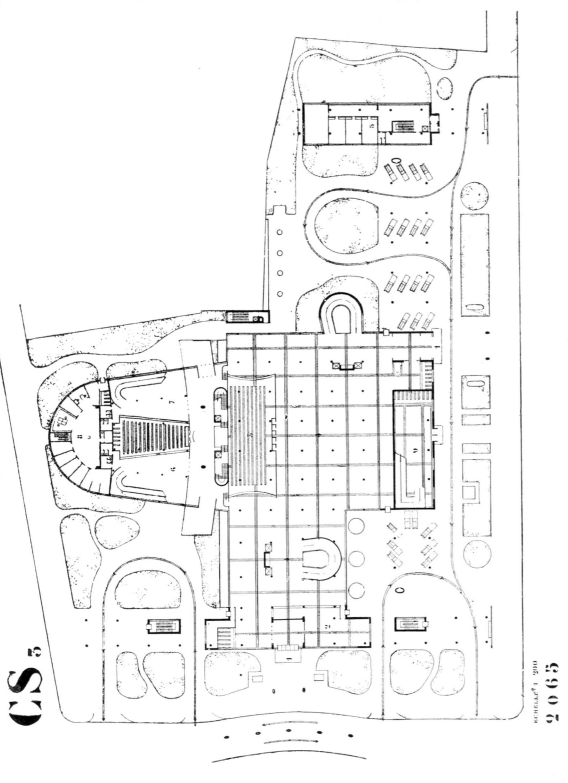

Here, the dynamic functions: distribution of sorts of traffic.
(Pilotis on the ground level.)

Here, the static function is expressed by offices, club and auditorium.
1928. Palace of Light Industry (first called the Centrosoyus) in Moscow. Now built.

Master plan for the urbanization of the City of Moscow.

In 1931, Moscow officials sent me a questionnaire, admirably thought out, about the city's reorganization. If only all cities would send out such questionnaires! Their lot would be improved.

The theoretical drawings of the "Radiant City" were made in order to answer this questionnaire. They form a theory of urbanization for modern times.

My "Answer to Moscow" caused an unexpected reaction: its technical aspects were hailed in flattering terms. But the cornerstone of my work was freedom of the individual, and this was held against me. Doctrinal vehemence prevented any worthwhile discussion. Capitalist? bourgeois? proletarian? My only answer is a term expressing my line of conduct and my ingrained revolutionary attitude: *human*. My professional duty, as architect and city planner, is to achieve what is *human*.

Charitable colleagues – Frenchmen, too, and far from being "Reds" – proclaimed to all who would listen or read, "that I wanted to destroy Moscow." Whereas they themselves, if only they were called upon, would, etc...

The plate which appears opposite (last in the "Radiant City" series), is not a program for Moscow's destruction but on the contrary, for its construction. It shows zoning and axes of movement along which the city could gradually achieve a position of supple ease, expansion without difficulty, and so forth. This plate shows a specimen of urban biology.

So far, only the International Congress for Modern Architecture, the C.I.A.M. (see page 18) has required its members to seek the lines of vital communication which can bring a city into efficient contact with its surrounding region. (A task which will fall to the 5th Congress.)

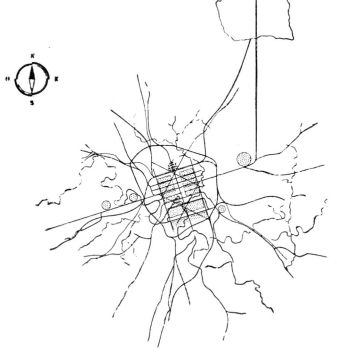

**APPLICATION TO MOSCOW**

Palace of the Soviets in Moscow (see pages 288-289).

The administration building, on the left, is independent of the ground. Not only is the ground freed but, moreover, the expanse of open space beneath the building forms a highly architectural frame for the landscape seen in the background.

On the right, impressive ramps lead the way to the open-air platform for 50,000 people.

By contrast, 15,000 can reach the main auditorium from ground level, by means of a continuous inclined plane, becoming concave until it reaches the seats. No stairways, not even a single step can be tolerated in a public building – and certainly not "monumental" stairways!

Here is where the 108-hectare site begins, an exquisite location on the Saël. The sky, the sea, the Atlas mountains – a natural treasure. But there will be nothing left of it, once you've built your 2,000 little cottages. This sketch gives a complete image of the future inhabitants' real needs. A dream? No, simply the particulars of the problem. At the same time, this is genuine regionalism, where the site, the topography, the climate govern the achitecture.

# 1932

# DOMAINE DE BADJARA (OUED OUCHAIA)

A private individual, M. Durand, of Algiers, was courageous enough to state: "I want to do things well. I will not sacrifice my splendid estate to the insensitive demands of brute money."

The site: 108 hectares, of hills and valleys, 20 minutes away from Algiers. To be turned into a garden city? No, modern city planning will find a solution.

Four buildings, for three hundred families each, will be given the best orientation. Three hundred superimposed villas, each with a living room lighted by a glass wall 4.50 meters high, a hanging garden, flowers and trees close at hand. The four big structures stand out boldly. A highway, with a garage and repair shops, links them to the road for Algiers.

DAL
3015

This is the answer: not for some privileged millionaire but for the person who could never afford to build his own little house. A dream come true, thanks to modern techniques and organization. The dream is even improved upon: communal services (cooperative food supply and housekeeping services) bring priceless luxury: the end of enslavement to household chores.

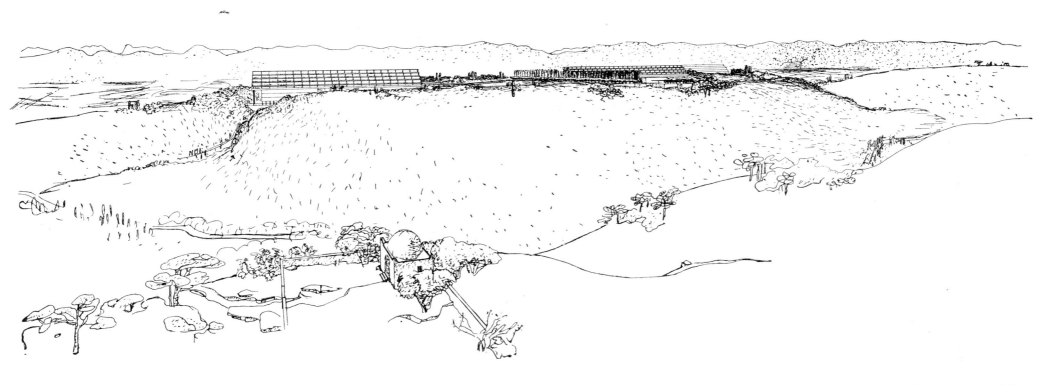

In the middle of the highway, food supply and housekeeping services. Along the length of each building, two systems of vertical transportation connect with two interior streets. Is this enough? This makes for three hundred separate villas, overlooking a horizon that gets wider the higher you go. The entire ground surface of the domain remains free. There are facilities for sports, and walks amidst a thoroughly natural setting. Deep in the valley, the sharecropping farms and part of the vineyards remain. To meet a possible (commercial) demand, five hundred plots for cottages are laid out along a simple boulevard, winding along the hillside. Horizontal boulevard, with villas above and villas below.

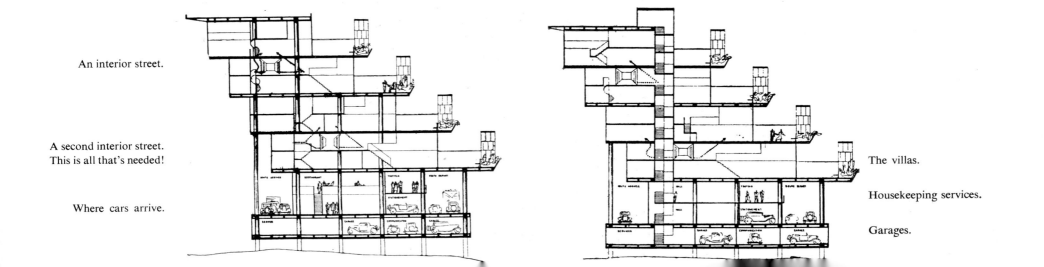

An interior street.

A second interior street.
This is all that's needed!

Where cars arrive.

The villas.

Housekeeping services.

Garages.

Southern façade
(parasol shape)

**D**AL 3051

Northern façade

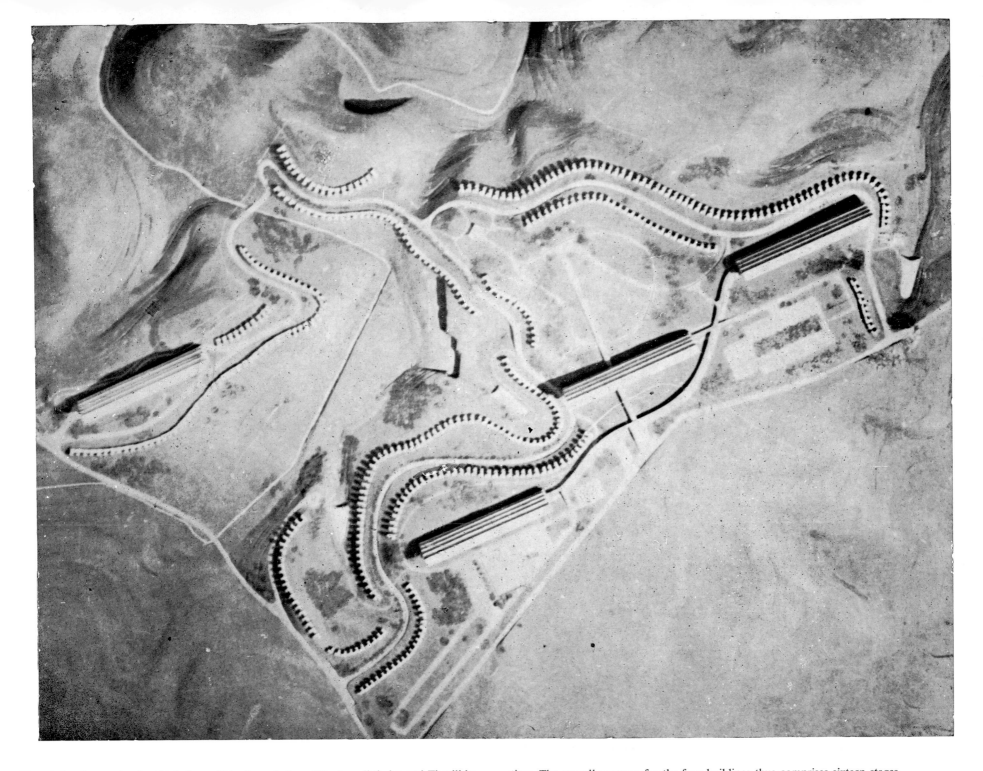

How I pity the people who think they will be freer, better off in these little houses! They'll be hugging the ground while their neighbors in the four big buildings can gaze upon vast horizons and benefit from communal services.

Because each building classifies vertical and horizontal traffic, it can be erected a quarter at a time. The overall program for the four buildings thus comprises sixteen stages.

In the foothills that actually overlap the buildings, three dams will be built, forming three swimming pools.

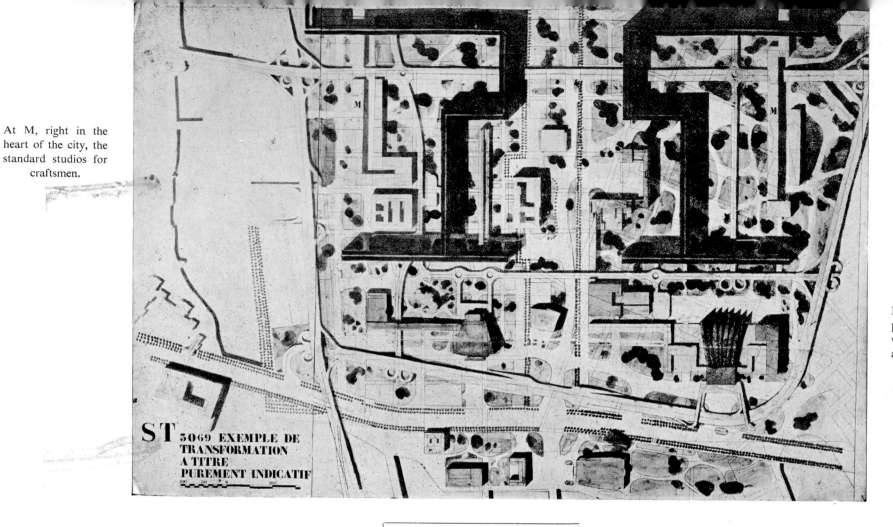

Housing *redent*

At M, right in the heart of the city, the standard studios for craftsmen.

The city's vertical axis, rid of heavy truck traffic, becomes a splendid promenade.

In the midst of parks, public buildings which exist or which are to be built.

ST 3069 EXEMPLE DE TRANSFORMATION A TITRE PUREMENT INDICATIF

Here is one of the prizewinners in the Stockholm contest: courtyards and corridor-streets. Can you imagine, in the 20th century, the automobile age, tearing everything down to build more corridor-streets, courtyards and homes facing north? (In this connection, see text on page 86.)

ST 3067

Norrmalm.

Sodermalm.

The gray spots stand for the sea which is everywhere and yet is never visible from the city.

Travel notebook
January, 1933:

"Big traffic arteries on the sides; hilltops = free, with curving *redents*.

"Create esplanades and artificial sites on the sea, for sports, restaurants, etc., and civic buildings. Airport too.

"They wanted to fill in the coves and bring down the hilltop and throw it into the water!

"The ground underwater is sturdy; depth 10 meters.

"May the 20th century city shine with spiritual brilliance like that of the King's Palace in 1700. A time of grave decisions!

"Principle: clean up the banks; plants; install sports areas from top to bottom of the hills. Crown the hills with curving *redents*. Pilotis everywhere. Skyline: avoid skyscrapers, but campaniles standing out clearly."

This clearly shows the immense promenade which would form the axis of Norrmalm.
Truck traffic is moved outside, to left and right.

# 1933. STOCKHOLM. URBANIZATION OF THE NORRMALM AND SODERMALM DISTRICTS

## MEMORANDUM ANNEXED TO THE PROJECT

1) After going to Stockholm to become acquainted with its present condition, the author tried to envisage its future. He decided that the subject of the competition (Nedre Norrmalm) was too localized and liable to paralyze the city's vital axis.

Project considered for first prize. New bottlenecks, corridor-streets, courtyards, homes facing north! And everything is torn down.

Such a flat, two-dimensional science! Alas, in officialdom, city planning remains a matter of two dimensions.

Pleasures of the landscape, of the sea which is everywhere? You'll go to the country to look for them, on Sundays!

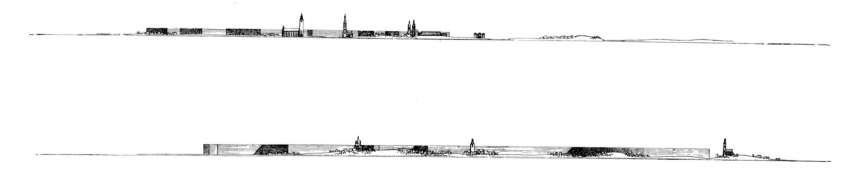

The whole of nature is revealed at every window in this gathering of homes and all along the sand beach which sets them off. The machine-age civilization brings new joys and solace. Nature and the city movingly integrated.

Thanks to modern techniques, my studies have led me to treat the very substance of the city – that is, the real volume of structures meant for housing – in a new way. Until now, since city planning was only two dimensional, the ground, whether flat or mountainous, was covered by a scab of houses, like a skin disease.

Whereas today, the very unevenness, the very vehemence of the ground is a source of beneficial calm, when seen in conjunction with the pure and uninterrupted pinnacle of the houses.

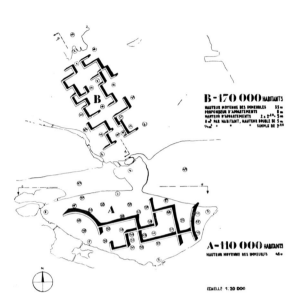

B - 170 000 HABITANTS
HAUTEUR MOYENNE DES IMMEUBLES 15ᵐ
PROFONDEUR D'APPARTEMENTS 5ᵐ
HAUTEUR D'APPARTEMENTS 2 à 2⁵⁰, 5ᵐ
8 m² PAR HABITANT, HAUTEUR DOUBLE DE 5ᵐ
SIMPLE DE 2.50

A - 110 000 HABITANTS
HAUTEUR MOYENNE DES IMMEUBLES 45ᵐ

ECHELLE 1:20 000

A veritable burst of light and space all around these *redents*. Everywhere parks go down the hills into the arms of the sea.

Suddenly, everything is melody, order, clarity. The city planner has sculpted something stupendous, magnificent; yes, sublime.

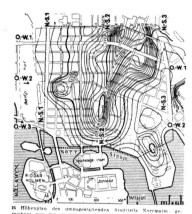

25 Höhenplan des umzugestaltenden Stadtteils Norrmalm gezeichnet von den Architekten Dr.-Ing. M. Säume und Dipl.-Ing.

And so, without causing any detour in the march toward progress ("big industry takes over building"), I have released the melody of the site, the true meaning of the ground, the intense expression of each place.

Modern city planning "sculpts" the site, making the outline and the modeling of the landscape appear. Silhouettes are eloquent and ever varied.
Sculptural "volume" has seized the city.
A (reduced) prototype of these plastic events already exists: the Vatican in Rome, particularly as seen from the Castel Sant' Angelo.

For it does not seem that the north-south axis should be given over to heavy traffic (multiple speeds, cars, trucks).

2) On the contrary: this median axis should no longer function as a rapid through passage. This function would be moved to left and right, to four north-south highways (4 – 1 – 2 – 5), plan S.T. 3067. Highways 1 and 2 would end at the intersection now being built (Slussen).

3) Transversal highways running east-west (3 – 8 – 7), would complete the network for heavy traffic.

4) Because of a doctrine of city planning, derived from his studies and from his travels to most of the major European and American cities, the author resolved that *his entry in the competition would be a general notion of urbanization, a program based on principle*. Of course such a project can merely suggest; the theories which it puts forward can be definitively applied only, in Stockholm itself, by Swedish specialists thoroughly familiar with the city's administrative and other local circumstances.

5) The project has been submitted as an overall plan (S.T. 3067), along with several tissue-paper drawings on top of one another (S.T. 3067 a, 3067 b, 3067 c, etc.), so as to show how the undertaking proceeds by successive stages and allow easy consultation of the regional map, scale 1/20,000, which was among the documents furnished to contestants.

6) *THEORY*. When considering the turbulence of today's cities, we must not confuse what is secondary with what is fundamental.

Although TRAFFIC is the critical factor afflicting all of our cities, it is still not the essential element in urban reform.

The fundamental element in a city is THE DWELLING.

First of all we have to LIVE! Traffic, as a function, is second to this one.

7) LIVING! DWELLING!

Perfect housing units, optimum living conditions – they outline an *entire program of organized construction under government supervision, or perhaps even launched by the government.*

The author is so convinced that THE HOME is what determines the city dweller's happiness, that he states the tasks to be accomplished in the following way:

8) *The materials needed for city planning are:*

the sky,

trees,

steel,

cement.

By this paradoxical listing, he hopes to stress the need to create sizeable open spaces. He arrives at a new conception of the modern city:

*"THE GREEN CITY"*.

9) The "Green City" is achieved by constructing edifices 50 meters high on the average; they form *redents* of housing *without a single courtyard*. Quite the contrary: each side of the *redent* looks over extensive parks.

These new districts can have a population density of 1,000 inhabitants per hectare. This *super-density* is calculated on the basis of a home (from the working-class to the luxury home) 4.50 meters high, with partial subdivision into two heights of 2.20 meters.

10) Included in the construction of such buildings is the creation of their interior streets and communal services (food supply, housekeeping, laundry, and so forth), organized perhaps as cooperatives.

11) These buildings take up, on the average, 12% of the ground. The remaining 88% is devoted to parks for relaxation and to playing fields.

*Sports are practiced at the foot of the house.*

12) The geographical and topographical conditions in Stockholm are such that these sports can be extended to include *aquatic sports*. All that is needed is to link residential districts to those for aquatic sports when the shoreline is rectified and the seafront boulevard laid out.

13) Since the apartment buildings are built on pilotis, the pedestrian may go where he likes; 100% of the ground is left free for the most complex network of pedestrian movement.

For Stockholm especially, this doctrine means that costly earthworks and earth removal can be avoided. The ground can remain in its natural, uneven state, varying from sea level (elevation zero) to elevations 19 and 35, at the summits of the two main urban agglomerations.

14) These methods *reinstate* the natural site in the city, making it an object of enjoyment for all the city dwellers. This factor seemed to be of prime importance.

15) Since the home itself is guaranteed optimum conditions of comfort, hygiene and well-being, all that remains is to complete the home by grouping in the appropriate place three elements intimately connected with the dwelling: the nursery, the kindergarten, and the primary school.

16) Once "living" and "dwelling" are taken care of, TRAFFIC must be urgently attended to.

17) Traffic must be divided into:

a) multiple speeds;

b) single speeds (pedestrians);

c) moderate speeds (access to public buildings and apartment houses).

18) Multiple speeds can be accommodated only by the construction of *highways raised on pilotis* and a strict minimum of contact with moderate speeds. This "A" network includes rational intersections like that already built at Slussen.

The first elements of this network to be constructed should be highways 1 and 2 on plan S.T. 3067 – here demolition would be easiest and efficiency most urgently needed.

There is no getting around one difficulty: it is impossible to have highway 2 continue across the Palace island, without canceling much of the beauty of the site. For this reason, highway 2 has been linked to 1 by an east-west branch. Heavy traffic will begin, therefore, at the island on which the Royal Palace stands, on highway 1.

At Slussen, this heavy traffic can continue north and south on highway 6, and east and west on highways 8 and 7. Ultimately, efforts at inter-suburban liaison can be furthered by the construction of highway 4, and possibly by 5 in the northern branch, which could be continued later. For the time being, transversal highway 3 stops where it runs into highway 2. Thereafter, the network becomes one of moderate traffic and simply uses the streets and avenues of the recently built eastern district.

In the future it will be easy to make connections with the airport and with the stadiums, both in this eastern region.

19) *Single speeds: network for pedestrians.*

The pedestrian should never have to meet high-speed automobile traffic, and even moderate-speed traffic only as seldom as possible. Of course this desirable state of affairs can be managed only when a district has been thoroughly reworked but it is not too early to adopt this goal.

If we build on pilotis and arrange apartment houses *en redent*, we can create a flexible network for pedestrian movement, by laying out diagonal and orthogonal paths through the parks.

20) *Moderate speeds.*

Cars should be able, upon leaving the throughways for highspeed traffic, to reach public buildings and apartment houses.

*Apartment houses are so conceived* that entrances are *spaced 200 meters apart.* Thus, the system of highways is simplified in the extreme, since it becomes independent of the layout of the houses. To reach the entrance of each house, it simply fans out into an *"auto-port"* or parking lot; *here and only here is where cars should go.*

As for public buildings, the highway network should be flexible enough to adapt itself to any particular case.

Any public building put up from now on can be required to place the automobile entrance on a different level from the pedestrian entrance and about 5 meters above the ground. *A ruling of this sort would bear fruit immediately.* And finally there must be boulevards which both pedestrians and cars could use at leisure and in perfect safety.

Boulevards for slow traffic: several essential axes where stores, cafés, clubs, etc. would be located.

21) The city is assured of contact with its suburbs through the extremities of the major highways.

22) Now that these vital functions (living, and getting about) have been outlined, we can consider at which points in the urban region they should be carried out.

The author feels that the enriching principle of the "Green City" *should eventually replace the paradox of garden cities.*

23) It is conceivable, in Stockholm, where nature is so accessible, that garden cities be harmoniously developed. But *there should be no question* of letting the 200,000 or 300,000 residents of the city itself continue to live like moles, *cut off once and for all from the region's natural beauty,* crammed into streets that have become too narrow to take traffic (and which the city itself is thinking of transforming) and clustered around gloomy courtyards.

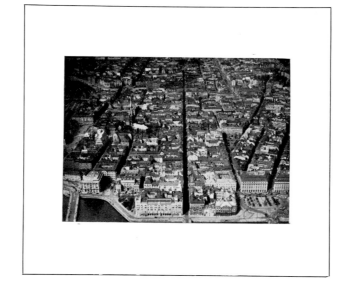

Living conditions of this sort are inhuman and the city's first care should be to improve them. This is why the author feels that instead of fleeing to the countryside and covering it with garden cities, *it is better to stay in the city* and to follow a rigorous program for demolition of undesirable districts.

In all honesty we must note, anyhow, that *a city's very existence consists of perpetual demolition and reconstruction.*

But when a city demolishes and rebuilds from day to day, *aimlessly,* and the authorities do nothing about it, this is a crime. For an adequate response to the new facts of city life, to speed and hygiene, requires the adoption of new methods and decisive programs.

24) But demolition *should imply valorization.* Modern building techniques allow a staggering increase in population density without compromising the conditions set out above.

25) *Now, if population density increases, the city shrinks and distances are lessened. This is the solution.*

26) If densities are increased, the *real estate value* of the ground is enhanced in direct proportion. Since these profits are brought about by the PLAN, under government leadership and supervision, they should by rights belong to those who made them possible: that is, to the government.

27) Accordingly, the author has looked for the solution to Stockholm's problem in the heart of the city. It is in zone B of the NEDRE NORRMALM district and zone A of the SODERMALM district that he has planned the demolition needed for proper traffic installations and the gradual construction of two new districts. District B will have a population capacity of 170,000; and district A, of 110,000. Plan S.T. 3063 shows how these figures were arrived at.

This is an unprecedented phase in the history of urban development; *but isn't that just the point? Isn't*

This proposal for Stockholm's urbanization expressed a new era, turned a new leaf. From then on, unprecedented urban events. I had been summoned to Stockholm and government leaders had begged me to submit an "idea" on the occasion of the international competition for the urbanization of the Norrmalm district.

I had annexed to my plans a report and 13 sheets of drawings in color, explicit and absorbing diagrams. In them lay the whole explanation of the new theory I was putting forth. Without these explanations, my project was incomprehensible.

Unlike the Antwerp jury which, in just a few hours, "ran through" several kilometers of plans, Stockholm took ten months to reach a decision.

But since the style of these 13 sheets might have "given me away," the judges covered them completely with white pasteboard – and in that state they were returned to me. This is the note I made at the time: "WHEN HONESTY BECOMES STUPIDITY!"

So the jury had not even been able to try to understand.

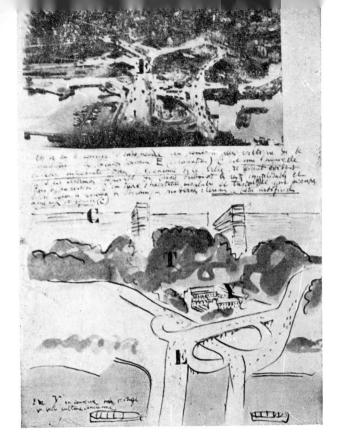

Important work has been courageously started at E, the most critical point in the traffic system. *The city's economy is thus placed on a new scale.*

We must not forget the heart of the question, which is DWELLING, and not, getting about. The latter is only a consequence of the former.

Dwelling means: a) *a sunny apartment;* the view from the apartment (sky, trees) = joy and dignity. b) *breathing:* system of exact air, replacing the inadequate notion of heating and ventilating. c) *household equipment:* through logical arrangement of the house, we make considerable saving on the volume of the dwelling. d) *freedom of the individual:* soundproofed apartments. e) *participation in group activities:* sports.

Stockholm is to have sports available at the foot of the house, and from there, direct access to aquatic sports in areas to be arranged when the outline of the docks is corrected.

*this phase proportional to contemporary needs and to the new factors which caused them?*

From now on city planning adopts a different stance. Once a science unfortunately limited to two dimensions, it becomes a three-dimensional science; it occupies space, both horizontal and vertical.

Whereupon new architectural phenomena appear. A calm and powerful architecture will replace the frightening chaos and the saddening monotony of today's cities. Men will be happy in their homes, and proud and enthused in the street.

The city will be beautiful, splendid.

For Stockholm, we can plan buildings which do not have to be more than 35 meters high; they can be erected *on the hilltops set back from the seashore.* From there they will command *views over every part of the horizon.* The center of the city, a spiritual gem, rich with the country's history, will retain its proportions. It will simply be cleaned and purged, little by little.

On the island of the Royal Palace, there will be nothing but vestiges of genuine historical value.

The highways and the network reserved to pedestrians are not all; there is the complete program to be realized. A sort of forum will descend from the north of Nedre Norrmalm all the way to Slussen, beyond the island of the Royal Palace. The forum consists of landscaped promenades and squares surrounded by low buildings of one or two stories built in tiers. They will frame the architectural landscape while providing convenient locations for cafés, restaurants, meeting halls, clubs and so forth.

This majestic way – where older buildings, easily respected, will also stand amidst parks – will be the scene of the city's civic and daily life.

To the south, opposite the castle, the forum will fan out and form two branches, east and west: *the seafront promenades* reaching into the country and going by the future aquatic sports facilities.

The residential district on Sodermalm island could be built very rapidly; to begin with, it could occupy the sites which are already free, especially to the south. Buildings will average 45 meters in height.

For both districts, Nedre Norrmalm and Sodermalm, we have planned to link the building entrances with the highways by *temporarily* using streets which already exist. Little by little, highways 5 meters from the ground could be built above them.

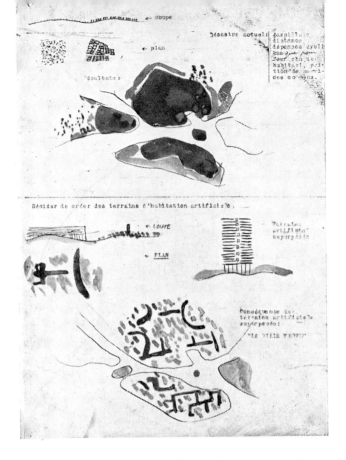

DWELLING: *necessary and sufficient functions,* expressing a new era, providing escape from the nightmare of the present.

THE GOVERNMENT'S REAL OBJECTIVE. Any initiative, any fragmentary task should be taken or undertaken for the sake of this objective and in its favor. Such is the task actually facing the government.

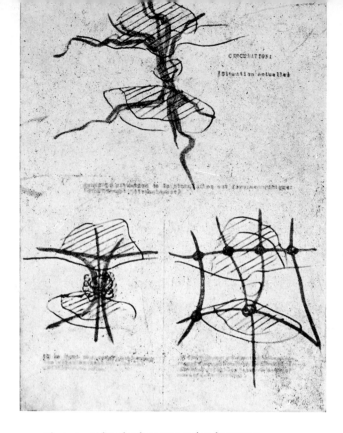

There must be absolute separation between:

a) the network for *high-speed traffic*

highways with $\begin{cases} \text{heavy vehicles: busses, trucks} \\ \text{streetcars} \\ \text{cars} \end{cases}$

b) the network for *pedestrians* (strollers)

\* \* \*

Public buildings, present and future, are situated along the pedestrian system.

So there must also be:

c) an *intermediary network*, branching off from the throughways, to reach these buildings at moderate speed.

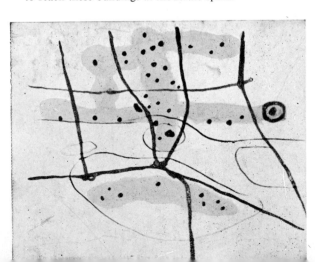

At 1, highways dip down to water level around the center of the city (Palace island).

At E, at the extremes, highways are on elevated viaducts, so as to leave clearance around the city's chief site: the quays and the Palace island.

CONCLUSION

This project and its accompanying explanations show that a contemporary city, with firm and farsighted leaders willing to innovate, can assure the happiness of each inhabitant by building a *Radiant City* which sums up the benefits to be derived from mechanical and industrial progress.

It also shows that a city's historical aspects can be safeguarded and, better still, enhanced and underlined.

And that civic spirit can find a new source of pride. A notion that is all the more striking in Stockholm, a city which has already managed to galvanize public opinion by keeping its Royal Palace intact and building its celebrated City Hall.

And how exceptional natural riches can be put to splendid use. When architecture creates in collaboration with natural beauty, the result is symphonic, the city acquires unspeakable brilliance. On the basis of these certitudes, of what he had done previously and of his long-term studies, the author of this project decided not to submit what the competition asked for: a localized solution for the Nedre Norrmalm district. Instead he availed himself of the permission given contestants to submit general principles.

Municipal authorities must realize that *only the modern techniques* which have revolutionized architecture *can right the social, material and spiritual life which they themselves have so radically upset.* The authorities must realize that we are equipped today to take far-reaching decisions, on the basis of overall plans and sound doctrine, and to inaugurate *the era of great public works. There is no time to lose.*

A clear distinction must be made between the city's various vertical and horizontal functions. Two-dimensional city planning is worthless.

The street has died. There are no more houses on the street; there are no more streets but instead:

a) a network for pedestrian movement, going in all directions, on the ground;

b) a network of highways 5 meters above the ground, to serve the dwellings;

c) a single network of major highways.

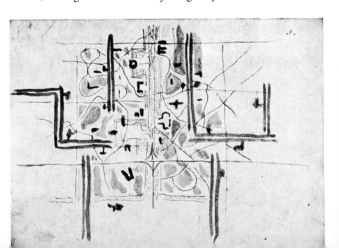

302

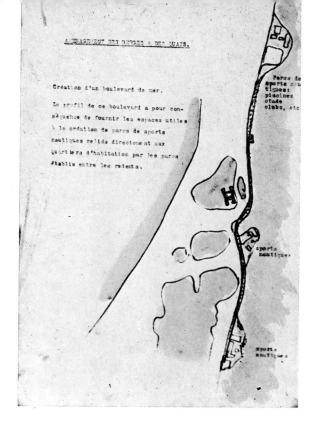

Improving the shore and quays (aquatic sports).

Big train stations are an illusion. A station is simply the scene of temporary passage.

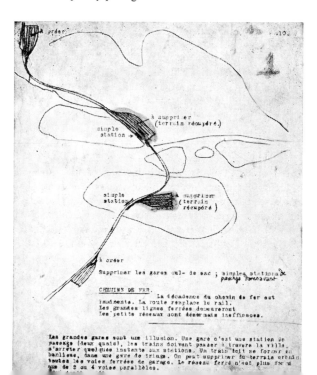

One of the most awkward problems in planning a living city concerns the space given over to craftsmanship. For even in this industrial age, craftsmen – whether in the realms of dressmaking and fashion, decoration, bookbinding, rug making and upholstering and the like, or in small national industries – will never disappear altogether.

Since these crafts are profoundly influenced by the life of the city, they should themselves *move into the city*.

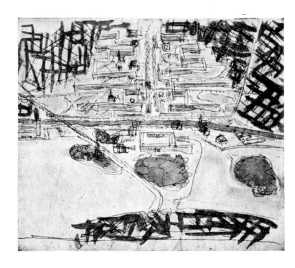

Little by little, the NORRMALM district is transformed. Its north-south axis becomes a grand promenade through the city, with cafés, clubs, stores, public buildings, etc.

Therefore the "Radiant City" provides a very special sort of facilities for craftsmen, that is: workshops and mills, of a standard mass-produced type that features a floor surface with maximum lighting, regularly spaced pillars, model apparatus, electric power.

Such matters as moving to new quarters or expanding should be achieved smoothly and automatically, without waste.

So plans S.T. 3067 and S.T. 3069 show one- and two-story buildings (at M) with warehouses (N). Since they use only electric power, these buildings are clean, and as architecturally valid as the apartment houses. The workshops are also convenient to stores and to the system laid out for pedestrians.

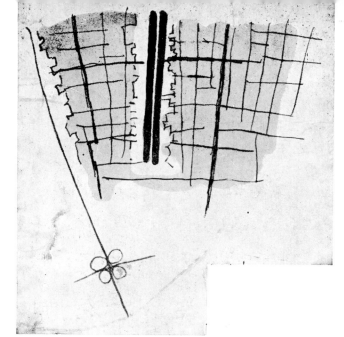

Cities die . . .

Every fifty years, or even more often, cities die.
They are demolished, they are rebuilt.

The new district perpetuates the spiritual tradition of the Royal Palace. Greenery comes back to the water's edge . . .

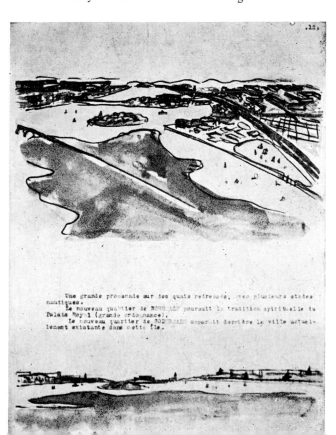

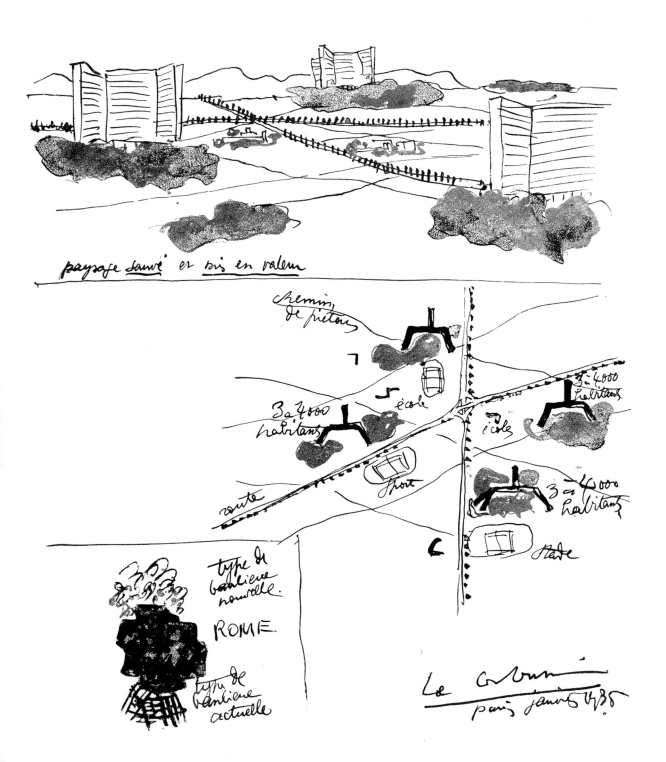

paysage sauvé et mis en valeur

chemin de piétons

3 à 4000 habitants

école

3 à 4000 habitants

école

route

Sport

3 à 4000 habitants

Sport

type de banlieue nouvelle.

ROME

type de banlieue actuelle

Le Corbusier
paris janvier 1935

# 1934
# SUBURB OF ROME

Letter addressed

TO HIS EXCELLENCY MR. BOTTAI
Governor of the City of Rome
ROME

. . . . . . . . . . . . . . . . . . . . . . . . .

The idea I mentioned at the beginning of this letter is the following: I was struck by the extent to which Rome, in expanding, devours its suburbs, in a splendid region of the finest, the most celebrated, the most moving landscapes. Wherever a house is built, the landscape is ruined and in this way Rome is gradually undermining the prestige of its site.

Now I am convinced that this site can be saved – if different methods are used – and its prestige given to the citizens of Rome as a bonus every day in the year.

The sketches I am enclosing are taken from my travel notebook; they will clearly explain the core of my idea.

Quite simply, my idea is to benefit from the modern techniques and very economical industrial methods which allow the construction of tall edifices. The communal services installed in each building make life much cheaper and more pleasant for the inhabitants. The buildings are placed far away from each other, yet occupy the ground with like density, so as to save great stretches of countryside. And the higher the floor, the more majestic will be the view from the apartment.

Among the most worthwhile results is that 80% of street- and road-building, including sewers and mains and upkeep, can be eliminated. The saving involved is immediately apparent.

Why aren't such ideas accepted? Because the teachings of the traditional schools and academies have had a deplorable effect. Yet I am sure that right now, Italy has reached a turning point, and that the healthy ideas of modern times can and should be welcomed there.

Believe me, my dear friend, cordially yours.

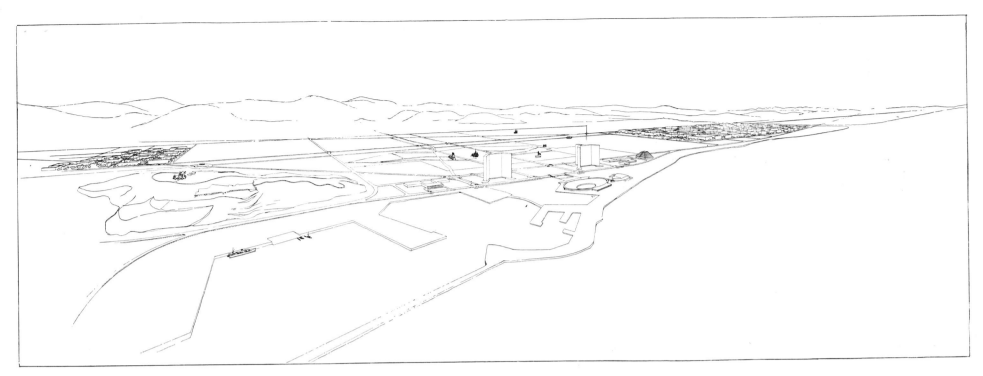

The new plan for the port, the Business City, and the major highways. To left and right, the two new districts, based on a mesh of 400 meters.

# 1932. THE "MACIA" PLAN FOR BARCELONA

In the spring of 1932, thanks to Luis Sert, who so lucidly directs the GATEPAC (Catalan group of the C.I.A.M.) in Barcelona, I was received by President Maciá.

For this farsighted man and his keen advisers, city planning and the future of the Catalan Republic went hand in hand.

I expounded my theories and voiced my admiration for Barcelona, both the city (geography makes it the appointed place for a capital city) and its natural splendors. I was optimistic: the city was intensely alive, its leaders youthful in spirit. At last, at one living point on this earth, modern times would find a haven.

President Maciá shared my enthusiasm.

In complete disinterestedness, we offered our services to the Catalan government. President Maciá accepted them and we immediately set to work.

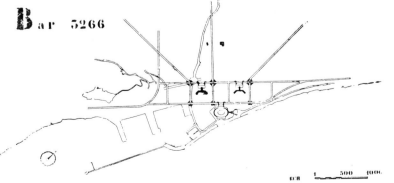

First of all, he requested me to lecture on my theories before city and state authorities and officials of the guilds and unions.

I lectured in the splendid Gothic Sala de Ciento, hung with tapestries, in the Palace of the Géneralidad, a place befitting solemn ceremonies.

We drew up a master plan for the development of Barcelona, an adequate plan whose effect could be guaranteed by the proper legislation. We did this work in full cooperation with the GATEPAC.

. . . . . . . . . . . . . . . . . . . . . .

Then the President died. Since he had been the father of the Catalan Republic, we asked that our plan be called the "Maciá" Plan for Barcelona.

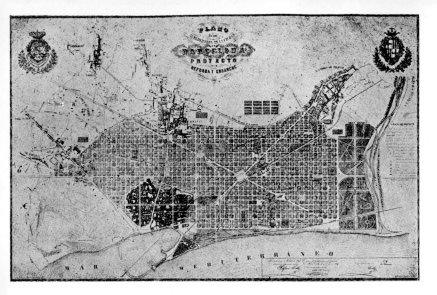

In the 19th century, when the monarchy gripped the somnolent city in a hand of iron, a remarkable plan was drawn on the basis of the famous "Spanish square" and a new city sprang up. A grandiose idea, an admirable achievement when you consider the thinking of the period. But cars did not exist then, nor did any of today's social problems.

Building lot:
"A WINDOW,
A TREE."
A temporary lot for auxiliary laborers from the country, it is based on the 400 m × 400 m unit of the road system. Although the buildings have only a raised ground floor and single story, the population density is 900 persons per hectare. Each home reconstitutes living conditions similar to those in the country.

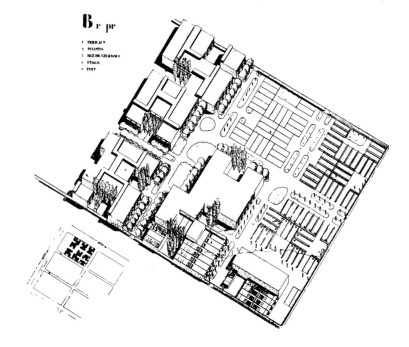

# MASTER PLAN FOR BARCELONA EXPLANATORY NOTES

Barcelona, February 20, 1933.

## LIST OF PLATES

### THE MASTER PLANS

1. ZONING
   Business City
   Civic center
   Present dwellings
   Future dwellings
   Commercial port
   Tourist port
   Free port (industry)
   Industry

2. PARCELING OUT THE LAND, NEW UNIT OF SIZE
   (module of 400 meters)

3. THE PORT
   Business City
   Tourists
   Commerce
   Free port (industry)
   Mills
   Heavy industry

4. TRANSPORTATION: a) RAILROADS
   Passengers
   Freight

5. TRANSPORTATION: b) HIGHWAYS
   Light vehicles
   Heavy vehicles

6. TRANSPORTATION: c) AVIATION
   Airport
   Air terminal

7. BATHING RESORT
   Rest zone

---

1) Cleaning the old city (Barrio Chino). First stage.

2) Cleaning the old city (Barrio Chino). Second stage.

---

Description of the project.

Drafts of decrees for application of the master plans.

PLATE I

CHAPTER I

# ZONING

## A) Business City

A zone 400 meters wide and 800 meters long, partly taken from the port and its sheds, is set aside for the *business city*. Its two office buildings will cover, on an average, 5% of the available area and will be 150 to 200 meters tall. They will be joined to a highway 5 meters above the ground, providing a perfect solution to automobile traffic and leaving the entire ground surface to pedestrians.

*Liaisons* (1) La Rambla. An axial artery in the extension of la Rambla de Cataluña; a Diagonal along the Paralelo and another along the route planned for the Via Meridiana. A highway (5) is to replace the present coastal railroad in the direction of Badalona. On the other side, the same highway serves the commercial and free ports.

## B) Civic center

Situated a) on the area to be reclaimed by demolishing the scum and slums of the 5th ward; b) on the Citadel's already existing parks.

*Liaisons.* La Rambla de Cataluña, Paralelo and Via Meridiana.

## C) The old city

Reform by stages; preservation of historic buildings. Will serve as instruction for the civic center (clubs, etc.). Hotels, stores, cafés, theaters, etc. System of small national handicraft industries, in the form of standardized workshops (vital activity in any city).

## D) The "Spanish square," 113 meters to a side.

Represents the present layout, dating from the 19th century.

*It must be changed.* By regrouping nine squares (three to a side) we arrive at the new unit of measure for modern traffic: a square 400 meters to a side. All that is built from now on in zone (D) should be built in accordance with this new module.

## E) New Free Port residential district

This district is based on the calle de Tarragona and the calle de Cortés. Layout using the square 400 meters to a side, ultimately to become housing *redents* with communal services. Can temporarily consist of one-story houses, for uneducated immigrant workers. Land is parceled out this way: grand avenues, 400 × 400. A median, lesser avenue, 200 × 200. In the other direction, three small streets, 133 × 133. Result: 6 plots measuring 133 × 200.

The expansion of this district, on the southwest side of the city, is limitless. But it should tend to extend northward, replacing the present "Spanish square" layout.

*Liaisons:* across a separation strip of greenery, direct contact with the commercial and free ports; to the northeast, by the avenida Cortés, the Consejo de Ciento.

## F) New residential district of the Besos

This district hugs the coast as well as the city, along the calle Luchana. Again, the layout uses the square 400 × 400. In the future it should be the site of important buildings with communal services. But like the Free Port district, it will probably be subdivided into 6 plots measuring 133 × 200, laid out on a square 400 × 400.

*Liaisons:* Direct contact with the San Andreú industrial zone through a separation strip of greenery along the calle Cortés-Consejo de Ciento.

## G) San Andreú industrial zone

It should not extend beyond the Via Meridiana and the calle Cortès.

## H) Free Port and industrial zone

Directly linked to the working class district across the green separation strip (Cortés-Consejo de Ciento) and to the Business City by the seafront highway.

## K) Commercial Port

Linked in the same ways.

## L) Tourist Port

Consists of part of the present port, with its commercial installations cleared away.

*Liaisons:* Direct contact with the Business City by way of La Rambla, the Paralelo, la Rambla de Cataluña, la Meridiana and the coastal road, with the civic centers, the old city, the residential zones and the interior, toward Madrid and toward France; also, by the Badalona highway, contact with the University City.

## M) Harbor for pleasure craft

Is constituted by the innermost part of the present port.

*Liaisons:* same as above.

## N) Trade Unions Hall

For the purpose of all popular demonstrations; situated at the very entrance to Barcelona, at the city's axial extremity and facing the sea, where all of the living forces of the city converge.

## O) University City

At one of the most beautiful points in the urban region, on the sea and in front of the coastal highway, in direct communication with the civic center and the Trade Unions Hall.

City walls: During the Renaissance.      In Roman times.

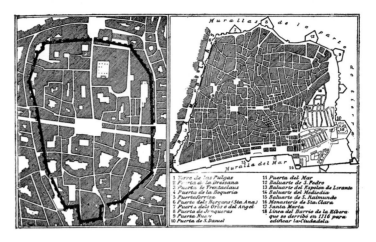

By purging the old city, we enhance its artistic and civic heritage.

Proposed improvement: a) The Barrio Chino is cleared away, leaving a site for the Civic Center.

Elsewhere, the picturesque streets are freed of automobile traffic and reserved for pedestrians. Within the remaining blocks: slums are cleared, handicraft industries installed, parks planted.

In this way the most worthwhile features of the old city are preserved.

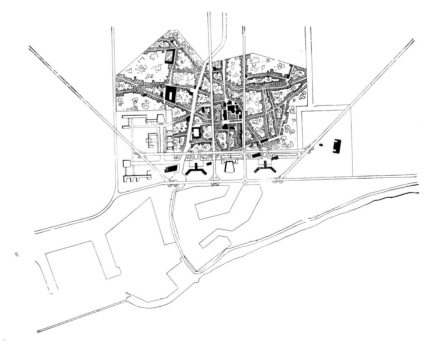

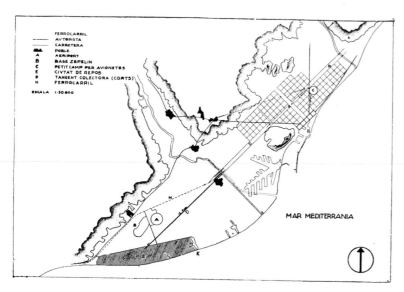

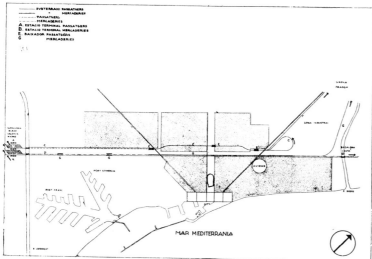

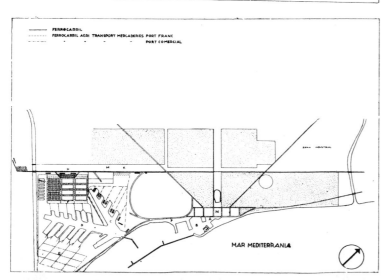

PLATE 2

CHAPTER II

*Parceling out the land:*

Establishment of a new unit of measurement, the square 400 meters to a side.

A) *"The Eixample"*

The 19th century "Eixample" was based on the square 113 meters to a side, before the days of automobiles. For horses, or pedestrians, the square of 113 meters was normal. But with the introduction of the automobile come multiple speeds, 20 times greater. Intersections every 113 meters constitute a danger or, at the very least, a permanent hindrance to traffic.

Result: for the moment we will have to work with this layout but make its replacement by the square of 400 meters compulsory. From now on all parcelings of land in this zone should be based on the new unit of measurement, as should all new contracts.

B) *Free Port residential district*

Its construction will be based on the square 400 meters to a side. The 19th century layout will be reformed through the gradual introduction of avenues forming the boundaries of the new square.

C) *The Besos residential district*

Same as (B).

D) *Business City*

Also laid out on the module of 400 meters, beginning at the two new residential districts named above and its natural junction with the axis of the Paseo de Gracia.

E) *The old city*

The old city will be purged from within, by use of the new unit of 400 meters, as in sectors (A) and (D).

G) *The great north-south throughway*

An axial zone for major traffic is created by the elimination of a line of 113-meter squares.

It is 183 meters wide: a 113-meter square, plus the width of the present avenida de Cortés (50 meters), plus the width of the calle Diputación (20 meters) between the Plaza de España and the Diagonal-Cortés-Meridiana intersection.

In the zone separating the Free Port and the Besos residential districts from the industrial zone, this throughway will be still wider, since a green separation strip must be made. Overall width: 316 meters.

H) *The great east-west throughway*

Created by eliminating two lines of 113-meter squares between the Rambla de Cataluña and Claris, this throughway reaches all the way to the ancient Roman city.

PLATE 3

CHAPTER III

TRANSPORTATION – The Port

C) *Commercial port*

We suggest that a commercial port be created next to the already planned free port. The commercial port would be an efficient modern operation.

*Liaisons.* For freight: by rail toward the interior and abroad; by highway toward the San Andreú industrial zone and all the outskirts of the city.

*Liaisons.* For people: by the seafront highway (P) to the Business City.

D) *Free port*

Its site is modified in the present project, allowing a rational arrangement of heavy industry (E) and mills (F).

*Liaisons.* Freight: by cable lift from the boats (at E) and loading onto trucks or trains (at H).

*Liaisons.* People: by the seafront highway (P) to the Business City.

G) Canals will be dug in the plain of the Llobregat to prevent flooding of the sites set aside for the free port's heavy industry.

B) *Port for tourist vessels*

Part of the present port is modified for this purpose.

This general sketch was made in Barcelona in 1932 in collaboration with members of the GATEPAC.

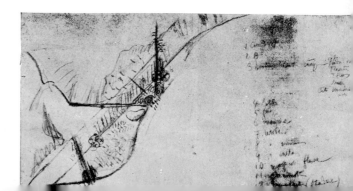

A) *Harbor for pleasure craft*

At the foot of the Business City, in the oldest basin.

## PLATE 4

### CHAPTER IV

### TRANSPORTATION – Railways

The fundamental need is to do away with the blind alley station (M.S.A. and North Station). The growth of automobile travel and transport by motor vehicles necessarily dooms many freight and passenger rail lines. Consequently, it would be wise to reduce the present network and divide it into clear categories: a) passenger traffic concentrated on the main lines (France, Madrid, Valencia); and b) freight traffic similarly concentrated. Trains bring freight across Barcelona from its origin in the interior (Tarragona, Lérida, Valencia, Bilbao) to the port, its destination. Or again, freight arrives from the commercial port to be transferred by train to its distant destination (Saragossa, Lérida, Bilbao, Valencia, France, etc.); c) Products of miscellaneous origin carried to the free port or the San Andreú industrial zone have the same region as their rail destination (Saragossa, Lérida, Bilbao, France, etc.).

C) *Products*

All raw or manufactured goods destined for nearby points. (The city itself, its suburbs and the province will use the network of motor-vehicle transport.) Therefore it is natural to cut out the coastal rail line to Badalona; its roadbed will be turned into a highway for heavy trucks. The same will be true of the line which leaves la Bordeta and goes toward the interior.

From then on, the railway network is reduced to a passenger line (c) with its sorting depot near the Llobregat river (A) and three through stations at convenient points in the city: Plaza de España (E), Paseo de Gracia (E), Diagonal Cortès (E). This is a one-way line, which loops back (after the Diagonal Cortès) toward Madrid and Valencia. It goes along the calle Aragon and the Consejo de Ciento.

The freight line also has a sorting depot next to the Llobregat (B) and spur tracks to the free port, the commercial port and into the San Andreú industrial zone.

## PLATE 5

### CHAPTER V

### TRANSPORTATION – Motor vehicles

*Heavy trucks*

Goods in transit for the suburbs or the prov-

inces are carried by trucks, channeled onto a highway system completely independent of that for through automobile traffic.

A) A route along the via Cortés serves the commercial and free ports; in one direction it leads to Tarragona (on the coast) and Lérida (in the interior) and in the other, toward France by way of Badalona. Beyond Badalona the roadbed of the coastal railroad which presently leaves the port reappears; in Chapter IV we mentioned that it would no longer be used as a railroad.
D) The main artery (A) which, at the Plaza de España, forks off for Lérida, follows the present route for Sans.
E) A second fork occurs at Diagonal-Cortés, to feed into the San Andreú industrial zone and the province of Gerona.
G) A direct link is established between Lérida-Tarragona and the Gerona road.

H-L-K-M-N-P-R-S

*Cars*

Elevated highways are built for cars.

R) *Main through route*

The city is "irrigated" by a main artery which is the Cortès-Consejo de Ciento route toward Valencia and the coastal road leading to France.
L) A diagonal serving the Business City in the direction of Madrid, and junction with the main through route Plaza de España (now the road for Sans).
K) A similar diagonal, Business City – Ribas road, and junction with the main through route at the Diagonal-Cortés intersection.
H) A route already exists, from the Business City to the via de las Cortés.
N) An adequate network for one-way traffic in the Business City.
P) The seafront highway, Business City – Commercial Port – Free Port.
M) On the roadbed of the former coastal railway, the highway linking the Business City – cliff road – Gerona – France.

## PLATE 6

### CHAPTER VI

### TRANSPORTATION – Aviation

A) *Airport*

It will be kept at the site that was recently chosen, 15 kilometers from the Plaza de Cataluña, and reached directly by the main through route. The airport constitutes the general headquarters for air traffic, and planes will find hangars and repair shops here.

B) *Zeppelin airport*

Next to the airport.

C) *Air terminal*

There will necessarily be an air terminal in the city.

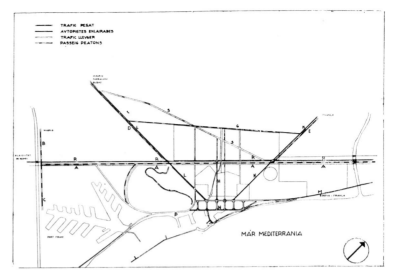

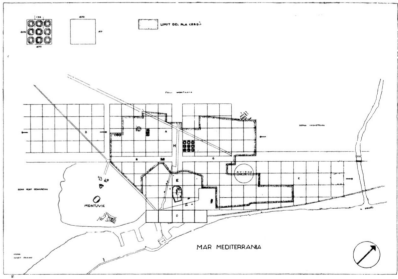

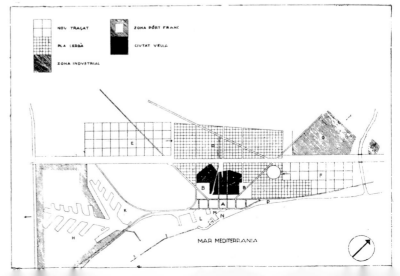

Nemours, July, 1934. A mayor, M. Llabrador, and two deputy-mayors, Pizzini and Besson. The city has a population of 3,000. It is sheltered by a rocky promontory; its clear layout dates from the French Conquest of about 1850. Like most of the Algerian cities laid out by the French Army at that time, it is well done, with discipline and order.

Now the railway from Fez, in Morocco, crosses the country and is to end at Nemours in a few months' time. A modern harbor is being built, on the left; steamrollers and cement mixers work noisily day and night. Mines are being opened in the hinterlands. Because of natural unevenness in the terrain, the Territoires du Sud are going to end at Nemours. The Cape railway has already been laid out (on paper) across Equatorial Africa; it could end at Nemours.

The three men responsible for this little city realize the magnitude of their task. They are thinking of the future, and they are taking action while the major cities of France are sinking into the disastrous condition resulting from lack of forethought.

In a word, the plan has been drawn up. The plan has been accepted.

And because at long last a modern plan, a vital element in the equipment of a machine-age civilization has been accepted and its validity officially recognized, then — then the moribund state of contemporary society appears, as cold as any verdict..

"Plans" bring contemporary society face to face with an ultimatum. (See page 318.)

# 1934. URBANIZATION OF NEMOURS
## (NORTH AFRICA)

(in cooperation with H. Breuillot, engineer in Algiers)

LEGISLATION THAT IS
        CREATIVE
        CONSTRUCTIVE
        HUMAN
        LYRICAL !

> "Born" architecture shares the integrity of nature. It exalts each site, opens the soul of the site to us, is embodied in the site. Architecture is nature itself through human creative force: farms in the Ile-de-France, houses in Brittany, *mas* in Provence, the Casbah in Algiers, the *isba*, the Norwegian peasant house, the Swiss chalet.
>
> But today, nature is despoiled by architecture. Money makes the laws and the result is vanity. Enough!
>
> *(Notebook*, 1934)

## URBANIZATION OF THE CITY OF NEMOURS
## MEMORANDUM ATTACHED TO THE PROJECT

As of September 20, 1934, the project includes the following plans and scale models:

No. 3,270   Plan of the first stage

No. 3,271   Plan of the second stage

No. 3,272   Plan of the third stage

No. 3,273   Plan for zoning

No. 3,274   Plan for rectification of the railway

No. 3,275   Plan for general expansion

No. 3,277   Legends.

A model on the scale of 1:5,000, showing the city at the final stage.

All of these plans are drawn to the scale of 1:5,000.

CHAPTER I

### TRAFFIC CATEGORIES

The following sorts of traffic are to be considered:

1) through traffic;

2) traffic within the port;

3) city traffic.

1) THROUGH TRAFFIC:

See plan No. 3,275. One road comes from Oran and after feeding into Nemours, should be able to join the road leading to Oudjda and the road to Tlemcen.

The Oran road, for the time being, enters Nemours from the east. After crossing the Oued, it would be shifted so as to join the road to Oudjda. It would fork off toward Tlemcen on the left bank of the Oued in accordance with what the Railroad Authority has already planned.

On plan No. 3,270, the first stage, the road is still laid out as the Railroad Authority has planned, while the road for Oudjda remains as it is today.

Beginning with the second stage, plan No. 3,271, there are rectifications in the curve of the portion of the road which goes to Oudjda. The road from Oran is also rectified, where it presently enters Nemours from the east, and its roadbed remains on the ground.

In the third stage, plan No. 3,272, the road from Oran, coming down the hills on the east, is elevated 12 meters above the ground level of the port. Since it runs above the port and the industrial city, it leaves the ground between them free of all traffic not directly concerning them. This elevated road, which has become a portion of the highway, touches the hill overlooking the projected sorting depot and gradually climbs to an elevation of 25 meters and there, just before forking off toward Oudjda and toward Tlemcen, it returns to ground level.

This third stage will be carried out when the industrial city has been created and the port has gone into full operation. To the east, the substructures of this highway 12 meters above the ground will be used as *souks*, and to the west, as warehouses.

In this way, there will be a completely independent system for through traffic, above the traffic involving the port and the industrial city and completely separate from ordinary traffic within the city. Speed limits on this through traffic (Oran, Oudjda, Tlemcen) can be removed.

2) TRAFFIC WITHIN THE PORT: The port includes tidal basins and breakwaters, railroad tracks, and the industrial city located on the estuary of the Oued. So there are several sorts of traffic: on the water, by rail, by road, and on foot.

a) *On the water.* The plans suggest places where new tidal basins and breakwaters could be created. Several possibilities are shown. Our study was not required to go into detail on this question, which is left up to the administration.

The Oued has been shown here diverted and channeled. There exist certain proposals for diverting the waters of the Oued, from its mouth to the estuary, either eastward beyond the plateau of Toouent, or westward, beyond the lighthouse rock. But this certainly does not in any way compromise the present project for urbanization.

b) *By rail.* The administration had had a plan drawn up; we were able to apply it completely, except for one minor, harmless alteration shown on plan No. 3,274. (The dotted line is the administration's plan; ours is shown in an unbroken line.)

Using the administration plan as a basis, the project includes a herringbone network serving the industrial city. The herringbone pattern allows us to take all the differences of level into account, from the lowest point, which is the industrial city, to the highest.

Only an aerial view, page 310, can reveal how the port should be laid out.

Zoning: from now on the city can take things in its stride. It will always be in good health. First 38,000 inhabitants, then 38,000 more, then another 40,000. Major through traffic (Algeria-Morocco) will never upset it.

Every sort of traffic is provided for.

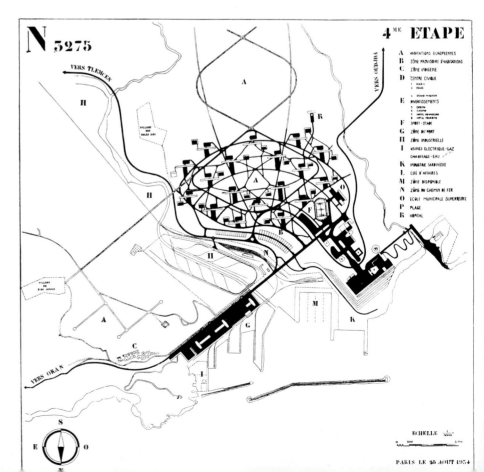

c) *By road*. This sort of traffic is summed up in an annular route serving the area set aside for the industrial city; see plan No. 3,275.

The same plan also suggests a branch from the highway, in the loop overlooking the sorting depot. This branch would go down the hillside in a northwesterly direction, to the new sardine canning industry.

d) *On foot*. Every part of the port and of the industrial city is accessible on foot. The connection between the two zones is made beneath the above-mentioned Oran-Oudjda-Tlemcen viaduct.

3) CITY TRAFFIC. A road system must lead to apartment buildings, the Civic Center, the Business City, and recreation and sports areas. We are talking about a specifically municipal system which, as we have said, we have protected from rapid through traffic (Oran-Oudjda-Tlemcen).

There are three sorts of municipal traffic.

a) Pedestrians;

b) Cars;

c) Mixed (cars and pedestrians).

On plan No. 3,275, the pedestrian system is indicated in yellow; the system for cars, in red; and the mixed system, in brown.

a) *Pedestrians*. Includes ramifications specially organized for the residential district: radiating roads; parallel belts of roads; diagonal roads in a diamond-shaped or hexagonal system. Each of these road complexes is joined to the great seafront boulevard which stretches all along the port from the lighthouse hill to the valley of the Oued El Bir.

This boulevard is set aside for pedestrians only. It comes down from the playing fields and Civic Center toward the port and crosses it on a viaduct six meters above the point of liaison between the industrial city and the port. From there, it takes the form of a ramp to go down onto the ground of the former city of Nemours, which will be transformed into a Business Center. The easternmost end of this pedestrian system reaches the El Bir valley, where the native community will be established.

It should be noted that this boulevard, instead of intersecting the road for Oudjda, actually passes above it.

b) *Cars*. We plan a diamond-shaped highway, to reach every one of the buildings in the Residential City. For each building, the highway branches off and leads to an "auto-port," or parking lot, at the foot of the building.

In the final stage, this diamond-shaped highway will be raised on stilts to a height of 5 meters above the ground, so that pedestrians will have complete freedom of movement and will never be in contact with automobile traffic (No. 3,275).

But in the second stage (No. 3,271), this highway is temporarily placed on the ground, although the foundations of the future elevated highway are taken into account.

Where this highway comes into contact with the major throughway – Oran, Tlemcen, Oudjda – there are rational junctions which do not disturb the through traffic.

By making this special system for cars entirely separate from the pedestrian network, we are in keeping with the most recent tendencies of city planning, by which the pedestrian is completely secure from the dangers of motor-vehicle traffic.

c) *Mixed: cars and pedestrians*. At certain specific points in the city, there can be a mixed system, wherever a number of cars, driving at a leisurely pace, need to approach public buildings and then park. We are thinking of the stadium, the Civic Center, the City Hall and Club, church, department store, theater or motion picture theater, casino and hotels (a hotel for transients, and another as a tourist resort).

We have employed special devices to allow cars to reach each of these urban centers.

4) STATION. a) Harbor station, trains and boats.

b) Bus station.

c) Airport.

a) Our project has respected the administration's plan and provides for a railroad station opening onto the port, on one side and, on the other side, onto the esplanade of the Business City.

b) Bus station. Planned as a platform on a level with the highway, and at right angles to the railroad station. Hence, convenient to every sort of traffic.

c) Airport. The question of an airport for Nemours is still not settled. But probably this airport, for planes and hydroplanes, will be located inland, about 12 kilometers from Nemours.

●

### CHAPTER II

ZONING

The elements to be considered are:

1) The port and the industrial city;

2) The sardine-canning industry;

3) Residence (Europeans and natives);

4) The Business City;

5) The Civic Center;

6) Amusements;

7) Expansion.

Zoning is established on plan No. 3,273.

1) *Port and industrial city.* The port has been planned so as to ensure that the road and rail approaches do not disturb the city's possible expansion. So its layout is merely a suggestion. (Several solutions.)

We have considered the possibility of developing, next to the commercial port now being installed, a free port, a naval base and an improved port for the sardine industry.

*The industrial city* should be strictly confined to the relatively flat lands which form the estuary of the Oued. Under no circumstances should new apartment buildings be erected on this zone (which appears in gray on the plan).

Site I, at the eastern tip of the port, is set aside for the electric power and gas plants.

*The sardine industry* could eventually be placed at the foot of the lighthouse rock, when the annexes to the port have been built and the rock hewn in such a way as to provide the necessary excavations for the port. This would furnish the flat surfaces needed for the sardine industry.

2) *Residential zone.* The great natural amphitheater facing the port, south of the present field of maneuvers, has been set aside for the residential zone. It rises from, roughly, 25 to 100 meters.

This site meets all the requirements for dwellings: it has a perfect north-south orientation *(we are in Africa)* and the finest view; it lends itself to traffic installations, joined to the vital elements of the future city.

The first residential zone covers 110 hectares, and is, in principle, set aside for Europeans.

So far there is no definitive municipal statute which legally defines the factors in the urbanization plan. Meanwhile, we have chosen two lots of land (at B, plan No. 3,272), one measuring 2.70 hectares and the other, one hectare, as a temporary residential zone. These two lots can be parceled out upon request and used for small structures which will, nonetheless, observe certain rules as to height and nearness.

This temporary zone is a sort of safety valve, making it possible to wait until there is definitive legislation on the subject.

At the eastern end of the present city of Nemours, sites have been chosen for a separate city for the indigenous population (C), covering an area of 6.60 hectares.

As far as both residential zones are concerned, the most recent advances in architecture and city planning can be put to work to secure all the benefits of progress for the City of Nemours.

3) *Business City.* We have assumed that the city cannot be developed further on its present site, since all the level ground available will be needed to create a port. Although the present city may last for some time yet, it will tend, circumstances permitting, to be replaced little by little by a Business City.

We have shown this Business City on plan No. 3,271, second stage, in the form of an office building which could be built progressively taller as needed. It would group all the premises necessary for doing business: offices, Chambers of Commerce, banks, and so forth. Later on, there could be an esplanade whose porticoes would shelter other offices, especially banks.

There will be very good connections between the bus station and the harbor station, on the one hand, and the Business City.

Moreover, the great boulevard for pedestrians ends at the Business City; in the future this boulevard will go on, toward the lighthouse rock, to serve the Civic Center and the residential zone. Plan No. 3,275 shows how the Business City could appear when completely developed.

4) The site for the *Civic Center* has been chosen on the lighthouse slope, in the loop of the Oudjda road, so as to be directly linked with the port, the industrial city and the residential zone. At this axial point will stand the City Hall and other public buildings, the church, the theater, motion picture-lecture hall, and the department store. This is a privileged site, admirably suited for a Civic Center.

5) *Amusements.* A hotel for transients could be built immediately at the northern tip of the lighthouse slope, overhanging the sea. The site is already directly linked to the major Oran-Tlemcen-Oudjda route. Later a resort hotel could be erected and, finally, a casino.

The stadium has been placed between the residential district and the Civic Center.

Measures have been taken for the creation of a beach in the little valley west of the lighthouse.

6) *The city's expansion* involves only the residential district, which will be able to spread south of the one already planned. There will be a traffic system analogous to the one serving the first residential district.

The Residential City, in the form of an amphitheater. Each home has the most advantageous installation and view. Here we have a new Casbah of Algiers, a Casbah of modern times, made of steel and cement. (See pages 320 and 233.)

So that nothing will be left to chance, we have counted on a possible expansion to the east, on the plateau of Sidi Amar. This eastern city would be linked to the residential district by a viaduct above the industrial city. If need be, and through the use of modern methods, the viaduct could be made to pay for itself, with its substructure rented out as housing.

7) *Communal protective zone.* On the assumption that zoning would be carried out exactly as stated above, it would be very wise to designate by law, starting right now, the zones which are unusable for any sort of construction whatsoever. In this way the city would not be defiled by deplorable enterprises. Since such zones would be officially called "communal," they are labeled CO on our plan No. 3,273.

●

CHAPTER III

STAGES

The plans have been drawn up in such a way as to make possible their gradual execution without undue haste, without upsetting people, and with respect for things as they are right now. But these plans do allow the City of Nemours to take steps as of now for the protection and allotment of its land, so that the city may face the future in the best of conditions.

On the left, the present city of Nemours, sheltered and sensibly laid out by the army in 1850. In the estuary in the middle, on either side of the Oued, the anarchy of modern times: everyone builds wherever he likes. Such freedom results in general coercion which, in turn, enslaves each individual.

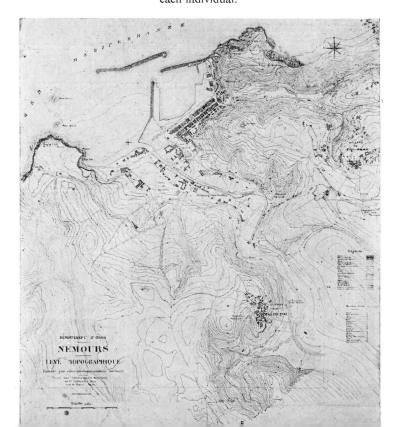

The new city. In the natural amphitheater: the residential zone; on the spur: the Civic Center and resort area.

| Resort area for tourists | | Gas and electricity | |
| Civic Center | Business City | Today's city | New city for indigenous population |
| Residential zone | Industrial City | | |

Estuary of the Oued-el-Bir,
where the industrial city is
to rise.

In conclusion: the 4th stage shows a complete city, with a European population of about 38,000 (A 1), which can be doubled (A 2) and even further extended (A 3). Armed with this plan the city's authorities can begin immediately to make their city secure for tomorrow and avoid the errors that crush most cities which develop without benefit of an overall view.

As these plans stand, they fully comply with the resolutions of the 4th International Congress for Modern Architecture, held in Athens in July, 1933. Its theme was: "Urbanization of the functional city."

•

As a (future) viaduct, the Oran-Oudjda-Tlemcen highway.

For rectification of the port, see page 310.

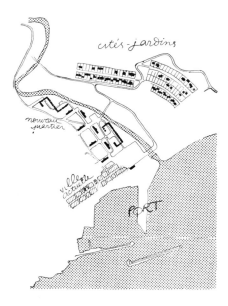

*cités-jardins*

*nouveau quartier*

*village actuel*

PORT

Nemours. Definitive plan, February, 1935. This is what the authorities CAN do today!

READER, stop and look a minute. This little sketch is the crux of the book. The officials of Nemours are in favor of the general plan for their city (see the preceding pages). They are enthused, willing, eager. . .

WHAT CAN THEY DO? This is what contemporary society can do: it can get everything ready to parcel out this little anachronistic garden city: 100 plots, 800 m² each, for a hundred isolated land owners. A hundred different and anarchic plots of land.

The officials of Nemours cannot carry out this PLAN!

Because the rules of society today are against the public good.

From the air, the land conquered by men and purchased by owners appears as countless strips. The new machines, which could be excellent helpers, are unusable, and unused. Men's arms are still weary with working the land. The mechanical revolution bears fruit – and the fruit withers unpicked.

But meanwhile there is a new economy, a new unity of products and machines. Man is excluded, crushed, famished, desperate. Nothing of this new phenomenon has been attuned TO HIM!

Algeria. On the plains of the Mitidja, at the foot of the Atlas mountains. From the beginning, because there was room on every side, the colonists drew a new sort of boundaries.

318

# 7th

## PART: RURAL REORGANIZATION

1. MY VILLAGE.
2. THE "RADIANT FARM."
3. REPLY TO THE PEASANTS.

# ¹ MY VILLAGE

No comment . . .

Do you know my village, on the main road? It's between two plateaus of farmland, at the bottom of a basin watered by three rivers, including the Sarthe, and it's charming – for people who like old things. An old church, old houses. Houses? No, they're "soues" as we say in the local dialect. Soue = pig-stye. One exception, and very much so: the school buildings.

Last winter, the floods nearly caused a real disaster; the village has been undermined by the water; in winter, half the place is swilling in it. It ought to be rebuilt.

How? Ought the main Caen – Bordeaux road to be moved? We need a solution soon; the houses are rotten – the road is dangerous for men. We ought to move the village up out of the water, then make a road up in the air to avoid the basin. If I go and tell the Mayor this he'll have me locked up as a madman. Yet it's high time it was done. The other day, a few kilometers away, there were people eating their dinner in a farm; the worm-eaten main beam broke: three dead and one seriously injured. Will we let them rebuild in the old style? Will we let them build another set of pig-styes? No.

We need a new village, but not a heap of cardboard boxes "cheaper by the dozen." So where is the architect who will build my village? We need people who know how to build.

Here are my ideas.

First, the public buildings: we can leave the church where it is; the tower is a thousand years old, it's been chiming out noon too long now to think of pulling it down.

A big central square: the SCHOOL, the community center, the CO-OP, the mechanic, the cartwright, the smith. Should we do away with the bars? Yes, as they are now; let them sell wine: wine never hurt anyone; but total suppression of spirits – I repeat, total.

What must the private houses be like? They can only be family units, or two to three households at the most: practical and comfortable; pure water, a big garden; we already have electricity; but for heaven's sake none of those awful barracks they're building just now outside le Mans.

I come back to the COMMUNITY CENTER. It must contain: the Council Chamber, the post office, the radio station, a meeting hall, a movie house and a library.

Not very complicated, but necessary.

The farms along the communal roads must also be rebuilt. But they must be proper FARMS. Who is going to build FARMS for us? Plenty of work there for teams of country laborers. I can't wait to see the first modern farm built.

At the moment, what we need are accurate plans and estimates. We're waiting for them. Make us a model of our future. You have created the "Radiant City" all right. Now do something about the Village, the Farm.

Norbert BEZARD
Agricultural laborer.

●

# 2. THE RADIANT FARM THE RADIANT VILLAGE
## 1933-1934

Norbert Bézard, an agricultural laborer in the Sarthe district, wrote me several letters quivering with impatience and saying, more or less: "Le Corbusier, don't just stay in the city! Do you think we can read the descriptions of your "Radiant City" without getting excited too? Why don't you give us some of your attention? Why don't you take a look at the country, at our farms, our fields, our villages . . . In my village, while one family was eating its dinner one evening, the main beam of the farm gave way, and the family was crushed. Every house here is threatened. The countryside is in the grip of tuberculosis. There is a fog of disease and despair eating away our very hearts, out here in the country. The French countryside is sick and dying. Corbusier, you must build us the "Radiant Farm," the "Radiant Village."

During these recent years of research, I had been forced to the conclusion that our cities are bulging with human detritus, with the hordes of people who came to them to try their luck, did not succeed, and are now all huddled together in crowded slums. I knew we should have to say to them one day: there is nothing more for you to do in the city; there is no place for you here; go back where you came from, back to the country. And in that way, the cities could be cleaned up.

I had also come to another conclusion: that the highway civilization now being created (the automobile, the truck) is opening up a whole new era; that the city and the country, long separated from one another by the railroad, their former harmonious relationship shattered by the railroad, could now be linked together once more in the normal way, thanks to the highway; that the nation's land could be adequately peopled, tilled with love again, and give good fruit; that the automobile would bring life back to the places that the railroad had cut off, and that a new relationship, a living and supple one, could be established between the city and the country, between the city dweller and the country dweller: a unity of spirit.

Norbert Bézard was still writing to me: "We want to have the same kinds of freedom as the man in the city; rescue us from our sooty old farm fireplace, the sign of our primitive state: our faces broiled by the fire, our backs icy from the damp in the house; we want radiators, and we shall throw anyone out who comes here telling us how much he loves the picturesque countryside and babbling on poetically about our "beautiful old fireplaces and quiet evenings in front of the hearth," without knowing a thing about it! We want houses on pilotis. Yes! Because we've had enough of standing with our feet in dung and mud, enough of damp beaten-earth floors that cripple us all with rheumatism. Give us windows, wide windows, so that we get sun in our farm. Take the dung away from in front of our table. Give us the means to be clean and healthy like people in the city. We want to wash!" Etc.

*Usés par l'âpre labeur des mines, par les rudes travaux ménagers, tous les membres de la famille Thaulez semblaient porter sur leurs épaules leur tragique destin.*

Work in the mines, work in the fields . . . collapsing houses, a life against all the deepest laws of nature . . .

Constantly, cold-bloodedly, on my journeys through our countryside, I am forced to observe to what extent our farms and villages are rotten with age. It is forced upon my attention that they are falling down; that they are dying; that the peasant leads a wretched life on his farm; that he is underprivileged in relation to the city dweller. Our farms and villages were all built two centuries ago, or even much longer ago than that. They are crumbling away.

From airplanes, I look down on infinitely subdivided, incongruously shaped plots of land. The more modern machinery develops, the more the land is chopped up into tiny holdings that render the miraculous promise of that machinery useless. The result is waste: inefficient, individual scrabbling.

The countryside is becoming deserted, the land is dying.

We therefore have a pressing duty: to turn our thoughts to the peasant; to use our *reason* to help him; to use our *love* to make him into a brother and not an underprivileged enemy.

*Rural reorganization!*

Reorganization of land distribution.

Revision of the peasant family's status with regard to the land.

We must create farms, tools, machinery, and homes conducive to a clean, healthy, well-ordered life. We must organize the village to fulfill its role as a center that will provide for the needs of the farm and act as a distributor of its products. We must face the fact that on this French soil of ours, rich in valleys, possessed of a complex subsoil, of such varied water sources, of sunlight so diversified in its effects by the accidents of our topography, of regional winds – we must face the fact that the tending of this soil is a multiple, various, precise, and ingenious business that requires constant initiative, invention, wisdom and attention. We must realize that in this matter of the countryside our concern must be, with only few exceptions, not to try and turn it into a sort of monopoly, to industrialize it according to some wholly theoretical formula, but to draw out of this rich and wonderfully varied land all sorts of products in all sorts of circumstances that are equally varied and particular. We must realize that individual initiative is the key to success here, and that though the steppes, or the pampas, or the savanna may be perfectly suited by nature to vast, one-crop forms of cultivation, the French countryside is much more suited to "garden" cultivation.

An examination of the problem leads clearly to a modern equation composed of two clearly definable terms: the family farm at the center of a land allotment proportioned to it, and the co-operative village – the heart of the peasant community.

But these things should be discussed by other people than myself.

I have drawn up plans for a family farm and for a co-operative village. A rural community, a basic cell, the key to agrarian reorganization.

The farms of the Toulouse region are built up from standard elements combined according to local requirements. They are precise tools. Everything about them is strict and pure. They are *true* objects. The resulting architecture is a marvel to behold.

A farm is not an architectural folly. It is a thing that resembles the products of *nature*, a thing that is rather like a humanized aspect of the earth itself: a kind of geometrical plant that is as intimately linked to the landscape as a tree or a hill, yet as expressive of our human presence as a piece of furniture or a machine.

So deeply is the farm's very being linked to the soil that even all on its own it can express and qualify the landscape it stands in.

And so, whether it be in Normandy, in the Toulouse region, in the Jura, or the Ile-de-France, the farm is like a natural presence on the land. It engages our sensibilities.

By what mysterious paths does our emotion reach the surface in this matter? By the path of truth. Nothing could be artificial here: everything is the harmonious expression of a complex of real facts: nature and man.

And the whole thing is so pure that any imitation of such a truth (a truth of yesterday) snickers like a filthy lie whenever people today content themselves, in the belief that they are being reverent, with copying the forms, or even the functions, of this thing *that is no longer of today*. Such make-believe, such face-pulling, such trumpery is immediately denounced by the country sky, by the realities of rural life, and by the verdict of *today*.

And a new truth can emerge only from the technical and spiritual revolution of modern times.

Technical, because it will be a solution provided for the problem of agricultural production by a collaboration between the peasant family and modern tools for working the land. Which implies an intimate symphony of sites, buildings, spaces, economic methods of transportation, appropriate dimensions, and efficient and rational siting. And surrounding the peasant's every action – whether working or resting – a body of mechanical and architectural equipment as impeccably efficient as the machinery that propells and sustains the aviator when his craft sweeps him up into the sky.

Spiritual, in that the goals assigned to this work are to feed mankind, to do good, to succeed, to help in the miracle of germination and fructification, to create pride in that work, and to incite in the peasant family an urge to become a thinking entity in the heart of modern society. An entity that will think with that special and precious quality found only in people who are in permanent contact with nature: her elements – the sun, the sky, the seasons; her flora and fauna; her laws.

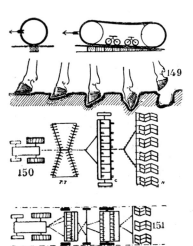

The principle of caterpillar traction has moved on from the battlefield into the wheatfield.

Technical and spiritual – this combination will extend from the individual family to the communal group, from the farm out into the fields, into the village, along the highway, the railroad, the canal.

It will be a reorganization of the modern age.

The peasant is no longer a "clodhopper" buried away in the solitude of his fields. He reads the newspaper; he is being kept informed and educated (for better or worse) by the radio; he has been brought into close contact with the city and the rest of the world by buses, by the railroad, by books. The peasant has complete political rights. He approves of the notion of a world divided into nations, then into regions. He feels he has a place in it. He can participate in the life of the world.

In his work, he needs the co-operation of others: there are certain machines, swift, but inaccessible because of their cost, that would make life easier for him. These machines will be acquired by the community and owned collectively; they will be there when needed, on his farm, to do the work that must be done. Other machines will remain in the village, again owned collectively, and at everyone's disposal. Organs indispensable to the safeguarding of his interests, to the rational utilization of the products of his work, must be created in order to prevent the fruits of his labor being wasted by chaos such as exists at present: a co-operative repair shop, a co-operative store (modern form of the fair), a co-operative silo – a means of safeguarding and preserving crops that will provide economic stability by safeguarding the individual peasant from speculators, money lenders and crooks.

Spiritual: the combination of individual farm with co-operative village is one that will direct men's thoughts toward others. Each peasant will be participating in the collective phenomenon: his community, the region, the nation, the world. In the village we shall build a "club," a place designed to house friendly meetings, or discussions, or contests; a place equipped to provide both general and specialized information: lectures, lantern slides, films, library. A place too where one can simply mingle with others who share the same local spirit, the spirit of that community. The community will have two living centers: the belly and the head, the silo and the club.

*　*　*

With Bézard's constant help, I spent six months gradually penetrating the secrets of rural life: the farm and the co-operative village – the community. It was a long, patient, meticulous process of assimilation.

It is easier (for people like me!) to approach the industrial problems of large cities than the complex annual deployment of work in the fields. Nevertheless, with modesty and perseverance, the vital functions were all eventually set out in their correct places and given their precise form on my drawing board.

Everything had been put together, classified, ordered, given the right dimensions, composed into a whole. Plans and sections. Though needless to say, no "façades"! And then, one fine day, we built a model of this well-ordered anatomy.

And there it was – the farm existed. A farm for the modern age. The prototype of the modern farm.

An organic, working, biological entity.

All around its buildings, through the open spaces of our imaginations, stretches the countryside: orchards, fields, roads, highways. In some places, the farm will be in a valley; in others, on the slope of a hill.

It is an integral part of the soil, of the region, of nature and of human work. It is alive!

And the co-operative village too, stretching all around the point where the local roads converge, is an embodiment of utility, of grace, of proportion, of purpose, of seemliness, of appropriateness.

*The term "co-operative village" is clumsy (1931); "co-operative center" is to be preferred (1964).*

*　*　*

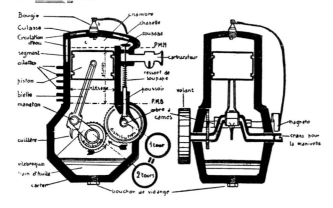

VIE ′A LA CAMPAGNE

Peasant, you are turning mechanic!
There are a lot of new things to learn!

And so, Norbert Bézard, agricultural laborer, thanks to you the first stage of this undertaking, the initial research and the creation of the *prototype*, has been accomplished. It is a very important stage. There may be errors in the results. But they will be corrected. The life of this modern age has been made visible in the result.

The peasant has become first cousin to the nearby inhabitant of the Radiant City. The Radiant Farm? Yes, perhaps it is!

Here are a few practical details of the Radiant Farm and the Radiant Village.

1. THE RADIANT FARM – In our agrarian reorganization, the farm constitutes our point of departure: the unit containing the individual family. To be properly tended, the land in France must benefit from the attentive activity of a family group attached to a particular locality and whose combined wisdom is applied to all the diverse circumstances determined by so complex a topography and so varied a climate.

The word family implies the word house. We therefore have to provide a house for our family. Not just any house, but a "*maximum*" house, one that will provide shelter not just for the family but also for its joys, its hopes, its individual undertakings – in a word, for everything that will give each hour of the day its full savor.

The farm as it is now, including the farmhouse, is hostile to these things; it lacks all contact with modern life; it is cut off from everything exciting and new; it is a leftover from the past.

The farmhouse of the Radiant Farm will therefore be hygienic; it will be gay, flooded with light, a piece of equipment that its occupants will be as glad to keep in good trim as modern man is to maintain an automobile or a tractor.

The peasants of the Sarthe laid down as a primary condition *that the house must be on pilotis*. Because they've had enough of the damp that surrounds and seeps into their present homes.

The house is not a human pig-stye thrown up in one corner of the farmyard. It is outside the farm, an independent housing unit that is nevertheless situated so as to command both the farm and the road leading up to it. It is at the vital nexus of all the farm traffic. It determines the axis on which the farm's work is based; it is the eye of the estate. From the house, high on its pilotis, one can look out on one side over the farmyard, on another over the orchard, on another over the flower garden, the kitchen garden and the poultry yard, and on the fourth and remaining side over the road leading off to the village.

During warm weather, in spring, summer and autumn, much of the domestic life of the farm will take place between the pilotis: the family will eat under the house, have a drink together under the house, rest, read the paper, see the end of the evening out underneath the house. During the day, the women will do their washing there.

It is an active, living area, in contact with the outside.

In winter, the living-room becomes the center of farm life. This living-room carries on the fundamental country tradition (combined kitchen and sitting-room); the mother and daughters are in the kitchen-living-room during the day, the men when they are relaxing.

The house is heated by modern equipment and not by the old-fashioned, dangerous open hearth. It is a single vessel designed to contain the entire family. Abundant light is provided by vast windows during the day and by electricity during the evening.

Radio, phonograph, newspaper, magazines, bookcases, etc.: the countryman is in touch with all that is going on in the modern world. From the living-room, his eyes can embrace the whole of his domain: North, South, East, West. This is a fact of great psychological importance.

The bedrooms open directly off the living-room: one for the mother and father, one for the girls, one for the boys.

Two bathrooms; one for the women, one for the men; both with showers. It is essential that "a good scrub" should become a natural function, and more than that – a pleasure. Not an unpleasant duty but a daily source of satisfaction. The old peasants may smile, shake their heads and shrug their shoulders. But the new generation will see to it.

The horse without hoofs.

The entire conception of this farmhouse is dominated by esthetic and ethical factors: light, cleanliness, immaculate domestic equipment. Once he has been provided with a tool so modern and so cleanly designed, the peasant will come to love it and look after it as well as he does his horse or his pig. In taking good care of his house he will also be taking good care of himself, and that is a first foundation for the essential joys of life.

RECAPITULATION: We must face the fact that our farmhouses at present are old and rotting implements incapable of unleashing the slightest enthusiasm. From the present state of mere subsistence, the countryman must progress to a desire to become an active being. So much for the farmhouse.

\* \* \*

Now the farm itself.

The men have come down from the house and have reached the farmyard gate. They walk through into a farmyard that has a concrete floor, is well drained, and is completely free from damp and standing water. No muck, no puddles, no dung. Along the right side of the yard is the equipment shed: light tractor, plough, weeder, dung-spreader, sower, roller, hay-mower, reaper and binder, the tedder, the hay-turner, the potato-planter and the potato-digger. Then the carts: a small two-wheeler and the big haycart. Then the automobile and the van. At one end, a workshop for the maintenance of all this machinery.

Opposite the equipment shed, along the other side of the yard, are the animal sheds. Each has an independent door into the yard that is used by the farmer but never by the animals: the animals themselves come and go through doors at the back that lead into the paddocks laid out for each separate species. Only the horses are allowed into the farmyard.

There are stables for the horses, then a shed for the sheep, then one for the pigs – which don't live at all "like pigs" – with a cement pond. On the other side of the stables there are the sheds for the cows, the calves, and the bull; then another for the bullocks.

Beyond the animal sheds, at the barn end, there is a room for the preparation of their food, a task that ought always to be carried out in controled conditions and with great care. One corner of it is equipped so that it can be used to sit up in if one of the animals is sick.

But we now have a transportation problem to consider: the regular handling of supplies and products. Purely manual means are insufficient. A rational and mechanical system of handling goods will supply this need: a rail running across the ceilings with hooks running along it on rollers. It will function rather like a miniature railroad track. It is designed with exact curves and crossings. Since the goods being moved will be hanging in the air, the ground will be left unencumbered. And physical effort will be reduced to zero.

People who live in towns have very little notion of the considerable work involved in running a farm. This work is a regular, daily matter; it begins anew every twenty-four hours, every morning as soon as the sun rises. And then, in addition, there are the great seasonal tasks: the harvest. Then, more than ever, we have to face a problem of rational goods' handling: transportation and storage.

I should add that all the animal sheds have been designed with identical main frame-works. Each shed is in the form of a curved roof running perpendicularly out from the farmyard wall, the roof being longer or shorter according to the number of animals to be housed. The equipment shed is also of the same basic construction. The barn, made

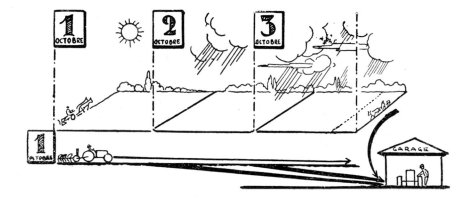

up of four of these curved roofs side by side, is also based on the same constructional unit, but raised on very high pillars. The whole farm has been designed so that the units can be mass-produced in a factory, then assembled on the site.

The barn is the farm's monument. Its dimensions are proportionate to the volume of the crops that will be stored there for whatever periods of time the alternation of good and bad weather renders necessary: once his harvest is under cover the farmer can breathe freely.

Some time later – on what precise day is not certain – the "*machine*" will arrive from the co-operative village to thresh the grain crops, bag the grain and bale the straw. The barn is designed to take 115 tons of wheat straw, 100 tons of oat straw. The fodder crops will be stored in a special silo and made into silage (80 tons). Beside the fodder silo there is also a beet silo and a potato silo. Part of the farm products will remain on the farm for consumption there; the remainder will be taken to the village when the time comes and stored in the big co-operative silos there until the opportune moment comes to sell them.

This brief account makes it plain that agricultural exploitation is fundamentally just a problem of *storing, handling and moving goods*. The physical effort involved should be reduced to a minimum.

It is therefore as difficult to establish a typical ground plan for a farm as it would be, should one wish to attempt it, to establish a typical ground plan for a city apartment. Though the latter is infinitely more arbitrary in essence than the typical plan for a farm can ever be. For a farm is a piece of equipment with precise functions.

The machine has now arrived to bring help – and chaos – to the rural economy. The physical form of the modern farm should be a rational creation in which all the elements present have been ordered according to their reciprocating relationships. The farm also enters into periodical contact with the co-operative village, via the use of collective machines and collective storage facilities.

\*   \*   \*

The orientation of the farm complex also plays a capital role. Sunlight is an essential, for the animals as well as for the men. It must therefore be present in abundance in both animal sheds and farmhouse! The axis of the farm will therefore run in a north-south direction: both the rising sun and the setting sun will thus shine into both farmhouse and farm buildings.

\*   \*   \*

2. THE RADIANT VILLAGE OR THE CO-OPERATIVE VILLAGE – Will the co-operative village be located on the side of the hill, where it will be bathed in sunlight as soon as the sun rises, where it will be surrounded by orchards and command a view across the whole countryside? Alas, no. Though such was the poetic hope of our friend Norbert Bézard.

No, the co-operative village too is fundamentally and inescapably a function of a transportation system, of storage needs, of merchandise handling problems.

We cannot consider, even for a moment, the idea of setting up a traffic system for heavy vehicles on the side of a hill. The difficulties inherent in the handling of heavily loaded trucks on any but a horizontal terrain rule that notion out immediately. A flat site is the primary condition of efficient transport. We therefore looked for a horizontal site to build our co-operative village on in Piacé: it is situated on the edge of the river and surrounded by a semicircle of hills. We grafted a branch road onto the national

Apotheosis of the horse! From now on he will browse in meadows of asphodel with the shades of Orpheus and Eurydice!

327

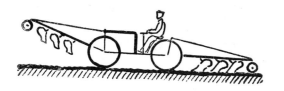

The new age

highway and had it lead directly down to our COMMUNAL SILO, the first building in our village. This silo is a mechanized construction – storage and product-handling – designed for the efficient loading and unloading of trucks.

A different section of road then leads on through the village to: THE SMITH, THE GARAGE, THE REPAIR WORKSHOP, THE COMMUNAL MACHINERY STORE. And also THE GAS STATION.

(On the subject of gasoline distribution, just one rather interesting remark: one's first reaction would be to set up one's gas station not in the village, away from the main highway, but on the contrary actually on the highway, where our branch road from the village leads into it. Thinking in terms of profit, since the profit motive is the foundation of our economy as it is at present, the manager of the gas station will say: if I put my station out on the highway then I shall get all my customers from the village plus the ones who are just passing through. Result: a bottleneck on the national highway and the necessity of setting up a home in a spot where it will be only partly productive from the point of view of the village: weakening of the village as a collective entity. The man in charge of the gas station must have other functions: he should also be the smith, or the repair mechanic. His job is not to waste his time on people driving past along the highway but to work for his fellow-villagers, to mend the machinery that comes in from the fifty farms dependent on the village. Setting up his gas station on the highway means the setting up of a parasitic function. But in the village, he will be fulfilling his proper function. This then is an example, one among many, of one of those particular moments when we have to choose between an obsolete economy and an economy of the future.)

The gas station will therefore be *in the village*.

Beyond, on the right, stands the co-operative supply building: dairy, bakery, grocery, fish counter, butcher's counter, deep-freeze, hardware, haberdashery, cobbler's, etc., etc. This is where all the goods bought collectively by the village, then stored in warehouses behind the display counters, are retailed to the peasants. Along the back of the building runs a loading and unloading platform at van height. The co-operative supply building, with its daily buying facilities, replaces the obsolete and poorly patronized weekly or bi-weekly village fair.

Further on is the small POST OFFICE building.

Then the SCHOOL.

Beyond that, on the right, stands another large building. It is the COMMUNAL SERVICES APARTMENT HOUSE, containing forty apartments that provide the inhabitants of the new village with all the benefits of modern technical progress: a new and youthful kind of domestic economy.

Why gather together these forty homes, formerly forty individual houses scattered through the old village, into a single apartment house? Because the peasants asked me to. The little cottage where one is really very uncomfortable, and which makes it impossible to derive the slightest profit from modern progress, is by no means entirely to their satisfaction, and they have heard people say that if you all organize yourselves together you can do better for yourselves. And they know for certain that people are better off in the towns. We city folk insist on believing that every village cottage is a nest of happiness; but that illusion tends to fade when you have to live in one three hundred and sixty-five days of the year, every year of a long life.

And so, in this new form, the housing for the villagers themselves is all together in one tall building.

At the far end of the village, in the axis of the main artery, the VILLAGE HALL, which contains the mayor's office and also that of the community's labor union. It is the manifest symbol of the communal reality.

Lastly, on the left, a new element in village life, the CLUB, which houses the library and an auditorium for lectures, plays, speeches, etc. The plays can perfectly well be put on by the peasants themselves – and not by delegates from the Comédic-Française (!). The Club looks out onto the sports grounds. It is the center of village pride, the seat of civic activity. Just as the commercial transactions of the old fair have been absorbed by the co-operative supply building, so its traditional parleyings will be given a new lease on life by the Club. Another affair altogether, and a much better bargain! Village life will become more intense, more active; the whole community will be woken up. The countryman will become one of the nation's active forces again. His intellectual participation is indispensable to the spiritual awakening of the whole country. The Club is the civic center of the new community.

Such is the face of the new co-operative village, implacably rational yet possessed also of a visible poetry. How much more dignified its aspect architecturally! The various elements that make it up are such that the co-operative village, in the midst of its meadows, on the bank of its river, surrounded by avenues of trees, will be a truly proud replacement for the obsolete village rotting with age nearby.

The buildings are as precise as their functions, they are all necessary and all adequate: it would be useless to do more, dangerous to do less. They are varied and full of character. They are the age we live in!

Since we are on the subject of the co-operative village, of a village for the modern age, of a reorganization of energies in the heart of a rural community, it will be of interest here to consider the results of an extremely valuable experiment that has been made quite recently, not far from Rome, in the Pontine Marshes. This land, once a region wholly in the grip of malaria and death, has been transformed into farmland of incomparable richness, and apart from the drainage and transportation systems so far created, apart from the farms with which the region has been covered, two new villages have also been built to date. The results of this experiment show that the will to attempt something new was there, but that success has not yet been achieved.

The first village, Littoria, provides extremely significant evidence of the confusion, disorder and incapacity displayed by our professionals when faced with a task of real depth, and also of the poverty of contemporary architecture. Littoria is nothing but a wretched little town of the "garden-city" type built in any and every style: the sewage from any architectural school.

The second, Sabaudia, is very different. Here, the first concern has been choice of site. Someone has picked out a spot that deserved to have a village on it: a spot, that is, from which the view will always be a comfort and a splendor. A very good start. Then, instead of allowing things to slide into an anarchic rush to get the place built, or into the grip of competing cliques, those in charge commissioned a team of young architects to build the entire village. So that what we find is a gentle poem, slightly romantic, full of taste, and a manifest sign of love. How different the atmosphere is from that in Littoria!

However, despite all this noble effort, the result is still not a village for the modern age: it is a dream, a dream of pastoral life just like the one that prompted Marie-Antoinette to build her Petit Trianon and dress up as a shepherdess.

But the story of the Pontine Marshes is not finished yet: there is a third village still to be built, the one that will be truly an expression of the modern age: Pontinia.

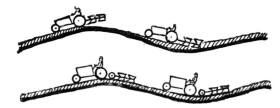

New techniques:
For the peasant too, the "step" of the horse has ceased to be the unit of space and time.

In order to explain what such a village could be, it is essential to insist on the necessity for basic constructional units as described in my own projects above: in the Radiant Farm and the Radiant Village, all the architectural units of the buildings envisaged conform to standard patterns and are designed to be produced by industrial methods. Neither the Radiant Farm nor the Radiant Village can suffer in its construction from the weaknesses or risks inherent in the use of local labor; we deliberately renounced the delights of village-style ingenuities in favor of Parisian teamwork. The Radiant Farm and the Radiant Village represent one of the most essential forms of production to which our national industry ought to be devoting itself. Everything in our countryside needs to be rebuilt! A gigantic industrial program! One that makes mass production inevitable. Mass production means standardization. And in order to standardize well, we must set about it with such a true architectural sense, such a love of proportions, such a respect for our raw materials, such a feeling for the human scale, that the units we produce in our factories, when they are assembled on the chosen site, will assume an authentically humanized aspect: beauty and utility combined in one form. My projects for the Radiant Farm and the Radiant Village have been designed so as to lend themselves to large-scale industrial mass production: the farm and village, having been built as prefabricated units in industrial centers, are then sent out, still in separate units, to their country destination, erected by specialized teams of workmen, then put at the peasants' disposal. A collaboration between the land and heavy industry.

Now, it remains to build such a farm. To see it standing there, out in the fields, at dawn, at noon, in the dusk; in the spring, the summer, the winter and the fall.

And also, Norbert Bézard, we have to build the "Co-operative Village", an elegant and joyful center for rural life.

Then the countryside will wake up again at last.

We whose task it is to plan great cities will then be able to demand of the authorities that they send a great many of those now crammed into urban slums back to the countryside.

For it will not be towards death that they are going. It will be towards a new joy in life.

*(Written in 1931.)*

Joy will return

# 3. REPLY TO THE PEASANTS

Friends,

The city cannot keep the city planner all to itself; the countryside is crying out for him too.

The country is the other city of tomorrow.

Our cities are crammed to the bursting point with parasitic elements of population. Our cities must be purged.

We cannot send these underprivileged groups of people back to the land unless we first redevelop our countryside.

The highway is our means of salvation. By means of the highway we can win back our country regions, all our country regions. And it is also by means of the highway that these country regions will be linked together.

Country life in France lies crushed beneath a dead weight of torpor; it needs to be endowed once more with those factors productive of an active social life that constitute the present attraction of our cities. The country must be "made" as joyful as the city.

The spirit of the age must reign over the entire country: why should the peasant, because of our negligence or idleness, remain as underprivileged as he now is? The man in the fields and the man in the factory must have the selfsame sunshine, whether of sky or spirit, shining onto their homes and into their hearts.

Twilight.

Orchard.

Animal enclosures.

Animal sheds.

Silos. Dung storage.

Approach road.

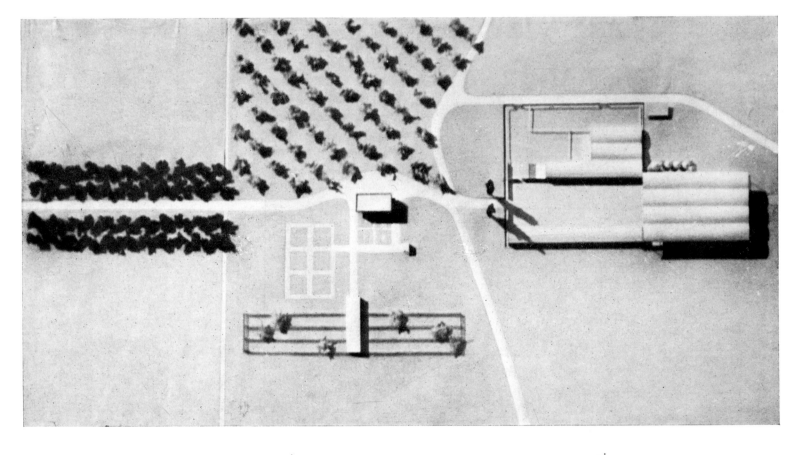

Barn open to the
concrete floored
farmyard.

Kitchen garden.

Poultry yard.

House with flower garden.

Machinery shed.

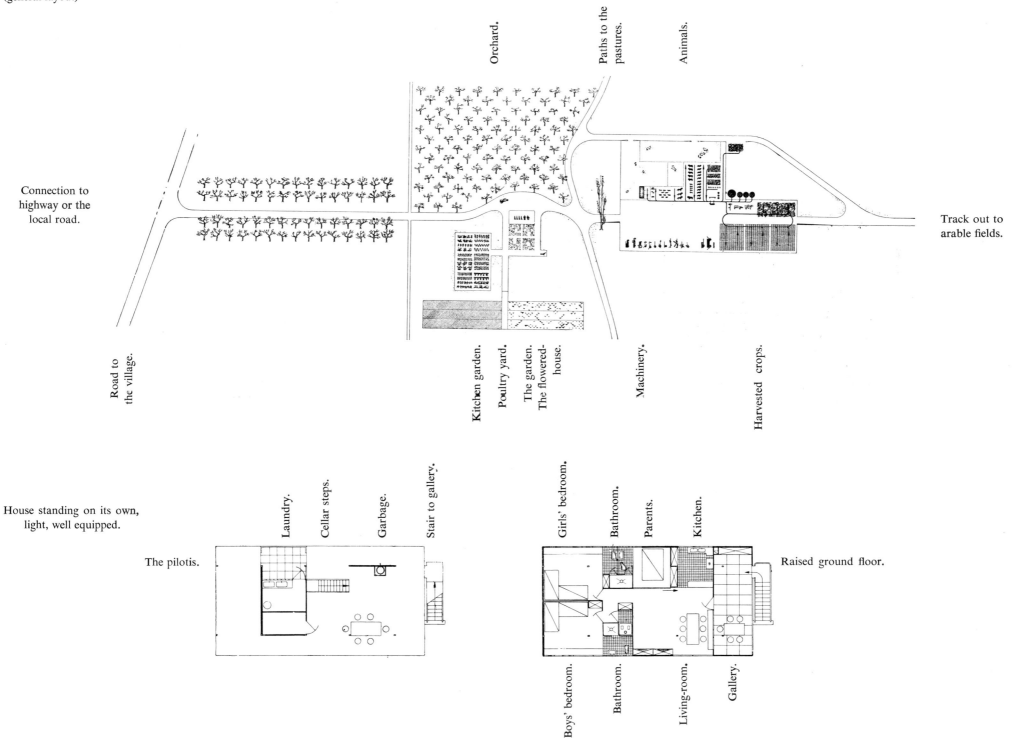

Connection to highway or the local road.

Orchard.

Paths to the pastures.

Animals.

Track out to arable fields.

Road to the village.

Kitchen garden.

Poultry yard.

The garden.
The flowered-house.

Machinery.

Harvested crops.

House standing on its own, light, well equipped.

Laundry.

Cellar steps.

Garbage.

Stair to gallery.

The pilotis.

Girls' bedroom.

Bathroom.

Parents.

Kitchen.

Raised ground floor.

Boys' bedroom.

Bathroom.

Living-room.

Gallery.

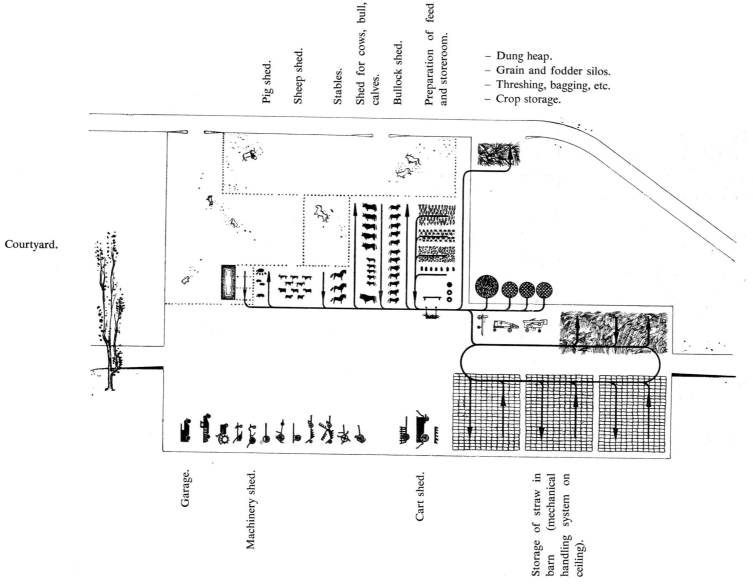

Pig shed.

Sheep shed.

Stables.

Shed for cows, bull, calves.

Bullock shed.

Preparation of feed and storeroom.

– Dung heap.
– Grain and fodder silos.
– Threshing, bagging, etc.
– Crop storage.

Courtyard.

It will be noted that the mechanical handling system can perform all the functions required of it.

Throughway forming axis of farm.

Garage.

Machinery shed.

Cart shed.

Storage of straw in barn (mechanical handling system on ceiling).

FARMYARD – Standardized metal girder construction: animal sheds to the left; machinery and carts to the right. At far end, the barn and silos. The yard floor is concrete; water drains away very quickly. The animal sheds are all independently extensible.

Animal sheds.

Barn.

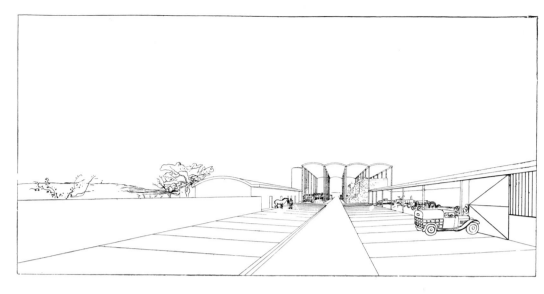

THE FARMHOUSE – Standardized and mass-produced construction susceptible of varying combinations. Under the house: stairs down to cellar, laundry, garbage chute from kitchen. The gallery is on the axis of the farm. The flower garden is in front of it, on the way to the kitchen garden and poultry yard.

Orchard.

Farmyard.

Cart shed.

Poultry yard.

House.

Our attitude towards the house was that it should be suitable for modern living. One must try to imagine the profound transformation that such architecture could produce in a peasant family's daily life.

It is something very like a *natural* event. Something like the humanized face of the land itself. A sort of geometrical plant as profoundly linked to the landscape as a tree or a hill, and as expressive of our human presence as a piece of furniture or a machine . . .

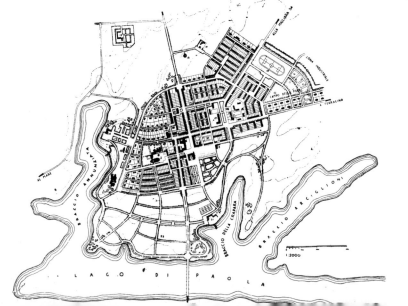

This is the plan of Sabaudia, the new village built in the h of the reclaimed Pontine Marshes area, just outside Rome. layout is sensitive and full of pretty intentions. But what I sho like to show here, by comparing Sabaudia with Piacé (on opposite page), is that Sabaudia is merely an artistic imitatio "lovely villages" all over the world, whereas Piacé is a piec equipment, a strict, pure, efficient, necessary and adequ creation – a rigorously defined and useful function. The equipn this modern age of ours needs.

Village Hall.     Communal apartment house.     Co-operative.

Rising in the midst of the countryside, with its ample transportation system, its airy buildings with their varied and characteristic outlines, thronged with its bustling peasants, the "radiant village" constitutes an outstanding architectural event capable of charging its site with strong and positive emotional power.

Connection to highway.

School    Post    Office    Smithy    Machinery repair shop    Co-operative silos    Gas station    Garage

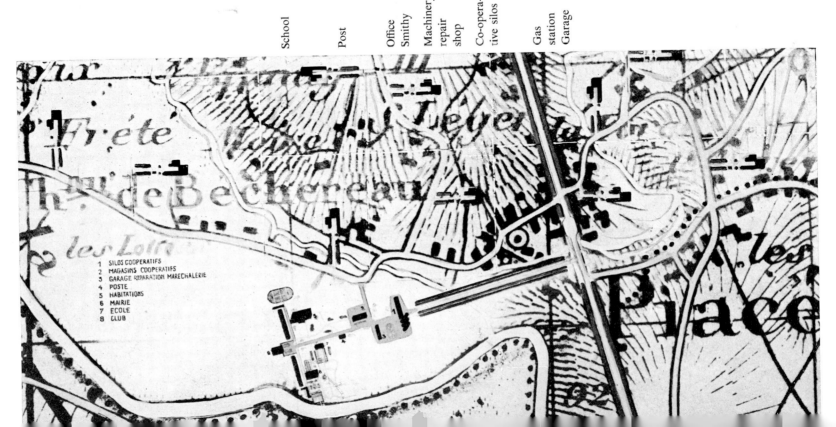

1  SILOS COOPERATIFS
2  MAGASINS COOPERATIFS
3  GARAGE REPARATION MARECHALERIE
4  POSTE
5  HABITATIONS
6  MAIRIE
7  ECOLE
8  CLUB

The new village that will replace the worn-out one.

Application to the village of Piacé (Sarthe).

the choice

L'ÉLOQUENCE

the grrrreat task ahead

Drawings by Mazerel published in the special issue of "PLANS": *War.*
*(These plates were made in 1935.)*

the fruits in their season.

# 8th PART: CONCLUSION

1. TOTAL PLANNING.
2. CONSTRUCTION THE BETTER CHOICE.

Little by little, the world is moving to its destined goal. In Moscow, in Rome, in Berlin, in the U.S.A., vast crowds are collecting around a strong idea.

"Modern society needs houses, parks and highways."

I should like to correct this to read: "Modern society needs housing, parks and highways."

I hadn't seen Freyssinet for years. Then he reappeared and told me all about the precise and very demanding research project in which he had been totally absorbed all that time: the discovery of a new material entirely different from any other already in existence, five or six times more resistant than the cements and steels now in use.

"I reached my goal. So now I'm looking around to see what I can use this discovery of mine for. And in my opinion, modern society needs housing, parks and highways."

What admirable powers of divination in this man of science, of precise and audacious calculations! At a single glance – in three words – he summed up the whole program of the modern age. Into that one short sentence he has crammed a vast wealth of poetry, of lyricism, of solidarity, of concern for mankind and the hearts of men.

And in his words I at once recognized an exact reflection of the conclusions to which I myself had been led by many years of meditation.

Finished, a savage era of civilization – that of money, money, money!
A hundred years: 1830-1930, the first era of the machine age.
Beginning today: the second era of the machine age, the era of harmony.

Man and nature.

Reader, perhaps you think that I am indulging in dangerous classifications? Take an airplane. Fly over our 19th century cities, over those immense sites encrusted with row after row of houses without hearts, furrowed with their canyons of soulless streets. Look down and judge for yourself. I say that these things are the signs of a tragic denaturing of human labor. They are the proof that men, subjugated by the titanic growth of the machine, have succumbed to the machinations of a world powered by money. The architects of the past hundred years did not build for men: they built for money.

Do you want a sign of a different kind? During the past two generations, the profession of architecture has undergone a transformation. Where before there were nothing but business men looking for good deals, now there are real hearts springing up on every side. And the coming generation feels itself bursting with faith and hope, already thrusting its hands into that generous trough filled with the raw clay of our future happiness: architecture and city planning. The indissoluble bond linking these two disciplines is a herald of the new age: individual creativity and collective action.

Money blocks our path, cruel and insatiable money.

We must kill off the old voracious and ruthless kind of money and create new, honest money, a tool to be used for the fulfillment of a wholly normal, wholly natural function – though today it still seems a fantasy: *to produce in order to consume.*

To consume what? Essential products:

> bread
>
> clothing
>
> housing
>
> and the spiritual fruits of life.

For us, here and now: housing – the roads that give access to that housing, and the landscape that surrounds it. "Housing, parks and highways!"

Our care and our concern, now deeply stirred, extends its embrace to the whole country at the same time. Oh, cities; oh, fields; oh, ports!

Our concern embraces you all with this clarion intent:

To rescue you from your nightmare.

To drive off the horrors that are smothering you.

To bring you the basic pleasures of life.

The farm, the village, the city: those are the objectives of our battle, the reasons why we have risen in arms.

Our farms and villages and cities are out of date, crumbling, old: so old that the mere sight of them is a stupefaction.

You have all been crushed by the machine age.

Before the advent of the machine, the village sat astride its stretch of road safe in its own purpose, a purpose much like the purposes of the two villages on either side.

And the farm, lying in the heart of the hard-tilled fields, supplied and nourished the village.

And what was the city like, good or bad? How do I know? But at least it was a whole century less old.

EXTRACT FROM A LETTER FROM COLONEL VAUTHIER
(of the defense against aerial warfare dep't.:)

"The authorities still believe that it is possible for aviation to find its own neat little place in our present life, juxtaposed to what already exists, when in fact it is exploding everything: our customs, our law, our economy."

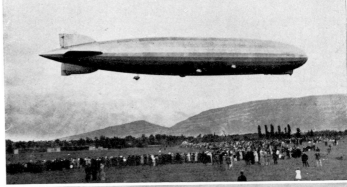

The new highways of the world.

341

Barcelona

New York

Buenos Aires

And in the last resort, what does it matter to me whether people were happy or unhappy before the machine came? One thing I am certain of: the vast and agonized labor of the 19th century and the dramatic explosions that have begun the 20th are the heralds of a new age of harmony and joy. Just as the premonitory gleams of dawn in the east, as night dies, leave no doubt about the imminent appearance of the sun, so a thousand signs and concrete events are now affirming the imminent birth of a new era.

At the end of a book as filled with details as this one, I feel able to proclaim, without pompous phrases, but with joy, the dawn of a new age.

I say: there is no modern housing. And yet there is enough too – there are samples, proofs that have sprung up in enough places for us to know objectively what modern housing is, for us to know that we should be happy living in it.

We know that it can be *manufactured;* that it would provide a vast and miraculous program for modern heavy industry; that once this program had been recognized (but what blindness everywhere!) all our workers and our factories would have work to do; that those workers would be working for themselves: housing for cities, for villages, for farms. The metal-producing industry, the construction plants, the laborers and the inventors, all would be fully occupied by this great task. Housing is a fruitful consumer product.

Worker and manager alike will know that they are working for their own happiness. The family provided with a magnificent daily environment – in city, and village, and farm! Consider what the difference will mean to them between our present dislocated organization of labor, the products of which are all intended for one caste – which is moreover incapable of undertaking their consumption – and this new, organized form of activity, now almost upon us, in which everyone will be able to feel himself both a producer and a consumer.

We shall see rising before us the noble pyramid of a new hierarchy of activities stretching ever upwards towards the conquest of quality. The program itself guarantees that there will be neither down-and-outs nor slaves.

Total planning. Who will be the first person in Authority to understand this necessity? Authorities in decay or authority reborn. This book is dedicated to Authority. With great serenity, I here affirm that it is on the "Plan" that the Authority we need will be founded.

*Waste*, that snickering and drunken tyrant, at present claims all our labor, all our sweat. Waste is strangling us, bewitching us, bogging us down, sucking us dry of all our substance. Already we are working for him six months out of every year! There are some mad folk who say: "Good old waste, you keep the world alive." Authority, it is up to you to see the truth of things, to contradict this folly, to stop this insane race into chaos once and for all.

The "Plan" kills waste.

No more waste: whereupon life will become a thing of dignity and sanity again. We shall always have enough emotional dramas in our lives to keep us alert and on our toes. But at the moment we have the drama of fighting for subsistence added to our usual ration of emotional drama, and that is why there are revolutions rumbling underground or exploding all over the place.

The "Plan" is revolutionary. We must accept the Plan and make it a reality: city, village, farm.

342

Total city planning. By means of a total gesture, of a universal undertaking, of a great plunge taken without a backward look, we shall make the new age a reality and provide ourselves with all the basic pleasures.

The only possible road is that of enthusiasm. Postulating the existence of a modern consciousness and awakening that consciousness in all mankind. Solidarity, courage and order. A modern ethic. Already we are hurtling forward into the modern adventure. You think the time is not yet ripe? What terrible sounds, what rendings, what avalanches must assail your ears then, before they will hear? The thunder now rolling around the world fills the heart of the coward with fear and the hearts of the brave with joy.

A new ethic has arisen to oppose the filth in which we are still being kept imprisoned by a dying status quo.

There is no need of either chimerical capital investments or new-fangled organizations. Everything we need already exists in the world: men, dedication, equipment. It remains only for a great breath of love to fling down the idol money, burst open all the doors, and set in motion all the energies of our hands, our machines, our spirits, and our hearts.

Let us soak ourselves in this idea: total city-planning for the good and dignity of all.

And to you, the idlers, the pleasure-seekers and the liars, you in your niches, conservatives and robbers, I say: tomorrow will see the necessary task accomplished.

We meanwhile, stubbornly and tenderly, will continue to *make Plans*.

*(Written in 1935.)*

Chaque année, la France dépense 12 milliards eu armements

•

When one is completely absorbed in the great modern purpose of architecture and city planning, then one is living, in heart and mind alike, a true life of PEACE: the peace that comes from struggle, from doing battle, from the daring, the disinterestedness, the enthusiasm and the faith that are needed to overcome people's ignorance and laziness. PEACE is *construction*. The means of acquiring authentic glimpses of happiness in life.

*War* is a stampede of uprooted human hordes, hordes of individual men helplessly caught up in a rushing torrent. They are called together and harangued; they are offered an antidote to their flagrant despair: action; plunder; conquest. It is a way of giving them hope (and a way of creating armies; of turning those men into cannon fodder).

## 2. CONSTRUCTION THE BETTER CHOICE

Once war has been declared, (oh, macabre irony!) the whole world suddenly finds that there is bread in the larder once more. Capital, man power, raw material, transportation, discipline – all these things are suddenly to be had in abundance. Production grows. It becomes vast, fantastic. A superhuman burst of energy. For five years the effort is maintained; it grows, it is titanic. It is a miracle; a thing of beauty worthy of the gods.

But no, you fool, it is GOLD that is leading this mad, satanic dance! It is DESTRUCTION . . .

There is a man who is not completely happy. On the verge of boredom almost. Then another man who is even less happy than the first. Then another, and another, etc.; millions of them. It's an odd thing; they're all a little hungry, or even very, because there's not enough work or because the product they make is selling badly. WAR! And everything is on the move again. Everyone is working; everything sells.

The economists know where and how and why things go badly here and there.

The sociologists measure these differences of voltage between human groups that are the cause of these thunderstorms. They tell us that we ought to set up transformer stations, as it were, between these groups, and control the currents.

The authorities . . . er, well . . .

The AUTHORITIES simply can't manage to understand how Diogenes came by his particular kind of wisdom, WHICH WAS KNOWING IN WHAT MAN'S HAPPINESS CONSISTS.

A man . . .

Millions of men . . .

Happiness?

Not in gold, nor in the pleasures we see unfolded on our movie screens.

But in a state of mental equilibrium.

A balance between ACTION and relaxation.

ACTION.

Well, being an architect and a city planner, I know that if we were to acquire a new awareness of life's realities, a modern consciousness, then innumerable sources of human covetousness could be removed without the slightest loss, and innumerable new sources of productive enterprise opened up.

What's to be done? Well, let us begin by comparing that racehorse there with this old cabhorse. Do they produce the same speed? Now compare all these men who've "had enough of it all" (because they've never managed to grasp and never will manage to grasp "what it's all about"), with the men they would become if they discovered one day, at last, that it had been decided to do something immense, something phenomenal, something unheard of and even undreamed of before, something that will bring them – and bring each one of them – HOPE, as well as other, measurable, true, tangible, effective things, thanks to which they will be able to keep a wife decently and bring up healthy children. Something that will bring them an advantage that touches the very essence of a man, that will touch each one of those millions of individuals who are so good at becoming soldiers and fighting wars: a task suited to their powers; a decent place to live, an active, strong, calm and human city. We must study the facts, put them in order, decide, and act. We must set out on the new adventure of organizing a modern world. We must take our decisions.

YES, AUTHORITY: decisions as pregnant with consequences as a declaration of war. A call to arms in the field of organization. Action and conquest. First of all, the mobilization of enthusiasm, that electric power source of the human factory. Then, all the other kinds of mobilization that enthusiasm will drive us on to. Mobilization of the land and the people and the production we need to make our plan a reality. Action. The advance. The great advance at least, once the plan is established.

Happiness lies in this imperceptible sway of the pendulum towards productive action.

Equipment: high command and army, machines and transportation, discipline – ALL EXACTLY THE SAME AS FOR WAGING WAR!

. . .. .. .. .. .. .. . .. .. .. .. .. .. . ..

Wide-eyed, one wonders: "Is it really so easy then, after all?": a simple decision of the mind, a simple movement of the pendulum towards the good side, towards the side of GOOD instead of the side of EVIL?

Simply choosing CONSTRUCTION instead of accepting DESTRUCTION.

Completed in March, 1935.

●

May this book find the way to men's hearts!

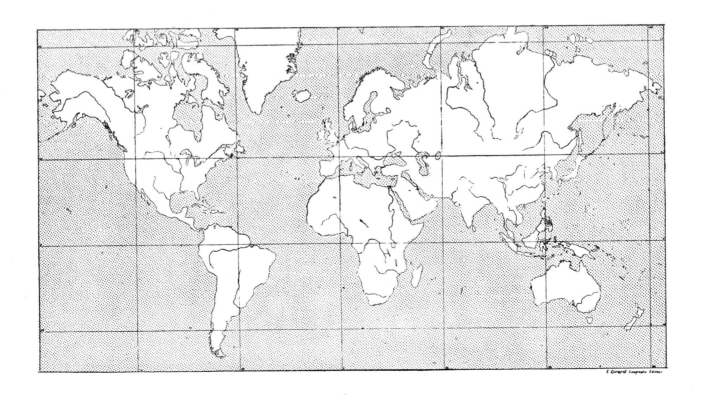

March 9, 1964

     I have just corrected the proofs of the reprint of this book: The Radiant City written between 1931 — 1933 and first published in 1935.

     Well, Mr. le Corbu, congratulations! You posed the problems of 40 years in the future 20 years ago! And you received your full and copious share of kicks in the backside for your pains!

     This book contains an impressive mass of meticulous and complete plans for new cities — plans that go from the detail to the whole, from the whole to the detail.

     You were told: No! You were treated as a madman! Thank you very much!

     Have you ever thought, all you ''Mister NOS!'', that these plans were filled with the total and disinterested passion of a man who has spent his whole life concerning himself with his ''fellow man,'' concerning himself fraternally. And for this very reason, the more he was in the right the more he upset the arrangements or schemes of others. He upset things. Etc. etc...

*Le Corbusier*

L—C

P.S. On pages 270 to 287 you will find the plan for Antwerp, an amazing total project put before the authorities during the Urban-planning Competition. Read it: you will find yourself in an Homeric world.

     This P.S. is also a coda.

May 27, 1964

L—C

*My thanks to Monsieur André Bloc, to whom we owe the recovery of the plates that were used for the printing of the first edition.*